CONTROVERSIES IN EQUAL PROTECTION CASES IN AMERICA

Controversies in American Constitutional Law

Series Editors:

Jon Yorke and Anne Richardson Oakes, Centre for American Legal Studies, School of Law, Birmingham City University, UK

Controversies in American Constitutional Law presents and engages with the contemporary developments and policies which mould and challenge US constitutional law and practice. It deals with the full spectrum of constitutional issues, publishing work by scholars from a range of disciplines who tackle current legal issues by reference to their underlying legal and political histories and the philosophical perspectives that they represent. Its cross-disciplinary approach encourages analysis of past, present and future challenges to the idea of US constitutionalism and the power structures upon which it rests. The series provides a forum for scholars to challenge the boundaries of US constitutional law and engages with the continual process of constitutional refinement for the protection of individual rights and liberties, within an evolving framework of legitimate government.

CALS promotes research, scholarship, and educative programs in all areas of US law, and is the home of the *British Journal of American Legal Studies*. Faculty members have extensive experience in submitting *amicus curiae* briefs to the United States Supreme Court and lower federal courts, and advising on criminal justice issues in many states. CALS coordinates the largest British law undergraduate internship program to the United States. Through this program, and members' research, CALS has created relationships with over 100 partners in over 25 states. CALS faculty advise public bodies, provide professional training, and speak at conferences across the USA.

Controversies in Equal Protection Cases in America

Race, Gender and Sexual Orientation

EDITED BY

ANNE RICHARDSON OAKES
Birmingham City University, UK

Routledge
Taylor & Francis Group
LONDON AND NEW YORK

First published 2015 by Ashgate Publishing

2 Park Square, Milton Park, Abingdon, Oxon OX14 4RN
711 Third Avenue, New York, NY 10017, USA

Routledge is an imprint of the Taylor & Francis Group, an informa business

First issued in paperback 2017

British Library Cataloguing in Publication Data
A catalogue record for this book is available from the British Library.

Library of Congress Cataloging-in-Publication Data
Controversies in equal protection cases in America : race, gender and sexual orientation / By Anne Richardson Oakes.
pages cm. – (Controversies in American constitutional law)
Includes bibliographical references and index.
ISBN 978-1-4094-5427-4 (hardback)
1. Discrimination–Law and legislation–United States. 2. Equality before the law–United States.
I. Oakes, Anne Richardson, editor.
KF4755.C664 2015
342.7308'5–dc23

2014044644

ISBN 978-1-4094-5427-4 (hbk)
ISBN 978-1-138-73217-9 (pbk)

Contents

Contributors

William D. Araiza is Professor of Law at Brooklyn Law School.

Mario L. Barnes is Professor of Law and Senior Associate Dean for Academic Affairs at the University of California, Irvine School of Law, with a joint appointment in Law & Criminology, Law & Society.

Erwin Chemerinsky is founding Dean and Distinguished Professor of Law, and Raymond Pryke Professor of First Amendment Law, at the University of California, Irvine School of Law, with a joint appointment in Political Science.

Pat K. Chew is Judge J. Quint Salmon and Anne Salmon Chaired Professor at the University of Pittsburgh School of Law.

John G. Culhane is Professor of Law at Widener University School of Law.

Haydn Davies is Director of Research in the School of Law at Birmingham City University.

Martha Albertson Fineman is Robert W. Woodruff Professor of Law at Emory University School of Law.

Patrick M. Garry is Professor of Law at the University of South Dakota.

Julie A. Greenberg is Professor of Law at Thomas Jefferson School of Law, San Diego.

Sora Han is Assistant Professor in the Department of Criminology, Law and Society, University of California, Irvine.

Ian F. Haney López is John H. Boalt Professor of Law at the University of California, Berkeley.

Jennifer S. Hendricks is Associate Professor at the University of Colorado Law School.

Laura A. Hernández is Associate Professor at Baylor Law School.

Anthony C. Infanti is Senior Associate Dean for Academic Affairs and Professor of Law.

Anne Richardson Oakes is Reader in American Legal Studies in the School of Law Birmingham City University, U.K.

Angela Onwuachi-Willig is Charles M. and Marion J. Kierscht Professor of Law at the University of Iowa College of Law.

Michael Paris is Associate Professor of Political Science at the College of Staten Island, City University of New York.

Janet W. Schofield is Professor of Psychology and Senior Scientist Emerita at the University of Pittsburgh and Professor and Senior Advisor at Royal Thimphu College in Bhutan.

Francisco Valdes is Professor of Law and Dean's Distinguished Scholar at the University of Miami School of Law.

Acknowledgments

The shifting landscape of equal protection during the preparation of this collection has presented considerable challenges to the contributors to this book. I would like to thank them for their flexibility and perseverance and general patience and good humour during what has turned out to be a more protracted process than originally envisaged.

I dedicate this book to my colleagues in the Centre for American Legal Studies, Birmingham City University in recognition of their friendship and support. My special thanks to my research assistants and former students, Daniel Gough and Amna Nazir, whose excellent work has been very much appreciated.

Chapter 1
Introduction: Equal Protection and the Problem of Identity

Anne Richardson Oakes

Famously dismissed as a "last resort" of constitutional lawyers[1] and "a dubious weapon in the armory of judicial review," the Equal Protection Clause of the Fourteenth Amendment, as Jacobus tenBroek predicted, did indeed come into its own.[2] *Brown v. Board of Education*, which tenBroek lived to see (he died in 1968 at the age of 59), has come to represent the clause's apotheosis but what would he have made of the controversies that followed? More than half a century later, current jurisprudence positions *Brown* in new contexts and at the center of new debates. Most recently, the possibilities of affirmative action for the benefit of racial minorities have been severely curtailed and the enforcement clause of the Voting Rights Act, one of the major victories of the civil rights era, has in effect been neutralized.[3] At the same time the Supreme Court led by Chief Justice Roberts has handed down decisions which herald new landmarks in the struggle for recognition of gay and lesbian rights. Specifically, the Court's apparent receptivity to anti-subordination arguments in the context of same sex marriage adds particular poignancy to those critics of its "colorblind constitution," who argue that the anti-classification principles in matters of race have little basis in the original meaning of the Fourteenth Amendment and that, in matters of race at least, equal protection jurisprudence is now mired in what looks like a dead-end.

Recruited by Thurgood Marshall to work on the historical origins of the post-civil war amendment, tenBroek's scholarship and that of his collaborator Howard Jay Graham, who wrote a substantial portion of the NAACP's final brief in *Brown v. Board of Education*, supported a historical narrative of equal protection as the constitutional vehicle for the nation's commitment to a founding promise of equality which was context specific.[4] The brief submitted to the Court on November 16, 1953 responded to specific questions posed by the deadlocked Vinson Court and was accompanied, in the form of a supplement, by Graham's analysis of the theoretical underpinnings of the Fourteenth Amendment.[5] Headed *An Analysis of the Political, Social, and Legal Theories Underlying the Fourteenth Amendment*, the supplement trenchantly located the origins of the Fourteenth Amendment in the anti-slavery sentiment that moved the members of the Thirty-Ninth Congress. The three clauses of Section One of the Fourteenth Amendment, Graham claimed, represented the "constitutionalization" of an "ethico-moral" commitment on the part of the Thirty-Ninth Congress to tackle race-based distinctions because these were a mark of caste and this was the legacy of slavery:

> The first Section of the Fourteenth Amendment did not spring full blown from the brow of any individual proponent. Primitive natural rights theories and earlier constitutional forms were the origins of its equal protection-due process-privileges and immunities trilogy. The occasion for the metamorphosis of moral premises to full-fledged constitutional status was the attack on the American system of slavery. During the

1 Buck v. Bell, 274 U.S. 200 (1927) (Holmes J.).

2 Joseph Tussman & Jacobus tenBroek, *The Equal Protection of the Laws*, 37 CALIF. L. REV. 341 (1949) (discussing interpretation of the Constitution's Due Process and Equal Protection Clauses and pointing out that the tide had been running against equality and in favor of due process).

3 Shelby County v. Holder, 133 S.Ct. 2612 (2013).

4 Felicia Kornbluh, Disability, *Civil Rights and Law: Jacobus tenBroek, Howard Jay Graham, and the New Politics of Equality in the Middle Twentieth Century* (Jan. 30, 2012) available at http://www.law.berkeley.edu/1108.htm.

5 Brief for the Appellants in Nos 1, 2 and 4, and for Respondents in No. 10 on Reargument, Brown v. Bd. of Educ., WL 48699, 199 (Nov. 16, 1953).

> long antislavery crusade, the trilogy became a form of shorthand for, and the spearhead of, the whole of the argument against distinctions and caste based on race.[6]

Pointing out that 10 of the 15 members of the Joint Committee on Reconstruction had antislavery backgrounds, Graham argued to the shared understandings of the men who formulated and submitted the Amendment. In their minds, the phrases "privileges and immunities," "equal protection," and "due process" had a shared and specific significance and this was opposition to slavery. Thus whilst equality as an absolute concept required that no legal recognition be given to racial distinctions of any kind, the all-important context was concern with caste and that "great reservoir of prejudice and evil" upon which racial distinctions drew. From this perspective "the notion that any state could impose such distinctions was totally incompatible with antislavery doctrine."[7]

Sixty plus years later, the authority of *Brown v. Board of Education* is unassailable but the correct interpretation of the underlying values of the Equal Protection Clause continues to generate heated debate. Nowhere is this more important than in the current arguments concerning the constitutionality of affirmative action. In *Parents Involved v. Community Schools*, Chief Justice Roberts memorably asserted that history would be heard.[8] His predecessor, Earl Warren, however, placed little weight upon history. The NAACP brief notwithstanding, the Chief Justice, in pragmatic fashion, recognized the limitations of appeals to history to solve the problems of today. Absent the ability to turn back the clock, he argued, what was important was the here and now; specifically the effect of segregated schooling needed to be addressed by reference to the "full development" of public education and "its present place in American life."[9] "Only in this way," he insisted, "can it be determined if segregation in public schools deprives these plaintiffs of the equal protection of the laws."[10]

This "proud ahistoricism" may be "one of *Brown's* most remarkable characteristics"[11] but in constitutional terms it was unusual and possibly regrettable. Judicial appeals to history can be important justificatory tools in legal argument but where the driving purpose is the largely rhetorical objective "of reassuring citizens that courts are acting consistently with deeply held values," historians warn us to approach with care.[12] "History teaches that history teaches nothing." Hegel's aphorism is well known[13] but as Professors Sarat and Kearns remind us, "law uses history to tell us who we are."[14] The current Chief Justice's rhetoric justifies a specific interpretation of the Equal Protection Clause which now invokes Justice Harlan's *Plessy* dissent to prohibit affirmative action in the name of a colorblind constitution which tolerates no classifications of race whether benign or malign. It is an interpretation which conceptualizes equal protection in terms of formal equality, with a commitment to the values of individual moral significance and equality of opportunity for all. These are values which resonate strongly with the national psyche but they are not immediately best-suited to assist those who seek to argue that unequal treatment can sometimes be constitutionally justified.

"All men," wrote Aristotle "think justice to be a sort of equality … . But there still remains a question: equality or inequality of what?"[15] In 1886, the Supreme Court in *Yick Wo v. Hopkins* ruled that "[t]he equal

---

6 *Id.* at 199.

7 *Id.* at 234–35.

8 Parents Involved in Cmty. Sch. v. Seattle Sch. Dist. No. 1, 551 U.S. 701, 705 2007):"when it comes to using race to assign children to schools, history will be heard."(Roberts C.J.).

9 Brown v. Bd of Educ., 347 U.S. 483, 492–93 (1954).

10 *Id.*

11 Christopher W. Schmidt, *Listening to History? Parents Involved and the Colorblind Constitution*, The Legal Workshop, Cornell Law Rev. Online (Apr. 30, 2009), available at http://legalworkshop.org/2009/04/30/listening-to-history-parents-involved-brown-and-the-colorblind-constitution#fn-1157–25.

12 Jack Rakove, *Fidelity through History*, 65 Fordham L. Rev. 1591(1997). *See* Laura Kalman, The Strange Career of Legal Liberalism, 180 (1996): "I doubt any historian considers the past authoritative. At best it may be edifying, but to the historian there are no 'lessons from the past.'"

13 Georg Wilhelm Friedrich Hegel, Lectures on the Philosophy of History (J. Sibree trans. 1914).

14 Austin Sarat & Thomas R. Kearns, *Writing History & Registering Memory in Legal Decisions & Practices: An Introduction*, in History Memory & the Law 5 (Austin Sarat & Thomas R. Kearns eds 2002).

15 Aristotle, The Politics, Book III Part xii (B. Jowett trans. 1885).

protection of the laws is a pledge of the protection of equal laws."[16] These words have never been controverted but as the subsequent debates concerning the scope and meaning of the Equal Protection Clause indicate, that conclusion was by no means inevitable. In the 1965 revised edition of his book *Equal under Law*, tenBroek, looking back at *Brown*, pondered the impact of the Court's decision in terms of the meaning of "equality." The sentence "[a]ll men are created equal" is not a declaration but an imperative, he asserted, which in Western European democracies in general and the United States in particular can have three possible dimensions. The first, "one for one" is directed towards political participation, is most commonly expressed in the slogan "one person, one vote" and comes down to this: "there are few differences among men that may be taken into account when considering their right to participate in the suffrage and those differences that may be taken into account must be carefully scrutinized for their relevance to the purpose of the suffrage."[17] The second, the "natural rights" model, however, references basic social contract ideas of inalienable rights, the institution of government to protect those rights; government by consent of the governed; and the right of the people to change that government, either by peaceful means or by revolution, whenever it fails to fulfill its purpose.[18] This version, he argues, in Declaration of Independence and abolitionist usage, was "almost exclusively substantive in character"—that is, the fundamental idea is the protection of natural rights, so that the Fourteenth Amendment confirms the duty of governments in this respect:

> The phrase "no state shall ... deny" therefore becomes a single command: Each state shall supply. And the whole clause is understood to mean: Each state shall supply the protection of the laws to men in their natural rights and the protection shall always be equal to all men. It was because the protection of the laws had previously been denied to some men that the word "equal" was used.[19]

His third model is the *Hopkins* equal treatment or anti-classification/non-discrimination definition which is neutral in the sense that it makes no assertions of specific rights but demands rather that the laws apply equally to all persons within the jurisdiction. It is this model of equality which now dominates equal protection jurisprudence but as tenBroek himself explained, if governments are to carry out what is arguably their primary function, that is, decision-making concerning the allocation of society's resources, then the exercise of some kind of discrimination in so doing cannot be avoided and we must be clear why exactly it is that some kinds of unequal treatment are more problematic than others. As Professor Brake reminds us, unequal treatment is only problematic when it is based on unacceptable criteria, but to the extent that these are socially determined and mutable over time, equality claims are "largely about challenges to existing social meaning" so that what is at stake is the place of the Constitution in the reconstruction of social relationships.[20]

"With all its blandness, simplicity, and technical imprecision, the *Brown* opinion of the Chief Justice contains the stuff of which history is made."[21] tenBroek's verdict works because, rather than in spite of, the open-texture of *Brown*. As James Boyd White reminds us, the law "is a not an abstract system or scheme of rules ... but an inherently unstable structure of thought and expression" which builds upon, reflects, and mediates underlying tensions not only between "ordinary language" and legal and other specialized discourses, but also "between language itself and the mute world that lies beneath it."[22] The current Chief Justice turns to history to authenticate a specific interpretation and validate a specific conclusion: the Equal Protection Clause of the Fourteenth Amendment "protect[s] persons, not groups";[23] "[t]he way to stop discrimination on the basis of race is to stop discriminating on the basis of race."[24] To his critics, he exploits *Brown*'s open-

---

16 Yick Wo v. Hopkins, 118 U.S. 356, 359 (1886) (Matthews J.).

17 Jacobus tenBroek, Equal under Law 19 (First Collier Books 1965) (1951).

18 *Id.* at 20–21

19 *Id.*

20 Deborah L. Brake, *When Equality Leaves Everyone Worse Off: The Problem of Leveling Down in Equality Law*, 46 Wm. & Mary L. Rev. 513, 566, 573 (2004).

21 tenBroek, *supra* note 16 at 24 (First Collier Books 1965) (1961).

22 James Boyd White, *An Old-Fashioned View of the Nature of Law*, 12 Theoretical Inquiries L. 381, 381 (2011).

23 *Id.* at 743 (quoting Adarand Constructors Inc. v. Peña, 515 U.S. 200, 227 (1995) (emphasis in the original).

24 *Id.* at 748.

texture and recasts its spirit to suit his own political vision, but his predecessor's success lay in his ability to capture a social and political imagination whose time had come. How history will view the Roberts Court remains to be seen but as the chapters in this collection reveal, the extent to which the Court's equal protection judgments adequately respond to perceptions of structural disadvantage and unjustified discrimination is very much a contemporary concern. Nowhere is this more pressing than in relation to those hot-button issues of contemporary America: race, gender, and sexual orientation.

This collection brings together contributors with a range of perspectives to interrogate the legal, theoretical, and factual assumptions which shape case law in these areas and to consider the extent to which they satisfactorily address contemporary concerns with social hierarchies and norms. The collection is divided into five parts and moves from the paradigm of race, the traditional concern of equal protection, to consider, via issues of gender and sexual orientation, the extent to which equal protection principles, despite, or indeed because of, their specific historical genesis, have contemporary resonance with and can be made to work for new and emerging minorities and groupings. The chapters foreground in different ways the connections between equal protection jurisprudence, discrimination in its contemporary manifestations, the implications of identity politics, and the moral and political conceptualizations of equality that represent the parameters of debate. They draw on historical analysis and disciplinary insights of the social sciences to bridge the gap between theory and practice, a characteristic endeavor of equal protection lawyering since Thurgood Marshall and his team first trialed the now more or less obligatory social science amicus curiae brief to success in *Brown*.[25] Notwithstanding the recent same sex marriage gains, the overall tone is bleak and generally realistic concerning the limits of constitutional litigation in general and the Equal Protection Clause in particular as mechanisms for achieving enduring social change.

The chapters begin with critical histories that set a pessimistic tone. Current race jurisprudence, argues Valdes, opening the collection, discloses a "judicially stunted" conception of equality" which turns its back on slavery as the original constitutional sin. The "unholy history" that emerges should "disabuse living Americans of any belief that judicial protection of equality is a front line of U.S. constitutionalism." Nevertheless, he argues, the extent to which "identity politics," by which he means the politics and ideologies of White supremacy, have shaped and continue to inflect Supreme Court race discourse, must be understood as a

> predicate for effective equality strategies going forward—strategies that appreciate the limits of law, and of adjudication in particular, and that include, but do not exaggerate, the role or potential of federal litigation and the judicial review power in ongoing struggles over constitutional equality (and democracy) in U.S. law and society over the course of a new millennium.[26]

The intuition that there must be a better prospect with which to go forward, of the possibility of a third reconstruction to undo "what the judges have done,"[27] tempers the underlying pessimism but for Han, in the chapter that follows, the escape from what she terms the "dead end" of the Equal Protection Clause lies not in constitutional jurisprudence, but in a psychological reawakening or reassertion of the "claim of the slave" in pursuit of a fugitive law of freedom. Han's critique of the Court's affirmative action and enforcement clause jurisprudence becomes a search for a critical knowledge of race and law via a methodology of learning through remembrance. An anamnesis of slavery, she argues, becomes a positive response to Derrick Bell's racial pessimism when it can ground a new racial politic centered on a narrative of racial identity mediated in terms of refusal of renunciation.

Both chapters, in different ways, bring into play what feminist scholar Linda Nicholson identifies as the contradictory stance in contemporary national discourse concerning the significance to be attached to identity differentiations and specifically those of race, gender, and sexual orientation. On the one hand, she argues:

25 It was actually Robert L. Carter, lead attorney for the plaintiffs in *Briggs v. Elliott*, 342 U.S. 350 (1952) (one of the five cases heard together in the U.S. Supreme Court under the name of *Brown v. Board of Education*) who secured the involvement of social scientists and particularly of Kenneth B. Clark, who provided evidence in the *Briggs* case on the negative effects of segregation on the psychological development of Black children.

26 Valdes, *infra*.

27 *Id.*

> race and gender are more than ever recognized as important phenomena of social life. In the 2008 presidential campaign, we constantly talked about both as influencing the outcome. We wondered whether Hillary Clinton's crying was helpful or not to her campaign for the Democratic Party's presidential nomination. We pondered how the racial remarks of Barack Obama's pastor might hurt Obama's chances. We talked about Clinton's appeal to older, white women and Obama's problems with older, white men. The topics of race and gender were all over the news, with few disputing the assumption that race and gender would in some ways affect the outcome. But, at the same time, even while we were making the above claims, we also kept saying that the era of identity politics was dead and that Americans were now in a "post" racial and "post" gender era. And now that that presidential race is behind us, we still continue to assume that race and gender profoundly influence social life even as we continue to proclaim that race and gender no longer matter.[28]

This confusion she attributes to the influence of "environmentalism," that is, the assumption that the categories of race and gender depict bodily and behavioral characteristics which are stable across time and social context. It is this assumption which drove twentieth-century challenges to racism and sexism but it did so in two mutually contradictory ways. On the one hand, the civil rights gains of the twentieth century were largely built on assumptions that denied the significance of racial and gender differences in favor of universalist assertions of the commonality of human needs and aspirations. On the other hand, it was disillusion with the ability of universalist discourses to tackle the structural mechanisms by which racism and sexism remained socially embedded that gave rise in the late 1960s and early 1970s to so-called identity politics or a politics based upon assertions of the significance of racial and sexual difference.[29]

As ideas concerning the "reality and importance of socially caused differences" have become more widely accepted, the result has been an unresolved tension between denial and acceptance of difference in discourse concerning the significance of race and gender which now increasingly extends to matters of sexual orientation.[30] Both however, depend upon Nicholson's "environmentalist" assumptions which modern science and cultural and psychoanalytical theory do much to challenge. In an influential lecture, Stuart Hall reminded his audience that although "one of those major concepts which organize the great classificatory systems of difference which operate in human society," in the absence of any sustainable biological or genetic account, race must be regarded as a "floating signifier."[31] By this he meant that "race" is a discursive construct, part of the "systems and concepts of a culture," of its "making meaning practices" which because they are culturally determined can never be "finally or trans-historically fixed."[32] Like all signifiers, that of race will be subject to what he describes as

> the constant process of redefinition and appropriation, to the losing of old meanings, and the appropriation and collection on contracting new ones, to the endless process of being constantly re-signified, made to mean something different in different cultures, in different historical formations, at different moments of time.[33]

The insight that matters of identity have a symbolic or linguistic dimension which is not constant but is mutable across time and context is not confined to race but has found particular resonance in relation to gender and sexual orientation in the work of Judith Butler.[34] Her analysis of identity as performance sees externalities of behavior and speech function not as reflections or expressions of that which is interior, but rather as processes of cultural signification because they acquire meaning via social interpretation. The recognition that the categorizations of identity in terms of race gender and sexual orientation do not represent fixed sets of attributes, in so far as it affords the possibility of "slide" or contextual fluidity, has the capacity to

---

28 Linda Nicholson, *Identity after Identity Politics*, 33 Wash. U. J.L. & Pol'y 43, 43–44 (2010).

29 *Id.*

30 *Id.*

31 Stuart Hall, *Is Race a Floating Signifier?* The Sage Anniversary Lecture and the Hayard Lecture Goldsmiths College/Lewisham Council (1996) (transcript available at www.mediaed.org/wp/transcripts).

32 *Id.* (emphasis in the original).

33 *Id.*

34 *See, e.g.*, the ground-breaker, Judith Butler, Gender Trouble: Feminism and the Subversion of Identity (1990).

break down binary oppositions which can be subversive and thus potentially personally liberating. However, the extent to which matters of race, gender and sexual orientation, all of which go to the heart of personal identity, should find constitutional recognition in a post-identity world is an issue that underpins much of contemporary equal protection discourse and becomes a unifying theme for this collection. Han's return to Bell's call for a reconstruction of identity raises directly the extent to which critical theory can set an agenda for political and thus legal practice.

Butler's emphasis on identity as discursively constrained has evoked the charge that her political agenda is underdeveloped. Martha Nussbaum's uncompromising critique still has the power to sting:

> What precisely does Butler offer when she counsels subversion? She tells us to engage in parodic performances, but she warns us that the dream of escaping altogether from the oppressive structures is just a dream: it is within the oppressive structures that we must find little spaces for resistance, and this resistance cannot hope to change the overall situation … .
>
> Isn't this like saying to a slave that the institution of slavery will never change, but you can find ways of mocking it and subverting it, finding your personal freedom within those acts of carefully limited defiance? Yet it is a fact that the institution of slavery can be changed, and was changed--but not by people who took a Butler-like view of the possibilities. It was changed because people did not rest content with parodic performance; they demanded, and to some extent they got, social upheaval.[35]

This is a critique that Butler herself should not accept. If there is no foundational ontology of identity but only normative injunctions "that [operate] insidiously by installing [themselves] into political discourse as its necessary ground," then the task of revealing, challenging, and reconfiguring those injunctions becomes a precursor to societal change and thus in and of itself a political activity.[36] Moreover, as Nicholson points out, the insight that Butler's ideas have significance to the social category of race is not to lose sight of what she terms the "social facticity and structural importance" of these categorizations nor "to deny that social meanings and social structures interact with each other in complex ways":

> When we recognize that the laws and institutions governing race and gender extend back within the United States to the very days of its founding, have had major social effects on the distribution of economic resources, as well as on many other aspects of social life, and that much of the legacy of those effects are still with us, then we must think of gender and race in social structural as well as in symbolic/linguistic terms and assess the specificity/pervasiveness of such structures as well as the specificity/pervasiveness of our understandings of race and gender.[37]

Professor Guinier's call for a new racial literacy with "the capacity to decipher the durable racial grammar that structures racialized hierarchies and frames the narrative of our republic" makes much the same point,[38] but as the chapters in Parts II and III of this collection consider, the prospects for an equal protection jurisprudence conceptualized in ways that can untangle the complex relationships between matters of identity and socio-economic circumstance remain bleak. Nowhere is this more contentious than in relation to the use of race-based remedies in a "post-racial era."

---

35 Martha Nussbaum, *The Professor of Parody*, The New Republic (1999) http://www.tnr.com/archive/0299/022299/nussbaum022299.html.

36 Butler, *supra* note 35 at 148.

37 Nicholson, *supra* note 29 at 73.

38 *See* Lani Guinier, *From Racial Liberalism to Racial Literacy:* Brown v. Board of Education *and the Interest-Divergence Dilemma*, J. Am Hist. 92 (2004); *Race and Reality in a Front-Porch Encounter*, The Chronicle of Higher Education (July 30 2008) available at http://chronicle.com/article/RaceReality-in-a/47509/.

Affirmative Action: The Problem of "Race" in a "Post-Racial Era"

For Haney López, writing in this collection, a court under the influence of "the most conservative cohort of justices in a century" stands accused of "judicial closed-mindedness [and] an unwillingness to engage with and thus potentially learn about the operation and evolution of an enduring form of injustice."[39] He argues that the "intentional blindness of [current jurisprudence] represents not a genuine application of equal protection law, but a successful effort by conservative judges to protect themselves from discomfiting evidence that racial mistreatment persists."[40] Willing to wound, though as yet not ready to strike, the Court masks "reticence in attacking civil rights" with "shrewd doctrinal maneuvering" which declines, for example, to prohibit affirmative action outright but nevertheless obstructed the challenged program on the ground that strict scrutiny was not applied strictly enough, or strike the key enforcement provision of the Voting Rights Act, but nevertheless "effectively gutted it" because "the prospects of Congress ... reaching a new accord regarding which states the Act covered are ... dim."[41]

As Paris suggests, the "doctrinal maneuvering" which has characterized the Court's responses to attempts to achieve a racially diverse student population stems from the opacity of a *Brown* mandate which used the language of discrimination but did not make clear whether this was always objectionable. "In the field of public education the doctrine of 'separate but equal' has no place."[42] So asserted the *Brown* court and the conclusion that separate educational facilities deprived the Black plaintiffs of the constitutional guarantee of the equal protection of the law was clear. The rationale, however, was not. To support its ruling, the Court gave three reasons. A dual system of education which separated children on the grounds of race violated the Equal Protection Clause of the Fourteenth Amendment[43] because: a) state-mandated separation of Black from White children offends the Constitution *per se*;[44] b) governmental discrimination by race causes psychological damage to Black children;[45] and c) governmental discrimination by race deprives Black children of the educational benefits of mixing with White children.[46] What the Court did not make clear was the mischief to which the constitutional guarantee is addressed. Specifically, it did not spell out whether the Constitution prohibits race-based classifications *per se* or merely those classifications that are invidious because they are mechanisms of racial subordination.

In the context of *Brown* itself, it did not need to do so; the separate provision of education required by Southern states in the first half of the twentieth century was part of a caste system which assigned subordinate status to African-Americans on the basis of their race or color.[47] From this point of view a dual system of education was necessarily invidious. For *Brown* supporters, this hardly needed stating.[48] Racial equality could not be accomplished whilst the races were separated so to prohibit discrimination was to promote integration.[49] As Thurgood Marshall later judicially explained, "unless our children begin to learn together, there is little hope that our people will ever learn to live together."[50]

---

39 Haney López, *infra*.

40 *Id.*

41 *Id.* at 44.

42 *Brown I*, 347 U.S. at 495.

43 U.S. Const., amend. XIV, § 1.

44 *Brown I*, 347 U.S. 483 (1954) at 495 "Separate educational facilities are inherently unequal."

45 *Id.* "To separate [children] from others of similar age and qualifications solely because of their race generates a feeling of inferiority as to their status in the community that may affect their hearts and minds in a way unlikely ever to be undone."

46 *Id.* citing *Sweatt v. Painter*, 339 U.S. 629 (1950), and *McLaurin v. Oklahoma State Regents*, 339 U.S. 637 (1950) regarding the "intangible" benefits for a law student of mixing with White students, that is, "his ability to study, to engage in discussions and exchange views with other students and, in general, to learn his profession."

47 *See generally* C. Vann Woodward, The Strange Career of Jim Crow (2001).

48 *See* James E. Ryan, *The Supreme Court and Voluntary Integration*, 121 Harv. L. Rev. 131, 152 (2007): ("[t]he assumption of those who argued for and supported Brown was that prohibiting segregation would lead to integration").

49 *See* J. Harvie Wilkinson III, *The Law of Civil Rights and the Dangers of Separatism in Multicultural America*, 47 Stan. L. Rev. 993, 994 (1995): "[t]he premise of Brown v. Board of Education was simple: Racial integration, or at least the end of the de jure segregation, would overcome the invidious failure of separatism."

50 Milliken v. Bradley, 418 U.S. 717, 783 (1974) (Marshall, J., dissenting).

After *Brown*, wrote civil rights attorney Robert L. Carter, it seemed certain that the civil rights fight had been won, but 50 years on, his confidence seemed misplaced.[51] The latent ambiguity in the reasoning sustains a different court with a new vision and a different language for the relationship between race and social justice and constitutes a fault line in the narrative of racial progress that was the promise of *Brown*. What the Constitution now requires is not integration but a society free from official and intentional classification on the grounds of race.[52]

The problem was apparent in the conceptualization of the *Brown* remedy.[53] Twelve months after the Court handed down its decision, *Brown II* directed federal courts to supervise implementation of the remedial process but was deliberately vague as to how this was to be done, and gave little guidance as to how judicial discretion was to be exercised.[54] Significantly, the words "segregation," "desegregation," and "integration" were not used. Instead, the formulations of the Court underwent a significant shift. What was at stake, said the Chief Justice, was "the personal interest of the plaintiffs in admission to public schools as soon as practicable on a nondiscriminatory basis."[55] The earlier ruling, he claimed, asserted "the fundamental principle that racial discrimination in public education is unconstitutional."[56] All legal provisions "requiring or permitting such discrimination must yield to this principle."[57]

For more than 10 years, Southern states, in opposition, relied upon these words to offer Black students facially neutral "freedom of choice" plans producing only minimal changes in the racial composition of the public school population until 1968 when the U.S. Supreme Court, in effect, acknowledged that "desegregation" required race-conscious integrative action.[58] Nearly 60 years later, however, a Supreme Court of a very different political persuasion relies upon the same words to justify its commitment to a symmetrical "color-blind constitution" which protects both Whites and Blacks from racial classification.[59] The effect is to separate equal protection jurisprudence from its contextual link with racial subordination and to define the current attempts of school districts to achieve an integrated student population as the pursuit of racial balance for its own sake, tantamount in Justice Thomas's terms to mere "classroom aesthetics" or the desire to have a classroom that looks a particular way.[60]

Within the constraints of the anti-classification model which now controls the Court's affirmative action jurisprudence, those who seek to persuade the Court that these programs continue to be a constitutionally appropriate response to a pattern of exclusion that is the legacy of discrimination must, first, explain exactly how race now operates to shape access to educational opportunity and thus institutional and political power and, second, demonstrate precisely how the programs in question will untangle and address the shifting variables of race, class, and geography. Decoded in this way and detached from constraints of biology and/or phenotype, the idea of race can become a powerful tool of social critique with the potential, when linked to

---

51 Robert L. Carter, A Matter of Law: A Memoir of Struggle in the Cause of Equal Rights 135 (2005); Robert L. Carter, *Public School Desegregation: A Contemporary Analysis*, 37 St L. U. L.J. 885, 885 (1993) ("With the 1954 declaration in *Brown v. Board of Education*, I believed the path was then clear for Black children to receive an equal education. My confidence in the inevitability of this result now seems naive").

52 *See* Parents Involved in Cmty. Sch. v. Seattle Sch. Dist. No. 551 U.S. 701 (2007).

53 *See, e.g.*, J. Harvie Wilkinson III, From Brown to Bakke 61–82 (1979).

54 Brown v. Bd. of Educ. (*Brown II*), 349 U.S. 294, 300 (1955).

55 *Brown II*, 349 U.S. at 300.

56 *Id.* at 298.

57 *Id.*

58 *See* Green v. Cnty Sch. Bd., 391 U.S. 430, 437–38 (1968) (noting that 10 years after *Brown*, a "freedom of choice" policy had made virtually no changes to the racial composition of the schools of New Kent County, VA, and quoting Griffin v. Cnty Sch. Bd. of Prince Edward Cnty, 377 U.S. 218, 234 (1964): "[t]he time for mere 'deliberate speed' has run out.". The language of the Court was guarded: "The views of the United States Commission on Civil Rights, which we neither adopt nor refuse to adopt, are as follows: 'Freedom of choice plans, which have tended to perpetuate racially identifiable schools in the Southern and border States, require affirmative action by both Negro and White parents and pupils before such disestablishment can be achieved.'" *Green*, 391 U.S. at 441 n.5.

59 Parents Involved in Cmty. Sch. v. Seattle Sch. Dist. No. 1, 551 U.S. 701 (2007).

60 *Id.* at 750 n.3 (Thomas, J. concurring).

issues gender and sexual orientation, for cross-racial coalitions to emerge.[61] Framing these issues in terms of the distribution of social goods requires the help of social science, but as Schofield and Chew in this collection point out, the Court's track record suggests that the impact in constitutional terms is unlikely to be great.

It is true that, as noted earlier, the use of the social science amicus curiae brief to inform the Court on social and economic matters has had some success in equal protection cases. In *Brown* itself, a social science amicus curiae brief testifying to the adverse psychological effects of segregation upon African-American children[62] apparently hit its mark when Chief Justice Warren's opinion for the Court referred in a footnote to some of the research.[63] Since then the methodological assumptions of the *Brown* research have been challenged,[64] the effect of the footnote much debated and the shifting focus of the Court's equal protection jurisprudence has made demands which social science has struggled to satisfy.[65] Most seriously, however, as Schofield and Chew suggest, the fact that the practice has become routine on both sides has generated a perception on the part of some members of the Court that the science itself is politicized to such an extent that its value has become undermined.

In *Parents Involved*, out of a total of 64 amicus curiae briefs, 27 made reference to or relied upon social science research.[66] Of these the majority, including one filed by 553 social scientists supported the school respondents with research documenting the educational benefits of racial diversity and the harms of racially isolated minority schools.[67] In the plurality opinion, the evidence was more or less completely ignored, but in the dissent of Justice Breyer and the concurrence of Justice Thomas we see two very different views of the extent to which questions of racial justice can be conceptualized in empirical terms.

For Justice Breyer, the Louisville and Seattle plans needed to be seen in a context of attempts to tackle racial justice conceptualized in terms of "segregation," "integration," and then "resegregation."[68] From

61 *See on this, e.g.*, Lani Guinier & Gerald Torres, The Miner's Canary: Enlisting Race, Resisting Power, Transforming Democracy, 14–16 (2002).

62 Brief for Appellants at 5, Oliver Brown, et al., Appellants, v. Bd. of Educ. of Topeka, KS et al., 347 U.S. 483 (1954) (No. 1).

63 Brown v. Bd. of Educ., 347 U.S. 483, 495 n.11 (1954) (*Brown I*).

64 *See* Roy L. Brooks et al., Civil Rights Litigation: Cases and Perspectives, 70 (3d ed. Carolina Academic Press 2005) (1950) (discussing research critical of the so-called "doll studies"). The "doll studies," conducted by Professor Kenneth Clark and his wife and fellow psychologist Mamie, claimed that Black children in New York when given a choice of playing with a Black or White doll showed a clear preference for the White doll. When asked to draw "the nice doll" the children again opted for the White. The Clarks drew the conclusion that Black children in a segregated school system suffered from a sense of self-rejection and a loss of self-worth.

Broadly, the criticisms are of methodology. Prof. Clark himself conducted the interviews with the children who participated in the doll studies, and the Clarks failed to indicate that the response of Black children in the North, who had not been subject to segregation, was not significantly different to that of Black children in the South who were. Deutscher and Chein were criticized for the biased nature of their survey sample. *See generally* Richard Kluger, Simple Justice: The History of Brown v. Board of Education and Black America's Struggle for Equality, 317–18 (Vintage Books ed., Random House 1975).

65 *Brown I*, 347 U.S. at 495 n.1.

66 *See* Race-Conscious Policies for Assigning Students to Schools: Social Science Research and the Supreme Court Cases, Nat'l Acad. of Educ. Comm. on Soc. Sci. Research Evidence on Racial Diversity in Schs. (Robert L. Linn & Kevin G. Welner eds, 2007), available at http://www.naeducation.org/Meredith_Report.pdf [hereinafter NAE Report] (reviewing briefs and social science research submitted in Parents Involved in Cmty. Schs. and Meredith v. Jefferson County Bd. of Educ.).

67 Brief of 553 Social Scientists as Amici Curiae in Support of Respondents, Parents Involved in Cmty. Schs., 551 U.S. 701 (2007) (Nos 05–908, 05–915), 2006 WL 2927079. The two principal opposition briefs filed separately by Professor Armor and associates Thernstrom and Thernstrom and Drs Murphy, Rossell and Walberg disputed these findings but on slightly differing grounds. *See* Brief of David J. Armor, Abigail Thernstrom, and Stephan Thernstrom as Amici Curiae in Support of Petitioners, Parents Involved in Cmty. Schs. v. Seattle Sch. Dist. No. 1, 127 S. Ct. 2738 (2007) (Nos 05–908, 05–915), 2006 WL 2453607; Brief of Amici Curiae Drs. Murphy, Rossell and Walberg in Support of Petitioners, Parents Involved in Cmty. Schs. v. Seattle Sch. Dist. No. 1, 127 S. Ct. 2738 (2007) (Nos 05–908, 05–915), 2006 WL 2459104. (discussed in Erica Frankenberg and Liliana M. Garces, *The Use of Social Science Evidence in Parents Involved and Meredith; Implications for Researchers and Schools*, 46 U. Louisville L. Rev. 703 (2008).

68 Parents Involved in Cmty. Schs. v. Seattle School Dist. No. 1, 551 U.S. 701, 864 (2007) (Breyer, J. dissenting).

this point of view, what he termed the "educational element" ("overcoming the adverse educational effects produced by and associated with highly segregated schools") and the "democratic element" ("producing an educational environment that reflects the 'pluralistic society' in which our children will live")[69] were not only intended to "improve the conditions of all schools for all students, no matter the color of their skin,"[70] but were integral to the "historical and remedial" attempt to overcome "the adverse educational effects produced by, and associated with, highly segregated schools."[71] Citing to the empirical evidence of researchers in support of the educational and democratic enhancements of integrated schooling,[72] Justice Breyer noted that there were competing views but concluded that the evidence was sufficiently weighty ("well established," "firmly established," and "strong") to permit a school board to make its own evaluative judgments without interference from the Court.[73]

For Justice Thomas, however, the absence of consensus on the part of the researchers was fatal. Noting that the claimed educational and democratic benefits of the race-conscious policies were not only not substantiated but in some cases positively controverted by the evidence, he reprised the oppositional stance that he had demonstrated in the precedent case concerning the admissions policies of the University of Michigan Law School.[74] The school boards, he said, were engaged in "classroom racial engineering."[75] This might be a fashionable solution to a particular social problem but constitutional adjudication could not depend upon "the mercy of elected government officials evaluating the evanescent views of a handful of social scientists."[76] "[T]he Constitution," he claimed, "enshrines principles independent of social theories" and those involving race were particularly suspect: "[if] our history has taught us anything, it has taught us to beware of elites bearing racial theories."[77]

The election in 2008 of a Black President was claimed to have inaugurated a new era—a post-racial era—in which the association of blackness with victim status no longer pertains and the role of race as an organizing social force has become much more nuanced so that the language of subordination is no longer required. In this new era, as Barack Obama proclaimed, "[t]here's not a Black America and White America and Latino America and Asian America; there's the United States of America."[78] If this is the language of post-racialism, it is remarkably close to that of the Roberts Court. In *Parents Involved* the Chief Justice cited with approval the words of Justice O'Connor: "[w]e are a Nation not of black and white alone, but one teeming with divergent communities knitted together by various traditions and carried forth, above all, by individuals."[79] Recognition by the Court of racial balancing or proportionality as constitutionally acceptable mechanisms of formulating and implementing social policy goals, he continued, "would 'effectively assur[e] that race will always be relevant in American life, and that the "ultimate goal" of "eliminating entirely from governmental decision-making such irrelevant factors as a human being's race" will never be achieved.'"[80] With these formulations, the message of the Roberts court is only thinly veiled: the time for remedying past social ills if not yet completely over, soon will be, and the nation and the Court must move on. To date only Justice Scalia has been direct on this point:

> [T]here can be no such thing as either a creditor or a debtor race .... To pursue the concept of racial entitlement—even for the most admirable and benign of purposes, is to reinforce and preserve for future mischief the way

69 *Id.*

70 *Id.* at 838–40.

71 *Id.*

72 *Id.* at 839–40.

73 *Id.*

74 Grutter v. Bollinger, 539 U.S. 306 (2003).

75 *Parents Involved in Cmty. Schs.*, 551 U.S. 701, 780 (Thomas, J. concurring).

76 *Id.* at 766.

77 *Id.* at 780–81.

78 Barack Obama, Keynote Address at the Democratic National Convention (July 27, 2004), available at http://www.barackobama.com/2004/07/27/keynote_address_at_ the_2004_de_php.

79 Parents Involved in Cmty. Schs. v. Seattle Sch. Dist. No. 1, 551 U.S. 701,730 (2007) (quoting *Metro Broadcasting, Inc. v. FCC*, 497 U.S. 547, 610 (1990) (O'Connor, J. dissenting).

80 *Id.* (internal citations omitted).

> of thinking that produced race slavery, race privilege, and race hatred. In the eyes of government, we are just one race here. It is American.[81]

The *Grutter* court was more circumspect[82] but the negative view of the relevance of race-based remedies, and the centrality of race as an organizing principle of social justice, which underpins them, clearly found resonance with state voters whose support, in Michigan, of a 2006 election ballot initiative banning the consideration of race in higher education effectively neutralized the impact of the Court's decision.

President Obama, the nation's first African-American President, has faced criticism for his refusal to use the language of race.[83] When the reality is that of White racial dominance, "color-blindness," it is said, becomes a legitimating ideology.[84] Post-racialism is dangerous not just because "it obscures the centrality of race and racism in society," and "serves to reinstate an unchallenged White normativity."[85] More problematic for those who challenge an unqualified narrative of racial progress is the issue of consensus; post-racialism "more effectively achieves what the Racial Backlash movement sought to do over two decades ago—forge a national consensus around the retreat from race-based remedies on the basis that the racial eras of the past have been and should be transcended."[86] If this is so, and the language of legal conservatism is indistinguishable from that of post-racialism, what should we say about the current Court's moral vision? Is the Court colluding in a denial of a legacy of Jim Crow which continues to make race a social reality in the United States or, in the same way as the jurisprudence of Earl Warren's court resonated with a racialized experience whose time for recognition had come, has it simply captured and given legal voice to the differently but now equally socially situated intuitions of ordinary people? And if the latter, how do we respond to Justice Breyer and those who use the language and principles of anti-subordination to advance the view that race and racism still function as key obstacles to equality in contemporary society?

In a recent analysis of the role of race in the criminal justice system, contributor Haney López has commented on a lack of receptivity on the part of White Americans to empirical evidence of racial injustice.[87] He concludes that "partly through colorblindness and partly through the accumulated weight of cultural beliefs and historical practices, most Americans accept that major American institutions are race-neutral so that the inequalities that they are prepared to recognize are regarded not so much a function of race but 'a legitimate feature of social reality.'"[88] He calls for "a countervailing narrative about race as a form of social stratification … to explain how racism actually functions in today's society."[89] He faces the problem that to an audience intuitively committed to the standpoint that society is constructed upon principles that are fundamentally fair, no kind of explanation or factual evidence is likely to be persuasive.[90]

---

81 Adarand v. Constructors, Inc. v. Pena, 515 U.S. 200, 438 (1995) (Scalia, J. concurring in part and concurring in the judgment).

82 Grutter v. Bollinger, 539 U.S. 306, 343 (2003) (O'Connor, J.: "[w]e expect that 25 years from now, the use of racial preferences will no longer be necessary to further the interests approved today.").

83 *See, e.g.*, the criticism that followed President Obama's renunciation of his former pastor, Reverend Jeremiah Wright (summarized in Sumi Cho, *Post-Racialism*, 94 Iowa L. Rev. 1589, 1604 n.35 (2009).

84 Ian F. Haney López, *Post-Racial Racism: Racial Stratification and Mass Incarceration in the Age of Obama*, 98 Cal. L. Rev. 1023, 1061 (2010). *See* Eduardo Bonilla-Silva, Racism without Racists: Color-Blind Racism and the Persistence of Racial Inequality in the United States (2003) (arguing that color-blindness operates as a key mechanism of what he terms "cultural racism": "Cultural racism is a frame that relies on culturally based arguments such as 'Mexicans do not put much emphasis on education' or 'blacks have too many babies' to explain the standing of minorities in society." *Id.*, at 28.

85 *See* Cho, *supra* note 83, at 1592–93 (2009) (arguing that "post racialism in its current iteration is a twenty-first century ideology that reflects a belief that due to racial progress the state need not engage in race-based decision-making or adopt race-based remedies, and that civil society should eschew race as a central organizing principle of social action").

86 *Id.*

87 Haney López, *supra* note 84, at 1064–69.

88 *Id.* at 1066.

89 *Id.* at 1068.

90 *Id.* at 1068 (2010).

The problem for the Court is similar. Whilst a view of social reality is a necessary component of constitutional adjudication, as Professor Dworkin has suggested, the persuasive impact of empirical evidence is always constrained by the underlying normative assumptions.[91] In *Parents Involved*, Justice Breyer called on the empirical findings of social science research in effect to substantiate the continuing effects of race in the context of education but, if Professor Lopez is correct, then this evidence will do little to overcome a basic intuition that the concepts of racism and racial injustice have outlived their usefulness in twenty-first-century America. New types of research into "implicit" or unconscious bias will face the same problem.[92] "Rightly or wrongly," observes Barack Obama, "white guilt has largely exhausted itself in America," and the automatic association of race with victim status now offends liberals and conservatives alike.[93] As I noted earlier, the preference for formal neutrality resonates strongly with values that are dear to the national psyche. When the popular assumption is that race is no longer an issue that needs to displace the default position of formal neutrality, then the Court's refocusing of equal protection jurisprudence represents a recognition of the need to reconnect with its wider audience which was arguably the message of its former Chief Justice. Justice Thomas has dismissed the pursuit of racial diversity as the "faddish slogan of the cognoscenti."[94] This might translate into the vernacular as "so much meaningless jargon." The Court is vulnerable to the criticism that its ability to avoid the conclusions of inconvenient empirical research is tantamount to disingenuity, but if popular acceptance is the key to its legitimacy, the Court must be able to justify its decisions in language that not only people can understand, but also in a way that is responsive to popular standards.

There is, however, a deeper problem for those who seek to persuade the justices to confirm a reality to the connection between race and the opening of the doors of opportunity. Professor Haney López has commented that minorities experience racism but "struggle to explain cogently how race continues to function so deleteriously in American life."[95] If an African-American has become the most powerful man in the world and race is no longer to be an automatic badge of victimhood, what then can we say about what it might mean and how can we conceptualize a connection between race and racialized inequalities in a way of which the Court can take note?

Fisher v. University of Texas was the first federal litigation challenging the use of race in university admissions since the Supreme Court's 2003 decision upholding the University of Michigan Law School's race-conscious admissions process in *Grutter v. Bollinger*.[96] Whilst the 2013 decision of the Supreme Court, as Barnes et al. in this volume have noted, was widely regarded as disappointing, the remarks of Circuit Judge Emilio Garza are flagged up here.[97] The Fifth Circuit by a majority found that the University of Texas plan was modeled on that upheld in *Grutter*, used race as only one factor, looked at applications as a whole in order to achieve the educational benefits of racial diversity, and for these reasons satisfied the constitutional requirements. In a lengthy special concurrence, agreeing with the result but dissociating himself from the reasoning, Judge Garcia commented as follows:

> The idea of dividing people along racial lines is artificial and antiquated. Human beings are not divisible biologically into any set number of races. A world war was fought over such principles. Each individual is unique. And yet, in 2010, governmental decision-makers are still fixated on dividing people into white, black, Hispanic, and other arbitrary subdivisions … .[98]

---

91 *See* Ronald Dworkin, *Social Sciences and Constitutional Rights: The Consequences of Uncertainty* in Education, Social Science and the Judicial Process 20–31 (Ray C. Rist and Ronald J. Anson eds, 1977).

92 *See* Anthony G. Greenwald and Linda Hamilton Krieger, *Implicit Bias: Scientific Foundations*, 94 Cal. L. Rev. 945, 951 (2006) (explaining that "implicit biases are discriminatory biases based on implicit attitudes or implicit stereotypes").

93 Barack Obama, The Audacity of Hope: Thoughts on Reclaiming the American Dream, 247 (2006). Cf. Clarence Thomas, *Victims and Heros in the "Benevolent State,"* 19 Harv. J.L. & Pub. Pol'y 671, 680–81 (1996) (arguing against "the modern ideology of victimology" whether manifested by Blacks or "angry white males").

94 Grutter v. Bollinger, 539 U.S. 306,350 (2003) (Thomas, J. dissenting).

95 Haney López, *supra* note 84, at 1069.

96 Grutter v. Bollinger, 539 U.S. 306 (2003).

97 Fisher v. Univ. of Texas, No. 09–50822 (5th Cir. Feb. 11, 2011).

98 *Fisher*, No. 09–50822, slip op. 86–87. Garza J. supported his assertion with footnoted references to academic sources concluding, "There is broad scholarly support for this proposition." *Id.*, at n.22.

As Stuart Hall reminded us, the loss of faith in a biological explanation of race has serious political implications; the disappearance of the reality of race as a "foundational guarantee" is "a very difficult truth to come to terms with amongst those people who feel [...] the reality of race gives a kind of guarantee or underpinning to their political argument and their aesthetic judgments and their social and cultural beliefs."[99] It is, of course, true, as Nicholson has observed, that social meanings are not confined "in the head only" but find reflection in the laws and institutions of the nation.[100] This means that even in its symbolic/linguistic conceptions, there can be an issue of "social facticity" about race that might ground a constitutional inquiry.[101] If this is to be conceptualized in equal protection terms and the Court is to be persuaded that racism and racist practices still constitute the lived experience of people's lives, then, I suggest, it can only do so as part of a national conversation still to be addressed on the relationship between racial identity in its various manifestations and those problematic areas for American political discourse, the twin issues of poverty and class.[102] Professors Barnes and Chemerinsky have commented elsewhere on the "improvised and largely impoverished" nature of constitutional jurisprudence in the area of socio-economic class.[103] However, when, as they observe, "society overall seems to have lost interest in the problems of the poor"[104] and the desirability of conceptualizing affirmative action in terms of class is itself not uncontested, this should not surprise.[105] Such counter-majoritarian credentials as the Court may have chosen to claim are necessarily limited by parameters of context and have arguably always been overstated; the Court "identifies and protects minority rights only when a majority or near majority of the community has come to deem those rights worthy of protection."[106]

Without a structural analysis of race that can connect with this wider debate, those who would criticize the conservative wing of the Roberts Court for its refusal to conceptualize the pursuit of racial diversity in a way that satisfies current equal protection formulations must be prepared to counter the argument that affirmative action programs not only deflect attention and resources from a national problem of increasing economic inequality, but also perpetuate a language of race and racial identity which is ideologically uncritical and for that reason itself inherently problematic in character.[107]

From Identity to Equality

Affirmative action programs are typically justified in terms of the desire to rectify systemic discrimination against disadvantaged groups which has effectively impeded their ability to participate fully in the social, economic, political, and cultural life of the community and on equal terms with all its members. As Hendricks, writing for this collection, observes, it is an irony (one of many) of equal protection doctrine that remedial sex/gender classifications are easier to justify than remedial or benign racial classifications. Justice Powell

99 Hall, *supra* note 31.

100 Nicholson, *supra* note 28, at 71–72.

101 *Id.*

102 *See* Walter Benn Michaels, The Trouble with Diversity: How We Learned to Love Identity and Ignore Inequality, 75–79 (2006) (arguing that "antiracism plays an essentially conservative role in American politics today." *Id.*, at 17).

103 Mario L. Barnes and Erwin Chemerinsky, *The Disparate Treatment of Race and Class in Constitutional Jurisprudence*, 72 Law & Contemp. Probs. 109, 110 (2009).

104 *Id.* at 125.

105 *Id.* at 124–5 (summarizing the arguments against substituting class-based affirmative action for race-based remedies and citing Deborah C. Malamud, *Assessing Class-Based Affirmative Action*, 47 J. Legal Educ. 452 (1997); Deborah C. Malamud, *Class Based Affirmative Action: Lessons and Caveats*, 74 Tex. L. Rev. 1847 (1996)).

106 Michael J. Klarman, *Rethinking the Civil Rights and Civil Liberties Revolutions*, 82 Va. L. Rev. 1, 18 (1996).

107 *See* Michaels *supra* note 103, at 75–79; Antonia Darder & Rodolfo D. Torres, After Race: Racism after Multiculturalism, 11 (2004) (explaining that "the power of racialized discourse 'allows elite groups to claim enlightened and meritocratic views, while applying racist definitions of social reality.' [...] Such forms [...] of racialized discourse effectively perpetuate [...] racialization—an ideological process of 'delineation of group boundaries and of allocation of persons within those boundaries by primary reference to (supposedly) inherent and/or biological (usually phenotypical) characteristics'") (internal citations omitted).

in *Bakke* explained the reason: the former do not share the same "lengthy and tragic history" as the latter so need not be regarded as inherently offensive. Moreover, he claimed, sex/gender classifications do not create the same "analytical and practical problems" as race classifications because "there are only two possible classifications" and thus "no rival groups" to claim entitlements.[108] Thirty years on, Hendricks observes, "the Court has not yet confronted cases involving intersexed or transsexual individuals under the Equal Protection Clause. It has barely scratched the surface of other claims involving individuals whose gender or sexual identity resists binary classification." Moreover, "[t]he Court's awkward stumbling in cases involving homosexuality does not bespeak a Court inclined to question its binary definition of sex."[109] As the contributors to Parts IV and V of this volume grapple with attempts to bring new groups with new and emerging claims of identity and disadvantage within the scope of the Equal Protection Clause, the central controversy of equal protection jurisprudence, namely the meaning of equality and how it is to be achieved, stands exposed.

This collection of chapters began with a critical history of equal protection and race under judicial review, described by its author Valdes as "the paradigmatic exemplar in U.S. nationhood of equality as jurisprudence." Of the term "paradigm," a dictionary search offers this: "a set of assumptions, concepts, values, and practices that constitutes a way of viewing reality for the community that shares them [...]."[110] Identity debates both organize and polarize these issues.As Professor Fineman, for this collection, observes,

> [o]ur understanding of equality and equal protection has been profoundly shaped by their twentieth century roots as a tool to end slavery and fight blatant forms of racial discrimination. The history of equality into protected classifications, therefore, both defines legal identities for some and also organizes us into political interest groups based on race, ethnicity, gender, and other identity characteristics.[111]

The view is often expressed that whilst equality may be a protean term, if substantive equality is to have meaning it must be something different to the equal treatment or anti-classification/antidiscrimination model which represents the Court's current preference. In other words it must both implicate the removal of barriers which exploit and oppress, and address or at least pay attention to the way in which resources, opportunities, and choices are socially distributed. In Joel Bakan's terms, "social equality" involves "an absence of major disparities in people's resources, political and social power, well-being, and [an absence] of exploitation and oppression."[112] In this sense it may well be the case that substantive equality is a matter for legislatures rather than the judiciary and that this is a view that is "deeply embedded in American equal protection jurisprudence,"[113] but the question is not whether the Court should change society but, rather, whether it can give society a chance to change itself. Most recently, from a different perspective, the same question cast in significantly broader terms has emerged: when the people of a state determine that social issues should not be addressed in a particular way and forbid the state to act, how should the Court respond?

Schuette v. Coalition to Defend Affirmative Action asked the Court to determine whether a state violates the Equal Protection Clause by amending its constitution to prohibit the use of race-conscious policies in public university admissions.[114] The amendment followed a successful voter-initiated ballot and is not confined to race but extends to discrimination against or preferential treatment in favor of any individual or group on the basis of race, sex, color, ethnicity, or national origin in the operation of public employment, public education, or public contracting.

---

108 Regents of the Univ. of Cal. v. Bakke, 438 U.S. 265, 302–03 (1978) (Powell J., announcing judgment). Justice Powell added that the perception of racial classifications as inherently odious stems from a "lengthy and tragic history that gender-based classifications do not share." *Id.* at 303.

109 Hendricks, *infra.*

110 http://www.thefreedictionary.com/paradigm.

111 Fineman, *infra.*

112 Joel Bakan, Just Words: Constitutional Rights and Social Wrongs, 47 (1997).

113 Eileen Kaufman, *Women and Law: A Comparative Analysis of the United States and Indian Supreme Courts' Equality Jurisprudence*, 34 Ga. J. Int'l & Comp. L. 557, 581 (2006).

114 Schuette v. Coalition to Defend Affirmative Action, Integration and Immigrant Rights and Fight for Equality by Any Means Necessary (BAMN), 134 S. Ct. 1623 (2014).

The Sixth Circuit, sitting *en banc*, struck down the amendment by an eight-to-seven vote. "The equal protection of the laws," they stated, "is more than a guarantee of equal treatment under existing law. It is also a guarantee that minority groups may meaningfully participate in the process of creating these laws and the majority may not manipulate the channels of change so as to place unique burdens on issues of importance to them."[115]

In the Supreme Court the political process argument received short shrift. Justice Kennedy, for the plurality, distinguished the precedents and upheld the amendment, asserting that "there is no authority in the Federal Constitution or in this Court's precedents for the Judiciary to set aside Michigan laws that commit to the voters the determination whether racial preferences may be considered in governmental decisions, in particular with respect to school admissions."[116]

Dismissed by the plurality and condemned by Justice Scalia as an unworkable exception that "nearly swallows the rule of structural state sovereignty,"[117] the political-process doctrine speaks to a model of equality that recognizes that equal treatment without a level playing field reinforces rather than displaces structural mechanisms of disadvantage. As President Lyndon B. Johnson so memorably explained, legal equity by itself does not wipe away the scars of exclusion. True equality requires true equality of opportunity but this requires "not just equality as a right and a theory but equality as a fact and equality as a result":[118]

> Men and women of all races are born with the same range of abilities. But ability is not just the product of birth. Ability is stretched or stunted by the family that you live with, and the neighborhood you live in--by the school you go to and the poverty or the richness of your surroundings. It is the product of a hundred unseen forces playing upon the little infant, the child, and finally the man.[119]

Fifty years on, the point is still the same: without an underlying constitutional infrastructure of substantive social and economic rights, access to the political process is not by itself a guarantee that social justice can be achieved.

As statistics of social inequality give the lie to the reality of the American dream of equal opportunity for all,[120] the claim is made that the absence from the U.S. Constitution of welfare rights or "physical needs rights," offering guarantees in relation to matters such as health, education, employment, and social security, and which "appear in some form in roughly 80% of the world's constitutions but have never attained constitutional status in the United States,"[121] threatens to leave U.S. citizens "bereft of the rights protections enjoyed by citizens of peer countries."[122] In this respect the apparent reluctance of the Supreme Court to participate in global dialog concerning the nature and scope of human rights norms may well leave the United States out of sync with an evolving global consensus, but as Valdes, in this collection remarks, "many Americans still believe, mistakenly, that judicial review is a primary or principal bulwark of constitutional equality rights."[123]

---

115 Coalition to Defend Affirmative Action, Integration and Immigrant Rights and Fight for Equality By Any Means Necessary v. Regents of Uni. of Mich., 652 F.3d 607, 474 (6th Cir. 2012) (Cole, Circuit Justice) (quoting *Washington v. Seattle Sch. Dist. No. 1*, 458 U.S. 457, 467 (1983); *Hunter v. Erickson*, 393 U.S. 385, 393 (1969)).

116 *Schuette*, 134 S. Ct. at 1638.

117 *Id.* at 1646 (Scalia J.).

118 President Lyndon B. Johnson's Commencement Address at Howard University: "To Fulfill These Rights" June 4, 1965 available at http://www.lbjlib.utexas.edu/johnson/archives.hom/speeches.hom/650604.asp.

119 *Id.*

120 According to an analysis of tax filings undertaken by U.C. Berkley Economics Professor Emmanuel Saez, Sept. 3 2013, IRC data show that income inequality in the United States has been growing for almost three decades. The income gap between the richest 1% of Americans and the other 99% widened to a record margin in 2012, the top 1% of earners collecting 19.3% of household income, breaking a record previously set in 1927. *See* Emmanuel Saez, *Striking It Richer: The Evolution of Top Incomes in the United States* (updated with 2012 Preliminary Estimates) (Sept. 3, 2013) available at elsa.berkeley.edu/~saez/saez-UStopincomes-2012.pdf.

121 *See e.g.*, David S. Law & Mila Versteeg, The Declining Influence of the United States Constitution, 87 N.Y.U. L. Rev. 762, 766–67 (2012).

122 Ann Elizabeth Mayer, *Reflections on the Proposed United States Reservations to CEDAW: Should the Constitution Be an Obstacle to Human Rights?* 23 Hastings Const. L.Q. 727, 728–29 (1996).

123 Valdes, *infra*.

Professor Martha Albertson Fineman, whose chapter brings this collection to a close, has recently commented on the limitations of equal protection guarantees shaped in antidiscrimination terms; "claims for nondiscrimination based on individual characteristics or statuses," she notes, "are inherently the products of their time and place; they arise during certain periods of history and are shaped in distinct political, cultural, and social contexts."[124] Thus even with the flexibility to add to or amend the categories of individuals and groups to be protected from hostile discrimination that now characterizes "more flexible" constitutions,[125] it is the so-called second-generation universal social or socio-economic rights that now find emphasis in the constitutional jurisprudence of other nations and international human rights treaties that "anchor and give substantive meaning" to equality guarantees.

Ever dismissive of the potential relevance of lessons from abroad, Justice Scalia memorably remarked that "every banana republic has a Bill of Rights." What is more important, he argued, "is the separation of powers and independent courts to enforce the rights of individuals."[126] If, as Valdes suggests, the lesson of the current Court's jurisprudence is that reliance on judicial review for equal protection of the laws invites "a false and dangerous complacency,"[127] then where might his "reformatory energies" be redirected? One solution could be to harness judicial attention to the task of improving the legislative process. As Fineman has observed, there is, at present, "no official, independent, funded body charged with making impact assessments on behalf of historically disadvantaged or particularly economically or socially sensitive individuals and groups … . Given the significance of the issues addressed by legislation […] some form of judicial oversight of the process of legislative deliberation might be warranted."[128]

As she concedes, however, without a fundamental change in attitudes towards the meaning of equality and the responsibilities of the state, the prospects for tackling, let alone eradicating, the institutional social and economic structures that underpin and perpetuate inequality will remain bleak. I give her the final word:

> If unfairness is the point and the objective is elimination of unwarranted discrimination that inhibits equality, why limit inquiry to personal characteristics such as race or gender? The affront to equality occurs not from the drawing of lines or distinctions in and of itself, but arises because of the resulting denial of access of opportunity or exclusion and isolation. The state should have a rigorous duty to ensure for everyone both equal protection of the law and equal opportunity to enjoy the benefits of society. If monitoring is restricted to rooting out discrimination against or stereotyping of personal characteristics, however, the state will only ever be able to partially achieve that objective. To reflect a rigorous commitment to equality it will be necessary to move beyond identities and beyond our current understanding of discrimination to a more universal perspective.[129]

---

124 Martha Albertson Fineman, *Beyond Identities: The Limits of an Antidiscrimination Approach to Equality*, 92 B.U. L. Rev. 1713, 1752 (2012).

125 She references Ernst-Ulrich Petersmann, *Time for a United Nations 'Global Compact' for Integrating Human Rights into the Law of Worldwide Organizations: Lessons from European Integration*, 13 Eur. J. Int'l L. 621, 631 (2002) ("EU law has evolved into a comprehensive […] system for the protection of civil, political, economic and social rights of EU citizens across national frontiers.") and cites to the jurisprudence of the European Court of Human Rights, the Canadian Charter of Rights & Freedoms, the South African Constitution, and the Equality Act of the United Kingdom. Fineman, at 1734.

126 *See* http://www.abajournal.com/news/article/scalia_bests_breyer_for_senate_zingers_asserts_every_banana_republic_has_a_/

127 Valdes, *infra.*

128 Fineman, *supra* note 124, at 1743,

129 Fineman, *infra.*

PART I
Equality and the Dead End of Equal Protection

Chapter 2
Original Sins, Continuing Wrongs: Equality, Democracy, and Supremacy in the U.S. Under Judicial Review

Francisco Valdes

> All men are created equal …
>
> —Declaration of Independence, 1776

> [The black man possesses] no rights which the white man [is] bound to recognize.
>
> —Dred Scott v. Sandford, 1857

Introduction

This foundational contradiction has framed and informed mainstream notions and politics of in/equality in U.S. law and society from before their beginning, and up to this very moment. American history—and current events—have oscillated and lurched across the spectrum of sociolegal possibilities bookended by these two poles. Judges—and other politicians—have been, and are, no exception. Indeed, in the United States, equality's fate seems structurally destined always to fall into the hands of the judges. In conformance with the politics of identity prevalent in the U.S. since before the Republic's founding, judicial review on the whole, and with a few hugely notable exceptions, has consigned equality to near oblivion. The resulting constellation of doctrinal fictions and other inventions forms the substance of constitutional equality's vexed fate under the rule of judicial review. The social and legal result has been an obstruction of justice.

More than a century ago, writing one of the earliest authoritative studies of the public legislative history leading up to the Fourteenth Amendment specifically, the then-Librarian of Congress began his detailed, comprehensive account with these prefatory words:

> The Supreme Court of the United States, [in its decisions in the *Slaughter House Cases* (1873), *Maxwell v. Dow* (1900) and the *Civil Rights Cases* (1883)] have given to the Fourteenth Amendment a meaning quite different from that which many of those who participated in its drafting and ratification intended it to have.[1]

As the twentieth century continued to unfold, the dismay already evident over this early judicial interventionism on behalf of legal racial supremacy continued and grew. Nearly a half-century later, in 1951, on the eve of a second national attempt at Reconstruction, a leading academic legal historian similarly observed:

> Is it anything less than a colossal historic irony that, after three times adopting a program to nationalize the natural rights of men—twice by solemn constitutional amendment (the Thirteenth and Fourteenth) and once by legislative enactment over a presidential veto (the Civil Rights Act of 1875)—(and) each time over the bitter criticism that it would destroy the federal system, the nation should then—particularly through the instrumentality of the Supreme Court—without benefit of formal repeal, adopt the objections and reject the program by refusal to carry it out?[2]

---

1 Horace Edgar Flack, The Adoption of the Fourteenth Amendment 7 (1908).

2 Jacobus TenBroek, The Antislavery Origins of the Fourteenth Amendment 204 (1951).

Equality's colossally ironic fate in the U.S. under judicial review continues to this very day, as shaped principally by the cultural, economic and legal politics of White supremacy and its needs or wants since before this nation-state's formal constitution.

The centrality of race, and specifically the racisms of White supremacy, in the fate of equality in the U.S. is no accident, nor mystery. Race has served as the U.S. equality paradigm because the safety and prosperity of White supremacy and its racial structuring of economically exploitative social class have been the paramount interests dictating the contours of liberty and democracy, as well as equality, since before the beginning. Racial equality politics have catalyzed tectonic changes in the political landscape of the entire country, and continue to hold sway over the country's fortunes and destiny. Moreover, as U.S. history illustrates time and again, racialized law and policy have been primary instruments for the establishment and enforcement of the social, cultural, economic, and other identitarian supremacies favored by the original ruling classes of U.S. settler society. Law—whether explicitly "racial" or not—therefore plays a consistently featured role in the re/production U.S. injustice and inequality.[3]

Understanding this historical coding, and its contemporary correlations or connotations, is not only a prerequisite to following the judicial politics of inequality as practiced today and presented below; it is particularly important because many Americans still believe, mistakenly, that judicial review is a primary or principal bulwark of constitutional rights protecting both (or either) equality and democracy. To be sure, the decade between the mid-1860s and mid-1870s during Reconstruction shows that federal judicial review can be a positive instrument in the implementation of pro-equality policy.[4] And of course a second pro-equality judicial interregnum also took hold a century later. Indeed, it is the iconic quality of the cases of the second Reconstruction—principally, *Brown v. Board of Education*—that explains much of the contemporary misperceptions that valorize federal judicial review as a bedrock guarantor of constitutional commitments to equality.

Some of the opinions issued during the 140 years between the fateful term of 1873 and the current 2013 term, which jointly have produced numerous anti-equality doctrines and results, are more transparently ideological than others. In some, dispassionate observers may find arguable merit, as defined by the norms and concerns of mainstream U.S. legal culture, whereas in others they might find very little, or none at all. In isolation, one or another of these judicial moves may be deemed minimally problematic, its pernicious consequences limited. But, as a whole, the still-accumulating effects of these opinions have been a racially ideological calibration of "liberty" and an anti-democratic subversion of "equality."

Overall, historical experience before *Brown*, as well as since, therefore should disabuse living Americans of any belief that judicial protection of equality or democracy is a consistent front line of U.S. constitutionalism. Instead, history teaches that reliance on judicial review for equal protection of the laws can invite a false and dangerous complacency; it invites a continual misdirection of reformatory energies. A critical understanding of judicial review's equality record is a predicate for effective equality strategies going forward—strategies that appreciate the limits of law, and of adjudication in particular, and that include, but do not exaggerate, the role or potential of federal litigation and the judicial review power in ongoing struggles over constitutional equality (and democracy) in U.S. law and society over the course of a new millennium.

This chapter outlines a critical history of equal protection under judicial review, the paradigmatic exemplar in U.S. nationhood of in/equality as jurisprudence. Highly abbreviated out of necessity, the main aim is to contextualize contemporary comprehension of the conceptual, doctrinal, and social quagmires resulting from this particular legal history in the search for reconstructive ways forward. In the longer term, the aim of this critically raced legal history is to contribute key antisubordination knowledge toward a final vindication of equal protection and substantive equality in the United States within, but also beyond, race cases.

---

3 Derrick A. Bell, Race, Racism, and American Law (6th ed. 2008).

4 Robert J. Kaczorowski, The Politics of Judicial Interpretation: The Federal Courts, Department of Justice & Civil Rights 1866–1876 (1985).

"States' Rights" and Equality: The Racial State and the State of Liberty

Reflecting the intricacy of founding formational politics, equality as a legal concept is both absent and omnipresent in American self-conception. Never mentioned in the text of the original Constitution by resort to repeated euphemism, the interrelated politics of slavery, liberty, and representation nonetheless were on everyone's mind at Independence Hall in Philadelphia. Indeed, the entire constitutional calculation at that time was to structure those politics for the future. For better or worse, it has and still does.

As is well known but rarely emphasized, in the U.S. the scope and reach of equality has always depended on the threshold act of defining the polity; put simply, those originally excluded were rendered marginal or even extraneous to the early formal development of equality as law. These original acts of constitutional exclusion and inequality undergirded the antebellum system of U.S. federalism with inter-locking structures of identity, property, and representation.[5] But within the polity as defined at any given moment, the idea of "freedom" or "liberty" entailed the notion of structurally *equal* liberties and freedoms; in the language of the common law, these were the "privileges and immunities" vested in polity members and "protected" equally for entitled members by "due process" (and other vested "rights") of the sovereign's law. Before and since 1776, this was the background legal normativity, rooted in still-formative common law traditions, that framed original conceptions and early developments in U.S. nation-building[6] and which the ending of the Civil War, and its postbellum codification of equal protection, was "intended" to reconfigure in limited yet fundamental ways. Thus, in practice "liberty" and "equality" were/are flipsides of the same normative coin; in this political framework, but only *within the polity*, equality of rights was/is the condition for (equal) liberty.

Nonetheless, in defining the polity to include only them, and people most like them, the original (White, male, propertied) settlers of the United States implanted a cancerous racism into the constitutional heritage, legal culture, and socio-economic architecture of the new nation-state. The contradiction of slavery in the name of liberty, designed to justify racial enslavement in the land of the free, originated in the naked politics of constitutional compromises—America's original sins. Afterwards, it was justified by stacking increasingly flimsy and self-serving rationalizations one upon another, oftentimes in the form of judicial opinions that purported to settle with principled reasoning the polarizing politics of in/equality empowered by those sins—America's continuing wrongs. Exhibiting the singular force of America's racial politics, judges on the whole have been collusive or worse in the still-stunted story of equality as a democratic and constitutional value in everyday U.S. life.

On the whole, and with some crucial reconstructive exceptions, U.S. judges have made an art of using common law techniques and tools to truncate and negate equality mandates enacted and re-enacted by local or national democratic majorities both before and after the Civil War amendments. Both before and after, "federalism" has provided the broad rubric for the dogged pursuit and defense of a mighty thing we aptly might call a one-way "Right to Discriminate" in favor of elites within the original exclusionary polity as an elemental aspect of American liberty. In the antebellum years, this mighty right was couched in the rhetoric of "states' rights"—a regime where "liberty" included the right to capture, exploit, injure, and enslave others, so long as they were Black. After the war, it remained couched in "states' rights"—this time, in the form of state or local "Black Codes" that tracked the substance and structure of the old "Slave Codes" prohibited by the Civil War amendments but blessed by the judges in the half century after the War through magical doctrinal maneuvers. Today, it still remains couched in the rhetoric of "states' rights"—now oftentimes cast juridically in the form of strategic colorblindness and a "new" federalism that remains faithful to the normatively antidemocratic, supremacist universe of the old South.

Under the terms of antebellum federalism and states' rights established effectively by judicial opinion in *Barron v. Baltimore* (1833),[7] local identity groups, frequently minorities, who had self-constituted the exclusionary local polity, now could act officially and constitutionally, even democratically, within the context of the Union, as the town or state, to do whatever they liked to normalize what was, in effect, a one-way

5 Robert Steinfeld, *Property and Suffrage in the Early American Republic*, 41 Stan. L. Rev. 335 (1989).

6 Earl M. Maltz, The Fourteenth Amendment and the Law of the Constitution (2003).

7 Barron v. City of Baltimore, 32 U.S. 243, 247–48 (1833).

"Right to Discriminate" vested originally, and ideologically, in some identities for sociolegal deployments against others.[8]

Though nowhere named or vested explicitly in the Constitution, this public and private Right to Discriminate at the very heart of the neocolonial racial order in the United States was brought into existence by the carefully calibrated interplay of at least four legal and constitutional actions.

The first was the structural and systemic set of compromises in Philadelphia resulting in a federal framework that, in conjunction with the specific compromises on slavery itself, tied policy to the protection of slavery at the national level. The second was the Slave Codes enacted by individual states, exploiting fully the privileges of federal union to leverage local politics into national policy, which made prey of Blacks, rendering them vulnerable to all kinds of injury with impunity; no legal recourse for abuse or injury existed precisely because of the specific disabilities imposed by the Slave Codes on victims of White supremacist exploitation, abuse, and harassment. The third was the combined and coordinated complex of public/private violence that characterized local governance across slave jurisdictions, and specifically the enforcement of racial slavery, in the antebellum period, which legalized racial domestic terrorism as state and local law enforcement policy. And finally, the fourth factor has been the judicial opinions which have shielded and fueled all of the above. As recounted below, unpacking and dismantling this formidable sociolegal edifice has proven elusive despite two momentous, sustained efforts to reconstruct original arrangements and emplace a plausible semblance of universal equality of individual liberty.

These reformatory cycles frequently are described as the "first" and "second" efforts to reconstruct the original constitutional framework for American federalism, which had been significantly skewed in 1787–89 in favor of political and constitutional protection of racial slavery as the price of ratification and nationhood. Ever since those original, sinful compromises, the general politics of federalism and nationhood can be tracked by the particular politics of protecting racial slavery and White supremacy. Whether explicitly or in code, successors-in-interest to original interests have recycled the same patterns, techniques, and rhetorics left unresolved in Philadelphia to sustain original colonial inequalities despite the passage of time and the asserted march of social and legal progress.[9]

Within this historical narrative, "equal protection" in the Fourteenth Amendment was literally and conceptually designed to disestablish White supremacy by constitutional mandate, and to shift the official "protection" of the law from the one-way Right to Discriminate toward the equally venerable common law ideal of universal equal treatment within the polity, through two key provisions of that Amendment. First, by expanding the polity, thus expanding the number of those vested with common law and other privileges and immunities. Second, by making the right to law's equal protection of those privileges and immunities express, thereby making the latter right—*equal* protection—explicit as a substantive individual right for the first time in the constitutional text. Underscoring both of these provisions is the choice to extend the right of equalized protection to all "persons" rather than just citizens. As widely well understood at the time, this shift unambiguously threatened the political and economic hegemony of whiteness in the U.S. because legal protection for one-way racist discrimination—as an indispensable element of White elites' "liberty"—was the very bedrock of White privilege, power, and property. Yet this was the overarching, basic, and original intent of the three constitutional amendments, and the multiple federal comprehensive civil rights statutes enacted to enforce them, in the decade between 1865 and 1875.

Of course, from the founding of the United States to the present, this original Right to Discriminate as social practice or legal rule clearly never was limited to race, even though in the United States it was contoured chiefly around White-over-Black racial agendas. Conspicuously, at the moment of founding, women, Indians, and selected religious traditions also were denied, by state law, the equal protection of its laws. Moreover, at that time, and in line with transplanted common law ideas, classes even formally within the polity also could be created to accord them lesser rights, so long as those within "separate" classes enjoyed "equal" rights. The "different" regimes of identity-related oppressions constructed for these overlapping groups shared many

8 Kenneth L. Karst & Harold W. Horowitz, *A Teleophase of Substantive Equal Protection*, 1967 Sup. Ct. Rev. 39 (1967).

9 Pamela Brandwein, Reconstructing Reconstruction: The Supreme Court and the Production of Historical Truth (1999).

important characteristics, yet they were not the same. Unlike hereditary racialized enslavement, the oppression of women, Indians, and religious minorities came to the United States with ready-made rationalizations and much-entrenched normalization refined by centuries of European endeavor and acculturation.

In the context of a new nation-state committed to the claim that "all men are created equal," the racialized hereditary enslavement specifically of Blacks *qua* Blacks, with no pre-existing blueprint in Anglo-Saxon legal tradition, required a justifying normative construct that rested on the conjunction of an old institution—slavery—and a relatively new construction: race.[10] The construction of antebellum federalism thus produced a legal, social, and political conflation of the two, succinctly expressed by judges in the form of law in an 1835 opinion from South Carolina: "it is hardly necessary to say that a slave cannot be a white man."[11] This thus became the formula for the institutionalization of hereditary racial subordination across much of the United States since its constitution.

Not only was essentialized race-based enslavement peculiarly at the very heart of national conception, but other profoundly racialized and racializing acts of lawmaking during the founding and formative years of the country helped to set the stage for the subsequent preservation of the *status quo* in strategic yet structural ways. Notably, these acts included the limitation on naturalized citizenship to "white" persons, enacted by the very first Congress and signed into law by George Washington as the Naturalization and Immigration Act of 1790. Later, this foundational restriction was reiterated in various statutory forms by successive generations of legislators until 1952, ensuring that, during the bulk of relevant history, American nation-building would be mostly White by brute force of law.

The ongoing reiterations of race-based slavery ranging from Black Codes, Jim Crow, and segregation to, today, the Orwellian logic of "reverse discrimination" provide key, paradigmatic, long-term examples of law's constitutional entanglement with race and, in particular, White supremacy in uniquely profound ways. The Chinese exclusion laws, Japanese internment, and dispossession laws, and similar acts of legal subordination designed to create and enforce racial hierarchy, further deepen and expand the history of racial ideology codified as law in incrementally coalescing these United States as a consciously and intentionally White nation-state. The dispossession and destruction of indigenous individuals and nations in explicitly racial terms is yet another example of this long and unique history. And the manipulation and exploitation of Latina/o communities or diasporas for cheap labor and other extractive, subjugating aims also is equally a part of the sorry but continuing history of White-identified Eurocentric racisms as central to the establishment and administration of the U.S. as a functional nation-state. Even the contemporary expression of this historical, traditional, neocolonial power structure to exert perpetual control over this nation-state—the culture wars discussed briefly below—are identity/color-centric, and waged still chiefly through the tools and techniques of law and policy, still mostly in the pursuit of original supremacies, and still coded typically with generalized invocations of liberty, democracy, and federalism.

Thus, whether focused on Black people, yellow people, red people, brown people, or other nonwhite people, the emergent neocolonial power structure of this country, generally transplanted to the U.S. from Europe, and mostly from England specifically, has been from its inception obsessively conscious of its own ethno-racial identity, and has used its original control over law relentlessly to ensure its racial supremacy politically, culturally, and economically. *Beginning with hereditary racial enslavement and the very first act of exclusion by Congress on immigration and naturalization, this pervasive racialism has policed the polity, demographics, and borders of the nation-state in resolutely racialized and re-racializing ways to build, law by law, and brick by brick, the edifice of white supremacy as integral to the sense of society stitching together the new nation-state. Consequently, predictably unsurprisingly, whiteness today retains its power to dominate both society and state.*

Through these repeated acts of *de jure* racialization to cohere a sense of *both* nation and state, the White elites and establishment of this country have fostered the quintessential racial state, which "employ[s] physical force, violence, coercion, manipulation, deceit, cajoling, incentives, law(s), taxes, penalties, surveillance, military force, repressive apparatuses, ideological mechanisms, and media—in short, all the means at a state's

10 Michael Omi & Howard Winant, Racial Formation in the United States: From the 1960s to the 1990s (2nd ed., 1995); Ian Haney-Lopez, White by Law: The Legal Construction of Race (10th ed., 2006).

11 State v. Cantey, 20 S.C.L. (2 Hill) 614, 616 (1835).

disposal—ultimately to the ends of racial rule … which is to say, to the ends of reproducing the racial order, and so representing for the most part the interest of the racial ruling class."[12] A more fitting description of the founding, origins, and development of the United States under the rule of law—and, more specifically, of the articulation of "equal protection" under the rule of judicial review—is difficult to imagine.

In this land assertedly of law and not men, forming itself under a pre-existing common law framework, it fell upon judges to explain and justify original sins of White supremacy, to fill the specific, gigantic gap allowing for racialized enslavement, exclusion, or subordination in the constitutional and legal foundations of a professedly freedom-loving country. Initially, therefore, their challenge was to explain, ameliorate, and navigate the gnawing effects of that original surrender. Later, their constitutional duty was to give full force and effect to the pro-equality reforms of two Reconstructions. Ultimately, their role must be to help the country move beyond the original confines of 1780s identity politics to help a multi-racial society with an increasingly nonwhite population engage with the unsustainability of its founding, existential contradictions. Instead, their chosen mission has been, and remains, the crafting and reinforcement of selective and formalistic boundaries around equality, only some of which can be explored here, that bolster and preserve original identitarian arrangements despite a Constitution dedicated to rights, privileges, and immunities for all. The result has been judicial negation of democratic reconstructive efforts to abolish the racial state and its constitutional underpinnings in the United States. The result, for the moment, is a neo-racial state.

Structural Equality and Minority Rule: Polity, Identity, Liberty and Exclusion

The customs and rules of the common law system created the cultural and political context not only for the development of law in the United States generally, but also specifically for the articulation of equality and related ideas by the settler elites who spearheaded the American Revolution and took control of the new nation-state upon independence from England. During this time, various conceptions of natural law and rights prevailed, even if they eluded fixed specificity or definition. Terms like "liberty" as well as "equality" were used frequently in the service of various political arguments, including in the Declaration of Independence, as well as in many of the subsequent political debates and judicial opinions interpreting constitutional meanings. This fluid universe of natural law and rights was the common normative well from which all sides in the U.S. political structure drew to reshape those concepts as applied in specific contexts under U.S. law.[13] This legacy produced the conceptual strands and tensions from which the framers of the Constitution proceeded, both in the late-1700s and in the mid-1800s.[14]

Notably, in the U.S. Declaration of Independence, "liberty and "equality" are textually, normatively, and functionally intertwined: "all men are created equal … with certain inalienable rights … life, liberty and the pursuit of happiness." The subsequent racialized severing of equality from liberty is, in effect, the history of constitutional in/equality. Thomas Paine captured this growing contradiction of slavery in the name of liberty in his first published article, asking original Americans, "with what consistency, or decency, they complain so loudly of attempts to enslave them, while they hold so many hundred thousands in slavery; and annually enslave many more, without any pretense of authority or claim upon them."[15] Awareness of this fundamental and untenable contradiction was so widespread that founding members of the new nation-state generally considered this peculiar institution to be their "communal sin."[16] And indeed, both original sins and continuing wrongs associated with social inequality in the U.S. have been communal in nature—inflicted through *both* public *and* private combinations of institutionalized racial power. Judges have been central to, but not alone in, this historic and continuing obstruction of justice.

---

12 David Theo Goldberg, The Racial State 109–10 (2002).

13 Maltz, *supra* note 6; Akhil Reed Amar, *The Bill of Rights as a Constitution*, 100 Yale L.J. 1131 (1991); Amar, *The Bill of Rights and the Fourteenth Amendment*, 101 Yale L.J. 1193 (1992).

14 Bernard Bailyn, The Ideological Origins of the American Revolution (1967).

15 Thomas Paine, *African Slavery in America*, Pennsylvania Journal & the Weekly Advertiser. Mar. 8, 1775 available at http://www.constitution.org/tp/afri.htm.

16 Alexander Tsesis, We Shall Overcome: A History of Civil Rights and the Law 28–30 (2008).

Given the identity politics of those times, this fundamentally conflicted dynamic required studied deflections. The uniquely existential contradiction of racial slavery in the state of liberty was the very compromise allowing political union for Whites. Thus, instead of a head-on articulation of a substantive individual equality right that might preclude that compromise, the structural elements of original equality under the United States Constitution are expressed through the combination of various textual provisions said to create a "system" of "checks and balances" that include the very "separation of powers" within the government as a whole. This initial version of "equality" aimed to structure and channel the politics of representative democracy in "the compound republic," but the anomalous effect was to place collectives—"factions"—at the center of society in the new land of emphatically individualized rights and liberties. This constitutional infrastructure, as a whole, thus formed a kind of structural equality, which was limited in various ways to the identity-based inner circle of the new society—the enfranchised polity—because it relied on a basic sense of political equality in the institutional workings of the new system to induce and maintain proper social order.

Limited by force of law to those individuals and factions included in the polity of a given state, these structural elements of original commitments to this kind of equality are exemplified by the one textual reference in the original constitutional text, providing that all constituent states are entitled to equal representation in the national senate. In other words, the structural elements of original in/equality effectively aimed to create a "level" playing field within a privileged polity for factual jockeying over powers' spoils; structural equality in the original Constitution sought to ensure roughly equalized access to political power within the original polity alone, and exclusively, while relegating by law other members of society to disposable and/or exploitable populations. More starkly, the structural (as well as substantive) components of this original, exclusionary in/equality are captured in the numerous, pivotal, and well-documented constitutional compromises, which never once mention race or slavery but which were at the heart of the sanitized yet compromised Constitution that set the stage for the politics of in/equality that overshadowed the formative years of the new nation-state.[17]

Importantly to the politics of structural equality and White supremacy in the establishment of a racial state in the new country, Philadelphia's compromises effectively and dramatically had inflated the political and economic might of slaver states and forces within the rules and mechanics of federal union. But the institutionalization and perpetration in the United States of hereditary racial enslavement, and later of Jim Crow apartheid, through local and state law was never a cleanly democratic or majoritarian enterprise. On the contrary, typically, local White minorities outnumbered by local Black populations but possessing a monopoly over physical violence, and hence over local government, imposed racial enslavement through minority tyranny.[18]

Thus, although today the three-fifths Clause of the original Constitution is decried as an affront to the human dignity of slaves and Blacks, it was much more than that. Its original calculations and multiplying dynamics provide a microcosm of antebellum federalism and explain why it would, but also could not, endure for long. It puts on display the predicament of structural in/equality in a racial state. It exposes how structural in/equality was customized to effectuate yet mask perpetual minority rule in the name both of liberty and democracy. It helps also to explain why strong remnants of the racial state endure even in an assertedly post-racial era.[19]

More particularly, this single clause gave to slavers representation both in the new Congress and in the Electoral College that was inflated by three-fifths of the population they had enslaved and excluded from the polity. This permanent representational advantage of the three-fifths compromise not only elevated the standing of slavers in the original Congress by a some 20 seats more than their actual voting population justified, but also granted Southern White slaver elites a permanent structural platform for national domination of constitutional politics, and for protection specifically of their ever-expanding Right to Discriminate.[20]

---

17 *See* William M. Wiecek, The Sources of Antislavery Constitutionalism in America, 1760–1848, 62–83 (1977); cf. Paul Finkelman who identifies 18 pro-slavery clauses in the original Constitution: Paul Finkelman, *Affirmative Action for the Master Class: The Creation of the Proslavery Constitution*, 32 Akron L. Rev. 423, 428–32 (1999).

18 Gabriel J. Chin & Randy Wagner, *The Tyranny of the Minority: Jim Crow and the Counter-Majoritarian Difficulty*, 43 Harv. C.R.-C.L. L. Rev. 65 (2008).

19 Leonard L. Richards, The Slave Power: the Free North and Southern Domination (2000); Sanford Levinson, Our Undemocratic Constitution: Where the Constitution Goes Wrong (and How We the People Can Correct it) (2008).

20 Tsesis, *supra* note 16, at 35.

This artificial hyperinflation of slaver power through the architecture of federal authority, and of "federalism" itself, constituted a permanent structural skew in the constitution of American democracy converting local racial minorities consisting of White elites into a controlling political bloc at the national level able to take control both of the Congress (through inflated representation), the executive (through correspondingly inflated representation in the Electoral College), and even the Supreme Court itself (through presidential control of judicial nominations). In these crucial formative times, slavers frequently controlled them all. In addition to controlling the sovereignty of their states, slavers and their allies thereby also controlled the process of federal lawmaking, as well as the subsequent processes of interpretation and enforcement.[21]

This much can be seen in the composition of the bench deciding the 1857 *Dred Scott* case, perhaps the exemplar constitutional opinion of the racial state under antebellum federalism, which then consisted entirely of pro-slavery appointees except for two: Benjamin Curtis and John McLean.[22] As illustrated by that infamous opinion and its progeny, this nearly hegemonic grip was reinforced in the antebellum years, as well as afterward, by ever-more-political judicial doctrines, fictions, and other devices constructed by successive generations of White appointees to the Supreme Court precisely through the constitutionalized workings of this slaver political hijacking to engineer both in/equality and "democracy" for the long term. These mutually reinforcing political dynamics and jurisprudential constructions became, during the antebellum years, the zealous guardians of the White-only Right to Discriminate in the name of liberty and democracy through the strategically particularized configuration of federal constitutionalism. Later, and ultimately, these and similar antebellum artifacts of structural in/equality were the institutionalized devices that the Civil War and reconstructed federalism were designed to reform, specifically yet fundamentally, in the mid-to-late 1800s.

Antebellum Federalism and the Right to Discriminate: Structural Equality's "Protection"

Because structural equality was limited to the members of a racially (and sexually and otherwise) exclusionary polity, this antebellum arrangement effectively erected an identity-based, one-way Right to Discriminate against those excluded from the polity, or subordinated within it by the traditions, customs, or logic of the common law inheritance, as modified by settler elites for their own personal and factional advantage and material convenience. Like all rules and rights, this one-way Right to Discriminate could be, and was, expressed in many different ways. For instance, both the Slave Codes before the Civil War and the Black Codes after it illustrate two then-common ways of imposing group-wide legal subordination—disabling classes of people from the legal capacity to make and enforce contracts, or disqualifying classes of people from instituting lawsuits or testifying in them; in effect, Black Codes were designed to reduce Black classes of persons to White prey at virtually the same levels of personal, social, and economic vulnerability imposed previously by antebellum slavery—except for the technical distinction of formal enslavement itself.

Paradigmatic of supremacist identitarian sociolegal regimes, the power of racial elites, whether majoritarian or minoritarian, to use their control of state or local sovereignties to create and maintain a sweeping social reality of systemic and institutionalized caste through "class legislation" or "special laws" was crisply noted, and heartily endorsed, by Roger Taney in his *Dred Scott* opinion. Writing for a bare five-judge majority in that case, he explained directly that recognition of Black citizenship was constitutionally impermissible in the U.S. because doing so would:

> … exempt them from the operation of the special laws [and give them the right] … to go where they pleased at every hour of the day of night without molestation, unless they committed some violation of law for which a white man would be punished … the full liberty of speech in public and in private upon all subjects upon which [the state's] own citizens might speak.[23]

21 Donald Robinson, Slavery in the Structure of American Politics 1765–1820 (1971); Daniel Walker Howe, What Hath God Wrought: the Transformation of America 1815–1848 (2007).

22 Tsesis, *supra* note 16, at 78.

23 Dred Scott v. Sandford, 60 U.S. 393, 416–17 (1857).

In other words, the results of the adjudication were explained—are explicable—chiefly by their perceived operational necessity to White supremacy in a racial state.

Underscoring the importance of the racially exclusionary polity at the state or local level as the lynchpin of antebellum federalism and structural in/equality, he continued:

> If persons of the African race are citizens of a state, and of the United States, they would be entitled to all of these privileges and immunities in every state, and the state could not restrict them: for they would hold those privileges and immunities under the paramount authority of the federal government, and its courts would be bound to maintain and enforce them, the Constitution and loss of the state to the contrary notwithstanding.[24]

This basic and coherent framing of constitutional equality, which the *Dred Scott* judged then promptly rejected in these very terms before the South lost the Civil War, was precisely the conception of "equal protection" for the "privileges and immunities" of all "persons" that the wording of the Fourteenth Amendment was designed specifically to secure after the North had won just a few years later. Speaking on the floor of the Senate in 1865, leading proponent Jacob M. Howard explained that the Fourteenth Amendment would abolish "all class legislation in the states and [do] away with the injustice of subjecting one caste of persons to a code not applicable to another."[25] For this reason the framers and advocates of the Fourteenth Amendment explicitly granted "equal protection of the laws" to all "persons" rather than citizens, even while expanding the polity through the granting of birthright citizenship at the same time; the Fourteenth Amendment and related lawmaking aimed in textual, conceptual, and functional terms to terminate entirely the Right to Discriminate, first, by extending the polity universally based on birth, thereby invalidating the exclusion of many from the polity under state laws blessed by the judges in *Scott*, and, second, by choosing to extend the "equal protection of the laws" not only to the expanded polity of all "citizens" but to all "persons" within the federal jurisdiction of the United States. The point was to withdraw law's "protection" from discrimination, and bestow it on equality, as a matter of constitutional mandate and policy. A more expansive extension of the common law equality principle hitherto limited to racial elites could not be framed in English.

Formal Democracy, Substantive Equality: National Reconstruction and "Equal" Protection

As in the original Constitutional Convention held in Philadelphia during summer 1787, calculated compromise was very much part of the drafting and ratification processes underlying each of the post-Civil War amendments, as well as the multiple major statutes based on them enacted through 1875. At each step, strategic rhetorical jockeying by skeptics and opponents repeatedly attempted to bog proponents down in the details of politically complicated scenarios calculated to chip away at support for the equality principle. At the same time, these debates occasioned multiple reiterations of core meanings and original intentions. Despite thickness and complexity, however, the record establishes a reasonably discernible central purpose articulated repeatedly by proponents of these reforms, who actually prevailed legislatively, as well as the opponents of those reforms, who ultimately prevailed judicially; moreover, their decade-long series of pro-equality measures add up to a reasonably discernable sense of policy and purpose. As summarized below, the postbellum reforms of the Reconstruction proceeded from a specific recognition that White power, especially in the South, would seek to "vex and oppress" new polity members, which prompted an array of constitutional and statutory bulwarks to protect equality from that danger.

On the day it convened, December 5, 1865, the Thirty-ninth Congress began working on the wording of the Fourteenth Amendment, generating at least 10 versions of the same basic concept. The recurrent idea, appearing in all their drafts, is that of "equal protection."[26] This baseline point is illustrated by the warnings of Senator Samuel Randall, opposing the Fourteenth Amendment: "The first section proposes to make an

24 *Id.* at 423.

25 Tsesis, *supra* note 16, at 102–03.

26 Jacobus tenBroek, *Thirteenth Amendment to the Constitution of the United States: Consummation to Abolition and Key to the Fourteenth Amendment*, 39(2) Calif. L. Rev. 171, 189–91 (1951).

equality in every respect between the two races, notwithstanding the policy of discrimination which has hitherto been exclusively exercised by the States."[27] This "policy of discrimination" at the state level provided formal legal protection for the private Right to Discriminate, and federal lawmakers like Randall plainly saw that undoing this combination of public policy and private rights in favor of legal discrimination and factional domination at the local or state level was the bottom-line purpose of the postbellum reforms constituting the Reconstruction.

Importantly, "Congress heard testimony from 125 witnesses, 89 of which confirmed the general hostility and frequent cruelty toward the Negro [that] characterized the attitude of Southern whites," and thus put into the record the social and legal conditions licensing the combination of private and public injury to Blacks. Consequently, "there can be little doubt not only that the members of the committee were aware of these individual violations but that the majority of the committee took pains to get them into the record—an odd procedure, to say the least, if they were not to be comprehended within the amendment which the committee was then perfecting."[28] The record makes abundantly clear that the framers of this constitutional Reconstruction knew from personal experience that these interlocking systems of social and legal subordination had been engineered incrementally by ruling racial factions, and sometimes even as minorities, across the states of the Confederacy with an original monopoly over violence, both public and private; since 1789, slaver elites had consolidated sweeping combinations of private and public coercion ranging from birth to death, tying identity to property and, ultimately, to destiny.[29]

Emphatically repudiating cramped or formalistic views of "equal protection" at the moment of its origin, leading architects and advocates of numerous reconstructive equality enactments made it ever-more clear that "equal protection" denoted a socially substantive state of affairs structurally and materially distinct from original and antebellum compromises. Made textually express for the first time in the Fourteenth Amendment itself, equality was to be a substantive individual constitutional right of all persons, secured and supplied by the positive protection of the law against public or private invasion, and not an abstracted theory of governmental and social structure, sapped by legal fictions that defied on-the-record social experience with structural in/equality. Thus, during the drafting process, the principal "father" of the Fourteenth Amendment specifically, John Bingham, phrased the meaning of "protection" explicitly this way:

> Suppose any person has acquired property not contrary to the laws of the state but in accordance with its law, are they not to be equally protected in the enjoyment of it, or are they to be denied all protection? That is the question, and the whole question, so far as that part of the case is concerned.[30]

Under this original, framing scenario, state inaction in the face of private injury would plainly constitute a denial of "equal protection." This hypothetical, among many others, illustrated the positive character of "protection"—the public protection of private enjoyment of private rights from all invasions, whether public or private. Recalling the sociolegal circumstances addressed by this constitutional policymaking helps to make complete sense of these particular, and expansive, legislative choices.

Given the extremely exclusionary antebellum polity, state and local "law" often enough was but an extension of minority elite preferences imposed on disenfranchised, disempowered majorities from above in the name of representative democracy. Never a majoritarian system or institution, slavers and slavery always relied on antidemocratic means to have their way; at that time, the very same people in control of the state legislatures oftentimes also were in control of the mob on the street, and of domestic terror groups like the Ku Klux Klan (KKK). When these persons acted, they sometimes wore a hood and other times a badge. Normatively and functionally, the formal distinction between "private" and "public" local action in the context of antebellum White supremacy was extremely unstable, and reliance on it foreseeably would help license supremacist politics and racist systems of inter-state subordination. Thus, it was clear to the framers and proponents of these structural legal reforms that their enactments must restrict the use of state action *and*

27 Tsesis, *supra* note 16, at 102–03.

28 tenBroek, *supra* note 26, at 186–87.

29 Adrienne D. Davis, *The Private Law of Race and Sex: An Antebellum Perspective*, 51 Stan. L. Rev. 221 (1999).

30 Maltz, *supra* note 6, at 68.

inaction to help impose or maintain private bigotry socially or legally: their "speeches indicate that the Equal Protection Clause is primarily a reference to the obligation of government to supply protection to men in their natural rights, and secondarily is a requirement that such protection, when supplied, must be equal to all."[31]

Therefore, postbellum notions of a complete displacement by the national government of state or local sovereignties was one of the false arguments activated by equality opponents to stir up fears, even as Framers and advocates repeatedly disclaimed any such purpose; certainly, reformers did not want to displace local power for themselves and communities, and knew that such a proposition would not sell publicly in any political quarter. They intended a revolution constitutionally, but one tailored to the erasure of structural racial subordination and establishment of substantive racial equality. For them, the first step was to withdraw formal and actual state solicitude for the Right to Discriminate completely, and instead shift the active protection of the law decisively in favor of the right to legal protection against inequality within an expanded polity. To this end, each of the three Civil War amendments, and the multiple major statutes enacted to enforce them, aimed to accomplish basically the same purpose, but with ever-greater specificity and force to overcome the massive resistance that each encountered, both socially and politically; the essentially constant goals motivating original reconstructive intentions focused on the withdrawal of *all* support, comfort, shelter, or legitimacy for the Right to Discriminate, and certainly no drafter ever declared that positive state discrimination was the only way possible for a state to "deny" to a "person" within the U.S. "the equal protection of the laws." All of this constricting surplusage was added years later by the judges, as discussed below.

To the Reconstruction's framers, however, "equal protection" secured the "liberty" of all members of an expanded polity to participate fully and peacefully in public life as economic, political, and social actors. Original intentions did not envision proactive racial integration or economic redistribution outright, but rather the affirmative ending of White-imposed isolation, subjugation, exploitation, domination, and stigmatization of Blacks in particular, but of all "persons" textually: "We now know that the equal protection clause was designed to invoke upon the states a positive duty to supply protection to all persons in the enjoyment of their natural and inalienable rights—especially life, liberty and property—and to do so equally."[32] Perhaps, in the end, the best evidence pointing to the original framers' intentions regarding the key provisions of the three constitutional amendments passed within a decade after the Civil War, starting in 1865, is found in the Congressional initiatives enacted by these very same lawmakers concurrently, which were specifically and explicitly intended to further these constitutional reforms.

Between 1865–75, a unique decade of interrelated constitutional and federal statutory lawmaking began with the passage of the Thirteenth Amendment prohibiting slavery anywhere in the United States, except as punishment for crime, and thus overturning all of the constitutional deals and accommodations embedded in the text of the original Constitution and subsequent judicial opining. The following year, Congress enacted the Civil Rights Act of 1866 to implement the new amendment by protecting the privileges and immunities of "freedmen" as previously recognized in the common law or legislatively, and as had been targeted for denial by the Slave Codes and, increasingly, by the Black Codes. This statutory protection applied both to private and public action, reflecting again the widespread concern for "private" mob violence that formed part of the ongoing resistance to the results of the Civil War. This initial postbellum amendment, coupled with this landmark enforcement bill, not only abolished slavery (except for criminal punishment) but also federalized the protection of individual civil rights nationwide for the first time—and specifically to guard all persons within the U.S. against anti-equality abuse professedly authorized by color of local law, whether purportedly democratic or not.

That same year, moreover, Congress also enacted the Slave Kidnapping Act of 1866 to protect freedmen from the established fugitive industry financed by slaver wealth and, within another year, also had enacted two additional statutes—the Peonage Act of 1867 and Judiciary Act of 1867—to further bolster the structure of federal legal protection for civil rights and enlist federal authority in the dismantling of the private-public complex fighting fiercely to preserve as much as possible their antebellum race-based privileges.[33]

---

31 tenBroek, *supra* note 26, at 207.

32 Joseph Tussman & Jacobus tenBroek, *The Equal Protection of the Laws*, 37(3) Calif. L. Rev 341, 341 (1949).

33 Tsesis, *supra* note 16, at 55.

These initial unprecedented reforms were opposed by claims that the 1866 Civil Rights Act could not be legislated under the Thirteenth Amendment, which opponents claimed applied narrowly, or strictly, only to slavery *per se*, and thus was unconstitutional. With massive resistance growing in the streets and public squares all across the Old Confederacy, reform leaders soon concluded that political prudence called for another amendment to re-enact the substance of the 1866 Act at a constitutional level. The next round of extraordinary legislative activity would fundamentally reform the antebellum social compact and include subordinated communities within its expanded scope and substance; after these reforms, "equal protection of the laws" would legally and constitutionally become "an integral part of the social compact-natural rights doctrine" derived from transplanted common law traditions.[34]

While tracking the substance of the 1866 statute, the Fourteenth Amendment in 1868 expressly granted birthright federal citizenship, federalized the protection of privileges and immunities, and guaranteed that this protection shall be equal to all persons under the law. Two years later, promoted by continuing and growing resistance to the Fourteenth Amendment and its application specifically to "political" rights and the franchise, the Fifteenth Amendment was enacted in 1870 to secure specifically the voting rights of racial out-groups. Thus, in the five years between 1865 and 1870, the nation had refashioned its federal system to codify the results of the Civil War in constitutional terms covering slavery, civil rights, citizenship, equality, and the franchise, and thereby to abolish all legal protection of the antebellum one-way Right to Discriminate.

Yet, resistance continued, both violent and institutional. Therefore, one year later, Congress enacted the Ku Klux Klan Act of 1871 explicitly to enforce the Fourteenth Amendment against the sort of organized private violence that White-on-Black terrorism had come to exemplify in the postbellum period. Then, immediately afterwards, Congress enacted the Civil Rights Act of 1870, under the new enforcement powers of the Fourteenth Amendment, in order to re-enact the 1866 bill and thereby remove any lingering question of its constitutional infirmity under the Thirteenth Amendment. This lawmaking represented the third direct congressional effort to enact essentially the same substantive policy to reconstruct federalism and establish equal protection for all persons in place of the antebellum Right to Discriminate based on exclusionary local polities with a violent monopoly over strategically unfettered "states' rights." The final and crowning effort to secure this first Reconstruction of federalism in favor of equality via multiple layers of national law came in 1875.[35] This expansive and comprehensive effort outlawed all private discrimination based on race, color, or previous condition of servitude in public accommodations, and additionally made violations a misdemeanor, while also providing injured persons with a private cause of action. Here, finally, was the comprehensive legal basis for a societal shift from the skews of structural equality focused on privileged factions to the substantively equalized "protection" of individual liberty, made expressly applicable to an expanded polity and community, under a thoroughly reconstructed federalism now protected by national authorities against local tyrannies, under both civil and criminal law.[36]

This postbellum vision of reformed equality was of course a limited one; it did not, for instance, extend to women *qua* women. Framed in the wake of a Civil War triggered by the social, economic, and constitutional politics of secession and nationhood over the structural future of the U.S. as a formally racial state, the public legislative history of the postbellum reforms shows a contextualized focus on racial equality in White-over-Black terms. However, and importantly for interpretive reasons, the framers of the Fourteenth Amendment chose not to so limit the text thus forged, opting instead to frame individualized equality rights beyond the immediate context of that historical moment. Within this basic framework of reconstructed federalism, states retained substantial discretion, albeit not unfettered impunity, to enact legislative schemes short of absolute equality across the social board. Fatally, but perhaps inevitably, the potential ambiguities inhering in this balancing act opened manifold opportunities for the perpetration of new wrongs, which were realized soon enough, and specifically by the judges in control of the Supreme Court, starting in the mid-1870s, just as the democratic reconstructive process was concluding.

---

34 tenBroek, *supra* note 26, at 198.

35 Civil Rights Act of 1875.

36 Harold Hyman & William Wiecek, Equal Justice Under Law: Constitutional Development 1835–1875 (1982).

Judging Equality: Defeating Democracy, Arresting the Law

While the number of opinions and variety of techniques used by anti-equality judges to truncate and negate reconstructive reforms in the decades following the Civil War are too many to detail here, key milestones bring into view how the postbellum phase of reactionary activism unfolded. Spanning three-quarters of a century, from the early-1870s to the mid-1950s, this period of equality adjudication drew from antebellum notions and rhetorics to block and dismantle the Reconstruction of federalism that the three amendments and the multiple statutes enacted for that singular purpose between 1865 and 1875 had sought to bring about. These cases, which begin even before those unique lawmaking efforts concluded, were part and parcel of the massive resistance engendered by these efforts and their objectives; while political terrorism and private/public violence re-enacted Slave Codes in the form of Black Codes, the judges constructed strategically formalistic doctrines and dogmas which protected, normalized, and legitimized those politics in the form of law. In the Jim Crow era that followed Reconstruction, the laws that they upheld through the doctrines they chose to spin could not have been better suited to the restoration of structural racial in/equality. Ultimately, the effect was to create a stunted kind of formal emancipation from formal enslavement that is reflected and refracted in the modern-day conception of "formal equality" that still defines the equal protection *status quo*.

In each, the "negative" right is only to be free of direct state action invidiously imposing a condition of *de jure* in/equality. Under this judicially contracted version of equal protection, only abstracted "opportunity" is formally protected; empirical social results cannot be consulted to measure opportunity's actual legal protection against continued or new acts of discrimination and, currently most significant of all, affirmative remedial actions to combat inequality's continuing manifestations are to be viewed as suspect. Without doubt, nothing could be further from original reconstructive intentions.

This judicial interventionism, began in earnest with the 1873 Supreme Court 5–4 *Slaughterhouse Cases* opinion, in which White butchers in New Orleans challenged, on the basis both of equal protection and of federal privileges and immunities, a state law establishing a monopoly in that industry within the city.[37] Adding supreme judicial muscle to the campaign of resistance already underway, the judges there opined that the Fourteenth Amendment "on the most casual examination of the language" applied chiefly, although perhaps not exclusively, to "the slave race"—to which the White butchers did not belong—and that the right to pursue a lawful occupation was not part of the "liberty" encompassed by the federal (as opposed to state) "privileges and immunities" protected by the Constitution. Insisting that a fundamental restructuring of antebellum federalism (and thus White supremacy) required more than the three constitutional amendments and numerous statutes that the first Reconstruction had provided, they declared that those exertions actually had changed nothing—except the technical abolition of "slavery." In one fell swoop, and with little reliance on any source resembling traditional law in a common law system, five judges in formal control of the nation's highest tribunal had ignored the plain meaning of constitutional text referring to "persons" and/or "citizens" and belatedly imposed substantive policy limitations on reconstructive lawmaking based on conclusory, generalized assertions of lawmaking purpose that in fact were inimical to its oft-stated and well-understood policy objectives, as well as its final wording.

A year later, the judges struck again, and again by just a bare majority, with their 5–4 1874 opinion deciding *United States v. Cruikshank*, in which KKK members convicted under the Civil Rights Act of 1870 were set free by the Supreme Court on the view that the Fourteenth Amendment supplied protection only "against the acts of the state government itself,"[38] thereby establishing a new limitation inimical to the goal and reach of postbellum equally lawmaking. After the judges' opinion in *Cruikshank*, the constitutional liberty of the KKK to terrorize local Black citizens seemly fully restored, so long as they pretended to be only a "private" group of individuals. Thus, less than a full decade after the end of historic reconstructive lawmaking efforts, the judges of those times already had managed to hollow out much of the practical effects originally intended for the Reconstruction of federalism and the constitutional shift toward substantive individual equality mandated by law after the Civil War.

---

37 The Slaughter-House Cases, 83 U.S. (16 Wall.) 36 (1872).

38 United States v. Cruikshank, 92 U.S. 542 (1876).

The triumph of this negation campaign, *The Civil Rights Cases* of 1883, again saw the judges employing the judicial review power to invalidate the crowning achievement of the previous decade—the Civil Rights Act of 1875, and specifically its prohibition of the private Right to Discriminate in all public accommodations. In these consolidated cases, defendants had been charged with denying Blacks access to hotels, theaters, railroad cars, and the like in states ranging from California to New York; "four of the five defendants did not even bother appearing to argue the case before the Court, but they nevertheless received a favorable ruling for their clients."[39] Blinding themselves to the fact that private actions and public codes worked together to control the same people in the same ways and through similar means after the Civil War—through Black Codes, as they had done before the Civil Wars with Slave Codes— the 1883 judges confirmed their *Cruikshank* interpretation that the reach of the Fourteenth Amendment extended only to state action, thus in effect resurrecting judicially the one-way Right to Discriminate despite so many acts of Congress intended to reach precisely the opposite result.

In the *Slaughterhouse Cases*, *Cruikshank*, the *Civil Rights Cases*, and other similar anti-equality adjudications of the latter 1800s that remain beyond the scope of this chapter,[40] the judges stepped beyond review and into revision. In choosing to do so, they established the basic judicial posture toward the first Reconstruction re-enacted by successive generations of appointees toward equality policy: reactionary activism dedicated to the revision of the postbellum reforms and to the negation or truncation of legal equality's social meaning. Over time, and on the whole, judicial appointees have been the most ardent, and certainly the most effective, protectors of the racial state. Judicial review has been their indispensable instrument.

Before the end of the century, then, judicial revisionism incrementally had culminated in the separate-but-equal fiction that protected not equality of liberty as a substantive individual right, but rather supremacist antebellum-style racial factionalism that legally coerced "separate" social spheres for Blacks and Whites by using, without any apparent sense of irony, the underlying fiction that both spheres of this racial division were materially, functionally, and hence constitutionally, equal. But as verified by the record facts of *Plessy v. Ferguson* in 1896,[41] in which racial segregation in rail transportation was squared with "equal protection" precisely on these non-credible terms, and by the documented facts of many other cases leading up to and following *Brown v. Board of Education* in 1954,[42] in which the same factually untenable fiction finally was rejected in the context of public education, places and facilities kept forcibly separate for nonwhites were certainly *never* even near to "equal" in fact to the comforts and advantages provided by Whites for Whites only. When the revisionist activists in *Plessy* and so many other similar cases made their choices to uphold this increasing flimsy ideological fiction in the name of the Fourteenth Amendment, they also surely knew the same—and not only because the record facts, and John Harlan's famous dissent, had put the factual specifics and power dynamics of social reality squarely in front of them.

Thus, barely 20 years after the postbellum reforms, judges of the late 1800s had pushed all that legislative and constitutional work aside to bless the materially unequal racial segregation documented in the *Plessy* record. Despite historically momentous and repeated democratic exercises to the contrary, postbellum appointees deployed judicial review to entrench legal and social antebellum race-based baselines repudiated by the framers of the constitutional and legislative provisions that those later judges professed to faithfully interpret and apply. Legal blindness, assiduously and strategically cultivated as jurisprudential method, promptly descended on justice to allow social and legal inequality to flourish under the calculated protection of state law in direct or effective contravention of repeated acts of Congress, as well as of the Constitution itself. Despite Harlan's powerful dissent in *Plessy*, as the nineteenth century prepared to set, the reconstructed Constitution had been forcibly blinded not to skin color but to social fact, a willful and strategic blindness still selectively cultivated by today's anti-equality activism.

In the first term of the new century, the judges thus were poised to invoke all the doctrinal truisms that their opinions had compiled since the 1870s in a case involving again, as occurred often since the *Slaughterhouse Cases*, both equal protection and privileges and immunities. Approving separate (non-racial) legal systems

39 Alexander Tsesis, The Thirteenth Amendment and American Freedom: A Legal History 69 (2004).

40 A more extensive and detailed account appears in Francisco Valdes, *Obstruction of Justice: Equality in the U.S. Under Judicial Review*, ____ Brit. J. Am. Leg. Studies (forthcoming 2016 _____).

41 Plessy v. Ferguson, 163 U.S. 537 (1896).

42 Brown v. Bd. of Ed., 347 U.S. 483 (1954).

for the free inhabitants of a single state, Utah in 1900, the judges reasserted in *Maxwell v. Dow* one of the many inaccurate propositions from the *Slaughterhouse Cases*: that the Fourteenth Amendment does not meaningfully protect any privileges and immunities apart from those pre-existing it. But then, on equality, the *Maxwell* judges added:

> We might go still further and say, with undoubted truth, that there is nothing in the Constitution to prevent any state from adopting any system of laws or judicature it sees fit for all or any part of its territory ... If diversities of laws and judicial proceedings may exist in the several states without violating the equality clause in the Fourteenth Amendment, there is no solid reason why there may not be such diversities in different parts of the same state.[43]

With this pithy additional pronouncement specifically on equal protection and criminal procedure, the judges showed the nation just how resurrected the states' rights regime of antebellum federalism now was, as the following passages of that remarkable 1900 opinion make clear:

> The Fourteenth Amendment does not profess to secure to all persons in the United States the benefit of the same laws and the same remedies ... For, as before said, it has respect to persons and classes of persons. It means that no person or class of persons shall be denied the same protection of the laws which is enjoyed by other persons or other classes in the same place and under like circumstances.[44]

As *Plessy*, *Maxwell*, and other similar opinions from those times demonstrate, reactionary judicial activism had succeeded by century's end to reconstitutionalize the use of class legislation within a single state—and, stunningly, in the name of deferring to democratic policymaking: by 1900, nearly three decades' judicial opining on equal protection had turned the Supremacy Clause of the original Constitution downside up, establishing situations in which the shifting results of putative democracy, whether local, state, or national, easily could trump bedrock principles of constitutional supremacy.

As these and similar postbellum judicial declarations officially congealed formally into "precedent," the judges in effect were constructing, brick by jurisprudential brick, an overarching separate-but-equal construct in the form of law increasingly adaptable to squaring equality with supremacy. Because of historical commitments to *stare decisis*, these early body blows to constitutional equality then continued to reverberate systemically throughout U.S. law and society, sending and normalizing strong ripples of antebellum preferences through modern culture. This toxic combination in the U.S. of common law tradition and White supremacy over time has served to impede retirement of the antebellum racial state despite its formal constitutional repudiation during the Reconstruction, and to protect instead the postbellum neo-racial version that continues to hold substantial sway over U.S. society and policy to this very day.

Interpretive Methods of Inequality: The Social Politics of "Strict Construction"

As outlined above, the judicial campaign to negate equality and obstruct justice relies on the manipulation both of method and of substance. Notions and techniques ranging from states' rights to legal blindness combine in myriad ways to suggest that hierarchy and equality are in normative and constitutional harmony. Another key method in the anti-equality toolkit has focused on controlling the very processes of constitutional interpretation in equality law and politics.

Original and antebellum constitutional debates over federal powers and "federalism" also had occasioned founding consideration of "strict construction" as a possible interpretive technique to be applied to constitutional text.[45] This technique posited the substantive premise that constitutional interpretation ought to proceed cautiously, and thus the text should be construed narrowly—strictly. In theory, strict construction

43 Maxwell v. Dow, 176 U.S. 581, 598–99 (1900).

44 *Id.* at 599.

45 Joseph M. Lynch, Negotiating The Constitution: The Earliest Debates Over Original Intent, 71–92 (1999).

of constitutional text may be seen as plausible, perhaps innocuous, especially in common law jurisdictions already accustomed to prudential thoughts like these. In practice, strict construction has been performed as identity politics in the service of original hierarchies while masquerading as neutral interpretive method.

Originally articulated as a fallback argument of antifederalist factions seeking to undermine the new government's powers after losing the ratification struggle over the original Constitution, "strict constructionism" has always served the same basic, political purposes: both to unite fears of centralized power that form part of the American common law legacy and to give some cover to otherwise naked identity politics that buttress the one-way Right to Discriminate. It thus lent itself to political and legal arguments in favor of selectively expansive "states' rights" in the antebellum years, as well as since, yet traveling mostly in one consistent direction: "states' rights" for states lining up with original inequalities, but, as noted earlier and illustrated vividly by the *Dred Scott* case, with very little of the same for states electing abolition of racial slavery specifically, and repudiation of White supremacy more structurally. Precisely because "states' rights" since the founding of the Republic has served as thinly disguised political code for White supremacy's social and legal protection by state (and federal) law, strict constructionism has been targeted chiefly and specifically at federal constitutional authority that might promote or protect equality's advance in the United States, increasingly becoming a ready implement in the postbellum anti-equality toolkit that remains in use to this day.

Juridically, therefore, "strict construction" often is found accompanied by corollary assertions of "states' rights," and each effectively employs the same basic rhetorical strategies developed over U.S. history by political factions since before 1789 that feared federal authority could interfere with local power hierarchies, beginning with the "antifederalists" of the eighteenth century and continued by the Jeffersonians during the period of Alexander Hamilton's influence in the George Washington administrations. Ironically, or perhaps not, key founders like Thomas Jefferson and James Madison belatedly became opposed to the strong federal government that they had helped to establish, but only when they felt a loss of personal control over it; this oppositional posture suited them only until they themselves were later elected President of that government, at which they time they no longer cared to be bound by a "strict construction" of the powers they then wielded. (As President, for instance, Jefferson certainly did not abide by a strict construction of his powers as he proceeded unilaterally to purchase the Louisiana territory form Napoleon's France, nor did he fret over it later.) Since these times, this fundamental type of strategic methodological inconsistency has characterized the practice of strict construction and the related cries of federalism and states' rights, both in and out of the courtroom, leaving political valence the only sure constant driving applications of this anti-equality trio.

No wonder, then, that this strategic pose and founding rhetoric were emphasized and thematized in the nineteenth century by minoritarian Southern local factions intent on preserving and expanding nationally slave interests throughout the United States. No wonder that this same line was continued during the post-Civil War Jim Crow era, and into the twentieth century, by the KKK and other "segregationists" who vowed to maintain the North American system of *de jure* apartheid until eventually producing the famous mid-twentieth century clashes between federal troops and state militias during the racial integration of southern schools following *Brown v. Board of Education*. More specifically even, as applied historically (and today), federalism, states' rights, strict construction, and their conceptual cousins (like modern-day originalism, discussed below) have been used strategically and selectively, yet quite ideologically consistently, to undermine national power under the two principal clauses of the Constitution employed during the earlier part of the same century by the federal government's elected branches to protect social, political, and economic underdogs from the traditional, neocolonial identity politics of ensconced racial elites: the Commerce Clause of Article I and Section 5 of the Fourteenth Amendment, as elaborated below.

Notably, however, strict interpretation as constitutional methodology was rejected explicitly, repeatedly, and authoritatively by the original generation of U.S. judges in some of the earliest landmark cases interpreting the Constitution and establishing judicial methods of constitutional construction. Those men were no more infallible than their successors, but in definitive cases known to all, like *Marbury v. Madison*, *McCulloch v. Maryland*, or *Gibbons v. Ogden*,[46] the judges of the founding generation were urged to construe the Constitution

46 Marbury v. Madison, 5 U.S. 137 (1803); McCulloch v. Maryland, 17 U.S. 316 (1819); Gibbons v. Ogden, 22 U.S. 1, 222 (1824).

strictly, and they declined emphatically, listing some of the method's obvious dangers to the viability of the new national government. For example, the influential Chief Justice, John Marshall, and his colleagues explained, at length, in the 1819 opinion deciding *McCulloch*, that a "strict" interpretive approach would exert a "baneful influence" on American constitutionalism, incrementally narrowing the scope of federal authority, and rendering the federal Constitution "a splendid bauble" but "incompetent" for national self-governance.

Instead they opted for an approach they called "fair" or "sound" constitutional interpretation. Thus, the threshold choice was understood as between "strict" vs. "sound" or "fair" construction. In the first-generation minds of judges like Marshall, "strict" signified unsound, unfair, incompetent.[47]

Five years later, in *Gibbons*, another early landmark case, first-generation judges expounded on this point further, in effect confirming that *McCulloch*'s foundational rejection of "strict" construction in favor of "sound" interpretation as adjudicatory method was neither inadvertent nor casual, nor to be ignored cavalierly by future generations of judges under the norms and rules of common law systems.[48]

Subsequent generations of federal judges have repeated the admonition, reminding the nation of its core insights. Thus, in 1952, as the second Reconstruction brewed, Felix Frankfurter explained:

> Deeply embedded ways of conducting government cannot supplant the Constitution or legislation, but they can give meaning to the words of a text or supply them. It is an inadmissibly narrow conception of American constitutional law to confine it to the words of the Constitution and to disregard the gloss which life has written upon them.[49]

After all this admonition and explanation, contemporary appointees who now opt to use the discredited methodology of supposedly "strict" constitutional construction do so for reasons other than interpretive necessity, utility, or legitimacy.

Historically, as noted above, this interpretative methodology was applied in a positively selective manner designed to yield legal consistency only in the form of particular anti-equality outcomes. More recently, as explained below in the discussion of modern-day anti-equality judging, the mantra of strict construction still is avidly urged, but only and increasingly in the interpretation of constitutional provisions thought to promote substantive equality—like "equal protection" included under the Fourteenth Amendment—while silently erased from consideration in the interpretation of other constitutional provisions thought to preserve original compromises and antebellum inequalities—like "states' rights" asserted under the Tenth Amendment. Today, as outlined further below, the White supremacism of strict construction is demonstrated under the banner of a "new" federalism applied one-sidedly only against federal power that is specifically supportive of civil rights for traditionally subordinated constituencies. Modern-day appointees still electing to deploy this particular anti-equality stratagem, like the stratagem of states' rights, or like that other interpretive technique—"originalism"—therefore choose to do so knowing all of this, and perhaps because of it, whether consciously or not, and whether acknowledged or not. To imagine otherwise is to impute fundamental ignorance of basic legal history and notions to professedly learned jurists.

Second Efforts and "New" Difficulties: Reconstruction, Resistance and Redux

In retrospect, the first attempt at reconstructing federalism in the nineteenth century established a dynamic that has been repeated since then along roughly similar lines: in order to address institutionalized inequalities at local and regional levels, national authorities enact protective measures until backlash and resistance at local levels eventually overwhelm the national will to reform, and ultimately clear political space for local and national restoration of the practices and incentives that had sustained the inequalities of the prior era/s. In this process, the deployment of the judicial review power to gut or outright invalidate legislative or constitutional reforms has been indispensable to redirecting the arc of postbellum history time and again. Thus, after a

47 *McCulloch*, 17 U.S. 399, 421.

48 Gibbons v. Ogden, 22 U.S. 1, 222 (1824).

49 Youngstown Sheet & Tube Co. v. Sawyer, 343 U.S. 279, 610 [1952] (Frankfurter, J. concurring).

near-century of negating and neutralizing the Reconstruction of federalism in favor of equality after the Civil War, the effective restoration of antebellum social, economic, and political conditions had been so successful that a new round of national reform erupted in the mid-twentieth century. Much like the first Reconstruction, the second was characterized by a brief period of extraordinary national initiative followed by the very same strategies of violent and institutional resistance, both private and public, that had proven so successful in undermining the first attempt a century before.

But unlike the first Reconstruction, which had been shaped mainly by White identity politics focused mostly on race and racisms internal to the United States, the second Reconstruction was driven both by "traditional" domestic racial frictions as well as by morphing geopolitical priorities shaped externally by the Cold War that followed World War II. Internally, the Black Civil Rights Movement created new political pressures and costs on the maintenance of White supremacy. Externally, the emerging politics of international competition between globalizing elites based in the United States and those based in the Soviet Union added another layer of new complexity, as U.S. national authorities found themselves forced to defend domestic racial apartheid specifically in the South while preaching freedom and democracy worldwide.[50] Realizing this racial "convergence of interests" in the midst of that uphill battle, by the mid-twentieth century national U.S. elites began to repudiate White supremacy formally, both legislatively and judicially, while pursuing a second reconstructive campaign on the remaining constitutional foundations of the first, even as these had been reconfigured by negative doctrinal convolutions, like the state action doctrine discussed above.[51] In part for these familiar reasons, the second Reconstruction has fared no better than the first: reformatory dynamics have followed the same basic sequence of Reconstruction and resistance resulting in redux.

This second Reconstruction was marked initially by landmark judicial rulings, like *Brown v. Board of Education* in 1954,[52] *Baker v. Carr* in 1962,[53] *Loving v. Virginia* in 1967,[54] and *Jones v. Alfred H. Mayer* in 1968,[55] all seeking to vindicate the original conception of equally protected individual rights embodied in the constitutional and statutory initiatives between 1865 and 1875. With equally landmark national legislation modeled on the initiatives of a century earlier, like the four Civil Rights Acts of 1956, 1957, 1960, and 1964, the comprehensive Voting Rights Act of 1965, the national Fair Housing Act of 1968, and even the Immigration Reform Act of 1965, Congress employed the same democratic structures and substance of the first Reconstruction to finally secure the original equality intentions of postbellum lawmaking: numerous federal civil rights laws focused on promulgating and enforcing socio-economic relations of legal equality within an expanded polity and diversified society. Moreover, the nation once again as a whole joined this second formal repudiation of White supremacy by law, enacting in 1964 another amendment to the Constitution, only the twenty-fourth in history, to prohibit expressly and positively voter suppression tactics still enabling minority White elites to control state governments under the type of judicial protection outlined above to enact and enforce state and local inequality. As in the first Reconstruction, these equality reforms formally redrew the U.S. social compact, but the judges yet again arrested the law; although the backlash opinions of the culture war cases like those discussed below are not limited to race and equality, they focus inordinately on second Reconstruction legal legacies because laws like these are the principal bulwarks protecting against a judicial or political restoration of antebellum-style society.

With opinions in contexts ranging from national security to higher education like *Korematsu v. United States* in 1944[56] to *Regents of the University of California v. Bakke* in 1978[57] that at once denounced racial in/equality while abetting the established normativity of White power and privilege, the original existential contradiction of U.S. nationhood was being updated for modernity. Reflecting the remains of the first

50 Mary L. Dudziak, Cold War Civil Rights: Race and the Image of American Democracy (2000).

51 Derrick A Bell Jr, *Comment, Brown v. Board of Education and the Interest-Convergence Dilemma*, 93 Harv. L. Rev. 518 (1980).

52 Brown v. Bd. of Ed., 347 U.S. 483 (1954).

53 Baker v. Carr, 369 U.S. 186 (1962).

54 Loving v. Virginia, 388 U.S. 1 (1967).

55 Jones v. Alfred H. Mayer, 392 U.S. 409 (1968).

56 Korematsu v. United States, 323 U.S. 214 (1944).

57 Regents of the University of California v. Bakke, 438 U.S. 265 (1978).

Reconstruction, the revival of equality by the second would now subject state-sponsored classifications that inflicted invidious discrimination on the basis of race to "strict" judicial scrutiny, and tolerate them only if deemed "compelling" and "narrowly tailored" by five of nine judges. The formal suspension, and hence formal absence, of positive *de jure* supremacy became the promised land of formal equality; the formally equalized restructuring of social opportunity was, itself, the formal realization of legal antidiscrimination, even if not a single fact actually changed on the ground. Instead of White supremacy thriving under the anti-equality doctrines of antebellum federalism, states' rights, and strict construction, White privilege now could continue structurally intact under the timid doctrines of formal equality and the antidiscrimination principle defining the second Reconstruction. But even these were too much to bear, as newfound concerns suddenly erupted over the anti-democratic implications of judicial review.

Directed specifically at *Brown* and overlooking the democratic lawmaking of the second Reconstruction, this "counter-majoritarian difficulty" emphasized that legislation is democratic, and therefore judicial review applied to invalidate such lawmaking, presumably as in *Brown*, is inherently antidemocratic. Thus, judicial invalidation of legislation, especially in the name of minority rights, thereby was said to trigger a "counter-majoritarian difficulty"—a difficulty of course enabled only by a premise that lawmaking through legislation is a democratic affair, an expression of popular will. Coupled with strategic assertions of (pro-equality) "judicial activism" and other strategically politicized slogans, this so-called difficulty and perceived lack of neutral principles—which overlooks the command of "equal protection" itself—have provided an exaggerated sense of justification during the latter half of the twentieth century for curbing even episodic judicial vindication of the original intentions and purposes behind the Civil War amendments and implementing federal legislation. Ironically, as previously noted, no such "difficulty" over politics and neutrality was widely trafficked a century earlier, when the judges were so busy coopting equality lawmaking following the Civil War.

Taking this historical irony to a completely different level is the fact that this newfound "difficulty" may be seen as rooted in New Deal critiques of judicial activism during the 1930s and beyond.[58] Facing the wholesale judicial invalidation of their legislative agenda despite securing landslide electoral victories, New Deal lawmakers from the President on down argued for judicial deference to democracy and majoritarianism—the will of the people. Yet the historical fact remains that this twentieth-century "difficulty" never posed a problem specifically in race cases when inequality was judicially upheld; the well-known and historically understood counter-majoritarian implications inherent in judicial review whenever it may be exercised became widely perceived and defined as a special species of difficulty only in the 1950s, when equality seemed to prevail in race cases. This belated counter-majoritarian difficulty took an inter-branch conflict over the historical debate on the proper balancing of democracy and judicial review that began even before *Marbury* was decided in 1803, and transformed it effectively into a key tool in the modern-day anti-equality arsenal. It quickly became the "central obsession of modern constitutional scholarship."[59]

By the mid-to-late 1970s, with the reactionary politics of anti-equality retrenchment and White backlash taking hold both politically and juridically,[60] activist judicial promotion of the reactionary "culture wars" was set to launch. Five professedly "strict constructionist" appointees chosen by Richard Nixon and Gerald Ford between 1971–75 were in operational control of the Supreme Court under a new Nixonian Chief Justice, Warren Burger. The Court was ready to begin rolling back, actively, the advances of the second Reconstruction, and to resume aggressively the historic judicial campaign against democratic equality policy. By the close of the 1980s, "liberal" precedents of the early second Reconstruction were increasingly being overturned, and doctrinal revision of "equal" protection was intensifying.[61]

---

58 Robert M. Cover, *The Origins of Judicial Activism in the Protection of Minorities*, 91 YALE L.J. 1287 (1982).

59 Barry Friedman, *The History of the Counter majoritarian Difficulty, Part One: The Road to Judicial Supremacy*, 73 N.Y.U. L. REV. 334 (1998).

60 Kimberlé Williams Crenshaw, *Race, Reform, and Retrenchment: Transformation and Legitimation in Antidiscrimination Law*, 101 HARV. L. REV. 1331 (1988); Kenneth L. Karst, *Religion, Sex, and Politics: Cultural Counterrevolution in Constitutional Perspective*, 24 U.C. DAVIS L. REV. 677 (1991); Keith Aoki, *The Scholarship of Reconstruction and the Politics of Backlash*, 81 IOWA L. REV. 1467 (1996).

61 MARK V. TUSHNET, A COURT DIVIDED: THE REHNQUIST COURT AND THE FUTURE OF CONSTITUTIONAL LAW (2005).

As promised in 1968, the anti-equality, anti-second Reconstruction opinions of the latter twentieth century begin promptly, effectively commencing in earnest during the second half of the 1970s, when the newly ensconced appointees began tinkering with "intent" as applied to state action in equality cases under the Fourteenth Amendment, and sometimes under related civil rights legislation. At that time, of course, the legacy of the common law provided much-refined definitions of intent founded on "foreseeability" as the basis of legal intentionality, developed in multiple bodies of well-established precedent ranging from contract to tort. More particularly, as noted above, the judges of the second Reconstruction had developed analytical frameworks for formal equality specifically in race equal protection cases that focused on "invidious" intent as the touchstone of constitutionally prohibited discriminations. Yet, succeeding judges later chose to ignore the sum of those institutional and intellectual legacies in favor of new intent definitions and gauntlets that predictably would undermine even the modest remaining systemic commitments to formal equality.

In *Washington v. Davis* (1976), the judges rebuffed equality claims pressed by Black public employees using statistical evidence of bias in employment practices that resulted in predictably skewed patterns correlated to race. Absent the holy grail of invidious intent, the racially skewed realities of the situation before them were attributed to the disparate impacts of neutral, unbiased, employment practices.[62] No intent, no invidiousness, no remedy, they opined. Then, just one year later, in the 1977 case of *Personnel Administrator of Massachusetts v. Feeney* in a gender inequality context they cemented the *Davis* approach with a remarkable conclusion: that a state law preference in favor of veterans for civil service positions did not manifest the necessary discriminatory intent despite the well-known and foreseeable correlation in that era between gender and the chosen statutory preference, when one gender was categorically forbidden by law from all military service.[63] Referring to intent's well-established legal meanings, the *Feeney* judges acknowledged it would be "disingenuous" to deny the statutory correlation of gender to employability in precisely the sense established by centuries of common law adjudication: "in the sense that [the selected statutory preference] was not volitional or in the sense that [the correlation of the selected preference to gender] was not foreseeable." They nonetheless did just that, summarily declaring:

> Discriminatory purpose [requires] more than intent as volition or intent as awareness of consequences. It implies that the decision maker [chose] or reaffirmed a particular course of action at least in part "because of" not merely "in spite of" its adverse effects upon an identifiable group.[64]

And thus a newly minted definition of "intent" loaded with evidentiary demands like never before was invented specifically for modern equality cases, instantly disadvantaging constitutional claimants, who in those days tended still to be from historically subjugated (nonwhite) groups. By 1977 *Feeney* and *Davis* thus stood as the twin pillars of a new Fourteenth Amendment intent requirement never envisioned by its creators, a free-floating standard so difficult to satisfy that anti-equality judges have since then been forced to relax it specifically for White claimants in 1980s and 1990s remedial discrimination (or "affirmative action") cases in order to be able to declare those particular claims meritorious, as elaborated below.

In the next two decades, the judges confirmed in place the now-familiar legal architecture of contemporary equal protection jurisprudence. From the late 1980s to the mid-1990s, anti-equality judges in "culture war" cases like *Croson* and *Wards Cove* imposed "strict scrutiny" on contemporary democratic efforts to vindicate the original intentions of the postbellum period, and to the same effect: negation and invalidation of substantive equality policy, and a relicensing of original sins and continuing wrongs. Along the way, and building on *Davis-Feeney*'s interpretive license, they managed to erase explicit discussion of "invidious" intent as a legal element for finding the malice necessary to constitute unlawful discrimination, and instead elected to impute or effectively assume such invidiousness only and specifically in remedial race cases pressed by White claimants to halt democratically adopted affirmative action policies.

Three 1989 rulings—*Antonio v. Wards Cove Packing Co., Inc.*, *City of Richmond v. J.A. Croson, Co.*, and *Patterson v. McLean Credit Union*—exemplify contemporary anti-equality judging, and its hostility to

62 Washington v. Davis, 426 U.S. 229 (1976).

63 Pers. Adm'r of Massachusetts v. Feeney, 442 U.S. 256 (1979).

64 *Feeney*, 442 U.S. 256, 258.

civil rights generally, while paying solemn lip service to the antidiscrimination principle at the base of formal equality.[65] The first two focus on race in antidiscrimination employment contexts, both under the Constitution and federal legislation, while the latter focuses on race and the Fourteenth Amendment in affirmative action nonfederal set-aside programs. In each case, the majority claimed faithful adherence to the antidiscrimination principle underlying formal equality and its remedial mandates. But, as Thurgood Marshall observed publically at the time, "the Court's approach to civil rights cases has changed markedly … It is difficult to characterize last term's decisions as a product of anything other than a deliberate retrenching of the civil rights agenda."[66]

Since this trio of rulings, and with the arguable exception of *Grutter v. Bollinger* in 2003,[67] only White people have prevailed on the merits before the Supreme Court under the federal Constitution's Equal Protection Clause, and in each instance to roll back "affirmative action" programs designed by local state or federal *majorities* primarily to undo White privilege. This stunning reversal in the legal and social application of the antidiscrimination principle, accomplished in significant part through repeated reversals of direct precedent, continues to negate equality claims in the twenty-first century through ways and means that correlate, in deed if not in words, closely to the color of the claimant's skin. As one scholar explains:

> Taken together, the Court's race decisions over the past few decades make it quite easy for white plaintiffs to make out a claim of reverse discrimination—to invalidate good faith legislative and executive efforts to make equality meaningful—but near impossible for minority plaintiffs to make out a claim of discrimination, even if the circumstances closely resemble traditional discrimination against minorities or pre-Brown segregation.[68]

To accomplish this remarkable inversion, "the Court has essentially established two distinct sets of rules, assumptions, and approaches that depend on whether Whites or minorities are claiming discrimination."[69] Defying most contemporary definitions of law, the result is a "dual system" of equality adjudication rather than a uniform, consistent body of rules applied equally to all discrimination claims. But blocking the first Reconstruction's use as the basis for a second was not all.

In addition to narrowing the federal power to promote equality generally, and racial equality specifically, in substantive terms under landmark reconstructive legislation, modern-day judges also have elected to tackle federal power to promote antidiscrimination as law and policy in more broadly structural terms, apart from their interventions in the structure and administration of formal democracy, and focusing chiefly on four constitutional provisions related to federalism. The first, Congressional power under the Commerce Clause of Article I, is the only one of the four found in the body of the original document. The other three are found in the amendments to the original: the Tenth Amendment, the Eleventh Amendment, and Section 5 of the Fourteenth Amendment, which contains its enforcement provisions. Only one of these four is explicitly linked to White supremacy—Section 5 of the Fourteenth Amendment—but all four play a key role in the promotion or inhibition of racial equality in general social terms. Signaling their ideological predispositions, modern anti-equality judges insist on a strict construction of the first and last, but a promiscuously open-ended approach specifically to the Tenth and Eleventh Amendments. The inconsistency of interpretive approaches is never acknowledged, much less explained even as the consistency of outcomes points to the hidden determinants directing the selectivity of anti-equality activism since the second Reconstruction.

As illustrated in the mid-1960s by early second Reconstruction landmarks like *Heart of Atlanta v. United States* and *Katzenbach v. McClung*, which had tested federal power over inter-state commerce to outlaw private discrimination (yet again),[70] the Commerce Clause, and Section 5, have proven to be the main sources of federal legislative authority over substantive civil rights law and national equality policy—over federal

65 Wards Cove Packing Co., Inc. v. Antonio, 490 U.S. 642 (1989; City of Richmond v. J.A. Croson, Co., 488 U.S. 469 (1989); Patterson v. McLean Credit Union, 491 U.S. 164 (1989).

66 Hon. Thurgood Marshall, Transcription of Remarks, Annual Judicial Conference, Second Circuit of the United States, 130 F.R.D. 165, 166–67 (1990).

67 Grutter v. Bollinger, 539 U.S. 306 (2003).

68 David Kairys, *A Brief History of Race and the Supreme Court*, 79(3) Temp. L. Rev. 751, 764–65 (2006).

69 *Id.*

70 Heart of Atlanta Motel Inc. v. United States, 379 U.S. 241 (1964); Katzenbach v. McClung, 379 U.S. 294 (1964).

authority to legislate the antidiscrimination principle into law, and to enforce the Equal Protection Clause of the Fourteenth Amendment, after the constraints imposed by opinions that are still generally regarded as legitimate precedent, like the 1873 *Slaughterhouse Cases* and the 1883 *Civil Rights Cases*. But using idiosyncratic reinterpretations of the Tenth and Eleventh Amendments, modern-day culture-war judges were prepared by the mid-1990s to begin in earnest to put an end to that. Two 1995 cases, *Adarand v. Peña* and *United States v. Lopez*,[71] mark the doctrinal ascendancy of this anti-equality structural effort to tightly circumscribe—strictly construe—federal legislative discretion over national policymaking under Section 5 and the Commerce Clause, respectively. Both also form part of the long litany of modern-day anti-second Reconstruction opinions issued by the "narrowest of margins and over spirited dissents."[72]

In *Adarand*, the judges overturned a key then-recent, pro-equality precedent—*Metro Broadcasting, Inc. v. FCC*—to subject for the first time ever Congress' use of remedial Section 5 powers to their "strict" judicial scrutiny, thus giving themselves new heightened powers broadly to invalidate civil rights legislation, while also simultaneously inhibiting general legislative capacity to use antidiscrimination law to root out socially entrenched racial realities that were historically instilled and valorized *de jure*.[73] In *Lopez*, they declared that Congress had no power to regulate guns around public schools under the Commerce Clause because, they asserted, gun control is not related to commerce, while under the Tenth Amendment gun regulation falls beyond federal reach.[74] Although *Lopez* itself was not an antidiscrimination suit, the generalized reduction of federal legislative power under the Commerce Clause came freighted with historical and potential significance for antidiscrimination law and policy, as was borne out during the next several terms.

The very next year, 1996, the judges were busy emplacing the related doctrinal conditions necessary for this sweeping reduction in the substantively remedial antidiscrimination powers of the federal government, as exemplified by their "new federalism" pronouncements in *Seminole Tribe of Florida v. Florida*,[75] another opinion supported only by the "narrowest of margins and issued over spirited dissents." There, five judges decided that Congress had no power under the portion of the Commerce Clause relating to "Indian tribes" to subject states to suits in federal court for violations of federal rights because their newly minted reinterpretation of the Eleventh Amendment clashed with, and trumped, Article I of the original Constitution. Congress therefore could not authorize suits against states under the Commerce Clause for violations of federal rights. Within a few short years, backlashing rulings like these had managed to begin sidelining the principal sources of federal antidiscrimination lawmaking employed during the past century to enact most of second Reconstruction statutes—thus bringing them all into arguable constitutional question.

In the first term of the new millennium, another quintet of anti-equality judges next pronounced, yet again over "spirited dissents," in *United States v. Morrison*,[76] that Congress could not, again under the Commerce Clause, enact the civil remedy provisions of the Violence Against Women Act, because violence against women—like gun control in *Lopez*—was, in their view, unrelated to "commerce." Moreover, Section 5 powers also failed here, the five judges declared in *Morrison*, because, in their view, the problem of "violence against women" simply did not merit the sort of policy response that Congress had enacted. Although a case focused on gender issues, *Morrison* provides a classic yet contemporary exemplar of judicial "legislation from the bench," and illustrates aptly the box into which contemporary judges have put federal civil rights power; the cumulative doctrinal valence of their 5–4 opinions in *Adarand, Lopez, Seminole Tribe, Morrison* (and other recent culture war cases) is designed to eviscerate the potential for either the Commerce Clause or Section 5 to serve as sturdy bases of federal pro-equality activity in the new millennium.

---

71 Adarand Constructors, Inc. v. Peña, 515 U.S. 200 (1995); United States v. Lopez, 514 U.S. 549 (1995).

72 Payne v Tennessee, 501 U.S. 808, 830 (1991) (Rehnquist C.J.) (describing general categories of precedents most suitable for overruling: constitutional cases, which unlike cases interpreting statutes cannot be corrected by Congress if they are in error; cases involving rules of evidence or procedural rights, in which people have no vested economic interest; and cases that have been decided "by the narrowest of margins, over spirited dissents challenging the basic underpinnings of those decisions."

73 *Adarand*, 515 U.S. 200; Metro Broadcasting, Inc. v. FCC, 497 U.S. 547 (1990).

74 United States v. Lopez, 514 U.S. 549 (1995).

75 Seminole Tribe of Florida v. Florida, 517 U.S. 44 (1996).

76 United States v. Morrison, 529 U.S. 598 (2000).

These and similar backlash rulings, all imputed to a "new" antebellum-style federalism, have asserted "for the first time since the founding of the Republic that Congress has no authority to subject a State to the jurisdiction of a federal court at the behest of an individual asserting a federal right"—an astonishing judicial assertion entailing wholesale reversals of longstanding precedent.[77] In other words, a bare majority of five judges effectively has announced in these remarkable opinions that Congress perhaps may pass its antidiscrimination and civil rights laws, but it cannot authorize suits by private citizens to enforce such concededly constitutional laws, nor to remedy their actual violation, because states, after all, have their "rights" too—one Civil War and two Reconstructions notwithstanding. To historically alert observers, these modern-day intonations eerily echo the claims, values, and logics of "nullification" federalism prior to the Civil War. With these and similar rulings of the new millennium, disregarding ancient common law tenets concerning precedent, injury, remedy, and equity, contemporary anti-equality appointees deny to the remedy the tools necessary to match and fit the harm, thus leaving in place the *de facto status quo* previously established and consolidated *de jure*.[78]

Deploying the federal judicial review power to prohibit the use of the Law to undo what the Law previously was marshaled to do, they invent modern implements of in/equality designed to play down the politics of contemporary judicial review in a very specific context: U.S. cultural warfare.

Culture by Law: Neo-Racial Democracy and Reactionary Judicial Activism

The "culture wars"[79] of the United States, brewing and waged since the New Deal, have taken a particularly severe turn since January 2009, when the United States inaugurated its first nonwhite President as the nation-state's 44th Chief Executive. This specific wave of backlash, and cultural warfare more generally, are best understood in proximate functional relationship to each other as expressions of the same anti-equality reactionism rooted in race-based liberty, race-centric democracy, and race-sensitive federalism that have undergirded White supremacy in the United States since the Republic's formal constitution. In this current historical moment, within the United States, this *kulturkampf* is seen in the form of neo-racial retrenchment from, and backlash against, "liberal" law and policy established specifically during the second Reconstruction, the Great Society, and the New Deal.

In U.S. law and jurisprudence, this culture war backlash, spearheaded through organizations like the Federalist Society, which was formed by now-prominent cultural warriors like Antonin Scalia and advanced by politicians like Richard Nixon, Ronald Reagan, and George W. Bush, has attempted to restructure the nation's perspective on its own values and history via a reconfiguration of the very structure of reconstructed federalism with the assistance of federal judicial appointees willing to compromise their responsibility for vindicating inconvenient constitutional rights. The use of judicial appointments to leverage electoral factional power therefore has two sides: backlash appointees serve both to reverse or limit inconvenient laws and precedents, as well as to shield new backlashing laws from meaningful judicial scrutiny. Even though the Constitution is designed to prevent factional overreaching and invidious lawmaking, backlash appointees at every level of the judiciary have re-interpreted statutes, precedents, doctrines, and the text itself to make sure that law licenses just that. In recent decades, as outlined below, reactionary judicial activism has combined with electoral backlash politics to effectuate a present-day neo-racial democracy through sustained cultural warfare.

By the early 1990s culture war appointees were ready to tackle directly race and its intersection with electoral politics—the focal point of the final postbellum amendment, a linchpin in reconstructive efforts to democratize the polity in politically empowering terms both locally and federally, and the solitary focus of the Twenty-Fourth Amendment's specific prohibition in 1964 of voter suppression tactics akin to those invented

---

77 Seminole Tribe of Florida v. Florida, 517 U.S. 44, 100 (1006) (Souter, J. dissenting).

78 Derrick Bell, Silent Covenants: Brown v. Board of Education and the Unfulfilled Hopes for Racial Reform (2004).

79 James Davidson Hunter, Culture Wars: The Struggle to Define America (1991); Paul Galloway, *Divided We Stand: Today's "Cultural War" Goes Deeper Than Political Slogans*, Chi. Trib, Oct. 28, 1992, at C1.

or developed by White factions throughout U.S. history to steal elections and formally mimic democracy. Several important judicial interventions during that decade, notably including another 5–4 bare majority over spirited dissents, *Shaw v. Reno*[80] in 1993, punctuated their efforts in voting rights cases. The pattern is fairly clear: whittle away methodically at federal civil rights legislation purposefully designed to help pry open the doors of the original political system propping up the United States as a racial state—legislation manifestly and plainly designed to enable the meaningful participation in formally "democratic" lawmaking of racial minorities traditionally excluded *de jure* and *de facto* from the electoral, and hence lawmaking, process since the days of antebellum slavery and federalism, and through the century of postbellum Black Codes.

The sociolegal background of these interventions is clear. After decades of poll taxes, literacy tests, and other devices employed by racial elites and factions in operational control of their states to deny in practice the formal right to vote to local racial out-groups, the Voting Rights Act of 1965 was enacted to lend significant federal weight to nonwhite rights to full and meaningful access to electoral power, including a mandate of no "retrogression" in gains. Since then, Congress repeatedly has re-enacted the landmark legislation by ever-greater bipartisan democratic margins. The pro-equality law worked to some extent, creating an unprecedented level of Black and other nonwhite elected officials, but as with other civil rights legislation throughout U.S. history, even meager social effects triggered traditionalist backlash.

Despite those modest gains, original and enduring patterns of racialized democracy have continued to structure U.S. electoral politics more broadly. In the most recent nationwide illustration of this phenomenon, the 2012 national elections, a majority of Whites chose to vote for one faction while the vast majority of nonwhites made the opposite choice: that year, 67 percent of Whites voted for the Republican candidate, while the Democrat was chosen by 93 percent of Blacks, 71 percent of Latinas/os, and 76 percent of Asian-Americans. These coded patterns of racial bloc voting are not new, but the identitarian polarization they represent has grown increasingly acute, widespread, and publically understood.[81]

In a rare moment of political candor, this thickly racialized, deeply entrenched, highly polarized pattern of color-coded bloc voting was cited by the "white party" in the wake of the 2012 presidential election as an increasingly existential issue for itself in a country still obsessed with race but turning significantly darker each electoral cycle. In a self-described post-election diagnostic, the party leadership issued a formal public report acknowledging that:

> The Republican Party must focus its efforts to earn new supporters and voters in the following demographic communities: Hispanic, Asian and Pacific Islanders, African Americans, Indian Americans, Native Americans, women and youth … Unless the RNC gets serious about tackling this problem, we will lose future elections; the data demonstrates this.[82]

When judicial appointees interpose the power of the tribunals they control to alter comprehensive and well-established legal frameworks responsive to these patterns, as five of them have chosen to do in the cases summarized here, they produce correspondingly racially inflected, anti-equality consequences—and they cannot but know it, as pointedly stressed by numerous spirited dissents and contemporaneous news accounts.[83]

Nonetheless, by the 2013 term a majority of the current Supreme Court appointees were prepared to embark on a surgical "demolition" of the Voting Rights Act. In another 5–4 opinion issued over spirited dissents, in *Shelby County v. Holder*,[84] five of today's incumbents invalidated Section II at the heart of

---

80 Shaw v. Reno, 509 U.S. 630 (1993).

81 Terry Smith, Barack Obama, Post-Racialism and the New Politics of Triangulation (2012); Dan Balz, *Obama's Re-Election, by the Numbers*, Wash Post, Nov. 8, 2012, at A24.

82 Republican National Committee, *Growth & Opportunity Project* (2013) http://goproject.gop.com/RNC_Growth_Opportunity_Book_2013.pdf.

83 Evan Thomas & Michael Isikoff, *The Truth Behind the Pillars*, Newsweek, Dec. 25, 2000, at 46; Richard L. Hasen, *Voter Suppression's New Pretext*, N.Y. Times, Nov. 16, 2013, at A19; David Zucchino, *Changes Loom for N.C. Electorate: Republican Leaders Are Pushing Measures That Could Negatively Affect Black Voters*, Los Angeles Times, Jun. 30, 2013 at 16; Charles M. Blow, *Carving Up the Country*, N.Y. Times, Jul 27 2013, at A19.

84 Shelby Cty. v. Holder, 570 U.S. ___ (2013).

the Voting Rights Act's statutory scheme. Known as the "pre-clearance" requirement, this core provision obligated certain jurisdictions, mostly in former slaver states, to secure approval from the U.S. Attorney General before altering state electoral rules or practices that undermine the equality objectives in voting rights mandated by the 1870 Fifteenth Amendment, by the 1964 Twenty-Fourth Amendment, by the 1965 Voting Rights Act itself, and by other expressions of formal public policy. Previously upheld by the Supreme Court more than once, this statutory pre-clearance requirement effectively had removed the upper-hand enjoyed by anti-equality forces ever since the Civil War, but *Shelby County*'s judicial signal was clear and its political cueing effective: within hours of this opinion's release, former slaver jurisdictions like Texas, Mississippi, Alabama, and North Carolina had re-enacted voter photo identification requirements, previously blocked by lower federal courts enforcing the VRA because of their disproportionate impact on Black (and brown) voters.[85] Within days, more had followed; by the end of 2013, 34 of 50 states had legislatively enacted similar identity-inflected voter suppression schemes with the exclusive support of political factions associated with this bare majority of judges—mostly (but certainly not exclusively) in former slaver jurisdictions.[86] Thus, within a year of the racially historic 2012 presidential election, the field of U.S. democracy had been re-leveled, and further skewed artificially, by this tight synchronicity of judicial and political action in preparation for power contests in 2014, 2016, and beyond.

Other milestones on the path from *Reno* to *Shelby County* were the decisions in *Bush v. Gore*,[87] perhaps the most egregious moment of judicial backlash activism in the area of democratic politics during this ongoing rollback of the second Reconstruction, and most recently *Citizens United v. Federal Election Commission*.[88] In *Bush*, a bare majority of judges associated with backlash factions and agendas declared in 2000 over extremely "spirited dissents" that the "equal protection of the laws" constitutionally prevented a state from counting legally cast popular votes in a presidential election that appeared poised to defeat the candidate of that narrow majority's preferred partisan faction.[89] In *Citizens United*, another bare majority declared in 2010—again over spirited dissents—that corporate entities are "persons" equivalent to "humans" under the First Amendment's free-speech provisions, thereby freeing from legal limits on contributions as well as disclosure requirements, the economic and racial elites who use Big Money institutions to buy national and local federal elections.[90] In each instance, "culture war" judges used federal judicial review instrumentally to dismantle the constitutional infrastructure of the second Reconstruction. Because electoral politics have tracked racial politics since before Philadelphia, these cases and opinions are thoroughly coded by the long and dense history of racialized obstructionism against every and all equality reform, practiced fiercely by White colonial and neocolonial settler elites, that always and still characterizes U.S. elections as those of a racial or neo-racial state.[91] The relentless judicial attack on the structure and administration of representative democracy through electoral politics illustrated by these and similar culture war opinions gradually has worked a subversion of democratic pro-equality legacies established both in the first and the second Reconstruction, as the outcomes and rationales of these and similar opinions manifest.

In historical perspective, this current attack is a sustained and determined intervention to reinflate the electoral power of identitarian and related neo/colonial elites that began with the three-fifths Clause of the original Constitution discussed earlier. If the bottom line is a judicial nullification of the reformed social compact constitutionalized after the Civil War and re-legislated a century later during the Cold War, none of the new doctrines and interpretive techniques are more potent than the legal ideology of "originalism."

85 Blow, *supra* note 88; Michael Cooper, *After Ruling, State Rush to Enact Voting Laws*, N.Y. Times, 6 July, 2013, at A9.

86 National Conference of State Legislatures, *Voter Identification Requirements* (Oct. 17, 2013). www.ncsl.org/research/elections-and-campaigns/voter-id.aspx.

87 Bush v. Gore, 531 U.S. 98 (2000).

88 Citizens United v. Federal Election Commission, 558 U.S. ___ (2010).

89 Thomas & Isikoff, *supra* note 88.

90 John Nichols & Robert W. Mccesney, Dollarocracy: How The Money And Media Election Complex is Destroying America (2013).

91 Smith, *supra* note 86.

Ideologies of Inequality: The Cultural Politics of "Originalism"

Unlike strict construction, today's conception of judicial originalism as legal method never surfaced as a mainstream aspect of early U.S. constitutionalism. Instead, the increasingly strident obsession with "original intent" that emerged during the latter part of the twentieth century is a key contemporary example of the extension of anti-equality history to the present. Like strict constructionism, judicial originalism purports to be a neutral methodology. Like strict constructionism, judicial originalism today is not. Like strict constructionism, judicial originalism today is an ideological implement for the practice of identity politics.

While several variants of "originalism" percolate in contemporary legal culture in general,[92] the label refers to the new viewpoint that would privilege "framers' intent" (and related historical indicia) as the first and best answer to all constitutional questions.[93] As Antonin Scalia, the most vocal proponent of this approach, has argued: "Now, my theory of what I do when I try to interpret the American Constitution is I try to understand what it meant, what it was understood to mean when it was adopted. And I don't think it changes since then."[94] This type of present-day judicial originalism consequently has been termed a "one-step" approach to the serious and complex business of constitutional interpretation.[95] All that is required is for today's appointees to appear to be peering back impartially into the distant past, re-enacting whatever choices they imagine might have transpired in that past.

Tellingly, however, early generations of federal judges—contemporaries of the framers—did not pursue original intention as jurisprudential method. Although they referred loosely and in passing, or rhetorically, to constitutional intentions, they did not attempt to sift through particular quotes or phrases from individuals for authoritative constitutional meanings. They did not profess to believe that intention was a source of constitutional interpretation trumping all others. They did not profess, nor practice, originalism as we know it today.[96] As we saw earlier, they professed instead, in the words of John Marshall, a "fair" and "sound" approach to the exercise of federal judicial review, especially in constitutional controversies.[97]

As practiced today, however, judicial originalism privileges a backward-looking analysis that eschews the attempt to account for complexity in the application of texts to accomplish intended goals under ever-changing circumstances. Rather than "interpret" the Constitution "with fidelity," this backward-focused approach omits the necessary "second step" in the process of interpreting or "translating" a text for practical application over time and circumstance—in much the same way that federal judges of all persuasions have been doing routinely since the time of John Marshall.

Aggravating the skewed ideological effects of modern-day judicial originalism is the additional insistence of its advocates that "history and tradition" must be measured at their most narrow or specific level of description, a practice likewise asserted to ensure the principled nature of constitutional interpretations. Another example of strategically "strict" construction, this additional layer of interpretive constriction would reduce the rights involved in *Brown v. Board of Education*, for instance, to the right of Black children to sit next to White children in public school classrooms. Under this approach, the answer to the issue in *Brown* would be simply no, simply because no exact "right" can be found in American neo/colonial history and tradition, even though the results mandated by postbellum equality reforms at both the statutory and constitutional levels are decidedly less clear.[98]

It may thus be the most supreme irony of all in the recent U.S. legal history of equality that judicial originalism's modern-day empowerment may be tied to *Brown* itself. There, the judges famously called for

92 Caleb Nelson, *Originalism and Interpretive Conventions*, 70 U. Chi. L. Rev. 519–98 (2003); Keith E. Whittington, *The New Originalism*, 2 Geo J.L. & Pub Pol'y, 599 (2004); Johnathan O'Neill, Originalism in American Law and Politics: A Constitutional History (2005).

93 Paul Brest, *The Misconceived Quest for the Original Understanding*, 60 B.U. L. Rev. 204–38 (1980).

94 Antonin Scalia and Stephen Breyer, Transcript, A Conversation on the Relevance of Foreign Law for American Constitutional Adjudication with U.S. Supreme Court Justices Antonin Scalia and Stephen Breyer (Jan. 13, 2005). http://www.wcl.american.edu/secle/founders/2005/050113.cfm.

95 Lawrence Lessig, *Fidelity in Translation*, 71 Tex. L. Rev. 1165 (1993).

96 Jack N. Rakove, *The Original Intention of Original Understanding*, 13 Const. Comment. 159 (1996).

97 McCulloch v. Maryland, 17 U.S. (4 Wheat.) 416, 417–18 (1819).

98 Michael McConnell, *Originalism and the Desegregation Decisions*, 81 Va. L. Rev. 947 (1995); Michael McConnell, *The Originalist Case for* Brown v. Board of Education, 19 Harv. J.L. & Pub. Pol'y (457) (1996).

additional briefing specifically on the intent of the framers of the Civil War amendments in relation to racially segregated public schools.[99] As has been suggested, "[t]he Court's request stimulated and gave a kind of official sanction to the search for original intent."[100]

But *Brown* also put judicial originalism's frailties on display. After asking for this briefing, the judges concluded the mountains of evidence indicative of collective lawmaking intent could be read in any number of ways and, more importantly, that the adjudication had to proceed under the facts of the present. Reflecting judicial notice of racial segregation's social and political role as an instrument of White supremacy, the judges famously declared that the practice plainly violated constitutional equality principles embodied in the Fourteenth Amendment and thereby showed that judicial originalism need not be ideologically rigid, nor specifically an ideology of inequality, as it has become.

Brown and numerous other cases show that judges can act in good faith when consulting historical materials for constitutional adjudication. *Brown* and other cases throughout U.S. history show that judges turn to various materials, including historical sources, without using any single one to eclipse or deride the rest, and as part of a larger analytical process aimed ultimately—supposedly—at effectuating the plain meaning of a final binding text in light of this contextualizing background information. That judicial originalism in the U.S. has become a political instrument in the legal resurrection of an antebellum-style social order is a testament to the larger and costly judicial devolution of the past several decades, which has taken place as the federal bench has became increasingly packed with partisan appointees as a key part of the culture wars.

While this phenomenon has yet to abate, prevailing proponents of judicial originalism strategically abandon their law office history when it suits them so to do. In cases like *Shelby County*, *Adarand*, and *Croson*, professed originalists expended little to no effort in discerning and implementing the fundamentally pro-equality intentions of the lawmaking generations who drafted and enacted the Thirteenth, Fourteenth, Fifteenth, and Twenty-Fourth amendments to the Constitution in the century between the 1860s and the 1960s. Nowhere did they concern themselves with the intentions of Reconstruction Framers like Bingham and his generation. Indeed, in their 5–4 majority opinion deciding *Shelby County*, a bare majority of the incumbent appointees, including conspicuous originalists, could not even bother themselves to formally cite any particular provision of the Constitution they deemed offended by the Voting Rights Act, or Section 2 of it, referencing only a recent previous opinion of their own as the sole authority for "demolishing" (as Ruth Ginsberg described in dissent) a key element of a historic, democratic equality law. A more striking contemporary example of personal usurpation under the guise of adjudication, rather than of principled interpretation or originalism, is difficult to identify.

Shelby County now stands as only the most recent example in a long and lengthening list of 5–4 outcomes issued over "spirited dissents" dedicated to backlash politics through the form of judicial opinion. As contemporary scholars observe, modern judicial originalism is comprehensible only as a twentieth-century invention tailored precisely to contemporary political struggles over identity, rights and power:

> The current ascendancy of originalism does not reflect the analytical force of its jurisprudence, but instead depends upon its capacity to fuse aroused citizens, government officials and judges into a dynamic and broad-based political movement. To understand originalism's power at the dawn of the 21st Century is to appreciate the ways in which originalism connects Constitutional law to a living, political culture and provides its proponents a compelling language in which to seek constitutional change through adjudication, as well as politics. Political proponents of originalism speak to and incite groups, in order to solidify their political mandates to reconstitute the Court. What is truly remarkable in assessing the performance of originalist judges (and here they speak specifically of Scalia and Thomas) is that they also engage in this same process of political mobilization. These two justices use their judicial opinions as conscious tools to excite the anger, fears and resentment of conservative constituencies and thus to fan the fires of political mobilization.[101]

99 Alexander M. Bickel, *The Original Understanding and the Segregation Decision*, 69 Harv. L. Rev. 1 (1955).

100 Herman Belz, *The Civil War Amendments to the Constitution: The Relevance of Original Intent*, 5 Const. Comment. 115, 122 (1988).

101 Robert Post & Reva Siegel, *Originalism as a Political Practice: The Right's Living Constitution*, 75 Fordham L. Rev. 566–67 (2006).

Modern-day, or one-step, originalism deploys a particular conception of "framers' intent" as an apparently neutral technique to disguise underlying ideological imperatives. Commingling this type of originalism with preexisting discourses surrounding states' rights, old and new federalism, selectively strict construction, strategic adjudicatory blindness, and other antebellum anti-equality conceptions or tactics, contemporary backlash judges, during the past two decades, have engineered a baroque doctrinal maze that makes sense only from the perspective of an actively reactionary, "anti-antidiscrimination" agenda:

> The consequence is not only an advantaging of whites, but a disadvantaging of blacks. Under *Adarand*, blacks and other racial or ethnic minorities are denied a legal privilege enjoyed by just about every other minority in the country ... Farmers can be given special governmental benefits. Large corporations can. Riparian landowners can. Victims of environmental damage can. Poor people, veterans, disabled people, railroad workers, ophthalmologists—just about any minority group can be singled out by law for special advantages in the allocation of governmental benefits or opportunities without running afoul of the Equal Protection Clause. But blacks cannot ...
>
> Everyone knows that the Equal Protection Clause was designed above all to ensure equal protection for blacks. The denial to black Americans, as a group, of legal rights or privileges enjoyed by any other group is the paradigmatic Fourteenth Amendment violation. Is this basic fact about the Fourteenth Amendment's meaning really reconcilable with a regime in which, alone out of almost every minority group in the country, blacks (and other racial minorities) are denied an important legal privilege—the privilege of being able to be singled out by law for specially favorable treatment in the allocation of governmental benefits or opportunities? How, then, can *Adarand* be taken seriously as a doctrinal elaboration of the Equal Protection Clause when it denies to blacks a privilege of legal protection enjoyed by so many other groups? ... If all this is true, the right response might not be to jettison the Court's case law, but to jettison the whole enterprise of taking constitutional doctrine seriously.[102]

The equality crisis fomented by judicial frustration of federal anti-discrimination policy for over a century, including multiple constitutional reforms, has thus led to the brink of a crisis over law's legitimacy—at least the legislative law of the judges. This brink is where the United States now stands poised as it peers past the furies of the present.

Nonetheless, one-step or modern-day originalists continue to insist that their approach constrains unprincipled exercises of public power, especially by "liberal" federal judges too keen on "rights." Conclusory claims of principled decision-making, as well as protracted defenses of those claims, remain typical of the virtues that originalists assert in support of their interpretive choices, even as today's appointees continue to act otherwise: more and more like "the most activist Supreme Court in history."[103] As the recent anti-equality cases show, judicial originalism and the identitarian ideologies it helps to mobilize and normalize today are a significant obstacle to a third Reconstruction—and this political reality is perhaps the greatest constitutional travesty of all, for a third effort toward constitutional equality should amount, in effect, to a final vindication of original intentions motivating the Framers of the first and second.

Conclusion

In 1952, while still under the long shadow cast by the judges in their postbellum opinions undoing the first Reconstruction, one astute observer commented:

> The legislative program of the post-Civil War days was premised on the belief that the fundamental rights of the individual should be defined and enforced by the federal government. But the Supreme Court has consistently

102 Jed Rubenfeld, *The Anti-Antidiscrimination Agenda*, 111 Yale L.J. 1170, 1177 (2002).

103 Thomas M. Keck, The Most Activist Supreme Court In History: The Road to Modern Judicial Conservatism (1st ed. 2004).

> refused to accept that premise. It has substituted its belief that civil rights lie within the realm of state power and that any federal attempt to encroach on that power is to be viewed narrowly and suspiciously. The Court has expressed its belief so many times that it would necessitate a judicial and constitutional upheaval of the first magnitude to undo what the Court has done.[104]

In the United States, these equality fundamentals have not changed since then, as the foregoing account only partially shows. Undoing what the judges have undone consequently remains the one great task of a third Reconstruction, and knowing this vexed history specifically of law, race, and equal protection under judicial review is a necessary, although insufficient, first step toward that "judicial and constitutional upheaval."

Judges, we have seen, hold the power to alter the course of U.S. social, legal, and political history. No doubt, whatever comes next in the continuing story of equality's history, both judges and identity once again will play central, perhaps determinative, roles. The question then is, which roles will they be?

Informed ideally by a critical and raced understanding of past and present, today's generation of pro-equality advocates must strive continually and increasingly to help ensure that future generations of Americans, including their judges, avoid another round of identity-based anti-equality distortions or deflections like those littering the history and lessons recounted here. The unresolved, unabated controversies over the meaning of constitutional equality in the United States will continue to afflict the country until the existential contradiction with which this Chapter opened is finally relinquished by society as a whole, but in particular by its judges. With this substantive, critically raced knowledge comes the future possibility of lasting judicial fidelity—and accountability to an informed public—in the interpretation and application of "equal protection of the laws" for all "persons" as mandated by the U.S. Constitution for nearly the past century and a half.

But, in addition to a well-informed public and a well-prepared judiciary, U.S. academics, researchers, and activists also have important roles to play that, in closing, must be brought into brief focus. Rather than be occupied mainly by the gyrations of doctrine that currently characterize judicial opining, academics and researchers can and must help to foster critical identity-conscious approaches to constitutional studies that unpack, contextualize, and transcend those gyrations, and which support intellectually the work of a third Reconstruction. Equally important, activists and organizers can and should help to foment diverse, identity-conscious coalitional networks, causes, and movements toward constitutional equality to support politically the work of future policymakers and judges tasked with equality's rightful, if belated, acceptance. Mindful of these closing notes, as well as of the reactionary noise of the moment, this chapter strives only to be a helpful part of the many efforts entailed by equality's proper constitutional recognition and substantive social vindication.

As the 150th anniversary of the Fourteenth Amendment approaches in 2018, critical knowledge of equality's racialized judicial history ideally will help beckon pro-equality Americans of all stripes, and their judges, to begin earnestly preparing, and bracing, to stand firmly and clearly for equality's coming of age. Hopefully, critical approaches to constitutional studies and practices will inspire and sustain principled solidarity toward equal justice for all. After one Civil War, two Reconstructions, a New Deal, a Great Society and unflinching backlash to any fraction of post-Philadelphia progress toward greater social equality, the future still depends on it.

104 Eugene Gressman, *The Unhappy History of Civil Rights Legislation*, 50 Mich. L. Rev. 1323, 1357 (1951–52).

Chapter 3
Equal Protection's Dead End, or the Slave's Undying Claim

Sora Han

> What is the word for bringing bodies back from water? From a "liquid grave"? […] I do an Internet search for a word or phrase for bringing someone back from underwater that has as precise a meaning as the unearthing contained within the word exhume. I find worlds like resurrect and subaquatic, but not "exaqua." Does this mean that unlike being interred, once you're underwater there is no retrieval—that you never "exhumed" from water? The gravestone or tombstone marks the spot of interment, whether of ashes or the body. What marks the spot of subaquatic death?
>
> NourbeSe Philip, Zong!, As told to the author by Setaey Adamu Boateng (2008)

> Slavery is still the touchstone for all of our discussions about race in America--as it should be, because race was born out of slavery. It is our nation's original sin. Through the telling and re-telling of the history of slavery, we judge our own responsibility for the continuing injustices of racial inequality.
>
> Ariela Gross, "When is the Time of Slavery?" (2008)

Introduction

In *Zong!*,[1] poet and lawyer, NourbeSe Philip, provides a stunning theoretical meditation on the eighteenth-century British decision, *Gregson v. Gilbert* (1783).[2] This famous case adjudicated an insurance claim of a slave cargo ship owner for approximately 150 enslaved Africans he threw overboard when his ship, "Zong," became lost at sea. According to maritime law, ship owners' cargo were insured for "loss" except by natural or voluntary causes, and thus the owner's fate stood in the balance between his judgment as murderer or as beneficiary. Yet, the decision about his wavering future, as perverse as these radically differing legal judgments might appear, depended upon a lost chorus of Black pleas and what that chorus might signify in a chain of legal reasoning charged to draw a line between legitimate commercial activity and criminal dealings in human bodies. The trial required that something be said about those 150 slaves, ordered to jump into the salty depths somewhere between the West Coast of Africa and Jamaica, and long gone to a "liquid grave" to which neither archived testimony nor the hermeneutics of language would allow for any return.

With the question of the slave's experience of a form of death so beyond the pale of the sociality of death that there is no word for an act that would allow us to return to them, Philip asks us to consider how we can know what happened aboard the Zong, in telling the "not-telling of the story that must be told." Noting the impossibility of marking a body in water, unlike the gravestone or tombstone or any other terrestrial practice that marks a body in land, she asks in the epigraph, "What marks the spot of subaquatic death?" And thus does this question drive Philip's literary descent into the opinion to create an unparalleled poetic work of justice from the words of law. In the splayed lyrics wrought from legal reason by Philip's onto-poetics of the slave ship, the spectral slave glints with every contact made between the sun and the ocean's infinite ripples.[3]

---

1 NOURBESE PHILIP, ZONG! (2008).

2 Gregson v. Gilbert, [1783] Doug, K.B. 232.

3 By "glint," I am referring to Lacan's famous story of his anxiety towards the tin can floating in the ocean when he tags along with a crew of fishers. This story would serve as an explanatory point of reference for developing his notion of the gaze, and the gaze's conceptual centrality to his eventual development of the register of the Real. THE FOUR FUNDAMENTAL CONCEPTS OF PSYCHO-ANALYSIS 95 (J.A. Miller ed., A. Sheridan trans., 1978).

Interestingly, and perhaps what we might take as a response to Philip's question, legal scholar and historian, Ariela Gross, describes slavery as a "touchstone."[4] The Merriam-Webster dictionary provides three definitions of the term. First, a black siliceous stone related to flint and formerly used to test the purity of gold and silver by the streak left on the stone when rubbed by the metal. Second, a test or criterion for determining the quality or genuineness of a thing. And third, a fundamental or quintessential part or feature.

Understanding slavery as a touchstone across these three meanings requires a knowledge of the world of the slave based on a form of law prior to and against which modern legal developments are cast in the spirit of *jus gentium* in particular, and the natural law tradition more generally. Slavery as touchstone denotes its infinite eventfulness, through which all other times of historicity and violence are experienced and judged. And while Philip's question suggests that only the ocean itself, and thus planetary life itself, can mark the millions lost during the Middle Passage, and thus, that everywhere and everything demands the telling of the untellable story, Gross by a sort of parallax view of slavery suggests that the unmarkable subaquatic deaths of the Middle Passage are our only path of ethical law and history. The path is the repetition of telling and judgment, a mimesis of narrative and moral failings, the justice of sliding into the "'improvisational immanence' that blackness is."[5]

These two points of meditation foreground the difficulty of entering into questions of history and justice through the law—a difficulty that becomes clear by the haunting of the present by specters of slavery and the insistent and ultimately unresolvable claims that were made as a result of the slave's status as both person and thing. And I open with them because what I would like to pursue in this chapter is *this* same difficulty, though in an *apparently* different doctrinal context and a different historical period. I stress here the difference between then and now perhaps might not be as different as we might hope because contemporary Equal Protection jurisprudence specifically, and Fourteenth Amendment jurisprudence generally, continue to struggle with how to address the claim of the slave that remains buried by a fundamentally defensive legal discourse.

Thus, my aim in this chapter will be to reveal how the *force* of this cataclysmic claim remains in Equal Protection jurisprudence, and to zero in on a radical alternative that comes into view with the foreclosed claim *of* the slave (to be distinguished from the various possible claims *to* the slave that Philip's reading of *Gregson* works against) as a touchstone for how to judge the value of any litigated gains or losses in contemporary Equal Protection jurisprudence. I do this by closely examining how the claim emerges in the most recent case in Equal Protection jurisprudence, *Fisher v. University of Texas, Austin*.[6] I then move into an examination of how the claim emerges within a broader landscape of Fourteenth Amendment jurisprudence, namely, the Supreme Court's recent decisions on Section 5 of the Fourteenth Amendment and the federalism issues resulting from Congress's enumerated power to legislatively enforce Section 1, which contains the Equal Protection Clause. This examination makes up the majority of the chapter's focus, to argue that the foreclosed claim of the slave between both Equal Protection and Section 5 doctrine must be read together to return to the possibility of a radical future for Fourteenth Amendment jurisprudence. It then concludes by revisiting Derrick Bell's philosophy of racial realism that continues to hold open this invitation.[7]

In short, this chapter is centrally concerned with the claim of the slave as neither the reproduction of the claimant's objecthood nor the validation of the claimant's subjectivity, but rather, with its enduring force against and in excess of the law's animation of rights through the protocols of judicial review. That is, the remaindered force of the claim of the slave compels us to ask anew: How should we generally understand

4 Ariela Gross, *When is the Time of Slavery? The History of Slavery in Contemporary Legal and Political Argument*, 96 Cal. L. Rev. 283 (2008).

5 Jared Sexton, *Ante-Anti-Blackness: Afterthoughts*, Lateral No. 1 (2012) (quoting Fred Moten, *Knowledge of Freedom*, 4(2) The New Centennial Rev. 269 (2004)).

6 Fisher v. Univ. of Texas, 133 S.Ct. 2411 (2013).

7 I am indebted to Mario Barnes for inviting me into a conversation about how to think differently about the Fourteenth Amendment. In particular, I leave a more nuanced legal-historical analysis of the Fourteenth Amendment's promise of equality in his expert hands. *See* his essay, co-authored with Erwin Cherminsky; Mario Barnes & Erwin Cherminsky, *The Once and Future Equal Protection Doctrine?*, 43 Conn. L. Rev. 1059 (2011), which readers should reference for all that they find lacking in my analysis. Instead, what I hope to add in this chapter is not a more coherent sense of historical and future development for Equal Protection jurisprudence, but explore the political significance of its decidedly uneven development through its color-conscious citational practices.

equal protection jurisprudence in our so-called post-civil rights, post-affirmative action, post-racial moment, particularly given the confused reality of so many identity-based legal campaigns arguing for and against this and that kind of reform to anti-discrimination law? Is the prohibition against discrimination still (if it ever was in the immediate aftermath of slavery's formal abolition) a meaningful way of understanding social identity, history, structures of power, and the democratic experiment? Can we sunder the seemingly inextricable relation between the law of anti-discrimination and the neoliberal grammar of free market values of individual opportunity, corporate diversity, and personal vindication? What new insights on social justice, legal practice and education, and democratic theory would a general understanding of race and Fourteenth Amendment jurisprudence provide us?

***Fisher* and the Dead End of the Equal Protection Clause**

The most recent Supreme Court decision on the constitutionality of affirmative action policy in higher education, *Fisher v. University of Texas, Austin*,[8] is as good a place to begin tracing the law's difficulties with encountering a present haunted by the claim of the slave. Specifically, the text of the decision raises quite accurately what Philip and Gross taken together argue about the impossibility and, thus, necessity of staging a reckoning between law and slavery that might open up onto an as-yet unforeseen and unprecedented justice.

We have only to scratch the surface of the decision, which enfolds the colorblind measuredness of Justice Kennedy's majority opinion and the color-conscious impatience of Justice Thomas's concurrence. By vacating the Fifth Circuit Court's ruling that UT Austin's policy was not in violation of the Equal Protection Clause as elaborated in *Grutter v. Bollinger*,[9] on the reason that the appellate court had not sufficiently reviewed whether UT Austin's policy was "narrowly tailored," Justice Kennedy avoided an actual finding on the substance of UT Austin's policy. Accepting the majority's judgment of the procedural inadequacy of the appellate court, Justice Thomas nonetheless wrote separately to beat the history of slavery and segregation into a bygone era.

The decision, then, simultaneously waits for the unfolding of a more precise application of Equal Protection doctrine on affirmative action and can't wait to be done with it altogether. Justice Kennedy is content to believe in the powers of judicial review to find some middle ground for strict scrutiny analysis in racial discrimination cases. At the end of his decision, we are left with this dubious belief when he opines that ideal judicial review would be neither "'strict in theory, but fatal in fact'" (quoting *Adarand Constructors, Inc. v. Peña*,[10] and *Grutter*[11]) nor, adding his own gloss on this famous dictum, "strict in theory, but feeble in fact."[12] We can put our own gloss on Justice Kennedy's play of dicta here to understand Justice Thomas, who in his turn, is anguished that judicial review of affirmative action policies continues to entertain any compelling interest that recognizes racial difference, including the compromised interest of diversity first affirmed in *U.C. Regents v. Bakke*[13] (1978). Justice Thomas's impatience, in other words, is with what he perceives to be the fact that judicial review has only ever been "strict in theory, *and* feeble in fact," instead of "strict in theory, *and* fatal in fact."

There is a profound agreement here about something tedious and ethically unfulfilling about strict scrutiny's balancing of ends and means to judge the constitutionality of racial discrimination under the Equal Protection Clause. And so while most if not all waited in anticipation for *Fisher*'s outcome to deliver the national debate over affirmative action into some sort of relief, the opinion marched on to the same monotonous beat established in *Bakke* and its sister cases, never to look back at the more fundamental question of whether strict

8 Fisher v. Univ. of Texas, 133 S.Ct. 2411 (2013).

9 Grutter v. Bollinger, 539 U.S. 306 (2003). *Grutter* was at the time the authoritative affirmative action ruling, which held that an admissions policy designed to create a "critical mass" of underrepresented minorities in furtherance of its educational purpose to maintain diversity in the student body passed strict scrutiny and, thus, did not violate the Equal Protection Clause of the Fourteenth Amendment.

10 Adarand Constructors, Inc. v. Peña, 515 U.S. 220 (1995).

11 *Id.*

12 *Fisher*, 133 S. Ct. 2411 at 2424.

13 Regents of the University of California v. Bakke, 438 U.S. 265 (1978).

judicial review was the proper standard of judging race-based remedial policies. Seemingly, to wake judicial review from its zombie-like commitment to diversity and its infinite policing of acceptable and unacceptable policies regulating racial difference, Thomas resurrected, true to form, the zombie of all legal zombies with the hopes of scaring judicial review straight.

This ur-zombie is the specter of the slave and her claim that was never given full standing in the wake of slavery's formal abolition and during the consolidation of a Jim Crow America. Let us look now at how this zombie comes to life. Of course, Justice Thomas is not concerned to actually hear this claim, let alone argue for its standing before the law. Instead, his indignation, again in its true form, insists that affirmative action's historical tradition is that of the "slaveholders"[14] and the "segregationists."[15] He calls to the mind of judicial review the sentimental discourse of slavery that imagined itself as a modern institution of enlightenment for the "'black race'"[16]; and also recalls the paternalistic discourse of segregation recorded in legal history by cases such as *Briggs v. Elliott* (1952)[17] and *Bolling v. Sharpe* (1954).[18] Here, he pleads, are our proper negative examples by which to reinvent strict scrutiny doctrine in affirmative action cases, if not all race discrimination cases brought under the Equal Protection Clause.

But the ur-zombie Thomas resurrects is not the slaveholder or the segregationist. It is, rather, a fundamentally problematic being in law, the "black race," from which such sentimental and paternalistic discourses came to life back then, and are given new life by Thomas now as he recites that discourse as a negative example. That is why as hard as Thomas works in his legal argument to suppress this ur-zombie and her claim without ground, it returns ineluctably. Neither he nor the law can escape it.

I am specifically referencing the arrival in the *Fisher* opinion, in the strange place of Thomas's reasoning against affirmative action, of the figure of W.E.B. Du Bois as the towering intellectual figure of modern thought's fundamental critique of a world built on slavery and capitalism. Here is where Du Bois enters:

> A century later, segregationists similarly asserted [as with the slaveholders] that segregation was not only benign, but good for black students. They argued, for example, that separate schools protected black children from racist white students and teachers. See, e.g., Brief for Appellees in *Briggs* 33–34 ("'I have repeatedly seen wise and loving colored parents take infinite pains to force their little children into schools where the white children, white teachers, and white parents despised and resented the dark child, made mock of it, neglected or bullied it, and literally rendered its life a living hell. Such parents want their child to "fight" this thing out,—but, dear God, at what a cost! ... We shall get a finer, better balance of spirit; an infinitely more capable and rounded personality by putting children in schools where they are wanted, and where they are happy and inspired, than in thrusting them into hells where they are ridiculed and hated.'") (quoting DuBois, Does the Negro Need Separate Schools? 4 J. of Negro Educ. 328, 330–31 (1935)).[19]

We can easily reveal the segregationist defendant's gross use and abuse of Du Bois in *Griggs* to stand their ground against the kind of national structural changes the Fourteenth Amendment promised as the echo of the slave's claim to freedom.[20] And I find it necessary here to reproduce what is cut from Du Bois in this legal history Thomas continues to write by his citation to *Briggs* as negative example. As Du Bois foresaw, "I

14 *Id.* at 2425. (Thomas, J., concurring).

15 *Id.* at 2426.

16 *Id.* at 2425 (quoting Paul Finkelman quoting pro-slavery Senator John C. Calhoun's famous 1837 speech, "The Positive Good of Slavery," in his critical study *see* PAUL FINKELMAN, DEFENDING SLAVERY: PRO-SLAVERY THOUGHT IN THE OLD SOUTH (2003)).

17 Briggs v. Elliot, 342 U.S. 350 (1952).

18 Bolling v. Sharpe, 347 U.S. 497 (1954).

19 *Fisher*, 133 S. Ct. 2411 at 2426.

20 *See* The Civil Rights Cases of 1883, 109 U.S. 3 (1883) Justice Harlan's understudied dissenting opinion in the *Civil Rights Cases of 1883*, where he asks: "If, then, exemption from discrimination, in respect of civil rights, is a new constitutional right, secured by the grant of State citizenship to colored citizens of the United States—and I do not see how this can now be questioned—why may not the nation, by means of its own legislation of a primary direct character, guard, protect and enforce that right? It is a right and privilege which the nation conferred." I will return to the significance of this question in the sections below.

know that this article will forthwith be interpreted by certain illiterate 'nitwits' as a plea for segregated Negro schools and colleges." And to these "nitwits," like the *Briggs* defendants and to all, including Kennedy and Thomas, who would fail to understand the fundamental issue underlying the Black struggle for education, he plainly states, "It is not. It is simply calling a spade a spade."[21]

What, then, is the spade Du Bois is calling a spade? It is the false choice of segregated or integrated schools determining and protracting the possible development of a knowledge based on "the fact that American Negroes have, because of their history, group experiences and memories, a distinct entity, whose spirit and reactions demand a certain type of education for its development."[22] Defending this "certain type of education" that he argues is more possible in committing to Black schools than in litigating school integration, he specifies, "In history and the social sciences the Negro school and college has an unusual opportunity and role. It does not consist simply in trying to parallel the history of white folk with similar boasting about Black and brown folk, but rather an honest evaluation of human effort and accomplishment, without color blindness, and without transforming history into a record of dynasties and prodigies."[23]

Ultimately, it is the possibility of "Sympathy, Knowledge, and the Truth" that Black schools promise, where "children are treated like human beings, trained by teachers of their own race, who know what it means to be Black in the year of salvation 1935."[24] And the political ramifications of developing this form of education, he explains, are clear and urgent, both domestically and abroad:

> Here, we have in America, a working class which in our day has achieved physical freedom, and mental clarity. An economic battle has just begun. It can be studied and guided; it can teach consumers' cooperation, democracy, and socialism, and be made not simply a record and pattern for the Negro race, but a guide for the rise of the working classes throughout the world … [Knowledge of] modern civilization would not only help them [Negroes] find their place in the industrial scene for their own organization, but also enable them to help Abyssinia, India, China, and the colored world, to maintain their racial integrity, and their economic independence. It could easily be the mission and duty of the American Negroes to master this scientific basis of modern invention, and give it to all mankind.[25]

I have tried to provide a basic sense of Du Bois's radical political recommendations in the context of the legal struggle for equal education that is cropped by his necessarily partial appearance in *Fisher*. The least we can do after reading *Fisher* is to echo Du Bois's own insistence against the "nitwits" of history. But, ultimately, I am after perhaps a more difficult task, which is to understand what about Du Bois's radical critique requires the segregationist and the neoconservative to reference Du Bois at all—just as we might ask why Thomas does not (not just in *Fisher*, but any other opinion he has written on the issue of racial discrimination) simply leave slavery and segregation to the dustbins of history and argue as a matter of doctrine why the diversity rationale does not qualify as a compelling interest under the Equal Protection Clause? What about the conservative course of doctrinal development in Equal Protection litigation is not enough to rest one's arguments in, and, instead, compels the recitation of the history of slavery and segregation and a radical knowledge embedded therein?

For now, I would like only to offer these questions, as there is not space here to fully elaborate on them. I note, however, that part of my argument here is that perhaps something is lost in developing a fuller knowledge of race and law when the primary focus of critical race theory has been to shift towards generating empirical studies of racial inequality that can help expand liberal legal reform strategies; and away from amplifying how the only way to think ourselves out of the dead end of both liberal and conservative legal development is to insist, as did Du Bois, on the claim of the slave that is always there, even in the most unlikely places, like in Thomas's opinion in *Fisher*.

---

21 W.E.B. Du Bois, *Does the Negro Need Separate Schools?*, 4 J. of Negro Educ. 335 (July 1935) (hereinafter *Separate Schools?*).

22 *Id.* at 333.

23 *Id.* at 334.

24 *Id.* at 335.

25 *Id.* at 334.

That is, perhaps Thomas's resurrection of the slave and her claim (for sure, only to degrade it) tacitly avows its truth as the law's foundational challenge. Thomas's recalcitrance toward the claim of the slave is a rejection that ultimately requires a latent recognition of it. In *Fisher*, this takes the form of Thomas's curious citation to a text in which Du Bois is faithfully asserting this claim unburdened by the limitations of the legal and political context of his day. "I am no fool,"[26] he warns, and by this warning echoes a historical reality in which the slave's claim rings true by every partial and failed address made to it. The slave as *the* undying legal personality of modern American law by virtue of its foreclosed claim to freedom, the ur-zombie as I characterized it earlier, is not simply an image that might potentially wake the law from its belief in multicultural diversity, as Thomas's wishes. We might instead approach this legal personality as a legal fact to the extent that it tends always to return in law, and carries with it the whole of freedom struggle that Du Bois has the penchant to perform in his political analysis, knowing full well the various political resistances to this performance.

I have tried to demonstrate how the claim of the slave surfaces today still, in perhaps the most pessimistic doctrinal arena, Equal Protection jurisprudence, where legal efforts to promote racial equality have historically taken place since the ratification of the Fourteenth Amendment. At the dead end of Equal Protection jurisprudence is, in fact, an alternative route of escape illuminated by this claim. For if the claim of the slave in *Fisher* makes clear that Equal Protection jurisprudence stagnates in a cesspool of strict judicial review, then it begs the question of how this would come to be by a constitutional amendment enacted at the wake of the Civil War so that no form of governance, no matter its jurisdictional authority, its function within a federal democracy, or history of political leadership, could undo the nation's decision to reconstitute itself in the image of a universal equality lifted from its social foundation in slavery?

The Doctrinal Landscape of Section 5 Anti-Discrimination Cases

Tellingly, the Fourteenth Amendment recognizes Congress's exceptional role in the nation's reconstitution by the language of Section 5, which declares that "The Congress shall have power to enforce, by appropriate legislation, the provisions of this article,"[27] including then, the Equal Protection Clause. Thus, to underscore the relevance of turning to Section 5 jurisprudence as a way to understand the dead end of Equal Protection jurisprudence, we should note a stark division in federal authority over the development of the various areas of Fourteenth Amendment law, in contrast to the general enforcement power specifically bestowed to Congress. Upon initial reading, the Fourteenth Amendment does not assign authority over Equal Protection issues as they arise as individual constitutional injury to the judiciary, and Equal Protection issues as they arise as the social effects of governance to Congress. But this is decidedly how federal authority has been divided. As we will see in this section, a deeper question about what kind of power-sharing between the federal branches—in the context of the Fourteenth Amendment, between the judiciary and legislative branches—was and is imagined to be possible is the broader doctrinal landscape in which Equal Protection jurisprudence must be understood.

And so while the move from examining the Supreme Court's decisions on equal protection claims in affirmative action to its decisions on federal anti-discrimination legislation seems abrupt, the point of making this leap is precisely to question why such a gap exists in Fourteenth Amendment doctrine at all. I do this not to ultimately argue that a proper interpretation of Section 5 would give Congress more authority to regulate private Equal Protection violations, though I certainly believe it is an important historical fact that Congress did attempt such legislation with the Civil Rights Act of 1875,[28] and that Congress argued for this particular interpretation of Section 5 at the close of the First Reconstruction. Again, as in the previous section, I am more interested in the judicial language that seals our current interpretation of Section 5 as the commonsense of Fourteenth Amendment law. For in the language, we can trace the success of this common sense not simply

26 *Id.* at 328.

27 U.S. Const. amend. XIV, § 5.

28 The Civil Rights Act of 1875, 43rd Congress, Session II, Chapter 114, accessed at http://www.constitution.org/uslaw/sal/018_statutes_at_large.pdf.

in the virtual legal impossibility of enacting today something like Congress's 1875 Acts, but in the foreclosed and returning claim of the slave.

Let us now turn to Section 5 jurisprudence. Robert Post and Reva Siegel provide an excellent roadmap for navigating the doctrinal landscape of recent Section 5 antidiscrimination cases. In "Equal Protection by Law: Federal Anti-Discrimination Legislation After *Morrison* and *Kimel*"[29] they argue that these two recent decisions' restricted interpretations of Congress's Section 5 legislative power signal a bleak future for federal anti-discrimination law more generally. They note, raising very reasonable if not urgent concerns in my mind, that these two decisions represent "the first time since Reconstruction that the Court has declared that Congress lacked power to enact legislation prohibiting discrimination."[30] They further argue that the Court's justification for such restricted interpretations of Section 5 powers, namely that Section 5 must be interpreted within a federalism framework balancing separation of powers, should determine Section 5's future and must be challenged by asserting that the proper framework is a recommitment to the general principle of equality the Fourteenth Amendment undeniably stands for.

I cannot offer a better historical account than Post and Siegel, and so recommend that readers consult their article in its entirety. For my purposes, however, I want to focus on their observation of a certain silence or ambiguity the Court bequeathed to the development of Fourteenth Amendment antidiscrimination law at the height of the Civil Rights Movement:

> The history of federal anti-discrimination law in the twentieth century features two momentous events. The first is *Brown v. Board of Education*, when the Supreme Court breathed new life into Section 1 of the Fourteenth Amendment. The second is the passage of the Civil Rights Act of 1964, the first major federal anti-discrimination legislation enacted since 1875. In debating and drafting the 1964 Act, Congress invoked its power under both the Commerce Clause and Section 5 of the Fourteenth Amendment. But when the Supreme Court came to determine the Act's constitutionality in *Heart of Atlanta Motel v. United States*, it shied away from a confrontation with its own Section 5 precedents, which dated from the first Reconstruction, and chose instead to build on the case law of the New Deal settlement, which ceded very broad powers to Congress to legislate under the Commerce Clause. It translated the question of congressional authority into the relatively simple issue of whether "Congress had a rational basis for finding that racial discrimination ... affected commerce."[31]

Section 5's silence in *Heart of Atlanta Motel v. United States* (1964),[32] then, continued to resound through the Court's subsequent decisions ratifying federal antidiscrimination law on Commerce Clause grounds, even though Congress continued to assert both Section 5 and the Commerce Clause for its authority. Over time, the Court's Fourteenth Amendment antidiscrimination decisions became split between a highly elaborated Section 1 substantive framework of relativized scrutiny and an obscuring neglect of Section 5's meaning and role in providing for equality. And between this split and uneven constitutional interpretation of the Fourteenth Amendment, the broad economic rationale of the Commerce Clause was firmly, if implicitly, set in place as Congress's sole authority to enact antidiscrimination legislation.[33]

We must note here two vital points about this history. The first is that the Court's priority of interpreting the Commerce Clause to the exclusion of Section 5 is symbolic of the law's general tendency to favor an economic rationale for enforcing equality, rather than a politically principled rationale. This is akin to the Court's investment in the political popularity (populism) of a New Deal ethos, and its divestment from the political unpopularity (radicalism) of the two Reconstructions preceding and succeeding the crisis of the

29 Reva B. Siegel & Robert Post, *Equal Protection by Law: Federal Antidiscrimination Legislation After Morrison and Kimel*, 110 YALE L.J. 441 (2000).

30 *Id.* at 443.

31 *Id.* at 447.

32 Heart of Atlanta Motel v. United States, 379 U.S. 241 (1964).

33 *See also* Robert C. Post & Reva B. Siegel, *Legislative Constitutionalism and Section Five Power: Policentric Interpretation of the Family and Medical Leave Act*, 112 YALE L.J. 1943 (2003), for another excellent article on Section 5, which explores the "separation of powers" framework that the Court has applied to limit Section 5 powers.

Great Depression. I refer to the radical approach to legal reform and constitutional interpretation marking the political ethos of nineteenth- and twentieth-century Reconstruction moments as "Reconstruction^2."[34] And the steady divestment from Reconstruction^2 has licensed an increasingly privatized approach to Equal Protection cases, and commercial approach in federal antidiscrimination cases. What many criticize today with respect to the Court's Equal Protection Clause jurisprudence as a neoliberalization of equality—following a political culture of promoting individual opportunity, business necessity, corporate diversity, choice and consent, freedom of expression, and any number of other liberal notions of democratic belonging over reparative notions of equality—is structurally foreshadowed in *Heart of Atlanta*'s quiet anti-Reconstruction^2 sensibility.

The second point to draw from Post and Siegel's history is that *Heart of Atlanta*'s precedent-setting interpretation of federal antidiscrimination law as an expression of Congress's authority over a national economic sphere is ancillary to the assumption that police powers (the regulation of social life and welfare) is purely within the states' jurisdiction.[35] Further, if the constitutional guarantee of equality is essentially both economic and social, *Heart of Atlanta* naturalized universal equality as a national economic phenomenon (read again here the template for the neoliberal subject of rights), only to set the stage then for any other more local commitments to equality (at state, municipal, administrative, and personal levels) as perversions of state power. The unspoken gutting of the CRA of 1964 through *Heart of Atlanta* reverberates today in the many arguments against any federal welfare reform initiatives, arguing that health care, housing, criminal justice, education, and so on, are all more effectively managed and innovated by states and their local authorities. The constitutional responsibility then of how to effectively ensure racial as well as other forms of equality literally falls through the glaring crack between a national economic sphere and a state-level social sphere.

Obviously, we need not accept this history as legal inevitability. However, we must accept that the very creation of federal antidiscrimination law in the wake of *Heart of Atlanta* reproduces a certain passivity towards guarding the legal openings of Reconstruction^2 and the vital task of imagining what kind of law would continue to hold them open. In other words, we are confronted now with the fact that the proliferation of federal antidiscrimination legislation (and variations of them at the state level) has also been a political demurring before the Court's hesitancy if not refusal in *Heart of Atlanta* to examine and overrule its precedent on Section 5, and more specifically, the ruling in the *Civil Rights Cases of 1883*.[36] I will return to this key issue later in the chapter, but for now we should rest here, as captured in *Heart of Atlanta*, with this image of federal antidiscrimination law that is at once actively promoting an economic rationale for antidiscrimination law and passively dishonoring a constitutional principle of redress to former slaves.

This is a "momentous" doctrinal event, as Post and Siegel rightly argue. At the same time, the jurisprudential landscape that emerges in *Heart of Atlanta*'s wake is decidedly complex, or perhaps more accurately put, obscurantist because of a certain theoretical common sense that such jurisprudence can and should be understood through rubrics of identity, social difference, and historical change that insufficiently account for the structure of American democracy founded upon a jurisdictional conflict between the states' police power and the federal government's enumerated powers. This founding jurisdictional conflict has been developed through three main constitutional provisions: the Eleventh Amendment, which provides for state sovereign immunity; the Interstate Commerce Clause of Article 1, which gives Congress power to regulate commerce; and Section 5 of the Fourteenth Amendment, which gives Congress power to enforce the principles of equal protection and due process. As a matter of the Constitution's history of amendment and ratification by the states, the first two provisions' antebellum development becomes complicated by the postbellum addition of the Reconstruction Amendments of which Section 5 of the Fourteenth Amendment is part. Again, I do not provide a narrative for this history, but note that the Civil War and the formal abolition

---

34 It is no small irony given Justice Thomas's Du Bois citation in *Fisher* that the paradigm-setting study of the First Reconstruction is W.E.B. Du Bois, Black Reconstruction (1935). *See also*, Eric Foner, Reconstruction: America's Unfinished Revolution (2002), which follows in Du Bois's intellectual spirit. C. Van Woodward would then conceptualize the Civil Rights Movement of the 1950s as a "Second Reconstruction," *see* C. Van Woodward, The Strange Career of Jim Crow (1955), which Manning Marable built upon, *see* Manning Marable, Race, Reform and Rebellion (1991).

35 *See generally*, Bryan Wagner, Disturbing the Peace: Black Culture and the Police Power after Slavery (2009).

36 The Civil Rights Cases, 109 U.S. 3 (1883).

of slavery should still shape our understanding of how these three provisions are and might be interpreted against and with each other.

The recent federalism cases addressing Eleventh Amendment limitations on Congress's legislative power include issues of tribal sovereignty, labor, and disability. In *Seminole Tribe of Florida v. Florida* (1996),[37] the Court found that Congress overstepped its legislative powers with the Indian Gaming Regulatory Act of 1988,[38] which allowed tribes to sue states in federal court if states did not enter into good faith negotiations. It reasoned that Congress's power, derived from Article 1's Indian Commerce Clause, could not abrogate state sovereign immunity by analogizing the Indian Commerce Clause with the Interstate Commerce Clause, and then finding that the Court's only relevant ruling in *Pennyslvania v. Union Gas Co.* (1989)[39] which affirmed Congress's abrogation power was in fact a weak plurality opinion with no majority agreement in the ruling's rationale. Overruling *Union Gas* as a radical and unsupported departure from its longstanding federalism jurisprudence beginning with *Hans v. Louisiana* (1890),[40] the Court applies the simplistic theory that no matter the subject matter and how completely it is vested under the authority of Congress (as in commerce with tribes), Congress may not allow private suits against nonconsenting states.[41]

Seminole Tribe would then be affirmed with respect to the Interstate Commerce Clause, when in *Alden v. Maine* (1999)[42] the Court found that federal legislation, in this case, the Fair Labor Standards Act, could not subject nonconsenting states to private suits for damages for violating overtime regulations either in federal or state courts because of the primacy of Eleventh Amendment sovereign immunity in the original unamended constitution. Particularly important in this case is the articulation by the majority that the spirit of the Eleventh Amendment is the preservation of the original federal structure that limits federal institutions to enumerated powers and leaves remaining governing powers to the states, and that protecting states from private suits is essential to maintaining this division of powers.

And finally we see in *Kimel v. Board of Regents of Florida* (2000)[43] and *University of Alabama v. Garrett* (2001)[44] the translation of the Court's deference to state sovereign immunity against Congress's Commerce Clause powers to Congress's Section 5 enforcement power under the Fourteenth Amendment. In these cases, the Court finds that although the Age Discrimination in Employment Act of 1967 and Americans with Disability Act of 1990, respectively, as enforcements of the Equal Protection Clause could be constitutional, this would depend on whether the specific enforcement mechanisms were "congruent and proportional" to the type of discrimination remedied or protected against. Since protection against age and disability discrimination only requires a rational basis, the Court finds that the intrusive abrogation of state immunity is incongruent with and disproportionate to the state duty owed to older or disabled citizens. In *Kimel* and *Garrett* we see that Eleventh Amendment immunity, while in theory subject to Section 5 of the Fourteenth Amendment, does not necessarily in fact mean that Congress's anti-discrimination legislation will prevail.[45]

So while in *Seminole Tribe* and *Alden* we see the Court recognize the priority of Section 5 over the Eleventh Amendment, in *Kimel* and *Garrett* we see that the Court subjects the potential effectiveness of Section 5 to a "congruence and proportionality" test derived from its Equal Protection Clause jurisprudence. From this perspective of Eleventh Amendment limitations on Congress's power to legislate, we should note

37 Seminole Tribe of Florida v. Florida. 517 U.S. 44 (1995).

38 Indian Gaming Regulation Act 25 U.S.C. §2701–21.

39 Pennsylvania v. Union Gas Co., 491 U.S. 1 (1989).

40 Hans v. Louisiana, 134 U.S. 1 (1890).

41 For a comprehensive analysis of Indian sovereignty at stake in and negotiated through the long-standing paternal relationship between the federal government and tribes represented by the IGRA, *see* Jessica Cattelino, High States: Florida Seminole Gaming and Sovereignty (2008).

42 Alden v. Maine, 527 U.S. 706 (1999).

43 Kimel v. Fla. Bd. of Regents, 528 U.S. 62 (2000).

44 Bd. of Trustees of the Uni. of Ala. v. Garrett, 531 U.S. 356 (2001).

45 *See* Tennessee v. Lane 541 U.S. 509 (2004), where the Court found that Eleventh Amendment immunity was validly abrogated by the ADA as an exercise of Congress's Section 5 power when a group of paraplegics sued the state for failing to make their courthouses accessible to them. This case, however, was based on the Court's analysis of the plaintiffs' Due Process claim, which requires "strict" scrutiny, and not an Equal Protection claim, which in this case would require only "rational" scrutiny.

the Court's attention to *how* Congress exerts its enumerated power—whether by the Interstate Commerce Clause, the Indian Commerce Clause, and Section 5 of the Fourteenth Amendment—is critical. What these three cases suggest is that neither a clearly enumerated federal power nor a clear intent by Congress to enforce equality can shift the Court's presumption of the supremacy of state sovereignty in a federal structure of governance.

If these Eleventh Amendment cases present a bleak picture, another line of cases more specifically developing the scope of Congress's Interstate Commerce Clause is similarly bleak. I highlight two cases: *U.S. v. Lopez* (1995),[46] limiting the Gun-Free School Zones Act of 1990; and *U.S. v. Morrison* (2000),[47] limiting the Violence Against Women Act of 1994 (VAWA). The Gun-Free School Zones Act made it a federal crime to possess a firearm in an educational environment, and the Violence Against Women Act allowed victims of gender violence to sue perpetrators in federal courts. Both cases represent the Court's turn towards a more stringent framework for determining whether the regulated activity has an effect on inter-state commerce. And the Court failed to see a "'substantial relation'"[48] between firearm possession and gender violence on inter-state commerce, and this heighted level of judicial demand for evidence of a link between the regulated activity and inter-state commerce has now displaced the prior "rational basis" threshold permitting Congress a wider scope of authority.

Morrison as the extension of the *Lopez* ruling requiring "substantial impact" into the antidiscrimination context is important to note. As Catharine MacKinnon perceptively observes in her article, "Disputing Male Sovereignty: On *United States v. Morrison*,"[49] this heightened judicial review applied to Congress's regulation of seemingly "noneconomic" activity is patently illogical: "it is unclear why the Court confines aggregation to activity considered commercial if substantiality of effect on commerce is what matters, yet if the commercial nature of the activity is what matters, why its effects need to be aggregated when they are direct."[50] She also goes on to discuss how not only it is problematic that such an illogical approach to Congress's Interstate Commerce power would be generalized, but also that it would build on this generalization to revive and reaffirm a problematic Section 5 jurisprudence. For *Morrison* not only affirms and curtails Congress's Interstate Commerce power, but it also curtails Congress's Section 5 power.

That is, if *Heart of Atlanta* is marked with a curious silence as to Congress's Section 5 power, *Morrison* is marked with a curious declaration that Congress's Section 5 power was also unconstitutionally used to enact the VAWA provision creating a federal cause of action between private individuals. The judicial invalidation of VAWA's provision on the right of victims to sue in federal court was based on restricted interpretations of both the Interstate Commerce Clause and Section 5 as sources of Congress's authority, while the judicial affirmation of the Civil Rights Act of 1964[51] in *Heart of Atlanta* required the affirmation of only one source of Congress's legislative authority. What is revealed here is an imbalance in how judicial review either affirms or strikes down antidiscrimination legislation. On the one hand, only one source of authority is needed for judicial review to affirm a policy, even if there are other sources that can strengthen that affirmation. On the other, all sources of authority must be limited for judicial review to strike down a policy, even if limiting only one would suffice to diminish Congress's authority. In other words, the Court's decision to strike down federal anti-discrimination legislation is more forceful than its decision to affirm. Or, stated another way, the Court's power to weaken the Fourteenth Amendment is in excess of its power to strengthen it. Its negative rulings have a scorched-earth effect on the Fourteenth Amendment jurisprudence, while its positive rulings have a humanitarian aid effect.

Before closing this section, then, let us briefly review the doctrinal landscape of Section 5 jurisprudence. In *Seminole Tribe*, *Alden*, and *Garrett*, we saw how issues of state sovereign immunity set the general scene

46 United States v. Lopez, 514 U.S. 549 (1995).

47 United States v. Morrison, 529 U.S. 598 (2000).

48 *Morrison*, 529 U.S. at 609 (quoting *Lopez*, 514 U.S. at 558–59).

49 Catharine A. Mackinnon, *Disputing Male Sovereignty: On United States v. Morrison*, 114 Harv. L. Rev. 135 (2000–01).

50 *Id.* at 147.

51 Civil Rights Act of 1964, Pub. L. No. 88–352, 78 Stat. 241 (codified as amended in scattered sections of 2 U.S.C., 28 U.S.C., and 42 U.S.C.).

for how Congress's authority under the Interstate Commerce Clause and Section 5 has remained incarcerated in a Hamiltonian philosophy of federalism. This philosophy animates state sovereignty with natural law from which the contract-based legal relationship between states births federal governmentality.[52] And it is consistently enacted across judicial review of the Indian Commerce Clause, the Interstate Commerce Clause, and Section 5 of the Fourteenth Amendment. With this political philosophy as the backdrop, the more specific development of a framework for delineating the commercial realm of Congress's Article 1 enumerated power of interstate regulation articulated in *Lopez* and *Morrison* appears as a kind of judicial functionalism in service of Hamiltonian federalism. Yet, even as *Morrison* serves as an important hinge between Interstate Commerce Clause and Section 5 doctrines, it at the same time, as I briefly noted, also reveals a profound asymmetry between judicial negation and affirmation of Congressional authority to legislate antidiscrimination policy.

We can now turn to the Court's contemporary approach to determining constitutional exercises of Section 5 power. The key case in this vein is *City of Boerne v. Flores* (1997),[53] which aside from its doctrinal significance as the case establishing the "congruence and proportionality" approach to Section 5, illuminates the ongoing drama between the judiciary and federal legislature over giving meaning to constitutional rights.[54] Indeed, *Boerne* must be read in its context as the judicial response to Congress's enactment of the Religious Freedom Restoration Act of 1993[55] (RFRA), which contravened the Court's ruling in *Employment Division v. Smith* (1990),[56] by legislating a "strict scrutiny" standard to be applied to any law that substantially burdened the free exercise of religion. In *Boerne*, the judicial authority to question and ultimately strike down the RFRA provision comes from the Court's division of the Fourteenth Amendment between substantive and procedural provisions. Under this framework, Congress can enact remedial or prophylactic legislation to address inequality, but only in such a way that is strictly an enforcement of a substantive right determined ultimately by the judiciary. Because the RFRA contained provisions for determining when the right to free expression was infringed, this was an unconstitutional encroachment of Congressional powers into the judicial domain.

The upshot of the *Boerne* "congruence and proportionality" approach, which is the current Section 5 framework, then, is to forever subordinate Congress's enforcement powers to judicial interpretations of what types of discrimination are actionable and what scale of judicial scrutiny should be applied to each type. Instead of arguing with these variable standards of judicial review, I want to simply point out that this framework is a type of power-hoarding by the judiciary as the ultimate purveyor of all rights, including personal rights of individuals, collective rights of groups, and jurisdictional rights of sovereign governing institutions. Further, *Boerne* crystallizes a profoundly specialized but nonetheless consistent doctrinal adherence across the decades since *Heart of Atlanta* to a notion of federalism that naturalizes the supremacy of state sovereignty over all other forms of sovereignty and divisions of power that inevitably exist in a political system (individual, tribal, supranational, and so on). To add to this unavowed antidemocratic form of judicial review, the many political struggles for civil rights and their various sources of injury and sites of recognition are strewn across these divisions of power and derivative sovereign entities that ultimately must submit to this, indeed, beguiling judicial power.

The Civil Rights Cases of 1883 as the Touchstone of Federalism

Section 5 jurisprudence is, within the larger doctrinal landscape I sketched above, wedged between fundamental federalist commitments to state sovereign immunity (Eleventh Amendment) and Congress's Commerce Clause powers (Art. 1). This is the result of the Court's adherence to a natural theory of states' rights that betrays its predisposition as the supreme appellate court of the land to jealously guard the power

52 *See for example*, Justice Kennedy's multiple references to THE FEDERALIST PAPERS, in *Alden v. Maine*, 527 U.S. 706 (1999), and in particular, his reference to The Federalist No. 81, depicting state sovereignty (716–17).

53 City of Boerne v. Flores, 521 U.S. 507 (1997).

54 On this drama, *see* Robert C. Post & Reva Siegel, *Protecting the Constitution from the People: Juricentric Restrictions on Section Five Power*, 78 IND. L.J. 1 (2003).

55 Religious Freedom Act of 1993, 42 U.S.C. § 2000bb—§ 2000bb-4.

56 Employment Division v. Smith, 494 U.S. 872 (1990).

to interpret and distribute rights and their jurisdictional limits. We could explain it as an effect of political pragmatism. Some body needs to decide conflicts of rights and jurisdiction, and our Constitution nominates the Supreme Court as the final guardian of this particular interpretive power. But if federal democracy's innovation as a form of governance is based in an unbendable general principle of power-sharing, and the power of interpretation is not just one power among others, but is the founding form of power that defines and limits the substance and scope of other powers, then we encounter a troubling structural impasse of democracy that emerges with the accumulation of this power in the judiciary. Political pragmatism then cannot fully explain why any one body need ever to have been nominated as the authority of this special power of interpretation constituting all other forms of power, instead of, keeping true to the principle of power-sharing, leaving it everybody.

Let us pursue another course of explanation, then, by examining how the structural impasse between federal power-sharing and judicial review as the exercise of this founding power of interpretation emerges in *Heart of Atlanta*. There, Justice Clark remarks that when the Court in *CRC 1883* declared certain provisions of the Civil Rights Act of 1875 unconstitutional, including the key provision that prohibited racial discrimination in "inns, public conveyances on land or water, theaters, and other places of public amusement,"[57] it did this by restricting Section 5 powers as well as noting that such restriction did not reach Congress's Commerce Clause powers because the 1875 Act did not invoke this latter authority. Justice Clark then goes on in *Heart of Atlanta*, "We, therefore, conclude that the *Civil Rights Cases* have no relevance to the basis of decision here where the [1964] Act explicitly relies upon the commerce power."[58] This is a most basic strategy of legal reasoning to distinguish the apparent similarity of a prior case to the present case under consideration in order to rule differently. In short, the Civil Rights Act in *CRC 1883* was an exercise of Section 5 only, while the Civil Rights Act in *Heart of Atlanta* was an exercise of both Section 5 and Commerce Clause powers, and, thus, it does not contradict legal rationality to affirm the 1964 statute and leave the invalidation of the 1875 statute undisturbed.

Another way to see this standard move of legal interpretation is that the opinion's declaration of *CRC 1883*'s limited irrelevance also implicitly recognizes the *CRC 1883* as general precedent for enacting the 1964 Act as an exercise of a commerce power understood in contradistinction to police power. In Justice Clark's discussion of why *CRC 1883* does not apply to the 1964 Act, we can literally trace *CRC 1883*'s dicta about Commerce Clause power as the basis of Congress's Civil Rights Act in 1964, and *Heart of Atlanta*'s acquiescence to the *CRC 1883*'s most troubling distinction between actionable public and unreachable private discrimination which becomes the basis for limiting Congress's Section 5 power. Glaringly present in Justice Clark's observation of *CRC 1883*'s limited irrelevance is the absent question of *CRC 1883*'s general relevance.

And this is the absent question that would return at the dawn of the twenty-first century. As Post and Siegel warn, the 2000 term marked the Court's shift from passive dishonoring to a more active retrenchment against (again) those openings created by Reconstruction². The silent assumption of *CRC 1883*'s general relevance, or we might say, archival status as authoritative law, is taken up explicitly in recent Section 5 jurisprudence, and most explicitly in *Morrison*. As I noted in the previous section, *Heart of Atlanta*'s curious silence as to Congress's Section 5 power in contrast to *Morrison*'s curious blast against Congress's Section 5 power is more than a sign of changing times. If we set aside for a moment the interminable calculus of social inequality and remedy, what shines through is *Heart of Atlanta*'s and *Morrison*'s shared indebtedness to *CRC 1883* as the touchstone of adjudicating the proper creative source of and limitation on civil rights.

There are many, many reasons why reading *Morrison* fills one with outrage and dread. In fact, the recent cases of rape and domestic violence—from the Steubenville case to the Marissa Alexander case, just to scratch the surface of public panic around sexual violence—seem to only confirm the inadequacy of the "congruence and proportionality" test that *Morrison* validates to the task of addressing the law's unavailability to victims of private and state violence.[59] But I would like to venture the argument that it is precisely the Court's reasoning that provides us with a knowledge of a fundamental challenge within the law, just barely discernible from the

57 Heart of Atlanta Motel v. United States, 379 U.S. 241, 250 (1964).

58 *Id.* at 252.

59 *See* Avital Ronel, *The Rhetoric of Testing*, *in* Stupidity, 95 (2002).

law's attempts to find a legal remedy for discrimination through a sophomoric sociology of gender violence.[60] MacKinnon has already analyzed this aspect of *Morrison*, and does a stunning job of challenging the Court's reasoning by using the same precedent the case relies upon to uphold VAWA. She also makes an observation somewhat in passing that I would like to extend, when she notes that "To invalidate the VAWA, the *Morrison* Court revitalized two post-Reconstruction rulings hostile to race and sex equality rights, the *Civil Rights Cases* and *United States v. Harris*, cases that had largely limited congressional exercise of Section 5 to official violations."[61]

The exact language through which this "revitalization" takes place can be found in the opening paragraph of Rehnquist's opinion:

> In these cases we consider the constitutionality of [VAWA], which provides a federal civil remedy for the victims of gender-motivated violence. The United States Court of Appeals for the Fourth Circuit, sitting en banc, struck down §13981 because it concluded that Congress lacked constitutional authority to enact the section's civil remedy. Believing that these cases are controlled by our decisions in *United States v. Lopez* (1995), *United States v. Harris* (1883), and the *In re Civil Rights Cases* (1883), we affirm.

Here, in this summary recitation of the case, we see the doctrinal convergence of a temporally transcendent scene of violence that slips in through the backdoor of the Court's commitment to federalism. Not only is the opinion's text perversely avoidant in its sociological demand for evidence of the problem of gender violence, but it is also perversely open here about how its interpretation of federalism is also a faithful demurring to the most disturbing and damning social violence haunting American democracy. In *Lopez*, *Harris*, and *CRC 1883*, all instances of federal antidiscrimination legislation, judicial interpretation and state police power converge as a form of federalist neglect towards Black life—the dark life of the urban center, life in the shadows of White mob violence, life on the other side of the track. This racial division in social life that is right there for our reading in this citational opening of Rehnquist's recitation is a poetic scene of racial and sexual violence.

This poetics, on my reading, is not about whether we can imagine the metamorphosis of VAWA's subject, detailed so meticulously by Kristin Bumiller in her book, *In an Abusive State*,[62] into the sexually degraded bodies haunting the failed justice of the Klu Klux Klan Act or Civil Rights Act of 1875 at issue in *Harris* and *CRC 1883*, respectively. It is about how the interminable calculus of the woman's violated body that *Morrison*'s analysis represents guards against the precedential poetics of a Black life in social death that *Lopez*, *Harris*, and *CRC 1883* are and will, as Rehnquist reasons, continue to be dispositive according to the "force of the doctrine of *stare decisis* behind these decisions."[63]

The structural impasse between federal power-sharing and judicial review as the exercise of this founding power of interpretation brushes up against the shadows of Reconstruction^2 which remains in the legal text a "fundamental antagonism."[64] With a certain protocol of reading, the Section 5 antidiscrimination doctrine that emerges at the turn of the century is ahead of the political curve, in a sense, interpreting the possible meanings of equality at a scale that is the condition of possibility for the various constituency-based political conflicts that characterize the post-civil rights era and its various identity-based legal reforms and academic fields of study.[65]

The signal Supreme Court cases I use above to sketch the doctrinal landscape of Section 5 jurisprudence take form through the foreclosed claims of Reconstruction^2 as *the* standard for judging civil rights cases and antidiscrimination reforms. This landscape both reflects the myriad identities that have taken advantage of the legal stage to claim their injuries over and against the claim of the slave; and the possibility of some other

60 The Court's full analysis of Section 5 is on 619–27, where the majority lays out why *CRC 1883* and *Harris* remain good law *see* United States v. Morrison, 529 U.S. 598, 619–27 (2000).

61 MacKinnon, *supra* note 39, at 156.

62 Kristen Bullimer, In An Abusive State: How Neoliberalism Appropriated the Feminist Movement Against Sexual Violence (2008).

63 United States v. Morrison, 529 U.S. 598, 622 (2000).

64 Frank Wilderson, III, Red, White and Black: Cinema and the Structure of U.S. Antagonisms (2010).

65 I elaborate on this "protocol of reading" in the final section of the chapter.

form of relation to be thought between those identities via the perpetual return of a Reconstruction^2 ethos. While it is popular to reduce the times of Reconstruction^2 to some simplistic notion of African-American or multicultural history, we find instead how the times of Reconstruction^2 consist precisely in a revitalized present in legal discourse, as we saw in the opening paragraph of *Morrison*, when the fundamental antagonism at the heart of federal antidiscrimination law between slavery and democracy erupts in legal reason. From this view, the times of Reconstruction^2 and its radical splaying of American law's philosophic traditions are always present, even as legal reason seduces its constituencies and parties into a national telos of multicultural inclusion away from the failures of the First and Second Reconstructions.

This telos of inclusion is precisely the politico-legal problem Wendy Brown identified in her well-known book, *States of Injury*.[66] There she raises the spectacle of a local law in Santa Cruz, CA, that taking the antidiscrimination claim to its limit, prohibits in addition to discrimination against legally recognized identities of difference (such as race, ethnicity, gender, ability, age, and so on), discrimination against "personal appearance," commonly referred to as "the 'purple hair ordinance' or the 'ugly ordinance.'"[67] What we have on the level of federal antidiscrimination law is something similar to this development at this local level, where antidiscrimination law has increasingly recognized (even if only to reject) forms of discrimination that exceed those social identities of difference that have memorialized histories of exclusion and oppression. We now have, for example, legal scholarship that is looking at the impact of personal appearance and identity performance in the workplace, that tries to understand how structural inequality and social categories are maintained at the micro-level of self-fashioning regulated by purportedly "race-neutral" policies.[68]

If this scholarship elaborates a certain empirical reality of how discrimination works, it nonetheless runs up against the judicially hoarded power to interpret power. Indeed, we saw the exercise of this power over the power of science supporting Congressional legislation in *Morrison*, but we have seen it in countless other cases, including the recent Voting Rights Act decision, *Shelby County v. Holder* (2013).[69] This suggests that we must accept that the power of empirical knowledge is subordinate to judicial interpretive power over power. We can regard this as either a profoundly pessimistic assessment, or a profoundly optimistic one.

That is, we know that institutional discrimination occurs oftentimes through "cognitive biases" absent outright malice, bigotry, or recognition of difference, and that this is the reason why identity-based antidiscrimination laws are in many instances ineffective. In response to this, conservatives call for the constitutional abolition of race-based equality measures,[70] and liberal/progressives call for the legal recognition of an alternative "implicit bias" understanding of legally actionable discrimination. Still, the emerging Section 5 jurisprudence seems to call for a third tack that requires neither the abolition of racial categories nor the pursuit of cognitive theories of discrimination.[71] Undoubtedly, the Rehnquist Court was central to normalizing a legal retrenchment against the times of Reconstruction^2. It is by this retrenchment's very reliance on raising the specter of a radical vision of civil rights as a negative reason for embracing both retractions and extensions of civil rights that I see the possibility for a new understanding of race and the Fourteenth Amendment unbound by identitarian (however intersectional they might be) politics, and properly oriented towards the legal present that Reconstruction^2 always returns. This radicalism is essentially given to us by the rotten core

66 Wendy Brown, States of Injury (1995).

67 *Id.* at 65–66.

68 *See, e.g.*, Devon Carbado & Mitu Gulati, Acting White? Rethinking Race in Post-Racial America (2013). Interestingly, Carbado published another book that same year, co-edited with Donald Weise, which recovers a dozen slave narratives about escaping slavery, *see* Devon Carbado & Donald Weise, The Long Walk to Freedom: Runaway Slave Narratives (2013). The split between empirical studies and historical studies of race, demonstrated by these two publications, is precisely what I am trying broach by tracing the force of the foreclosed claim of the slave in the doctrinal landscape of Section 5 jurisprudence.

69 570 U.S._ (2013).

70 *See, e.g.*, Project for Fair Representation, http://www.projectonfairrepresentation.org/ (last visited Nov. 15, 2013).

71 Critiques of the former approach are abundant. A thorough argument of the limitations of this latter approach to reforming equal protection doctrine can be seen in; Mona Lynch, *Institutionalizing Bias: The Death Penalty, Federal Drug Prosecutions, and Mechanisms of Racialized Punishment*, 41 Am. J. of Crim. L. 1 (2013).

of what Rehnquist in *Morrison* described as "the enduring vitality of the *Civil Rights Cases* and *Harris*."[72] To be clear, their vitality comes from the undying question of how civil rights are to attach to freedpersons, and the force of the slave's claim as judicial review's deconstruction. It is a vitalism that is contained in the citational practices of an essentially conservative judicial power, at the same time that it compels another protocol of reading through and against judicial rationality.

What form of justice does *CRC 1883*'s fugitive claim call forth, as it echoes across the landscape of Section 5 jurisprudence? And is the possibility of posing a question about this claim's fugitivity precisely why the claim returns, however obliquely, whenever we are lost in the sea of legal calculation and distributive justice? This is not Rehnquist's question, but is the question that his recitation of precedent in *Morrison* allows us to ask. It is not Thomas's question, but is the question that his unsightly recitation of precedent in *Fisher* allows us to ask. And finally, this is not the law's question, but is the question that the law's unsightly recitation of the Fourteenth Amendment allows us to ask.

Towards a Fugitive Law of Freedom: Bell's Invitation

In bringing this chapter to a close, I would like to return to Derrick Bell's philosophy of racial realism as a form of thought that calls for the recognition of *CRC 1883*'s echoic claim I attempted to trace in the preceding sections. This of course provokes us to contemplate the purported pessimism of Bell's philosophy, and as what I provisionally designate as "pessimism+." Indeed, in the 1992 preface to his *Faces at the Bottom of the Well*, he writes: "The challenge throughout has been to tell what I view as the truth about racism without causing disabling despair."[73] Not "*disabling* despair," but then what *other kind of despair* might his thought be promoting? He goes on to draw from Paulo Freire, Albert Camus, and Frantz Fanon in order to delineate something we might think of as a *productive* despair, or what each of these authors in their own language have theorized as *freedom*. Specifically, Bell references a rich and provocative passage from Fanon that I want to look at closely. I am quoting Bell's discussion of Fanon's *Black Skin, White Masks* (1967) here:

> Fanon argued two seemingly irreconcilable points, and insisted on both. On the one hand, he believed racist structures to be permanently embedded in the psychology, economy, society, and culture of the modern world—so much so that he expressed the belief "that a true culture cannot come to life under present conditions." But, on the other hand, he urged people of color to resist psychologically the inheritance they had come into. He insisted, despite pages of evidence suggesting the inviolability of the racial order, that "I should constantly *remind myself* that the real *leap* consists in introducing invention into existence. For the world through which I travel, I am endlessly creating myself."[74]

Bell's emphasis remarks how Fanon might have had to remind *himself* that: "For the world through which I travel, I am endlessly creating myself." David Marriott, Fanon's most dedicated reader today, also remarks on this self-reminding, pointing to the "peculiar anamnesis" contained in Fanon's assertion: "'I am not the slave of the Slavery that dehumanized my ancestors.'"[75] Perhaps Bell's emphasis also bespeaks a reminder to *himself* of the truth of a Fanonian political reality, or what Bell would improvise as his own theory of racial realism, and what he would live out in his person through open invitations to a collective life lived *in* freedom struggle, as opposed to a progressive movement beyond it.

This trace of self-reminding across Bell and Fanon (and Marriott) is an insistence of an "organic" force, or the "+" of my designation of racial realism as "pessimism+," that is produced in the "peculiar anamnesis" of "Slavery." Extending the classical Platonic notion of anamnesis that designates a transformative process of learning through remembrance, it's as if Bell via Fanon turned this classic notion into a racial politic. This

---

72 United States v. Morrison, 529 U.S. 598, 624 (2000).

73 Derrick Bell, Faces at the Bottom of the Well, vix (1992).

74 *Id.* at x, first emphasis, "*remind myself*," is Bell's; second emphasis, "*leap*," is Fanon's.

75 David Marriot, Haunted Life: Visual Culture and Black Modernity 235 (2007) (quoting Fanon, Black Skin, White Masks, 230).

kind of study is also what is at stake in Du Bois's defense of Black schools, to come back full circle to my discussion of Du Bois mediated performance in *Fisher*, when he states that "Negroes must know the history of the Negro race in America, and this they will seldom get in white institutions … They ought to study intelligently and from their own point of view, the slave trade, slavery, emancipation, Reconstruction, and present economic development."[76]

The "+" is not power that is taken, or power that is bestowed, or power that is exchanged, or power that is shared. It is not a possessible power, but an irreducible *force* in the infinite depths of self-fashioning where no "good choices" are available, which is to say, the position of complete powerlessness and dishonor. Thus, in order that Fanon should remind himself that the only thing that matters politically is this invention of existence, he proclaims: "One duty alone: That of not renouncing my freedom through my choices."[77] When we hear as Bell did the rhythm of this refusal of renunciation in its infinite expressions, then *there* is the radical chance for something other in the world of judicial review. All other recognitions of freedom loop endlessly, which is to say, they seek only to reform *this* world.

What might we say, do, or think if we start not with division but with a thought of the whole? The claim of the slave which comes from the force of refusing to renounce freedom? What if the various constituency-based legal reform movements as political and intellectual formations have already met at the level of prophesy and in the revelatory space of a law in the interstitialities of federalism the foreclosed claim of the slave reveals, are already an "ensemble,"[78] as Fred Moten might describe it? This question that becomes possible by the force of the claim of the slave is ultimately a Moten-esque formulation: whether we can "faithfully reclaim the honor of the whole, an honor which is real only within the complex, radical, and realist attention and devotion we pay to the world,"[79] instead of simply taking measure of and compensating for all our incompletenesses. *This* law, what we can call a *fugitive law of freedom*, is what becomes possible at the dead end of the Equal Protection Clause, and where we always must begin our descent into a critical knowledge of race and law.

76 *Separate Schools? supra* note 21, at 333.

77 Frantz Fanon, Black Skin, White Masks 229 (1967, trans. Charles Lam Markmann).

78 The idea of the ensemble, then, is what provides my protocol of reading in this chapter. Moten describes it "as something out-from-outside, other than the other or the same, something unbound by their relation or nonrelation, and situated at an opening onto the site of the intersection of the knowledge of language (as prayer, curse, narrative [*récit* or recitation]) and the knowledge of freedom (as both a negative function of the experience of oppression and the trace of an 'innate endowment that serves to bridge the gap between experience and knowledge …')." *See* Fred Moten, *Knowledge of Freedom*, 4(2) The New Centennial Rev., 269, 281 (2004).

79 *Id.* at 280.

PART II
The Formulae for Stasis

Chapter 4
Equal Protection as Intentional Blindness

Ian F. Haney López

> The Court that refused to see inequality … would be making the only kind of law that can be warranted outrageous in advance—law based on self-induced blindness, on flagrant contradiction of known fact.
>
> —Charles Black[†]

Introduction

Since the end of the civil rights era in the early 1970s, the emancipatory potential of the Fourteenth Amendment has been thoroughly undone. Today, its guarantee of "equal protection" no longer promotes reform but rather protects the racial *status quo*. This undoing has spanned four decades, with sharp plunges followed by ever-lower plateaus. These reversals have come in two principal areas: in how the Supreme Court evaluates claims of discrimination against nonwhites, an area governed by intent doctrine; and in how it regards affirmative action designed to ameliorate racial inequality, where the Court draws on colorblindness.

We find ourselves in a renewed period of rapid devolution. In the next few months and years, scholars will react to these changes, a few extolling and most bemoaning them, many focusing on distinct cases and some seeing overarching patterns. Yet almost all will accept as the foundation for their engagement the basic division in equal protection between intent and colorblindness. This chapter seeks instead to understand the present and near future by revising our understanding of the past. In this vein, it offers a wholly new conception of the relationship between discriminatory intent doctrine and colorblindness.

The pronounced tendency to regard these doctrines as fundamentally distinct is understandable, for not only do they operate in different domains, they seem to be mirrored inversions of one another. Colorblindness applies to affirmative action because it expressly uses race; intent doctrine sweeps up allegations of discriminatory treatment where race is almost never explicitly referenced. Colorblindness denies that the state's purposes can be discerned; intent doctrine makes proof of malice indispensable. Colorblindness consistently imposes the most stringent form of scrutiny; intent cases always default to the most lenient form of constitutional review. Plaintiffs challenging affirmative action under colorblindness virtually always win; parties challenging discrimination under intent doctrine almost invariably lose.

Yet despite these dramatic dissimilarities, intent and colorblindness are profoundly connected. How could they not be? The contemporary versions of these doctrines were elaborated at the same time, by the same Justices, and to the same ultimate effect: to defeat challenges to, and remedies for, discrimination against nonwhites.

Moreover, for both doctrines, the basic method was and is the same: to deny that context matters. In declaring that only one form of intent counts—malice—discriminatory intent doctrine excludes most evidence of continued discrimination against nonwhites, whether rooted in history, contemporary practices, or social science. It thus blinds the courts to the obvious truth that forms of discrimination have evolved since the civil rights era, and no longer exclusively take the form of hooded bigotry. Likewise, in pronouncing that motives are unknowable and hence irrelevant, colorblindness similarly closes the courthouse doors to evidence of a changing context, in this case the rise of efforts by state actors to use race to break down inequality and to foster integration. Colorblindness fundamentally ignores the victories wrought by the civil

[†] Charles Black, *The Lawfulness of the Segregation Decisions*, 69 Yale L.J. 421, 426 (1960).

rights movement itself, which moved the country from one seeking to enforce racial supremacy to one hoping for its eradication.[1]

We should no longer conceive of equal protection as divided between intent and colorblindness. Instead, we should understand it as unified under what might best be termed "intentional blindness." Combining the names of the two doctrines, this portmanteau expresses the marrow of the Court's racial jurisprudence—which seems intentionally blind to racial context.

This chapter first examines equal protection before the advent of colorblindness, when one doctrine—discriminatory intent—applied to both express and non-express uses of race. The chapter then details the heretofore unrecognized symbiosis between colorblindness and intent: colorblindness arose in response to intent doctrine, especially as applied to affirmative action; and in turn, colorblindness impelled intent doctrine toward a monocular focus on malice. It then traces the rise and application of malicious intent across the 1980s, reconsidering the actual operation of malice doctrine to offer a damning indictment heretofore missing from the literature. Virtually all of intent doctrine's critics accept that today's intent standard actually searches for illicit motives. This is evident in the two primary critiques they lodge. Either the critics reprove an exclusive focus on conscious animus that imperils attention to unconscious bias. Or they remonstrate that requiring proof of malice disables the courts from remedying entrenched disadvantage. In either event, they chide the Justices for not easily improving intent doctrine by updating its conception of cognition and broadening its focus from mindsets to structures. Yet in both cases, these critics assume that the malice test is in fact geared to searching for illicit motives.

Upon re-examination, however, the conservative Justices may have repeatedly exhorted proof of malice, but they showed no interest in parsing mental states. Instead, their demands seemed geared to closing the courthouse doors to evidence showing continued racial hierarchy. To make this point as powerfully as possible, this chapter asks how the malice test would resolve a challenge to Jim Crow segregation. It argues that the malice test would fail to arrive at the correct result even in a case like *Brown v. Board of Education*—the paradigmatic equal protection case of the twentieth century.

Finally, this chapter brings the analysis up to the present, demonstrating the consolidation of intent and colorblindness after the 1990s. This consolidation occurred in two senses: first, in terms of the emergence of a solid bloc of conservative Justices who repeatedly voted to ignore racial discrimination and to strike down affirmative action; and second, in terms of a striking convergence between the doctrines themselves.

A last introductory word: this chapter focuses on doctrine, but it is not a doctrinal article. Instead, it takes doctrine seriously in order to lay bare the racial politics of the conservative Justices who have reversed equal protection over the last four decades. This story could be told much more simply in terms of elections and judicial appointments. In this version, equal protection's transmogrification since the 1970s follows most fundamentally from a backlash against civil rights manipulated by demagogic politicians, and resulted in the election of presidents, and in turn the appointment of Justices, hostile toward racial progress.[2] Those Justices who consistently refused to find discrimination against nonwhites, or to support affirmative action programs, were prepared to reach those results without doctrine or evidence on their side. Crucially, though, they were also quick to craft doctrines and evidentiary standards that confirmed their favored outcomes, and it is here that the story becomes complicated, widely misunderstood, and critically important. True, malice doctrine and colorblindness were not engines for rolling back civil rights, so much as a dissimulating gloss. Over time, however, this gloss has hardened into a strong protective carapace. So long as colorblindness and discriminatory intent remain misunderstood as separate and plausible doctrines, it will be all but impossible to understand ongoing devolutions in the Court's racial jurisprudence. Charles Black in 1960 described the refusal to see racial inequality as self-induced blindness. Colorblindness and intent doctrine are the bandages the Justices use to blind themselves to continued racism against nonwhites, and also to hide from public view their ferocious disfigurement of equal protection.

---

1 Except, of course, when it uses evidence of racial progress as an excuse to demolish antidiscrimination law, as in the recent Voting Rights Act case. *Shelby County v. Holder*, 570 U.S. __ (2013).

2 I trace how politicians have exploited hostility toward civil rights, and toward racial minorities more generally, in Dog Whistle Politics: How Coded Racial Appeals Have Reinvented Racism and Wrecked the Middle Class (forthcoming, 2014).

Contextual Intent, Discrimination, and Affirmative Action

In the stock story regarding intent, the prime villain is a 1976 case, *Washington v. Davis*.[3] In the 1980s, the leading treatise on constitutional law summarized *Davis* in the following terms: "In essence, *Washington v. Davis* announced that henceforth every lawsuit involving constitutional claims of racial discrimination directed at facially race-neutral rules would be conducted as a search for a bigoted decision-maker."[4] In so writing, Laurence Tribe accurately captured the state of intent doctrine at that date. But he was wrong to impute this structure to *Davis*, and wrong not once but twice.

To begin with, *Davis* did not require a search for a bigoted decision-maker, but instead envisioned a weighing of the totality of the circumstances. Rather than inventing intent doctrine, *Davis* helped formalize the Court's basic approach to allegations of discrimination in place since *Brown v. Board of Education* struck down segregated schools in 1954. During the civil rights era, the Court evaluated the general purposes behind challenged government actions using a broadly inferential approach, rather than through a hunt for bigots. Sometimes this inferential process reflected little more than judicial notice of race relations. At other times, the Justices relied on a more focused examination of surrounding racial patterns, including through the invocation of social science. Whatever the combination, the point is that the Court did not demand direct proof of subjective mindsets. Instead, findings of discriminatory purpose reflected inferences drawn from the challenged action as well as the surrounding context—in a phrase popular with the Court, from the "totality of the circumstances."[5] Just so in *Davis*, where the Court held that "[n]ecessarily, an invidious discriminatory purpose may often be inferred from the totality of the relevant facts."[6]

Next, Tribe erred in suggesting that, under *Davis*, intent applied to "claims of racial discrimination directed at facially race-neutral rules"—that is, that intent doctrine did *not* apply when the state expressly used race. On the contrary, up through *Davis* and just beyond, equal protection's evaluative approach did not turn on whether the challenged government action expressly invoked race. Indeed, illustrating this, *Davis* itself presumed that the intent test applied to race-conscious state action. Immediately after announcing the need to show an invidious purpose, the Court explained: "This is not to say that the necessary discriminatory racial purpose must be express or appear on the face of the statute."[7] *Davis* thus assumed that the intent test applied to express uses of race, and clarified that it might *also* apply to race-neutral practices. By offering this clarification, *Davis* pointed back toward a basic fact that is now virtually forgotten: the Jim Crow cases expressly mandating segregation constituted the quintessential intent cases.

If Tribe's treatise misrepresented *Davis*, it nevertheless correctly described intent doctrine as it stood in the late 1980s. To contrast the two distinct versions of intent doctrine, distinguish "contextual" from "malicious" approaches. Where contextual intent focused on motives only in the loosest sense and emphasized instead a broadly informed inferential approach to evaluating possible discrimination, today's malice doctrine declares direct proof of injurious motives a prerequisite—and concomitantly declares contextual evidence irrelevant. Understanding the shift from contextual to malicious intent, in turn, requires understanding the strengths of contextual intent, and more generally the relationship between malicious intent and colorblindness.

Contextual intent, as its name implies, asked courts to consider the larger context in which challenged actions occurred. This allowed courts to discern racial discrimination even when it did not take the form of archetypal Jim Crow segregation. More strikingly, however, it also provided a ready means to distinguish oppressive uses of race from remedial ones—in other words, contextual intent provided a means to uphold affirmative action.

A year after *Davis*, the Court decided *United Jewish Organizations of Williamsburgh, Inc. v. Carey*,[8] or *UJO*, involving a decision by the New York legislature to create two majority-minority districts in the Williamsburgh area of Brooklyn. *UJO* thus involved what Justice William Brennan characterized as the use

3 Washington v. Davis, 426 U.S. 229, 242 (1976).

4 Laurence Tribe, American Constitutional Law 1509 (2nd ed. 1988).

5 White v. Regester, 412 U.S. 755, 769 (1973).

6 *Davis*, 426 U.S. at 242.

7 *Id.* at 241 (emphasis added).

8 United Jewish Org. of Williamsburgh, Inc. v. Carey, 430 U.S. 144 (1977).

of "race-centered remedial devices."[9] The decision was nearly unanimous, though various rationales were advanced. Two Justices applied *Davis* directly: "Under the Fourteenth Amendment the question is whether the reapportionment plan represents purposeful discrimination against White voters. *Washington v. Davis*."[10] Three others used an intent analysis, though without specifically citing *Davis*. Because the "plan represented no racial slur or stigma with respect to whites or any other race," they concluded, "we discern no discrimination violative of the Fourteenth Amendment."[11] Justice Brennan concurred but hesitated to fully endorse the intent analysis, lest this suggest that merely rational review would suffice. For Brennan, even remedial uses of race carried sufficient risks to warrant a more searching, though not strict, review.[12] Sifting through these rationales, a surprising result emerges: five Justices—and not just any five, but White, Stevens, Rehnquist, Stewart, and Powell, all of whom with the exception of White would soon support the rise of colorblindness—thought that race-conscious remedies should be treated just like every other use of race and evaluated for an intent to harm. To reiterate, in *UJO* those Justices poised to embrace colorblindness concluded that in the absence of any intent to harm, affirmative action was constitutional. What a brief, remarkable moment. In the first case to squarely address the constitutionality of a race-conscious remedy, the Court for the last time found affirmative action lawful by asking whether there was an intent to harm whites.

Colorblindness and Malice

UJO seemed to serve as a wake-up call to the racially conservative Justices. That decision warned (or from a different perspective promised) that race-conscious remedies, when reviewed for discriminatory intent, would be readily upheld. Betraying dissatisfaction with that result, the next year in *Bakke* five Justices voted to restrict affirmative action.[13] Yet, likely reflecting their holding just the prior year, four avoided the constitutional question altogether. Standing alone, Lewis Powell experimented with a constitutional argument. Powell started by rejecting colorblindness, at least when defined as a *per se* prohibition on any use of race.[14] In its place, though, Powell established the fundamentals of modern colorblind analysis: not automatic invalidity but its close cousin, the application of the highest level of constitutional hostility to all express uses of race—which is to say, to affirmative action.[15]

Though Powell initially attracted no other votes for this perversion of equal protection, two years later Stewart and Rehnquist exploited the opening when they dissented in a 1980 case upholding a minority set-aside in federal construction contracts.[16] For the first time, conservative Justices declared that the "constitution is color-blind," employing John Marshall Harlan's famous aphorism from his dissent in *Plessy v. Ferguson*.[17] Yet, this position, adopted by only two Justices, still seemed so bizarre that the majority opinion began: "As a threshold matter, we reject the contention that in the remedial context the Congress must act in a wholly 'color-blind' fashion."[18] It would take another nine years before a majority of the Justices consolidated behind colorblind logic as a basis for overturning an affirmative action program. In 1989 five Justices in *City of Richmond v. Croson Co.* used colorblindness to strike down a race-conscious remedy.[19] Since *Croson*, colorblindness has become dominant on the Court, striking down remedial program after program, even if typically only with the votes of a bare majority of five Justices.

9 *Id.* at 169 (Brennan, J., concurring).

10 *Id.* at 179 (Stewart, J., concurring).

11 *Id.*

12 *Id.* at 170–75 (Brennan, J., concurring).

13 Regents of the Univ. of Cal. v. Bakke, 438 U.S. 265, 272 (1978).

14 *Id.* at 284–85.

15 For a full discussion of *Bakke* and the rise of colorblindness, *see* Ian Haney López, *"A Nation of Minorities": Race, Ethnicity, and Reactionary Colorblindness*, 59 STAN. L. REV. 985 (2007).

16 Fullilove v. Klutznick, 448 U.S. 448, 522–23 (1980) (Stewart, J., dissenting).

17 *Id.* at 522.

18 *Id.* at 483.

19 City of Richmond v. Croson Co., 488 U.S. 469 (1989).

It is into the colorblindness timeline that one must place the origins of malicious intent. Just a year after *Bakke*, in *Personnel Administrator of Massachusetts v. Feeney*, five conservative Justices began to rework intent doctrine.[20] Strikingly, they did so in direct reliance upon Powell's colorblind reasoning—making *Feeney*, not *Croson*, the first case by a decade to assemble a majority behind colorblindness. Extending Powell's analysis in *Bakke*, *Feeney* split equal protection into the separate domains now taken for granted, one governing affirmative action and the other discrimination against nonwhites. In turn, this schism contributed directly to the rise of the malicious intent rule requiring the nearly impossible proof of malice.

In *Feeney*, even the majority recognized that Massachusetts conferred on veterans "a well-nigh absolute advantage" in the competition for civil-service positions.[21] For any available job, the state ranked applicants according to their score on a competitive exam but placed veterans above all others: the lowest-scoring veteran took his place above the highest-scoring nonveteran. As the Court observed, because 98 percent of veterans were male, "[t]he impact of the veterans' preference law upon the public employment opportunities of women has thus been severe."[22] To challenge this system, Helen Feeney invoked the contextual intent approach formalized in *Davis*. She especially emphasized the concurrence by Stevens, who had urged attention to "objective evidence of what actually happened rather than evidence describing the subjective state of mind of the actor. For normally the actor is presumed to have intended the natural consequences of his deeds."[23]

But the majority did not begin by addressing intent. Rather, *Feeney* used Powell's equal protection story in *Bakke* to rewrite the Fourteenth Amendment in terms of a basic concern with the act of classification. "Most laws classify," Stewart began, observing that equal protection generally required that distinctions among classes be subjected to no more than rational review—the standard asking only whether the government has a conceivable legitimate interest.[24] "Certain classifications, however, in themselves supply a reason to infer antipathy. Race is the paradigm."[25] In this narrative, the simple use of race without more triggered constitutional suspicion. "A racial classification, *regardless of purported motivation*, is presumptively invalid and can be upheld only upon an extraordinary justification."[26] *Feeney* pretended to reach back to *Brown v. Board of Education* for this radical proposition.[27] Yet clearly the appropriate citation was Powell's lone opinion in *Bakke*. Only a year after that case—and a full decade before *Croson* would see five Justices say the same to strike down an affirmative action program—*Feeney* assembled five votes for the rule that all uses of race, even if remedial, were "presumptively invalid."

Only after announcing a mechanical distrust of any use of race did *Feeney* address intent doctrine. It did so by recasting intent doctrine as the flip side of colorblind doctrine's automatic hostility to express uses of race: now, absent a reference to race, even government action that disproportionately harmed nonwhites would be presumptively constitutional. The express use of a racial classification became the crucial pivot. In effect, *Feeney* built on *Bakke* to bifurcate equal protection into two domains with two dramatically different presumptions of constitutionality.

In the first domain, all racial classifications merit the highest level of constitutional suspicion. Stewart cast colorblindness as skepticism of any "racial classification, regardless of purported motivation." This put a universal spin on the point, as if colorblindness stood in opposition to every use of race whether propelled by invidious or benign motives, whether Jim Crow or affirmative action. But colorblindness—arising in the late 1970s—stood in opposition to Jim Crow only in its own mythos. In reality, opposition to every use of race meant hostility toward race-based remedies. Powell introduced colorblind logic in *Bakke* in 1978 primarily to evade the thrust of *UJO*. Stewart endorsed anticlassification reasoning in *Feeney* and then immediately seized upon colorblindness to condemn affirmative action in employment in 1980 and 1981. Once five Justices came to this position in *Croson*, colorblindness went on to strike down myriad remedial measures but applied in

20 Personnel Adm'r of Mass. v. Feeney, 442 U.S. 256 (1979).
21 *Id.* at 264.
22 *Id.* at 270, 271.
23 Washington v. Davis, 426 U.S. 229, 253 (1976) (Stevens, J., concurring).
24 *Feeney*, 442 U.S. at 272.
25 *Id.* at 272.
26 *Id.* (emphasis added).
27 *See id.* (citing *Brown*).

only *one* case involving the mistreatment of nonwhites—and that over the strenuous objections of Clarence Thomas and Antonin Scalia, two of the most vociferous proponents of colorblindness.[28] The colorblind claim to oppose any government use of race is misleading, for in practice colorblindness opposes race-conscious remedies and nothing more.

Meanwhile, in the second domain, facially race-neutral laws merit almost complete constitutional deference. But there is obfuscation here too. After *Feeney*, the "neutral" laws presumed to be constitutional unless malice could be shown never involved government action that *helped* minorities; those laws were examined skeptically under colorblindness. And these "neutral" laws never involved the supposed mistreatment of whites. There have been no cases alleging the use of race-neutral devices to discriminate against whites. Instead, the fruitless search for invidious intent has only been required in challenges to government practices imposing disproportionate harm on nonwhites. Almost complete deference to government action applies only when minorities, not whites, allege racial discrimination.

Thus, in one domain of equal protection, extreme suspicion reigns, and in the other, virtually complete abdication prevails. Abstractly, these two domains correspond to facially racial and facially neutral government actions. In reality, they correspond to affirmative action and disproportionate harm to nonwhites. Affirmative action receives fatal-in-fact review; harm to nonwhites is treated with lenient indifference.

Feeney, of course, is not commonly known as a colorblindness case, but rather as the case that first announced, notoriously, that intent required a showing that the state pursued the challenged action "at least in part 'because of,' not merely 'in spite of,' its adverse effects."[29] That is, *Feeney* defined "intent" as acting not just in full awareness of impending harm but out of a desire to cause such harm. Reva Siegel, among others, understands the Court to have demanded proof of conscious antipathy, something approaching malice: "[I]n *Feeney*, the Court asked plaintiffs to prove that legislators adopting a policy that would foreseeably injure women or minorities had acted with the express purpose of injuring women or minorities—in short, a legislative state of mind akin to malice."[30]

In reconsidering contemporary intent doctrine, we must recognize its close symbiosis with colorblindness. Colorblindness arose in response to contextual intent, in particular to its propensity to uphold affirmative action. In turn, the malice test developed as a mirror to colorblindness, deeming all facially race-neutral government practices presumptively innocent and imposing an egregiously high burden to prove otherwise. *Bakke* elevated affirmative action into a singular threat to equality. *Feeney* rendered discrimination against vulnerable groups a marginal problem. Once embraced as a way of thinking about equality, colorblindness both legitimized and impelled a highly restrictive approach to proving discrimination against nonwhites.

That said, *Feeney* remained a transitional case. Marking an abrupt rupture from past decisions, it endorsed the colorblind reasoning first proposed by Powell the year before in *Bakke*, and dramatically narrowed the meaning of intent to a mindset akin to malice. Yet harkening back to prior intent cases, *Feeney* used contextual evidence to decide whether or not the requisite intent existed. The next year, the Court would begin to impose on plaintiffs not only the onerous need to prove malice, but the impossible challenge of doing so through direct evidence regarding the thinking of identified individuals. It is important to note that *Feeney* did not take that second step, but remained open to inferences drawn from a totality of the circumstances. This bears emphasis not only because it confirms the settled nature of intent doctrine's previous method, but also because *Feeney*'s continued reliance on contextual evidence marked the emergence of a remarkable double standard. Beginning the next year, conservatives on the Court would disparage and reject all but direct evidence to prove animus against nonwhites. But pursuant to *Feeney*, they would continue to draw contextually based inferences of innocence to *defeat* claims of discrimination.

Feeney reversed the logic of earlier cases, which had held that in some cases disproportionate harm to nonwhites was so extreme as to compel an inference of invidious intent. *Feeney* declared instead that a self-

---

28 *See* Johnson v. California, 543 U.S. 499 (2005) (holding that colorblind reasoning requires strict scrutiny of the practice of segregating prisoners).

29 *Feeney*, 442 U.S. at 279.

30 Reva Siegel, *Why Equal Protection No Longer Protects: The Evolving Forms of Status-Enforcing State Action*, 49 Stan. L. Rev. 1111, 1135 (1997).

evidently legitimate purpose defeated evidence of discrimination.[31] Ignoring the possibility of mixed motives, the majority declared that the presence of a single, obvious nondiscriminatory rationale insulated government action by foreclosing the possibility that discriminatory purposes also played some role. A defensible preference for veterans, *Feeney* reasoned, "necessarily compels the conclusion that the State intended nothing more than to prefer 'veterans.' Given this finding, simple logic suggests than an intent to exclude women from significant public jobs was not at work in this law."[32] In dissent, Thurgood Marshall offered the obvious retort: "That a legislature seeks to advantage one group does not, as a matter of logic or of common sense, exclude the possibility that it also intends to disadvantage another."[33] The malice cases that followed *Feeney* would demand that plaintiffs directly prove intent, as if they were deeply concerned with the actual—and necessarily multiple—motivations of individuals. But contrarily, these cases also drew on *Feeney*'s new rule that the presence of a single, legitimate government purpose, discerned generally from the context surrounding the challenged policy, would warrant an unimpeachable inference of innocence. The malice test developed as a rule banning contextual proof of discrimination, while at the same time allowing contextual exonerations.

1980–87: Malice Applied

The malicious intent test as a bar on claims of mistreatment came into full force almost immediately. This is not to suggest that, after *Feeney*, the Court demanded direct proof of animus in every case alleging discrimination against nonwhites. On the contrary, whether in terms of affirmative action or racial discrimination, a high level of doctrinal instability marked equal protection during the 1980s. Nevertheless, equal protection has since consolidated around the malicious intent test, warranting a special focus on the logic of the cases that developed this approach.

The year after *Feeney*, the Court heard *Mobile v. Bolden*.[34] Mobile, Alabama, employed citywide elections for choosing commissioners. Given prevalent racism, although African-Americans constituted 35 percent of the city's population, they were consistently outvoted—a pattern that resulted in no blacks being elected to the city commission since its establishment in 1911. The trial and appellate courts held that Mobile engaged in unconstitutional discrimination by maintaining an electoral system that virtually guaranteed the perpetual exclusion of African-Americans from local government—and, indeed, that operated to ensure the defeat of even those White politicians seen as more sympathetic to the Black third of the population.[35]

In reversing the trial and appellate courts, *Mobile* first reiterated *Feeney*'s logic regarding exculpatory inferences. The majority seemed reassured that the at-large electoral structure applied across the country.[36] *Mobile* then weighed each bit of evidence adduced to show racial mistreatment, though piecemeal and seriatim rather than holistically. This technique of evidentiary disaggregation, which would become routine in malice cases, elicited a strong objection from *Davis*'s author, who correctly pointed out that it violated the spirit of the contextual approach: "By viewing each of the factors relied upon below in isolation ... the plurality rejects the 'totality of the circumstances' approach we endorsed in ... *Washington v. Davis* and *Arlington Heights*, and leaves the courts below adrift on uncharted seas with respect to how to proceed on remand."[37]

The most lethal innovation came, however, in measuring each piece of the disassembled evidence for what it could prove regarding the existence of a subjective mindset of malice. *Mobile* neatly disposed of every probative iota by declaring it individually incapable of showing the actual thinking of an identified state actor. The district court had stressed continued Jim Crow patterns in *Mobile*. It documented at length the exclusion of African-Americans from municipal boards, the relegation of blacks to menial government jobs, the preservation of overwhelmingly White fire and police departments, and allegations of widespread police

31 *Feeney*, 442 U.S. at 275.
32 *Id.* at 277.
33 *Id.* at 282 (Marshall, J., dissenting).
34 Mobile v. Bolden, 446 U.S. 55 (1980).
35 Bolden v. City of Mobile, 423 F. Supp. 384, 387–89 (S.D. Ala. 1976).
36 *Mobile*, 446 U.S. at 59–60.
37 *Id.* at 103 (White, J., dissenting).

brutality that included complaints of mock lynchings.[38] Waiving away this evidence, the opinion rejoined: "[E]vidence of discrimination by White officials in Mobile is relevant only as the most tenuous and circumstantial evidence of the constitutional invalidity of the electoral system under which they attained their offices."[39] Clarifying exactly why such evidence was "tenuous and circumstantial," *Mobile* explained that the district court failed "to identify *the state officials whose intent it considered relevant* in assessing the invidiousness of Mobile's system of government," adding that "the actions of unrelated governmental officials would be, of course, of questionable relevance."[40] The case took a similar stance toward "the substantial history of official racial discrimination in Alabama."[41] It declaimed: "[P]ast discrimination cannot, in the manner of original sin, condemn governmental action that is not itself unlawful. The ultimate question remains whether a discriminatory intent has been proved *in a given case*. More distant instances of official discrimination ... are of limited help in resolving that question."[42] Finally, *Mobile* used the same technique to respond to Marshall's dissenting insistence that "historical and social factors" were indispensable to comprehending Mobile's longstanding exclusion of blacks from political power. The decision flatly declared, "these gauzy sociological considerations have no constitutional basis."[43] It continued: "[I]t remains far from certain that [such considerations] could, in any principled manner, exclude the claims of any discrete political group that happens, for whatever reason, to elect fewer of its candidates than arithmetic indicates it might."[44]

Mobile constituted the first race case to demand proof of a particular actor's invidious intent. This demand rendered constitutionally irrelevant racism's peculiar history in the Deep South, as well as contemporary manifestations of White-over-Black hierarchy. Past discrimination offered only "limited help," meriting derision as merely the distant stain of "original sin."[45] "Historical and social factors" dwindled to "gauzy sociological considerations [without] constitutional basis."[46] Meanwhile, ongoing racism perpetuated by Mobile's government became "tenuous and circumstantial" and "of questionable relevance."[47] Having shorn the city's actions of history and contemporary context, the Court insisted that there was no way to distinguish the perpetual exclusion of blacks from the occasional political losses suffered by other random groups "for whatever reason."[48] In its first iteration, the demand for proof of specific intent worked principally to deprecate the contextual evidence theretofore elemental in proving discriminatory intent.

The next year in *Memphis v. Greene*, largely the same Justices repeated this analysis when blessing a Southern city's decision to close a public street between a White and a Black neighborhood.[49] Built as a segregated enclave in the years before World War II, the Hein Park subdivision in Memphis remained all-White when in 1970 its residents sought to block off the street passing from an adjoining, predominantly Black area.[50] Officials favoring the closure publicly emphasized the safety of children, neighborhood tranquility, vehicular speed, and litter. Opponents challenged it as an obvious racial affront.[51]

Again, the Court used the existence of legitimate governmental purposes to impugn the possibility that animus also operated. And again it resorted to the malicious intent test to disregard contextual evidence. The majority stressed that only the motives of the city officials named in the suit, not of the White voters pressuring them to wall off their neighborhood, should be considered. "We must bear in mind that respondents have sued the city, the Mayor, and the City Council and its chairman. Therefore, we must focus on the

38 *Bolden*, 423 F. Supp. at 388–92.
39 *Mobile*, 446 U.S. at 74.
40 *Id.* at 74 n.20 (emphasis added).
41 *Id.* at 74.
42 *Id.* (emphasis added).
43 *Id.* at 75 n.22.
44 *Id.*
45 *Id.* at 74.
46 *Id.* at 75 n.22.
47 *Id.* at 74.
48 *Id.* at 75 n.22.
49 Memphis v. Greene, 451 U.S. 100 (1981).
50 *Id.* at 103 (1981).
51 *Id.* at 143 n.9 (Marshall, J., dissenting).

decisions of these public officials, and not on the actions of the residents of Hein Park."[52] The Court similarly dismissed evidence of racial prejudice in Hein Park and Memphis generally. After conceding that "the pre-World War II development of Hein Park may well have been influenced by the racial segregation which was then common, and the record contains evidence that racial prejudice still exists in Memphis,"[53] the Court nevertheless concluded that such evidence had little bearing on whether "the City Council's action *in this case* was racially motivated."[54] Having narrowed the constitutional question to animus on the part of the named parties, and then only as immediately related to the challenged street closing, the Court confidently asserted, "there is *no* evidence that the closing was motivated by *any* racially exclusionary desire."[55]

Perhaps the most outrageous example of malicious intent during this period came in the infamous Georgia death penalty case, *McCleskey v. Kemp*.[56] Proof regarding the racially discriminatory application of Georgia's capital sentencing came in two forms: the Baldus study, the most comprehensive statistical analysis of capital sentencing undertaken to that point; and a detailed history, dating back to slavery's reign, laying bare Georgia's exceptional willingness to execute African-Americans. Brennan in dissent reprised both sorts of evidence at length. He devoted four pages to parsing the Baldus study, demonstrating how "the statistical evidence in this case … relentlessly documents the risk that McCleskey's sentence was influenced by racial considerations."[57] Brennan then turned to the historical record, and beginning with slavery traced over another four pages the workings of a "dual system of crime and punishment" that had long reserved the harshest penalties for blacks thought to have transgressed racial supremacy through violence against whites.[58] Brennan acknowledged that this history did not conclusively prove discrimination against McCleskey himself; nevertheless, he insisted on its relevance in evaluating a claim of discrimination in Georgia's application of the death penalty.[59]

The Court in a 5–4 decision written by Powell used malicious intent to reject the pertinence of both the sociological and historical evidence. As in *Mobile* and *Memphis*, the decision began with general inferences tending to expiate the state. For instance, the majority suggested that the need for discretion in capital sentencing or McCleskey's underlying crime—not discrimination—explained the case.[60] Then, turning to McCleskey's burden in proving discrimination, Powell shifted away from general inferences, with italics to emphasize the point: "[T]o prevail under the Equal Protection Clause, McCleskey must prove that the decision-makers in *his* case acted with discriminatory purpose."[61] Powell then immediately put the writing on the wall, stating that McCleskey "offers no evidence *specific to his own case* that would support an inference that racial considerations played a part in his sentence. Instead, he relies solely on the Baldus study."[62] At that point, Powell paused to suggest several reasons why, in general, statistical analyses should not figure in the death penalty context. Once Powell redefined discriminatory purpose as malicious intent, however, the admissibility of statistical analyses became a red herring. Even if admitted, statistics could never "*prove*," as Powell demanded with italics, "that race was a factor in McCleskey's particular case."[63] The posture of the case required the Court to accept the validity of the Baldus study.[64] The majority seemed to respond that though valid, the study was irrelevant: the study proved nothing because it proved nothing specific to "McCleskey's particular case."[65] Powell summed up: "[W]e hold that the Baldus study is clearly insufficient to support an inference that any of the decision-makers in McCleskey's case acted with discriminatory purpose."[66]

52 *Id.* at 114, n.23.
53 *Id.* at 116, n.27.
54 *Id.*
55 *Id.* at 114 (emphases added).
56 481 U.S. 279 (1987).
57 *Id.* at 325–28 (Brennan, J., dissenting).
58 *Id.* at 328–34.
59 *Id.* at 332.
60 *Id.* at 294–95, 311 (discretion); *id.* at 306 (underlying conviction).
61 *Id.* at 292.
62 *Id.* at 292–93 (emphasis added).
63 *Id.* at 308.
64 *Id.* at 291 n.7.
65 *Id.* at 308.
66 *Id.* at 298.

Powell separately considered McCleskey's historical argument, measuring Georgia's long romance with White supremacy only for what it could prove regarding the mental states of contemporary legislators. Citing *Feeney*, Powell insisted that no constitutional harm could arise simply by virtue of the Georgia legislature's maintenance of a death penalty regime that it knew to a moral certainty disproportionately executed blacks.[67] McCleskey's burden was to demonstrate that contemporary legislators consciously pursued this racially murderous end. To meet this burden of proving current malice, history would avail very little. Powell relegated his discussion of Georgia's painful past to a single short footnote that readily dismissed this material, rendered all the more marginal through the use of scare quotes. "McCleskey relies on 'historical evidence' to support his claim of purposeful discrimination by the State. ... But unless historical evidence is reasonably contemporaneous with the challenged decision, it has little probative value."[68] Powell reiterated: "Although the history of racial discrimination in this country is undeniable, we cannot accept official actions taken long ago as evidence of current intent."[69] Powell did not otherwise engage the stained history narrated in detail by Brennan's dissent. Instead, in an echo of *Mobile* and *Memphis*, Powell avowed that "[t]here was *no* evidence ... that the Georgia Legislature enacted the capital punishment statute to further a racially discriminatory purpose."[70] Having used the alchemy of malice to transmute Georgia's history into "no evidence," Powell declared that "we will not infer a discriminatory purpose on the part of the State of Georgia."[71]

Betraying Brown with Self-Induced Blindness

McCleskey cast into sharp relief the near impossibility of demonstrating racial discrimination. Malicious intent managed to reduce to "no evidence" even a sophisticated statistical study confirmed by, and confirming, obvious historical and sociological patterns of entrenched racism. It is no wonder the demand that evil intent be specifically proved has been widely criticized as making discrimination claims extraordinarily difficult to win. Rather than repeating this damning point, however, this Part offers two new critiques. First, it argues that these cases exemplify an antidiscrimination doctrine so onerous it likely would not detect impermissible mistreatment even in situations of Jim Crow segregation. In short, the malice test would likely uphold segregation in a case like *Brown v. Board of Education*. Second, this Part argues that as it evolved in *Mobile* and afterward, malicious intent did *not* develop to discern mindsets. Rather, malice developed primarily to disparage evidence of discrimination's persistence.

Brown v. Board of Education has emerged as the metric for measuring modern equal protection. No contemporary theory of equal protection is legally or morally legitimate if it would not produce the correct result in that case. Indeed, *Brown* is taught in law schools, and perceived by the public, as the paragon of just legal decision-making. Imagine, then, a court approaching the sort of discrimination overturned in *Brown*, but constrained by the limitations imposed by *Mobile* and its progeny. Would a judge employing a malice approach be able to rule school segregation unconstitutional?

To begin with, there would have been few rank expressions of animus by responsible government officials to put before the Court. In 1954, George Wallace was not yet standing in the schoolhouse door ranting "segregation forever," and White mobs were not yet hurling spittle-laced invective on Black children being marched into White schools between phalanxes of soldiers. Those explosive images of racial hate lay in the future, as the response to *Brown* and civil rights activism. Instead, public discourse came in the quiet susurrations of entrenched hierarchy, the calm tones of a social oppression so thoroughly and completely enforced it could be presented as with the consent and for the benefit of the subjugated. Clarence Thomas recently emphasized that racial oppression wraps itself in velvet, and did so even during the heyday of Jim Crow.[72] The quotes he garnered from the government officials supporting segregation in *Brown* are instructive here. South Carolina

67 *Id.*

68 *Id.* at 298 n.20.

69 *Id.*

70 *Id.* at 298 (emphasis added).

71 *Id.* at 299.

72 Parents Involved in Cmty. Schs. v. Seattle Sch. Dist. No. 1, 551 U.S. 701, 778, n.27 (2007) (Thomas, J., concurring).

publicly declared itself "confident of its good faith and intention to produce equality for all of its children of whatever race or color. It is convinced that the happiness, the progress and the welfare of these children is best promoted in segregated schools."[73] Virginia crowed that extensive research proved the beneficence of segregation: "Our many hours of research and investigation have led only to confirmation of our view that segregation by race in Virginia's public schools at this time not only does not offend the Constitution of the United States but serves to provide a better education for living for the children of both races."[74]

In 1962, eight years after *Brown*, famed constitutional scholar Alexander Bickel raised exactly the question posed here. If the constitutional standard of discriminatory intent reduces to actual motives, how is one to prove the existence of animus among legislators claiming to act out of benevolence for the benighted Negro? In Bickel's language:

> Who is to say that the majority of a legislature which enacts a statute segregating the schools is actuated by a conscious desire to suppress and humiliate the Negro? Who is to say that for many members more decent feelings are not decisive—the feeling, for example, that under existing circumstances Negro children are better off and can be more effectively educated in schools reserved for them exclusively, and that this is the most hopeful road to the goal of equality of the races under law?[75]

Malicious intent analysis struggles to pierce assertions of kindness—especially where those may well be rooted in genuinely held beliefs about the altruism of racial oppression, beliefs potentially shared by members of the bench and academy.

Not only would the malice standard require animus, but it would also require *direct* proof of individual mindsets, while mandating indifference to the abundant contextual evidence demonstrating the discriminatory purposes behind school segregation. Such contextual evidence lay manifest in the systematic material harm done to Black children—inferior school buildings, truncated curriculums, tattered or missing text books, dilapidated grounds and facilities. And it lay bare in the larger context, in local patterns of racial degradation and stigmatized separation, a social order founded on racial hierarchy, and a history of racism running directly from Jim Crow back to the black codes and from there to slavery. In other words, proof of purposeful mistreatment lay plain for all to see—but in exactly the historical and contextual evidence eschewed by *Feeney*, *Mobile*, *Memphis*, and *McCleskey*. Clarence Thomas compiled the soothing words of segregation's supporters, quoted above, to bolster the colorblind thesis that invidious and benign motives cannot be distinguished. But the distinction between Jim Crow and affirmative action is unknowable only if one abjures all attention to context—exactly as malicious intent demands. Laboring under the injunction that animus be proved, and handicapped by the putative irrelevance of actual harm, a court using the malice approach would have found itself blind to what all could see. A court so bound would have struggled to declare discrimination in whites-only schools unconstitutional. Some may object that the intent test should not apply to Jim Crow, for express racial classifications are covered by colorblindness. But this merely accepts post-*Feeney* mythmaking. In fact, as discussed, in dismantling *de jure* segregation the Court used precisely a contextual search for intent. Today's iteration of intent, in contrast, would have blinded courts to proof of segregation's evil. Put bluntly, malicious intent fails the *Brown* test. There could hardly be a more profound indictment of contemporary intent doctrine.

Yet for however devastating this point, care must be taken not to overly emphasize malicious intent's shortcomings as a means for detecting discrimination. If anything, this critique is too generous. To stress malice doctrine's failure to find discrimination risks giving malicious intent doctrine too much credit—for it assumes that this doctrine actually aims to fight discrimination. It does not. Rather, malicious intent developed as a technique for *not* finding discrimination. At root, the conservative Justices used the malice test to defend themselves from evidence tending to show discrimination against nonwhites.

Powell's demand for direct proof of animus allowed the quick disposal of the Baldus study, and so might be thought critical to the rejection of McCleskey's discrimination claim. But the malice test proved merely

73 *Id.* (citation omitted).

74 *Id.* (citation omitted).

75 Alexander Bickel, The Least Dangerous Branch: The Supreme Court at the Bar of Politics 61–62 (1962).

expedient, not necessary. Using the same statistical and historical evidence, McCleskey challenged Georgia's capital regime under both the Fourteenth Amendment's guarantee of equal protection as well as the Eighth Amendment's prohibition of cruel and unusual punishment. While intent doctrine applied for proving an equal protection violation, the standard under the Eighth Amendment was different, requiring instead a probabilistic inquiry into whether capital punishment was in general "irrationally imposed."[76] As a result, the majority in its Eighth Amendment analysis had no choice but to engage the statistical evidence. It was forced, for instance, to grapple with the fact that the Baldus study showed that for African-Americans convicted of murder, those who killed whites were *22 times* more likely to be sentenced to die compared to those with Black victims.[77] Unable to sidestep the study's substance, Powell nevertheless easily dismissed it. In the course of single paragraph he described the numbers as indicating "at most … a discrepancy that appears to correlate with race"; shifted to the even more nebulous language of "apparent disparities" and "imperfections"; and then announced "we decline to assume that what is unexplained is invidious."[78]

The Eighth Amendment claim acts as a kind of litmus test for what the conservative Justices thought of the Baldus study. Without that claim, one could argue that the majority dispatched the Baldus study because the malice standard required them to do so. But their treatment of the Eighth Amendment argument shows that even when they had no legal reason, such as the malice doctrine, for giving the study's evidence of rampant discrimination no legal weight, they still disparaged it. With a depressing economy of words, Powell neutralized the report in a quick slide from "discrepancy" through "apparent disparity" and "imperfection" to the merely "unexplained." Required by Eighth Amendment to confront disturbing evidence, the majority simply dismissed its damning thrust.

The sense that the malice test did not drive the results finds additional support insofar as the Court *never* investigated the thinking of contemporary government officials charged with mistreating nonwhites. There is not a single case in which the Court examined a contemporary state actor's subjective purpose to discriminate against nonwhites. True, the Court in 1985 arguably employed malicious intent to strike down an Alabama felony disenfranchisement law.[79] But in that case the Court probed the mindset of defendants long since dead, the attendees at a 1901 Alabama constitutional convention at which even Rehnquist conceded the "zeal for white supremacy ran rampant."[80] Also, as shall be detailed later, the Court in the 1990s did focus on motives to find unconstitutional discrimination—but only when overturning *remedial* efforts, not in cases involving the racial mistreatment of nonwhites. To reiterate, though the Court claimed to require proof of malicious intent, in no case alleging discrimination against nonwhites did the Court parse the precise mindsets of contemporary government officials. This goes beyond the claim, also true, that no decision ever employed malicious intent to strike down racial mistreatment by current officials.[81] The point here is more denunciatory than that. It is that in no case, win or lose, did the Court ever even *look* at the actual motives of today's government officials. Malicious intent doctrine simply never operated to investigate motives.

From *Feeney* to *McCleskey*, the prevailing Justices refused to credit claims of group mistreatment. Faced with compelling contextual evidence showing discrimination, they did not *refute* this material—they simply refused to engage it. They did not grapple in any meaningful way with the sexism in civil service employment in *Feeney*, the mock lynchings by the police in *Mobile*, the lily-white demographics in *Memphis*, or the history and killing numbers in *McCleskey*. Instead, they invoked malice to nimbly declare such evidence constitutionally irrelevant. In *Mobile*'s pithy formulation, "these gauzy sociological considerations have no constitutional basis."[82] Ultimately, this is a story of judicial closed-mindedness, of an unwillingness to engage with and thus potentially learn about the operation and evolution of an enduring form of injustice.

76 McCleskey v. Kemp, 481 U.S. 279, 328 (1987) (Brennan, J., dissenting).

77 *Id.* at 286.

78 *Id.* at 312–13.

79 Hunter v. Underwood, 471 U.S. 227, 230 (1985).

80 *Id.*

81 After *Mobile*, the few cases finding racial discrimination against nonwhites came when the Court employed a contextual intent approach, typically over the strong objection of those favoring the malice standard. See Rogers v. Lodge, 458 U.S. 613 (1982), Batson v. Kentucky, 476 U.S. 79 (1986), and Miller-El v. Dretke, 545 U.S. 231 (2005).

82 Mobile v. Bolden, 446 U.S. 55, 75 n.22 (1980).

The intentional blindness of the malice test represents not a genuine application of equal protection law, but a successful effort by conservative Justices to protect themselves from discomfiting evidence that racial mistreatment persists.

In closing the courthouse doors, did the conservative Justices do so out of ignorance about pervasive discrimination, or instead with awareness that racial mistreatment remains ubiquitous in American life? For Warren McCleskey, executed in 1991, the question hardly seems to matter. For those seeking immediate succor from the courts, the bottom line is their barred doors. Nevertheless, in fathoming the politics behind the doctrine, it seems a pressing issue whether malice doctrine emerged out of incomprehension about racism, or instead came despite awareness that discrimination continued.

The evidence suggests the latter. Powell, for instance, sometimes evinced a sophisticated conception of discrimination. Consider his engagement with discrimination in *Bakke*. There, Powell ruled that attempting to remedy discrimination did not constitute a compelling government interest capable of justifying affirmative action.[83] In so concluding, however, he exhaustively detailed various theories of racial mistreatment, ranging from harm to individuals, to group disadvantaging, to the relatively automatic operation of cultural biases.[84] Perhaps, as in *Bakke*, Powell in *McCleskey* fully understood the thrust of the Baldus study that relentlessly documented the influence of race on who lived and died at Georgia's hands, and nevertheless set this bitter truth to the side. If so, Powell did not adopt the malice standard out of personal ignorance, but rather in derogation of his own belief that various forms of racial discrimination likely continued. (Some years after retiring from the bench, Powell came to regret his vote in *McCleskey*, concluding that the death penalty should be held unconstitutional. Though one might hope that, even if late and sorry, Powell at last acknowledged the fatal racism in capital punishment, in fact Powell's principal objection lay elsewhere. According to his biographer, "For Powell ... [the] death penalty should be barred, not because it was intrinsically wrong but because it could not be fairly and expeditiously enforced. The endless waiting, merry-go-round litigation, last-minute stays, and midnight executions offended Powell's sense of dignity and his conception of the majesty of the law."[85])

If a disheartening suspicion of knowing indifference toward pervasive racial discrimination is tentative with respect to Powell, it seems entirely warranted against Antonin Scalia. In an internal memo supporting a draft of the *McCleskey* opinion, Scalia acceded to the majority's demand for proof of malice. Nevertheless, he made clear he did not believe there was *insufficient* proof regarding racial mistreatment. On the contrary, Scalia acknowledged that unconscious racial antipathies permeated Georgia's criminal justice system, from juries to prosecutors. From Scalia's point of view, however, unconscious racism was simply an "ineradicable" reality that the courts should ignore. Challenging the opinion's thin pretense that no correlation with race could be discerned, Scalia stated baldly: "I do not share the view, implicit in the opinion, that an effect of racial factors upon sentencing, if it could only be shown by sufficiently strong statistical evidence, would require reversal."[86] For Scalia, the issue was not a lack of proof of systemic bias, but its legal irrelevance. "Since it is my view that the unconscious operation of irrational sympathies and antipathies, including racial, upon jury deliberations and (hence) prosecutorial decisions is *real ... and ineradicable*, I cannot honestly say that all I need is more proof."[87] For Scalia, racism is simply part of the world in which we live, and law has no role to play, even when the stakes include state decisions to kill.

Intentional blindness, not unfortunate ignorance, more aptly characterizes the racial jurisprudence of the Supreme Court's conservatives. They seem to understand that racism is a pervasive problem, and yet oppose using the courts and the Constitution to contribute to the solution.

83 Regents of the Univ. of Cal. v. Bakke, 438 U.S. 265, 307–09 (1978).

84 *Id.* at 306 n.43.

85 John C. Jeffries, Jr., Justice Lewis F. Powell, Jr: A Biography 452 (1994).

86 Memorandum to the Conference Re: No. 84–6811, McCleskey v. Kemp, January 6, 1987 (Scalia, J.), reprinted in Erwin Chemerinsky, *Eliminating Discrimination in Administering the Death Penalty: The Need for the Racial Justice Act*, 35 Santa Clara L. Rev. 519, 528 (1995).

87 *Id.*

Intent *In* Colorblindness, Intent *As* Colorblindness

Two years after *McCleskey*, *City of Richmond v. Croson Co.* marked the arrival of colorblindness as a doctrine commanding the allegiance of a majority of the Justices.[88] The next year, in a last gasp, William Brennan and Thurgood Marshall voted together to uphold a race-conscious remedy one final time.[89] When Brennan and then Marshall left the Court in 1990 and 1991, their departures facilitated the consolidation of intentional blindness.

On one level, the instability of the previous period gave way to repeated holdings in favor of malice as well as colorblindness. After 1991, with very rare exceptions the Court consistently applied the malice test to find no discrimination, and struck down all race-conscious remedies.[90] On another level, doctrinal consolidation also occurred. Colorblindness and malice increasingly melded. To begin with, colorblindness adopted the evidentiary techniques of malice, dismissing evidence of discrimination against nonwhites while inferring White innocence. More strikingly, colorblindness also colonized the intent test, turning it into an ersatz colorblindness rule. It did so by shifting the focus of the intent doctrine from a search for malice, which is to say a conscious intent to harm, to a search for a conscious decision to use race.

Mobile boldly declaimed: "[G]auzy sociological considerations have no constitutional basis."[91] As demonstrated, it meant that proof of discrimination against nonwhites would have to be direct. Inferences of innocence, on the other hand, could be loosely based, say on the need for discretion in death sentencing, concerns over traffic, the widespread use of at-large elections, or a legitimate desire to help veterans. Colorblindness would import this double standard into cases evaluating affirmative action. Judgments favoring whites would rest on loose inferences and unexamined suppositions, even as nonwhites would be forced to prove with specificity prior discrimination in order to show that affirmative action was warranted.

With a population over half Black, Richmond, Virginia, had for years allocated over 99 percent of its construction contracts to White-owned firms.[92] Aiming to break this pattern, in 1983 the Richmond City Council adopted a set-aside program to channel construction dollars to minority-owned businesses.[93] Writing for the new colorblind majority, O'Connor stressed the risks of discrimination—against whites—associated with affirmative action. To show this sort of mistreatment, O'Connor did *not* examine actual motives, as virtually the same Justices had recently insisted in *McCleskey* would be required to prove discrimination. At no point did the Court parse the intentions of the Richmond City Council; indeed, as Marshall noted in dissent, there was no "direct evidence that the city council's motives were anything other than sincere."[94] Rather, O'Connor employed inferential techniques, relying on contextual generalities. For instance, she insinuated the possibility of self-dealing by an empowered majority (blacks) at the expense of a disempowered minority (whites) by stressing that blacks accounted for half of Richmond's population and five of the nine city council members.[95] The other Justices who wrote separately in favor of colorblindness joined in this profound suspicion. Stevens referred repeatedly to whites as "the disadvantaged class," and worried that the set-aside program "might be nothing more than a form of patronage."[96] Kennedy lamented that "[w]e are left with an ordinance and a legislative record open to the fair charge that it is not a remedy but is itself a preference which will cause … corrosive animosities."[97] Scalia warned against "the enactment of a set-aside clearly and

88 488 U.S. 469 (1989).

89 *See* Metro Broadcasting Inc. v FCC, 497 U.S. 547 (1990) (upholding a preference for racial diversity in broadcast licenses).

90 For the few exceptions, see Easely v. Cromartie, 532 U.S. 234 (2001) (O'Connor shifting to uphold use of race in majority-minority districting); Grutter v. Bollinger, 509 U.S. 306 (2003) (O'Connor shifting to uphold affirmative action in higher education); and Miller-El v. Dretke, 545 U.S. 231 (2005) (O'Connor and Kennedy shifting toward contextual intent to uphold jury exclusion claim).

91 Mobile v. Bolden, 446 U.S. 55, 75 n.22 (1980).

92 City of Richmond v. Croson Co., 488 U.S. 469, 479–80 (1989).

93 *Id.* at 477–8.

94 *Croson*, 488 U.S. at 546 (Marshall, J., dissenting).

95 *Id.* at 495.

96 *Croson*, 488 U.S. at 516 n.9 (Stevens, J., concurring).

97 *Id.* at 519–20 (Kennedy, J., concurring).

directly beneficial to the dominant political group, which happens also to be the dominant racial group."[98] As in *McCleskey*, *Memphis*, *Mobile*, and *Feeney*, one sees a contextual approach to evaluating discrimination—but one available only to buttress intuitions of White innocence, and in the line of cases that followed *Croson*, White victimization.

In contrast to the loose inferences regarding the mistreatment of whites, the colorblind affirmative action cases demand exacting proof of prior mistreatment against nonwhites. Affirmative action would be justified, these decisions hold, only if structured to remedy "identified discrimination" (or, in the higher education setting, to promote diversity).[99] But as it turns out, identified discrimination functions similarly to malicious intent: first, as a basis for rejecting contextual evidence; and second, as a receding mirage.

Croson represents the first majority adoption of the "identified discrimination" test, casting this in contrast to "societal discrimination." Ostensibly, the latter was "an inadequate basis for race conscious classifications," while the former "can support and define the scope of race-based relief."[100] But what would be required to establish the requisite discrimination? Ambiguity surrounded "identified discrimination."

Ultimately, however, this ambiguity mattered little. Identified discrimination paralleled malicious intent in operating like an unreachable standard against which each piece of evidence was to be separately measured, found wanting, and quickly dismissed. In *Croson*, the local and state contractors' associations were almost all White. Repeating the technique of evidentiary disaggregation from the malice cases, O'Connor rejoined: "[S]tanding alone this evidence is not probative of any discrimination in the local construction industry."[101] A city council member testified to pervasive discrimination in the local, regional, and national construction field. O'Connor declared, "[t]hese statements are of little probative value in establishing identified discrimination in the Richmond construction industry."[102] Congress had found nationwide racial discrimination in construction. But, O'Connor insisted, "[t]he probative value of these findings for demonstrating the existence of discrimination in Richmond is extremely limited."[103] "In sum," she concluded, "none of the evidence presented by the city points to any identified discrimination in the Richmond construction industry."[104] As with malicious intent, the identified discrimination standard neatly absolved the Court of having to engage with the contextual evidence that demonstrated ongoing patterns of racial stratification. In the former capital of the Confederacy—a city half Black but where 99 percent of the municipality's construction dollars went to White-owned firms the conservative Justices could perceive no evidence of discrimination against nonwhites.

Identified discrimination parallels malicious intent not only in dismissing probative evidence, but also in receding as a mirage. Just as the Court has never found the subjective intent required to strike down contemporary discrimination against nonwhites, the Court has never found the identified discrimination that would justify an affirmative action program. Marshall's dissent in *Croson* gave special attention to its status as the first case in which the majority used colorblindness to justify strict review of race-conscious remedial measures. Insisting that "[a] profound difference separates governmental actions that themselves are racist, and governmental actions that seek to remedy the effects of prior racism,"[105] Marshall reiterated his admonition in *Fullilove* that "[remedial] programs should not be subjected to conventional 'strict scrutiny'—scrutiny that is strict in theory, but fatal in fact."[106] O'Connor dismissed this charge: "Nothing we say today precludes a state or local entity from taking action to rectify the effects of identified discrimination within its jurisdiction."[107] Two decades later and counting, we know this to be false. There is no case in which the Court

98 *Id.* at 524 (Scalia, J., concurring).

99 In addition to crafting "diversity" as a justification for affirmative action in the university setting, in *Bakke* Powell introduced the term "identified discrimination." Regents of the Univ. of Cal. v. Bakke, 438 U.S. 265, 307 (1978).

100 *Croson*, 488 U.S. at 497.

101 *Id.* at 503.

102 *Id.* at 500.

103 *Id.* at 504.

104 *Id.* at 505.

105 *Id.* at 551–52 (Marshall, J., dissenting).

106 *Id.* at 552.

107 *Id.* at 509.

has upheld a race-conscious remedy because it responds to identified discrimination. A Supreme Court finding of either malicious intent or identified discrimination remains a purely theoretical proposition.

Colorblindness absorbed the evidentiary techniques of malicious intent—and then it colonized the doctrine itself, resulting in a monocular focus on express uses of race. In 1993, the Court in *Shaw v. Reno* overturned a congressional district expressly drawn to include a majority of African-American voters.[108] Acting under pressure from the Department of Justice, North Carolina had begun to remedy a history of political disempowerment by creating majority-minority districts, leading to the state's first Black congressional representatives since Reconstruction.[109] Despite the urging of the White challengers, O'Connor sidestepped an outright application of colorblindness. Instead, she turned to the intent test, and in particular to the Tuskegee gerrymandering case, *Gomillion v. Lightfoot*.[110] In doing so, however, O'Connor encountered a major problem. As a contextual case, *Gomillion* had asked whether the facts warranted a judicial inference of a harmful purpose. Here, in the remedial context, no purpose to harm whites existed.

O'Connor responded by reinterpreting *Gomillion*, introducing a nonsensical distinction between purpose and motive. O'Connor asserted that the relevant inquiry was whether there existed a "purpose" to use race. If so, O'Connor declared, the underlying "motive" was irrelevant. "*Gomillion*," O'Connor claimed, stood for the proposition that "district lines obviously drawn for the *purpose* of separating voters by race require careful scrutiny under the Equal Protection Clause regardless of the *motivations* underlying their adoption."[111] "Purpose" here seemed to mean an intent to use race; it no longer referred to an intent to harm. Moreover, the new "classificatory intent" would be read directly from conduct. Thus, *Shaw* announced a Fourteenth Amendment claim against a majority-minority district if a court could detect "an *effort* to segregate voters into separate voting districts because of their race."[112] In effect, the new intent test abandoned any concern with intentions, whether labeled purposes or motives. Instead, it was solely concerned with the express use of a racial classification. Classificatory intent operated directly as a colorblindness rule.

Applying this new version of intent doctrine, *Shaw* staged an elaborate charade. The majority purported to carefully scrutinize the challenged district for telltale signs that race had been considered, when all candidly admitted race-conscious decision-making. As Justice White said in dissent, "[t]he State has made no mystery of its intent, which was to … improv[e] the minority group's prospects of electing a candidate of its choice."[113] Over the next several years, as the Court entertained further challenges to majority-minority districts, this charade grew in comedic proportion. In 1995, Kennedy parsed racial demographics, district shape, and procedural history in attempting to discern whether Georgia had used race to fashion a majority-minority district.[114] Here again the Justices otherwise inclined to demand proof of malice against nonwhites were content to employ a contextual approach to measure potential discrimination against whites. Even more farcical, after this arduous peregrination through contextual evidence, Kennedy capped the case by exclaiming that Georgia had "admitted" and "conceded" race-conscious motives.[115] Indeed, Kennedy found an admission of classificatory intent in the very brief Georgia submitted to the Supreme Court, wherein it confessed "a desire by the General Assembly to create a majority black district."[116] The next year, when *Shaw* returned to the Court a second time, Rehnquist too marshaled the confessions of state actors.[117] Richest of all, Rehnquist cited as evidence of classificatory purpose White's dissent in the first iteration of that case, where White had complained that the state had "made no mystery of its intent to … improv[e] the minority group's prospects."[118] The hitherto fruitless search for illicit purposes was suddenly fecund, detecting evidence of discriminatory motives even in briefs to the Court and the arguments of fellow Justices.

---

108 509 U.S. 630 (1993).
109 *See id.* at 676.
110 *Id.* at 644–45.
111 *Id.* at 645.
112 *Id.* at 658.
113 *Id.* at 666 (White, J., dissenting).
114 Miller v. Johnson, 515 U.S. 900, 917–18 (1995).
115 *Id.* at 918.
116 *Id.*
117 Shaw v. Hunt, 517 U.S. 899, 906 (1996).
118 *Id.*

Intent doctrine as a search for animus had long since atrophied in its ability to detect racial discrimination. And as a search for the intentional use of race, it proved similarly feeble in protecting nonwhites. Yet once transformed into a search for classificatory intent, this doctrine gained renewed vigor and sprung to the task of finding unconstitutional action—in the effort to promote racial justice.

Yet even as the *Shaw* line of cases seemed to herald the full ascent of colorblindness, these decisions also revealed some hesitancy, especially on O'Connor's part. In *Shaw*, the challengers had urged that the majority-minority districts be reviewed as racial classifications immediately meriting strict scrutiny.[119] O'Connor was deeply sympathetic, seeing in every governmental use of race a threat to the unity of nation.[120] Yet she did not adopt a formal anticlassification rule. Partly this reflected the history of gerrymander cases coming under intent doctrine. But it also likely reflected a fear that directly applying a colorblind rule would have imperiled *every* majority-minority district, a result O'Connor expressly disclaimed.[121] Though the *Shaw* cases converted intent into an ersatz colorblindness rule, they did so in a way that preserved modest flexibility. The comedic search for intentional uses of race, as well as additional doctrinal innovations carving out other limiting factors, provided a modicum of discretion otherwise unavailable under rigid colorblind logic.[122] Colorblindness as the automatic application of fatal-in-fact review is severely procrustean. At the very moment in the 1990s that support for colorblindness consolidated on the Court, Justices like O'Connor and occasionally Kennedy seemed to pull back a bit from its most extreme implications. The consolidation of colorblindness, tempered by modest reticence to push its logic imperially outward, defined the period preceding the 2005 ascendance of Chief Justice John Roberts and the rise of the most conservative cohort of justices in a century.

Colorblindness Rex: Parents Involved and Ricci

Today, reticence in attacking civil rights has evaporated. We are once again in a period of rapid devolution, though this is somewhat masked by shrewd doctrinal maneuvering. In *Fisher v. University of Texas*, for instance, the Court declined to prohibit affirmative action in higher education outright, but nevertheless overturned the challenged program on the ostensible ground that strict scrutiny was not applied strictly enough.[123] Likewise, in *Shelby County*, a 5–4 conservative bloc left intact the key enforcement provision of the Voting Rights Act, but rejected Congress's determination regarding which states the Act covered.[124] Because the prospects of Congress soon reaching a new accord regarding coverage are so dim, this effectively gutted the Voting Rights Act without directly saying so. These cases differed from the intent and colorblindness cases insofar as they largely eschewed a discussion of those rules and instead rested on different and more technical doctrinal bases. Nevertheless, they bore key similarities. First, both decisions emphasized a purported lack of evidence: *Fisher* bemoaned that Texas did not do enough to prove that non-racial alternatives had been exhausted, despite a carefully detailed plan; and *Shelby* dismissed Congress's evaluation of a voluminous evidentiary record that ran to 15,000 pages, substituting its own judgment that little justified the legislature's coverage formula. Second and more fundamentally, from behind a legal façade these decisions continued to war against civil rights.

Beyond this seeming continuity, however, the Roberts Court seems determined to more fully enforce past colorblind reasoning—indeed, to expand its reach. This is evident in the logic, if not necessarily the results, of major decisions from 2007 and 2009.

In *Parents Involved in Community Schools v. Seattle School District No. 1*, the 2007 Seattle and Louisville school integration cases, the Court reprised the basic anti-contextualism of colorblindness.[125] For instance,

119 Shaw v. Reno, 509 U.S. 630, 641–42 (1993).

120 *Id.* at 647.

121 *Id.* at 642.

122 *See, e.g.*, *Miller*, 515 U.S. at 916 (disfavoring intentional uses of race if race a "predominant" factor); *Shaw*, 509 U.S. at 644 (disfavoring those districts having a "bizarre" shape).

123 Fisher v. University of Texas, 270 U.S. __ (2013).

124 Shelby County v. Holder, 270 U.S. __ (2013).

125 Parents Involved in Cmty. Schs. v. Seattle Sch. Dist. No. 1, 551 U.S. 701 (2007).

Roberts dismissed the school districts' efforts to preserve integration as "directed only to racial balance, pure and simple."[126] Caricaturing integration as solely concerned with racial balance derogated the many values and aspirations animating the long struggle against continued and even resurgent racial segregation in both Seattle and Louisville. Meanwhile, the four dissenters seemed to be talking to themselves in presenting evidence of increasing resegregation in the nation's schools, wasting their time on material the majority treated as no more than "gauzy sociology."[127] The dissenters pounded out detailed local histories of segregation and its evils, ultimately filling nearly 20 pages in the *United States Reports*, but seemed unheard by an indifferent majority disdainful of appeals to "original sin."[128]

More ominously, the Court seemed to contemplate that colorblind ignorance should apply every time a government actor expressly considered race, a possibility that would extend to general policymaking and data collection.[129] Kennedy concurred separately to pointedly warn against the rigid application of a colorblind rule to all general uses of race,[130] and Breyer in dissent spelled out the range of policies under threat.[131] Yet Roberts, writing for three other Justices, refused to disavow the possibility that they might soon construe colorblindness to prohibit government decision-makers from merely considering how race continues to function.[132]

If *Parents Involved* portends the forced imposition of racial blindness on policymakers, *Ricci v. DeStefano* threatens legislative efforts to curtail discrimination by governments as well as public sphere actors.[133] The 2009 New Haven firefighters case effectively replayed the fight between malicious and contextual intent, though this time recast as a conflict between disparate treatment and disparate impact in the context of federal antidiscrimination law. At least since 1971, there have been two routes for proving unlawful racial discrimination under Title VII: one depending on relatively direct proof of intentional bias (disparate treatment) and the other allowing inferences of mistreatment on the basis of contextual evidence, including disproportionate harm to nonwhites (disparate impact). In 2009, *Ricci* pitted these approaches against each other. Writing for the Court, Kennedy construed disparate treatment as forbidding any race-based decision-making; that is, he dramatically shifted disparate treatment from a concern with discrimination to a colorblind focus on the mere use of race.[134] Kennedy then cast this prohibition on considering race as a major limitation on the core of the disparate impact approach, attention to racial context. In effect, the conservative Justices ruled 5–4 that considering racial impact in order to avoid potential discrimination itself constituted racial discrimination. That bears repeating, though the logic induces vertigo: to consider race, even in order to avoid discrimination, *is* discrimination.

Under the malice and affirmative action cases discussed in this chapter, when nonwhites allege mistreatment, equal protection blinds *courts* to their evidence.[135] *Parents Involved* potentially heralds the imposition of racial blindness across government policymakers generally. And *Ricci* arguably goes even further in exporting intentional blindness. Because *Ricci* hijacked a federal antidiscrimination statute, its reach extends to all of those institutions, public and private, covered by that law. Thus, *Ricci* proposes that federal, state, and local governments, as well as other public sphere actors like employers, landlords, and schools, all blind themselves to persistent racial discrimination—and even more perversely, that they do so at the precise moment they seek to combat racial discrimination. A colorblind Fourteenth Amendment may soon come to require, across the whole nation governed by law, only one test for racial discrimination: malicious intent. If it does, malicious intent will continue to work as it has in the courts: as a sure route to finding no discrimination, and as an excuse for intentional blindness toward evidence of continued racial stratification.

126 *Id.* at 726.

127 *See Parents Involved*, 551 U.S. at 869–72 (Breyer, J., dissenting).

128 *Id.* at 804–23.

129 *Id.* at 745.

130 *See id.* at 787–90 (Kennedy, J., concurring).

131 *See id.* at 828–29 (Breyer, J., dissenting).

132 *See id.* at 745.

133 Ricci v. DeStefano, 129 S.Ct. 2658 (2009).

134 *Id.* at 2673.

135 Indeed, *Washington v. Davis* specifically noted that Congress retained the power to address racism in ways beyond what equal protection directly proscribed—including disparate impact approaches, and presumably affirmative action as well. 426 U.S. 229, 248 (1976).

Chapter 5
Judging Opportunity Lost: Race-based Affirmative Action and Equality Jurisprudence After *Fisher v. University of Texas*

Mario L. Barnes, Angela Onwuachi-Willig, and Erwin Chemerinsky

> You do not take a person who, for years, has been hobbled by chains and liberate him, bring him to the starting line of a race and then say, "you are free to compete with all others," and still justly believe you have been completely fair … This is the next and the more profound stage of the battle for civil rights. We seek not just freedom but opportunity … not just equality as a right and a theory, but equality as a fact and equality as a result.
>
> Lyndon B. Johnson, Commencement Address, Howard University, June 4, 1965[1]

Introduction

Within United States history, social and judicial understandings of the Constitution's pronouncement, "[N]or shall any State … deny to any person within its jurisdiction equal protection of the laws," have been deeply conflicted when applied to the concept of race. For example, in 1896, in the case of *Plessy v. Ferguson*, the U.S. Supreme Court held that state laws requiring racially segregated public accommodations did not violate the Equal Protection Clause of the Fourteenth Amendment.[2] This endorsement of segregation as being consistent with the goals of equality, however, was famously revisited in 1954, in *Brown v. Board of Education*, where the Court struck down *Plessy*'s "separate but equal" mandate.[3] In so doing, the Court signaled that the language of the Fourteenth Amendment should be understood as rejecting state-enforced racial segregation as constitutionally permissible. As shifting as the Court's treatment of race has been, these two cases reflect the Court dealing with programs designed to disadvantage racial minorities. Even more controversial in our country's recent history, however, have been state considerations of race that have advantaged members of certain discrete minority racial groups. These programs, which have been constructed for myriad purposes including remedying past racial exclusion to fostering racial inclusion and diversity, have typically come to be referred to as affirmative action.[4]

Concerns about the fairness of race-based affirmative action programs have been the subject of much scholarly debate from a wide range of political perspectives.[5] Moreover, citizen attitudes toward such

1 Lyndon B. Johnson, "To Fulfill These Rights," commencement address at Howard University, June 4, 1965, in *Public Papers of the Presidents*, vol. II, entry 301, 635–40 (1965).

2 Plessy v. Ferguson, 163 U.S. 537, 544 (1896) (holding in a 7–1 majority opinion that the Fourteenth Amendment was meant to ensure political rather than social equality).

3 Brown v. Bd. of Educ. of Topeka, 347 U.S. 483, 494–46 (1954).

4 Affirmative action programs typically include women and minorities, but this chapter will primarily address race-based benefits programs. Including an analysis of the interrelation of race and gender in affirmative action would be ideal, but it would also be too complicated to capture in this limited format, especially since White women—who, as a group, have historically benefited from such programs—have often been plaintiffs in cases challenging race programs. *See* Michele Goodwin, *The Death of Affirmative Action?* 2013 Wis. L. Rev. 715, 721–22.

5 A number of scholars have argued that affirmative action programs are an important remedial tool for ensuring equality for women and minorities. *See, e.g.*, William Bowen and Derek Bok, The Shape of the River (2000) (an empirically focused defense of the use of race-conscious admissions programs in education); Ruth Colker, *Anti-Subordination Above All: Sex, Race and Equal Protection*, 61 N.Y.U. L. Rev. 1003 (1986); Christopher Edley, Jr, Not All Black and White: Affirmative Action, Race, and American Values (1998) (defense of affirmative action from a social justice perspective). On the other side of the debate, scholars have argued that affirmative action is ill-advised, race-based discrimination. *See, e.g.*,

programs are often contradictory.[6] While arguments against affirmative action have been ostensibly fueled by contemporary commitments to "colorblindness" and "post-racialism,"[7] a significant substantive debate has centered on whether courts should consider state considerations of race for affirmative action programs to be as suspect as invidious racial classifications.[8] Opinions on this topic have been shaped by whether the Equal Protection Clause is interpreted to require all people to be treated the same or whether it should be understood as a guarantee of equal opportunity.[9] This is essentially the distinction to which President Johnson alluded in the quotation at the beginning of the chapter. Within the scholarly discourse, this distinction has also been described as a difference illuminating an "anti-classification" versus an "antisubordination" approach to equal protection.[10] While two authors of this chapter have previously written that the Fourteenth Amendment should be interpreted in light of the goal of the Reconstruction amendments to make freed slaves full citizens, we now advance a more contemporary approach to constitutional interpretation. We suggest that with regard to race-conscious affirmative action, courts should guide their consideration by what role law ought to play in mitigating long-term, structural disadvantages maintained through race now functioning as caste within the U.S.

In this chapter, we shall provide an overview of the rise, and, perhaps, approaching demise of race-based affirmative action programs in the U.S. Within the areas of employment and contracting, governmental considerations of race-based benefits have already been severely curtailed through state executive orders,[11] ballot initiatives,[12] and direct legal challenges to state and federal programs. In fact, education is the only real

---

Stephan & Abigail Thernstrom, *Reflections on the Shape of the River*, 46 UCLA L. Rev. 1583 (1999) (reviewing William Bowen and Derek Bok, The Shape of the River (2000)) (arguing that Bowen and Bok's analysis of affirmative action rests upon faulty empirical data and flawed conclusions); Terry Eastland, *The Case Against Affirmative Action*, 34 Wm. & Mary L. Rev. 22 (1992) (arguing against affirmative action as a remedial tool because it violates the country's commitment to "colorblind law"). A number of critiques have also questioned whether affirmative action programs and policies obscure more important questions about how race figures in conversations about merits and desert. *See, e.g.*, Richard Kahlenberg, The Remedy: Class, Race and Affirmative Action (1996) (advocating class-based affirmative action); William J. Wilson, *Race and Affirming Opportunity in the Barack Obama Era*, 9 Du Bois Rev. 5–16 (2012) (using, as one example, a program initiated at the University of California, Irvine after Proposition 209 went into effect, to argue for "affirmative opportunity" premised upon flexible, merit-based criteria rather than race).

6 For example, a recent survey of attitudes regarding affirmative action indicated that 68 percent of Americans favor programs to remedy past discrimination, but 64 percent of respondents reject the use of race-based preferences in education admissions. Ironically, 38 percent of persons who reject race-based admissions claim to otherwise support affirmative action. *See*, *Americans Divided Between Principle and Practice on Affirmative Action, Divided on DOMA*, Public Religion Research Institute Survey (May 30, 2013), http://publicreligion.org/research/2013/05/may-2013-religion-politics-tracking-survey/.

7 Colorblindness is often linked to Justice Harlan's call in the *Plessy* dissent for a society that does not use race to punish its citizens; it has now been used to refer to a society not "seeing" color or race. Post-racialism is an extension of this concept—a declaration that America has moved beyond race as a salient structure. *See for example*, Mario L. Barnes, Erwin Chemerinsky and Trina Jones, *A Post-Race Equal Protection*, 98 Geo. L.J. 967 (2010); and Sumi Cho, *Post-Racialism*, 94 Iowa L. Rev. 1589, 1593–1600 (2009).

8 One justice surmised in an educational affirmative action case that the purpose of the Fourteenth Amendment is to eradicate invidious discrimination as opposed to limiting the diversity goals of affirmative action programs. Defunis v. Odegaard, 416 U.S. 312, 334–35 (1974) (Douglas, J., dissenting) (dismissing the case as moot because the petitioner was later admitted to the University of Washington Law School, which first denied the petitioner's application).

9 *See* Angela P. Harris, *Equality Trouble: Sameness and Difference in Twentieth-Century Race Law*, 88 Cal. L. Rev. 1923, 1929–30 (2000).

10 *See, for example*, Jack Balkin & Reva Seigel, *The American Civil Rights Tradition, Anticlassification or Antisubordination?*, 58 U. Miami L. Rev. 9 (2004) (parenthetical information?); Colker, *supra* note 5; Reva Seigel, *Equality Talk, Antisubordination and Anticlassification Values in the Struggle Over Brown*, 117 Harv. L. Rev. 1470 (2004).

11 *See, e.g.*, Florida Exec. Order No. 99–281 (1999) (implementing Governor Jeb Bush's "One Florida Initiative," which effectively ended affirmative action in university admissions and state employment and contracting).

12 With Proposal 209, California voters banned affirmative action in employment, contracting, and education in 1996. The ban has been twice upheld by federal courts. *See* Coal. to Defend Affirmative Action v. Brown, 672 F.3d 1128 (9th Cir. 2012); Coalition for Economic Equity v. Pete Wilson et al., 110 F.3d 1431 (9th Cir. 1997). Michigan's Proposition 2 created a similar ban. *See* Coal. to Defend Affirmative Action, Integration & Immigrant Rights & Fight for Equal. By Any

area where there is still some modest room to consider race-conscious assignments plans.[13] Although, recent Supreme Court cases have both curtailed how race can be used and set the stage for the future revisiting of this last domain of race-conscious consideration.[14]

In this chapter we will primarily analyze the Court's history of applying the Equal Protection Clause to governmental programs that have sought to consider race as a factor in awarding educational, employment, and contracting opportunities. Initially, we will review the origins of such programs. We will then focus primarily on the area of education and assess what the Supreme Court's opinions in the most recent educational affirmative action case—*Fisher v. University of Texas*—portend for the viability of affirmative action moving forward. In so doing, we will question what these education cases reveal about the Court's understanding of race as a social construct and suggest how this understanding resulted in *Fisher* being a missed opportunity for the Court to substantively address how equal protection jurisprudence should be reconciled with race-based decision-making.

A Brief History of Affirmative Action

The Executive Genesis of Affirmative Action

In 1961, President John F. Kennedy issued Executive Order 10925, which created the Committee on Equal Employment Opportunity (CEEO), in part, to "recommend additional *affirmative steps* which should be taken by executive departments and agencies to realize more fully the national policy of nondiscrimination" and mandated government contractors to "take *affirmative action* to ensure that applicants are employed, and that employees are treated during employment, without regard to their race, creed, color, or national origin."[15] This mandate to contractors was reiterated in 1965, when President Johnson superseded Kennedy's Order with Executive Order 11246. Johnson's Order abolished the CEEO while passing on some of its functions to the Equal Employment Opportunity Commission, included Kennedy's affirmative action language, and also empowered the Secretary of Labor to ensure contractor and agency compliance. However, Johnson's Order went further by requiring government contractors, except where exempted due to factors such as numbers of workers or size of the contracts, to post notices of non-discrimination to workers, unions, and subcontractors, to include non-discrimination clauses within contracts, and to file compliance reports with the Labor Department.[16] This Order directly influenced what explicitly became recognized as affirmative action during the Nixon administration. Based on Executive Order 11246 and a local plan originally introduced in 1967, the city of Philadelphia, in consultation with United States Department of Labor, adopted the aptly named Revised Philadelphia Plan on June 27, 1969. That plan not only prohibited government contractors

Means Necessary v. Regents of Univ. of Michigan, 701 F.3d 466 (6th Cir. 2012) cert. granted, 133 S. Ct. 1633, 185 L. Ed. 2d 615 (U.S. 2013). *See also infra* notes 42–43.

13 *See, e.g.*, Parents Involved in Cmty. Sch. v. Seattle Sch. Dist. No. 1, 551 U.S. 701, 787–88 (2007), (Kennedy, J., concurring) (joining plurality decision to strike down race-based considerations for integration plans in Seattle and Louisville, but allowing that race might still be considered for such purposes); Grutter v. Bollinger, 539 U.S. 306 (2003) (reaffirming the *Bakke* plurality's approval of the consideration of race based upon its value to diversity within education as a compelling interest which may survive strict scrutiny).

14 *See* Fisher v. Univ. of Texas at Austin, 133 S. Ct. 2411 (2013) (vacating a lower court award of summary judgment to the state and returning to the 5th Circuit a case involving race-conscious college admissions, for the application of strict scrutiny consistent with the decision in *Grutter*); *Parents Involved*, 551 U.S. at 730–32.

15 Exec. Ord. No. 10925, 26 Fed. Reg. 1977 (March 6, 1961) (emphasis added). Some have argued, however, that the earliest forms of legislation committed to race-conscious remedy took place during Reconstruction. *See, e.g.*, Carl E. Brody, Jr, *A Historical Review of Affirmative Action and the Interpretation of Its Legislative Intent by the Supreme Court*, 29 Akron L. Rev, 291, 294 (1996) (claiming that the Freedman's Bureau legislation of the mid-1890s was designed to remedy the ills of slavery); James E. Jones, Jr, *The Genesis and Present Status of Affirmative Action in Education: Economic, Legal and Political Realities*, 70 Iowa L. Rev. 901, 904 (1985) (citing the NAACP's amicus brief in *Bakke*, which similarly advanced this point).

16 Exec. Order No. 11246, 3 C.F.R. 1964–65 (1965).

from discriminating on the basis of race but also specifically required them to create goals for hiring African-American employees in order to ameliorate systemic and historic discrimination practiced in certain trade unions. In August of 1969, President Nixon additionally issued Executive Order 11478, which required equal employment opportunity for federal employees to be achieved through a "continuing affirmative program in each executive department and agency."[17] These affirmative approaches to ensuring opportunities quickly spread to other cities and states. The U.S. Comptroller General initially issued a report indicating such plans violated Title VII of the Civil Rights Act of 1964, but President Nixon lobbied Congress to reject these findings.[18] Additionally, the plans were presumed to be constitutional when the Supreme Court refused to grant certiorari to a Third Circuit case, holding that the Revised Philadelphia Plan neither violated the Title VII nor the Fifth Amendment Due Process Clause,[19] and later upheld a program which reserved 50 percent of the openings in a training plan for African Americans.[20]

Growing Pains: Affirmative Action Backlash in the Courts

The era of affirmative action programs being viewed as consistent with the constitutional protection of equality was decidedly short-lived. Less than 10 years after the implementation of the Revised Philadelphia Plan, a plurality opinion in *Regents of the University of California v. Bakke* signaled that the Court was loath to view affirmative action programs as restoring equality for minorities who had suffered past discrimination. Rather, such plans were instead considered as reverse discrimination against groups not favored by such programs.[21] *Bakke* did not directly discuss government employment and contracting and only struck down the use of race-conscious quotas in higher education admissions. In fact, in the years immediately following the *Bakke* decision—in cases worth additionally noting because they did not employ strict scrutiny—the Court upheld two minority set-aside programs in employment.[22] Within a decade after the *Bakke* decision, however, the understanding of remedial race-conscious set-asides as unconstitutional also invaded employment and contracting cases.

In a set of cases looking at affirmative action within the employment and government contracting arenas—*Wygant v. Jackson Board of Education* (1986),[23] *City of Richmond v. J.A. Croson Co.* (1989),[24] *Adarand Construction v. Pena* (1995)[25] are most representative—the Supreme Court systematically exhibited hostility toward affirmative action by requiring strict scrutiny analysis for all government race classification cases, demanding a strong basis in evidence to justify remedial race-based decision-making, and adopting "colorblindness" as a prevailing perspective for analyzing equal protection claims.[26]

---

17 Exec. Order No. 11478, 3 C.F.R. 803 (1969).

18 *See* Patricia A. Carlson, Adarand Constructors, Inc. v. Pena: *The Lochnerization of Affirmative Action*, 27 St. Mary's L.J. 423, 431 (1996).

19 Contractors' Ass'n of E. Pennsylvania v. Schultz., 442 F.2d 159 (3rd Cir. 1971). While the Fifth Amendment does not include an equal protection clause, the Court has read this protection into the amendment to prevent there being a disjuncture between the Fifth and Fourteenth Amendments. *See* Bolling v. Sharpe, 347 U.S. 497, 489–90 (1954).

20 United Steel Workers of America, AFL-CIO-CLC v. Weber, 443 U.S. 193, 208 (1979) (overturning a 5th Circuit holding that the program violated Title VII).

21 Regents of the Univ. of California v. Bakke, 438 U.S. 265 (1978). Justice Powell wrote the Court's opinion and was joined by four justices to pronounce a special admissions program at the University of California, Davis Medical School that reserved 16 seats per year for minority applicants—some of whose entry test scores were lower than candidates rejected in the regular admissions program—to be unconstitutional and a violation of federal law. *Id.* at 271.

22 *See* Fullilove v. Klutznick, 448 U.S. 448, 492 (1980) (upholding as lawful a section in the Public Works Employment act of 1977 that required state and local recipients of federal funds to use 10 percent of their funding to procure services from among designated minority groups) *Weber*, 443 U.S. at 208.

23 Wygant v Jackson Bd. of Educ., 576 U.S. 267 (1986).

24 City of Richmond v. J.A. Croson Co., 488 U.S. 469 (1989).

25 Adarand Construction v. Peña, 515 U.S. 200 (1995).

26 On colorblindness as "mythologized racial justice," see Jerome M. Culp, Jr, *Colorblind Remedies and the Intersectionality of Oppression: Policy Arguments Masquerading as Moral Claims*, 69 N.Y.U. L. Rev. 162 (1994).

In *Wygant*, a plurality decision that addressed the constitutionality of a race-conscious layoff provision in a collective bargaining agreement, five Justices agreed that the provision violated the Equal Protection Clause. The case also produced five votes for a "strong basis in evidence" standard to justify the use of race-conscious remedies. Justice Powell, writing for the Court, also proposed that strict scrutiny apply to any governmental classification or preference based on racial or ethnic criteria.[27] In the *Croson* case that followed, the Court adopted Justice Powell's strict scrutiny suggestion, at least for racial classifications used by individual states.[28] Much of the dicta in the opinion relied upon Powell's *Bakke* opinion and suggested that racial classifications could unfairly burden Whites as well as minorities.[29] Additionally, while the Court indicated that remedying specific past discrimination could be a compelling interest, it rejected general societal discrimination as sufficient to meet the test.[30] Finally, in *Adarand* the Court struck down a federal government program that created financial incentives for general contractors to hire subcontractors who were "socially and economically disadvantaged."[31] For some subcontractors, establishing disadvantage included considerations of race.[32] The Court essentially extended the approach from *Croson* of applying strict scrutiny to all state uses of racial classifications to the federal government.

Affirmative Action Backlash via Voter-led Initiatives

In addition to the aforementioned Court cases, the backlash against affirmative action expanded to include a series of states banning considerations of race in public education, employment, and contracting. The University of California Board of Regents was an early proponent of discontinuing considerations of minority status in education, eliminating affirmative action in higher education admissions in 1995. This policy shift was followed in the same year by then Governor Pete Wilson's executive order eliminating affirmative action in state employment.[33] In 1996, Proposition 209, which was approved by 54 percent of California voters, banned minority group considerations in public education, employment, and contracting through an amendment to the state Constitution.[34] Styled as a civil rights initiative, Proposition 209 proclaimed that states shall "not discriminate against, or grant preferential treatment to" any person in employment, education, or contracting, based on "race, sex, color, ethnicity, or national origin."[35] The Proposition became a model for anti-affirmative action ballot initiatives in other states including Washington State's Initiative 200, Nebraska's Initiative 424, Amendment 46 in Colorado, and Proposal 2 in Michigan, all of which employed similarly universalist language.[36] The proposals passed in each state but

---

27 *Wygant*, 576 U.S. at 272 74.

28 *Croson*, 488 U.S. at 493. For states, then, the Court rejected the notion that racial considerations could be regarded as "benign."

29 A former law professor and current Associate California Supreme Justice, however, has argued that claims that affirmative action deprives White applicants are based on distortions of statistical truth. Goodwin Liu, *The Causation Fallacy:* Bakke *and the Basic Arithmetic of Selective Admissions*, 100 Mich. L. Rev. 1045, 1055 (2002).

30 *Croson*, 488 U.S. at 496–97. The Court then struck down the city of Richmond's minority set-aside program and remanded the case back to the Circuit to apply strict scrutiny.

31 Adarand Construction v. Peña, 515 U.S. 200, 207 (1995). With regard to the decision to apply strict scrutiny to federal programs considering race, *Adarand* expressly overruled the approach followed in *Metro Broadcasting, Inc. v. Fed. Commc'n. Comm'n*, an earlier case where the Court had applied intermediate scrutiny in upholding a federal government program considering racial set-asides, which the Court described as "benign." *Id.* at 227.

32 *Id.* at 207.

33 *See* U.C. Berkeley Thelton Henderson Center for Social Justice, Proposition 209 and Public Employment: Trends in Workforce Diversity 5 (2008).

34 *Id.* Ward Connerly, a member of the U.C. Board of Regents, spearheaded repeal of affirmative action within the U.C. system, then championed not only Proposition 209, but similar initiatives in other states. *See Ward Connerly's Falling Star*, 43 The Journal Of Black Issues In Higher Education 26, 26–29 (2004).

35 Erwin Chemerinsky, *The Impact of the Proposed California Civil Rights Initiative*, 23 Hastings L. Q. 999, 1004 (1996).

36 *See* Kim West-Faulcon, *The River Runs Dry: When Title VII Trumps State Affirmative Action Law*, 157 U. Pa. L. Rev. 1075 (2009).

Colorado.[37] While the Sixth Circuit Court of Appeals overturned Michigan's law,[38] the U.S. Supreme Court recently reversed the lower appellate court. Applying the so-called "political process" doctrine articulated in cases such as *Reitman v. Mulkey*,[39] *Hunter v. Erickson*,[40] and *Washington v. Seattle School District No. 1*,[41]—all of which had previously disallowed race-based discrimination in various segments of public life based on voter preferences—the Roberts Court determined that racial groups could not be presumed to share common political perspectives and that it would be risky for the Court to decide "the policy realms in which certain groups—groups defined by race—have a political interest."[42] Rather than seeing Proposal 2 and the resulting amendment to the Michigan Constitution as inflicting injury upon, or alienating minorities from the political process, the Court, instead, stated:

> For reasons already discussed, *Mulkey*, *Hunter*, and *Seattle* are not precedents that stand for the conclusion that Michigan's voters must be disempowered from acting. Those cases were ones in which the political restriction in question was designed to be used, or was likely to be used, to encourage infliction of injury by reason of race. What is at stake here is not whether injury will be inflicted but whether government can be instructed not to follow a course that entails, first, the definition of racial categories and, second, the grant of favored status to persons in some racial categories and not others.[43]

Based upon the *Schuette* holding, even if future federal courts uphold as constitutional state university policies that include race-conscious decision-making in admissions, voter initiatives may be used to overturn these policies. Given, however, that only a small number of states have passed such initiatives thus far, race-conscious admissions plans in education potentially remain viable as long as they otherwise comport with U.S. Supreme Court's current standards for such programs, which are next discussed.

The Last Remaining Vestiges of Affirmative Action (For Now)

In *Bakke*, race-conscious set-asides in higher education admissions programs were held to violate the Equal Protection Clause, but 5 Justices also preserved the idea that because achieving diversity among the student body involved a compelling state interest, race could be considered as a "plus" factor in creating diversity in admissions.[44] In *Grutter v. Bollinger*, a Justice O'Connor-led majority reaffirmed what has come to be referred to as "the diversity rationale" articulated in *Bakke* whilst upholding the constitutionality of a race-conscious admissions process at the University of Michigan Law School, which considered race as one factor in a

37 Nebraska and Washington both passed the initiatives with 58 percent of the votes. Ward Connerly's group attempted similar initiatives in Oklahoma, Arizona, Missouri, but they failed. *See* Naomi Zeveloff, *Amendment 46 to Repeal Affirmative Action Loses Despite Hefty Odds*, Colorado Independent (Nov. 7, 2008), http://coloradoindependent.com/14699/amendment-46-to-repeal-affirmative-action-loses-despite-hefty-odds.

38 *See supra* note 12 (6th Circuit 8–7 en banc majority holding that Proposal 2 violated the Equal Protection Clause by "reorder[ing] the political process in Michigan to place special burdens on minority interests.").

39 Reitman v. Mulkey, 387 U.S. 369 (1967) (a 5–4 decision upholding a California Supreme Court decision that struck down a voter initiative, which would have changed the state constitution to allow residents to discriminate in contracts for the sale, lease or rent of property).

40 Hunter v. Erickson, 393 U.S. 385 (1969) (8–1 decision overturning as a violation of the Equal Protection Clause, a change to the Akron, OH, city charter, that prevented the City Council from implementing any ordinance to address discrimination in housing without the approval of the majority of the voters of Akron).

41 Washington v. Seattle Sch. Dist. No. 1, 458 U.S. 457 (1981) (a 5–4 decision holding that a voter initiative that blocked the implementation of Seattle's mandatory busing plan violated the Equal Protection Clause).

42 Schuette v. Coalition to Defend Affirmative Action, 134 S.Ct 1623 (2014) (Kennedy J., authoring a 6–2 opinion overturning a 6th Circuit decision striking down Proposal 2 and the resulting Amendment 26).

43 *Schuette*, 134 S.Ct. at 1637–38.

44 Regents of the Univ.of California v. Bakke, 438 U.S. 265, 311–14 (1978). Although scholars have contested whether the meaning of the diversity rationale is clear. *See* Devon W. Carbado, *Intraracial Diversity*, 60 UCLA L. Rev. 1130, 1144 (2013).

highly individualized admissions process.[45] In that decision, Justice O'Connor, however, also opined, "We expect that 25 years from now, the use of racial preferences will no longer be necessary to further the interest approved today."[46] Based on the Court's opinion in *Fisher v. University of Texas*—another case involving race-conscious higher education admissions standards—it appears we may not have to wait until 2028 for a new determination on the efficacy of affirmative action. Although *Fisher*, itself, did not overrule *Grutter* or ban affirmative action in educational admissions, the *Fisher* majority refined *Grutter*'s meaning, both increasing the likelihood of *Grutter* being a less effective tool for protecting race-conscious admissions and of other such cases being appealed to the Court.

Fisher v. University of Texas and Affirmative Action—Missed Opportunities in Substance and Process

The facts of the *Fisher* case were fairly simple. In 2008, petitioner Abigail Fisher was denied admission to the University of Texas, Austin, through a two-pronged admissions system. The largest portion of Texas undergraduates is admitted via the race-neutral practice[47] of taking the top 10 percent of Texas high school students. To ensure diversity, a smaller number of students (25 percent) are admitted via a race-conscious review.[48] Although Fisher was admitted to another Texas campus and ultimately enrolled at Louisiana State University, she sued the University and school officials, alleging that the University's use of a race-conscious system violated the Equal Protection Clause.[49]

The *Fisher* majority opinion was written, not surprisingly, by Justice Kennedy. What was surprising was that it was a 7–1 decision with only Justice Ginsburg dissenting, given the Court's current thin conservative majority that often produces 5–4 decisions on cases involving hot-button social issues.[50] With regard to affirmative action, in particular, opponents of affirmative action thought that there might be five votes in *Fisher* to overrule, or greatly narrow, *Grutter v. Bollinger*. Justices Scalia, Kennedy, and Thomas dissented in *Grutter*. Chief Justice Roberts wrote an opinion in *Parents Involved in Community Schools v. Seattle School Dist. No. 1*, which Justice Alito joined, which said that the Constitution requires the government to be colorblind and that rejected diversity in the classroom as a compelling government interest.[51] Put another way, Justice Alito's replacing Justice O'Connor, the author of the Court's opinion in *Grutter*, led many to believe that there could be a majority to overrule *Grutter*.

Rather than substantially revisiting *Grutter*'s core points, seven justices voted to return the case to the Circuit Court for further proceedings. The scope of their decision, however, was very narrow. The Court focused its opinion on the lower court's application of the narrow tailoring prong of strict scrutiny. The Court called for "careful judicial inquiry" into whether acceptable diversity could be achieved without using race, requiring courts to determine whether there were no race-neutral alternatives.[52] With this focus, we next argue, the Court both ignored significant issues of process and substance. Specifically, we argue that based on precedent addressing remedies for denied University applicants, the Court should not have heard Fisher's complaint, and

45 In the same term, the court found the University of Michigan undergraduate admissions system's consideration of race to be unconstitutional. Gratz v. Bollinger, 539 U.S. 244, 251, 281 (2003) (finding that the points awarded to race in the admissions system involved no individual assessment and almost always made the difference for the admissions decision).

46 Grutter v. Bollinger, 539 U.S. 306, 330–31 (2003).

47 As discussed below, whether the plan is, in fact, race neutral is a point of contestation. *See infra* notes 75–81 and accompanying text.

48 Erwin Chemerinsky, *What's Next for Affirmative Action*, ABA Journal (Aug. 6, 2013, 8:25 AM), http://www.abajournal.com/news/article/chemerinsky_whats_next_for_affirmative_action/.

49 Fisher also claimed violations of 42 U.S.C. §§ 1981 and 1983, and Title VI of the Civil Rights Act of 1964.

50 In the term in which *Fisher* was decided, there were several such opinions. *See* Vance v. Ball State University, 133 S. Ct. 2434, 2454 (2013) (5–4 Justice Alito decision narrowing the definition of who can be treated as a supervisor under Title VII); Univ. of Texas Southwestern Med. Ctr v. Nassar, 133 S. Ct. 2517, 2533 (2013) (5–4 Justice Kennedy decision requiring Title VII retaliation plaintiff's to prove but-for causation for their claims); and Shelby Cnty. v. Holder, 133 S. Ct. 2612, 2631 (2013) (5–4 Justice Roberts decision striking down Section 4 of the Voting Rights Act).

51 Parents Involved in Cmty Sch. v. Seattle Sch. Dist. No. 1, 551 U.S. 701, 702–04 (2007).

52 Fisher v. Univ. of Texas at Austin, 133 S. Ct. 2411, 2420 (2013).

that the majority, concurrences and dissent, failed to use the *Fisher* case as a meaningful opportunity to explicate Equal Protection Doctrine as a function of the lived experiences of racial minorities within this country.

Why Fisher *Never Should have Been Heard: Precedent and Process Limits for Denied Applicants*

It is absolutely clear that the Supreme Court never should have heard or decided *Fisher* because it lacked jurisdiction. It is not even a close question. In other affirmative action cases involving higher education, like *Regents of the University of California v. Bakke* and *Grutter v. Bollinger*, the plaintiffs were seeking injunctive and declaratory relief. But Abigail Fisher was not; since she graduated from Louisiana State University in 2012, she no longer had a claim for an injunction or a declaratory judgment. She had no desire to return to college. Her only remaining claim was for $100 in money damages, $50 for her application fee, and $50 for her housing deposit. Nor was this a class action suit or a suit with any other remaining plaintiffs.[53]

The problem was that the defendants named in the suit were the University of Texas, a state university, and its officers who were sued in their "official capacity." The law is clear that the Eleventh Amendment and sovereign immunity bar suits for money damages against a state government or its officials who are sued in their official capacity for a constitutional violation.[54] It is that clear and simple. No other defendants were named and those who were named could not be sued in federal court because of the Eleventh Amendment.

Moreover, it is questionable whether Fisher had standing to bring the claim. Her injury, a loss of money for the application and housing fee, was not caused by the University of Texas' affirmative action plan. She surely would have applied anyway. In fact, in *Texas v. Lesage*, the Court expressly distinguished between an affirmative action case seeking an injunction, or prospective relief, as opposed to one seeking only money damages. The Court declared:

> Of course, a plaintiff who challenges an ongoing race-conscious program and seeks forward-looking relief need not affirmatively establish that he would receive the benefit in question if race were not considered. The relevant injury in such cases is the inability to compete on an equal footing. But where there is no allegation of an ongoing or imminent constitutional violation to support a claim for forward-looking relief, the government's conclusive demonstration that it would have made the same decision absent the alleged discrimination precludes any finding of liability.[55]

In the federal district court, Texas demonstrated that Fisher would not have been accepted to the University even if she had a perfect Personal Achievement Score.

Put another way, standing to sue in federal court requires that a plaintiff allege and prove an injury that was caused by the unconstitutional policy. Abigail Fisher's remaining injury for which she is suing is the loss of $100 in her application fee. That harm, however, was not caused by the University of Texas' affirmative action plan. She surely would have applied to the school even if the affirmative action plan did not exist.

It is puzzling that the University of Texas did not do more to emphasize this in its brief and argument to the Court. It is raised in a long footnote—footnote 7 on pages 16 and 17 of its brief to the Supreme Court. The footnote cites to an article by Adam Chandler that develops the jurisdictional points in detail.[56] But that's it. Of course, the Court is supposed to raise problems with jurisdiction, which include the Eleventh Amendment and standing, on its own. The Court didn't even acknowledge these jurisdictional obstacles. It appears that its desire to decide the issue caused it to ignore that it was required to dismiss the case.[57]

---

53 Originally, *Fisher* included co-plaintiff Rachel Michalewicz, who was also admitted to and enrolled at a school other than the University of Texas, Austin; unlike *Grutter*, *Fisher* involved no claims on behalf of future applicants. *See* Adam D. Chandler, *How (Not) To Bring an Affirmative-Action Challenge*, 122 Yale Online J. 85, 86–88 (Oct. 1, 2012), http://www.yalelawjournal.org/the-yale-law-journal-pocket-part/supreme-court/how-(not)-to-bring-an-affirmative%11action-challenge/ (similarly arguing that the case could have been rendered moot had the University returned the application fees).

54 *See* Scheuer v. Rhodes, 416 U.S. 232, 241–43 (1974).

55 Texas v. Lesage, 528 U.S. 18, 21 (1999).

56 *See* Chandler, *supra* note 53.

57 On remand, the Fifth Circuit acknowledged the jurisdictional issues, but declined to decide the case on standing grounds. Fisher v. Univ. of Texas, Austin, 758 F.3d 633, 640 (5th Cir. 2014).

The Fisher *Majority and Missed Opportunities for Addressing the Lived Experience of Race*

Beyond narrowing how strict scrutiny is applied and ignoring procedural constraints, the Supreme Court repeatedly missed opportunities to challenge assumptions about race and its relevance to the everyday lives of applicants that are widely held by White people in our country. By so doing, the Court essentially defined the experiences of Whites in the United States as the normative standard by which all college and university applicants and thus all affirmative action programs should be evaluated. The end result? The Court both reinforced and fortified White privilege with the *Fisher* majority.

For example, while detailing its precedents in the affirmative action arena, the Court proffered a statement about "race" that tends to comport primarily with the actual lived experiences of Whites in our country. Specifically, the Court asserted:

> Justice Powell's central point … was that this interest in securing diversity's benefits, although a permissible objective, is complex. "It is not an interest in simple ethnic diversity, in which a specified percentage of the student body is in effect guaranteed to be members of selected ethnic groups, with the remaining percentage an undifferentiated aggregation of students. The diversity that furthers a compelling state interest encompasses a far broader array of qualifications and characteristics of which racial or ethnic origin is but a single though important element … To be narrowly tailored, a race-conscious admissions program cannot use a quota system," but instead must "remain flexible enough to ensure that each applicant is evaluated as an individual and not in a way that makes an applicant's race or ethnicity the defining feature of his or her application."[58]

Implicit in these statements is the notion that race does not play a defining role in the actual lives of university and college applicants. Such statements assume that race has no meaning in real life other than to work as a plus or minus during the admissions process. Indeed, these statements assume that race plays no role but the role that applicants and admissions officers choose to assign to it.

Yet, as Professors Michael Omi and Howard Winant convincingly reveal in their book *Racial Formation in the United States: From the 1960s to the 1990s*, "[f]rom the very inception of the Republic to the present moment, race has been a profound determinant of one's political rights, one's location in the labor market, and indeed one's sense of 'identity.'"[59] In other words, race has never represented a mere decorative symbol for individuals in our society; instead, race has always carried with it real substantive consequences for the lives of people of color, who generally endure some form of racial subordination on a regular, if not everyday, basis. As Professors Richard Delgado and Jean Stefancic have pointed out, unlike for most Whites, who generally do not "have to think about race,"[60] race and racism "[s]till, by every social indicator … continue […] to blight the lives of people of color, including holders of high-echelon jobs, even judges."[61] Indeed, for most people of color in the United States, particularly Black Americans and Latinos, race has involuntarily become a defining feature in their lives.[62]

For this reason, when the Court failed to acknowledge the real meaning of race, racism, and their consequences in the United States, it essentially solidified what Professors Devon Carbado and Cheryl Harris have identified as a racial preference in favor of Whites in the admissions game.[63] After all, as Carbado and Harris pointed out in reference to the tasks of writing and evaluating personal admissions essays, to assume that race has no meaning or consequence in people's lives and thus should not be a part of their applications

58 Fisher v. Univ. of Texas at Austin, 133 S. Ct. 2411, 2418 (2013) (quoting Regents of Univ. of California v. Bakke, 438 U.S. 265, 315 (1978)).

59 Michael Omi & Howard Winant, Racial Formation in the United States: From the 1960s to the 1990s 1 (1994).

60 Richard Delgado & Jean Stefancic, Critical Race Theory: An Introduction 11 (2nd ed. 2012). *See also* Barbara J. Flagg, *"Was Blind, But Now I See": White Race Consciousness and the Requirement of Discriminatory Intent*, 91 Mich. L. Rev. 953, 969 (1993).

61 Delgado & Stefancic, *supra* note 60.

62 *Id.* at 1–2.

63 *See* Devon W. Carbado & Cheryl I. Harris, *The New Racial Preferences*, 96 Cal. L. Rev. 1139, 1148, 1168 (2008) (arguing that a mandate to ignore race in admissions ends up "conferring a preference for applicants for whom race does not matter").

unfairly assumes that one can intelligently speak of herself and her life without regard to race. While the requirement to completely avoid race in describing one's self and one's potential contributions to a school may make sense for most Whites, who, due to skin color, view and think of themselves as raceless,[64] it makes little sense for people of color for whom race often plays a part in every social interaction.[65] In sum, "the life story of many people—particularly with regard to describing disadvantage—simply does not make sense without reference to race."[66] When each of the opinions failed to acknowledge how race is a central and defining feature in the lives of many people of color, the Court accepted, without challenge, that a person of color can describe, explain, or make sense of his or her existence without any account of race and thus missed an opportunity to derail White privilege.

More than that, the Court missed an opportunity to highlight how failures to account for race in admissions evaluations can actually discount the actual achievements of a candidate of color in the admissions process.[67] For example, in its facts section, which by definition is supposed to merely describe the situation at hand, the Court described the University of Texas' Personal Achievement Index, which in conjunction with the Academic Index, was used to evaluate applicants who did not earn admission under the Texas Ten Percent program, stating:

> This Personal Achievement Index (PAI) measures a student's leadership and work experience, awards, extracurricular activities, community service, *and other special circumstances that give insight into a student's background. These included growing up in a single-parent home, speaking a language other than English at home, significant family responsibilities assumed by the applicant, and the general socioeconomic condition of the student's family.*[68]

By detailing the University's factual assertions that factors such as growing up in a single-parent home or speaking a language other than English can provide useful insights into a person's background and thus their potential contributions to an institution, the Court acknowledged, to some extent, that the evaluation of an applicant's leadership, awards, and extracurricular activities, for example, is contextual. After all, many of us would consider a student's achievement in becoming her school's best fiction writer to be more impressive (assuming no other differences, which we admit is a big assumption) if that student were a non-native English speaker rather than a native speaker. Similarly, a student's significant achievements in being elected and serving as a strong leader in many activities at her school would be even more impressive to us if that student grew up in a poor single-mother household that required her to work 20 hours per work on top of her academics and activities than if that student grew up in a wealthy household and did not come with such burdens.

64 Flagg, *supra* note 60, at 970 ("White people externalize race. For most whites, most of the time, to think or speak about race is to think or speak about people of color, or perhaps, at times, to reflect on oneself (or other whites) in relation to people of color. But we tend not to think of ourselves or our racial cohort as racially distinctive. Whites' 'consciousness' of whiteness is predominantly *unconsciousness* of whiteness.").

65 *See* Delgado & Stefancic, *supra* note 60, at 1–2 (briefly discussing how microaggressions can "mar the days of women and people of color" and referring to microaggressions as "dispiriting transactions"); Derald Wing Sue, Microaggressions in Everyday Life: Race, Gender, and Sexual Orientation 5 (2010) (defining microaggressions as "brief and commonplace, daily, behavioral and environmental indignities, whether intentional or unintentional, that communicate hostile, derogatory, or negative, racial, gender, sexual-orientation, or religious slights and insults to the target person or group.").

66 Carbado & Harris, *supra* note 63, at 1148 (highlighting how essays written by President Barack Obama and Justice Clarence Thomas, for example, would make little sense if race were ignored or if President Obama or Justice Thomas were assumed to be White). For example, in discussing how a portion of Justice Thomas's autobiography would be distorted without acknowledging race and its saliency in his life, Professors Carbado and Harris note:

"In Thomas's case, that history of disadvantage is also racial. It would be virtually impossible for him to tell the story of his background without reference to race. His story would be both incomplete and incomprehensible. The difficult position Thomas finds himself in here exposes the problem of formally removing race from an admissions process against a social backdrop in which race both matters and is cognizable." *Id.* at 1186.

67 Angela Onwuachi-Willig, *"I Wish I Were Black" and Other Affirmative Action Tales*, Chron. Higher Educ. (Oct. 28, 2013), http://chronicle.com/article/I-Wish-I-Were-Black-and/142561/.

68 Fisher v. Univ. of Texas at Austin, 133 S. Ct. 2411, 2415–16 (2013).

Nevertheless, the Court missed the opportunity to take this understanding even further by exploring and explicating how race may often further contextualize each of these judgments during the admissions process. For instance, if one tacks on the fact that the high-achieving, fiction-writing student (above) is of Mexican descent and speaks Spanish as her first language, as opposed to, for example, being of French descent and speaking French as her first language, one should likely consider the extreme prejudices and presumptions of incompetency and criminality that are generally imposed on Latinos who are of Mexican descent in evaluating her achievements.[69] More so, one should consider and give the student credit for the extra focus, skill, and hard work that it must have taken that student in order to overcome those stereotypes and prejudices in achieving her literary accomplishments. Or add the fact that the student in a single-parent home lives with her Black mother. That fact, too, adds important dimensions to understanding the particular applicant's story, as the public has historically as well as presently had different perceptions of single mothers, particularly if they require any government assistance or if they are Black or Latino as opposed to White.[70] In sum, in both instances, added racial details give a fuller picture of the student's background—their personal achievement index—and thus their merits for admission; the two cannot be separated, and trying to separate them actually undercuts the significance of the different applicants' achievements by failing to take into account the race-related obstacles that they had overcome. For instance, would it make sense to ignore the fact that a student had become the first African-American student body president at a predominantly White institution—how he was able to visualize and then achieve that goal despite never seeing any role models in that position or how he overcame what may have been a historically hostile school environment to persuade enough White students to vote for him? Indeed, as many scholars have pointed out, evaluating Justice Thomas's achievements from elementary school until his appointment to the Supreme Court and even his performance on the Supreme Court is impossible without taking race, racism, and their effects on him into account.[71] Based on his autobiography, which is filled with references to how race influenced his life and the race-based obstacles, including hostilities that he had to overcome, Justice Thomas, too, at least implicitly agrees.[72]

On top of that, the Court missed the opportunity to confront perhaps the most offensive assumption behind challenges to race-based affirmative action: the notion that Whites, not people of color, naturally belong in the seats at these public institutions, institutions meant to serve the public within the state, regardless of the state's demographics. The Court missed this important opportunity when it described what it believed to be an increase in the African-American and Latino student populations at the University of Texas, Austin, since the Fifth Circuit's last affirmative action decision in *Hopwood v. Texas* in 1996, without any reference to the ways in which the demographic picture of the state had changed in that 10-year period. The Court provided:

---

69 *See* Neil Gotanda, *A Critique of "Our Constitution Is Colorblind,"* 44 Stan. L. Rev. 1, 6 (1991) ("Any trace of African ancestry makes one Black. In contrast, the classification white signifies 'uncontaminated' European ancestry and corresponding racial purity. The socially constructed racial categories white and Black are not equal in status. They are highly contextualized, with powerful, deeply embedded social and political meanings."). *Mary Romero, State Violence and the Social and Legal Construction of Latino Criminality: From El Bandido to Gang Member*, 78 Denv. U. L. Rev. 1081, 1083-85 (2001) (discussing how Black and Latino youth are viewed as "superpredators" and how this designation is "socially constructed through a racial lens—the lens that reflects the images of White middle class youth as 'our' children and Latino adolescent males as violent, inherently dangerous, and endangering").

70 *See, e.g.*, Martha Fineman, The Neutered Mother, The Sexual Family, and Other Twentieth Century Tragedies 107 (1995) ("[I]n the public's mind, and despite overwhelming evidence to the contrary, the face of poverty has increasingly become that of a single mother, particularly the African-American single mother."); Kevin R. Johnson, *Public Benefits and Immigration: The Intersection of Immigration Status, Ethnicity, Gender, and Class,* 42 UCLA L. Rev. 1509, 1542–44 (1995) (asserting that there is an assumption that many welfare recipients are Mexican immigrant mothers); *see also* Angela Onwuachi-Willig, *The Return of the Ring: Welfare Reform's Marriage Cure as the Revival of Post-Bellum Control*, 93 Cal. L. Rev. 1647, 1665–73 (2005) (highlighting how Black mothers, specifically Black welfare mothers, are stereotyped and demonized); Adrien Katherine Wing & Laura Weselmann, *Transcending Traditional Notions of Mothering: The Need for Critical Race Feminist Praxis*, 3 J. Gender Race & Just. 257, 274 (1999) ("The law's preference for stay-at-home mothers never applied to Black mothers.").

71 *See* Angela Onwuachi-Willig, *Using the Master's "Tool" to Dismantle His House: Why Justice Clarence Thomas Makes the Case for Affirmative Action*, 47 Ariz. L. Rev. 113 (2005) (using Thomas's life, including the race-based obstacles he faced, to highlight why the Justice is a good example of affirmative action working in the right manner).

72 *See* Carbado & Harris, *supra* note 63, at 1174–86, 1195–99 (examining excerpts from Justice Thomas's autobiography and explicating how his narrative makes little sense without attention to race).

> The University's revised admissions process, coupled with the operation of the Top Ten Percent Law, resulted in a more racially diverse environment at the University. Before the admissions program at issue in this case, in the last year under the post-*Hopwood* AI/PAI system that did not consider race, the entering class was 4.5% African–American and 16.9% Hispanic. This is in contrast with the 1996 pre-*Hopwood* and Top Ten Percent regime, when race was explicitly considered, and the University's entering freshman class was 4.1% African–American and 14.5% Hispanic.[73]

The Court, however, is factually wrong in one important respect. The measure for the increase in students of a particular racial group at a public university cannot simply be determined over a 10-year period by the rise in numbers alone—that is, unless the percentages of each racial group in that state remained the same over that 15-year period. In Texas, the demographics of the state changed significantly during that time, particularly with the Latino population, which, as the University asserted, exploded during that time period. For instance, in 2004, Latinos made up 34.2 percent of the state's population as compared to just 25 percent in 1996.[74] In this sense, the Court missed the opportunity to challenge deeply held assumptions by many Whites about belonging in the United States more generally, and, specifically, at the University of Texas, Austin.

In essence, the Supreme Court's assumptions about race in *Fisher*, or rather what seemed to be its adoption of Petitioner Abigail Fisher's assumptions about race in her briefs, only worked to reinforce White privilege by identifying the experiences of Whites as the normative standard by which all others will be evaluated. In so doing, the Court ended up "conferring a preference for applicants for whom race does not matter,"[75] very few of whom would be people of color. In all, the Court failed to challenge White privilege and the type of colorblind rhetoric that works to reify current racial hierarchies by seeing and acknowledging the meaningfulness of race within the admissions scoring process at the University of Texas, Austin.

Fisher*'s Modest Dissent and Justice Thomas' Misplaced Analogies*

In *Fisher*, Justice Ginsburg dissented and Justices Thomas and Scalia wrote separate concurring opinions. Each of these opinions could have moved equality jurisprudence forward by clarifying how race-conscious admissions practices should be reconciled with modern conceptions of equal protection. We argue next that Justice Ginsburg missed this opportunity, Justice Scalia wholesale rejected it, and Justice Thomas confused the contemporary equality conversation by relying significantly on ahistoric analogies in his analysis of the University of Texas' use of race. Taken together, these opinions have not provided particularly balanced or nuanced approaches to assist in deciding future cases.

Justice Ginsburg: dissenting without raising the race question

The majority's avoidance of substantive questions regarding the acceptable contours of constitutionally sound considerations of race in admissions was not remedied by the other opinions in *Fisher*. Justice Scalia's one-paragraph opinion need not be discussed at length because he merely wrote to state that the Court was not asked to overturn *Grutter*—a result he supports and many commentators predicted when *Fisher* was granted certiorari. In dissent, Justice Ginsburg, by contrast, claimed that the Fifth Circuit opinion was compliant with the *Grutter* decision. While she did not provide detailed support for this claim, it matters because it is a direct challenge to the majority's controlling argument—that *Grutter* commends a more robust application of the "narrow tailoring" prong of strict scrutiny.

Justice Ginsburg's more significant, and perhaps more controversial point in dissent, was that it was misguided for the majority to frame the debate over the University of Texas program as involving a choice between race-conscious admissions and the Top Ten Percent Plan. Specifically, she stated, "I have said before and reiterate here that only an ostrich could regard the supposedly neutral alternatives as race unconscious,"[76]

---

73 Fisher v. Univ. of Texas at Austin, 133 S. Ct. 2411, 2416 (2013).

74 U.S. Census Bureau, The American Community—Hispanics 2004, American Community Survey Reports, Feb. 2007, at 6, http://www.census.gov/prod/2007pubs/acs-03.pdf.

75 Carbado & Harris, *supra* note 63, at 1168.

76 Fisher v. Univ. of Texas at Austin, 133 S. Ct. 2411, 2433 (2013) (Ginsburg, J., dissenting).

and "it [the Top Ten Percent Plan] was adopted with racially segregated neighborhoods and schools front and center stage."[77] According to Justice Ginsburg, then, the Top Ten Percent Plan is not truly a "race neutral" program. This claim acknowledges that ostensibly race-neutral admissions practices have likely been so labeled to achieve diversity in the wake of court decisions invalidating explicitly race-conscious methods.[78] This claim, however, complicates the judicial landscape moving forward. On the one hand, her pronouncement is designed to influence future cases by pointing out the fallacy of the Court attempting to argue race-conscious admissions are unnecessary given the availability of race-neutral alternatives. Consistent with her *Gratz* dissent, this argument is made to advocate for transparent considerations of race in admissions.[79] This argument, however, also has a potential downside. As others have previously written, if the intent behind the Top Ten Percent Plan was always to improve minority enrollment then it should be subject to strict scrutiny rather than rational basis.[80] This claim seems somewhat crazy-making when one considers cases where the Court has ignored evidence of disparate racial impact for constitutional claims because the government actions or relevant statutory language were facially neutral and the Court was not willing to infer a discriminatory purpose.[81] In the future, however, critics are likely to cite to Justice Ginsburg's dissent as a reason to interrogate admissions plans based on their presumed improper purpose rather than their facial neutrality.[82]

The fact that one's argument may be coopted for a purpose one does not intend is not necessarily a reason to avoid speaking one's truth. With regard to Justice Ginsburg, however, it might also have been helpful had she included in the dissent either a more particularized defense of why the Texas plan was sufficiently narrowly tailored, or otherwise addressed the continuing constitutionality of race-conscious decision-making in this area. *Grutter* itself was a Justice O'Connor opinion that borrowed the diversity rationale from *Bakke* and premised the importance of diversity, in part on its importance to business and military interests.[83] It would have been much more useful to future cases, if Justice Ginsburg had spent some time describing the forces that make race-conscious admissions necessary and why these programs remain consistent with the goals of equal protection.

Had she been so inclined, Justice Ginsburg could have also pointed out for the Court that not only is it hard to separate race from the Texas Ten Percent Plan, in light of residential segregation and thus school segregation in Texas (as well as most other cities and towns in the United States), but it is hard to separate race and the consequences of our social structure of race from the lives of many people of color, which in turn makes it impossible to evaluate the application of any student or any person's life without taking race into account. As Professor Neil Gotanda once explained in his seminal article, *A Critique of "Our Constitution Is Colorbind"*: "[A]ny revised approach to race and the Constitution must explicitly recognize that race is not a simple, unitary phenomenon. Rather … race is a unique social formation with its own meanings, understandings, discourses, and interpretive frameworks. As a socially constructed category with multiple meanings, race cannot be easily isolated from lived social experience."[84]

---

77 *Id.*

78 For example, the Top Ten Percent plan was formed in the wake of Hopwood v. Texas, 78 F.3d 932 (5th Cir. 1996), which struck down race-conscious admissions in the Fifth Circuit. *See* Kim Forde Mazrui, *The Constitutional Implications of Race-Neutral Affirmative Action*, 88 GEO. L.J. 2331, 2232–33 (2000).

79 Like Justice Ginsburg, others have argued that the more formulaic consideration of race at issue in *Gratz* was superior to the individualized review approved in *Grutter*. Ian Ayres & Sydney Foster, *Don't Tell, Don't Ask: Narrow Tailoring After* Grutter *and* Gratz, 85 TEX. L. REV. 517, 519–20 (2007).

80 *See* Brian Fitzpatrick, *Can Michigan Universities Use Proxies for Race After the Ban on Racial Preferences?*, 13 MICH. J. OF RACE AND L. 277 (2007); Mazrui, *supra* note 77, at 2388 ("[T]he use of race-neutral classifications as a proxy for racial minorities as a proxy for diversity would also involve a discriminatory purpose").

81 *See, e.g.*, Washington v. Davis, 426 U.S. 229 (1976); McCleskey v. Kemp, 481 U.S. 279 (1987).

82 *See, e.g.*, Ilya Somin, VOLOKH CONSPIRACY (June 24, 2013, 12:41 PM), Fisher, *the Texas Ten Percent Plan, and "Race-Neutral" Alternatives to Affirmative Action*, http://www.volokh.com/2013/06/24/fisher-the-texas-ten-percent-plan-and-race-neutral-alternatives-to-affirmative-action/.

83 Grutter v. Bollinger, 539 U.S. 306, 308 (2003).

84 Gotanda, *supra* note 68, at 63.

Justice Thomas: concurring through the lens of (contested) history

Unlike Justice Ginsberg's dissent, Justice Thomas's concurrence provides a detailed account of how race-based affirmative action should be reconciled with our Fourteenth Amendment equality mandate. He concurs in the judgment because he agrees that the Fifth Circuit incorrectly applied strict scrutiny, but writes separately to assert race-based affirmative action is categorically unconstitutional. Most of his opinion, however, centers on justifying the overturning of *Grutter*. Justice Thomas believes very few governmental considerations of race should withstand judicial review. He would support the use of racial classification to support "pressing public necessity."[85] He states this standard was met by the national security concerns at stake in *Korematsu*—concerns that have now been largely debunked. Per *Richmond v. Croson*, he also endorses race considerations to remedy past discrimination where there is a strong basis in evidence supporting the need of the program.[86] This standard, however, is unlikely to be met without specific proof of continuing discrimination being carried out by an identifiable actor. Given his beliefs about the very limited ways the State can or should consider race, Justice Thomas argues then that *Grutter* radically departs from an acceptable standard.

Justice Thomas expands his attack on *Grutter* through comparisons to other cases and circumstances where he believes race has been improperly considered. His analogies, however, were somewhat controversial. He first attacks the concept of the diversity rationale itself, by citing to *Brown v. Board of Education* for the proposition that "the argument that education benefits justify racial discrimination was advanced in support of racial segregation in the 1950's ..."[87] He then goes on to compare contemporary supporters of affirmative action with segregationists and claims that their specific justifications—claims related to creating leaders, improving interracial relations, and understanding such practices as temporary—are substantially congruent.[88] He makes a final historical analogy when he argues the near impossibility of discerning when race-based decisions help or hurt minorities. To his mind, affirmative action advocates who claim such programs involve so-called benign considerations of race are in league, historically-speaking, with slave-holders and segregationists who claimed racial segregation was beneficial for Black children.[89] He then articulates a modern example of the harm such programs produce for minorities by citing to studies of "mismatch"—negative consequences and stigma produced from underprepared minority students being admitted into elite institutions.[90] For many, Justice Thomas's concurring opinion was ahistorical, misleading, and rife with contradictions. Indeed, his opinion was so filled with contradictions that there are too many to discuss in this short chapter, but we highlight just a few examples of his inconsistencies.

First, even as he compared the arguments of segregationists to the supporters of affirmative action, he simultaneously referenced research concerning the mismatch theory, a theory that posits that Blacks and Latinos would perform better in college and beyond if they went to schools for which their scores indicated they would be better matched. Justice Thomas and other proponents never raise any concerns about "mismatched" White students under this theory.[91] Moreover, they fail to acknowledge that advocating mismatch theory too involves discrimination. It is discrimination for which Justice Thomas draws no comparisons to the actions

85 Fisher v. Univ. of Texas at Austin, 133 S. Ct. 2411, 2423 (2013) (Thomas, J., concurring) (quoting Korematsu v. U.S., 323 U.S. 214, 216 (1944)).

86 *Id.* at 2423.

87 *Fisher*, 133 S. Ct. at 2424 (Thomas, J., concurring).

88 *Id.* at 2426.

89 *Id.*

90 *Id.* at 2431–32.

91 *See generally* Richard Sander, *A Systemic Analysis of Affirmative Action in American Law Schools*, 57 Stan. L. Rev. 367 (2004). Within legal academia, Sander's theory has been significantly criticized. *See, e.g.*, Ian Ayres & Richard Brooks, *Does Affirmative Action Reduce the Number of Black Lawyers*, 57 Stan. L. Rev. 1807 (2005) (refuting Sander's claim that mismatch, which is fueled by affirmative action, leads to less Black lawyers); David Wilkins, *A Systematic Response to Systematic Disadvantage: A Response to Sander*, 57 Stan. L. Rev. 1915 (2005). Additionally, there are other university admissions policies, such as legacy programs that favor the children of alumni, which create types of advantage for applicants that go largely uncontested by the Court. Based purely on the racially disproportionate numbers of Whites who have attended college throughout U.S. history—numbers themselves influenced by opportunities being foreclosed to minorities until quite recently—the legacy privilege confers a benefit that is racialized without ever being considered in this way.

of segregationists, even where they would be equally germane, since proponents support mismatch theory precisely because they deem the type of discrimination it performs to be "best" for minorities.

Second, Justice Thomas's declarations in his concurring opinion failed to account for the realities of race even as he has previously employed them in opinions and his own writings such as his autobiography. For instance, in his *Fisher* concurrence, Justice Thomas proclaimed, just as he did in *Grutter*, that "[t]here is no principled distinction between the University's assertion that diversity yields educational benefits and the segregationists' assertion that segregation yielded those same benefits."[92] Yet, years before during a conference on *Missouri v. Jenkins*, Justice Thomas once made a statement that seems to reveal that he at least intuitively realizes the distinctions between the two. He announced to his colleagues: "I am the only one at this table who attended a segregated school."[93] In fact, of course, he was not the only one of the justices to have attended segregated schools, because all or nearly all of his colleagues at the time had attended all-White schools, which, too, are segregated. The fact of the matter is that intuitively, Justice Thomas understood that his experience—his type of segregation—was not the same as his colleagues' because of the unequal resources and the stigma that attached to such inequities. Indeed, the next comments by Justice Thomas demonstrated as much, for he continued:

> And the problem with segregation was not that we didn't have white people in our class. The problem was that we didn't have equal facilities. We didn't have heating, we didn't have books, and we had rickety chairs. All society owed us [were] equal resources and an equal opportunity to make something of ourselves. … The evil of segregation was that black students had inferior facilities, not that they were denied the chance to go to school with white students. … All my classmates and I wanted … was the choice to attend a mostly black school or mostly white school, and to have the same resources in whatever school we chose.[94]

This point, or even this sentiment, is arguably the most significant missed opportunity of all in the *Fisher* opinions: the missed opportunity to link the segregation and discrimination that Justice Thomas experienced with the segregation and discrimination that Heman Sweatt, whose grandfather was a slave, had experienced before him when he fought to gain admission to the University of Texas Law School to the very different, but still sad discrimination that so many students of color as well as White students are experiencing today. As the Sweatt family highlighted in its amicus brief: "Public schools in Texas's major cities are even more highly segregated [today]. In 2011–12, only 8.1% of all students in the 279-school Houston Independent School District were white. At Jack Yates High School, from which Heman Sweatt graduated, only 6 of the 1,179 students that year—or 0.5%—were white, and 91.7% were African American."[95]

The family further explained that such racial segregation in public schools is not what the Court envisioned when it asserted in *Sweatt v. Painter* that "that education 'cannot be effective in isolation from the individuals and institutions with which the law interacts'; it 'cannot be removed from the interplay of ideas and exchange of views with which the law is concerned.'"[96] Such interplay and exchange, the Sweatt family maintained, requires consideration, not avoidance of race, and such considerations of race, they explained, are distinct from the considerations of race that nearly prevented Heman Sweatt from obtaining admission to the University of Texas Law School in 1950. For, "[s]tigma attaches not when one is recognized as a member of a racial or ethnic group; stigma attaches when one is seen as nothing more."[97]

Clearly, Justice Thomas believes racial classifications are never benign and that history is relevant to exposing the dangers of state considerations of race in education. The problem is that he ignores his personal history, and uses history more generally to suggest only that justifications for considering race that were once advanced by segregationists share some commonality with the arguments of proponents of affirmative

92 *Fisher*, 133 S. Ct. at 2428 (Thomas, J., concurring).

93 Jeffrey Rosen, *Moving On*, New Yorker, Apr. 29 & May 6, 1996, at 66, available at http://archives.newyorker.com/?i=1996–04–29#folio=066.

94 *Id.*

95 Brief of the Family of Heman Sweatt as *Amicus Curiae* in Support of Respondents, at 30.

96 *Id.* at.17 (quoting Sweatt v. Painter, 339 U.S. 629, 634 (1950)).

97 *Id.* at 37.

action. Unlike the Sweat family, he sees no meaningful difference in using race as a tool for inclusion or to segregate, despite the historical significance of the Fourteenth Amendment's intended purpose of integrating freed slaves into society. Also absent from his analysis are any references to generations of institutional racialized inequalities—inequalities not likely remediable with either of the race-conscious standards Justice Thomas claims are acceptable under precedent. For example, scholars have described the dangers of only regarding racial inequality as produced through the willful actions of self-motivated individuals, rather than considering the "historical-structural, state-based account."[98] Specifically, they argue, "As this historical narrative suggests, federal social policies have combined with White control of labor markets to promote White accumulation of economic advantages while contributing to Black disaccumulation through segregation and disinvestment."[99] This history of racialized distribution of resources continues to create material deficits in the lives of minorities, especially Blacks.[100] Given his penchant for connecting present considerations of race to the past, the question the proponents of affirmative actions should pose to Justice Thomas is why is it unconstitutional for the state to more broadly consider race-conscious remedies, today, where history reveals longstanding, race-conscious origins to the problems?

The Viability of Race-based Affirmative Action Moving Forward

In economic theory, an opportunity loss is the value of a lost chance or profit foregone through actions taken that did not permit it to be realized. Similarly, with *Fisher*, the opinions resulted in lost opportunities arising from the Court's failure to resolve critical questions relevant to the future of race-based affirmative action in education. A number of these questions—such as the resolution of jurisdictional issues, what constitutes a critical mass for diversity purposes, and whether plans such as the Top Ten Percent plan will continue to be treated as race-neutral moving forward—may be litigated in future cases. As for the remand in the *Fisher* case, the Fifth Circuit Court of Appeals kept the case rather than returning it to the district court. In a 3–1 decision, the court once again affirmed the lower court's ruling, and found that Texas' race-conscious admissions plan was constitutional even under the stricter form of review directed by the U.S. Supreme Court. Relying heavily on the facts that Texas' admission plan considers race as part of a holistic approach and that diversity cannot be achieved without this consideration, Circuit Judge Higginbotham wrote for the court:

> Yet the backdrop of our efforts here includes the reality that accepting as permissible policies whose purpose is to achieve a desired racial effect taxes the line between quotas and holistic use of race towards a critical mass. We have hewed this line here, persuaded by UT Austin from this record of its necessary use of race in a holistic process and the want of workable alternatives that would not require even greater use of race, faithful to the content given to it by the Supreme Court. To reject the UT Austin plan is to confound developing principles of neutral affirmative action, looking away from *Bakke* and *Grutter*, leaving them in uniform but without command—due only a courtesy salute in passing.[101]

98 Michael K. Brown & David Wellman, *Embedding the Color Line: The Accumulation and the Disaccumulation of Opportunity in Post-Civil Rights America*, 2 DuBois Review 187, 189 (2005); John A. Powell, Racing to Justice: Transforming Our Conceptions of Self and Other to Build an Inclusive Society 81 (2013) ("Privilege is distributed and mediated through structures, language, power and institutions that always outrun the control of any given individual.").

99 Brown & Wellman, *supra* note 97, at 201. *See also* William Julius Wilson, *Structural and Cultural Forces that Contribute to Racial Inequality*, *in* More than Just Race: Being Black and Poor in the Inner City 1–24, 17 (2009) ("One of the effects of living in racially segregated neighborhoods is exposure to group-specific, cultural traits … that emerged form patterns of racial exclusion and that may not be conducive to factors that facilitate social mobility"); Thomas W. Mitchell, *Destabilizing the Normalization of Rural Black Land Loss: A Critical Role for Legal Empiricism*, 2005 Wis. L. Rev. 557 (tracking government's differential financial treatment across race of rural southern landowners and the high resulting levels of black land loss).

100 *See, e.g.*, Barnes, Chemerinsky & Jones, *supra* note 7, at 981–92 (detailing racial gaps in income, wealth accumulation, home ownership, educational attainment, and treatment within the criminal justice system).

101 Fisher v. Texas, No. 09–50822, *43 (5th Cir. Jul. 15, 2014).

The Fifth Circuit's new opinion, however, has only set the stage for a return of this case to the U.S. Supreme Court. Upon its return, it is likely that the conservative wing of the Court will call for *Grutter* to be overruled. Our hope for the Supreme Court or any court considering such cases, however, is that they will come to grips with the myriad ways that race shapes opportunities and outcomes in American life. To do so, courts will need to do much more than merely question whether racial classifications may operate in a manner that is benign. Instead, courts will have to concern themselves in a more robust way than they previously have with the societal deficits of those who have been marked by minority racial status and how these deficits are reproduced through institutional and structural, rather than merely individual decisions. With regard to expanding the scope of its analysis, it means courts will need to pay closer attention to population demographics, statistics reflecting the continuing consequences of racial segregation in America, and how belonging to a minority racial group creates challenges relevant for deciding the merits of distributing opportunity. Neither *Fisher*, *Schuette*, nor *Shelby County v. Holder*[102]—another recent case but in the voting rights area, where the Court seems to underestimate the influence of America's history of racism on contemporary life—provide reasons for proponents to hope that affirmative action programs will survive moving forward. Real change will only occur when the terms of the debate shift, likely through appointments that disrupt the Supreme Court's current conservative majority, in a manner that allows for interpretations of equality under the Fourteenth Amendment that do not require dissimilar life circumstances to be treated as if they are the same. While this may contradict conservative commitments to "colorblindness," we believe the following concept of that term is preferred:

> I do not even want to insist that the ideal government would at all times and at all places be entirely blind to color ... What is needed, rather, is the development of a better grammar of race, a way through which we can at once take account of it and not punish it.[103]

---

102 Shelby Cnty., Ala. v. Holder, 133 S. Ct. 2612 (2013).

103 Stephen L. Carter, Reflections of an Affirmative Action Baby 227–28 (1991).

Chapter 6
The Troubled Adolescence of City of Boerne v. Flores

William D. Araiza

City of Boerne v. Flores,[1] the case enunciating the modern standard governing Congress's power to enforce the Fourteenth Amendment,[2] turned 16 in 2013. As with many 16-year-olds, it is unsettled. In a way roughly akin to a child's sometimes-painful development of a distinct personality, early consensus about *Boerne*'s "congruence and proportionality" standard[3] gave way to conflicts about its proper application. Until recently, though, this disagreement was outweighed by a basic template: legislation enforcing rights the Court itself viewed as fundamental would satisfy that test, as would legislation enforcing the equality rights of groups the Court itself had held merited heightened judicial protection. Regardless of other disagreements, during *Boerne*'s first decade one could confidently predict a Court majority for such results.

No more. Starting in 2009 with the modern Court's first abortive encounter with the Voting Rights Act (VRA),[4] and continuing three years later with its invalidation of part of the Family and Medical Leave Act (FMLA),[5] and the year after with its strike down of the VRA's pre-clearance coverage provisions,[6] enforcement legislation benefitting suspect classes and fundamental rights has been susceptible to judicial strike-down. The VRA and FMLA cases turn on different aspects of the congruence and proportionality test.[7] In the VRA cases, the Court first doubted, and then outright found lacking, a factual predicate of pervasive racial discrimination in voting justifying the sovereignty burdens the VRA imposed on a select group of states. In the FMLA case, a plurality of the Court was simply unconvinced that the statute's self-care provision effectively deterred sex discrimination, the law's avowed aim.

The Court's doubts about these laws' factual and policy bases reflect a pattern that will likely recur with increasing frequency. Stubborn discrimination, or discrimination that takes subtler forms, will prod Congress to enact, respectively, stronger or more indirect remedies that will test the Court's willingness to defer to Congress's judgments about their need or effectiveness. At the same time, as antidiscrimination laws successfully suppress the most obvious instances of the targeted discrimination, challengers will continue arguing, as they argued with the VRA, that those laws have succeeded so completely that they have become unnecessary, and thus unconstitutional. These challenges will force the Court to decide how much latitude to accord congressional policy judgments about the need for a particular enforcement statute.

These new ambiguities have joined older ones lurking beneath the surface of the Court's seemingly predictable applications of *Boerne*. Most notably, the Court has mistaken its own institutionally limited

1 521 U.S. 507 (1997).

2 U.S. Const. amend. XIV§ 5 ("The Congress shall have power to enforce, by appropriate legislation, the provisions of this article [of amendment].").

3 The standard requires enforcement legislation to be "congruent and proportional" to the injury sought to be prevented or remedied. *See Boerne*, 521 U.S. at 520. The test has been understood to authorize Congress at least some latitude to enact prophylactic legislation that goes beyond providing remedies for actual constitutional violations. *See, e.g.*, Kimel v. Bd. of Regents, 528 U.S. 62, 88 (2000).

4 Northwest Austin Mun. Util. Dist. No. 1 v. Holder, 557 U.S. 193 (2009). For convenience, references to the VRA should be understood as limited to that statute's preclearance provisions, unless the context clearly indicates otherwise.

5 Coleman v. Court of Appeals of Maryland, 132 S.Ct. 1327 (2012).

6 Shelby County v. Holder, 133 S.Ct. 2612 (2013).

7 There remains some ambiguity about the applicability of the congruence and proportionality test to the VRA, given the statute's foundation in both the Fourteenth and the Fifteenth Amendments. In *NAMUDNO* the Court, as part of its avoidance of the constitutional issue, expressly refrained from deciding the standard of review governing the VRA's constitutionality. *See* 557 U.S. at 204. In a cryptic footnote, the *Shelby County* Court observed that *NAMUDNO* "guides our review under both [the Fourteenth and the Fifteenth] Amendments." 133 S.Ct. at 2622.

application of the Equal Protection Clause for the actual constitutional standard against which enforcement legislation should be tested for congruence and proportionality. For example, in *Board of Trustees v. Garrett*,[8] the Court considered a challenge to enforcement legislation benefitting disabled persons, a group it had previously deemed a non-suspect class. The rough approximation of its jurisprudence noted earlier predicts that the Court would strike such legislation down—as indeed it did. However, in *Garrett* the issue was complicated by the ambiguous constitutional status of that earlier suspect class determination. *Garrett*'s response to this complexity was simply to deny it.

That denial no longer suffices. The tension between understanding suspect class decisions as true constitutional interpretations and as applications of sub-constitutional decisional heuristics will continue bubbling up. Emerging identity groups will continue to raise equality claims that, because of their political, doctrinal, or practical complexities, the Court will be tempted to vindicate on narrow grounds, without adding to the now-calcified list of official suspect classes. Those groups will also continue advocating for statutory remedies, including enforcement legislation. Judicial review of that legislation will place the Court in the same situation it found itself in in *Garrett*. If the Court continues to deny the contradiction *Garrett* papered over, its enforcement power decisions will become ever-less predictable and credible.

The Court's 2013 decision in *United States v. Windsor*,[9] striking down Section 3 of the Defense of Marriage Act (DOMA), exacerbates this problem. *Windsor* applied an unusual methodology that ignores the standard equal protection tools underlying the Court's application of the congruence and proportionality test. It thus raises a fundamental challenge to Enforcement Clause doctrine. To the extent the Court employs *Windsor*'s method in future equal protection cases, this challenge will only grow.

Thus, the congruence and proportionality standard faces several difficult years. This chapter examines whether, like most adolescents, it will grow out of that troubled period into a mature adulthood or remain mired in teenage awkwardness. Part I begins this examination by exploring the early history of the standard, from its inception in *Boerne* to *Tennessee v. Lane*,[10] the 2004 case that, in retrospect, marked the close of the doctrine's first phase. Part II picks up the story. It begins by explaining how the doctrine's first phase has set the Court on a collision course with legislation addressing emerging groups' equality claims. It then considers the Court's confrontations with the VRA and the FMLA's self-care provision. It explains how these cases pose an additional challenge for the Court, one traceable to the doctrine's imperative that the Court second-guess Congress's policymaking. Part III considers how the Court can resolve these challenges, consistent with *Boerne*'s judicial supremacy foundation. Part IV concludes by speculating on the Court's likely path.

Part I Early Growing Pains

Boerne commanded agreement across the Court's ideological spectrum.[11] As a statement of judicial supremacy in matters of constitutional interpretation, it appealed to both wings of the Court, each of which had reasons to favor such supremacy when it suited their other goals. Soon, however, the consensus began to crack.

The First Applications

In the first set of post-*Boerne* cases the disagreement turned on whether Congress had identified sufficient unconstitutional conduct to justify the enforcement statute. In *Florida Prepaid Postsecondary Education*

---

8 531 U.S. 356 (2001).

9 133 S.Ct. 2675 (2013).

10 541 U.S. 509 (2004).

11 Six justices joined the majority opinion. In addition, Justice O'Connor would have joined the majority had she agreed with the Court's resolution of the underlying Fourteenth Amendment issue, and Justice Breyer agreed with at least some of her views. Only Justice Souter expressed no opinion on the enforcement power question. No justice expressed active opposition.

Expense Board v. College Savings Bank,[12] a five-justice majority struck down an enforcement statute abrogating state sovereign immunity from patent infringement suits. The Court concluded that Congress had amassed an insufficient record of state government patent violations depriving patent holders of their property.[13] One year later, in *Kimel v. Florida Board of Regents,*[14] the Court rejected the Age Discrimination in Employment Act (ADEA) as legislation enforcing elderly employees' equal protection rights. The same five justices that formed the *Florida Prepaid* majority similarly concluded in *Kimel* that Congress lacked an adequate record of unconstitutional age-based employment discrimination by states.

In addition to finding the record inadequate, *Kimel* introduced another concept that became crucial in later enforcement power cases. Before examining Congress's record for evidence of unconstitutional state action, the Court canvassed its own age discrimination jurisprudence. It noted that age discrimination merited the lowest level of equal protection scrutiny—as a non-suspect classification, it received only rational basis review. This lower level of judicial protection provided what Justice O'Connor called "the backdrop"[15] for the Court's evaluation of Congress's evidence. Essentially, the Court's deferential attitude toward age discrimination raised the hurdle Congress faced in justifying the ADEA as enforcement legislation. As Justice O'Connor explained, an enforcement statute was less likely to be congruent and proportional to the underlying constitutional violations it targeted when it targeted a constitutionally inconsequential problem. Since, according to the Court, age discrimination was so rarely unconstitutional, for Congress to demonstrate a record of *unconstitutional* age discrimination it had to show not just a pattern of age discrimination *per se*, but a pattern so irrational or infused with animus that those examples would have failed even rational basis review.

The *Garrett* Synthesis

These two doctrinal strands—the requirement that Congress demonstrate a pattern of unconstitutional conduct, and the Court's use of its own equal protection doctrine as the benchmark for identifying that conduct—combined in the next case to establish the Court's post-*Boerne* template. In *Board of Trustees v. Garrett*[16] the same five-justice majority from *Florida Prepaid* and *Kimel* rejected the enforcement power foundation of the employment provisions of the Americans With Disabilities Act (ADA). At first blush, *Garrett* maps neatly onto *Kimel*. In both cases, the Court considered discrimination to which the Court accorded only rational basis scrutiny, and concluded that Congress had not demonstrated a pattern of discrimination that would fail such review.

However, closer inspection reveals that *Garrett* presented the Court with a more difficult problem. First, in enacting the ADA, Congress amassed a far more extensive record than that supporting the ADEA. Second, the Court's disability discrimination jurisprudence was more ambivalent than its age discrimination counterpart. Sixteen years before *Garrett*, in *City of Cleburne v. Cleburne Living Center*[17] the Court had struck down an instance of disability discrimination. However, determining *Cleburne*'s relevance to the ADA's congruence and proportionality itself posed a difficult problem, because of *Cleburne*'s own ambiguity. On the one hand, *Cleburne* held that disability discrimination merited only rational basis review, thus suggesting that *Cleburne*'s facts constituted the rare example of state conduct so arbitrary or infused with animus that it failed even that low level of scrutiny. On the other hand, the Court's ostensible rational-basis review looked suspiciously strict: the Court imposed evidentiary burdens on the government defendant, and reviewed its justifications with a skepticism inconsistent with traditional rational basis scrutiny. Further complicating the picture, *Cleburne*'s rationale for denying the intellectually disabled suspect class status focused heavily on

12 527 U.S. 627 (1999).

13 The statute invalidated in *Florida Prepaid* sought to enforce a Due Process Clause right. However, as the text explains, the Court's analysis is relevant for congressional power to enforce equal protection.

14 528 U.S. 62 (2000).

15 528 U.S. at 86.

16 531 U.S. 356 (2001).

17 473 U.S. 432 (1985).

the practical difficulties lower courts would face if the Court granted that status, rather than on the actual likelihood that disability discrimination posed a serious risk of unconstitutionality.

Garrett's response to these two complications revealed the depth to which the dominant five-justice coalition had committed itself to a strict application of the congruence and proportionality standard. First, the Court was exceptionally grudging in its review of Congress's factual record. Most notably, it restricted the range of relevant evidence to instances of employment discrimination by state governments that a court would likely judge unconstitutional. While at first blush reasonable, these limitations betrayed the majority's insistence on limiting the effective scope of the enforcement power. For example, the Court justified its refusal to consider discrimination committed by sub-units of state governments on the ground that such sub-units are not protected by Eleventh Amendment immunity. But this explanation conflates the scope of Eleventh Amendment immunity with the scope of Congress's power to enforce the Fourteenth Amendment; indeed, it also perhaps revealed the Rehnquist Court's real agenda of protecting states' sovereign immunity at any cost.[18] Eleventh Amendment immunity is surely a major factor in considering the *practical* importance of the enforcement power, since that power constitutes Congress's most important regulatory tool allowing it to abrogate state sovereign immunity. But no logically necessary relationship connects the two.

Garrett's other restrictive glosses on Congress's record trigger similar doubts. For example, it insisted that the only relevant evidence consisted of discrimination so severe as to likely be judged unconstitutional if challenged in court. That insistence explicitly linked the fate of enforcement legislation to the Court's own willingness to strike down government action as violating the Equal Protection Clause. This linkage might make sense if the Court's own equal protection doctrine extended to the full scope of the equal protection guarantee. In that case, the Court would simply be reiterating *Boerne*'s insistence on distinguishing between legitimate congressional enforcement of the Fourteenth Amendment and illegitimate congressional interpretation. The problem, however, is that judicial doctrine often stops short of enforcing the full limits of the Fourteenth Amendment. Instead, the Court often—and sometimes explicitly—shrinks from applying the Amendment to its full limits, based on concerns about judicial competence and the appropriate judicial role.

Garrett itself illustrates this dynamic. As noted above, one challenge *Garrett* posed to *Kimel*'s template lay in the fact that the Court had previously sent conflicting signals about the constitutional status of disability discrimination. In *Cleburne*, while the Court held that the disabled receive only rational basis scrutiny, its application of that standard suggested it was actually performing more stringent review. Thus, the core constitutional status of disability discrimination, and with it, how much latitude Congress possessed to combat the problem, remained unclear.

This problem was compounded by a second facet of *Cleburne*. *Cleburne*'s refusal to accord heightened scrutiny to disability classifications stemmed largely from concerns about courts' institutional competence. The *Cleburne* Court worried that courts applying heightened review to disability classifications could not competently distinguish between when differential treatment reflected animus or irrationality and when instead it reflected appropriate judgments about the concededly real differences distinguishing the disabled from mainstream society. It also expressed concern that a decision to grant suspect class status to the disabled would open the floodgates to similar demands from other groups who, according to the Court, occupied a similar social position. These concerns suggest that the Court's decision to apply rational basis review reflected not the true meaning or full extent of the Equal Protection Clause, but rather judicial recognition that courts lacked the capability to fully enforce that provision.

Despite *Cleburne*'s ambiguities, the *Garrett* Court perceived no serious problem citing *Cleburne* as support for its skeptical review of the ADA. It described *Cleburne* as applying standard rational basis scrutiny, and brushed aside any suggestion that *Cleburne*'s institutional competence concerns supported greater congressional latitude to enact enforcement legislation benefitting a group whose constitutional status was ambiguous. Describing the disabled as a group discrimination against which triggered no special level of judicial scrutiny, *Garrett* proceeded to draw a precise analogy between the ADA and the ADEA that the Court had so easily dispatched in *Kimel*.

18 *See, e.g.*, David Getches, *Beyond Indian Law: The Rehnquist Court's Pursuit of State's Rights, Color-Blind Justice and Mainstream Values*, 86 Minn. L. Rev. 267, 320–21 (2001) (finding support for this hypothesis).

Temporary Equilibrium: Applying the *Garrett* Synthesis

The next enforcement power cases confirmed *Garrett*'s lessons, even while reaching the opposite result. First, in *Nevada Dept of Human Resources v. Hibbs*,[19] the Court upheld as valid enforcement legislation the FMLA's family-care leave provisions, which provided employees with uncompensated leave to care for sick relatives. The FMLA suffered from some of the same problems that afflicted the ADA: a somewhat spotty record of state violations of the underlying constitutional right the statute sought to enforce, and findings that were either compiled by a Congress previous to the enacting one or found by a private body, whose conclusions were never translated into formal legislative findings.

Nevertheless, the Court upheld the law, on a 6–3 vote that included two members of the *Florida Prepaid-Kimel-Garrett* majorities. Writing for the Court, Chief Justice Rehnquist stressed the Court's recognition of the importance of the sex equality right the FMLA sought to enforce. As the Chief Justice recognized, the Court had long accorded sex discrimination heightened judicial scrutiny. For him, this fact distinguished the FMLA from both the ADEA and the ADA. As he explained, because the FMLA targeted a right the Court itself had identified as constitutionally significant, Congress faced an easier task in demonstrating the existence of constitutional violations justifying the statute's remedial measures.

The other major case decided during this phase of *Boerne*'s evolution reinforced the doctrinal trend visible since *Kimel*, but also introduced a new element. In *Tennessee v. Lane*,[20] the Court confronted another title of the ADA, addressing public accommodations, in a case brought by two disabled persons who, because of their disabilities, were unable to access part of a state courthouse. Writing for the same *Hibbs* majority (except for Chief Justice Rehnquist, who dissented), Justice Stevens stressed that courts had recognized the constitutional right at issue—the right to access the judicial process—as fundamental.

Justice Stevens's move had two consequences. First, it allowed him to apply *Hibbs*'s statement that enforcement legislation targeting a constitutionally significant right enjoys more deferential scrutiny of its factual foundations. Second, it allowed him to describe this application of the statute as congruent to the underlying right. Indeed, he argued, the fit was tight: the ADA required that owners of public accommodations make "reasonable modifications" to allow disabled access, a mandate that closely tracked the constitutional requirement imposed on states to make their judicial processes accessible.

However, in order to trigger this analysis Justice Stevens had to make two preliminary moves. First, he had to identify the right at issue as the due process right to access the judicial process, rather than disabled persons' equal protection rights. The Court had previously recognized the first of these rights as fundamental; by contrast, *Garrett* had dismissed the latter as constitutionally insignificant. Characterizing the right as the due process right to judicial access cleared the way for Justice Stevens to cite *Hibbs*, not *Garrett* or *Kimel*, as the relevant precedent.

But the focus on that right was not self-evident from the statute. After all, the ADA's public accommodations provisions address public accommodations generally, not courthouses in particular. Thus, in a second move, Justice Stevens characterized the case as considering the enforcement power foundation of the ADA's public accommodations provisions *as applied to courthouse access*. This statutory parsing provoked a sharp retort from Chief Justice Rehnquist, writing for three of the four dissenters. He argued that this move pre-determined the outcome of the congruence and proportionality test, by excising any non-courthouse applications of the statute from the denominator of the proportionality fraction. Indeed, he argued, Justice Stevens' move would always result in a finding that the challenged statute was congruent and proportional, since the statute's sweep would be compared only to applications (here, courthouse access) directly relevant to the case before the court.

One last point about this phase of the congruence and proportionality test's evolution requires notice. Until *Lane*, no justice had expressed disagreement with the congruence and proportionality test, even if the justices regularly disagreed on its application. That consensus cracked in *Lane*, where Justice Scalia wrote a solo dissent abandoning the test. He criticized it as "flabby" and enmeshing the Court in an unseemly

19 538 U.S. 721 (2003).
20 541 U.S. 509 (2004).

review of Congress's "homework,"[21] that is, its fact-finding record. He argued that, with the exception of race, which he described as a central concern of the Fourteenth Amendment's framers, the Enforcement Clause did not give Congress the latitude to do more than prescribe penalties for actual constitutional violations. With that exception, he therefore defected from even theoretical agreement that Congress enjoyed the power to enact prophylactic legislation proscribing constitutionally permissible conduct in order to deter constitutional violations.

Lane closed the first phase of *Boerne*'s evolution. It solidified the apparent rule of thumb in which the level of judicial protection of a right largely determined the result of Enforcement Clause analysis. At the same time, *Lane* revealed the underlying tensions in the justices' understanding of the congruence and proportionality standard, and, indeed, about that standard's basic correctness. After *Lane* the Court did not face a difficult Enforcement Clause issue for several years.[22] When it did, those tensions widened, and threatened even the tentative consensus that had developed up to that point.

Part II Awkward Adolescence

After 16 years, *Boerne*'s doctrinal template faces significant pressure. This Part explains how particular types of enforcement legislation, either already enacted or likely to be enacted soon, challenges that template. It also describes how three recent cases have already widened the cracks in the Court's Enforcement Clause jurisprudence. Taken together, these challenges have seriously unsettled the Court's tentative post-*Boerne* equilibrium.

Emerging Groups and the Suspect Class Problem

The Court's practice of according skeptical review to enforcement legislation benefitting non-suspect classes triggers the critique that it confuses the Court's suspect class jurisprudence with core constitutional law. This critique explains the Court's suspect class jurisprudence as merely a decisional aid that helps it identify equal protection violations within the confines of its limited institutional competence.[23] Thus, it argues that the Court's jurisprudence should not play its current outsized role in Enforcement Clause analysis. Rather, Congress, as the institution best situated to make the value choices equal protection demands, should enjoy significant latitude to conclude that certain types of discrimination are either irrational or based on animus, and thus appropriately targeted by enforcement legislation.[24] The Court's suspect class jurisprudence, while clearly relevant, should provide only a starting point for Enforcement Clause analysis.

The Court has refused to accept this reasoning. Instead, it has largely[25] relied on the benefitted group's suspect class status as a major determinant of enforcement legislation's constitutionality. This juricentric approach to the congruence and proportionality standard has already caused the Court difficulty. Most prominently, the Court in *Garrett* provided only a brief and unconvincing response to the argument that its earlier decision in *Cleburne* effectively acknowledged room for Congress to enact aggressive enforcement legislation targeting disability discrimination.[26]

---

21 *Id.* at 558.

22 In *United States v. Georgia*, 546 U.S. 151 (2006), a unanimous Court agreed that the ADA's public services provisions constituted valid enforcement legislation if the conduct complained of itself violated the Fourteenth Amendment.

23 *See, e.g.*, *Windsor*, 133 S. Ct. at 2716 (Alito, J., dissenting) ("The modern tiers of scrutiny … are a heuristic to help judges determine when classifications have that fair and substantial relation to the object of the legislation" required by equal protection) (internal quotation omitted).

24 For a fuller version of this argument, see William D. Araiza, *New Groups and Old Doctrine: Rethinking Congressional Power to Enforce the Equal Protection Clause*, 37 Fla. St. L. Rev. 451 (2010) (hereafter "New Groups").

25 The qualifier refers to the Court's decisions in *Coleman* and the VRA cases. *See infra*. Part II.

26 *See supra* Part I.

This problem will only grow as the Court confronts equality claims pressed by emerging groups, such as those demarcated by sexual orientation, genetic make-up, or obesity (all groups that either have recently won significant equality legislation or have come close). These groups will likely confront a Supreme Court that is unwilling to grant them suspect or quasi-suspect class status. The reasons for this reticence vary. The Court may believe (as it confessed in *Cleburne*) that suspect class status is too blunt an instrument to judge classifications that may be appropriate in some circumstances but not others. Relatedly, it may believe that some decisions are simply not amenable to the purpose and fit inquiries that flow from a given answer to the suspect class question.[27] Or it may believe (again as *Cleburne* explained) that granting suspect class status to such groups will open the floodgates for analogous groups to demand similar protection. Finally, the answer may simply be that the Court has sworn off creating new suspect classes—not an unreasonable suspicion, given that it last granted such status over 30 years ago, even while finding equal protection violations in several instances of discrimination against an ostensibly non-suspect class.[28]

The Court's treatment of sexual orientation illustrates the problem. The Court has never expressly accorded sexual orientation the status of a suspect or quasi-suspect classification. Yet it has now twice ruled in favor of equality claims raised by gay rights advocates. The first of these victories—the 1996 case of *Romer v. Evans*—featured an opinion that at least partially followed the template of standard equal protection analysis, even if its application of rational basis scrutiny was unusually muscular and even if it featured as an alternative rationale an innovative, if under-theorized, discussion of the law's *per se* violation of equal protection principles. *Romer* did not engage the suspect class question—an omission that is at least arguably legitimate given its decision that the challenged law failed even rational basis review. Nevertheless, its failure even to acknowledge the possibility of such status remains remarkable, and at least something of an innovation in equal protection doctrine.[29]

The Court's second sexual orientation equality case, *United States v. Windsor*, strayed even farther from the standard doctrinal template. Even more than *Romer*, the *Windsor* Court abandoned traditional equal protection review. Like *Romer*, *Windsor* ignored the suspect class question. But *Windsor* failed even to inquire whether the law (Section 3 of DOMA) had a reasonable fit with a legitimate government purpose, instead directly examining Congress's motives in enacting Section 3. If *Romer* and (especially) *Windsor* are any guides, future discussion of sexual orientation at the Supreme Court will feature holistic, *ad hoc* reasoning rather than the rigid, if predictable, path of suspect class (or even "fit") analysis.

If the Court's refusal to explicitly accord heightened scrutiny to sexual orientation classifications comes to characterize its general equal protection treatment of new equality claimants, then it will have trapped itself in a box of its own making once it confronts enforcement legislation benefitting those groups. Under the post-*Boerne* template, a refusal to accord heightened scrutiny would likely undermine the Enforcement Clause foundation of legislation such as the Genetic Information Non-Discrimination Act (GINA) and the proposed Employment Non-Discrimination Act (ENDA) protecting LGBT employees against job discrimination.

Such results would be anomalous. A significant number of lower courts have ruled in favor of victims of sexual orientation discrimination,[30] as has the Supreme Court, now on two occasions. But if the Court remains faithful to its post-*Boerne* template—and, in particular, to *Garrett*'s treatment of *Cleburne*—it will accord substantial weight to its own suspect class determination about the beneficiary group, despite judicial recognition that some sexual orientation discrimination violates the Constitution. Similarly, judicial approval

27 *See, e.g.*, United States v. Windsor, 133 S.Ct. 2675, 2716 (2013) (Alito, J., dissenting) ("Our equal protection framework … is a judicial construct that provides a useful mechanism for analyzing a certain universe of equal protection cases. But that framework is ill suited for use in evaluating the constitutionality of laws based on the traditional understanding of marriage, which fundamentally turn on what marriage is.").

28 *See Cleburne*, 473 U.S. 432 (mentally retarded); Romer v. Evans, 517 U.S. 620 (1996) (gays, lesbians, and bisexuals); Allegheny Pittsburgh Co. v. Webster County, 488 U.S. 336 (1989) (recent purchasers of property); *see also* Dept. of Agriculture v. Moreno, 413 U.S. 528 (1973) ("hippie communes").

29 Cf. Heller v. Doe, 509 U.S. 312 (1993) (acknowledging the argument that the mentally disabled should be a suspect class, but refusing to address it); Richmond v. J.A. Croson Co., 488 U.S. 469 (1989) (considering the argument that race-based affirmative action should receive a lower level of scrutiny than outright racial exclusion); City of Cleburne v. Cleburne Living Center, 473 U.S. 432 (1985) (considering the suspect class status of the mentally retarded).

30 Araiza, "New Groups," *supra* note 24, at 471.

of GINA's constitutionality as enforcement legislation would presumably encounter the same suspect class-based objection, despite the apparently broad political consensus that genetic discrimination is fundamentally unfair and thus violates equal protection's core command.[31]

These problems will only become more intractable if the Court's underlying equal jurisprudence continues to evolve in the direction of *Windsor*'s direct, particularized inquiry into legislative intent that abjures not just suspect class doctrine but even the "fit" analysis that has characterized equal protection review since the end of the *Lochner* era. This dynamic could yield the ironic result that enforcement legislation benefitting a given group could be struck down, even in the face of a broad social consensus condemning such discrimination—and, indeed, even though federal courts themselves had compiled a record striking down such discrimination as violating equal protection's core prohibition on animus-motivated government action. More conceptually, it would create a situation where judicial doctrine the Court has largely abandoned—suspect class analysis—nevertheless played a major role in preventing Congress from enforcing equal protection rights the Court itself had recognized as legitimate and serious. Finally, and perhaps most seriously, it would cement *Garrett*'s mistake of testing enforcement legislation against the wrong legal standard—indeed, a standard that is not itself constitutional law.

The Measurement Problem: Prophylactic Legislation and the Problem of Legislative Success

The Court's three most recent Enforcement Clause cases have posed a separate set of questions, by forcing the Court to make quintessentially policy-type judgments. In *Coleman v. Court of Appeals of Maryland*[32] the Court had to consider whether enforcement legislation employing nuanced methods to combat discrimination was effective enough to be constitutionally valid. In *Northwest Austin Municipal Utility District No. 1 v. Holder* ("*NAMUDNO*")[33] and *Shelby County v. Holder*,[34] the Court had to consider an equally policy-heavy question: whether a previously upheld enforcement statute had so succeeded at eradicating the targeted discrimination that it was no longer necessary, and thus no longer constitutional. These cases pose what can be called "the measurement problem"—that is, the problem inherent in courts basing constitutional decisions on their estimation of a statute's effectiveness. This is a serious problem, distinct from the suspect class problem described above. Like that previous problem, it is likely to recur.

Coleman

In *Coleman* a five-justice majority held that the FMLA's "self-care" provision, which allowed workers unpaid leave to care for the employee's own illnesses, exceeded Congress's enforcement power. Writing for a plurality of four of those justices, Justice Kennedy concluded that the self-care provision was not congruent and proportional to the sex discrimination it ostensibly targeted. The provision's defenders argued that it equalized the burdens male and female employees imposed on their workplaces, by providing a sex-neutral leave benefit that counteracted women's perceived tendency to predominate in taking other types of FMLA leave, in particular, family care leave. Rejecting that argument, Justice Kennedy concluded that the evidence showed that men and women generally took only a few days of self-care leave every year, an amount he stated would not significantly equalize the sex-disparate burden FMLA family-care leave was perceived to impose on employers. Justice Scalia, while agreeing that the self-leave provision exceeded Congress's enforcement power, refused to join the plurality's congruence and proportionality analysis, adhering to his abandonment of that test in *Lane*.

In response, Justice Ginsburg, writing for the dissenters, recounted a detailed history of women's rights advocates seeking to equalize employment opportunities for women by the provision of sex-neutral leave.

31 Araiza, "New Groups," *supra* note 24, at 457–58. Approval of GINA as valid enforcement legislation would also run into the problem of the lack of a clear record of actual discrimination based on genetic make-up. *See, e.g.*, Culbreth v. Wash. Area Metro. Trans. Auth., 2012 WL 959385 (D. Md.) (relying on this objection to reject GINA as enforcement legislation).

32 *Supra* note 4.

33 *Supra* note 5.

34 *Supra* note 6.

She described the self-care provision as a form of double prophylaxis. The FMLA's family-care provisions, she explained, were thought likely to redound to women's detriment, as employers responded to them by discriminating against female employees and applicants on the theory that women were more likely to take such leave. Thus, it was thought, adding to the FMLA a grant of self-leave, which women and men took in equal measure, would mitigate the statute's perceived provision of female-identified job benefits that rendered women less attractive as employees.

NAMUDNO and Shelby County

In *NAMUDNO* and *Shelby County* the Court first came close to confronting the constitutionality of the VRA's pre-clearance provisions and then squarely confronted the issue, striking down the coverage formula on which those provisions rested. Those provisions require certain jurisdictions to obtain prior federal approval for ("preclear") any change to their structure or voting procedures, to ensure that it does not impair minorities' voting rights. The jurisdictions subject to those provisions were identified based on a several-decades-old statutory formula. However, the statute allows jurisdictions to "bail out" of coverage if they demonstrate non-interference with minority voting rights, and also provides for a non-covered jurisdiction to be "bailed-in" if a federal court decides that it has impaired voting rights.

The pre-clearance provisions cut deeply into covered jurisdictions' sovereignty, interposing federal authorities between them and their sovereign functions of structuring themselves and their elections. On the other hand, the VRA was designed to prevent racial discrimination in voting—a combination of the Constitution's most prominent equality rule with perhaps its most important right. The complexity posed by this juxtaposition was exacerbated by the fact that 43 years earlier the Court had upheld the pre-clearance provisions' constitutionality as legislation enforcing the Fifteenth Amendment.[35] In response, the plaintiff jurisdictions argued that the VRA's very success in eradicating racial discrimination in voting rendered it no longer necessary, and hence an unconstitutional intrusion on state sovereignty. Thus, *NAMUDNO* and *Shelby County* posed the question, previously unconsidered in the Court's post-*Boerne* jurisprudence, of when previously appropriate enforcement legislation became obsolescent because of its very success in resolving the problem it originally targeted.

In *NAMUDNO* the Court declined to reach the constitutional question. Nevertheless, it expressed unease about the pre-clearance provisions' sovereignty intrusion in light of the argument that they had largely succeeded in eradicating the targeted discrimination. Four years later, in *Shelby County*, the Court acted on its unease. In a 5–4 vote Chief Justice Roberts, who wrote the *NAMUDNO* majority opinion, struck down the pre-clearance provisions' coverage formula. He argued that the formula, which had not been altered for 40 years, no longer reflected differences between states experiencing serious racial discrimination in voting and states with better voting rights climates. Citing improved minority voting statistics in the covered jurisdictions, he concluded that the coverage formula no longer reflected "current political conditions."[36] In response to the dissent's argument that other data reflected continued differences between covered and non-covered jurisdictions with regard to voting rights, he concluded that, however convincing the evidence might be—a question on which he expressed some exasperation[37]—there did not exist the "pervasive" and "flagrant" discrimination that existed when the VRA was enacted in 1965.

The Complexity of Modern Enforcement Clause Challenges

Coleman and the VRA cases reflect the types of issues the Court will likely face more and more frequently when deciding enforcement power challenges. The FMLA's self-care provision exemplifies a double-prophylaxis

35 Katzenbach v. S. Carolina, 383 U.S. 301 (1966).

36 133 S. Ct. at 2628.

37 *See id.* at 2629 ("The court below and the parties have debated what [the] record shows—they have gone back and forth about whether to compare covered to noncovered jurisdictions as blocks, how to disaggregate the data State by State, how to weigh § 2 cases as evidence of ongoing discrimination, and whether to consider evidence not before Congress, among other issues.").

approach to equality issues. It thus goes beyond both the direct enforcement legislation the Court encountered in cases such as *Kimel* and *Garrett*, and the single prophylactic approach of the FMLA's family-care leave provision upheld in *Hibbs*. The self-care provision posed difficult evidentiary questions—for example, how employers perceived sex-based differentials in employee use of FMLA leave—and evaluative questions—for example, whether the sex parity with which men and women took self-care leave meaningfully counteracted those perceptions.

Measuring the extent to which enforcement legislation addressed the targeted constitutional violation has always constituted an important part of congruence and proportionality review. Indeed, the Court's acknowledgement that stubborn constitutional problems justify aggressive enforcement legislation[38] necessarily requires the Court to review the relationship between the constitutional problem and the legislative remedy. However, more nuanced legislative attempts to deter subtler constitutional violations stretch the Court's authority and expertise to perform that measurement, as compared with the task of evaluating legislation that, like the ADA and the ADEA, straightforwardly attack explicit discrimination.

For its part, the Court's treatment of the VRA highlights the difficulty posed by *Boerne*'s requirement that remedial legislation target an actual problem. As Part I explained, in prior cases reviewing equality-enforcing legislation, the seriousness of the constitutional problem, and thus Congress's latitude in attacking it, posed a question whose answer flowed primarily from the Court's own doctrine. The VRA was enacted to combat racial discrimination, which judicial doctrine has long considered the most serious constitutional equality problem. However, the VRA confronted the Court, for the first time in the *Boerne* era, with legislation that assertedly had corrected the wrong. Thus, the case deviated from the prior template, in which judicial doctrine largely determined the allowable breadth of the statute. Rather, *NAMUDNO* and *Shelby County*, like *Coleman*, required the Court to engage in both empirical measurements and judgments about those measurements' policy implications. Those types of judgments quite arguably exceed the legitimate scope of judicial resolution.

Part III A Path to Maturity

The issues discussed above illustrate the challenges facing the Court in applying the congruence and proportionality test to equality-enforcing legislation. First, emerging groups' equality claims will strain the Court's application of that test, at least to the extent it continues to ground its analysis in the benefitted group's suspect class status. Second, the FMLA's self-care provision demonstrates the difficulty posed by prophylactic legislation that either attacks discrimination indirectly or attacks subtler forms of discrimination. Finally, the Court's doubts about the continued need for the VRA's pre-clearance provisions reflect the problem posed when once-necessary enforcement legislation is claimed to have succeeded, and thus to have obsolesced itself.

Each of these issues poses different problems for Enforcement Clause doctrine. The first highlights the difficulties caused when the Court bases that doctrine on a rigid understanding of its underlying equal protection jurisprudence—a jurisprudence that *Cleburne*, *Romer*, and *Windsor* reveal as much more nuanced than the Court's Enforcement Clause cases suggest. The second and third issues illustrate the challenge inherent when courts review legislative policymaking. The FMLA example requires judicial measurement of the legitimate breadth of enforcement legislation, while the VRA requires judicial measurement of a statute's success. Both tasks strain courts' competence and authority. All of these issues transcend the cases and illustrations discussed above. They will continue to pose difficulties for the Court as it struggles to apply *Boerne*'s judicial supremacy principle to both new types of enforcement legislation and legislation addressing an evolving social landscape.

These issues highlight the need for the Court to apply the congruence and proportionality standard with increased nuance and understanding of the proper judicial and congressional roles in enforcing the Fourteenth Amendment's broad but vague guarantees. The rigidity of the Court's Enforcement Clause doctrine requires the Court to confront its understanding of the constitutional status of its suspect class determinations. The measurement problems illustrated by *Coleman* and the VRA cases require the Court to assess Congress's and

38 *See, e.g.*, *Kimel*, 528 U.S. at 88 ("Difficult and intractable problems often require powerful remedies").

its own expertise and authority to make those measurements, and the Court's appropriate role in reviewing Congress's determinations.

Doctrine's Proper Role

The Court's Confusion

A fundamental problem with the Court's application of the congruence and proportionality test has been the Court's insistence on treating its own equal protection doctrine—in particular, the suspect class status of the group benefitted by the legislation—as largely determinative of equal protection's requirements. *Garrett* and similar cases illustrate how severely this approach limits Congress's role in enforcing the Equal Protection Clause.

Despite its limiting effect, the Court's approach might make sense if its suspect class jurisprudence reflected actual constitutional meaning. In that case, the Court would simply be implementing *Boerne*'s insistence that Congress respect constitutional meaning when it acts to enforce that meaning. But that jurisprudence does not reflect actual constitutional meaning. The Court developed suspect class analysis as part of its post-1937 repudiation of the close judicial scrutiny the *Lochner*-era Court accorded much economic and social legislation. Its response to that era—to presume the constitutionality of most legislation produced by a fair and open legislative process—made sense for a Court that was seeking a more modest role appropriate for its non-elected and non-policymaking role. Nevertheless, this approach to judicial review reflects equal protection's underlying requirements only indirectly, through the prism of political process analysis. Such analysis does not, and does not purport to, reveal equal protection's actual meaning.[39]

Thus, the Court commits a fundamental error when it over-relies on suspect class analysis to determine how carefully to review enforcement legislation. Beyond the bare fact of its mistakenness, this approach also exacts practical costs. Most notably, it significantly reduces Congress's latitude to participate with the Court in the process of constitutional construction by perceiving and attacking irrational or animus-based discrimination against groups that, for prudential reasons, the Court has declined to label suspect classes. As revealed most clearly by *Garrett*, the Court's refusal to accord that status leads it to react skeptically to any congressional attempt to remedy discrimination against that group. The prospect of the Court greeting ENDA with similar skepticism is troubling for anyone concerned with doctrinal coherence. Such skepticism would present the bizarre picture of judicial skepticism about a congressional attempt to remedy the same type of discrimination the Court itself has twice described as violating a core constitutional rule—all because of the Court's prudential decision not to consider whether sexual orientation is a suspect class.

The modern Court's abandonment of suspect class analysis and history of denying suspect class status for prudential reasons, when combined with its insistence on tying judicial scrutiny of enforcement legislation to a group's suspect class status, creates a formula for stasis. Under this approach, the Court's limited ability to protect the full measure of equal protection's guarantee cabins Congress's latitude to largely the same degree. It locks Congress into the same institutionally limited perspective on equal protection that marks the Court's suspect class jurisprudence. This approach disrespects any comparative expertise and authority Congress may possess to perceive and counteract irrational or animus-based discrimination.[40]

More conceptually, the Court's linkage of suspect class status to congressional enforcement power leads the Court to test the constitutionality of enforcement legislation against the wrong standard—the Court's own prudence and competence-grounded suspect class jurisprudence, rather than equal protection's underlying command. As the Court has noted, that command is exceptionally broad, embracing all classifications[41] and any

39 *See supra* note 23.

40 *See* William D. Araiza, *Deference to Congressional Factfinding in Rights-Enforcing and Rights-Limiting Legislation*, 88 N.Y.U. L. Rev. 878, 887–93 (2013) (hereafter "Deference") (explaining the expertise and authority-based justifications for deference to congressional fact-findings in enforcement legislation).

41 Indeed, the Court has interpreted the clause to guard against discrimination based not only on group membership, but also based on a so-called "class of one" theory: Village of Willowbrook v. Olech, 528 U.S. 562 (2000).

benefit or burden the government bestows or imposes.[42] The sheer breadth of that guarantee, when combined with the logical emptiness of the requirement of equal treatment,[43] led the Court—quite reasonably—to decide equal protection claims based on the mediating principles reflected in *Carolene*'s tiered scrutiny structure. But by tying Congress's enforcement authority to that same structure, the Court has mistaken *Carolene*'s shadow of equal protection law for the real thing.

The Way Forward

At first blush, fixing this problem appears straightforward. The Court simply has to recognize that its institutionally limited application of the Equal Protection Clause does not fully exhaust its meaning, and acknowledge that sometimes Congress enjoys superior expertise and/or authority to instantiate the Court's own expansive interpretation of the Clause. But this seemingly simple response raises a host of follow-on issues. Most notably, the Court's expansive understanding of the Clause's scope means that a significant congressional role in enforcing it beyond judicial applications could lack a stopping point. If equal protection's fundamental requirement is that government not classify arbitrarily or with malice, then allowing congressional enforcement power to extend beyond the Court's *Carolene*-based decisional rules could allow Congress exceptional latitude to enact a broad variety of enforcement legislation. Such a result risks granting Congress an unreviewable enforcement power that could easily become a *de facto* power to interpret the Constitution.

These concerns highlight the imperative for conceptually sound yet practicably workable limits on Congress's enforcement authority. Setting those limits requires the Court to both demarcate the proper sphere of that authority, and apply appropriate deference to congressional judgments supporting enforcement legislation. These requirements interact closely. Demarcating the proper sphere for congressional enforcement authority requires the Court to identify the underlying requirements of equal protection (even if those requirements sometimes elude complete judicial application). Once it does so, and can therefore test the particular enforcement legislation against the proper legal standard, it must then consider the appropriate deference to accord Congress's determinations supporting that legislation.

The first of these tasks is largely accomplished. As noted earlier, the Court has understood the Equal Protection Clause as a broadly applicable rule against arbitrary or animus-based classifications. At times, the Court has further specified the law of equal protection. It has decided, for example, that the unequal distribution of certain fundamental rights requires heightened judicial review.[44] Similarly, it has decided that racial classifications are strongly disfavored, and require both a compelling justification and the exhaustion of other policy tools.[45] These principles are more than decisional rules—the legal analysis inherent in identifying the rights subject to equal protection's fundamental rights strand and the Court's rejection of political process theory in judging race classifications make this clear.

These general rules thus demarcate the boundaries of Congress's enforcement power. But their very generality requires us to consider how carefully the Court should review enforcement legislation. The breadth and scope of the equal protection guarantee and the vagueness of the arbitrariness limitation it imposes on state action threaten to provide Congress nearly unlimited enforcement authority. This prospect requires the Court to articulate and apply meaningful deference standards governing its review of congressional determinations that state conduct violates these rules egregiously enough to warrant a federal legislative response.

A full discussion of such deference standards would far exceed this chapter's scope.[46] However, some basic principles can be set forth. First, the Court must recognize that determinations of arbitrariness and

---

42 *Compare, e.g.*, Raoul Berger, Government by Judiciary 169–92 (1977) (arguing that the Fourteenth Amendment simply aimed at constitutionalizing the rights protected by the Civil Rights Act of 1866); John Harrison, *Reconstructing the Privileges or Immunities Clause*, 101 Yale L.J. 1385, 1433–51 (1992) (arguing that the Equal Protection Clause is fundamentally about the requirement that government provide equality in the protection for rights, rather than in the rights themselves).

43 *See* Peter Westen, *The Empty Idea of Equality*, 95 Harv. L. Rev. 537 (1982).

44 *See, e.g.*, Reynolds v. Sims, 377 U.S. 533 (1964) (right to vote).

45 *See, e.g.*, *Croson, supra* note 29.

46 For a fuller treatment, *see* Araiza, "Deference," *supra* note 41.

animus rely heavily on moral judgments. Just as groups do not naturally exist, but instead are created by humans making moral determinations that certain individuals are relevantly similar or dissimilar,[47] so too determinations of a classification's arbitrariness and animus are fundamentally normative. Congress, as the institution whose numerosity, national scope, and constantly renewed popular mandate render it the best spokesperson for the moral views of the American people, is best suited to determine whether a classification fails this basic test of equal protection. Courts should accord significant respect to those determinations.

Nevertheless, courts retain a significant role in reviewing such judgments. In particular, they should investigate whether a social consensus does in fact exist regarding the claimed arbitrariness or malice. For example, courts should consider whether other important social institutions—corporations, unions, schools, other civil society groups, and even state and local governments themselves—have reached a consensus about the discrimination in question. Indeed, judicial decisions—both the Supreme Court's and others'—also constitute relevant inputs, with the important caveat that in this role they carry no inherently greater weight than any other institution's decisions. This inquiry would examine whether society has in fact reached a consensus that such discrimination fails the arbitrariness-animus test. Such review must ultimately be deferential, in recognition of Congress's superior authority to receive society's signals and, based on those signals, draw conclusions about a given classification's social meaning. But that review must also be meaningful, to ensure that the enforcement legislation under review reflects an actual social consensus, rather than an idiosyncratic legislative victory won by a group which has not yet successfully made its case to American society.

Enforcement legislation may also rest on more quotidian foundations, such as factual findings and evaluations of those facts. The next section considers the appropriate judicial role when reviewing such congressional determinations.

Stubborn Discrimination and Successful Attacks: The Measurement Problem

The Problem

If legislation such as GINA and ENDA illustrate the doctrinal problem raised by the Court's post-*Boerne* jurisprudence, *Coleman* and the VRA cases illustrate its fact-finding and policymaking problems. Those cases illustrate situations that are likely to become more common in the future: congressional attacks on stubborn, nuanced, or "second-generation" discrimination, and claims by states that legislation once necessary to attack discrimination have succeeded so completely that they have become unnecessary, and thus exceed Congress's enforcement power.

These situations are closely related. For example, claims that an enforcement statute has become unnecessary may be countered by arguments that the discrimination has become more nuanced, thus justifying either the existing challenged legislation or even stronger remedies. Most importantly for our purposes, what unites these phenomena is the burden they place on courts to review Congress's policy judgments—for example, that stubborn or evolving forms of discrimination require stronger or more nuanced legislative responses, or that facial impressions that the statute has succeeded are misleading, or hide latent discriminatory tendencies likely to re-emerge if the statute is struck down.

This problem arguably poses a more intractable issue than the doctrinal problem triggered by the Court's misguided insistence on basing review of enforcement legislation on its own suspect class jurisprudence. That earlier problem, while conceptually fundamental, can be remedied relatively easily by the Court clarifying the proper legal standard against which to test enforcement legislation. By contrast, "the measurement problem" requires the Court to decide how carefully, and by what means, to review Congress's judgments about matters such as the effectiveness of legislation in attacking discrimination, the degree of success such legislation has achieved, and the likelihood of backsliding in its absence.

Reviewing such judgments presents the Court with significant difficulties. Those measurements reflect a combination of empirical findings (for example, the relative rate at which men and women use particular types

---

47 *See* Laurence Tribe, *The Puzzling Persistence of Process-Based Constitutional Theories*, 89 YALE L.J. 1063, 1074 (1980).

of FMLA leave), predictions (for example, the impact sex-neutral self-care leave has on equal employment opportunity) and evaluative judgments (for example, the extent to which the VRA has permanently eradicated racial discrimination in voting). Second-guessing Congress on such matters both taxes courts' competence and stretches their authority.[48] Empirical facts may present less of a problem, to the extent they are objectively verifiable—although complex policy facts remain difficult to uncover competently through the litigation process. However, predictions and evaluations, to the extent they rest on ideological pre-commitments, are quite challenging for courts to review legitimately, given Congress's superior authority to reflect the ideological commitments of the American people.

The measurement problem offers courts a choice between reviewing the substance of congressional judgments, or the process by which Congress reached them. Both paths are fraught with hazard. As discussed above, review of the substance of Congress's findings stretches courts' competence and authority to their outer limits. For example, in *Coleman* the plurality simply refused to believe that men's and women's presumed equal use of FMLA self-care leave would meaningfully mitigate the gender-disparate effects of FMLA family-care leave. That sort of doubt constitutes little more than disagreement with the statute's policy wisdom.

Review of the process by which legislation is enacted, to ensure that Congress carefully considered the underlying policy issues, is similarly problematic. Such review would enmesh the Court in a thicket of difficult questions. How much deliberation would be appropriate? By whom—both houses, the relevant committees, or some other bodies? More conceptually, a focus on deliberation assumes an understanding of the legislative process in which open-minded legislators sincerely engage and base their voting decisions on the factual record developed during formal legislative proceedings. Competing understandings of that process, in which legislators reflect and advocate for exogenous constituent, contributor, party leader, or lobbyist preferences, paint a very different picture, in which deliberation on the record is largely irrelevant.[49] Perhaps we might prefer the first of these understandings. Indeed, analysis in some post-*Boerne* cases reflects an assumption that this prior picture is accurate.[50] But that is surely a contested proposition.[51]

Given these difficulties, it is unsurprising that Justice Scalia criticized the congruence and proportionality test as "flabby" and "a standing invitation to judicial arbitrariness and policy-driven decisionmaking."[52] Indeed, in *Coleman* he trenchantly observed that both the plurality and dissenting opinions "seem[ed] to [him] a faithful application of [the Court's] congruence and proportionality jurisprudence."[53] Future cases will likely yield similarly plausible dueling opinions. As discrimination evolves from explicit, facial exclusions toward nuanced, second-generation-style variants, congressional judgments supporting enforcement legislation will similarly become more focused on policy-inflected questions of need and effectiveness. For example, the FMLA's defenders described its self-care leave provisions as a prophylactic measure to lessen employers' perceptions that FMLA leave primarily benefitted women, thus making them more costly as employees. The causal chain connecting such facially equal benefits and Congress's discrimination-fighting goal was simply too "overly complicated" and "unconvincing" to satisfy the plurality.[54] By contrast, it seemed plain to the dissenters. A clearer example of "judicial arbitrariness and policy-driven decisionmaking" could hardly be imagined.

---

48 For a fuller discussion of the concepts of competence and authority as they relate to judicial deference to congressional judgments, *see* Araiza, "Deference," *supra* note 41.

49 *See, e.g.*, Douglas Laycock, *A Jurisprudence of Errors*, 107 MICH. L. REV. 1169, 1175 (2007) ("often [legislators] are locked into positions by ideology or political pressure before the hearing ever begins"); *id.* ("Most of the real discussions in which legislators 'find' facts occur *ex parte* and off the record.").

50 *See, e.g.*, *Garrett*, 531 U.S. at 37–371 (discounting some evidence supporting the ADA's Enforcement Clause foundation because the information was developed by a private task force and not incorporated into Congress's formal findings).

51 *See, e.g.*, Philip Frickey & Steven Smith, *Judicial Review, the Congressional Process, and the Federalism Cases: An Interdisciplinary Critique*, 111 YALE L.J. 1707, 1730 (2002) ("In our view of the state of political science, no theory of legislative decisionmaking exists that is capable of addressing the issues adequately.").

52 Tennessee v. Lane, 541 U.S. 509, 557–8 (2004) (Scalia, J., dissenting).

53 132 S. Ct. at 1338 (Scalia, J., concurring in the judgment).

54 132 S. Ct. at 1336.

Similar difficulties attend judgments whether enforcement legislation has succeeded so completely and permanently as to become unnecessary and, hence, unconstitutional. Judging the success of an antidiscrimination law requires much more than simply examining whether the particular types of targeted discrimination continue to occur. For example, the statute's prohibitions may force discrimination into subtler forms. That phenomenon would require a reviewing court to determine whether those responses themselves constituted unconstitutional discrimination of the sort condemned by the Constitution, and whether the statute was effective in eradicating them.

Indeed, a statute's success in eradicating explicit, first-generation discrimination does not necessarily guarantee that even such egregious conduct has permanently vanished. For example, judges in a post-*NAMUDMO* case considering the constitutionality of the VRA's pre-clearance provisions sparred over the argument that, without those provisions, previously eradicated first-generation discriminatory devices would return. A judge skeptical of that claim cited the oral argument in *NAMUDNO*, where Chief Justice Roberts ridiculed such a claim, not on the specific facts of the VRA but as a general matter, on the ground that such assertions were fundamentally unverifiable.[55] As a retort to the Chief Justice, one might agree with his assessment about such claims' unverifiability, but question whether it justified a refusal to defer to Congress's contrary judgment.

Deference to Congressional Measurements

Thus, the measurement problem poses significant difficulties for judicial review of enforcement legislation. The Court cannot easily avoid this problem, as the congruence and proportionality standard necessarily requires the Court to review Congress's factual support for enforcement legislation. If that test is to survive, the Court must develop a methodology for such review that is both effective and legitimate in light of each institution's relative competence and authority.

Any such methodology must recognize the difficulties measurement issues pose for courts. First, such issues necessarily involve matters of degree—for example, the extent to which the FMLA's provision of sex-neutral self-care leave mitigates employers' perceptions that FMLA leave is primarily a women's benefit. Such judgments of degree necessarily involve line-drawing, a quintessentially legislative exercise. Hence, when a court disagrees with the legislature's line—as the plurality did in *Coleman*—it exposes itself to Justice Scalia's charge of arbitrariness. Concededly, judicial decisions often take the form of a pronouncement that, in effect, the legislature has simply taken one step too far.[56] But such conclusions—reflected in proportionality and balancing methodologies more generally—necessarily elicit this objection.[57]

If proportionality review does in fact raise concerns of judicial overreaching, one obvious mitigation measure consists of limiting the effect of such review by confining judicial strike-downs to rare occasions. Thus, one response to the objection is to adopt a default position of deference. Of course, deference standards raise their own concerns about arbitrariness, given their necessarily non-mechanical quality. Nevertheless, judicial deference to congressional measurement judgments would go a long way toward mitigating this problem.

One way to make such deference more concrete is to tie the review standard to the type of judgment under review. As Justice Scalia noted in critiquing the congruence and proportionality standard, judicial review of Congress's enforcement legislation "homework" enmeshes the Court in policymaking.[58] His solution to that critique was to cut back severely on the enforcement power, by confining Congress's ability to enact prophylactic legislation to situations of racial discrimination. Such a blunderbuss answer has little in logic to

55 *See Shelby County*, 679 F.3d at 898 (Williams, J., dissenting) (quoting Tr. of Oral Arg. at 28, *NAMUDNO* (No. 08–322) (statement of Chief Justice Roberts) ("Well, that's like the old—you know, it's the elephant whistle. You know, I have this whistle to keep away the elephants. … Well, there are no elephants, so it must work.").

56 Perhaps the classic statement of this principle is Justice Holmes's pronouncement that "if regulation goes too far it will be recognized as a taking." Pennsylvania Coal v. Mahon, 260 U.S. 393, 415 (1922).

57 *See, e.g.*, Harmelin v. Michigan, 501 U.S. 957, 986 (1991) (criticizing Eighth Amendment proportionality review as fundamentally subjective). Unsurprisingly, *Harmelin*'s critique of proportionality review was written by Justice Scalia.

58 *See supra* note 52.

recommend it, given the Court's expansive understanding of equal protection.[59] Moreover, it exacerbates the exclusion of Congress from the joint task of implementing constitutional meaning.

However, Justice Scalia's framing of the issue suggests a better solution. Understanding statutory measurements as policymaking suggests that the Constitution delegates to Congress the authority to make them. Of course, judicial review of such policymaking remains; indeed, it constitutes a basic component of our system. But courts should not reverse such policymaking unless it is arbitrary.[60] Such a standard respects both congressional and judicial authority, because it reflects Congress's policymaking discretion, but also because it recognizes that legal reasoning is largely incapable of justifying judicial line-drawing.[61] This standard thus allows a meaningful and logically justifiable role for judicial review of such judgments, reducing the disrespectful and inappropriate judicial second-guessing of congressional handiwork that Justice Scalia rightly criticized in *Lane* and *Coleman*.

Part IV Toward Adulthood?

It is too early to know whether the congruence and proportionality test will grow out of its adolescent awkwardness. Perhaps a series of embarrassing confrontations with popular enforcement legislation will convince the Court to correct its course, much as a teenager's painful encounters with adult situations sometimes trigger emotional growth. However, any such optimism must be tempered by recognition of the Court's continued insistence on judicial supremacy in stating constitutional meaning. One can certainly envision an adjustment to *Boerne* that respects judicial supremacy while nevertheless according Congress its due as a partner in the project of constitutional construction. However, the Court's willingness to cripple the VRA, a crown jewel of the Second Reconstruction, suggests that it may be over-optimistic to think that the current Court is willing to engage in a more nuanced examination of its and Congress's respective roles. This is especially so given that the results under its current approach track so closely its apparent preferences for limiting federal power, and especially for protecting states' freedom from federal oversight.[62] In this area as in others, substantive change may have to await change in the Court's composition.

59 *See supra* notes 42–43.

60 Particular components of that policy decision—for example, Congress's findings of empirical fact—may call for more aggressive judicial review. *See* Araiza, "Deference," *supra* note 41 (arguing that empirical facts should be subject to more searching judicial review than other types of congressional findings).

61 *See* Araiza, "New Groups," *supra* note 24, at 513 (discussing this argument).

62 *See supra* note 18; *see also, e.g.*, National Federation of Ind. Business v. Sebelius, 132 S. Ct. 2566 (2012) (rejecting the Affordable Care Act's Medicaid expansion provisions' condition on state receipt of Medicaid funds, as unduly coercing states).

PART III
Racial Justice in Education

Chapter 7
Racial Liberalism and School Desegregation Jurisprudence: Notes Toward a More Usable Past

Michael Paris

Introduction

When it comes to struggles for racial justice, federal equal protection doctrine has reached a dead end. "Colorblind constitutionalism," a weapon deployed to undercut even modest racial reforms, now approaches a complete formal-legal victory. How did we get here?

In this chapter I suggest a line of analysis that explores the relationship between racial liberalism—a connected body of ideas about race, racism, and racial justice—and the trajectory of federal equal protection doctrine.[1]

I follow Gordon Silverstein's account of the juridification of American politics to argue that legal doctrine and judicial policymaking are much like a game of *Scrabble*, with earlier key moves shaping, without tightly determining, the subsequent language and path of the law as well as subsequent reform ideas and strategies. As Silverstein puts it, in such a game "players start with a blank board, and the first player can head off in any direction she chooses. But slowly, over the course of the game, the players often end up in one corner of the board, whereas another part of the board is totally empty."[2]

Although somewhat reductionist, Silverstein's analogy is a useful way to think about the evolution of school desegregation jurisprudence. *Brown*, with its many possible meanings and futures, represents the first tiles in the game. *Green*, not *Milliken*, is the most significant narrowing case. Then, finally, with *Parents Involved in Community Schools* (*PICS*), we end up buried and gasping for air in one cramped corner of the board, one defined by the legalistic logic of intentionally discriminatory acts and the evil of racial classifications *per se*. Another quadrant concerned with "equal educational opportunities" is sparsely populated, while still another that might have been dedicated to fighting racial subordination is entirely blank. What proponents of school desegregation need now are new ideas and strategies—some of which might be informed by forgotten past moments and turning points—deployed on a new institutional game board.

More broadly, I argue that racial liberalism powerfully shaped the Court's desegregation jurisprudence; that this doctrine was on the wrong path as early as 1968; that these particular and far from inevitable doctrinal developments were then easily absorbed and coopted by conservative opponents of racial justice; and that, indeed, we might even say that the central commitments of colorblind constitutionalism were already imminent within racial liberalism and liberal court "victories."

The first section sets the table with a brief sketch of racial liberalism, the second traces the Supreme Court's school desegregation jurisprudence from *Brown* to *PICS* and connects it to racial liberalism, and the third turns to the search for alternative arguments and strategies. In the end, I will suggest that the remaining proponents of school desegregation should look first to the contributions of their most powerful critic (Derrick Bell) for insights, and next to state constitutionalism and state courts as a viable path to the revival of their seemingly lost cause.

1 My thinking about racial liberalism, legal doctrines, and the evolution of politics and policy has been influenced by Daniel Hosang-Martinez's essay about school desegregation battles in California, and especially in Los Angeles. *See* Daniel Hosang-Martinez, *The Triumph of Racial Liberalism, The Demise of Racial Justice*, in RACE AND AMERICAN POLITICAL DEVELOPMENT 288 (Joseph Lowndes, Julie Novkov & Dorian T. Warren eds, 2008).

2 *See* GORDON SILVERSTEIN, LAW'S ALLURE: HOW LAW SHAPES, CONSTRAINS, SAVES AND KILLS POLITICS (2009), at 66.

Racial Liberalism

Historian Thomas Sugrue has given us a magisterial treatment of "the forgotten history of the Civil Rights Movement" outside the former Confederacy.[3] One central theme in Sugrue's account is the ascendance between 1940 and 1960 of a particular liberal view of race and racism. This view, for which I use the shorthand "racial liberalism," emphasized "racism as a moral and psychological problem: One in the hearts and minds of misguided whites … Eliminating inequality was a matter of changing attitudes and beliefs; institutional change would follow."[4]

Gunnar Myrdal's *An American Dilemma* and Gordon Allport's *The Nature of Prejudice* were perhaps exemplary texts that embodied and promoted racial liberalism.[5] Myrdal famously argued that the "dilemma" was fundamentally a moral one involving the basic contradiction between widely endorsed American ideals—the American Creed of "liberty, equality, and fair opportunity for everybody"—and American practices. As Stephen Steinberg has noted, Myrdal's master frame tended to reduce "racism to the level of beliefs that whites hold about blacks." Race was a matter of irrational fear and prejudice on the part of Whites.[6]

This moral focus on White prejudice was only one side of racial liberalism, however. The other was a deep concern—one might even say an odd fascination—with the psychological damage that racism did to Blacks. Both sides, irrational prejudice and stigmatization, were further developed in Allport's important book. Racism as White prejudice was most manifest in laws and practices guaranteeing segregation in residential neighborhoods and schools. Segregation stigmatized Blacks. Forced separation meant isolation, and isolation created an inferiority complex and low self-esteem. Damaged Black psyches could give rise to dysfunctional attitudes and values, which could easily congeal into specific, pathological cultural adaptations to oppressive conditions.

Irrationality and stigmatic harm. These two ideas capture the essence of the racial liberal view of the nature of racism and its primary effects. Following Guinier and Torres, we can call this view "race as irrational stigmatization."[7] What links the two sides of racial liberalism is what Myrdal, Allport, and many others after them posited as a "vicious circle." As it was with slavery, so it was with Jim Crow, and now with the ghetto: prejudice and discrimination have their intended effects; they degrade, dehumanize, and debilitate. Those effects can then be observed and invoked as facts confirming the rationality of the prejudicial attitudes and values in the first place.[8]

This analysis had powerful implications for racial liberal goals and strategies. The overall goal of racial liberalism was of course racial integration in all walks of life. Racial mixing was always and everywhere the remedy for the disease. Why? As Allport put it, in lines that are still often cited by liberal proponents of school desegregation, "inter-group [inter-racial] contact" on "equal-status terms" would disabuse Whites of their irrational fears and convince Blacks of their basic humanity and equality. For Whites, what was essentially a phobia could be met and dissipated in much the same way that all phobias are: the patient would be exposed to that which is irrationally feared, and thereafter the patient would learn that the anticipated ill-effects did not follow. These social processes of enlightenment were not automatic, of course; they had to be carefully managed or they could go terribly wrong. But research showed that interracial contact reduced prejudice and discrimination, improved race relations, expanded opportunities for minorities, and so on.

And how would the desired racial integration come to pass? The liberal view of social change matched the diagnosis. It was generally a technocratic, top-down approach. "Moral leaders" should emphasize the proper,

---

3 Thomas Sugrue, Sweet Land of Liberty: The Forgotten Struggle for Civil Rights in the North (2008).

4 Sugrue, *supra* note 3, at xxvi.

5 Gunnar Myrdal, with the assistance of Richard Sterner & Arnold Rose, An American Dilemma: The Negro Problem in Modern Democracy (1944); Gordon Allport, The Nature of Prejudice (1954).

6 Stephen Steinberg, Turning Back: The Retreat From Racial Justice in American Thought and Policy (1995). On Myrdal, *see also* Walter Jackson, Gunnar Myrdal and America's Conscience: Social Engineering and Racial Liberalism, 1938–1987 (1990).

7 Lani Guinier & Gerald Torres, The Miner's Canary: Enlisting Race, Resisting Power, Transforming Democracy (2002), at 13.

8 Steinberg, *supra* note 6, at 39. See also, Allport, *supra* note 5, at 472 (remedial legislation needed to break "vicious circles").

widely endorsed values and disseminate rational arguments in support of integration. Moral exhortation was invariably supported by copious references to social science research, with a heavy accent on social psychology.[9] The emphasis on social psychology arises from and reinforces the "black victimization" side of the liberal case for integration. In portraits of damaged victims, racial liberals found an emotion-laden way to appeal to Whites' moral conscience.[10] If forced separation caused damage psyches and pathological cultural adaptations, then integration would heal the wounds though "exposing" Blacks to mainstream cultural norms and opportunity structures.

Over time, racial liberals' preferred institutional mechanism for policy change became courts (sometime thought to be the forum of principle) and administrative agencies (sometime thought to be the forum of enlightened expertise). The resort to courts and administrative agencies is most often attributed to the hopelessness of a political process marked by hostility against "discrete and insular minorities." However, there is also a strong affinity between racial liberalism's conception of race and racial justice and the seeming attractiveness of social change imposed by judicial or administrative decree. If irrational prejudice was at the heart of the problem, then the imposition of change from above was seen as no problem at all, provided that it could be had. Indeed, liberal reformers often preferred it to the messiness and unpredictability of democratic mobilization and protest. Allport himself often referred to it as "the *fait accompli*." If there is too much public argument or discussion in advance of change, then irrational fear and loathing prevail; in advance, Whites typically protest vociferously. However, once change backed by "vigorous leadership" is imposed, reality takes over and White protest and resistance quickly subsides. People quickly get used to it.[11]

Racial liberalism first arose to combat biological determinism. In that role it was an insurgent doctrine. Its basic antidiscrimination principle has underwritten a great deal of racial progress. However, whatever one makes of our current situation, there is not much dispute that residential and school segregation are two tightly connected areas in which racial liberalism largely failed. The racial ghetto and all that it means—for policing and mass incarceration, for housing, for the experience of community and the quality of life, and for schooling in a political democracy—remains for us to confront in some way.

Is there a viable alternative to racial liberalism? Throughout his book, Sugrue contrasts racial liberalism with many alternative views linked only by a felt sense of what racial liberalism lacked. The critics generally held that American racism was more systemic than racial liberalism allowed, that it was deeply "embedded in American economic, legal, and political institutions." Race was better understood as a powerful but also a highly flexible marker tied in some way to phenotype but more fundamentally to group identity, relational power, and unequal social positions. For these critics, the alteration of power relationships and winning economic resources would do more to change hearts and minds than would any appeal to conscience or intercultural education programs ever could. What was required was the stuff of group conflict over political power—political organization and mobilization, alliances with other subordinated groups and, as A. Phillip Randolph put it, "pressure, more pressure, and still more pressure." Here, positive group identity and distinctive cultural forms could and should be viewed as a vital resource for struggle, not as something to repress or downplay or get beyond.[12]

In the U.S. Supreme Court's equal protection jurisprudence, it was the liberal view of race and racial justice that eventually prevailed, and this was nowhere more apparent than in the highly contentious matter of school desegregation.

---

9 In his 1979 Introduction to a new edition to Allport's *The Nature of Prejudice*, Kenneth Clark wrote that "Allport and Myrdal personify the insistence that thoughtful, moral, rationalistic social scientists must be the contemporary custodians of such enduring human values as justice—and that trained human intelligence is an important weapon in the ongoing struggle against ignorance, superstition, and injustice." Kenneth Clark, *Introduction* to Allport, *supra* note 5, at x.

10 For contemporary examples of the presentation and use of damage imagery, *see* Jonathan Kozol, Savage Inequalities (1991); Susan Eaton, The Children in Room E-4: American Education on Trial (2006). For a critical evaluation of damage imagery, *see* Daryle Michael Scott, Contempt and Pity: Social Policy and the Image of the Damaged Black Psyche, 1880–1996 (1997). The problem raised by such appeals is of course the age-old problem of white paternalism.

11 Allport, *supra* note 5, at 274–75; 471; 510.

12 Sugrue, *supra* note 3, Chapter 2. *See also* Michael Omi & Howard Winant, Racial Formation in the United States: From the 1960s to the 1980s (1994); Stephen Steinberg, Race Relations: A Critique (2005); Guinier & Torres, *supra* note 7; Howard Winant, The World Is a Ghetto: Race and Democracy Since World War II, 34–38 (2004).

School Desegregation Jurisprudence from *Brown* to *PICS*

The Court's opinions in *Brown I* and *II* could plausibly read in several different ways. The precise nature of the wrong, the right, and the remedy were all opaque. The story of the political resistance and intransigence in the South that followed the Court's decision has been told many times and need not be rehearsed in detail here. In *Brown II*, the Court never used the words "segregation" or "desegregation." Rather, it offered several formulations sounding in racial neutrality and delegated authority to school districts and federal district courts to manage some sort of transition away from legally mandated segregation to some unspecified state of affairs that was not that. "With all deliberate speed," a phrase that highlighted the pace of change, got all the attention, but the foundational issues (for example, "why was legal segregation wrong?") went unexamined. The Court evaded the deeper questions for over a decade, and when it did finally address them, it gave us the wrong answers.[13]

In the South, the big game of whack-a-mole came to an end with the Civil Rights Act of 1964, which put coercive federal power behind the quest to eliminate separate schooling mandated by law, and the Elementary and Secondary Education Act of 1965, which vastly enhanced federal aid to education and thereby provided administrators with financial leverage to bring about change. In 1965 and again in 1966, the Office of Civil Rights (OCR) issued guidelines on student assignment policies. The latter set of rules included numerical goals for desegregation.[14]

Outside the South, interestingly, *Brown* reinvigorated longstanding civil rights struggles for equal educational opportunity. As current civil rights historians show us, these were typically grassroots efforts grounded in an antisubordination perspective. Here, the subordinated group demands that the dominant group cease and desist from policies and practices that relegate the subordinated group to inferior resources (broadly understood) and second-class citizenship. Integration *per se* was not the point. When these claimants resorted to courts and administrative agencies, as they often did, they did so in conjunction with a broad array of political strategies and tactics, including social protest.[15] We can glimpse the future of school desegregation jurisprudence in the defensive response of non-Southern officials. New terminology, sounding in racial liberalism and racial neutrality, entered the lexicon of debate. "*De facto*" segregation was a world apart from the "*de jure*" kind. Whites and Blacks went to different schools, to be sure, but not because they were assigned on the basis of race, but rather because they lived in different "neighborhoods." And who under the sun could fathom the causes of residential segregation? And wasn't "segregation" itself the wrong term, implying as it did that someone was doing something wrong to someone else? If the racial population of a school did not match that of a district or region, then might it not be more accurate to say that the school was "racially imbalanced"? Racial balance might be a good policy idea, perhaps, but surely there was no constitutional mandate for "racial balancing for its own sake." That would be inconsistent with the foundational proposition that race is an irrational and stigmatizing category, would it not?

From 1966 on, the story of the Court's school desegregation jurisprudence is best understood as one about the official rejection by liberals on the Court of "equal educational opportunity" and/or "antisubordination" justifications for racially integrated schooling in favor of a form of legalism that was not only arid, but pernicious. Once we have the doctrinal path clearly in view, we are then in a better position to pursue harder questions about the relationship between legal doctrines, on one hand, and cultural understandings and political struggles, on the other.

---

13 This paragraph draws on R. Shep Melnick, The Civil Rights State, forthcoming (2015). A great account of the many plausible meanings of *Brown I* can be found in What *Brown v. Board of Education* Should Have Said: The Nation's Top Legal Experts Rewrite America's Landmark Civil Rights Decision (Jack M. Balkin, ed., 2001).

14 For a treatment of *Brown* and its consequences for politics, *see* J. Harvie Wilkinson III, From *Brown* to *Bakke*: The Supreme Court and School Desegregaton: 1954–1978 (1977).

15 *See* Sugrue, *supra* note 3, Chapter 6 (especially the discussion of local activism and litigation in New Rochelle, New York). *See also* Theoharis, *"I'd Rather Go to School in the South": How Boston's School Desegregaton Complicates the Civil Rights Paradigm*, in Freedom North: Black Freedom Struggles Outside the South, 1940–1980 (Jeanne Theoharris & Komozi Woodard eds 2005); Adina Back, *Exposing the "Whole Segregation Myth": The Harlem Nine and New York City Segregation Battles*, in Theoharis and Woodard eds, *Id.*

A significant and largely forgotten moment in this trajectory from open possibilities to narrow legalism can be marked by the transition from Judge John Minor Wisdom's opinion in *United States v. Jefferson County* (1966) to Justice Brennan's opinion for the Court in *Green v. County School Board* (1968). The issue in *Jefferson County* was the constitutional adequacy of "freedom of choice" plans in seven consolidated cases from Alabama and Louisiana. Writing for a panel of the Fifth Circuit Court of Appeals, Judge Wisdom began with the proposition that *Brown* promised Black children "equal educational opportunities with white children in a racially nondiscriminatory public school system."[16] Affirmative steps would be required to "disestablish segregation." Indeed, Wisdom wrote, here "desegregation" and "integration" should be used "interchangeably." The Southern "dual system" had to be converted to a "unitary, nonracial (nondiscriminatory) system—lock, stock, and barrel: students, faculty, staff, facilities, programs, and activities." The reason for the transformation was "to offer educational opportunities to all on equal terms."[17] Wisdom would then go on to constitutionalize the numerical goals of OCR's 1966 Guidelines. He flatly rejected the school districts' contention that racial integration was not mandatory.

What has been largely forgotten is Wisdom's wide-ranging argument about why this was so. Over the course of his opinion, Wisdom moved seamlessly from his opening focus on equal educational opportunity to the deeper ground of anti-caste subordination. Several times, he called the Southern political and cultural system what it was—"apartheid." *Brown*, he argued, was also about how Blacks were harmed "collectively" when "the state, by law *or by custom*, operates segregated schools or a school system with uncorrected segregation effects."[18] What was the nature of this collective harm? Wisdom gave the following answer, which, it seems to me, could very well apply to our current ghettos and ghetto schooling:

> Denial of access to the dominant culture, lack of opportunity in any meaningful way to participate in political or other public activities, the stigma of apartheid condemned by the Thirteenth Amendment are concomitants of the dual educational system. The unmalleable fact transcending in importance the harm to individual Negro children is that the separate school system was an integral element in the Southern States general program to restrict Negroes as a class from participation in the life of the community, the affairs of the State, and the mainstream of American life: Negroes must keep their place.[19]

This was why, Wisdom continued, the Court in *Bolling v. Sharpe*, the District of Columbia case, "concluded that racial classifications in public education were so unreasonable and arbitrary as to violate due process," quite "beyond any question of psychological harm or denial of educational opportunities to the individual ..."[20] What was really at stake here, then, was nothing less than "the right of Negroes to national citizenship, their right as a class to share in the privileges and immunities only white citizens had enjoyed as a class." Invoking the first Justice Harlan's dissent in *The Civil Rights Cases* (1883), Wisdom wrote that the Civil War Amendments "created an affirmative duty that the States eradicate all relics, 'badges and indicia of slavery,' lest Negros sink back into 'second class' citizenship."[21]

Wisdom could have ended his argument here, but he did not. The antisubordination foundation of his argument led directly to the question of collective (government) responsibility for so-called *de facto* segregation. That concern pointed sharply up toward the non-South, and Wisdom did not shy away from going there. The law on the question of *de facto* school segregation in the non-South was highly unsettled, but for Wisdom *Brown* at least entailed a presumption of a "duty to integrate." Although strict and inflexible racial balancing was not required,

16 372 F.2d 836, 845 (5th Cir. 1966).

17 *Id.* at 847.

18 *Id.* at 866.

19 *Id.*

20 *Id.* at 871–72. In light of Wisdom's appeal to *Bolling* and due process, it is interesting that Martha Minow's commentary on *PICS* urges advocates to "try due process" as a doctrinal framework "more in line with equal opportunity." The claim would be that "racially segregated schools" are "an arbitrary deprivation of liberty, unrelated to a proper government objective." Martha Minow, *"A Proper Objective": Constitutional Commitment and Educational Opportunity After* Bolling v. Sharpe *and* PICS, 55 How. L.J. 575 (2012).

21 *Jefferson County*, 372 F. 2d 873.

"integration [was] an educational goal to be given a high, high priority among various considerations involved in the proper administration of a school system beset with *de facto* segregated schools." Nationwide, racially separate schools were just part of a vast, interlocking, mutually reinforcing complex of ideas and institutions that secured racial subordination. That past, Wisdom seemed to be saying, should never be forgotten.[22]

In *Green v. County School Board of New Kent County* (1968), the Supreme Court sets off in a radically different direction on the *Scrabble Board*.[23] This case involved the rural Virginia school district of New Kent County. The district had 1,300 students, of whom 740 were Black and 550 were White, and it operated two K-12 schools, one for Whites and one for Blacks. Because there was little residential segregation, a zoning policy that sent students to the nearest school would have desegregated the district. After plaintiffs filed suit in 1965, the lower courts approved a "freedom of choice" plan that had resulted in 115 Black students transferring to the White school, and no Whites transferring to the Black school.[24]

Justice Brennan's opinion for a unanimous Court in *Green* began not with *Brown I*, as Wisdom had, but with *Brown II*. The question was whether the district's freedom of choice plan complied with the duty "to achieve a system of admission to public schools on a nonracial basis."[25] *Brown* had outlawed the "pattern of separate 'white' and 'Negro' schools ... established under compulsion of state law," Brennan wrote. The duty was therefore to effectuate a transition from a "dual system" to "a unitary, nonracial system of public education." Desegregation remedies had to touch every facet of the system, not just the students but also "faculty, staff, transportation, [and] extracurricular activities and facilities." These remedies would be imposed to create a system "without a 'white' school or a 'Negro' school, but just schools."[26]

That Brennan borrowed liberally from Wisdom's phrasings makes it easy to miss the complete erasure of Wisdom's moral and constitutional foundations. If we think of the two opinions as plastic relief maps, with *Green* overlaid on *Jefferson County*, then the only thing left of *Jefferson County* after *Green* is the remedial rulebook. In place of Wisdom's antisubordination perspective, *Green* substitutes the tort-like logic in which an identifiable wrongdoer commits a discrete act that causes some consequence. The wrong must then be remedied by a finite decree restoring some (in this instance mythical) *status quo ante*.

Wisdom had figured separate schools "by law or custom" as just a key piece in a total system of racial subordination. In his *Jefferson County* opinion, "dual" and "unitary" took on meaning in light of the underlying recognition of a history of White supremacy. This sense of the wrong and therefore sense of purpose might have guided approaches to remedies and the compromises and difficulties inevitably attendant to their implementation. Keeping group power and group inequality in mind might have mitigated the extent to which some of the later purported remedies for racial injustice tended to, themselves, embody racism and disadvantage Blacks. *Green* intimated that judging the adequacy of a remedy was no more complicated than viewing race as phenotype and counting the number of Black and White bodies housed under one school roof. In a deep sense, the proffered purpose of desegregation (to undo specific discriminatory acts) was absurd. Because the real purpose remained hidden (or perhaps no one real purpose existed), the contours of any "transition" from dual to unitary remained opaque.

Green did "do something," however. It made many existing judicial decrees in the South, considered "by the numbers," legally insufficient, and it sparked an intense six-year period of conflict over schools, courts, and racial justice, nationwide. In the South, the NAACP Legal Defense and Education Fund (LDF) and Department of Justice reopened scores of cases, and by 1972 the South was more desegregated than any other region of the country. The most important desegregation battles occurred in America's large cities.

Swann v. Charlotte-Mecklenburg[27] further embedded the legal logic of *Green*. The LDF had filed *Swann* in 1965. The case was unusual in that city and county had merged into one school district in 1960, for reasons having nothing to do with race. The new district was vast. It covered 550 square miles, operated 107 schools, and served 84,000 students. Of these students, 71 percent were White and 29 percent were Black. The initial

22 *Id.* at 875.
23 391 U. S. 430 (1968).
24 *Id.* at 432–33.
25 *Id.* at 432.
26 *Id.* at 435, 437, 438, 442.
27 402 U.S. 1 (1971).

round of litigation had resulted in some desegregation. Still, when the LDF moved to reopen *Swann* in light of *Green*, over half of the district's 24,000 Black students still attended 21 schools in the central city that were 99–100 percent Black. The pattern of residential segregation was common nationwide.[28]

In March 1970, Federal District Judge James McMillan asked the district to submit a new desegregation plan. He ended up relying on his own expert and imposing an order requiring desegregation secured by extensive two-way busing. In May, the Fourth Circuit reversed McMillan. It held that he went too far in ordering desegregation at the elementary school level. The Supreme Court granted certiorari in June, and issued its decision in April of 1971.

The question before the Court in *Swann* was whether the trial judge had exceeded his remedial authority. In a unanimous opinion nominally authored by Chief Justice Burger, but in which Justice Brennan played a large role, the Court answered "no." Scholars are generally critical of Burger's opinion; one calls it "somewhat schizophrenic" and another "one of the most confused opinions ever produced."[29] Although the opinion is indeed rife with vague and contradictory statements, two things are very clear: the wrong is the intentional segregative act and the remedy is by-the-numbers racial mixing. Neoconservative scholars generally argue that *Green* and *Swann* transformed *Brown* by turning its non-discrimination principle into a mandate for racial integration. But Burger's opening lines in *Swann* defined the situation before the Court this way: "*Swann* and its companion cases arose in states having a long history of maintaining two sets of schools in a single system deliberately operated to carry out a government policy to separate people solely because of their race. That was what *Brown* was all about."[30] It is only old-fashioned, Jim Crow racism that offends the Constitution. Burger's most important lines were these:

> School authorities are traditionally charged with broad power to formulate and implement education policy, and might well conclude, for example, that, in order to prepare students to live in a pluralistic society, each school should have a prescribed ratio of Negro to white students reflecting the proportion for the district as a whole. To do this as an educational policy is within the broad discretionary powers of school authorities; absent a finding of a constitutional violation, however, that would not be within the authority of a federal court. As with any equity case, the nature of the violation determines the scope of the remedy.[31]

The point is not that the phrase "the violation determines the scope of the remedy" necessarily limits what "intent" amounts to, or the scope of remedies. The Court's expansive understanding of both violation and remedy in *Keyes* belies that notion. Rather, the point is that "the why" of it all has been resolved once again against both the contested substance of equal educational opportunity and the contested history of racial subordination and its relevance. Nothing whatsoever was said about educational harms and benefits or our history of racial injustice.

With the table thus set, Burger goes on to offer his schizophrenic effort to define "with more particularity the responsibilities of school authorities in desegregating a state-enforced dual system in light of the Equal Protection Clause."[32] But there is really a much deeper schizophrenia here. On one hand, the Court is saying that there is no constitutional right to "racial balance." This comment foreshadows the Court's later, constant refrain that "racial balancing for its own sake" is "patently unconstitutional" (as if anyone ever would pursue "racial balancing for its own sake"). On the other hand, because the Court's notion of violation (wrong) is historically thin and far removed from social realities, it seems that the Court itself is requiring lower courts to engage in "racial balancing" not for any great or important reason, but almost simply for its own sake. Of

28 This discussion of *Swann* relies on the Court's opinion, *id.* as well as BERNARD SCHWARTZ, SWANN'S WAY: THE SCHOOL BUSING CASE AND THE SUPREME COURT (1986).

29 JAMES E. RYAN, FIVE MILES AWAY, A WORLD APART: ONE CITY, TWO SCHOOLS AND THE STORY OF EDUCATIONAL OPPORTUNITY IN MODERN AMERICA 31, 79–81 (2010) ("schizophrenic") and MELNICK, *supra* note 13 (forthcoming) ("confused"). We now know that the opinion was "the product of a long, torturous, and even comical effort to extract a unanimous ruling from a deeply divided court" (MELNICK, citing SCHWARTZ, *supra* note 28).

30 *Swann*, 402 U.S. 5–6.

31 *Id.* at 16.

32 *Id.* at 18.

course, the proffered reason is to "correct the wrong." But no one could really believe that there were any tight connections going from segregative acts, to causation, to remedies undoing the wrong. Soon many people, many African-Americans included, could not quite see the point of rigid racial balancing remedies, either.

Swann made busing a central issue on the national agenda.[33] After *Swann*, all eyes turned to whether all-out desegregation via busing would come to the non-South. Perhaps the most avid and astute Court-watcher at the time was President Nixon. Nixon's public comments after *Swann* perfectly illustrate how liberal legal doctrine strengthened the hand of conservatives in their quest for a colorblind constitution. Although the final closing down of open doctrinal possibilities would not come until the Court's decision in *Keyes* in June 1973, Nixon's appropriation of legal concepts and categories reveals much about the trajectory of law and politics.

Nixon's approach hinged crucially on the *de jure/de facto* distinction. As early as March 1970, in response to Judge McMillan's order requiring extensive busing in Charlotte, Nixon issued a carefully considered written statement. He wrote that: "[t]he constitutional mandate will be enforced." But he went on to stake his initial claim about the nature of this mandate. It was one guaranteeing fair, unbiased treatment, but not "any compulsory busing beyond normal geographic school zones for the purpose of achieving racial balance." "To the extent possible," he added, "the neighborhood school concept should be the rule." Nixon went farther. He linked this position with a broader vision of American society. He stated:

> In speaking of "desegregation" or "integration," we often lose sight of what these mean within the context of a free, open, pluralistic society. We cannot be free, and at the same time be required to fit our lives into prescribed places on a racial grid—whether segregated or integrated, and whether by some mathematical formula or by automatic assignment. Neither can we be free, and at the same time be denied because of race—the right to associate with our fellow citizens on a basis of human equality.[34]

Nixon thus laid claim to *Green*'s understanding of wrong and remedy. As between the two, controlling the notion of "the wrong" is obviously more important than debates over remedies. The wrong, Nixon argues, is racial classification itself; indeed, our very freedom is threatened if the government places us on a "prescribed" place on "a racial grid." It comes almost as an afterthought that the government must also ensure that a "right to associate" is not irrationally denied on the basis of racial prejudice. Although it was not much perceived at the time, Nixon actually ended up getting much of what he wanted in from the Court in *Swann*.

In April 1971, when reporters asked Nixon for a reaction to the Court's decision, Nixon specifically referred back to his March 1970 statement and highlighted what he rightly perceived as hardening of legal doctrine based on the *de jure/de facto* distinction. He had, he said, long opposed "busing for the purpose of achieving racial balance" and supported the "neighborhood school." But now that the Court had spoken on the permissible scope of remedies, he would follow the law. Indeed, he said, "no one is above the law." Translation: "If the Court says that it is the law, I will enforce it. If you do not like it, blame the Court, don't blame me."[35] Nixon was then happy to step aside while a bi-partisan consensus emerged in Congress over the latter half of 1971 against busing to achieve integration. In September of that year, he nominated Lewis Powell and William Rehnquist to serve on the Court.

But then developments in the lower courts provided Nixon with another golden opportunity to, all at once, claim the mantle of legality, appeal to White working-class resentments, and profess his concern for the minority poor. In Richmond, Virginia, in January 1972, District Court Judge Robert Merhige issued a 325-page opinion ordering consolidation of Richmond with two surrounding suburban districts.[36] After concluding

---

33 Within months of *Swann*, lower courts ordered more extensive busing in many districts that were clearly guilty of *de jure* segregation, including Little Rock, Arkansas, Tampa and Jacksonville, Florida, Columbia and Savannah, Georgia, Louisville, Kentucky, Prince George's County, Maryland, Oklahoma City, Oklahoma, Memphis and Nashville, Tennessee, Dallas, Fort Worth, and Waco, Texas, and Norfolk, Virginia. Melnick, *supra* note 13.

34 This discussion of Nixon's strategy relies on McMahon's masterful account of Nixon's strategies in relation to law and courts. Kevin J. McMahon, Nixon's Court: His Challenge to Judicial Liberalism and Its Consequences (2011), at 84, 100.

35 *Id.* 105 (citing President Nixon's press conference of April 29, 1971).

36 This discussion of the Richmond case relies on Ryan's detailed account. Ryan, *supra*, note 29.

that *Brown* stood for a right to equal educational opportunity, Merhige found that, in a "bi-racial community," "meaningful integration" was an essential element of that right. Although Merhige offered several justifications for consolidation, this key one did not hinge on a predicate finding of intentional segregation on the part of the suburbs. Like Wisdom's argument in *Jefferson County*, Merhige's pointed sharply to the non-South.[37] Around the same time, in Detroit, Michigan, District Court Judge Stephen Roth was moving toward consolidation of the city schools with 53 suburban districts.

Nixon seized the moment. He used a nationally televised address to urge Congress to adopt anti-busing measures. The matter was now "urgent," Nixon said,

> because of a number of recent decisions of the lower Federal courts. Those courts have gone too far in some cases beyond the requirements laid down by the Supreme Court in ordering massive busing to achieve racial balance. The decisions have left in their wake confusion and contradiction in the law; anger, fear, and turmoil in local communities; and, worst of all, agonized concern among hundreds of thousands of parents for the education and safety of their children who have been forced by court order to be bused miles away from their neighborhood schools.

The "vast majority of Americans, white and black," he added, "feel strongly that the busing of school children away from their own neighborhoods for the purpose of achieving racial balance is wrong." Nixon's attack on busing came couched in concern for the minority poor. Congress should also spend more money to improve ghetto schools. James Ryan calls this "Nixon's Compromise": "students in the city would remain in the city and not be permitted to attend suburban schools; in exchange for staying put, they would get more resources."[38]

Nixon's turning of the tables was remarkably astute. It prefigured the world of race and equal protection doctrine that that we inhabit today. One central idea here is that liberals favor pursuing racial balance for its own sake. What makes this facially strange idea plausible is the liberals' reduction of race to phenotype, prejudice, and stigma. If liberals think race amounts to skin color and prejudice, then it follows that they think racial mixing produces racial justice. They want racial balancing not for no reason, as Nixon alleges, but for reasons that run back to the older, Jim Crow form of racism. These reasons would become increasingly weak as time went on. It then becomes easier and easier to say that liberals favor racial balancing for its own sake. Nixon added another constant theme of subsequent Supreme Court opinions—namely, the claim that liberals who pursue race-conscious policies are, themselves, mindlessly fostering racialist thinking and racial divisiveness and balkanization. They are to blame for White resentments and heightened racial conflict.[39]

The Court's next major pronouncement on school desegregation came in *Keyes*. The posture of *Keyes* on appeal forced the Court to confront the validity of the *de jure*/*de facto* distinction. It had to either reaffirm or abandon it. When the Court initially voted in the case in January 1973, Burger, Powell, and Rehnquist indicated that they would affirm the Tenth Circuit and hold that desegregation should be required only for the Park Hill area, the only neighborhood for which intentional segregation had been proven. The other justices "coalesced around the views of Justice Brennan." Brennan, it has been reported, liked to greet his new law clerks by asking them what the most important rule of law was, and then holding up five fingers, by which he meant five votes. The important thing for this liberal justice was the result, and not the legal justification for the result. The Court's decision process in *Keyes* illustrates this view perfectly.[40]

---

37 In the Denver, Colorado case, *Keyes v. School District No. 1*, District Court Judge William Doyle had embraced "equal educational opportunity" as the basis for ordering district-wide desegregation in a large, urban district. 313 F. Supp. 61 (D. Colo. 1970). I return to *Keyes* below.

38 Nixon, quoted in McMahon, *supra* note 34, at 108. (Nixon's "Address to the Nation on Equal Educational Opportunities and School Busing," Mar. 16, 1972). See also Ryan, *supra* note 29, at 4–5; 94–98.

39 *See* Reva B. Siegel, *From Colorblindness to Anti-Balkanization: An Emerging Ground of Decision in Race Equality Cases*, 120 Yale L.J. 1278 (2011).

40 John C. Jeffries, Jr., Lewis F. Powell: A Biography 292 (1994) ("coalesced around Justice Brennan"). Jeffries describes the Court's decision process in Keyes in detail. For "Brennan and five votes," see Silverstein, *supra* note 2, at 69.

Brennan's draft opinion, which would eventually command the Court, rejected the trial judge's claim that there was a positive right to "equal educational opportunity."[41] The touchstone of a constitutional violation would remain "purpose or intent to segregate." However, Brennan noted, the lower courts had not applied "the correct legal standard." A proper analysis, Brennan argued, required a two-step process that entailed shifting burdens onto the defendants' shoulders. First, a finding of intentional segregation in a substantial part of the district would impose a burden on defendants to rebut a strong presumption in favor of the conclusion that the segregation was systemic. Defendants would have to show that the parts of the system were really isolated from each other. If they could not, then the system would be deemed a "dual system," and, as in *Green* and *Swann*, an "all-out effort to desegregate" should follow.[42] Moreover, even in the unlikely event that a district met this first burden, Brennan continued, the finding of intentional segregation in a substantial part of the district still cast a shadow over any circumstantial evidence with respect to the rest of the district. The finding had "probative value" in assessing official intent elsewhere in the system.

Justice White recused himself (his old law firm in Colorado had once represented the school district), Justice Powell determined to draft his own opinion, concurring in the result but dissenting in part, and Justice Blackmun withheld his vote until he saw both the Brennan and Powell drafts. Brennan did not yet have his five votes.

Powell's view was not grounded in the country's history of racial subordination or in a positive right to equal educational opportunity. Rather, it was mostly grounded in his anger at sectional hypocrisy and his concerns about the potential counter-productivity of rigid racial balance remedies in general and busing in particular. His basic point was that what was fair for Charlotte should be fair for Denver.

Powell argued that the existence of racial separation in the schools, without regard to its cause, could trigger a judicial inquiry into whether school officials were "operating a genuinely integrated school system." Powell was exceedingly vague about what a district would have to show to meet this test, or about how this inquiry would then differ from the Court's focus on intentionally segregative acts. Moreover, Powell was careful throughout his opinion to emphasize that his analysis applied only *within* a school district, and not across districts. Finally, even if a violation were found, remedies would have to be "reasonable," by which Powell meant the result of "a balanced evaluation of the obligation of public school boards to promote desegregation with other, equally important educational interests," like "the neighborhood school concept."[43]

We now know that there may have been five, or perhaps even six, votes on the Court in *Keyes* for abandoning the *de jure/de facto* distinction. When Justice Brennan saw Powell's draft, he immediately circulated a memo stating that he would be happy to recast his majority opinion, and, indeed, to start the analysis where Powell said it should start. However, Brennan made it clear that he could not simply accept Powell's view of "neighborhood schools" and opposition to busing. Not surprisingly, Powell never responded to Brennan's invitation to negotiate over legal doctrine and remedies. Like his "diversity" rationale in *Bakke*, the doctrinal gymnastics that he proffered in *Keyes* were just instrumental, if not somewhat "tongue-in-check." For his part, Brennan then stood pat on the firmer legal foundation built up in *Green* and *Swann* based on intentionally segregative acts, and on his five votes.[44]

All of its flaws notwithstanding, one cannot help but wonder about what kind of life Powell's framework might have had, quite beyond the intentions of its author. The very vagueness of Powell's conception of wrong and remedies might well have led to different contests over them. Powell's view might have been more welcoming to liberal arguments about racial isolation and its consequences, for example. It might have opened up a new quadrant on the *Scrabble* board. But it was not to be. For instrumental reasons, the liberal majority on the Court opted for the well-worn doctrinal path.

---

41 413 U.S. 189, 208 (1973). No opinion in *Keyes* mentions the case, but in *San Antonio v. Rodriguez* (handed down in March 1973), a five-justice majority, led by Justice Powell, was in the process of rejecting that claim. 411 U.S. 1 (1973).

42 *Id.* at 199–202.

43 *Id.* at 226–28 ("duty to operate integrated school system"); at 226 ("within districts"); at 236 ("reasonable" remedies); at 242–48 (importance of neighborhood schools).

44 Alan David Freeman, *Legitimizing Discrimination Through Anti-Discrimination Law: A Critical Review of Supreme Court Doctrine*, 62 MINN L.R. 1049 (1978), at 1101 n.214. (Powell's opinion "gains a tongue-in-cheek character"); JEFFRIES, *supra* note 40, at 302–05.

Milliken v. Bradley (1974), the Detroit busing case, brings the "uncertainty" era of school desegregation jurisprudence to a close. *Milliken* is best seen *not* as most current liberal proponents of school desegregation see it, but rather simply as the last nail in the coffin. There is a virtual consensus among current racial liberals that the Court (and federal courts generally) were staunch allies in the battle for desegregation until President Nixon appointed four justices and the Court changed direction in *Rodriguez* and *Milliken*. On this view *Milliken* was a great, history-changing decision. *Milliken* is really the wrong target, however. The problems, which should never be viewed as limited to just the contours of legal doctrine, ran much deeper than the rise of the Nixon 4 and the failure to get a fifth vote in *Milliken*.

The Detroit case followed a trajectory similar to that of several non-Southern cases.[45] Complicated local- and state-level political battles led the school board to embrace a modest desegregation plan in April 1970. Nevertheless, White resistance to even this degree of change was immediate and widespread. White citizens staged boycotts, ousted liberal school board members, and secured a state law repealing the local plan. The NAACP filed *Milliken* in August 1970.

Equal protection doctrine was in flux. It is worth noting that this legal uncertainty allowed the NAACP to construct an antisubordination argument in court. Its case had two components, a housing case and a school case. Taken together, the two prongs of their case showed that the vast majority of White residents regarded Blacks as an inferior order of beings, beings unfit to live with, unfit to go to school with, unfit to associate with—in a word, unfit for equal citizenship.

District Court Judge Stephen Roth was so moved by these presentations that the idea for metropolitan-wide relief initially came not from the plaintiffs but from him. He went on to hold additional hearings on consolidation and to issue his order for metropolitan-wide relief in March 1972. With the suburbs now participating in the case, defendants appealed. In December 1972, a panel of the Sixth Circuit affirmed Judge Roth's decision and order. In June 1973, the full Sixth Circuit, sitting *en banc*, also affirmed Roth.[46] The Supreme Court heard arguments in *Milliken* in February 1974, and issued its 5 to 4 ruling in July.

Chief Justice Burger's opinion for the Court appealed to *Swann*'s key statement about violation and remedy. As with "any equity case," Burger wrote, "the nature of the violation determines the scope of the remedy." The violation was "intra-district," and therefore any remedy had to be limited to Detroit. The focus of the courts below, Burger added, had shifted to the suburbs "only because of their conclusion that total desegregation of Detroit would not produce the racial balance which they perceived as desirable." The lower courts sought a prescribed ratio of roughly 20 to 30 percent of Black students at each school. But *Swann* held that there was no constitutional right to any prescribed racial balance. Inter-district remedies would be appropriate only after a showing that the state or suburbs had intentionally caused urban-suburban segregation. School district lines were not mere matters of political convenience. Local control of education was a "deeply rooted" tradition, one of constitutional significance.

Milliken completed the doctrinal trajectory that began with *Green*. David Kirp once offered this comment:

> The Supreme Court's decision to discuss the issue entirely in terms of numbers—racial balance substituting for historically rooted understandings of racial justice, on one hand, and educationally-rooted understandings of equal opportunity on the other—proved to be a fatal misrepresentation of the problem.[47]

After *Keyes*, the law required advocates to engage in "tedious historical digs" to find intentional segregative acts.[48] After *Milliken*, there was little hope that racial balance remedies, with or without compensatory funding, could work. The violence in Boston was an extreme example, but by the late 1970s a sense of futility had set in.

---

45 This discussion of *Milliken* relies primarily on Joyce Baugh, The Detroit Busing Case (2011). *See also* Ryan, *supra* note 29.

46 Both the panel and the *en banc* court set aside the relevance of Judge Roth's findings about intentional government acts producing housing segregation. This enabled the Supreme Court to ignore this strand of argument in its decision in *Milliken*.

47 David L. Kirp, *Retreat Into Legalism: The Little Rock School Desegregation Case in Historic Perspective*, Ps 30 Pol.Sci. & Pol 443, 446 (1997).

48 *Id.*

The Supreme Court next issued a series of inconsistent rulings in separate desegregation cases from Dayton and Columbus, Ohio.[49] It also signed off on substituting money for racial balancing in a second appeal in the Detroit case.[50] And then it abandoned the field for over a decade, issuing no school desegregation rulings between 1979 and 1991.

As Desmond King and Rogers Smith have recently argued, in the late 1970s a new alignment of competing racial coalitions was fast taking shape on the terrain of racial liberalism.[51] The Court's equal protection doctrine reflected and helped constitute the new common sense about law and racial justice. In *Washington v. Davis* (1976), *Village of Arlington Heights v. Metropolitan Housing Development Corp.* (1977), and *Personnel Administrator v. Feeney* (1979), the Court's majority came down firmly in favor of a narrow intent standard for the Equal Protection Clause. This turn made it more difficult to challenge facially neutral policies with disparate racial consequence, but easier to attack race-conscious measures designed to correct past wrongs.[52]

In his controlling concurrence in *Regents v. Bakke* (1977), Justice Powell succeeded in promoting four ideas that would be crucial to the new order of equal protection.[53] First, he argued, all racial classifications should be greeted with skepticism by the courts. Second, Powell made the case for ruling history out of bounds as a legal justification for race-conscious measures. Third, in Powell's hands, race and ethnicity were flattened (he used the terms interchangeably). We were in fact "a nation of minorities." Fourth, in education, now, in addition to the interest in the largely fictional idea of correcting the discrete effects of identified acts of racial discrimination, governments could have a compelling interest in securing the educational benefits of "diversity."

The cultural power of the diversity rationale, which is, in truth, substantively rather weak and often simply incoherent, perhaps stems from its seamless continuity with racial liberalism. It is, as Sugrue writes, simply a variation on the self-same underlying "hearts and minds" view of race and racism.[54] Racial diversity becomes good for many of the same reasons that racial integration was good. The arguments for racial diversity often appeal to the same language of social psychology. The only difference is that now "cultural differences" are to be recognized and valued, and not washed away. As it was with an earlier generation's case for racial integration, so it is now with the modern case for diversity. Diversity breaks down racial stereotypes, fosters interracial tolerance and understanding, and promotes a more equal, integrated society in the future.

The rise of Ronald Reagan brought an aggressive colorblind constitutionalism into the heart of American national government, particularly the federal judiciary. The results could be seen in *Croson* (1989), *Adarand* (1995), *Hopwood* (1996), and the anti-affirmative action ballot initiatives, starting with California's Proposition 209 in 1996.[55]

The mid-1990s marked the beginning of the end for school desegregation as well. Various parties—sometimes school districts, sometimes aggrieved White parents, and even occasionally, as in Louisville, aggrieved Black parents—began to bring challenges to race-conscious student assignment or admissions policies in K-12 public education. Challenges proceeded along two tracks. The first one involved the dissolution of desegregation decrees and the ending of judicial oversight in proceedings seeking declarations of "unitary status."[56] After such a declaration, districts were free to return to neighborhood zoning and the increased school segregation entailed therein, and many did just that.

49 *Dayton Bd. of Educ. v. Brinkman*, 433 U.S. 406 (1977) [*Brinkman I*]; *Dayton Bd. of Educ. v. Brinkman*, 443 U.S. 526 (1979) [*Brinkman II*]; *Columbus Bd. of Educ. v. Penick*, 443 U.S. 449 (1979).

50 *Milliken v. Bradley*, 433 U.S. 267 (1977) [*Milliken II*].

51 Desmond S King & Rogers M. Smith, Still A House Divided: Race and Politics in Obama's America (2011).

52 *Washington v. Davis*, 426 U.S. 229 (1976), *Village of Arlington Heights v. Metro. Housing Dev. Corp.*, 429 U.S. 252 (1977); *Pers. Adm'r v. Feeney*, 442 U.S. 256 (1979).

53 *Regents of the Univ. of California v. Bakke*, 438 U.S. 265 (1978).

54 Sugrue, *supra* note 3, at 507–09.

55 *Richmond v. J.A. Croson Co.*, 488 U.S. 469 (1989); *Adarand Constructors, Inc. v. Peña*, 515 U.S. 200 (1995); *Hopwood v. Texas*, 78 F.3d 932 (5th Cir. 1996).

56 In three decisions issued between 1991 and 1995, the Supreme Court sent strong signals to lower courts to end judicial supervision of district policies that had often persisted for decades. A finding of unitary status meant that remedial measures had removed "all vestiges" of official discrimination "to the extent practicable." *Bd. of Educ. of Oklahoma City v. Dowell*, 498 U.S. 237 (1991); *Freeman v. Pitts*, 503 U.S. 467 (1992); and *Missouri v. Jenkins*, 515 U.S. 70 (1995).

The second track involved school districts previously released from judicial supervision or never subject to it that wanted voluntarily to take race into account to promote integration. These cases pitted an older settled law that had held that voluntarily undertaken desegregation initiatives were permissible, against the more recent political and legal assault on race conscious measures in all of their forms. White challengers brought several cases, seven of which reached the federal courts of appeal between 1998 and 2005.[57] As a general matter, lower courts invalidated race-conscious measures before the Court's decisions in *Gratz/Grutter* (2003), and upheld them thereafter on the basis of *Grutter*'s reaffirmation of Powell's reasoning in *Bakke*. After *Grutter*, the debate narrowed to how the K-12 public school setting was like and unlike higher education in terms of the nature of diversity itself and its purported educational benefits. The Court's decision in *PICS* does not finally resolve the debate, but districts' room for voluntary maneuver grows ever narrower.

Proponents of the race-conscious measures at issue typically invoked the conservative tradition of judicial deference to democratically elected, local officials and the value of local control in education. They also pointed out that if diversity mattered in higher education, then it mattered even more for young children with young hearts and minds. Finally, they said, unlike in the higher education context, in the K-12 setting no one was denied a coveted place as the result of race consciousness. Public school integration benefitted everyone and harmed no one. Opponents argued that "true diversity" in *Bakke* and *Grutter* encompassed much more than mere "racial diversity." Racial diversity was but one component of true diversity, the pursuit of which absolutely required treating persons as persons, and not members of, or stand-ins for, some rigid notion of groups and group identity. Without an individualized decision process, the pursuit of diversity always amounted to racial balancing for its own sake, with its threat of embedding racialist thinking in institutions and policies and fostering racial divisiveness.

Rather than wade far into the details of these cases, I conclude this section with a few thoughts and comments about what they really show us. What is on view here is nothing if not the historical exhaustion of racial liberalism in the area of school desegregation. Three difficulties in particular stand out.

First, one is struck in almost all of these cases by the triviality of the policies at issue. Nothing large or transformative was at stake. In most of these cases, school districts were just tinkering at the margins with the racial compositions of a few schools. The policies' very triviality undermined the ability to defend them, for it implied that their proponents could not really have been all that serious about fighting racial isolation or securing racial integration. Second, and more importantly, we can see the inadequacy of racial liberalism's view of race as phenotype, plus stigmatization. It is that view of race and racial justice that gave us the ultimate goal of racial integration, and now gives us the diversity rationale. These cases show us that the diversity rationale is inadequate for the pursuit of racial justice, and just how easily and plausibly it can be turned into just "racial balancing for its own sake." Third, these cases, and particularly the Louisville case, at least raise the question whether the participation and views of marginalized racial groups have been neglected by the current proponents of school desegregation.

Wessmann v. Gittens and *Parents Involved in Community Schools* [PICS] ("the Seattle case") illustrate the first two difficulties. *Wessmann* involved a challenge to the Boston School District's use of racial preferences in the admissions process for its most prestigious elite high school, Boston Latin. The school district awarded half of all seats strictly according to grades and a score on a standardized test, and half by a formula tied to the racial composition of the district as a whole. Students did not receive individualized consideration. Some White students with higher grades and test scores could be denied admission in preference to members of racial minority groups with lower ones. Sarah Wessmann was such a student. She sued the district alleging a violation of the Equal Protection Clause.

57 The cases came from Boston, Massachusetts: *Wessmann v. Gittens*, 160 F.3d 790 (1998) (1st Cir.); Arlington, Virginia: *Tuttle v. Arlington Cnty. Sch. Bd.*, 195 F.3d 698 (1999) (4th Cir.); Montgomery County, Maryland: *Eisenberg v. Montgomery Cnty. Pub. Sch.*, 197 F.3d 123 (1999) (4th Cir.); Rochester, New York: *Brewer v. West Irondequoit Cent. Sch. Dist.*, 212 F.3d 738 (2000); Lynn, Massachusetts: *See Comfort v. Lynn Sch. Comm.*, 418 F.3d 1 (1st Cir. 2005) (*en banc*); Louisville, Kentucky: *McFarland v. Jefferson Cnty. Pub. Sch.*, 416 F.3d 513 (2005) (6th Cir.) (affirming, without opinion, the reasoning of the district court in *McFarland v. Jefferson Cnty. Pub. Sch.*, 330 F. Supp. 2d 834 (2004)); and Seattle, Washington: *Parents Involved in Cmty. Sch. v. Seattle Sch. Dist. No. 1*, 426 F.3d 1162 (2005) (*en banc*) (9th Cir.)

The district defended its policy by invoking the diversity rationale. The federal district court upheld the affirmative action policy on that basis, but the Fourth Circuit Court of Appeals reversed. In his opinion for the panel, Judge Selya wrote that "few would gainsay the attractiveness of diversity." However, the court had to look beyond abstractions to "the concrete workings of the policy." The "devil was in the details."[58]

The policy, Judge Selya noted, categorized students by race and then used a proportional representation scheme to allocate some of the coveted seats. "Diversity" rapidly melted into mechanical racial balancing. The district's own analysis showed that using only the composite score for grades and test scores, without the racial preferences, would cut the number of Black and Hispanic students admitted in half, but together they would still constitute 15–20 percent of the student body. This percentage would pale in comparison to their overall percentage of district students (73 percent), and also in comparison also to their overall percentage of the applicant pool. But could the district easily defend a need for 35 percent Black and Hispanic enrollment, as opposed to 20 percent, if its interest was in the educational benefits of diversity? Why isn't a school that is 10 percent Black, 10 percent Hispanic, 40 percent Asian-American, and 40 percent White a racially diverse school?

In his concurring opinion in Wessmann, Judge Boudin was refreshingly candid. The district, he wrote, was really engaged in "a thoughtful effort to assist minorities historically disadvantaged while, at the same time, preserving the essentially competitive character of the schools in question. So viewed," he concluded, "there was no misfit between problem and remedy." The only misfit was with the requirements of law, as dictated by Bakke, Croson, and Grutter.[59]

The Seattle case exposes the same problems of triviality, race viewed as phenotype, and the inadequacy of the diversity rationale. Although Seattle had a long and complicated history of school desegregation struggles and policies, vigorous racial integration was mostly dead before Parents Involved began.[60] In 1998, the district adopted an open choice policy for its 10 high schools. Any rising ninth grader could apply for admission to any school, and could list schools in order of preference. If a particular school was both oversubscribed and racially out of balance, then the district used a series of tiebreakers to allocate the scarce seats. A high school was out of balance if its White/nonwhite student population varied by more than 10 percentage points from the White/nonwhite ratio for the district as a whole. As of 2000–01, 41 percent of Seattle's 46,000 students were White, and 59 percent were nonwhite (23.8 percent were Asian-American; 23.1 percent were African-American; 10.3 percent were Latino; and 2.8 percent were Native American). For oversubscribed, "out of balance" schools, the district looked first to whether the applicant had a sibling at the school, next to racial composition, and finally to residential proximity to the school. Typically, the sibling tiebreaker accounted for 10 percent of the placements at the oversubscribed schools, as did the racial tiebreaker, and residential proximity accounted for all the rest, or 80 percent.

In the summer of 2000, when Jill Kurfirst's son Andy Meeks was not accepted into Ballard High School's Biotechnology Career Academy, she joined with Parents Involved in Community Schools to sue the district. In 2000–01, four high schools were both oversubscribed and out of racial balance: Ballard, Nathan Hale, Roosevelt, and Franklin. According to the district, the racial tiebreaker meant that Ballard received 107 more nonwhite students than it otherwise would have, Nathan Hale 27 more, and Roosevelt, 82 more. Franklin received 89 more White students than it otherwise would have.[61]

The partisans of colorblindness had a field day with Seattle's policy. First, the conservative challengers pointed out, in order to operate its racial tiebreaker, the district would have to have some way of classifying individual students by race. Seattle handled that problem they way we typically handle it nowadays, by "self-identification." But in tried and true bureaucratic fashion, Seattle officials dutifully provided for the

58 *Id.* at 797–98.

59 *Id.* at 810.

60 For histories of school desegregation in Seattle, see Laura Kohn, Priority Shift: The Fate of Mandatory Busing for School Desegregation in Seattle and The Nation (1996) and Jennifer Hehnke, The Politics of Racial Integration in the Seattle Public Schools: Discourse, Policy, and Political Change, 1954–1991 (unpublished Ph.D. thesis, University of Oregon, Eugene, OR.).

61 *Parents Involved in Cmty. Sch. v. Seattle Sch. Dist. No. 1*, 551 U.S. 701, 713, 714 (2007).

contingency of racial non-self-identification. And so there it was on page six of the aggrieved White parents' main brief to the Supreme Court:

> For purposes of this [racial] preference, a student is deemed to be of the race specified in her registration materials. When initially registering for Seattle's public schools, parents must identify the race of each child by using codes on a form … If a parent declines to specify a race, the child is assigned a race by the District, based on a visual inspection of the parent or student.[62]

Although there is no indication in *PICS* that the district ever did assign a student to a race by visual inspection, it is still jarring to see the contemplation of it.[63] This extreme example is problematic not because racial categorization is *inherently* demeaning and divisive, but rather because it is a telling example of what Guinier has aptly called "racial illiteracy." It "misreads" race by neglecting that fact that race is more varied and fluid than in past eras, and that mechanisms of racial subordination grew ever-harder to name, understand, and challenge. Race as phenotype (with or without the visual inspection) overlooks altogether the place- and resource-based material inequalities that continue to constitute race and to make it matter for life chances and equal standing in the community.[64]

The White parents opening salvo about race by visual inspection set the stage for a scathing attack on what their brief several times called the district's pursuit of increased "skin pigmentation diversity." Once again, the goal of diversity was easily transformed into racial balancing for its own sake. Seattle used a mechanical "white vs. nonwhite" distinction, even though the nonwhites in the district were comprised of several different groups. If the policy was really about the educational benefits of diversity, then should not the district be paying attention to these differences? As Chief Justice Roberts twice pointed out in his opinion, under Seattle's policy a high school in which 50 percent of the students were White and 50 percent were Asian-American would be considered racially balanced, while a much more diverse school with 20 percent Whites, 25 percent African-Americans, 25 percent Latinos, and 30 percent Asian-Americans would not be.[65] In his dissent, Justice Breyer called this hypothetical "fanciful," but it does go to the heart of the trouble with diversity here. Oversubscribed Seattle schools were already quite diverse, and this would be true without the racial tiebreaker. Seattle could not very well defend its policy in terms of eliminating or even reducing "racial isolation" because its policy left two Seattle high schools (Cleveland and Rainier Beach) with student populations that were 90 percent or more minority, and disproportionately poor.[66]

Chief Justice Roberts was also able to use comparisons to the Louisville desegregation policy to drive home his point. In Louisville, the Jefferson County Public School District (JCPS) student population was roughly 66 percent White and 34 percent Black. JCPS used a controlled choice policy implemented so as to make sure that the racial composition of each non-magnet school came within a 15 percent band of the racial demographics of the district as a whole. Under its policy, no school could have a Black population of less than 15 percent or more than 50 percent. Obviously, the White student population of a school could range from 85

---

62 Appellant-Petitioner's Brief, *Parents Involved in Cmty. Sch. v. Seattle Sch.Dist. No. 1*, No 05–908, at 6 (hereinafter "Petitioner's Brief").

63 Lest anyone think the prospect fanciful, racial assignment by visual inspection actually did occur in *Brewer*, a case arising in Rochester, New York. There, the officials running an inter-district transfer policy had a *de facto* policy of limiting urban-to-suburban transfers to minority students, and suburban-to-urban ones to white students. Jennifer Haak was a white Rochester student who sought to transfer to a suburban district. Eventually, one suburb (West Irondequoit) accepted her. She even successfully completed an interview at the receiving school. Apparently, the school leaders were unaware of racial policy. But then a program administrator observed her at a subsequent orientation meeting, saw that she looked white, checked her self-identification on file with the Rochester district (which confirmed her sense that Haak was white), and then informed her guardian (Brewer) that Jennifer was not eligible for the program because only minority students could transfer out of Rochester. Brewer sued. The district court struck down the program as not narrowly tailored. The Second Circuit reversed and remanded for a full hearing. The school officials then settled with the plaintiff. *Brewer*, 212 F.3d 738 (2000).

64 Lani Guinier, *From Racial Liberalism to Racial Literacy:* Brown v. Board of Education *and the Interest Convergence Dilemma*, 91 J. Am Hist. 92 (2004). *See also* Elizabeth Anderson, The Imperative Of Integration (2010).

65 *Parents Involved in Cmty. Sch.*, 551 U.S. 701 at 724.

66 Petitioner's Brief, *supra* note 63, at 14.

to 50 percent. Roberts could thus ask why the pursuit of "diversity" and its purported educational benefits in Seattle meant that the White population of a high school there could not drop below 30 percent, whereas in Louisville it could not drop below 50 percent. In Louisville, a school could have as few as 15 percent minority students, but in Seattle it could have no fewer than roughly 50 percent. No one could ever show any tight connection between any particular racial mix of students and the purported benefits of diversity. The problem in court at least is with the diversity rationale itself.[67]

The Louisville case, *Meredith v. Jefferson County Public School District*, was significantly different from the other voluntary integration cases in several ways.[68] However, whatever the differences between the Louisville case and other voluntary integration cases, Jefferson County Public School's policies and its defense of them shared the same, underlying, and highly problematic view of race as phenotype, plus stigmatization, that we find in the other cases. Once we scratch the surface of the Louisville case, we can see this problematic conception of race at work. We can also see strong evidence that, as a result of this conception of race, the district had neglected the concerns and values of large segments of the African-American community.

White parents denied transfer applications filed *Meredith* in 2002. However, this dispute really began much earlier, in the mid-1990s, with the grievances of a group of African-American parents. They were specifically upset with the way the racial balance guidelines operated to exclude Blacks from a desirable magnet program geared toward careers in law at Louisville's Central High School. In 1994, the district actually removed 10 Black students from the school to keep it within the guidelines. During the summers of 1995 and 1996, hundreds of Black students, many of whom lived near Central, received rejection letters noting that rejection was based on the district's need to "keep all schools within racial compliance." Many of them, like Dionne Hopson, were assigned to far-away schools in predominantly White, working-class areas. Hopson's assigned school was 12 miles from her home. The African-American parents formed CEASE, "Citizens for Equitable Assignment to School Environment."[69]

As Garland shows, CEASE activists were not opposed to the ideal of integration, but, like many African-Americans before them, they objected to many features of "the way desegregation had been carried out—with the closure of black schools, the firing of black teachers, and the one-way system of busing black children ..."[70] Tellingly, for high school placements, only predominantly Black neighborhoods were designated as satellite zones, which required residents to be transported to schools outside of their neighborhoods. The burdens of integration were not equally shared.[71]

Of course, the views of CEASE parents were hotly contested within Louisville's African-American community. African-Americans had generally supported the district's desegregation program through the mid-1990s. CEASE wanted to end the racial guidelines and busing, but at the same time claimed that racism was a deep, structural feature of the JCPS. Whites, they said, were the ones who got to make the choices. Other groups of Black parents formed and stepped forward to defend the district's integration policies, and thus to oppose CEASE, but they agreed with CEASE that the district had failed to address such issues as academic tracking and the exclusion of Black students from its "Advanced Program."

CEASE had a hard time finding a lawyer willing to take on their cause. Eventually, they found Teddy B. Gordon, a White local lawyer who was less than experienced in handling civil rights litigation. CEASE sued the district in federal court, alleging that its denial of access to Central High School on the basis of race violated the Equal Protection Clause. The case came before Federal District Court Judge John G. Hayburn. After a trial in 1999, Judge Hayburn determined that prior rulings had not actually released the district from judicial supervision. CEASE and Gordon then sought a declaration of unitary status. With this new case

---

67 *Parents Involved*, 551 U.S. 701 at 726–28.

68 This account of the background of the Louisville case is based on Sarah Garland, Divided We Fail: The Story of an African American Community That Ended the Era of School Desegregation (2013).

69 *Id.* at 19–30. In his fine book on the Kansas City, Missouri case, Joshua Dunn describes a similar dynamic in which large segments of the African-American community experienced a lack of voice, a lack of representation, and also objected to the denial of material opportunities (exclusion from magnet schools) in service of racial mixing as an end in itself. Joshua Dunn, Complex Justice: The Case of *Missouri v. Jenkins* (2008).

70 Garland, *supra* note 69, at x, 153.

71 *Hampton v. Jefferson Cnty. Bd. of Educ.*, 72 F. Supp. 2d 753 (2000) (*Hampton I*).

pending, Judge Hayburn urged JCPS leaders and CEASE to enter into settlement negotiations. Garland reports that JCPS board members and officials were rigidly committed to their racial balance guidelines:

> CEASE offered to drop the suit if the school district allowed 150 additional black students to enroll at Central and created law and medicine magnets elsewhere to accommodate additional applicants. They also asked that 200 more black students be admitted to the district's best-performing schools ... The school board refused the proposal. CEASE reduced its request to 75 additional black students at Central. The school board again refused, arguing that letting one school go out of balance would open the door to requests from every school in the district.[72]

Judge Hayburn ended up finding that JCPS's use of rigid racial balance guidelines at magnet schools violated the Equal Protection Clause. He also declared the district "unitary," and opined that JCPS was free to pursue any constitutional student assignment policies that it wanted to.[73] The JCPS then continued its managed choice program, with the preexisting racial guidelines.

White parents then filed suit, challenging the district's denial of their transfer applications because of its adherence to these guidelines. The policies at issue were not trivial. The JCPS had long pursued policies that secured racial mixing at the building level, and this in a large district (97,000 students) encompassing both urban core and outlying suburban areas. Desegregation proponents had long trumpeted Louisville as an under-recognized success story. In June 2004, relying on the Court's opinion in *Grutter*, Judge Hayburn held that the district had a compelling interest in operating racially integrated schools, and that its policies were narrowly tailored to achieving that goal. He found more than enough evidence of the educational and social benefits of integration. In 2005, the Court of Appeals affirmed Hayburn's decision.[74]

In its decision in *PICS*, the Court ruled that JCPS could no longer classify students by race and then make that classification relevant to an individual student's assignment to a school or program. However, not much changed in Louisville. The JCPS simply revised the core of its program, which already relied on zoning and clustering, by using neighborhood-level data about race, poverty, and parent education levels. The new plan "closely resembled the old one." It "divided the city and suburbs into two regions, A and B," defined by these three factors. "Region A encompassed most of the city's black neighborhoods, while B encompassed most of its white areas." Students were now classified not by race, but by whether they lived in region A or region B. Schools were now required to draw between 15 and 50 percent of their students from region A.[75]

Some Notes on Reviving the Anti Subordination Case for School Desegregation

In this chapter, I have offered a sketch of the evolution of equal protection doctrine in school desegregation cases, one colored by a focus on the significance of racial liberalism in shaping the path of the law. I have argued that a doctrinal "closing down" of possibilities began with *Green* and was fully completed before *Milliken*. I have also suggested that conservatives opposed to racial reform easily coopted and reframed liberals' moral and legal arguments. Although, in current discourse, these two ideological positions (racial liberalism and racial conservatism) do indeed yield different legal and policy prescriptions, what they share in terms of conceptions of "race" and "racial justice" is perhaps more important.[76] On this view, *PICS* represents not so much a triumph of racial conservatism over racial liberalism, but rather a logical endpoint of racial liberalism itself. *PICS* is just the latest (and perhaps next to last) tile in a game a *Scrabble* that started to go awry when the liberals on the Court opted for legalism over substance.

72 Garland, *supra* note 69, at162.

73 Hampton v. Jefferson Cnty. Pub. Sch., 102 F. Supp. 2d 358, 364, 368 n.19, 368–69 (2000) (*Hampton II*).

74 McFarland v. Jefferson Cnty. Pub. Sch., 330 F. Supp. 2d 834 (2004). The Court of Appeals affirmed without writing its own opinion. It simply referenced and endorsed Hayburn's opinion.

75 Garland, *supra* note 69, at 190.

76 I draw here, again, on Hosang-Martinez, *supra* note 1.

What is to be done? One plausible response to these developments would be to give up on school desegregation and instead pursue other reforms that might improve education for poor, minority children, such as enhanced educational funding or charter schools. This, however, would be a grave mistake. In education, cross-race, cross-class desegregation is the only possibly viable reform that attacks rather than accepts the racial ghetto. Racial subordination is now much less a matter of White animosity or prejudice than place-based racial construction, exclusion, and containment. Certainly, a lack of good jobs, segregated housing patterns (and how markets reproduce them), and policing and criminal justice policies all probably play a larger role in the modern contours of racial subordination, compared to public schooling. But separate and unequal schooling, too, is an important part of the new "post-racial" reality. Moreover, compared to other domains, schooling in the United States is a relatively open space for oppositional politics, given its public nature and its place in the mythology of the American Dream.

In any event, in education, as the remaining proponents of desegregation continue to argue, desegregation promises to do the most work in undermining racial inequalities, if only it could be had. As one proponent of desegregation once put it, we face here a paradox of "best policy, worst politics."[77] In my view, the puzzle is not only how to get from here to there, but also why proponents of desegregation have not devoted much more time and energy to thinking about how to get from here to there. I conclude with some political and strategic observations about how the cause of desegregation might be revived, which, in turn, demonstrate that racial liberalism itself has helped generate the current ideological and strategic straightjacket.

We can begin this quest for a revival with Derrick Bell's longstanding critique of school desegregation litigation. In the mid-1970s, it seemed to Bell that school desegregation litigation had gone off the rails. In an essay published in 1976 in *The Yale Law Journal*, he rose to his feet to object.[78] To the great consternation of his erstwhile colleagues, Bell argued that at least some of the new difficulties could be traced to the civil rights litigators themselves. He urged them to rethink their ideological commitments and related legal and political strategies. Both the virtues of Bell's critique and its defects can inform a search for new possibilities today.

Bell's critique of how school desegregation litigation had come to be conducted had three interrelated components: lawyers and clients; liberal reformers' conception of their cause; and liberal reformers' conception of the role of law and courts in struggles for change.

In reform litigation, the attorney-client relationship raises thorny questions about interest representation, citizens' participation, and lawyers' accountability to clients or constituents for the positions they take in court. In the mid-1960s, Bell argued, although views about desegregation and inequality within the African-American community grew ever-more diverse, the mainstream civil rights lawyers continued to assume the unquestioned authority to speak for all. They often preferred "nominal" or "phantom" plaintiffs who played no role in shaping litigation strategies or their coordination with extra-judicial political efforts.

Bell made this attorney-client dynamic the heart of his analysis, which he misconstrued as a problem of legal ethics. All else equal, the active involvement of ordinary citizens in commissioning and controlling their lawyers is to be preferred to lawyers acting on their own, but not because it is unethical for lawyers to act on their own (in fact, they do that all the time), but because citizen participation makes success in both court and politics more likely. Change on behalf of the have-nots generally requires political mobilization, and litigation can sometimes help foster that. This is true, whatever the goal of litigation. But here we should note that the cause and its justifications are one thing, and the attorney-client relationship that forms in pursuit of the cause is another. The mainstream lawyers that Bell criticized believed in and pursued a political position that, as I have suggested above, reflected and projected the basic assumptions of racial liberalism. This view was just one among many in the urban centers in the mid-1960s. Bell made a valuable point about these lawyers' tendency to take a top-down, technocratic, "we-know-what's-best" approach to reform litigation, but his real

---

77 Jennifer Hochschild, *Is School Desegregation Still a Viable Policy Option*, 30 PS: Pol. Sci. & Pol. 458 (1997).

78 Derrick Bell, *Serving Two Masters: Integration Ideals and Client Interests in School Desegregation Litigation*, 85 Yale L.J. 470 (1976). From 1960 to 1966, Bell worked as a staff attorney for the NAACP LDF; he worked mainly on school desegregation cases in the South. From 1966 to 1968, he worked for the Department of Health, Education and Welfare's Office of Civil Rights. Bell reiterated and deepened his critique over subsequent decades. *See* Bell, And We Are Not Saved (1987), Chapter 4; Derrick Bell, Silent Covenants: *Brown v. Board of Education* and the Unfulfilled Hopes for Racial Reform (2004).

problem was with their ideological stance (their conception of the cause) and their concomitant theory of how change could be brought about.

The liberal reformers, Bell argued, had a particular conception of the cause. They were, he said, religiously devoted to "unconditional integration." The goal of integration as an end in itself led readily to an uncritical acceptance of the rigid racial balance remedies forthcoming from the courts. Desegregation "by-the-numbers" had for them taken on a symbolic importance all out of proportion to its consequences, in terms of both group empowerment and educational results. Bell charged that, for the mainstream lawyers, the "actual presence of white children was essential," and *Brown* stood for "desegregation, not education."[79] For Bell, by contrast, the ultimate goal had to be "educational improvement." It was already clear that Black communities were bearing the brunt of the burdens of desegregation remedies.[80] But aside from these difficulties, Bell argued that integrationists had lost sight of "the real evil of pre-*Brown* schools: the state supported subordination of blacks in every aspect of the educational process." Legally mandated separation was just the most glaring manifestation of pervasive subordination. "Educational improvement" (whatever that turned out to mean) had to be seen as a key means to the larger goal of ending racial subordination.

Let us pause for a moment to consider this key term in Bell's lexicon, and in this chapter, "racial subordination." One might plausibly say that it is both vague and emotive, more a proclamation of political identity and commitment by one who uses it than a useful starting point for analysis and strategy. By contrast, with Bell, we might say that the claim that existing institutional arrangements reflect and foster racial subordination is indeed a useful starting point precisely because it stakes a claim about justice and fairness as between (quite roughly defined) groups; it is a claim made by one group (the subordinated) against another group (the dominating). It calls our attention to intertwined group positions and relational power—perhaps even to structures of inequality that can reproduce themselves quite well without the presence of much racial prejudice and discrimination—and it diverts our initial attention at least from racial liberalism's fascination with White attitudes and Black stigmatization. It says, as Judge Wisdom said, that one group is doing something to, or enjoying something in relation to, another group, and that that is just plain wrong.

Bell moved directly from his insistence on "subordination" and "antisubordination" as starting points to an objection to the mainstream lawyers' use of what one scholar subsequently called "damage imagery" to portray the harm done to minority children and thereby to evoke White sympathy.[81] Portrayals of harm, often in "lurid detail," covertly classed Blacks "as undesirable objects of interaction."[82] The mainstream lawyers were making too much peace with the racism they purported to fight. They misunderstood both the nature of the problem and the depths of the political struggle needed to combat it. The struggle had to be waged broadly, on both cultural and structural fronts at once, as well as in court.

Bell's targets had responses to this objection, and to his credit he included them in two long footnotes.[83] For these advocates, racial mixing was the only way to break out of the iron grip of racial categorization and stigmatization. Separate but equal was, after all, inherently unequal. For Bell, the easy acceptance of the idea that separate Black institutions were inherently degrading was, itself, inherently degrading. Contrary to what the Court said in *Brown*, Blacks were not a "damaged race" and separation itself was not an injury. This dispute, which yesteryear's discourse took up as "integrationism" versus "separationism," is, admittedly, rather old news. For my purposes, however, there are two important implications of this dispute between Bell and the integrationists over race and stigmatization.

First, I think it makes sense to see Bell as objecting primarily to racial liberalism. In the context of the mid-1970s, he naturally saw the goal of school desegregation as a necessary entailment of this ideological position, which he found objectionable. He therefore promoted an alternative goal ("educational improvement") and alternative means to it, such as enhanced school funding and political empowerment through Black control of governance structures. However, it seems to me that one can embrace Bell's critical stance toward racial

79 Bell (1976), *supra* note 79, at 477–78; 482.

80 See Bell (1987), *supra*, note 79, at 104–05; Bell (2004), *supra* note 79, at 112–25.

81 *See* Darly Michael Scott, Contempt and Pity: Social Policy and the Image of the Damaged Black Psyche, 1880–1996 (1997).

82 Bell (1976), *supra* note 79, at 479 n.12.

83 *Id.* at 480 n.32, 492 n.64.

liberalism and integrationism and yet still endorse a struggle for the goal of desegregated schools. In principle, there is no inherent connection between an anti-subordination perspective on race and Bell's rejection of the goal of desegregation. Indeed, desegregation may well be the reformist measure in education that promises to do the most work in education because it rejects a key practice involved in keeping poor, minority students in their place. If such a struggle were justified in the broader language of anti-subordination, would subordinated citizens be more likely to embrace it?

Second, and relatedly, Bell seemed troubled also by the practical political implications of racial liberalism's emphasis on irrationality and stigmatization. He seemed to be calling for recognition of the positive side of racial identity, the varied and valued cultural forms that emerged out of experiences of racial oppression, as well as the existential liberation arising out of struggles embracing positive racial consciousness and solidarity.[84] The liberal focus on educational and psychological harms, on damage imagery, was perhaps not conducive to inspiring effective action by those being wronged. It was not an honorable stance from which to go forward with a demand for justice. This point directs our attention not simply to the ultimate goal and how it is justified, but also to processes of political and legal change.

The last component (of three) of Bell's critique had to do with the liberal reformers' conception of law, politics, and actual processes of change. He argued that the mainstream litigators had come to over-rely on litigation and court decisions, to the neglect of community organizing, mobilization, and protest. Here, Bell astutely picked up on an emerging realistic critique of "legalism," a view that Stuart Scheingold had just then explicated as "the myth of rights."[85] "Law and lawyers," Bell wrote, "had received too much credit" for the reforms won since *Brown*. Because these lawyers had not given favorable structural conditions and grassroots mobilization and pressure their due, they failed to appreciate the potential ancillary and indirect benefits of litigation activity. "[T]he attorney must be more than a litigator," Bell said. Litigation should be used "as a community organizing tool, an educational forum, a means of obtaining data, a method of exercising political leverage, and a rallying point for public support."[86]

With the great benefit of hindsight, we can see that there were two main problems with Bell's analysis, and highlighting these, too, can help point a way forward. One problem was that Bell treated the three elements of his critique (attorney-client, liberal integrationism, and law, politics and change) as an undifferentiated whole. It was true historically (at least since the mid-1960s) that, with the NAACP and LDF's efforts, a top-down approach to the lawyer-client relationship, a commitment to racial liberalism and integrationism, and a legalistic approach to law and change all went hand-in-hand. Bell's view of them as such, then, made perfect sense. But my point here is that there are no necessary connections among them. For example, one could easily imagine an instrumental case for desegregation as the best means to other ends, like Bell's "educational improvement," and, indeed, that is how most liberals seek to make the case for desegregation today, even if their arguments still include too much talk about what the poor lack. But the proponents of such an effort could follow Bell's advice about the attorney-client relationship (assuming that litigation will be part of the struggle), and, relatedly, about how to understand the role of law and courts in processes of change, and yet still jettison his rejection of school desegregation *tout court*.

Another problem with Bell's analysis involved his realistic approach to legal doctrine and its significance in reform struggles. This view of legal doctrine as insignificant window dressing never allowed for the potential malleability of legal concepts and categories or the creative processes through which actors can sometimes create and advance new legal norms and meanings. Therefore Bell's view made no room for an inquiry into the connection between the specific content and character of legal claims, on one hand, and possibilities for political organization and mobilization, on the other.

For those interested in reviving the cause of school desegregation, what lessons follow from these discussions of the evolution of equal protection doctrine and the virtues and defects of Bell's critique of liberal reform efforts?

A revived case for school desegregation would recognize the limits of racial liberalism while at the same time acknowledging the difficulty of formulating actionable claims pointing beyond it. It would seek to move

84 For a discussion of positive race consciousness and oppositional politics, see GUINIER & TORRES, *supra* note 7.

85 Bell (1976), *supra* note 79, at 513 n.137.

86 *Id.* at 513.

quickly past race as phenotype, irrational fear and prejudice, and stigmatization, to an account of racialized injustices linked to unequal wealth and power, and the connections between durable inequalities and place. The problem is not that we must find a way to include poor, minority kids in what the middle class now rightly and justly enjoys; the problem is structural. The privileges of some depend structurally on the exclusion and suffering of others. Such a case would make racial subordination and the honor of resisting it central to the cause. It would emphasize equal citizenship and belonging, and downplay or avoid damage imagery or the celebration of "diversity." It would hold, with Judge Wisdom, that those consigned to ghetto schools are being wronged because they are clearly being denied access to equal participation in the life of the community; they are being denied access to knowledge, to social networks, and to a fair chance at human flourishing. It would hold, in short, that when it takes the form of ghetto schooling, *de facto* segregation is now the moral equivalent of what *de jure* segregation once was, and it should be resisted with the same fervor.

Such a rhetorical stance might have important strategic implications for organizing and mobilizing those being taken advantage of. I assume that the organization of ordinary citizens and bottom-up pressure from them will be a necessary part of any effort that threatens White privilege and opportunity hoarding, even if bottom-up pressure alone is often not sufficient. In any event, it is clear that school officials in charge of educational bureaucracies (the "policy audience" for most current liberal policy commentary) cannot be expected to do more than tinker at the margins with population counts and then wax eloquent about the benefits of diversity. They have neither the incentives nor institutional capacities to do more than that, unless they are pressured to do so.

Admittedly, the history of the troubled crusade for school desegregation might lead to despair about the prospects for mobilizing citizens to fight for it, or for securing official institutional support. However, I suggest that there may be some latent, overlooked opportunities lurking within American political institutions.

For example, Desmond King and Rogers Smith have developed an interesting framework for understanding race and politics in the United States. They begin with the idea of "competing racial policy alliances." Such an alliance is a coalition comprised of "leading political figures, governing institutions they have occupied, and politically active groups." Alliances "compete in multiple arenas for political support." A great virtue of this approach is its injunction to take into view, all at once, ideas (especially ideas about race), economic interests, and the institutional locations where ideas and interests find homes. Over the course of American history, Smith and King show "different governing institutions have been controlled by proponents of different racial policies." The American state is not a unitary "racial state," but rather a highly fragmented one. Fragmentation generally works against the interests of the have-nots, but it can also present actors with openings and opportunities.[87]

If there is a political-institutional space for the revival of school desegregation today, then it must be American state-level politics, and especially state constitutionalism and state courts. State politics and state constitutional processes have long been alternative forums for the development of insurgent political movements and policy innovations. Moreover, struggles for new state constitutional provisions or the reinterpretation of existing constitutional texts have often successfully pressed for the recognition of positive rights—demands that governments act to protect citizens from threats from unrestrained capitalism or from the degradations of impoverishment.[88]

Over the past generation, as the conservative racial coalition has come to dominate the federal judiciary, liberal interests and projects have increasingly turned to state constitutional arguments and processes. This turn to state-level processes has been most apparent in education, and particularly in the area of school finance. Since the early 1970s, reformers have mobilized around the presence of both equal protection and education language in state constitutions. These school finance reform litigation efforts have succeeded in over half the states, resulting in judicial endorsements of a right to "equal educational opportunity" or an "adequate education." The development of a fundamental, positive right to an equal or adequate education at

87 King & Smith, *supra* note 52.

88 *See* Emily Zackin, Looking for Rights in All the Wrong Places: Why State Constitutions Contain America's Positive Rights (2013); Sanford Levinson, *Courts as Participants in "Dialogue": A View from American States*, 59 Kan. L. Rev. 791 (2011); Kathleen Sullivan, *"From States' Rights Blues to Blue States' Rights,"* 75 Ford. L. Rev. 799 (2006).

the state level presents an opportunity for new arguments and strategies in pursuit of school desegregation.[89] The antisubordination-based claim that the existence of ghetto schools violates a fundamental right could begin anew under state law, with new possibilities (new games of *Scrabble*?) for doctrinal innovation under state constitutions.

Consider first a little noticed blip in *PICS*, the Seattle case. After the district court granted the school district's motion for summary judgment, White parents appealed to the Ninth Circuit. It initially reversed, but then upon reconsideration decided to certify important state-law questions to the Washington Supreme Court: (1) whether the state's Initiative 200 ("I-200"), a popularly enacted statutory version of California's Prop. 209, banned Seattle's modest use of race in student assignments,[90] and (2) if it did, then whether I-200 ran afoul of Article IX of the state constitution.[91]

The Washington State high court ultimately held that, properly interpreted, I-200 banned only programs providing preferences for the less qualified over the more qualified ("stacked deck" programs), and not race-conscious but "neutral programs" that "treat all races equally and do not provide an advantage to the less qualified, but do take positive steps to achieve greater representation of underrepresented groups" ("reshuffle" programs).[92] However, along the way, the court strongly intimated that Article IX might well be construed to "mandate integrated schools," if "it is determined that in a contemporary setting *de facto* segregated schools cannot provide children with the educational opportunities necessary to equip them for their role as citizens ..."[93]

This intimation of a positive right to equal educational opportunity that entails cross-race, cross-class desegregation actually finds official endorsement in another case litigated in the State of Connecticut. *Sheff v. O'Neill* began in the mid-1980s when a coalition of national civil rights groups joined forces with local activists in Hartford, the state's largest city and its capitol. The lawyers argued that racial isolation and concentrated poverty deprived Hartford school children of their right to equal educational opportunity under the state constitution. At the outset, and throughout the long, tortuous course of litigation and implementation, the plausibility of this claim depended on state constitutional law made in the state's school finance litigation in the 1970s. In 1996, the Connecticut Supreme Court sided with the civil rights groups. It held that the state constitution "requires the legislature to take affirmative responsibility to remedy segregation, regardless of whether it has occurred *de jure* or *de facto*." The court did not say that there was a right to integration, but only that there was a right to equal educational opportunity that was not "substantially impaired" by racial isolation. Of course, when the decision issued, it articulated constitutional norms that were largely unenforceable. However, the ensuing 18 years have witnessed several reform laws, five trips back to court, two consent agreements—one in 2003, and one in 2008—and some actual school desegregation. The case has resulted in several new inter-district schools that provide glimpses of the kind of power sharing and better educational outcomes needed to resist racial subordination.[94]

---

89 On school finance litigation, *see* Douglas Reed, On Equal Terms: The Constitutional Politics of Equal Opportunity (2001); Michael Paris, Framing Equal Opportunity: Law and the Politics of School Finance Reform (2010); and Ryan, *supra* note 29.

90 I-200 in pertinent part provides that "The state shall not discriminate against, or grant preferential treatment to, any individual or group on the basis of race, sex, color, ethnicity, or national origin in the operation of public employment, public education, or public contracting." The measure, endorsed by Washington voters in 1998, is codified at Wash. Rev. Code, Section 49.60.400.

91 Article IX of the state constitution in pertinent part provides: "It is the paramount duty of the state to make ample provision for the education of all children residing within its borders, without distinction or preference on account of race, color, caste, or sex," and, further, that "The legislature shall provide for a general and uniform system of public schools." *Parents Involved*, 137 F. Supp. 2d 1224 (W.D. Wash., 2001) (summary judgment for district); *Parents Involved*, 285 F.3d 1236 (2002) (reversing District Court); 294 F.3d 1082 (2002) (withdrawing prior opinion and certifying questions to state supreme court).

92 *Certification From the United States Court of Appeals for the Ninth Circuit in* Parents Involved in Cmty. Sch. v. Seattle Sch. Dist. No. 1, 72 P.3d 151.

93 *Id.* at 162–63.

94 *Sheff v. O'Neill*, 238 Conn. 1 (1996). My brief discussion of *Sheff* is based on my ongoing research on the case, which has included extensive document analysis and interviewing.

Sheff is an important model, for several reasons. First, it stands as the only currently valid judicial decision in the United States in which a court has dispensed with the *de jure/de facto* distinction. In Connecticut, and in no other state, government officials have an affirmative legal obligation to care about racial isolation and poverty in education, and to pursue inter-district desegregation. Second, and equally important, a study of legal and political mobilization in *Sheff* would reveal that reformers were at least to some extent cognizant of prior problems with desegregation litigation, and they conducted themselves accordingly. The *Sheff* lawyers organized and represented a multi-racial group of live constituents and plaintiffs. Indeed, these lawyers engaged in a two-year process of community education and organizing before the case was even filed in 1989. Just as Derrick Bell had suggested, moreover, the *Sheff* reformers' focus was primarily on "equal educational opportunity"; metropolitan-wide desegregation was proffered to minority groups as simply far and away the most effective means to this end. Finally, a study of *Sheff* can teach us much about the processes through which lawyers and activists can sometimes create new legal meanings out of a particular set of authoritative materials and the negotiation of local political contexts.

With *Sheff*, we are still left with a slow pace of change determined by deep structural constraints. But like the Washington high court's opinion in *PICS* itself, *Sheff* shows us that there may well be institutional channels for revisiting past wrong turns, starting new doctrinal games of *Scrabble*, and imagining a different future for racial justice in public schooling in America.

Chapter 8
Supreme Court Opinions on Equal Protection in Education and Their Use of Social Science Research

Janet W. Schofield and Pat K. Chew

As part of the series of constitutional amendments adopted in the years immediately following the Civil War, the Fourteenth Amendment to the U.S. constitution, adopted in 1868, was intended to require the states to treat former slaves as full citizens and to provide them with due process and equal protection under the laws.[1] This was a dramatic change for individuals who just a few years before had been legally denied the most fundamental human rights and treated as the property of others. But, the meaning of this amendment as applied to various realms of social life changed over time as the U.S. evolved in many areas including its demographic composition as well as its norms and beliefs regarding how members of different groups should be treated and what they are like.

This chapter traces the history of the application in Supreme Court opinions of one of the basic clauses of the Fourteenth Amendment, the Equal Protection Clause, to two issues that caused great controversy in the U.S. in the twentieth century and that are still controversial today—school desegregation and affirmative action in educational institutions. We focus on these two areas because they both, in different ways, deal with the implications of the Equal Protection Clause for the racial/ethnic composition of educational institutions. Also, although they are generally thought of as different areas of litigation, the issues dealt with have become increasingly similar. In addition, we discuss more briefly the extent to which social science has figured in opinions handed down by the Supreme Court in such cases as well as changes over time in the utilization of social science theory and research.

Equal Protection and School Desegregation

Supreme Court cases pertaining to the issue of racial segregation in school systems in which the Equal Protection Clause has figured prominently span more than 100 years. Here, we summarize landmark cases in this area, focusing on the changing conceptions of the requirements of the Equal Protection Clause. Rather ironically the first case we discuss, which in 1896 laid the legal basis for the development of separate school systems serving White and African-American students, apparently had little to do with schools, as it concerned the segregation of railroad passenger cars. Demonstrating the dramatic way that American jurisprudence pertaining to equal protection for members of different racial/ethnic groups has evolved, this section of the chapter ends with a case that concerns whether pre-collegiate educational systems may take account of race in *voluntary* efforts to *increase* diversity within their schools.

In the first case considered here, *Plessy v. Ferguson*,[2] the issue at hand was a Louisiana state law that required railroads operating there to provide separate train cars for Whites and African-Americans, or at least to provide sections within train cars separated by a partition.[3] The law provided that railroads could be punished for not providing separate facilities and that passengers refusing to sit where instructed by the

1 U.S. Const. amend. XIV.
2 163 U.S. 537 (1896).
3 *Id.* at 540–41.

conductor could be fined or jailed.[4] The only exception to the requirement for separate seating was for "nurses attending children of the other race."[5]

The Court, in a decision written by Justice Brown, maintained that the requirement for separate seating on trains within Louisiana did not violate the Equal Protection Clause as long as equal facilities were provided to members of both groups.[6] Interestingly, the Court noted that the Supreme Court of Massachusetts had earlier let the School Committee in Boston provide separate schools for White and African-American children and that such a practice was quite widespread, being found even in the nation's capital.[7] The basic argument put forward in *Plessy v. Ferguson* was that "Laws permitting, and even requiring ... separation ... do not necessarily imply the inferiority of either race."[8] The majority opinion maintained, "The underlying fallacy ... consist(s) in the assumption that the enforced separation of the two races stamps the colored race with a badge of inferiority. If this be so, ... [it is] solely because the colored race chooses to put that construction upon it."[9] Further, it argued that both groups were treated equally as both were required to sit in the sections set aside for them.[10] The Court distinguished between political equality, which it said was required by the Equal Protection Clause, and social equality, which it opined could "neither be accomplished nor promoted by laws."[11] In a spirited dissent, Justice Harlan pointed out that although the law applied equally to members of both groups, "[e]very one knows that the statute in question had its origin in the purpose ... to exclude colored people from coaches occupied by ... white persons"[12] so that the law interfered with the personal freedom of one group of citizens, a situation not consistent with the Equal Protection Clause. He went on to argue that such arbitrary separation of citizens "is a badge of servitude wholly inconsistent with the civil freedom and the equality before the law established by the constitution."[13]

The separate but equal doctrine reigned for over 50 years. However, the 1954 *Brown v. Board of Education* case flatly rejected it.[14] In this case, it was decided that denying African-American children admission to White schools under laws requiring or permitting segregation by race was inconsistent with the Equal Protection Clause, even if schools attended by the African-American plaintiffs were equal to those attended by White children with regard to factors such as facilities, curricula, and teachers' salaries.[15] A major rationale presented to justify the about-face was that public education played a dramatically different role in the U.S. at the time of *Brown* than when the Fourteenth Amendment was passed, or even when *Plessy v. Ferguson* was decided. Chief Justice Warren wrote for the Court that "Today, education is perhaps the most important function of state and local governments,"[16] in contrast to earlier times when state-supported education was neither as widespread nor as necessary for success in life. However, this opinion also picked up on Justice Harlan's argument in his dissent in *Plessy v. Ferguson* that separation solely because of group membership "generates a feeling of inferiority."[17] It then argued that such a feeling was likely to affect the motivation of African-American children to learn, thus slowing their development and depriving them of crucially important benefits.[18] The opinion succinctly concluded that "in the field of public education the doctrine of 'separate but equal' has no place" and that such segregation deprives children of equal protection.[19] Given the magnitude of this change

4 *Id.* at 541.

5 *Id.*

6 *Id.* at 548.

7 *Id.* at 544.

8 *Id.*

9 *Id.* at 551. When quoting from Court opinions we use the group descriptors found there. Elsewhere we use terms for various groups widely accepted at the time this chapter was written.

10 *Id.* at 549.

11 *Id.* at 551.

12 *Id.* at 557.

13 *Id.* at 562.

14 347 U.S. 483 (1954).

15 *Id.* at 493.

16 *Id.*

17 *Id.* at 494. *See also Plessy*, 163 U.S. at 563.

18 *Brown*, 347 U.S. at 494.

19 *Id.* at 495.

and its inconsistency with customs and norms in many parts of the U.S., as well as the great extent to which local districts control education there, it is hardly surprising that in response to tremendous resistance and delay a second *Brown* decision in 1955 instructed lower courts to "require (a) … prompt and reasonable start toward full compliance" with the earlier ruling.[20]

The difficulty of gaining timely compliance with the *Brown* decisions is illustrated by *Green v. County School Board of New Kent*,[21] decided 14 years after *Brown I* in 1968, and *Alexander v. Holmes Country Board of Education*,[22] decided a year later in 1969. In the former, a county had taken no action for more than a decade after Brown to disestablish a dual school system in which African-American students from all over the district were bused to one elementary school with African-American staff and all the White elementary students were bused to another school with White staff.[23] When action was finally taken, a "freedom of choice" plan was developed under which students could apply to attend whichever elementary school they wished.[24] But, after three years not a single White child had enrolled in the African-American school, which continued to serve 85 percent of the African-American students.[25] Based on *Brown II* which required dismantling dual systems with "all deliberate speed,"[26] this decision said that achieving equal protection by dismantling dual systems was an "affirmative duty"[27] and that dual school systems must "take whatever steps might be necessary to convert to a unitary system in which racial discrimination would be eliminated root and branch."[28] Thus, providing the *opportunity* for African-American students to attend a White school was not enough. The district was responsible for implementing a plan that dismantled its previously existing dual system and eliminated current segregation stemming from earlier segregation. Whereas both the *Brown* decisions highlighted the need for considering feasibility and local conditions, this decision emphasized a requirement for immediate progress and measurable results. Similarly, the *Holmes* case called for immediate termination of dual school systems, reflecting the adage that justice delayed is justice denied.[29]

Delay and opposition to the dismantling of dual school systems led to substantial involvement of the lower courts in deciding whether school systems were complying with the law. Indeed, where systems were obdurate, lower courts often assumed the responsibility of drawing up desegregation plans for them to follow, commonly using court-appointed experts. Both court-ordered and district-developed plans spurred litigation given the controversial nature of the issue. In 1971 in *Swann v. Charlotte- Mecklenburg Board of Education*, the Supreme Court turned "to the problem of defining with more particularity the responsibilities of school authorities in desegregating a state-enforced dual school system in light of the Equal Protection Clause."[30] For example, it concluded that limited use could be made in planning of desired ratios of students from different backgrounds,[31] that the existence of a few one-race schools within a district was not in and of itself indicative of continuation of a dual system,[32] and that the pairing of schools that required busing of students from their neighborhood to more distant locations to achieve desegregation was acceptable.[33] Charlotte-Mecklenburg, like the school districts in the earlier landmark cases, at one point had a state-sanctioned dual school system, although segregated housing patterns also contributed to the school segregation remaining at the time of this litigation. Interestingly, the majority opinion in this case specifically indicated that it was not ruling on the question of whether state action by authorities other

20 Brown v. Bd. of Educ. of Topeka, 349 U.S. 294, 300 (1955).
21 391 U.S. 430 (1968).
22 396 U.S. 19 (1969).
23 *Green*, 391 U.S. at 432–33.
24 *Id.* at 433–34.
25 *Id.* at 441.
26 *Id.* at 436.
27 *Id.* at 437.
28 *Id.* at 437–38.
29 *Holmes*, 396 U.S. at 20.
30 402 U.S. 1, 18 (1971).
31 *Id.* at 25.
32 *Id.* at 25–26.
33 *Id.* at 28–29.

than the school system (such as those concerned with housing issues) that led to segregated schools would suffice to require school system action to desegregate.[34]

The *Keyes v. School District No. 1* case decided in 1973 saw two extremely important developments.[35] First, earlier cases had dealt specifically with the rights of White and African-American students, ignoring those from other backgrounds. In Denver, the district involved in the case, roughly 20 percent of the students were Hispanic, 14 percent African-American and 66 percent White.[36] Writing for the majority, Justice Brennan concluded that Hispanics constituted an identifiable class for purposes of equal protection, saying "that they suffer from the same educational inequities as Negros and American Indians" and that the combined percentage of African-Americans and Hispanics should be considered in deciding whether schools were segregated.[37] This expansion of the groups covered in school desegregation cases was potentially very important from a practical perspective, given the large and growing number of Hispanics in numerous cities across the U.S. during the last half of the twentieth century and at the beginning of the twenty-first century.

Secondly, and also importantly differing from earlier landmark desegregation cases, a formal dual school system like those typically found in Southern states before *Brown* never existed in Denver.[38] Earlier opinions had emphasized the existence of formal dual school systems, creating what was called *de jure* segregation, as the government action that violated the right to equal protection and hence that had to be remedied by desegregation plans. Yet, the majority opinion in *Keyes* held that "where plaintiffs prove that the school authorities have carried out a systematic program of segregation affecting a substantial portion of the students ... it is only common sense to conclude that there exists a predicate for a finding of the existence of a dual school system."[39] In other words, a formal dual school system did not need to exist to create a duty to desegregate. Rather, showing that school authorities engaged in activities intended to create segregation in substantial parts of the school system would be enough to require desegregation. Perhaps not surprisingly, given the implications of the *Keyes* decision and the fact that it substantially changed the "rules of the game" regarding which groups could be considered in desegregation litigation and what kinds of actions were sufficient to open districts to the possibility of court-ordered desegregation, the *Keyes* decision was far from unanimous.

Less than a year later in another important case, *Milliken v. Bradley I*, the Court decided that a District Court could not order a multi-district solution to desegregating the Detroit city schools, even though that appeared to be the only way to have African-American students in Detroit attend schools with any significant number of White students and the Detroit district had been shown to have discriminated in the past, making it subject to a desegregation order.[40] The reasoning underlying this decision was that there was no evidence in the record that the other districts involved in the proposed multi-district desegregation plan had themselves discriminated or that the discrimination that had occurred within Detroit had produced a segregative effect in them.[41] Thus, it was seen to be inappropriate to require other districts to participate in a desegregation plan designed to solve Detroit's problem. Also, in a follow-up decision, *Milliken v. Bradley II*, the Court determined that the state of Michigan could be required to pay for various educational programs included in a desegregation plan for Detroit developed by the District Court as long as those programs were tailored to remedy the consequences of the constitutional violation, saying "the Constitution is not violated by racial imbalance in the schools, without more."[42] *Milliken I* and *II* had huge practical implications, because the demographic composition of many American cities was such that without involving surrounding heavily White suburban districts many cities would have school populations that were heavily minority.

---

34 *Id.* at 23.
35 413 U.S. 189 (1973).
36 *Id.* at 195.
37 *Id.* at 197.
38 *Id.* at 198.
39 *Id.* at 201.
40 418 U.S. 717, 745 (1974).
41 *Id.*
42 Milliken v. Bradley, 433 U.S. 267, 280 n.4 (1977).

Two major cases in the early 1990s, *Board of Education v. Dowell*[43] and *Freeman v. Pitts*,[44] ushered in a new era in desegregation litigation in which school districts began to be released from desegregation orders. In the former, Justice Rehnquist, writing for the majority, concluded that once equal protection violations had been remedied by a school district's good faith compliance with a desegregation degree and the vestiges of earlier discrimination had been eliminated to the extent practical, the district should be released from the earlier desegregation order.[45] Similarly, in *Freeman v. Pitts* the Court decided that a Georgia school district that had been determined to have eliminated discrimination in four areas of its operation, but which had not yet eliminated discrimination in faculty assignment or resource allocation, should be released from court supervision in the areas in which it had eliminated discrimination.[46] The Court's opinion in both cases reiterated that racial imbalance between schools in a district in and of itself was not a reason to keep a district under a desegregation order. Even districts with a substantial number of heavily segregated schools could be released partially or completely from court supervision in realms where they no longer discriminated, as long as the remaining imbalances were most likely due to "private" decisions rather than to district action and experience suggested the district had acted in good faith to change discriminatory practices.

These two cases were followed a few years later by one challenging a court-ordered response to prior equal protection violations that went further than many earlier responses, which had focused more on achieving racial balance within schools in a given district through activities such as pairing schools or busing students. Specifically, in *Missouri v. Jenkins* (1995) the fundamental questions related to equal protection were whether the District Court could order the state of Missouri, which had maintained a dual school system, to pay for efforts to make the formerly segregated Kansas City schools attractive to White students living outside the district as a means of desegregating that school system, and whether it could order state funding for activities such as pay raises for virtually all Kansas City school district employees.[47] In addition, there was argument regarding whether that court could order the state to pay for programs designed to increase achievement in the city school district.[48] The Court's opinion on these matters, written by Justice Rehnquist, held that the District Court's plans to make the Kansas City schools attractive to students from other districts as a way of enhancing racial balance in the city schools was beyond the scope of its authority, since the original violation was an intra-district one and there was no showing that the district's behavior had directly caused segregation in surrounding districts.[49] Furthermore, Missouri was not held responsible for funding the school system.[50] Both of these outcomes rested on the principle that desegregation remedies are designed only to restore the victims of discrimination to the place they would have been without the discrimination and that the scope of a remedy must directly reflect the constitutional violation.[51]

The most recent major Supreme Court case closely related to desegregation at the pre-collegiate level, *Parents Involved in Community Schools v. Seattle School District*, reflects continuing public skepticism about the value of racial diversity in schools, especially when it comes at the cost of individual preferences in other regards.[52] Although this case, decided in 2007, is often thought of as a desegregation case, conceptually it merges with the affirmative action cases to be discussed, because the dispute concerned the legality of districts that were not under desegregation orders taking affirmative steps to foster diversity in their schools. In this case, Seattle, which was never subject to a desegregation order, and Louisville, which had been declared unitary just a year earlier, were sued by citizens who felt that these districts were voluntarily doing too much to racially balance their schools.[53] Specifically, in different ways each school district considered the racial balance in a school in deciding whether students from different racial backgrounds who wished to attend it would be

43 498 U.S. 237 (1991).
44 503 U.S. 467 (1992).
45 *Dowell*, 498 U.S. at 249–50.
46 *Freeman*, 503 U.S. at 490–91.
47 515 U.S. 70, 80 (1995).
48 *Id.* at 100.
49 *Id.*
50 *Id.*
51 *Id.* at 89.
52 551 U.S. 701 (2007).
53 *Id.* at 709.

admitted there.[54] Justice Roberts, writing for the majority, averred that any governmental action that considers individuals' race in making decisions regarding benefits or burdens requires "strict scrutiny" which means that the action must be narrowly tailored to attain a compelling state interest.[55] He argued that the actions of these two districts clearly did not pass that test, distinguishing between the situation in these districts and that in the affirmative action case to be discussed below, *Grutter v. Bollinger*.[56] His opinion also stressed the fact that when these suits were brought, neither city was required to undertake actions to desegregate their schools, thus making their consideration of race particularly problematic.[57] The very clear intention of the programs in both cities was to promote racial balance, not to discriminate against minority students. However, his opinion stressed, as had earlier ones, that racial balance in and of itself is not a constitutionally supported goal.[58]

In striking contrast, Justice Breyer's extended dissenting opinion in this case, in which three other justices joined, argued that the Equal Protection Clause does not prohibit consideration of race when it is intended to *include* rather than to *exclude and subordinate* minority group members.[59] He argued that given that the Court decided in *Grutter* that the University of Michigan law school demonstrated a sufficiently compelling interest in a diverse student body to justify some consideration of race in its admissions process that a compelling interest in the same goal followed *a fortiori* in this case.[60] He also argued that the procedures challenged in the two school districts were, in fact, more narrowly tailored than the plan allowed by the Court in *Grutter*.[61]

The preceding discussion reveals a striking evolution in the understanding of the requirements of the Equal Protection Clause with regard to the provision of schooling to students of different backgrounds over about a century. In 1896, the earliest case used that clause to justify segregation in public facilities as long as those facilities were equal. Roughly 50 years later, the "separate but equal" doctrine it propounded was flatly overturned in *Brown I*. Cases in the following decades explored the limits of the federal courts' power to prescribe various kinds of remedies for school segregation. In the 1980s and 1990s, cases also began to delineate the conditions under which school systems could be *freed* from earlier desegregation orders. The *Seattle* case in 2007 dealt with whether school districts' voluntary efforts to increase diversity that accomplished this by considering students' race were constitutional. Thus, it reflected both major changes in the behavior of school districts and continuing public reluctance to embrace the value of diversity when achieving it conflicts with specific individual interests.

The Role of Social Science in Major Supreme Court Desegregation Cases

It is hardly surprising that social science did not figure at all in *Plessy v. Ferguson*. When that case was heard in 1896, the social sciences were in their infancy. Interestingly, however, statements in that case regarding issues amenable to investigation by social scientists are inconsistent with later social science findings. For example, writing for the majority, Justice Brown asserted "The argument also assumes that social prejudices may be overcome by legislation … We cannot accept this proposition."[62] Yet, there is evidence that, over time, a change in the laws regarding racial segregation can indeed result in changed attitudes as well as changed behavior.[63]

Indeed, *Brown I*, roughly half a century later, is often said to be notable as an early example of the deep involvement of social scientists in litigation reaching the Supreme Court.[64] According to what Mody

54 *Id.*

55 *Id.* at 720.

56 *Id.* at 723–25; *see also* Grutter v. Bollinger, 539 U.S. 306 (2003).

57 *Id.* at 753–54.

58 *Id.* at 726.

59 *Id.* at 830.

60 *Id.* at 837.

61 *Id.*

62 *Ferguson*, 163 U.S. at 551.

63 Thomas F. Pettigrew, *Racial Change and Social Policy*, 441 Annals Am. Acad. Pol. & Soc. Sci. 114, 119 (1979).

64 James R. Acker, *Thirty Years of Social Science in Supreme Court Criminal Cases*, 12(1) Law & Pol'y 2 (1990); Wallace D. Loh, Social Research in the Judicial Process 44 (1984); Michael Rustad & Thomas Koenig, *The Supreme Court and Junk Social Science: Selective Distortion in Amicus Briefs*, 72 N.C. L. Rev. 110 (1990).

characterizes as the "conventional narrative," the Court not only mentioned this evidence, but *relied* on it in making this historic decision.[65] For example, Justice Breyer, in the years before he joined the Supreme Court, referred to the Court's "use of social science evidence … to determine a question of law" in *Brown I*.[66] Consistent with this view is the language of part of the Court's *Brown I* opinion which made claims that read very much like conclusions from social science:

> To separate them (African-American students) from others of similar age and qualification solely because of their race generates a feeling of inferiority as to their status in the community that may affect their hearts and minds in a way unlikely ever to be undone. … Segregation … in public schools has a detrimental effect upon the colored children … the policy of separating the races is usually interpreted as denoting the inferiority of the negro group. A sense of inferiority affects the motivation of a child to learn.[67]

However, another school of thought in legal scholarship contends that claims that *Brown I* turned on social science evidence misread the situation.[68] Indeed, Mody argues that the social science studies were cited in this case primarily to bolster the legitimacy of the Court's decision, which the justices anticipated would be extremely unpopular, both because it went against existing social customs in many parts of the country and because it suggested a "living Constitution" rather than an "originalist" approach to deciding the case.[69]

The contentious issue of the role that social science played in *Brown I* is complex and cannot be resolved in the space available here. However, Mody makes quite a convincing case that social science played a smaller role in the decision than that with which it is usually credited. But, even if its role was primarily a legitimizing one as Mody contends, it was not unimportant. Public acceptance of unpopular decisions is not guaranteed, although it is fundamental to the American system of government. So, even if the social science studies cited only let the justices feel more confident that their decision would ultimately be accepted, such a contribution was noteworthy.

A considerable body of desegregation research conducted by social scientists emerged between the late 1960s and the mid 1970s,[70] the period during which school desegregation began on a wide scale.[71] Cases decided early in this period, such as *Green v. County School Board of New Kent*[72] and *Alexander v. Holmes County Board of Education*,[73] made essentially no use of such research, although the former did cite some U.S. Civil Rights Commission research on the effectiveness of freedom of choice plans, after saying specifically that it neither adopted nor refused to adopt the views expressed therein. *Swann v. Charlotte-Mecklenburg Board of Education* cited various facts and figures regarding the demographic composition of the relevant school district, as did many other cases. It also contained information on the amount and distance of busing that occurred in the relevant district with and without racial balance as a goal.[74] However, it did not cite social science research, in spite of its suggestion that the age of students was "probably" the pre-eminent factor to be weighed in deciding on whether the time or distance of transportation planned to achieve desegregation was

65 Sanjay Mody, Brown *Footnote Eleven in Historical Context: Social Science and the Supreme Court's Quest for Legitimacy*, 54 Stan. L. Rev. 793, 795 (2001–02).

66 Steven Breyer, *What Researchers Need to Know About Law and the Courts, Remarks from Panel Discussion in Washington D.C. Conference on the Use/Nonuse/Misuse of Applied Social Science Research in the Courts* (Oct. 9, 1978), *in* The Use/Nonuse/Misuse of Applied Social Research in the Court 76 (Michael J. Saks & Charles H. Baron eds, 1980).

67 *Id.* at 494.

68 William E. Doyle, *Can Social Science Data Be Used in Judicial Decisionmaking?*, 6 J.L. & Educ. 16 (1977); William Taylor, *The Supreme Court and Recent School Desegregation Cases: The Role of Social Science in a Period of Judicial Retrenchment*, 42 Law & Contemp. Probs. 37, 39 (1978).

69 Mody, *supra* note 65, at 793.

70 Janet W. Schofield & Leslie R. Hausmann, *School Desegregation and Social Science Research*, 59 Am. Psychologist 538 (2004).

71 Gary Orfield & John T. Yun, Resegregation in American Schools 12 (1999), *retrieved from* http://civilrightsproject.ucla.edu/research/k-12-education/integration-and-diversity/resegregation-in-american-schools.

72 391 U.S. 430 (1968).

73 396 U.S. 19 (1969).

74 402 U.S. 1 (1971).

great enough to put children's health or education at risk, a suggestion on which developmental psychologists might have been able to shed some light.[75]

The majority opinion in *Keyes v. School District No. 1* also made essentially no use of social science data, although a U.S. Commission on Civil Rights report dealing with the situation of Hispanics in the U.S. was cited, as were demographic data on the composition of the Denver school system and particular schools within it.[76] However, Justice Powell's opinion, concurring in part and dissenting in part, quoted the work of sociologist Karl Taeuber to the effect that segregation was a fact of life in virtually all American cities no matter what the local laws or policies.[77] Justice Powell used this to support his contention that it was time to end the distinction between *de jure* segregation, which is that caused by state action intended to segregate, and *de facto* segregation, which is that caused by the preferences and actions of private individuals. Both the difficulty in determining intent and the disadvantaged position of minority children who happen to have been born in *de facto* segregated systems rather than in previously *de jure* segregated systems figured in his argument. He also cited the testimony of a sociologist who served as an expert witness earlier in this case as well as a social scientist's study of the neighborhood school concept.[78]

The opinions in *Milliken v. Bradley I* and *II* did not explicitly cite social scientific studies, although they did not refrain from making statements on topics about which social science has a lot to say. For example, Justice Marshall's dissenting opinion in *Milliken II* made the following statement "Children who have been thus educationally and culturally set apart from the larger community will inevitably acquire habits of speech, conduct and attitudes reflecting their cultural isolation … [this] can affect any children who, as a group, are isolated by force of law from the mainstream."[79] *Milliken I* also made reference to expert testimony given to the District Court regarding White flight, the departure of Whites from central city areas to surrounding suburban districts.[80] The degree to which and the circumstances under which desegregation actually contributes to White flight became a topic of heated controversy and considerable research within the social scientific community shortly after that.[81] However, relatively little of that work had been published at the time this opinion was written.

Like most other previous cases, the majority opinion in *Board of Education v. Dowell* did not explicitly cite social science research.[82] However, Justice Marshall's dissent, in which two other justices joined, referred back extensively to *Brown I*, including the famous "hearts and minds" quote and asserted that Brown was based on "recognition of the particular social harm that segregated schools inflict" on African-American students.[83] It also mentioned two earlier Supreme Court cases asserting a causal connection between school segregation and housing segregation, without citing specific studies supporting that link.[84] Finally, in buttressing its argument that stigmatic injury associated with segregation should be considered in cases involving the possible dissolution of desegregation decrees as a vestige of earlier discrimination, it cited two papers suggesting that predominately minority public schools have fewer resources than others.[85]

The social science-related issue featuring most prominently in *Freeman v. Pitts* was the relation between school and housing segregation.[86] Justice Kennedy's majority opinion, with which others concurred, cited

75 *Id.* at 31.

76 413 U.S. 189 (1973).

77 *Id.* at 223 n.9.

78 *Id.* at 241 n.20; *see also* Meyer Weinberg, Race & Place: A Legal History of the Neighborhood School (1967).

79 433 U.S. 267, 287 (1977).

80 418 U.S. 717, 732–33 (1974).

81 David Armor, *White Flight and the Future of School Desegregation*, *in* School Desegregation: Past, Present, and Future (Walter G. Stephan & Joe Feagin eds, 1980); James S. Coleman, Sara D. Kelly & John A. Moore, Trends in School Desegregation, 1968–73 (1975); Reynolds Farley, Toni Richards & Clarence Wurdock, *School Desegregation and White Flight: An Investigation of Competing Models and Their Discrepant Findings*, 53 Soc. Educ. 123 (1980); Thomas F. Pettigrew & Robert L. Green, School Desegregation in Large Cities: A Critique of the Coleman "White Flight" Thesis (1976).

82 498 U.S. 237 (1991).

83 *Id.* at 257.

84 *Id.* at 264–65.

85 *Id.* at 260 n.5.

86 503 U.S. 467 (1992).

a study to support the District Court's conclusion that housing segregation in the relevant district was not caused by school district policies but by private action.[87] In his concurring opinion, Justice Scalia emphasized the difficulty of determining whether demographic patterns years or even decades after a desegregation order are a vestige of earlier state action, especially given that the Court had not clearly described how such vestiges could be determined.[88] He basically argued that with passing time it becomes untenable to presume that current racial disparities are the consequence of earlier state action.[89] Thus, in the near future he would shift the burden of proof to plaintiffs, who presumably would need to present empirical evidence of that connection.[90] In sharp contrast, Justice Blackmun's concurrence suggested that the policies of the DeKalb County School District might have contributed to residential segregation, citing several studies suggesting an interactive effect between school and neighborhood segregation, and pointing out possible avenues of connection between school policy and residential segregation that the District Court neglected to explore before, determining that no part of the current racial imbalance in the schools flowed from earlier *de jure* discrimination.[91]

Rather ironically, *Missouri v. Jenkins* spawned an opinion in this area containing both the most extensive citation of social science studies in desegregation cases since *Brown I* and the most clear cut rejection of the utility of the social sciences in the Court's opinions in this area.[92] Specifically, in concurring with Justice Rehnquist's majority opinion, Justice Thomas argued that *Brown I* was based "on the principle that the government must treat all citizens as individuals, and not as members of racial, ethnic or religious groups."[93] After attacking the validity of the studies cited in *Brown I*, he cited numerous studies to support his contention that "there simply is no conclusive evidence that desegregation either has sparked a permanent jump in the achievement scores of black children, or has remedied any psychological feelings of inferiority black schoolchildren might have had."[94] Emphasizing his distrust of social science, he opined that the counts should not accept "the unnecessary and misleading assistance" of the field,[95] warning lower courts against being swayed by social science's "easy answers."[96]

The most recent major case related to school desegregation, *Parents Involved in Community Schools v. Seattle School District*, is strikingly different from most preceding ones in that social science figures in it much more prominently, although it got essentially no notice in Justice Roberts's plurality opinion.[97] His only mention of it was to note that the *amici* briefs, some of which discussed a large number of social science studies, were not in agreement with regard to the possible benefits of racial diversity for academic or social outcomes.[98] He also indicated there was no need to deal with this issue because the procedures in question were not constitutional, as they were not "narrowly tailored" to achieve any such possible benefits.[99]

In contrast, both Justice Thomas's concurring opinion and Justice Breyer's dissenting opinion cited numerous studies.[100] Justice Thomas again expressed his distrust of social science, citing studies primarily in an effort to illustrate their inconclusiveness and to discredit the way in which they were used in Justice Breyer's opinion. In addition, he critiqued Justice Breyer's dissent for maintaining that the social science evidence is strong enough to let a democratically elected school board argue that racial balance is a compelling interest.[101]

87 *Id.*

88 *Id.*

89 *Id.* at 501–3.

90 *Id.*

91 *Id.* at 513 n.2.

92 515 U.S. 70 (1995).

93 *Id.* at 120.

94 *Id.* at 120 n.2.

95 *Id.* at 121.

96 *Id.* at 122.

97 551 U.S. 701 (2007).

98 *Id.* at 726.

99 *Id.*

100 Julie M. Morgan & Diana Pullin, *Social Science and the Courts: Challenges and Strategies for Bridging Gaps Between Law and Researcher*, 39(7) EDUCATIONAL RESEARCHER 8 (2010).

101 *Id.*

However, he also used the results of research to support a point he wished to make about the possibility of high achievement in all African-American schools.[102] Justice Breyer's opinion is striking in that, unlike most of the other desegregation cases in which social science has been cited, he included tables of data from social science studies and discussed the actual findings of several studies with considerable specificity. For example, when arguing that school districts have a compelling interest in racial diversity he cited roughly a dozen studies, quoting two sentences from one and reporting results from others.[103] In fact, some of the opinion reads as if it could have been taken from a social science review of the literature. Justice Breyer acknowledged that there was not complete unanimity in social science findings regarding the benefits of diversity in the schools, but concluded that "[i]f we are to insist upon unanimity in the social science literature before finding a compelling interest, we might never find one."[104]

Equal Protection Law and Affirmative Action Cases

The legal history of equal protection challenges to affirmative action programs in education is largely captured in four U.S. Supreme Court cases. This jurisprudence evolved in cases challenging university-level student admissions programs, beginning with *Regents of the University of California v. Bakke*[105] in 1978 and followed 25 years later with the *Grutter v. Bollinger*[106] and *Gratz v. Bollinger*[107] cases in 2003. *Fisher v. University of Texas*,[108] a decade later in 2013, completes this quartet of landmark cases, although in that case the Court arguably leaves the interpretation of equal protection law less certain than earlier rather than more certain.

In *Bakke*, Allan Bakke, a White male and twice rejected applicant for admission, sued the Medical School of the University of California at Davis, claiming that its admissions program violated his equal protection rights.[109] Under the regular admissions procedure, except as indicated below, the school summarily rejected applicants with an overall undergraduate grade point averages falling below 2.5/4.0. Each member of the 5–6 member admissions committee then rated the remaining candidates on a scale of 1 to 100 based on academic and nonacademic factors. All the ratings were added together to provide a "benchmark score" used to rank these applicants.[110]

Applications from candidates who indicated they wanted to be considered as "economically and/or educationally disadvantaged" or as members of a "minority group" were given to a separate admissions committee.[111] This committee used a similar evaluative process as the regular admissions committee, except that candidates did not have to meet the 2.5 GPA cutoff. This committee's top choices were given to the general admissions committee, who admitted them up to a number designated by faculty. In the two years at issue, the designated number constituted 16 percent of the entering class.[112]

Bakke was considered under the general admissions program and rejected. In both years, applicants were admitted under the special admissions program with lower benchmark scores than Bakke's.[113]

Justice Powell announced the judgment of the Court, although no other Justice joined him.[114] Given this "fractured" decision, the precedential value of Powell's opinion was at first not clear. However, subsequent

102 *Id.* at 761.
103 *Id.* at 815, 839–40.
104 *Id.* at 839.
105 438 U.S. 265 (1978).
106 539 U.S. 306 (2003).
107 539 U.S. 244 (2003).
108 133 S. Ct. 2411 (2013).
109 *Bakke*, 348 U.S. at 277–78.
110 *Id.* at 273.
111 *Id.* at 274.
112 *Id.* at 275.
113 *Id.* at 276.
114 The *Bakke* decision contains six opinions, none of which commanded a majority of the court. *Id.* at 269.

Supreme Court cases confirmed that Justice Powell's opinion provided the authoritative legal framework for equal protection analysis in this area.[115]

Justice Powell began with certain threshold issues. He confirmed that racial or ethnic classifications are not *per se* invalid under an equal protection analysis, although they would be considered "suspect" classifications.[116] He further confirmed that all persons "seeking protection from official discrimination,"[117] including White males, have equal protection rights, noting however that the original focus of the Fourteenth Amendment was "the freedom of the slave race."[118]

Moving to the substantive equal protection analysis, Justice Powell laid out a two-pronged inquiry for justifying the use of a suspect classification and surviving an equal protection review:[119]

1. The state must show that it has a constitutionally permissible and substantial purpose or interest; and
2. The state must show that its use of race was necessary to fulfilling that interest.

Thus, if the University's purpose was only some specified percentage of admissions on the basis of race, without more, the admissions policy would be "facially invalid."

Instead, the university argued that it satisfied the first prong of the analysis because its admissions policies had numerous substantial goals; and that its use of race was necessary to fulfill those goals.[120] While acknowledging these varied institutional goals,[121] the Court focused most on the school's goal of a diverse student body.

This goal, Justice Powell indicated, was clearly a "constitutionally permissible goal for an institution of higher education," further linking it to the university's academic freedom to make its own judgments on selection of its student body.[122] Further, he elaborated on the pedagogical and political benefits of a diverse student body. Citing a report by the President of Princeton University, he noted: "The atmosphere of 'speculation, experiment and creation'—so essential to the quality of higher education—is widely believed to be promoted by a diverse student body."[123] And citing *Keyishian v. Board of Regents*, Justice Powell observed "It is not too much to say that the 'nation's future depends upon leaders trained through wide exposure' to the ideas and mores of students as diverse as this Nation of many peoples."[124]

While concluding that the school's goal satisfied the first prong of his analysis, Justice Powell was critical of its methodology in fulfilling its goal, thus questioning whether the school could satisfy the second prong.[125] The reservation of a specific number of seats for minority students in the entering class misconceived the goal: "The diversity that furthers a compelling state interest encompasses a far broader array of qualifications and characteristics of which racial or ethnic origin is but a single though important element."[126] The setting aside of a specific percentage of seats for minority students was problematic. Students who are nonminority were "totally excluded" from these seats, no matter how strong their qualifications, including their own potential for contribution to educational diversity.[127] This was a disregard of their individual rights without the necessary justification, and therefore invalid under the Fourteenth Amendment.

While the court could have simply invalidated the Davis' program, without more, it instead decided to provide guidance on what would be a constitutionally permissible race-conscious admissions policy. Using

115 *See Grutter*, 539 U.S. at 323.
116 *Bakke*, 348 U.S. 287–91.
117 *Id.* at 292.
118 *Id.* at 291.
119 *Id.* at 305.
120 *Id.* at 305–06.
121 *Id.* at 307.
122 *Id.* at 311–12.
123 *Id.* at 312 (quoting William G. Bowen, *Admissions and Relevance of Race*, PRINCETON ALUMNI WKLY., Sept. 26, 1977, at 7, 9).
124 *Id.* at 313 (quoting Keyishian v. Board of Regents, 385 U.S. 589, 603 (1967)).
125 *Id.* at 315.
126 *Id.*
127 *Id.* 319–20.

the Harvard College admissions policy as a model, going so far as appending the official policy to his opinion, Justice Powell described its key attributes: no set target-quotas for any racial group (or any other specified group); race or ethnic background can be a "plus" in a particular applicant's file, yet do not insulate the individual from comparison with all other applicants; and flexible consideration of all "pertinent elements of diversity" in light of the particular qualifications of each candidate.[128] This kind of "individualized" consideration of each candidate would mean, for instance, that a rejected nonminority applicant would have "combined qualifications, which may have included similar nonobjective factors" that did not outweigh those of other accepted applicants.[129] Her or his qualifications would have been weighed fairly and competitively and without a basis to complain of unequal treatment under the Fourteenth Amendment.

The Supreme Court waited 25 years after *Bakke* to revisit the meaning of equal protection in university affirmative action policies.[130] In 2003, the University of Michigan was the defendant in two cases: in *Grutter v. Bollinger*, denied applicants sued the law school, a graduate level professional school,[131] and in *Gratz v. Bollinger*, denied applicants sued the undergraduate college.[132]

In *Grutter*, a White female applicant, Barbara Grutter, challenged the race-conscious admissions policy at Michigan's law school as violative of the Equal Protection Clause.[133] Michigan Law School has a highly competitive admissions process with only about 10 percent of applicants matriculating. Admissions officials evaluate each applicant based on all the information in the file, including a personal statement, letters of recommendation, an essay describing how the applicant will contribute to the life and diversity of the school, undergraduate grades, and law school admissions test scores.[134] While the law school's admissions policy affirms its commitment to racial and ethnic diversity with special reference to the inclusion of African-Americans, Hispanics, and Native Americans and notes the relevance of enrolling a "critical mass" of underrepresented minority students, it also focuses on academic ability.[135] The faculty intentionally crafted a policy that it believed complied with the *Bakke* requirement. As evidence of its consideration of many forms of diversity, the law school frequently accepted nonminority applicants with grades and test scores lower than underrepresented minority applicants and other nonminority applicants who were rejected.[136]

Justice O'Connor delivered the opinion of the Court. She began by stating the key legal issue: whether diversity is a compelling interest in selecting applicants for admission to public universities?[137] By doing so, she focused her analysis on the first prong of the strict scrutiny review, laying out the most current interpretation of this requirement. Ultimately, the Court upheld the law school admissions policy and concluded that it did not violate the Equal Protection Clause, satisfying both the requirements of a compelling government interest and a narrow tailoring of the use of a racial classification.[138]

The *Grutter* decision strongly endorsed Justice Powell's opinion in *Bakke*, calling it the "touchstone for constitutional analysis of race-conscious admission policies" and the model for universities designing their own admissions policies post-*Bakke*.[139] Justice O'Connor particularly zeroed in on Justice Powell's discussion in *Bakke* of the goal of a diverse student body.[140]

The *Grutter* Court confirmed that the law school's goal of obtaining "the educational benefits that flow from a diverse student body" clearly satisfied the requirement of a compelling state interest.[141] It deferred to the law school's professional judgment that diversity is indeed essential to its educational mission, noting that

128 *Id.* at 317.
129 *Id.* at 318.
130 *See Grutter*, 539 U.S. at 323.
131 *Grutter*, 539 U.S. at 311.
132 *Gratz*, 539 U.S. at 244.
133 *Grutter*, 539 U.S. at 316.
134 *Id.* at 314.
135 *Id.* at 316.
136 *Id.* at 314.
137 *Id.* at 322.
138 *Id.* at 343.
139 *Id.* at 323.
140 *Id.* at 324.
141 *Id.* at 330.

the law school policy promotes cross-racial understanding, helps to break down racial stereotypes, and enables students to better understand persons of different races. Justice O'Connor further noted the many amicus briefs offering substantiation.[142] Significantly for our purposes, she expressly acknowledged: "In addition to the expert studies and reports entered into evidence at trial, numerous studies show that student body diversity promotes learning outcomes, and 'better prepares students for an increasingly diverse workforce and society.'"[143] The law school also emphasized that a "critical mass" of minority students was necessary, claiming that the "diminishing force of ... stereotypes ... cannot [be] accomplish[ed] with only token numbers of minority students."[144]

Justice O'Connor completed the Court's review of the law school's admissions program by assuring that it was narrowly tailored—to "ensure that 'the means chosen 'fit' th[e] compelling goals so closely that there is little or no possibility that the motive for the classification was illegitimate racial prejudice or stereotype.'"[145] Like the Harvard plan, it did not operate as a quota, but made flexible use of race as a plus factor. Some attention to numbers without more did not transform it into a rigid quota, as illustrated by the varying number of underrepresented minority students who enrolled in the law school from year to year. There was a highly individualized holistic review of each applicant regardless of his or her race, so that race was not the defining feature of the application.[146]

Finally, Justice O'Connor indicated that race-conscious admissions policies be limited in time and used no longer than necessary to meet a compelling state interest. "We expect that 25 years from now, racial preferences will no longer be necessary."[147]

The Supreme Court in *Gratz v. Bollinger* found the undergraduate admissions process for the University of Michigan's College of Literature, Science and the Arts (LSA) problematic, in contrast to its finding regarding the law school admission process.[148] White applicants Jennifer Gratz and Patrick Hammacher applied, were denied admission, and subsequently sued the University for violation of their equal protection rights under the Fourteenth Amendment.[149] Justice Rehnquist delivered the opinion of the Court. He began by confirming once again that the use of race in admissions decisions should be "strictly scrutinized," thus requiring "narrowly tailored" measures for the furthering of compelling government interests.[150] While the *Grutter* case particularly explored the meaning of compelling government interests, the *Gratz* case focused mostly on the meaning of "narrow tailoring."

Justice Rehnquist referred to Justice Powell's recognition in *Bakke* that an applicant's race might be a plus factor if the admissions process was flexible enough to allow individualized consideration of each applicant.[151] The LSA process, however, did not allow such individualized consideration. Beginning in 1998, LSA admissions counselors used a "selection index" on which an applicant could score a maximum of 150 points, with 100 points guaranteeing admission. Points were based on a broad range of academic factors, with up to 110 points possible for academic performance and up to 40 points possible for nonacademic factors such as an outstanding essay, leadership activities, or public service.[152] As described by Justice O'Connor in her concurring opinion, applicants automatically received a 20-point bonus if they were members of an underrepresented minority group, attended a predominantly minority or disadvantaged high school, or were

142 *Id.*

143 *Id.* (quoting Brief of American Educational Research Association et al. as Amici Curiae Supporting Respondents at 3, Grutter v. Bollinger, 539 U.S. 306 (2003) (No. 02–241)).

144 *Id.* at 333.

145 *Id.* (citing Richmond v. J.A. Croson Co., 488 U.S. 469, 493 (1989)).

146 *Id.* at 337. Furthermore, narrow tailoring only requires a serious and good faith consideration of workable race-neutral alternatives; it does not require exhaustion of every conceivable race-neutral alternative. *Id.* at 339. The law school adequately considered race-neutral alternatives that might produce critical mass without forcing the school to abandon the academic selectivity that is the cornerstone of its educational mission. *Id.*

147 *Id.* at 343.

148 *Gratz*, 539 U.S. at 250–51.

149 *Id.* at 252.

150 *Id.* at 270.

151 *Id.* at 270–71.

152 *Id.* at 277–78.

being recruited for athletics.[153] In addition to this numerical calculation, an admissions counselor could "flag" an applicant's file for further review, although it was unclear how frequently this flagging occurred.[154]

The policy's automatic distribution of 20 points to every "underrepresented minority," Justice Rehnquist concluded, did not provide individualized consideration.[155] Moreover, this procedure has the effect of making "the factor of race ... decisive" for every minimally qualified minority candidate.[156] He also contrasted Michigan's program with that of Harvard's, as described in *Bakke*, where the "critical criteria are often individual qualities or experience *not dependent upon race but some sometimes associated with it.*"[157] Thus, Michigan's use of race in its undergraduate admissions policy was not "narrowly tailored" to achieve its compelling interest in diversity, and hence violated the Equal Protection Clause.[158]

Only a decade after *Grutter* and *Gratz*, the Supreme Court heard another affirmative action case, *Fisher v. University of Texas*.[159] Two Texas residents, Abigail Fisher and Rachel Michalewicz, were denied admission to the University's undergraduate program in 2008. They subsequently claimed they were discriminated against on the basis of race in violation of their equal protection rights.[160] Following *Grutter* and *Gratz*, the university considered two components in their admissions process. The first was an Academic Index (AI), reflecting an applicant's test scores and academic performance in high school. The second was a Personal Achievement Index (PAI), considering a number of factors including an applicant's leadership, work experience, extra-curricular activities, and other circumstances giving insight into a student's background. The student's race was included in the PAI. While race was not assigned an explicit numerical value, it is "undisputed that race is a meaningful factor."[161] The Court further noted that the university moved to this "race-conscious" admissions process in substantial reliance on a study concluding the lack of "critical mass" of minority students.[162] In addition to this admissions process based on an applicant's PAI and AI, the state legislature also created the Top Ten Percent program, which granted automatic admission to any public state college, including the university, to all students graduating in the top 10 percent of their high school class.[163] Both the District Court and the Court of Appeals for the Fifth Circuit had upheld the university's admissions process as constitutional.

Justice Kennedy began the Supreme Court's review of the Texas admissions process by noting the applicability of the *Bakke*, *Gratz*, and *Grutter* cases and confirming the strict scrutiny standards articulated in those cases. He concluded, however, that the Fifth Circuit had not applied a sufficiently demanding strict scrutiny review of the university's process.[164]

In remanding the case back to the appellate court, Justice Kennedy clarified the strict scrutiny analysis, noting distinctions that earlier Supreme Court cases did not highlight. In particular, he differentiated between the kinds of judicial review required in the two prongs of the strict scrutiny inquiry. In the first prong dealing with compelling interest, the court can give substantial deference to the university's judgment that a diverse student body is essential to its educational mission, so long as there is a "reasoned, principled explanation" for that decision.[165] In the second prong dealing with narrow tailoring, however, the court should not defer to the university. The courts, not university administrators, must ensure that the way the university has chosen to accomplish its purpose is specifically and narrowly framed.[166] "This involves a careful judicial inquiry into whether a university could achieve sufficient diversity without using racial classifications."[167] The

153 *Id.*
154 *Id.* at 256.
155 *Id.* at 271.
156 *Id.* at 272.
157 *Id.* at 272–73.
158 *Id.* at 270.
159 Fisher v. University of Texas, 133 S. Ct. 2411 (2013).
160 *Id.* at 2417.
161 *Id.* at 2416.
162 *Id.*
163 *Id.*
164 *Id.* at 2421–22, 631 F.3d 213 (5th Cir. 2011), *cert. granted*, 132 S. Ct. 1536 (2012).
165 *Id.* at 2419.
166 *Id.* at 2420.
167 *Id.*

reviewing court must ultimately be satisfied that "no workable race-neutral alternatives" would accomplish the university's purpose. If a nonracial approach … could promote the substantial interest about as well and at tolerable administrative expense," … "then the university may not consider race."[168]

Justice Kennedy concluded, however, that the Fifth Circuit did not engage in this "searching" strict scrutiny examination. Instead, Kennedy continued, the Fifth Circuit was overly deferential to the way the university crafted its admissions policies, requiring only that the university's decision to use race as a factor in admissions was made in good faith.[169] Signaling that the current application of equal protection law in this context as illustrated in the Fifth Circuit opinion is insufficiently demanding, Kennedy concluded, "Strict scrutiny must not be strict in theory but feeble in fact."

Surprisingly, the Supreme Court declined to demonstrate this more "searching" review of Texas' admissions policies, thus declining an opportunity to more fully articulate its position on affirmative action in university admissions. Instead, it remanded the case to the Fifth Circuit to determine if the Texas admissions processes are constitutionally permissible under the Supreme Court's newly pronounced "correct analysis."[170]

The Role of Social Science in Major Supreme Court Affirmative Action Cases in Higher Education

While the desegregation cases have a much longer history, the affirmation action in higher education cases cover a comparatively short and modern 35-year span beginning with the *Bakke* case in 1978 and now including the *Fisher* case in 2013. During approximately the same time period, courts have incrementally increased their use of social science research in their legal analysis.[171] This upward trend is mirrored in the affirmative action cases described above.[172]

While the use of social science research was negligible in *Bakke* in 1978, its use in *Grutter* in 2003 was notable. Advocates for the University of Michigan's position, spearheaded by Michigan social scientists such as Richard Lempert and Patricia Gurin, linked the school's legal arguments to social science research.[173] For instance, the Court was provided with substantial research on the educational benefits of a diverse student body, including increased cross-race understanding and decreased stereotyping among students, hence better preparing them as leaders in a diverse workplace and society. Researchers also emphasized the importance of having a critical mass of minority students in order to achieve these benefits.[174]

Indeed, a wide range of groups offered the *Grutter* court an avalanche of amicus curie briefs, many of which relied on social science research.[175] Amherst College's brief, for instance, described "exhaustive and careful research" by William Bowen and Derek Bok on the negative effects on minority enrollment if the consideration of race in the admissions process is eliminated, particularly at the highly selective schools.[176] The American Educational Research Association (AERA) brief described its "deep seated interest in the accurate representation of relevant research addressing the educational benefits of student body diversity in higher

---

168 *Id.*

169 *Id.*

170 *Id.* at 2421.

171 James R. Acker, *Social Science in Supreme Court Cases and Briefs: The Actual and Potential Contribution of Social Scientists as Amici Curiae*, 14 Law & Hum. Behav. 25 (1990); Rosemary J. Erickson & Rita J. Simon, The Use of Social Science Data in Supreme Court Decisions 1–2 (1997).

172 Faye J. Crosby et al., *Understanding Affirmative Action*, 57 Ann. Rev. Psychol. 585, 588–95 (2006) (describing social scientists' contributions to demonstrating the need for affirmative action).

173 *See, e.g.*, Patricia Gurin, Expert Report, Gratz et al. v. Bollinger et al., No. 97–75321 (E.D. Mich.); Grutter et al. v. Bollinger et al., No. 97–75928 (E.D. Mich.); Richard O. Lempert, David L. Chambers & Terry K. Adams, *Michigan's Minority Graduates in Practice: The River Runs Through Law School*, 25 Law & Soc. Inquiry 395 (2000).

174 *See* Gurin, *supra* note 165.

175 http://www.vpcomm.umich.edu/admissions/legal/gru_amicus-ussc/um.html, providing over 60 briefs in support of the University of Michigan.

176 Brief of Amherst et al. as Amici Curiae Supporting Respondents at 12–13, Grutter v. Bollinger, 538 U.S. 306 (2003) (Nos. 02–241, 02–516).

education."[177] While noting that much of the research had been generated in only the past few years, "the consistency of the findings in demonstrating the educational benefits of diversity is impressive."[178] The AERA brief noted research by a range of social scientists including Patricia Gurin,[179] Gary Orfield[180] and Dean Whitla.[181]

The Court did not ignore this abundance of social science research. Justice O'Connor expressly noted in her *Grutter* opinion the following uses of social science research and experts:

- "The District Court heard extensive testimony from Professor Richard Lempert, who chaired the faculty committee that drafted the 1992 policy."[182] Lempert is a sociologist from the University of Michigan whose research focuses on the application of social science research to legal issues.[183]
- "In addition to his testimony at the trial, [Kent] Syverud submitted several reports on the educational benefits of diversity. Syverud's testimony indicated that when a critical mass of underrepresented minority students is present, racial stereotypes lose their force because nonminority students learn there is no 'minority viewpoint' but rather a variety of viewpoints around minority students."[184]
- "Relying on data obtained from the Law School, petitioner's expert, Dr. Kinley Larntz, generated and analyzed 'admissions grids' for the years in question (1995–2000). These grids show the number of applicants and the number of admittees for all combinations of GPAs and LSAT scores. Dr. Larntz made 'cell-by-cell' comparisons between applicants of different races to determine whether a statistically significant relationship existed between race and admission rates."[185] His conclusion was that "membership in certain minority groups 'is an extremely strong factor in the decision for acceptance'" but that "race is not the predominant factor in the Law School's admission calculus."[186]
- "Dr. Stephen Raudenbush, the Law School's expert, focused on the predicted effect of eliminating race as a factor in the Law School's admission process. In Dr. Raudenbush's view, a race-blind admissions system would have a 'very dramatic,' negative effect on underrepresented minority admissions."[187] Raudenbush is a faculty member in the sociology department at the University of Chicago, whose work focuses on the sociology of education.[188]

In preparation for the Supreme Court's deliberations in the recent *Fisher* case and Texas' race-conscious admissions policy, social scientists again marshaled an abundance of research. While this work dealt with many of the same topics noted in *Grutter*, these materials included the substantial research published since then. Given University of Texas' Ten Percent Plan, the materials also developed further the inadequacy of race-neutral alternatives for achieving a more diverse student body and the corollary educational benefits.

The Brief of the American Education Research Association (AERA) as *Amici Curiae* in support of Respondents University of Texas illustrates the kind of materials prepared for the case.[189] It organized relevant social science research around two prominent legal arguments: first, that the university has a compelling governmental interest in student body diversity; and second, that the university's admissions policy is narrowly tailored.

---

177 Brief of American Educational Research Association et al. as Amici Curiae Supporting Respondents at 1–2, Grutter v. Bollinger, 539 U.S. 306 (2003) (No. 02–241).

178 *Id.* at 2.

179 *Id.* at 5.

180 *Id.* at 17.

181 *Id.*

182 *Grutter*, 539 U.S. at 319.

183 UNIVERSITY OF MICHIGAN LAW SCHOOL, http://web.law.umich.edu/_facultybiopage/facultybiopagenew.asp?ID=159 (last visited Sept. 9, 2012).

184 *Grutter*, 539 U.S. at 319–20.

185 *Id.* at 320.

186 *Id.*

187 *Id.*

188 UNIVERSITY OF CHICAGO, http://sociology.uchicago.edu/people/faculty/raudenbush.shtml (last visited Sept. 9, 2012).

189 Brief of American Educational Research Association et al. as Amici Curiae Supporting Respondents, Fisher v. Univ. of Texas, 631 F.3d 213 (5th Cir. 2011) (No. 11–345).

This brief first provided research demonstrating that student body diversity leads to significant educational benefits in several ways:[190]

1. By promoting cross-racial understanding and reducing prejudice;
2. By improving students' cognitive abilities, critical thinking, and self-confidence;
3. By promoting civic engagement and skills needed for professional development and leadership; and
4. By improving classroom environments.

The brief also demonstrated the harms associated with tokenism, racial isolation, and stereotyping.[191] In addition, it laid out the research indicating that claims that minority students are harmed by race-conscious admissions are without a strong empirical foundation.[192]

Second, the AERA brief documented the research supporting the legal conclusion that the University of Texas' policies are narrowly tailored.[193] It particularly supported the argument that "critical mass" is not a fixed percentage and should be assessed by the university in evaluating the educational benefits of diversity.[194] Finally, it describes the research indicating that race-conscious admissions are necessary to complement the University of Texas' Top Ten Percent plan.[195]

Another illustrative brief, the one submitted by the American Social Science Researchers as Amici Curiae in Support of Respondents, is impressive both for its content and for the broad base of its submitters.[196] Collectively, the submitters include 444 researchers from 42 states and from 172 educational institutions and research centers. Their work crosses many disciplines, including education, psychology, sociology, demography, economics, political science, and history.[197]

Though organized a little differently from the AERA brief, the topics covered are similar. They include:

1. Why classroom diversity is essential to achieve higher education's compelling educational benefits (for example, promoting learning outcomes, enhancing the content of class discussions, and motivating students to work with peers from other racial groups);[198]
2. How racially integrated classrooms help to reduce stereotype threat, which is a physiological response that limits the performance of racial minorities;[199]
3. The importance of a critical mass of students in the classroom to leverage the educational benefits of diversity;[200]
4. Why the Top Ten Percent plan is inadequate for producing a sufficiently diverse learning environment,[201] and how other race-neutral plans are similarly inadequate;[202] and
5. How declines in racial diversity harm the quality of education for all students.[203]

Despite all of this proffered social science research, Justice Kennedy's majority opinion in *Fisher* did not refer to any of it. Except for a brief reference to Texas' use of empirical observations to explain the need for

190 *Id.* at 6–16.
191 *Id.* at 18.
192 *Id.* at 24.
193 *Id.* at 32.
194 *Id.* at 33.
195 *Id.* at 35.
196 Brief of American Social Science Researchers as Amici Curiae in Support of Respondents, Fisher v. Univ. of Texas, 631 F.3d 213 (5th Cir. 2011) (No. 11–345).
197 *Id.* at 1.
198 *Id.* at 5.
199 *Id.* at 8.
200 *Id.* at 6–7.
201 *Id.* at 13.
202 *Id.* at 22.
203 *Id.* at 31.

a "critical mass" of minority students,[204] the opinion does not refer to any social science research. While this may seem surprising at first glance, it is consistent with Kennedy's focus on rearticulating the strict scrutiny standard but not actually applying that standard to the facts in the case. The Fifth Circuit, in its remanded review of the facts, however, will likely refer to social science research in determining whether Texas has any race-neutral alternatives to its current race-conscious admissions policies in achieving its diversity goals.

Interestingly, Justice Thomas in a concurring opinion did refer to a range of non-legal sources. In explaining his position that higher education's use of race in admissions is categorically prohibited by the Equal Protection Clause, he refers to social science studies and empirical observations, as well as a range of other historical and philosophical analyses.[205] In contrast to much of the social science research offered by defenders of affirmative action, Justice Thomas utilizes these sources to attack it. Justice Ginsburg in her dissenting opinion also refers to amicus briefs which incorporate social science research, although she refers to these in explaining her position that Texas was in compliance with *Grutter* and that the Fifth Circuit properly concluded the same.[206]

Discussion and Conclusions

Interpretation of the Equal Protection Clause in cases related to race and education has clearly evolved substantially. One has only to compare the issues litigated and the reasoning of the Supreme Court opinions discussed here to see that. The *Plessy v. Ferguson* case, at the close of the nineteenth century, legitimized the enforcement of separate but equal facilities for Whites and African-Americans, referring specifically to the existence of segregated schools as support for the acceptance of such an interpretation of the Equal Protection Clause. Fifty years later, the Court unequivocally decided in *Brown I* that separate could not be equal with regards to schooling children, even though there was enough resistance to this idea that the *Brown II* was necessary to move schools districts towards compliance with *Brown I*.

Roughly 25 years after the *Brown* decisions, attitudes had changed enough that the University of California at Davis had instituted an admissions policy designed to make sure that at least a modest number of African-Americans were admitted to its medical school. Although, in *Bakke*, the Court found that the university's specific approach to achieving this goal to be inconsistent with equal protection, it proactively provided guidance on what would be a constitutionally permissible race-conscious admissions policy designed to increase the probability of a diverse student body.

Desegregation litigation remained active in the late twentieth century as school districts fought to be freed from desegregation orders. However, acceptance of the idea of racially and ethnically diverse schooling increased dramatically during that period. Indeed, by the beginning of the twenty-first century, in *Grutter*, the Court gave its imprimatur to a policy designed to increase the number of minority group members admitted to the University of Michigan's law school, accepting the argument that the university had a compelling interest in having a diverse student body. However, it found a somewhat different procedure developed for the same purpose by the University of Michigan's College of Literature, Science and the Arts (LSA) unconstitutional, because unlike the Law School's procedure which individually considered applicants and used race as a "plus factor," it was a less individualized process that automatically assigned a given number of points to minority group members.

The role of social science in Supreme Court decisions related to equal protection in education also changed notably over this same time period, although it still remains quite modest. Not surprisingly given the dearth of social scientific work available in the late 1890s, no mention was made of it at all in *Plessy v. Ferguson*. The *Brown I* decision broke new ground for Supreme Court decisions with its citation of numerous social science studies.[207] Like *Bakke* in 1978, many of the desegregation decisions handed down between *Brown I*

204 *Fisher*, 133 S. Ct. at 2416.

205 *Id.* at 2431–32 (Thomas J., concurring).

206 *Id.* at 2433 n.1 (Ginsburg J., dissenting).

207 Rustad & Koenig, *supra* note 64, at 110.

and 1990 made relatively little use of social science studies. But, as in other areas of litigation,[208] more recent Supreme Court cases dealing with equal protection issues in education have made greater mention of social science than earlier ones, even though in some cases it was featured only to disparage its findings or to dispute its relevance.

Two questions arise from this brief summary of the use of social science research in the cases discussed here. First, why has reference to it in Supreme Court opinions involving equal protection in education increased, although not necessarily in a clear linear manner? Second, why is this research still used such a relatively modest amount in comparison to the current size of the social science enterprise? Before turning to these questions, it should be pointed out that although we have been discussing the "use" of social science in Supreme Court decisions, that term actually covers a variety of things, from the setting of context, to the establishment of general facts about the way individuals and the society function, to the determination of specific information related to the particular case being decided, to the determination of legal conclusions. In addition, determining the actual amount of use is not easy.[209] Justices may well be influenced by amicus briefs without citing them or specific studies mentioned in them, in which case their use is not apparent, although it has occurred. In other situations, Justices may "use" social science research to support a conclusion by citing it in an opinion, whereas in reality that opinion may be based on other considerations as has been suggested with regard to *Brown I*.[210]

Although use is hard to determine exactly, explicit citation of social science studies has increased in the area under discussion enough so that discussion about why this has happened is worthwhile. One obvious reason for the increase in the use of social science research in the areas reviewed here is the tremendous increase in the amount of relevant information available as the growth of research funding and the work force in the social sciences expanded so dramatically in the latter half of the twentieth century. So, for example, in the decade immediately after *Brown* an average of five papers per year relating to school desegregation were published in the core psychological literature. By the 1970s, that average had roughly quadrupled.[211]

However, other factors seem likely to have contributed importantly to the increased use of social science in Supreme Court opinions as well. One important contributor to this trend appears to be the extent to which social scientists themselves have produced and/or compiled research intended to be directly pertinent to issues on which the Supreme Court decisions are likely to turn. Indeed, the historic first use of social science input in *Brown I* was far from an accident. It occurred in a case in which a group of social scientists worked closely over a couple of years with NAACP lawyers. Together, they examined the questions that the Supreme Court had posed as the basis for the re-argument of the cases gathered together under *Brown I* to determine the social science issues inherent in them. Social scientists then attempted to answer some of those questions by conducting research and gathering reports from individuals participating in relevant situations,[212] submitting these as an appendix to the appellants' briefs in *Brown I*.

Since the end of the 1970s such focused efforts to produce social science directly relevant to legal issues has become increasingly common and significant. For example, in the late 1970s the National Review Panel on School Desegregation research was set up specifically to bring together lawyers, judges, and scholars involved in desegregation research both in order to help make such research more pertinent to legal issues and to bring relevant knowledge to the attention of the legal community.[213] Flowing out of this effort, among other things, were papers on the role that social science played in Supreme Court decisions and the factors promoting and inhibiting such use, which provided analyses of the situation useful to those wishing to understand how

208 James R. Acker, *Social Science in Supreme Court Cases and Briefs: The Actual and Potential Contribution of Social Scientists as Amici Curiae*, 14 Law & Hum. Behav. 25 (1990); Rosemary J. Erickson & Rita J. Simon, The Use of Social Science Data in Supreme Court Decisions 1–2 (1997).

209 John Monahan & Lauren Walker, *Judicial Use of Social Science Research*, 15(6) Law & Hum. Behav. 571 (1991); Ronald G. Roesch, Stephen L. Golding, Valerie P. Han & N. Dickon Reppucci, *Social Science and the Courts: The Role of Amicus Curiae Briefs*, 15 Law & Hum. Behav. 2–3 (1991).

210 Loh, *supra* note 64, at 79.

211 Schofield & Hausmann, *supra* note 70, at 538.

212 Kenneth B. Clark, *The Background: The Role of Social Scientists*, J. Soc. Issues 2 (1953).

213 Betsy Levin & Willis D. Hawley, *Foreword*, 42(3) Law & Contemp. Probs. 2 (1978).

to increase social science's role.[214] In the mid-1990s, a political scientist and a lawyer jointly set up the Harvard Civil Right Project (later called the Civil Rights Project/Proyecto Derechos Civiles at UCLA) that commissioned more than 400 studies and a dozen or more books on topics related to civil rights, including both school desegregation and affirmation action.[215] One of the specific missions of this organization was to provide intellectual capital pertinent to legal issues.[216]

Not only has more research relevant to issues being litigated been produced. In addition, organized efforts to bring this work to the attention of the Supreme Court in a way that will be effective have increased. Specifically, increasing numbers of social scientists have become involved in the submission of amicus briefs as litigation relating to equal protection in education has evolved. To illustrate, the social science amicus brief in *Brown I* in 1954 was signed by 32 individuals, the similar briefs in both *Freeman v. Pitts* and *Missouri v. Jenkins* were signed by just over 50 social scientists, and that in *Parents Involved in Community Schools v. Seattle* was signed by more than 550 individuals. Furthermore, whereas professional associations such as the American Psychological Association (APA) and the American Educational Research Association (AERA) did not submit amicus brief in the early cases, they have participated in more recent cases such as *Parents Involved in Community Schools v. Seattle* and *Grutter v. Bollinger*. Indeed, whereas the American Psychological Association filed only one amicus brief in all of the 1960s, it filed over three dozen such briefs dealing with a wide variety of topics between 2000 and 2010. These briefs routinely cite many dozens of studies, providing the Court with ready access to relevant research.

In addition, some professional associations representing researchers, such as the AERA, have begun to weigh in on issues under consideration by the Supreme Court in other ways, such as holding press briefings on relevant research.[217] To the extent that these are successful in gaining coverage in the news media, they have the potential to influence the justices directly as well as indirectly through their impact on public opinion. Such approaches may have an impact, as Ellsworth and Getman suggest that social science research is most influential in legal decision-making when its conclusions are so broadly accepted that they become truisms.[218] Other work suggests that when research is reported in the popular press or bears the imprimatur of a professional organization, it is more likely to be used than otherwise.[219]

The second question raised above, why social science research has played what many see as a relatively minor role in Supreme Court decisions, has been the focus of considerable prior discussion and analysis[220] and space constraints require that it is only touched on briefly here. Possible reasons for this modest use are numerous. First, as Justice Thomas has pointed out, conflicting results are quite common, making it difficult (especially for those not familiar with the methodological canons of social science and the intricacies of complex statistical analyses) to judge the validity of different conclusions. This point is well illustrated by the fact that although 32 social scientists signed the social science brief submitted in *Brown I*, the former

214 Betsy Levin, *School Desegregation Remedies and the Role of Social Science Research*, 42(4) Law & Contemp. Probs. 1 (1978); William L.Taylor, *The Supreme Court and Recent School Desegregation Cases: The Role of Social Science in a Period of Judicial Retrenchment*, 42(4) Law & Contemp. Probs. 37 (1978); Mark G. Yudof, *School Desegregation: Legal Realism, Reasoned Elaboration, and Social Science Research in the Supreme Court*, Law & Contemp. Probs. 57 (1978).

215 Sam Dillon, *New Home and Issues for Civil Rights Project*, N.Y. Times, Nov. 30, 2008, http://www.nytimes.com/2006/11/ 30/us/30ucla.html?_r=0.

216 The Civil Rights Project, Proyecto Derechos Civiles, http://civilrightsproject.ucla.edu/.

217 http://www.aera.net/SearchResults/tabid/10042/Default.aspx?Search=amicus+brief; http://www.aera.net/SearchResults/tabid/10042/Default.aspx?Search=press+briefing.

218 Phoebe C. Ellsworth & Julius. G. Getman, *Law and Social Science Decision Making*, *in* Law and the Social Sciences 1 (Leon Lipson & Stanton Wheeler eds, 1986).

219 Gary B. Melton, *Bringing Psychology to the Legal System: Opportunities, Obstacles, and Efficiency*, 42(5) Am. Psychologist 488 (1987).

220 Levin, *supra* note 203; John Monahan & Laurens Walker, *Social Science Research in Law: A New Paradigm*, 43(6) Am. Psychologist 465 (1988); Taylor, *supra* note 203; Linda R. Tropp, Amy E. Smith & Faye J. Crosby, *The Use of Research in the Seattle and Jefferson County Desegregation Cases: Connecting Social Science and the Law*, 7(1) Analyses Soc. Issues & Pub. Pol'y 93 (2007); Yudof, *supra* note 203.

head of APA Henry Barrett testified in favor of maintaining school segregation.[221] It is also illustrated by the contentious discussion in the decades following *Brown I* regarding whether the studies cited there were of sufficient quality to justify their use and whether or not their conclusions were correct.[222]

Second, and related to the preceding point, research is an enterprise intended to provide new information and to produce new insights. The culture of science is one that expects to see change on many fronts and which values such change as progress. While law also recognizes that change and progress are inevitable and valuable, it counters this recognition with an emphasis on stability and the importance of predictability.[223] Thus, concerns are often expressed about basing decisions on social scientific conclusions that may change over time.[224] However, a social scientist reading Supreme Court opinions is struck both by the many assumptions about social life and processes the justices make as well as reliance on "common sense."[225] Since both assumptions about social behavior and about what constitutes "common sense" change over time, it is unclear why they should constitute a better basis for decision-making than social science data. Perhaps they are just less recognized as open to change than data produced as part of a scientific process that documents and highlights such change.

Third, social science findings may well be specific to a given place and time, not so much due to progress in understanding, which was just discussed, but due to changed social circumstances.[226] However, the law needs to apply broadly across geographical regions, demographic groups, and the changing culture of different eras. Fourth, the accepted standard of social scientists is objectivity whereas legal argument is based on an advocacy model which legitimates choosing the information one wishes to emphasize to favor one's side while discounting the relevance of and highlighting weaknesses in the opponent's evidence. For example, social scientists striving to be as fair as possible may include caveats pointing out a minor weakness in their research, but this caveat may be exploited by lawyers in a legal argument in a way completely unintended and unanticipated by the social scientist. This contrast between social science and law norms poses real challenges for social scientists preparing amicus briefs,[227] discouraging some social scientists from getting involved in this kind of activity. Finally, strong data about particular issues may not be available at the time a decision is made. As in the case of the earliest litigation in which the issue of "white flight" figured, sometimes legal decisions stimulate subsequent research or occur while such research is in progress rather than when a large and reliable body of pertinent research is readily available.

In conclusion, this analysis of the evolving interpretation of the Equal Protection Clause as it applies to issues of race and education highlights the remarkable changes that have occurred during the course of just over a century. Analysis of major Supreme Court decisions in this area suggests that social science has played an increasing role in such decisions, although much remains to be learned about the exact nature and size of its impact, including the extent to which it truly affects the justices' thinking as opposed to serving primarily to buttress decisions made on other grounds. It seems very likely that the increased efforts to produce research specifically pertinent to issues under litigation, as well as to bring such information to the attention of the Supreme Court and the general public, have contributed to increased use of such work. It also seems likely that efforts to do both of these things will continue and even increase as the social sciences continue to expand and mature. However, it is also clear that social science research will remain only one of many often competing considerations that will vie for attention as the justices weigh the complex issues before them and make decisions that both reflect and shape the society in which they live.

---

221 Thomas F. Pettigrew, *Justice Deferred: A Half Century After* Brown v. The Board of Education, 59(6) AM. PSYCHOLOGIST 522 (2004).

222 Stuart W. Cook, *Social Science and School Desegregation: Did We Mislead the Supreme Court?*, 5 PERSONALITY & SOC. PSYCHOL. BULL. 420 (1979); Stuart W. Cook, *The 1954 Social Science Statement and School Desegregation: A Reply to Gerard*, 39(8) AM. PSYCHOLOGIST (1984); Harold B. Gerard, *School Desegregation: The Social Science Role*, 38(8) AM. PSYCHOLOGIST 869 (1983); Walter G. Stephan, *School Desegregation: An Evaluation of Predictions Made in* Brown v. Board of Education, 85(2) PSYCHOL. BULL. 217 (1978).

223 Tropp et al., *supra* note 209, at 110.

224 David. L. Faigman, *To Have and Have Not: Assessing the Value of Social Science to the Law as Science and Policy*, 38 EMORY L.J. 1042 (1989); Tropp et al., *supra* note 209, at 110.

225 Pettigrew, *supra* note 210, at 522.

226 Kenneth J. Gergen, *Social Psychology as History*, 26(2) J. PERSONALITY & SOC. PSYCHOL. 309 (1973).

227 Rustad & Koenig, *supra* note 64, at 119.

Chapter 9
The State's Compelling Interest in Substantive Equality

Jennifer S. Hendricks

Does the state have a legitimate interest in promoting substantive race and sex equality? In the 2007 case *Parents Involved in Community Schools v. Seattle School District No. 1*,[1] a plurality of the U.S. Supreme Court answered this question in the negative, at least as to race. To do so, the plurality exploited an area of confusion in equal protection doctrine: in several cases, the Supreme Court has held that existing conditions of inequality cannot justify particular racial remedies, such as quotas. The *Parents Involved* plurality argued that, therefore, existing conditions of inequality cannot justify *any* race-conscious remedy and are of no legitimate concern of the state. In other words, complete colorblindness is the only acceptable stance, and the current fact of racial inequality is constitutionally protected from state intervention.

When state actors seek to advance the cause of racial equality, the Supreme Court has long exhorted them to do so in ways that do not require the classification of individuals according to race. One would think that the legitimacy of such measures and of their goal—increased racial equality—would be obvious, but the *Parents Involved* plurality called them into question.[2] This chapter demonstrates one way in which the plurality's position is contrary to precedent. First it shows that the Court has allowed the state to pursue sex equality by a variety of means, even when similar strategies are impermissible with respect to race. Second, it shows that the key difference between these race and sex cases is not that racial equality is a less worthy constitutional goal but that the Court is uncomfortable with classifying individuals according to racial labels. Race-conscious remedies for inequality that do not involve individual classification are thus constitutionally valid.

Two Kinds of Affirmative Action

The phrase "affirmative action" most often calls to mind race- or sex-specific preferences in hiring or in university admissions. When the Supreme Court has struck down those kinds of affirmative action programs, it has often held out the alternative of facially neutral strategies for meeting the state's goals.[3] Increasingly,

1 551 U.S. 701 (2007). *Parents Involved* struck down voluntary plans for racial integration in school districts in Seattle and Louisville. In Louisville, the voluntary plan was a continuation of court-ordered desegregation plans that had been in effect from 1975 until 2000. *Id.* at 715–16. Seattle had never been subjected to a desegregation order but had begun voluntary measures in 1963 and expanded on them in part to settle desegregation lawsuits. *Id.* at 712; *id.* at 807–13 (Breyer, J., dissenting).

2 In addition to joining the *Parents Involved* plurality, Justice Scalia laid out a case against race-conscious state action in his concurring opinion in *Ricci v. DeStefano*, 557 U.S. 557 (2009).

3 *See, e.g., Parents Involved*, 551 U.S. at 789 (Kennedy, J., concurring in part and concurring in the judgment) (proposing site selection, design of attendance zones, resource allocation, and recruitment of faculty and students). Justice Kennedy's short and sparse opinion for the Court in *Fisher v. University of Texas*, 133 S. Ct. 2411 (2013), arguably takes a similar approach, implicitly endorsing "race-neutral" policies like the Texas Ten Percent Plan. *See infra* notes 4–9 and accompanying text (describing the Ten Percent Plan and the senses in which it is and is not race-neutral). These sorts of purportedly race-neutral methods are not necessarily available or effective to integrate many school districts. *See also* Derek W. Black, *The Uncertain Future of School Desegregation and the Importance of Goodwill, Good Sense, and a Misguided Decision*, 57 Cath. U. L. Rev. 947, 980–82 (2008) (explaining why race-neutral measures such as site selection will not achieve integration and stating that Justice Kennedy's suggestion that they could "underestimates reality"); James E. Ryan, *The Supreme Court and Voluntary Integration*, 121 Harv. L. Rev. 131, 138–39, 144–49 (2007) (assessing the impact of and remaining alternatives after Parents Involved and noting, for example, that much existing segregation is between rather than within school districts). But see Kimberly Jenkins Robinson, *The Constitutional Future of Race-*

as the federal courts and many states have restricted the use of traditional affirmative action, institutions have turned to these alternative, facially neutral means for increasing diversity and providing equal opportunities.

One well-known example of race-neutral, but race-conscious, affirmative action is the Texas Ten Percent Plan. The Ten Percent Plan guarantees admission to any public college for students in the top ten percent of any Texas high school's graduating class.[4] At the K-12 level, school districts have experimented with income-based instead of race-based busing.[5] Schools, employers, and governments bidding out contracts have expanded recruitment efforts to target minority applicants.[6]

Justice Ginsburg has pointed out that "only an ostrich could regard the[se] supposedly neutral alternatives as race unconscious."[7] The Ten Percent Plan assumes the existence of racially segregated high schools and exploits that segregation to attain racially diverse university admissions without explicitly referring to race. "It is race consciousness, not race blindness, that drives such plans," which therefore "suffer from 'the disadvantage of deliberate obfuscation.'"[8]

For purposes of this chapter, however, the key difference between these programs and traditional preferences is that the alternative programs seek to ameliorate inequality and segregation without facially classifying *individuals* by race.[9] Traditional preferences depend on identifying individual applicants who belong to particular disadvantaged groups. The alternative strategies either operate more diffusely or capitalize on correlations that are created by existing conditions of inequality. Although these policies are facially neutral, they are adopted with the hope that they will lead to greater diversity within institutions and equality across society. The purpose is thus to combat structural inequality.

In the oral argument of the *Parents Involved* case, several justices inquired about the status of facially neutral policies adopted for the purpose of achieving racial diversity in the schools.[10] Justice Kennedy posed

---

Neutral Efforts to Achieve Diversity and Avoid Racial Isolation in Elementary and Secondary Schools, 50 B.C. L. Rev. 277, 336–45 (2009) (canvassing race-neutral alternatives and suggesting they could be somewhat effective); Jefferson County Public Schools, No Retreat: The JCPS Commitment to School Integration (2008), http://www.jefferson.k12.ky.us/Pubs/NoRetreatBro.pdf (summarizing Louisville's new student assignment plan and describing the community as "resolved and united in its desire to integrate our schools without using an individual student's race"). *See also* Daniel Kiel, *Accepting Justice Kennedy's Dare: The Future of Integration in a Post-PICS World*, 78 Fordham L. Rev. 2873 (2010) (evaluating *Parents Involved* and Louisville's new plan).

4 Tex. Educ. Code Ann. § 51.803(a) (Vernon 2007). The Texas plan was adopted in response to the Fifth Circuit's pre-*Grutter* decision that affirmative action was unconstitutional. *See* Hopwood v. Texas, 78 F.3d 932, 962 (5th Cir. 1996); *see also* Fisher, 133 S. Ct. at 2416 (describing the Ten Percent Plan).

5 *See* Evan Osnos, *Schools Find New Route to Diversity; New Integration Plans Use Income to Place Pupils*, Chi. Trib. Jan. 28, 2002, at N7; *see also* Lauren E. Winters, *Colorblind Context: Redefining Race-Conscious Policies in Primary and Secondary Education*, 86 Ore. L. Rev. 679 (2007) (arguing that school districts should use socioeconomic status to assign students to schools).

6 *See* David Benjamin Oppenheimer, *Understanding Affirmative Action*, 23 Hastings Const. L.Q. 921, 929–32 (1996) (describing self-study, outreach, and counseling as methods for increasing diversity in schools and workplaces); Michelle Adams, *The Last Wave of Affirmative Action*, 1998 Wisc. L. Rev. 1395, 1401–07 (1998) (describing a range of facially neutral but race-conscious measures to increase diversity in government programs, businesses, and schools).

7 *Fisher*, 133 S. Ct. at 2433 (Ginsburg, J., dissenting).

8 *Fisher*, 133 S. Ct. at _2433 (Ginsburg, J., dissenting) (quoting Gratz v. Bollinger, 539 U.S. 244 (297–98) (Souter, J., dissenting)).

9 Whether the plans are effective for this purpose or are unacceptable for other reasons remains open. *See, e.g.*, *Fisher*, 133 S. Ct. at _ (citing statistics about minority admissions at the University of Texas, comparing the Ten Percent Plan favorably to earlier practices that explicitly took race into account); Marta Tienda & Sunny Xinchun Niu, *Capitalizing on Segregation, Pretending Neutrality: College Admissions and the Texas Top 10% Law*, 8 Am. L. & Econ. Rev. 312 (2006) (finding that the Texas plan facilitated some minority enrollment in selective institutions but failed to sustain minority admissions rates at the flagship schools); *see also* Gratz v. Bollinger, 539 U.S. 244, 303 n.10 (2003) (Ginsburg, J., dissenting) (pointing out that percentage plans depend on continued segregation in K-12 schools and encourage students to stay in low-performing schools and take easy courses); Robert J. Delahunty, *"Constitutional Justice" or "Constitutional Peace"? The Supreme Court and Affirmative Action*, 65 Wash. & Lee L. Rev. 11, 37–41 (2008) (arguing that affirmative action is itself a conservative, privilege-preserving response to racial inequality).

10 *E.g.*, Transcript of Oral Argument at 4–5, *Parents Involved*, 551 U.S. 701 (No. 05–908) (Kennedy, J.) (site selection); *id.* at 6 (Scalia, J.) (magnet schools); *id.* at 18 (Roberts, J.) (sites and magnet schools); *id.* at 19 (Kennedy, J.) (site selection).

the hypothetical of a school district deciding where to build a new school. In light of existing segregation in housing, one location would result in a racially diverse school, while the other would contribute to the *de facto* segregation of the schools. Could the school district choose the former, because it wants racial diversity? Counsel for the plaintiffs said that it could not, because any race-related motive for state action is forbidden.[11] Although no member of the Court appeared to support this position at oral argument, the four-justice plurality ultimately endorsed it. The court thus came within one vote of holding that the government had no legitimate interest in striving for racial equality and integration.

That one vote belonged to Justice Kennedy. Justice Kennedy wrote separately and distanced himself from the plurality on this point, emphasizing his discomfort with racial classifications of individuals but also the importance of racial equality and integration. Examining cases involving sex equality confirms that the latter concern is firmly grounded in precedent.

"Only One Equal Protection Clause":[12] Existing Inequality and the Sex Cases

Just as "[t]here is only one Equal Protection Clause,"[13] there is only one underlying doctrinal structure for equal protection cases. Doctrinal shifts in one context carry over into others.[14] The outcome of the struggle over the legitimacy of the goal of racial equality necessarily affects whether the government can properly seek sex equality as well. Similarly, cases in which the Court allowed the state to pursue the goal of sex equality demonstrate that the *Parents Involved* plurality was wrong to claim that substantive racial equality is an illegitimate goal.

In the context of sex classifications, the state may seek to overcome not only societal discrimination against women but even what the Court perceives as women's inherent biological disadvantages. The key doctrinal reason why governments have such leeway with respect to sex is that classification of individuals according to sex, rather than race, is not troubling to the Court.[15] Isolating that factor clarifies the error in the *Parents Involved* plurality's rejection of the state's compelling interest in equality.

The Sex Classification Cases

One of the ironics of equal protection doctrine is that it is easier to justify remedial sex classifications than to justify remedial or benign racial classifications.[16] Doctrinally, this discrepancy is a function of the lower level of scrutiny for sex classifications.[17] Because of this reduced scrutiny, the state has more leeway to

11 Transcript of Oral Argument at 5, 7, *Parents Involved*, 551 U.S. 701 (No. 05–908).

12 Craig v. Boren, 429 U.S. 190, 211 (1976) (Stevens, J., concurring).

13 Craig v. Boren, 429 U.S. 190, 211 (1976) (Stevens, J., concurring).

14 *See generally* Serena Mayeri, *Reconstructing the Race-Sex Analogy*, 49 WM. & MARY L. REV. 1789 (2008) (describing the ways in which race and sex cases have influenced each other).

15 *See infra* notes 29–34 and accompanying text.

16 *See* Mary K. O'Melveny, *Playing the "Gender" Card: Affirmative Action and Working Women*, 84 KY. L. REV. 863, 864–65 (1996). ("Ironically, the unwillingness to employ strict scrutiny for gender-based classifications means that, under the Court's most recent rulings on affirmative action issues, affirmative action programs for women may survive challenge where comparable race-based programs will not. Or, to put the issue another way, White men may look to greater constitutional protections from race-based affirmative action plans (however well-intentioned) than exist for women challenging programs that discriminate based upon sex.") (footnote omitted).

17 *See* Craig v. Boren, 429 U.S. 190, 197–98 (1976) (adopting the intermediate standard of review for sex classifications). Intermediate scrutiny requires that the state action be substantially related to an important state interest, *id.*, as opposed to strict scrutiny's requirement that state action be narrowly tailored to a compelling state interest, Johnson v. California, 542 U.S. 499, 505 (2005). *See also* United States v. Virginia, 518 U.S. 515, 524 (1996) (formally adhering to intermediate scrutiny for sex classifications); Nguyen v. INS, 533 U.S. 53 (2001) (demonstrating that *United States v. Virginia* had not ratcheted up review of sex classifications by applying extremely deferential review to a sex classification clearly rooted in stereotypes).

shape gender relations than race relations. Of course, the state may use this leeway to perpetuate stereotypes and inequality. The state may also, however, try to improve the relative status of women, including through affirmative action programs.[18]

A striking example of a remedial sex classification was the compensatory social security program upheld in *Califano v. Webster*.[19] Under the program, women and men were subject to different rules for calculating their social security benefits. The result was higher benefits for a woman than for a man with the same earning history. The Supreme Court had no trouble accepting the important state interest justifying this outcome: "[r]eduction of the disparity in economic condition between men and women caused by the long history of discrimination against women."[20] Less dramatically, the same state interest has justified affirmative action for women in areas such as public employment, which has proceeded with far less controversy than what swirls around race-based affirmative action.[21] Equal protection analysis that takes into account the need to combat existing inequality is thus well established in the field of sex classifications.[22]

Importantly, the gender differential in *Webster* was intended to redress *private* discrimination in employment. There was no suggestion that Congress was at fault or had itself violated the Equal Protection Clause by, say, failing to outlaw discrimination by private actors.[23] The inequality that justified this sex classification is thus analogous to the structural inequality that the *Parents Involved* plurality called into question as a justification for race-conscious action. It is the sort of inequality that does not meet the test for state action and thus does not trigger a judicial remedy under the Equal Protection Clause. Nonetheless, Congress had a legitimate interest in redressing the existing inequality. Congress's ability to favor women in the benefits calculation was contingent on that inequality. The *Parents Involved* plurality's refusal to apply the same analysis to remedies for racial inequality is inconsistent with the Court's willingness to apply this analytical structure to the remediation of sex inequality in *Webster*.

Of course, there are differences between race and sex—in doctrine and in reality—that might explain different outcomes. It is difficult to imagine the Court upholding a compensatory social security system similar to *Webster* but designed to compensate individual members of racial minorities for private employment discrimination.[24] A racial *Webster* would apply a different level of scrutiny. Breaking down the analysis,

---

18 *See, e.g.*, Johnson v. Santa Clara County Trans. Agency, 480 U.S. 616 (1987) (upholding a sex-based affirmative action program against a Title VII challenge).

19 430 U.S. 313 (1977) (per curiam).

20 *Califano*, 430 U.S. at 317.

21 *See* Debra Frazese, *The Gender Curve: An Analysis of Colleges' Use of Affirmative Action Policies to Benefit Male Applicants*, 56 Am. U. L. Rev. 719 (2007); O'Melveny, *supra* note 14, at 864–65. *But see* Celia M. Ruiz, *Legal Standards Regarding Gender Equity and Affirmative Action*, 100 Ed. L. Rep. 841, 844 (1995) (discussing the Sixth Circuit's application of strict scrutiny to sex-based affirmative action in order to eliminate this anomaly). In the educational context, some institutions now engage in "reverse" affirmative action in order to maintain parity between male and female admissions. *See* Frazese, *supra* (arguing that such policies are unconstitutional because they are based on stereotypes and unsupported by any pedagogical objective).

22 The Supreme Court regularly cites *Webster* and the state interest in redressing past economic discrimination against women when cataloguing acceptable governmental uses of sex classifications. *See, e.g.*, United States v. Virginia, 518 U.S. 515, 533 (1996); Miss. Univ. for Women v. Hogan, 458 U.S. 718, 728 (1982); *see also* Orr v. Orr, 440 U.S. 268, 280 (1979) (citing *Webster* with approval).

23 While the Equal Protection Clause might have been read to require Congress or the states to enact non-discrimination laws, the Supreme Court has never gone down that road. Cf. Laurence H. Tribe, American Constitutional Law 1695 n.16 (2nd ed. 1988) (suggesting that in *The Civil Rights Cases*, 109 U.S. 3 (1883), the Supreme Court should have held that Congress had power to intervene under Section 5 of the Fourteenth Amendment when a state had repealed its common law rule of equal access).

24 It is perhaps even more difficult to imagine that Congress would enact such a program. In addition to the doctrinal factors discussed in the text, a third reason that such a program would be neither enacted nor upheld is that redistribution of wealth on the basis of sex is much less radical than redistribution on the basis of race. Wealth is typically held by families, which are mixed-sex far more often than mixed-race. For those who were dependent on social security for survival, the sex differential upheld in *Webster* probably helped some older women get by. Given, however, that social security pays more to higher earners, the primary beneficiaries of the differential would have been the families of relatively prosperous, mostly White women.

however, reveals that the difference cannot lie in the legitimacy or weight of the state interest in ameliorating racial inequality as compared to sex inequality. Rather, the difference lies in what the Court considers acceptable means for ameliorating different kinds of inequality.

Judicial scrutiny of sex classifications is, at least in theory, less intense than scrutiny of race classifications in two ways. First, a race classification must serve a "compelling" state interest, while a sex classification need serve only an "important" state interest.[25] Second, the means of achieving the state interest must be appropriate: if the means include a race classification, it must be "narrowly tailored" to the state interest.[26] A sex classification need only be "substantially related" to the state interest or, when the Court is feeling particularly hostile to sex classifications, have an "exceedingly persuasive" justification.[27] If a racial *Webster* would come out differently, then the difference must lie either in the state interest asserted or in the means used to effectuate that interest.

The Supreme Court has never provided a comparative analysis of the difference between "important" and "compelling" state interests. Indeed, it has barely distinguished between those categories and other legitimate state interests. Most legitimate state interests seem capable of being deemed at least important, with the sole exception of mere administrative convenience.[28] While the "compelling" category may yet turn out to be narrower than the "important" category, the state interest in fighting inequality is obviously the wrong place to draw that line. To hold that equality is an important but not compelling goal *under the Fourteenth Amendment* would be bizarre, even where the equality sought is more positive and substantive than the negative right to equal treatment enforced by the Court. Equally strange would be to hold that racial inequality was a lesser concern than sex inequality under that Amendment. Thus, if race and sex cases have different outcomes, it cannot be because of the formal difference between "important" and "compelling" state interests.

The Supreme Court has similarly failed to explicate the difference between "narrowly tailored" and "substantially related" means for achieving state interests by way of race or sex classifications. One of the reasons, however, that sex classifications trigger a lower level of scrutiny is that the Court does not consider the government's classification of an individual as female or male to be inherently offensive. In *Bakke*, Justice Powell explained that sex classifications do not create the same "analytical and practical problems" as race classifications because "there are only two possible classifications" and thus "no rival groups" to claim entitlements.[29] Thirty years later, the Court has not yet confronted cases involving intersexed or transsexual individuals under the Equal Protection Clause. It has barely scratched the surface of other claims involving individuals whose gender or sexual identity resists binary classification. The Court's awkward stumbling in cases involving homosexuality does not bespeak a Court inclined to question its binary definition of sex.[30]

Lower court cases reflect a similar insistence on the binary determinability of sex. In Title VII cases, courts faced with questions about "correct" racial classification have in recent years fallen back on social reality and perception rather than purportedly scientific definitions of race.[31] Not so for sex classifications.

25 *See* Johnson v. California, 543 U.S. 499, 505 (2005) (strict scrutiny); Craig v. Boren, 429 U.S. 190, 197–98 (1976) (intermediate scrutiny); United States v. Virginia, 518 U.S. 515, 524 (1996) ("exceedingly persuasive justification").

26 *See Johnson v. California*, 543 U.S. at 505.

27 *See* U.S. v. Virginia, 518 U.S. at 524; *but see* Nguyen v. INS, 533 U.S. 53, 78–80 (2001) (O'Connor, J., dissenting) (complaining that the majority had abandoned the "exceedingly persuasive" requirement).

28 *See Craig*, 429 U.S. at 197–98 (noting prior rejection of state interests in reducing probate court workload and administrative ease and convenience).

29 Regents of the Univ. of Cal. v. Bakke, 438 U.S. 265, 302–03 (1978) (Powell, J., announcing judgment). Justice Powell added that the perception of racial classifications as inherently odious stems from a "lengthy and tragic history that gender-based classifications do not share." *Id.* at 303.

30 *See* Oncale v. Sundowner Offshore Servs., Inc., 523 U.S. 75 (1998) (holding that same-sex sexual harassment can be actionable under Title VII, but failing to provide useful guidance for determining when such harassment is "because of sex," as required by the statute). On the question of when adverse action is "because of sex," *see generally* Jennifer S. Hendricks, *Women and the Promise of Equal Citizenship*, 8 Tex. J. Women & L. 51, 85–91 (1998) (discussing "animus based on gender" under the Violence Against Women Act and "because of sex" under Title VII as applied to sexual harassment cases).

31 *See, e.g.*, Al-Khazraji v. St. Francis College, 784 F.2d 505, 514–18 (1986) (invoking congressional intent to hold that an Arab plaintiff could proceed with a race discrimination claim under 42 U.S.C. § 1981, regardless of whether Arabs were "taxonomically Caucasian").

In cases ranging from discrimination to the validity of marriages, courts have insisted on a binary, biological definition.[32] Although this approach is unrealistic and harmful in many contexts,[33] its prevalence illuminates equal protection doctrine: sex cases demonstrate what courts and other state actors may do in the face of historic and persisting inequality when the classification itself is not deemed pernicious.

Because of the tolerance for individual classification, a variety of means remain open to a state actor seeking to ameliorate sex inequality. In contrast, to implement a *Webster*-like program for race, Congress would have to define each person's race with the precision of Jim Crow.[34] That act of classification—not the state interest in equality—is what distinguishes *Parents Involved* from *Webster*.

The Real Differences Cases

The binary sex classification is so untroubling to the Supreme Court that purportedly innate sex differences can justify sex classifications in the law. While laws based on "real differences" often perpetuate archaic stereotypes, they can also reflect state efforts to promote sex equality. For example, a state can require employers to provide pregnancy leave to their employees,[35] and Congress enacted the Family and Medical Leave Act in part to help level the playing field for working women.[36] As with affirmative action, the Supreme Court has never held that governments are *required* to take these steps toward substantive equality.[37] But unlike the race-based affirmative action cases, the "real differences" cases have easily permitted governments to choose accommodation of "women's differences," which the Court perceives as inequality imposed by nature. In the absence of an inherently pernicious classification, the state is free to seek affirmative, substantive equality. The real differences cases thus further demonstrate that the *Parents Involved* plurality's rejection of the state interest in equality is unfounded in prior equal protection jurisprudence.

Sylvia Law and Ann Freedman first identified the real differences cases as those in which the Supreme Court invokes natural sex differences to justify different legal treatment of men and women.[38] Of course, the Court's perception of which differences are natural has changed over time. In the infamous *Bradwell v.*

---

32 *See generally* Julie Greenberg, *Defining Male and Female*, 41 Ariz. L. Rev. 265, 292–325 (1999) (surveying cases illustrative of "law's insistence on clinging to a binary system that traditionally ignores the importance of self-identification").

33 *See* Elizabeth Reilly, *Radical Tweak: Relocating the Power to Assign Sex*, 12 Cardozo J.L. & Gender 297, 301–07 (2005) (summarizing literature about the effects on individuals of medical and legal enforcement of binary sex categories).

34 In fact, to accurately reflect past discrimination, Congress might well adopt definitions of race from the very laws that structured *de jure* segregation. Cf. Plessy v. Ferguson, 163 U.S. 537, 541–42, 549, 552 (1896) (discussing Homer Plessy's claim to a property right in whiteness); Loving v. Virginia, 388 U.S. 1, 5 n.4 (1967) (quoting Virginia's statutes defining race).

35 *See* Calif. Fed. Savings & Loan Ass'n v. Guerra, 479 U.S. 272 (1987), discussed *infra*.

36 29 U.S.C. §§ 2601–54 (2008).

37 *See* Sylvia Law, *Rethinking Sex and the Constitution*, 132 U. Pa. L. Rev. 955, 962 (1984) (cataloguing the real differences cases); *see also* Nguyen v. INS, 533 U.S. 53 (2001); United States v. Virginia, 518 U.S. 515 (1996). In all of these cases, the Supreme Court either upheld the government's policy or (in *United States v. Virginia*) struck down a policy treating women and men differently because the Court rejected the government's claim that they were differently situated. The Court has never struck down a policy of facial sex-neutrality (no matter how superficial, *see* Geduldig v. Aiello, 417 U.S. 484 (1974)) because it failed to account for biological difference. *Cf.* Califano v. Webster, 430 U.S. 313, 320 (1977) (stating that Congress's change of heart—repealing the sex-differential in the social security rules—did not affect the Court's analysis of whether Congress had the power to enact the differential).

38 Law, *supra* note 37, at 962; Ann E. Freedman, *Sex Equality, Sex Differences, and the Supreme Court*, 92 Yale L.J. 913 (1983). They identified the following as real differences cases: Michael M. v. Super. Ct., 450 U.S. 464 (1981) (statutory rape a crime only when committed by male against female); Rostker v. Goldberg, 453 U.S. 57 (1981) (male-only registration for the draft); Dothard v. Rawlinson, 433 U.S. 321 (1977) (exclusion of women from contact jobs in prisons); Gen. Elec. v. Gilbert, 429 U.S. 125 (1976) (exclusion of pregnancy from disability benefits policy offered by a private employer); Schlesinger v. Ballard, 419 U.S. 498 (1975) (separate rules for male and female officers under navy's up-or-out policy); Geduldig v. Aiello, 417 U.S. 48 (1974) (exclusion of pregnancy from the disability benefits policy offered by a public employer); Cleveland Bd. of Educ. v. LaFleur, 414 U.S. 632 (1974) (mandatory pregnancy leave).

Illinois,[39] the Court perceived men and women as differently situated, by biology and the "law of the Creator," with respect to the practice of law.[40] Purported natural differences also justified early labor restrictions for female workers when men's labor was still subject to *Lochner v. New York*.[41] More recently, the Court has been receptive to real differences arguments only when the link to reproductive biology is more direct.[42] In *Michael M. v. Superior Court*, for example, the Court accepted women's vulnerability to pregnancy as a justification for sex-specific statutory rape laws.[43] In *Dothard v. Rawlinson*, the Court equated femaleness with rapeability to justify restricting employment opportunities for female prison guards.[44]

The most infamous of the real differences cases is *Geduldig v. Ailleo*.[45] *Geduldig* involved a comprehensive short-term disability policy for state employees in California. The Court held that the exclusion only of pregnancy from coverage under the policy was not sex discrimination. The policy, said the Court, did not distinguish between women and men but between "pregnant women and nonpregnant persons."[46] The Constitution did not require the state to make up for what the Court perceived as a natural disadvantage in the labor market.

Other cases, however, show that the state *may choose* to enact laws to promote sex equality in the face of sex differences. After the Court extended *Geduldig*'s cramped conception of sex discrimination to Title VII,[47] Congress responded with the Pregnancy Discrimination Act (PDA).[48] The PDA defines discrimination "because of sex" to include discrimination because of pregnancy, and it requires that employers treat pregnancy the same as any comparable physical condition.[49] The PDA thus protects women not just from irrational discrimination based on pregnancy but also from indifference to pregnancy's effect on their ability to work.[50]

The State of California went even further than the PDA, affirmatively mandating childbirth-related maternity leave, even for employees who were not protected against any other short-term disabilities.[51] The Supreme Court upheld this statute in *California Federal Savings and Loan Association v. Guerra* (*CalFed*),[52] in which an employer argued that the California law constituted both sex discrimination and pregnancy discrimination. The employer pointed out that the maternity leave requirement contradicted the PDA's insistence that pregnancy be treated "the same as" other comparable conditions. Looking to congressional intent, the *CalFed* Court read "the same as" to mean "no less favorably than." The state was thus given a choice: it could seek substantively equal outcomes in the face of natural difference, or it could allow natural differences to translate into unequal outcomes.

A common denominator of the real differences cases is that, regardless of whether the classification is challenged by a male or female party, the justifying biology—susceptibility to pregnancy or rape—is

39 83 U.S. (16 Wall.) 130 (1872) (holding that state could exclude women from practice of law).

40 *Bradwell*, 83 U.S. at 142.

41 198 U.S. 45 (1905) (striking down maximum hours laws for (presumably male) bakers); *see* Muller v. Oregon, 208 U.S. 412 (1908) (upholding maximum hours law for women working in laundries).

42 United States v. Virginia, 518 U.S. 515 (1996) (striking down a male-only admissions policy for a public, quasi-military college), is an example of a failed modern attempt to restore the real differences category to its former scope. *See* 518 U.S. at 540–41 (summarizing the state's argument about women and men having different "tendencies" that require different pedagogical approaches).

43 *See Michael M.*, 450 U.S. at 471–73 (Rehnquist, J., plurality opinion).

44 *See Dothard*, 433 U.S. at 336 ("The employee's very womanhood would thus directly undermine her capacity to provide [security]"). By conceding that the sex differences relied upon in these more recent cases are more closely connected to biology than those in *Bradwell*, I do not mean to imply that they are not also based on stereotypes or gender hierarchy. *See generally* Law, *supra* note 37 at 1014 n.217 (citing *Dothard* and *Rostker* for the point, "There is substantial evidence that the judiciary is not able to distinguish between biology and the social consequences attached to it").

45 417 U.S. 484 (1974).

46 *Geduldig*, 417 U.S. at 496 n.20.

47 *See* Gen. Elec. v. Gilbert, 429 U.S. 125 (1976).

48 42 U.S.C. § 2000(e)(k).

49 *Id.*

50 *Cf.* Cleveland Bd. of Educ. v. LaFleur, 414 U.S. 632 (1974) (holding that mandatory pregnancy leave for a teacher still able to work was impermissible).

51 *See* West's Ann. Calif. Gov. Code § 12945 (2005).

52 479 U.S. 272 (1987).

constructed as the natural disadvantage of women.[53] States have the option either to entrench the existing disadvantage *or* to counteract it with the force of law. The real differences cases thus share the same analytical structure as cases like *Webster*, with the purportedly natural disadvantage of biology playing the role of structural inequality. Cases like *CalFed* show that states may legitimately promote substantive equality even when existing inequality is deemed to be caused not by discriminatory state action or even by diffuse societal discrimination, but by nature itself.

The shared structure of *Webster* and the real differences cases can also be seen in how lawyers define the category of real differences cases. Two cases involving the exclusion of women from combat service in the military are routinely classified as real differences cases.[54] The difference—the combat exclusion—was clearly *de jure*. What mattered, however, was that, like structural inequality or biological sex differences, the combat exclusion was unquestioned in the context of the litigation. Because an admitted inequality was beyond the Court's power to remedy, the state had the option to level the playing field or to leave it askew.

The military cases are the only modern real differences cases that do not claim to rest strictly on biology. *Rostker v. Goldberg* upheld male-only registration for the draft.[55] *Schlesinger v. Ballard* upheld the navy's policy of giving women extra time to achieve promotion under the up-or-out policy.[56] Both cases were premised on the unchallenged exclusion of women from combat positions. In *Rostker*, women's exclusion from combat was the purported reason for excluding them from the draft, since Congress believed a draft would most likely seek combat troops.[57] In *Ballard*, exclusion from combat and sea duty limited women's ability to acquire the prerequisites for promotion; the navy allowed them extra time to make up for its own discriminatory policy.[58]

Rostker and *Ballard* are consistently classed with the real differences cases, even though they are based not on biological differences but on the military's explicit, sex-based exclusion of women from combat.[59] Analytically, then, *Rostker* and *Ballard* show that what makes a difference "real" is that the law takes it as a given. No party in *Ballard* or *Rostker* challenged women's exclusion from combat.[60] This failure made the fact that women did not serve in combat, even though clearly a function of law, just as "real" as the differences that the Court saw as imposed by nature in cases like *Michael M.*, *Dothard*, and *Geduldig*. A real difference is simply one that the Court can not (or will not) order to be changed.[61]

This analytical structure unites the real differences cases with the explicitly remedial cases involving social security, affirmative action, and integration. In all of these cases, the Court's analysis takes some social fact of inequality—structural race or sex inequality, biological sex differences, or the combat exclusion—as

53 As the prison context of *Dothard v. Rawlinson* should have helped make clear, vulnerability to rape is not a biologically determined sex characteristic. *See* Catharine A. MacKinnon, *Reflections on Sex Equality Under Law*, 100 YALE L.J. 1281, 1305–06 (1991) ("Men can be raped, and sometimes are. That alone should suggest that the overwhelming numbers of women in the rape victim population expresses inequality, not biology."). It is also not obvious that potential for pregnancy should be constructed as a vulnerability rather than as an ability.

54 *See* Rostker v. Goldberg, 453 U.S. 57 (1981); Schlesinger v. Ballard, 419 U.S. 498 (1975).

55 453 U.S. 57 (1981).

56 419 U.S. 498 (1975).

57 *See Rostker*, 453 U.S. at 76. The more likely reason for excluding women from registration, over the protest of military officers who testified in favor of registering women, was the political desire to maintain an ideology that looks to the male military to protect the women and children at home.

58 *See Ballard*, 419 U.S. at 508.

59 *See*, *e.g.*, Law, *supra* note 37, at 962 (listing real differences cases). Although many would surely argue that the combat exclusion itself was justified by biology, the Court has not confronted that claim because the exclusion was unchallenged in both cases. Moreover, biology has not changed in recent decades, but the combat exclusion has nearly disappeared. The justifications for what remains have more to do with the behavior of male troops than with women's abilities.

60 *See Ballard*, 419 U.S. at 508 (noting that plaintiff did not challenge combat and sea duty restrictions); *Rostker*, 453 U.S. at 83 (White, J., dissenting) ("I assume what has not been challenged in this case—that excluding women from combat positions does not offend the Constitution."). Although the issue was not raised, the majority in *Rostker* clearly would have upheld the combat exclusion.

61 Cf. Girardeau A. Spann, *Affirmative Inaction*, 50 How. L.J. 611, 636–39 (2007) ("A baseline is something that separates the factors that a court actively considers from the factors whose validity a court assumes without examination.").

a given for purposes of the litigation. Because that social fact is treated as unproblematic under the Equal Protection Clause, the state is under no duty to try to change it. But because that social fact creates conditions of actual inequality, the state has a legitimate interest in change if it chooses to try.

Because the analytical structure is the same, the plurality view in *Parents Involved* threatens not only remedial efforts that involve race-conscious state action but also those that involve sex classifications and even sex-conscious social policy. For example, under *Geduldig*, the PDA and the California maternity leave statute arguably do not contain sex classifications. Because pregnancy is not a sex classification, special protection for pregnancy fails to trigger heightened review, just as the targeted exclusion failed to trigger heightened review in *Geduldig*. However, both the PDA and the California law were adopted to give women a relative advantage, as compared to a *status quo* in which disfavored treatment of pregnancy was legal. Altering the playing field in women's favor was a motivating factor for the legislation.

Similarly, in the past, the Supreme Court has endorsed the use of facially gender-neutral policies that Congress intends to promote sex equality. Both the Violence against Women Act (VAWA)[62] and the Family and Medical Leave Act (FMLA)[63] are textually gender-neutral; both were enacted and the FMLA was upheld by the Supreme Court as an attempt to achieve greater substantive equality for women.[64] To uphold the FMLA on this basis, the Court had to strain to identify a pattern of state action unconstitutionally discriminating against female employees that corresponded to the remedy provided by the FMLA.[65] A more honest assessment of the FMLA is that its purpose was to alter the playing field: to restructure employment markets to accommodate employees with caretaking responsibilities, in large part in order to achieve greater substantive sex equality.

If eliminating *de facto* racial inequality and segregation is not a legitimate state interest, it is hard to see how the government would fare much better in claiming an interest in restructuring employment markets to facilitate greater achievement by a naturally less-suited class of people (such as women who have or plan to have or might accidentally have children). A Supreme Court prepared to constitutionalize *de facto* racial segregation would not necessarily balk at doing the same for gender hierarchy.[66] Conversely, as things now stand, the real differences cases underscore that rejecting equality as a compelling state interest would be an abrupt departure from existing law.

The Critical Role of Individual Racial Classification

Despite the clear state interest in promoting equality in the sex cases, the race cases have long shunned any state interest in promoting general racial equality against the forces of "societal discrimination." This rejection of societal discrimination as a justification for racial classifications must be understood in context. In his foundational opinion in *Bakke*,[67] Justice Powell said that responding to societal discrimination, for which the university's medical school was not specifically responsible, could not justify affirmative action in the school's admissions program.[68] The Court has generally adhered to Justice Powell's position with respect to affirmative action programs and has held that generalized societal discrimination could not justify minority set-asides in government contracting.[69] Nonetheless, the Court's more recent cases also indicate that structural

62 Violent Crime Control and Law Enforcement Act of 1994, Pub. L. No. 103–322, 108 Stat. 1796 (1994) (codified in scattered sections of 8, 18 & 42 U.S.C.).

63 29 U.S.C. §§ 2601–54 (2006).

64 *See* Nev. Dep't of Human Res. v. Hibbs, 538 U.S. 721 (2003).

65 *See Hibbs*, 538 U.S. at 728–32. While Congress certainly had evidence of sex discrimination, including discrimination with respect to parental leave, the FMLA's affirmative requirements for family and medical leave go well beyond remedying anything that the Supreme Court would have found to be unconstitutional sex discrimination.

66 The main reason one might expect them to balk is non-doctrinal and is that White male members of the Court may have greater empathy with, for example, the plight of professional women. *See* Joan C. Williams, *Hibbs as a Federalism Case, Hibbs as a Maternal Wall Case*, 73 U. Cinn. L. Rev. 365, 374–75 (2004) (describing Chief Justice Rehnquist's experiences caring for his wife when she was ill and helping his daughter, a lawyer and single mother, with child care).

67 438 U.S. 265 (1978).

68 *Bakke*, 438 U.S. at 307–10 (Powell, J., announcing judgment).

69 Adarand Constructors, Inc. v. Pena, 515 U.S. 200, 227 (1995).

inequality has a role to play in evaluating the constitutionality of affirmative action. The real fault line in the race cases is not the goal of promoting equality but the means: classification of individuals according to race.

In both *Grutter* and *Gratz*, the University of Michigan was careful not to propound societal discrimination as its justification for affirmative action, relying instead on its interest in having a diverse student body for educational purposes. This strategy reflected the fact that Justice Powell's *Bakke* opinion had become the "touchstone for constitutional analysis of race-conscious admissions policies."[70] Accordingly, a defense based on societal discrimination would have been doomed.

Nonetheless, *Grutter*'s famous sunset clause indicates that existing inequality played a role in the Court's analysis. The university's primary interest was in having a diverse student body. Existing conditions of inequality made that goal difficult to achieve using its traditional admissions criteria. The Court acknowledged the existence of social inequality *and* the fact that this inequality had an adverse effect on the educational interest in diversity.[71] In the absence of affirmative action, the university would have not only reflected but perpetuated the unequal *status quo*. Inequality thus served as a second-order justification for affirmative action. The sunset clause expressed the hope that this background inequality, and thus the need for affirmative action, would be eliminated within a generation. (After all, the law school's educational interest in a diverse student body would not become more or less compelling with the passage of time.) The sunset clause was thus an implicit acknowledgement that the Court's application of the Equal Protection Clause depended on the current fact of structural inequality.[72]

In addition, the state interest in diversity itself contained an implicit equality component. Although the law school emphasized the educational benefits of diversity, the Court spoke also of the social benefits of diversity in the professions.[73] The law school needed a diverse student body not only because students would learn better but also because it was necessary, for society's sake, "that the path to leadership be visibly open."[74] The law school's affirmative action program was permissible, in part, because it would help remedy the stratification produced by the mechanisms of structural inequality.[75]

In *Grutter*, then, structural inequality played a background role, somewhat obscured by the educational interest in diversity. *Bakke* and its progeny mean at most that eliminating inequality, *by itself*, is not a compelling state interest *sufficient to justify traditional affirmative action programs*. That is not the same as saying that eliminating inequality is never a compelling state interest.[76] The two steps of strict scrutiny are not so isolated from each other that the acceptability of the means cannot affect whether a particular interest is deemed compelling.[77] The Court's fundamental objection to affirmative action is not to the goal—whether that be diversity or equality, both of which the Court invoked in *Grutter*—but to the means.

---

70 *Grutter*, 539 U.S. at 323.

71 *See Grutter*, 539 U.S. at 328 (recognizing the law school's compelling interest in a diverse student body), 338 (stating that minority applicants are "less likely to be admitted in meaningful numbers on criteria that ignore [their] experiences" attributable to "our Nation's struggle with racial inequality").

72 *See* Michelle Adams, *Stifling the Potential of Grutter v. Bollinger: Parents Involved in Community Schools v. Seattle School District No. 1*, 88 B.U. L. Rev. 937, 938–39, 950–53 (2008) (discussing the non-pedagogical aspects of *Grutter*'s diversity rationale); Kevin R. Johnson, *The Last Twenty Five Years of Affirmative Action?*, 21 Const. Comment. 171, 173 (2004) (noting that the sunset clause implies a remedial or equality-seeking rationale in tension with the diversity rationale highlighted by the Court).

73 *See Grutter*, 539 U.S. at 332.

74 *Grutter*, 539 U.S. at 332.

75 Cf. Johnson, *supra* note 72, at 173.

76 It also does not rule out the possibility that even traditional affirmative action programs would be permissible for the purpose of eliminating inequality on a showing that other means were ineffective.

77 *See* City of Cleburne v. Cleburne Living Ctr., Inc., 473 U.S. 432, 455 (1985) (Marshall, J., concurring in part and dissenting in part); San Antonio Indep. Sch. Dist. v. Rodriguez, 411 U.S. 1, 98–99 (1973) (Marshall, J., dissenting) (both arguing that the Court in truth applies a multi-factored sliding scale analysis when analyzing equal protection claims); *see* Andrew M. Siegel, *Equal Protection Unmodified: Justice John Paul Stevens and the Case for Unmediated Constitutional Interpretation*, 74 Fordham L. Rev. 2339 (2006); Suzanne B. Goldberg, *Equality Without Tiers*, 77 S. Cal. L. Rev. 481 (2004) (focusing particularly on Grutter and Gratz); Leslie Friedman Goldstein, *Between the Tiers: The New[est] Equal Protection and Bush v. Gore*, 4 U. Pa. J. Const. L. 372 (2002).

Traditional affirmative action programs promote equal opportunity by classifying individuals on the basis of race and using those classifications to distribute benefits. It is primarily this act of classification, not the state interest in equality, to which the Supreme Court has usually objected.[78]

The Court's discomfort with racial categorization was apparent even as it upheld the University of Michigan's law school admissions program. One of the more frustrating aspects of the *Grutter* and *Gratz* decisions was the Court's apparent preference for obscurity in the decision-making process of an affirmative action program. The Court preferred the law school's "holistic" approach that did not assign numerical values to race or other elements of diversity, rather than the undergraduate point system.[79] As Justice Ginsburg argued, "If honesty is the best policy, surely Michigan's accurately described, fully disclosed College affirmative action program is preferable to achieving similar numbers through winks, nods, and disguises."[80]

Two factors are likely to have driven the Court's preference for the opaque rather than the transparent process. First is a preference for suppressing controversy and conflict.[81] If there are to be racial preferences in admissions, better that they be obscured so that no one can say for sure what effect they had, and fewer feelings will be hurt.[82]

Second is the Court's discomfort with the mere act of classifying individuals by race. To classify individuals by race, the government must have a definition of race, something the Supreme Court has not had to confront since it rejected Homer Plessy's claim that he was White.[83] Slavery, Jim Crow, and legal segregation all required an official system for stamping each person with a racial label, often using the infamous "one drop of blood" rule.[84] A point system for affirmative action admissions requires each person to be classified, even if not necessarily under the same rule.[85] Under a holistic system, the classification can be fudged. The increasing proportion of the

78 *See* Parents Involved in Cmty. Schs. v. Seattle Sch. Dist. No. 1, 551 U.S. 701, 796–97 (2007) (Kennedy, J., concurring in part and concurring in the judgment); *see also* Andrew M. Carlon, *Racial Adjudication*, 2007 BYU L. Rev. 1151, 1159–60.

79 *See* Grutter v. Bollinger, 539 U.S. 306, 334–39 (2003) (favorably describing the law school's program and concluding that it was narrowly tailored); Gratz v. Bollinger, 539 U.S. 244, 270–74 (2003) (concluding that the undergraduate point system was not narrowly tailored).

80 *See Gratz*, 539 U.S. at 305 (Ginsburg, J., dissenting).

81 *See* Delahunty, *supra* note 9, at 69 (arguing that the Court's strategy has been to pursue a brokered peace by allowing limited affirmative action rather than choosing between competing visions of racial justice) ("The opacity of the law school's race-conscious admissions process was its virtue, the transparency of the college's admissions process was its vice. Opacity in this context mutes racial envy and antagonism, transparency breeds them."); cf. Laurence H. Tribe, *Erog v. Shub and Its Disguises: Freeing Bush v. Gore From Its Hall of Mirrors*, 115 Harv. L. Rev. 170, 287–88 (2001) (discussing the Court's reaction to the perceived chaos of post-2000 election Florida and concluding, "To judge from what this Court does, not what it says, high on [its] list of values is the preservation of a stable order and of an appearance of regularity. Low on that list is an energized, politicized, unruly electorate struggling to find its way toward concrete outcomes ..."); Planned Parenthood of Se. Pa. v. Casey, 505 U.S. 833, 866–69 (1992) (arguing that vociferous popular protest against Roe v. Wade, 410 U.S. 113 (1973), was all the more reason to reaffirm rather than overrule it) (discussed in Tribe, *supra*, at 289–90).

82 *Cf.* Richard A. Primus, *Equal Protection and Disparate Impact: Round Three*, 117 Harv. L. Rev. 293 (2003) (arguing that *Ricci v. DeStefano*, 557 U.S. 557 (2009), as well as *Grutter* and *Parents Involved*, could be read to prohibit affirmative action measures that have "visible victims").

83 *See* Plessy v. Ferguson, 163 U.S. 537, 541–42, 549, 552 (1896) (holding that the state could choose how to define race for purposes of its Jim Crow laws).

84 *See, e.g.*, Loving v. Virginia, 388 U.S. 1, 5 n.4 (1967) (quoting Virginia statutes defining *White persons* as those with "no trace whatever of any blood other than Caucasian," with a minor exception designed to "honor[] the descendants of John Rolfe and Pocahontas").

85 Most affirmative action programs rely on self-identification, a system which has generated surprisingly little controversy (at least to the point of inspiring litigation) over the correctness of those self-designations. *See* Carlon, *supra* note 78, at 1164–65 (noting that there are few documented instances of "abuse" of affirmative action by non-minorities); *see, e.g.*, Fisher v. Univ. of Tex., 133 S. Ct. 2411, _ (2013) (stating that the Texas affirmative action plan "asks students to classify themselves from among five predefined racial categories"). (Slightly more common are disputes over "close cases," such as whether a person of Arab descent is "white." *See id.*; Al-Khazraji v. St. Francis Coll., 784 F.2d 505, 514–18 (1986) (invoking congressional intent to hold that an Arab plaintiff could proceed with a race discrimination claim under

population who check "other" when asked their race can, in fact, be treated as individuals rather than forced into one of a few categories. A holistic system avoids the potential for litigation in which a court is asked to decide whether the government has applied the wrong racial label to a modern-day Homer Plessy.

The *Parents Involved* opinions highlighted the evils of individual racial classifications. The plurality framed its holding as concerned with the distribution of "burdens or benefits on the basis of individual racial classifications."[86] Justice Kennedy criticized the Seattle school district's "blunt distinction between 'white' and 'nonwhite,'" which tells "each student he or she is to be defined by race."[87]

The weight this concern should receive is certainly open to debate.[88] It is, however, a legitimate concern that is important to the Court's swing vote. It is therefore worth isolating the effect of the racial classification problem, in order to avoid over-generalizing the Court's existing precedents. That is, the Court's hostility to racial labels should not be allowed to taint the state interest in equality. In the interplay of state interests with narrow tailoring that is strict scrutiny, equality may be a compelling state interest even if it is not always strong enough for the Court to allow individual classifications as the means to achieve it.

The Court's aversion to racial classifications makes it inappropriate to allow the affirmative action cases to stand for the general proposition that equality is not a compelling state interest. The Court's rejection of societal discrimination as a compelling interest should be understood in context. The affirmative action programs struck down in *Gratz* and *Bakke* required classification of individuals into fixed racial categories. In contrast, the Court's acknowledgement of existing inequality played at least some role in upholding the law school's program in *Grutter*, which avoided strict racial categories. *Grutter* and *Gratz*, then, should be understood as leaving open the possibility of structural inequality as a compelling state interest.

In *Parents Involved*, although Justice Kennedy agreed with the plurality on the outcome, he sided with the dissent on the question of the state interest: he accepted that the claimed state interest in avoiding racial isolation was compelling.[89] His objection to the schools' plans came at the second step of the strict scrutiny analysis, the requirement of narrow tailoring. The substance of that objection was to the state's classification of individuals by race: "[O]fficial labels proclaiming the race of all persons in a broad class of citizens ... are unconstitutional as the cases now come to us."[90]

Justice Kennedy's point of disagreement with the plurality thus made explicit what had been implicit in prior affirmative action cases. The Court's seeming protestations to the contrary notwithstanding, the state *has* a compelling interest in combating the unequal *status quo*. In crafting policy to serve that interest, however, some means are more acceptable than others, and individual racial labels must be kept as a last resort.[91]

Interestingly, Justice Kennedy's opinion progressed from a *Grutter*-like diversity rationale to equality concerns as he discussed different kinds of state action. When discussing acceptable state interests for individual

---

42 U.S.C. § 1981, regardless of whether Arabs were "taxonomically Caucasian"). For an example of what the Supreme Court presumably wants to avoid, see Edward C. Thomas, *Racial Classification and the Flawed Pursuit of Diversity: How Phantom Minorities Threaten "Critical Mass" Justification in Higher Education*, 2007 BYU L. Rev. 813 (2007) (arguing that universities that fail to establish and enforce precise racial definitions have failed to narrowly tailor their affirmative action programs to their interest in diverse student bodies).

86 Parents Involved in Cmty. Schs. v. Seattle Sch. Dist. No. 1, 551 U.S. 701, 720 (2007).

87 *Parents Involved*, 551 U.S. at 787–9 (Kennedy, J., concurring in part and concurring in the judgment).

88 *See, e.g.*, *Parents Involved*, 551 U.S. at 867 (Breyer, J., dissenting) ("This is not to deny that there is a cost in applying 'a state-mandated racial label.' But that cost does not approach, in degree or in kind, the terrible harms of slavery, the resulting caste system, and 80 years of legal racial segregation.") (quoting *id.* at 797 (Kennedy, J., concurring in part and concurring in the judgment)).

89 *See Parents Involved*, 551 U.S. at 783–84, 797–98 (Kennedy, J., concurring in part and concurring in the judgment) (summarizing disagreement with plurality); *id.* at 787–88 ("The plurality opinion is too dismissive of the legitimate interest government has in ensuring all people have equal opportunity regardless of their race.").

90 *Parents Involved*, 551 U.S. at 782 (Kennedy, J., concurring in part and concurring in the judgment). *See* Joshua O. Oluwole & Preston C. Greene III, *Parents Involved and Race-Conscious Measures: A Cause for Optimism*, 26 Buff. Pub. Int. L.J. 1, 27–28 ("[W]hat Justice Kennedy condemns is not typing by race, but rather *individual* typing by race.").

91 *See Parents Involved*, 551 U.S. at 790 (Kennedy, J., concurring in part and concurring in the judgment) ("And individual racial classifications employed in this manner may be considered legitimate only if they are a last resort to achieve a compelling interest.").

classifications, he spoke in terms of diversity, and squarely within the race-as-ethnicity perspective.[92] From this perspective, race is one of many personal characteristics that make up the range of human experience, but it does not necessarily implicate a hierarchy.[93] Ian Haney López has chronicled how this conception of race promotes a doctrine of strict colorblindness at the expense of other Fourteenth Amendment values, particularly the elimination of racial subordination.[94] Justice Kennedy's critique of the Seattle plan fits squarely within this tradition.[95] His main objection to the Seattle plan was to its "blunt distinction between 'white' and 'nonwhite,'" which failed to account for substantial racial and ethnic diversity in the "nonwhite" category.[96] When Justice Kennedy discussed the educational benefits of diversity, racial difference was merely a matter of perspective, not hierarchy.

When he turned, however, to the question of alternative, race-conscious integration measures, Justice Kennedy spoke the language of equality. He opened with a nod to racial progress that acknowledged "the flaws and injustices that remain" and the need for "assurance that opportunity is not denied on account of race."[97] The state interest at stake was the government's interest in "ensuring all people have equal opportunity regardless of their race."[98] He took on the plurality's invocation of Justice Harlan's dissent in *Plessy v. Ferguson*, explaining that "our Constitution is colorblind" must be read in context.[99] He summed up his disagreement with the plurality as follows: "To the extent the plurality opinion suggests the Constitution mandates that state and local authorities must accept the *status quo* of racial isolation in schools, it is, in my view, profoundly mistaken."[100] Justice Kennedy thus made clear that he supports state efforts to reduce structural inequality, but only if racial labels are avoided.

The claim that societal discrimination is not a compelling state interest has been repeated so often in affirmative action cases that it has taken on a life of its own. It has thus become capable of threatening not only programs that depend on facial classifications but even race-neutral forms of affirmative action. At the same time, however, the Supreme Court's own reasoning has invoked the state's interest in equality and demonstrated that the real objection is to means that rely too heavily on individual racial classifications. Under *Grutter/Gratz* and *Parents Involved*, the act of racial classification, not the desire to reduce inequality, is what created problems under the Equal Protection Clause. The sex cases, which eliminate this classification problem but are otherwise analytically the same, prove that the Court's complaint has never been with the legitimacy of the state interest in equality. Despite all the inveighing against racial balancing, the problem in *Parents Involved* was not in the fact that racial balance was *sought* but in how it was achieved. The government can legitimately

92 *See* Ian Haney López, *"A Nation of Minorities": Race, Ethnicity, and Reactionary Colorblindness*, 59 Stan. L. Rev. 985, 1006–11 (2007) (describing the development of an ideology that treats race as a form of ethnicity).

93 *See* Haney López, *supra* note 92, at 990 (arguing that the ethnicity perspective "suggested that racial subordination was largely past and that social inequalities, if any, reflected the cultural failings of minorities themselves.").

94 *See* Haney López, *supra* note 92, at 990 ("[M]y primary aim in this Article is to demonstrate that race-as-ethnicity provided the first coherent intellectual justification for reactionary colorblindness."); *id.* at 1011–12 (arguing that "ethnicity operated [to depict] affirmative action, not as a needed national response to racial subordination, but instead as the sort of group rent-seeking one would expect in the context of ethnic group competition"; *see also* Alan David Freeman, *Legitimizing Racial Discrimination Through Antidiscrimination Law: A Critical Review of Supreme Court Doctrine*, 62 Minn. L. Rev. 1049 (1978) (arguing that colorblindness represents the perpetrator's perspective in discrimination law).

95 Cf. Heather K. Gerken, *Justice Kennedy and the Domains of Equal Protection*, 121 Harv. L. Rev. 104, 108 (2007) (referring to the "anti-essentialist boilerplate" in Kennedy's opinion).

96 *Parents Involved*, 551 U.S. at 787 (Kennedy, J., concurring in part and concurring in the judgment).

97 *Id.*

98 *Id.* at at 788.

99 *Id.* at 788; Plessy v. Ferguson, 163 U.S. 537, 559 (1896).

100 *Parents Involved*, 551 U.S. at 788 (Kennedy, J., concurring in part and concurring in the judgment). This statement also serves as an appropriate rejoinder to Justice Thomas's invocation of another famous line, paraphrasing, "The Fourteenth Amendment does not enact the dissent's newly minted understanding of liberty."). *Id.* at 767 n.15 (Thomas, J., concurring); Lochner v. New York, 198 U.S. 45, 75 (1905) (Holmes, J., dissenting) ("The Fourteenth Amendment does not enact Mr. Herbert Spencer's *Social Statics*."). Of course, the *Parents Involved* dissent would not have enacted any particular understanding of liberty or equality; it would merely have permitted the people of Seattle and Louisville to pursue their understanding. It was the *Parents Involved* plurality that, like the *Lochner* Court, sought to constitutionalize a particular social theory (in both cases, maintain a status quo of unequal power and protect it against legislative interference).

seek racial integration, but it must try to do so without stamping each person with a racial identity.[101] Subject to limits that reflect that concern, the state has a compelling interest in overcoming structural inequality. The *Parents Involved* plurality's attempt to brand that interest as illegitimate is as false to precedent as it is to the Fourteenth Amendment itself.

101 *See Parents Involved*, 551 U.S. at 790 (Kennedy, J., concurring in part and concurring in the judgment).

PART IV
The Possibilities of Equal Protection

Chapter 10

Ball of Con(stitutional)Fusion: The Supreme Court's Evolving Gay Rights Jurisprudence

John G. Culhane†

Introduction

The United States Supreme Court is on the precipice of deciding whether same-sex couples have a constitutional right to marry. In a quartet of cases from Kentucky, Tennessee, Ohio, and Michigan, the Court seems poised to decide that laws restricting marriage to a man and a woman treat gay and lesbian couples unfairly.[1] While it is impossible to predict the rationale the Court might use to decide the case, it is clear that the Court's evolving jurisprudence on LGBT rights has seeded the ground in ways helpful to the movement.

How did we reach this point? It might be best to start in 2013, and then to spin backward through time.

In June 2013, the United States Supreme Court issued two decisions that accelerated movement toward full marriage equality for these couples. In *Hollingsworth v. Perry*, the Court effectively threw out California's Proposition 8, thereby reinstating the marriage rights of gay and lesbian couples in the nation's most populous state.[2]

Of even greater significance, though, was the Court's decision in *United States v. Windsor*[3] striking down the most significant piece of the federal Defense of Marriage Act ("DOMA").[4] The law had denied federal recognition to same-sex couples, even those validly married in their home states. That action has led to further positive developments for same-sex couples, as federal administrative agencies have extended many of the most substantial federal benefits to married same-sex couples living in states that don't recognize such marriages. Especially noteworthy are decisions allowing couples to file federal joint tax returns,[5] permitting citizens to sponsor their non-U.S. resident spouses into the country,[6] and extending benefits to spouses of members of the military.[7]

---

† Professor of Law and Co-Director, Family Health Law & Policy Institute, Widener Law Delaware; contributing writer, *Slate Magazine*. The author would like to thank his colleague Erin Daly, his research assistant James Saintvil, and—for their endless patience—his family.

1 The four cases were decided by the court in one opinion, DeBoer v. Snyder, 772 F.3d 388 (6th Cir. 2014), cert. granted and cases consolidated, Bourke v. Beshear, 135 S. Ct. 1041 (2015). Most predict that the Court will rule in favor of the couples. *See, e.g.*, Garrett Epps, The Odds of Marriage Equality, Atlantic, Jan. 16, 2015, at http://www.theatlantic.com/politics/archive/2015/01/same-sex-marriage-supreme-court-scotus/384618/ ("[I]f I were a bookie, I'd make marriage equality an odds-on favorite.").

2 133 S.Ct. 2652 (2013).

3 133 S.Ct. 2675 (2013).

4 The Defense of Marriage Act (DOMA), 110 Stat. 2419, contained two operative provisions, each of which was set forth in a different part of the U.S. Code. Section 2, which was not challenged in *Windsor*, allows states to refuse to recognize same-sex marriages performed in other states. 28 U.S.C. § 1738C (2013). Section 3, which was the section the *Windsor* Court struck down, created a federal definition of "marriage" by amending the Dictionary Act. That amendment explicitly declared that, for all federal law purposes, marriage was limited to "one man and one woman as husband and wife," and further that "the word 'spouse' refers only to a person of the opposite sex who is a husband or wife." 1 U.S.C. § 7 (2013).

5 IRS Revenue Ruling 13–17, Aug. 29, 2013, available at http://www.irs.gov/pub/irs-drop/rr-13-17.pdf (explaining rule and justification).

6 See Statement by Director of Homeland Security Janet Napolitano (and FAQs), at: http://www.uscis.gov/portal/site/uscis/menuitem.eb1d4c2a3e5b9ac89243c6a7543f6d1a/?vgnextoid=2543215c310af310VgnVCM100000082ca60aRCRD&vgnextchannel=2543215c310af310VgnVCM100000082ca60aRCRD (last visited Oct. 8, 2013).

7 For a comprehensive discussion of this issue, see *Military Spousal Benefits*, HRC, at http://www.hrc.org/files/assets/resources/Post-DOMA_MilitarySpousalBenefits_v3.pdf (last visited Oct. 8, 2013). This was one area of the law that

At the state level, the movement toward marriage equality had until recently been less successful, but recent developments buoyed proponents' hopes that final victory is in sight. After a two-decades-long, uninterrupted drumbeat of failure at the ballot box, in 2012 advocates won victories in three states.[8] In addition to the Proposition 8 win mentioned above, in 2013 seven additional states moved into the marriage equality column.[9] After clerks in New Mexico began issuing licenses to same-sex couples, in late 2013 the New Mexico Supreme Court held that same-sex couples had the right to marry.[10] With that decision, the number of jurisdictions within the U.S. recognizing same-sex marriages had climbed to 18 by year's end.[11]

Then, mostly because of *Windsor* itself, 2014 saw an explosion in the number of states recognizing the marriage rights of same-sex couples. Lawsuits alleging that state laws barring recognition of same-sex marriages erupted in every state.[12] As of early 2015, several federal appellate courts had decided in favor of marriage equality, with only the Sixth Circuit's 2–1 decision to the contrary.[13] And officials in at least two states (Oregon and Pennsylvania) decided not to appeal decisions striking down their laws.[14] Thus, on the eve of the Supreme Court's decision in the consolidated cases from the Sixth Circuit, 37 states (and the District of Columbia) recognized the marriages of gay and lesbian couples.[15]

The path for these suits has been paved in three layers. First, since 2003 state courts have been issuing decisions recognizing that same-sex couples have a constitutional right to marry. Second, the Supreme Court's decision in *Windsor* is so broadly written that it provides plenty of useful language for lower federal courts and state courts to use in declaring state "mini-DOMA" laws invalid. Third, the political climate surrounding marriage equality has shifted seismically, especially in the past few years. Now, consistent majorities of Americans favor granting same-sex couples full marriage equality.[16] No one can reasonably think that judges are unaffected by this constellation of developments—including the political realities. In fact, the Supreme Court itself might have obliquely signaled in *Hollingsworth* that the movement toward equality might one day provide it with the national consensus needed to spur it to the conclusion that same-sex couples have a constitutional right to marry.[17]

---

was clearly going to change once DOMA fell, because those in the military are federal employees. The Secretary of Defense said as much in a Memorandum issued while DOMA was still good law. *See* Memorandum for Secretaries of the Military Departments Acting Under Secretary of Defense for Personnel and Readiness, Feb. 11, 1013, available at http://www.defense.gov/news/Same-SexBenefitsMemo.pdf.

8 *See* Walter Olson, *Republicans Helped Same-sex Marriage Win at the Polls*, Wash. Post, Nov. 30, 2013, at http://articles.washingtonpost.com/2012–11–30/opinions/35584970_1_sign-that-gop-voters-marriage-ban-mitt-romney (discussing wins in Maine, Maryland, and Washington, and the defeat of anti-equality amendment in Minnesota).

9 The states are Delaware, Minnesota, Rhode Island, Illinois, Hawaii, New Jersey, and New Mexico. See http://www.freedomtomarry.org/pages/history-and-timeline-of-marriage (last visited Jan. 31, 2014).

10 Griego v. Oliver, ___ P.3d ___, 2013 WL 6670704 (N.M. 2013).

11 These include 17 states and the District of Columbia. For a useful and reliably updated tally of state laws recognizing or forbidding same-gender unions, *see* http://gaymarriage.procon.org/view.resource.php?resourceID=004857 (last visited Jan. 31, 2014).

12 For a reliably updated tracking of these cases, the Freedom to Marry website is an excellent source. *See* http://www.freedomtomarry.org/litigation (site visited July 3, 2014).

13 *See* n. 1 supra. The four circuit court cases ruling in favor of the couples are: Kitchen v. Herbert, 755 F.3d 1193 (10th Cir. 2014); Bostic v. Schaefer, 760 F.3d 352 (4th Cir. 2014); Baskin v. Bogan, 766 F.3d 648 (7th Cir. 2014); Latta v. Otter, 771 F.3d 456 (9th Cir. 2014).

14 See http://www.freedomtomarry.org/litigation/entry/pennsylvania (summary of Pennsylvania cases) and http://www.freedomtomarry.org/litigation/entry/litigation-in-oregon (summary of litigation in Oregon) (sites visited July 3, 2014).

15 *See* National Status Map, Marriage Equality USA, at http://www.marriageequality.org/national_maps (site visited April 10, 2015).

16 A 2014 Washington Post-ABC News poll put the support/oppose numbers at 59–34 percent, which probably represents the high-water mark on this issue. The poll is available at: http://www.washingtonpost.com/page/2010–2019/WashingtonPost/2014/03/05/National-Politics/Polling/release_301.xml. For an up-to-date list of relevant polls, with links, visit http://www.marriageequality.org/national-polls (last visited July 3, 2014).

17 Toward the end of the oral argument, Justices Kennedy and Sotomayor wondered whether the Court had taken the case before the issue of marriage equality had worked through enough states. Justice Sotomayor asked: "If the issue is letting the States experiment and have more time to figure out its direction, why is taking a case now the answer?" A narrated transcript can be found at http://www.oyez.org/cases/2010–2019/2012/2012_12_144 (comment heard at the 73:31 mark).

Two principal arguments have been advanced in service of the right of gay and lesbian Americans to marry a person of the same gender.[18] First, the denial of marriage licenses is said to violate their fundamental right to marry. That right has been clearly established by the Supreme Court in several cases as subsumed under the liberty promised by the Due Process Clause of the Fifth and Fourteenth Amendments to the U.S. Constitution. Second, as the term "marriage *equality*" suggests, proponents have argued that to deny same-sex couples the right to marry is to deprive them a right that opposite-sex couples enjoy, thereby making them unequal, also in violation of the Fourteenth Amendment.

The equality argument has been in ascendance, both as a litigation strategy and as the principal ground of decision in many of the cases. *Windsor* itself makes it easy to understand the appeal of this approach. The plaintiff, Edith Windsor, was legally married to Thea Spyer under New York law. But when Spyer died, Windsor, as inheritor of Spyer's estate, was saddled with a tax bill of more than $350,000.[19] Had Spyer been a man, Windsor would have owed no federal estate taxes because of a spousal exemption that—because of the Defense of Marriage Act—was available only to opposite-sex couples. It would be hard to discern a clearer case of inequality, and the Supreme Court took the occasion to inter the law. One need not resort to more abstract arguments about fundamental rights and the ill-understood concept of "substantive due process" when a much simpler and more intuitive path to success is at hand.

Yet *Windsor* contains another important truth, one that has been more fully developed in a few state courts. The equality argument is so strong in part precisely because it is closely braided to the argument from fundamental rights. Together, these arguments form an alloy that is harder and more durable than their simple addition would suggest.

Relying heavily on state court decisions that preceded *Windsor*, this chapter explores the developing jurisprudence of marriage equality. For reasons that will become clear, an important part of this discussion is the movement by a few state courts toward recognition that discrimination based on sexual orientation warrants a high degree of scrutiny from reviewing courts. The state courts have proceeded in roughly three ways. There is insight to be found in each of these approaches, and all will be explored.

The discussion then turns from these state cases to *Windsor*, an analytically undernourished decision that can be fleshed out by more complete discussion of the Court's own earlier cases, and by reference to the state cases that are its intellectual progenitors. Although they are using somewhat different analyses and legal tools, the Supreme Court and these state courts are developing a body of law that acknowledges the dignity and full citizenship of gay and lesbian persons through a constitutional fusion of equality and fundamental rights. This emerging approach can be helpful not only to same-sex couples seeking to marry, but to any group that can convince the Court that a particular law contributes to their relegation to second-class status. In short, the Court seems to be in the midst of recognizing a broader, antisubordination principle.

Equality and Sexual Orientation: Contextualizing the State Cases

The Supreme Court's jurisprudence of equality might uncharitably be called a mess, at least when it comes to the treatment of sexual orientation. In general, laws challenged as depriving a group of people of their right to equality under the law are evaluated quite deferentially; if the law is said to have a rational basis, it will be upheld.[20] But laws that burden a fundamental right, or that target certain groups, are evaluated against much

18 This chapter is not centrally concerned with the rights of the transgendered to marry, but a brief note on the topic is in order. With laws in place restricting marriages to two people of the opposite sex, state courts have engaged in lengthy and confusing discussions about how to characterize the sex of transgendered people. In a few distressing decisions, courts have ignored even complete transitions (and, in one case, an amended birth certificate) and found that the genetic sex controlled; in other cases, the courts have reductively looked at the anatomical features of the transgendered person. The result has been that some transgendered people have been able to marry; others, not. One of the happy effects of marriage equality is that any two otherwise qualified adults will be able to marry, regardless of sex—thereby solving the problems that members of the transgendered community face in attempting to marry the person of their choosing.

19 United States v. Windsor, 133 S. Ct. at 2682. The details are more fully set forth in a profile of Windsor that ran in the New Yorker. *See* Ariel Levy, *The Perfect Wife*, New Yorker, Sept. 30, 2013, at 54.

20 *See* Heller v. Doe, 509 U.S. 312, 320 (1993).

tougher standards. Discriminations based on race are policed to determine whether they meet a strict scrutiny analysis: do the laws advance a compelling state interest, and is there no less restrictive alternative that might have been used?[21] When a law discriminates on the basis of gender or legitimacy, the scrutiny is only slightly lower: laws must further an important government interest, and be substantially related to that interest.[22] Recently, and controversially, the Court appears to have ratcheted up this so-called "intermediate scrutiny" even further, stating that laws discriminating on these bases need an "exceedingly persuasive" justification.[23] Together, these latter two standards are often referred to as "heightened scrutiny," and laws challenged under either of them usually fail.

In deciding whether laws targeting a particular group are to be assessed under a heightened scrutiny standard, the Court has examined several factors relating to that group. First, is the group politically powerless? Second, have members of the group historically been discriminated against? Third, is membership in the group immutable (as is the case with race)? And finally, do the laws targeting the group relate to the ability of the group's members to contribute to society?[24]

Surprisingly, the Supreme Court has never directly answered the question whether sexual orientation discrimination should be judged under a heightened scrutiny standard. Indeed, the Court has rarely even addressed the issue. In a 1985 dissent to the denial of a certiorari petition, Justice Brennan made the case for considering sexual orientation to be a suspect class.[25] And when the Court granted the petition for review in *Windsor*, it was widely expected that it would address the issue of heightened scrutiny, but it did not.[26] Mostly, there has been silence.

That silence notwithstanding, the Court has issued two major decisions in favor of the LGBT community that are grounded in equal protection, and another that eschewed equal protection only because the Court thought that a decision on that basis would not have been strong enough![27] Before considering those decisions, it will be useful to consider the development of equal protection law as applied to the marriage equality cases in state courts. These contain important tools for understanding how the Supreme Court is moving in this area.

State supreme courts have issued decisions in the marriage equality cases that have applied different, often creative, approaches to the issue of equal protection. A couple of states have used a flexible approach that led to advances just short of full marriage equality. Another held for full marriage equality under a form of rational basis analysis that was more searching than the usual inquiry under that standard. And most recently, a few states have applied heightened scrutiny to laws that discriminate based on sexual orientation. These results will turn out to be important in assessing the development of the Supreme Court's equal protection jurisprudence.

Marriage Equality Before Heightened Scrutiny

In 1999, the Vermont Supreme Court decided *Baker v. State*.[28] There, same-sex couples had challenged their exclusion from marriage under the state's common benefits clause, which is analogous to the Equal Protection Clause of the U.S. Constitution. Perhaps because of the difficulty of the issue before it, or perhaps because of

21 *See* Clark v. Jeter, 486 U.S. 456, 461 (1988).

22 *See* Craig v. Boren, 429 U.S. 190 (1976).

23 The phrase was used in Mississippi Univ. for Women v. Hogan, 458 U.S. 718, 724 (1982), and has been used by the Court since then; notably, in United States v. Virginia, 518 U.S. 515 (1996).

24 These considerations are pieced together from statements by the Supreme Court, notably in Lyng v. Castillo, 477 U.S. 635, 638 (1086) and Frontiero v. Richardson, 411 U.S. 677, 686 (1973).

25 Rowland v. Mad River Local Sch. Dist., 470 U.S. 1009 (Brennan, J., dissenting from denial of petition for certiorari).

26 Cf. United States v. Windsor, 133 S.Ct. at 2706 (Scalia, J., dissenting) (the "opinion does not resolve and indeed does not even mention what had been the central issue in this litigation: whether, under the Equal Protection Clause, laws restricting marriage to a man and a woman are reviewed for more than mere rationality").

27 The cases are discussed in more detail *infra*, during the discussion of the *Goodridge* and *Windsor* cases.

28 744 A.2d 864 (Vt. 1999).

a concern that considering sexual orientation a suspect class could have unforeseen consequences, the court expressly abandoned its previous use of the tripartite classification for evaluating equal protection challenges, and announced that, going forward, it would examine challenged laws to determine whether they bear "a reasonable and just relation to the governmental purpose." This question was to be answered "consistent with the core presumption of inclusion," aided by consideration of several factors. For present purposes, chief among these is "the significance of the benefits and protections of the challenged law."[29]

The court found that same-sex couples could not be excluded from the benefits and rights of marriage, but ordered a surprising remedy; while the legislature would be required to grant gay and lesbian couples these benefits and rights, it would not be required to issue them marriage licenses.[30] Lawmakers were instead invited to construct a parallel institution. This they did in short order, and the civil union was born.[31] Although the court articulated prudential reasons for stopping short of ordering the remedy the plaintiffs sought, it seems reasonable to conclude that considering the "significance of the benefits and protections" as a central factor in assessing constitutionality also supported this creative but limited remedy. Once the court ordered the benefits equalized, the residual unfairness of fencing same-sex couples out from the *institution* of marriage itself led to the civil union under the flexible equal protection standard that the court had just adopted.[32]

My argument that a departure from the tripartite analysis leads to the "virtual marriage" status of the civil union is supported by the decision of the New Jersey Supreme Court in *Lewis v. Harris*.[33] New Jersey is similar to Vermont in that these two states are among a very few that do not begin by classifying equal protection cases into two or three classes, and then applying different tests based on that classification. Indeed, New Jersey's test bears a striking resemblance to Vermont's. The court has weighed "three factors: the nature of the right at stake, the extent to which the challenged statutory scheme restricts that right, and the public need for the statutory restriction."[34] Applying that standard, the court surgically separated the benefits of marriage from the title, and then held that the residual rights of the same-sex couples at stake—to have their relationships called "marriage"—was not important enough (to be blunt) to tip the balance of the factors in their favor.[35] Thus, the *Lewis* court gave the legislature the same remedial option as had the *Baker* court, and the result was the same: civil unions.[36]

In sum, in the *only* two states considering the same-sex marriage issue that use a general balancing test for equal protection challenges, the courts have focused on rights and benefits "only" and have given their legislatures the wiggle room needed to enact civil union compromises. But given what other state courts were doing at the time—especially in 1999, when *Baker* was decided—the civil union represented a substantial step forward for gay and lesbian couples seeking legal recognition of their unions.

Until 2008, all other state supreme court cases to consider equal protection challenges to the marriage laws used rational basis analysis. In all but one case, the result was defeat for the same-sex couples seeking to marry. The one case that found for the couples was able to see a dimension of the Supreme Court's decisions in two cases involving sexual orientation that the other courts missed.

---

29 *Id.* at 879. The other factors are: "(2) whether the omission of members of the community from the benefits and protections of the challenged law promotes the government's stated goals; and (3) whether the classification is significantly underinclusive or overinclusive." *Id.*

30 *Id.* at 886 ("We hold only that plaintiffs are entitled … to obtain the same benefits and protections afforded by Vermont law to married opposite-sex couples. We do not purport to infringe upon the prerogatives of the Legislature to craft an appropriate means of addressing this constitutional mandate … .").

31 Vt. Stat. Ann. Tit. 15 § 1201 et seq. (repealed, 2009). For a compelling account of the political and cultural struggle that culminated in the civil union law, *see* David Moats, Civil Wars (2004).

32 It might also be relevant that the guarantee of equality in Vermont is phrased in terms of "common benefits." The word benefits arguably calls to mind a more tangible set of entitlements than what is comprehended under the term "equality."

33 908 A.2d 196 (N.J. 2006).

34 *Id.* at 212.

35 *Id.* at 221 ("Under our equal protection jurisprudence, [p]laintiffs' claimed right to the name of marriage is surely not the same now that equal rights and benefits must be conferred on committed same-sex couples.").

36 *Id.* at 221–22.

In Washington,[37] New York,[38] and Maryland,[39] courts applied rational basis analysis in a conventional way, and thereby found legislative justification for restricting marriage to same-sex couples. Both decisions articulate extreme deference to legislative classifications; as the Washington Supreme Court put it, "the court may assume the existence of any conceivable set of facts that could provide a rational basis for the justification,"[40] even if those facts formed no part of legislative purpose. And both the New York and Washington courts found such a basis in the odd idea that the legislature might have wanted to encourage "responsible procreation" through marriage.[41]

In telling contrast stands the opinion of the Massachusetts Supreme Judicial Court in *Goodridge v. Department of Public Health*.[42] In a decision that augured *Windsor*, the court gave eloquent expression to foundational principles of dignity and equality before presenting a more straightforward (if not overly deferential) application of the rational basis test. At the outset—before even summarizing the facts and procedural posture of the case—the court contextualized the discussion that followed with the pronouncement that the "Massachusetts Constitution affirms the dignity and equality of all individuals. It forbids the creation of second-class citizens."[43] Exclusion from marriage, the court continued, "is incompatible with the constitutional principles of respect for individual autonomy and equality under the law."[44]

Moving further into the decision, the court pushed the discussion of the intangible benefits of marriage ahead of a long list of the legal rights associated with it, thereby emphasizing the importance of "the decision whether and whom to marry" as "among life's momentous acts of self-definition."[45] That act of self-definition is compromised if "a State [wields] its formidable power to regulate conduct in a manner that demeans basic human dignity … ."[46] Here, the court cited the then-recent decision in *Lawrence v. Texas*,[47] in which the Supreme Court had held that laws criminalizing same-sex intimacy were obnoxious to the liberty guaranteed by the Fourteenth Amendment.[48]

It did not escape notice by one of the dissenting justices that the court's lengthy foregrounding of the state's asserted justifications for excluding same-sex couples from marriage was hardly typical of the kind of rational basis analysis in which the court then engaged.[49] Yet by so doing, the court was able to link back from the justifications to the broader points it had made earlier about the second-class citizenship implied by exclusion from marriage, and then to circle back to connect its discussion of the specific justifications to its earlier, general points about disrespect and subordination.

---

37 Anderson v. King County, 138 P.3d 963 (Wash. 2006).

38 Hernandez v. Robles, 855 N.E.2d 1 (N.Y. 2006).

39 Conaway v. Deane, 932 A.2d 571 (Md. 2007).

40 *Anderson*, 138 P.3d at 980.

41 *Id.* at 982–84; *Hernandez*, 855 N.E.2d at 21–22. This argument is so silly that it scarcely warrants response, but if one were needed, New York's Chief Justice Kaye obliged: "Properly framed, the question before us is not whether the marriage statutes properly benefit those they are intended to benefit … but whether there exists any legitimate basis for *excluding* those who are not covered by the law." *Hernandez*, 855 N.E.2d at 27 (Kaye, C.J., dissenting) (emphasis in original).

42 798 N.E.2d 941 (Mass. 2003).

43 *Id.* at 948.

44 *Id.* at 949.

45 *Id.* at 955.

46 *Id.* at 958, n.17.

47 539 U.S. 558 (2003).

48 This case is discussed in more detail *infra*, as part of the analysis of *Windsor*.

49 "Although ostensibly applying the rational basis test to the civil marriage statutes, it is apparent that the court is in fact applying some undefined stricter standard to assess the constitutionality of the marriage statutes' exclusion of same-sex couples. While avoiding any express conclusion as to any of the proffered routes by which that exclusion would be subjected to a test of strict scrutiny—infringement of a fundamental right, discrimination based on gender, or discrimination against gays and lesbians as a suspect classification—the opinion repeatedly alludes to those concepts in a prolonged and eloquent prelude before articulating its view that the exclusion lacks even a rational basis … . In short, while claiming to apply a mere rational basis test, the court's opinion works up an enormous head of steam by repeated invocations of avenues by which to subject the statute to strict scrutiny … ." *Goodridge* at 980–81 (Sosman, J., dissenting).

One example of the court's treatment of the state's justifications will suffice to illustrate the point. After demolishing the state's argument that marriage "provides a favorable setting for procreation," the court went further and attached its conclusion to the Supreme Court's statement in *Romer v. Evans*,[50] where an amendment to the Colorado state constitution that ruled out laws to protect the LGBT community from discrimination was struck down because it "identifie[d] persons by a single trait and then denie[d] them protection across the board."[51] Doing so, the *Goodridge* court held, "confers an official stamp of approval on the destructive stereotype that same-sex relationships are ... inferior to opposite-sex relationship and not worthy of respect."[52]

In concluding, the court stated: "The marriage ban works a deep and scarring hardship on a very real segment of the community for no rational reason. [This] suggests that the marriage restriction is rooted in persistent prejudices against persons who are (or who are believed to be) homosexual."[53] In this language one detects traces of both equality and fundamental rights.

Thus, among the several state supreme courts to have faced the marriage equality issue before 2008, the results were decidedly mixed. Courts either used a flexible standard to fashion a compromise (in New Jersey and Vermont), or reflexively fell back on rational basis analysis and capitulated to plainly absurd arguments. Only the *Goodridge* court looked more deeply into the justifications than is typical in cases decided under the rational basis analysis, and there found ... nothing. We will have occasion to revisit *Goodridge* as part of the discussion of *Windsor*, because in some ways *Goodridge* is the intellectual progenitor of the more recent case.

But in general, it is not surprising that the tide began to swell in favor of marriage equality only when courts turned to the more searching analysis commanded by the "heightened scrutiny" standard. The California Supreme Court became the first to do so in its 2008 decision, *In Re Marriage Cases*.[54]

Heightened Scrutiny Analysis in State Court Marriage Equality Decisions

The California court's decision in *In Re Marriage Cases* is worth close analysis, because it connects the rationale for applying a higher level of scrutiny to the specific ways in which the law deprived same-sex couples of both equality and a fundamental right. As we shall see, moreover, the court's rhetoric, if not precisely its *ratio decidendi*, rings strongly through Justice Kennedy's decision in *Windsor*. But the California Supreme Court was much clearer and cleaner in its analysis than the U.S. Supreme Court.

When *In re Marriage Cases* came before the California Supreme Court in 2008, California had moved, through a series of incremental steps, from a limited domestic partnership law to a statutory scheme that essentially mirrored marriage.[55] Like the more recent civil union status,[56] this law conferred all the rights and benefits of marriage but pointedly withheld the name. In a 4–3 decision, the court held that this two-tiered system violated the state's constitutional guarantees of both substantive due process and equality, and that same-sex couples were entitled to marriage licenses.[57]

Under California precedent, the inquiry into whether a class should be entitled to heightened scrutiny is a distillate of the factors the U.S. Supreme Court uses in making the same determination. As the *In Re Marriage*

50 517 U.S. 620 (1996).

51 *Romer*, 517 U.S. at 623.

52 *Goodridge* at 962.

53 *Id.* at 968.

54 183 P.3d 385 (Cal. 2008).

55 This progression is discussed in detail in In re Marriage Cases. *Id.* at 413–18.

56 I have discussed the civil union in previous articles. *See* John G. Culhane, United States v. Windsor *and the Future of Civil Unions and Other Marriage Alternatives*, 59 Vill. L. Rev. Tolle Lege 27 (2013); John G. Culhane, *Civil Unions Reconsidered*, 26 J. Civil R. & Econ. Dev. 621 (2012): John G. Culhane, *The Short, Puzzling(?) Life of the Civil Union*, 19 B.U. Pub. Int. L. J. 1 (2009).

57 When Proposition 8 was enacted later that year, the result was to return California to the domestic partnership scheme. The subsequent, successful challenge to Proposition 8 under the U.S. Constitution, Hollingsworth v. Perry, 570 U.S. ___ (2013), has been well chronicled and has somewhat overshadowed the bold decision in *In Re Marriage Cases*, but the case is discussed here because of its thoroughly reasoned argument in support of equal marriage rights for same-sex couples, because of its adoption of a strict scrutiny standard of review, and because of its influence on subsequent cases.

Cases court stated, the two crucial requirements for suspect class status are that the characteristic in question "[1] bear[s] no relation to a person's ability to perform or contribute to society, and [2] [is] associated with a stigma of inferiority and second-class citizenship, manifested by the group's history of legal and social disabilities."[58]

My reading of the case is that domestic partnership status, in an odd way that the court itself only obliquely acknowledged, impelled the court towards recognizing sexual orientation as a suspect class. The second requirement, as noted above, seems to have been created with just this sort of marriage/domestic partnership statutory classification in mind. Why withhold a name, and nothing else, if not to remind gays and lesbians of their inferiority and disfavored status? And few would argue that, whatever the advances today, gays and lesbians have not suffered "a history of legal and social disabilities." In a related way, the "virtual equivalence" of domestic partnerships, coupled with the panoply of other rights and protections afforded over time to gays and lesbians—and, significantly, their children—demonstrates that the "characteristic" is unrelated to their ability to contribute to society. Thus, the first requirement for suspect class status is also met, and also tied to the domestic partnership/marriage divide.

The determination that sexual orientation is a suspect class is closely interwoven with the court's extended discussion of how the challenged exclusion offends both the fundamental right to marriage and equal protection. The clearest evidence for these interconnections appears in a general discussion that precedes the court's more thorough consideration of these two constitutional issues. Noting that the right to marry and establish a family is fundamental, the court states that a "core element" of that right entails according the family relationships of gay and lesbian couples "dignity and respect equal to that accorded other officially recognized families, and assigning a different designation for the family relationship of same-sex couples while reserving the historic designation of 'marriage' exclusively for opposite-sex couples poses at least a serious risk of denying the family relationship of same-sex couples such equal dignity and respect."[59]

Note the close correlation between the quoted language and the second requirement for suspect class status—that the characteristic defining the class is "associated with a stigma of inferiority and second-class citizenship." The equal protection/due process/strict scrutiny circle the California Supreme Court has created might be phrased as follows:

> Since marriage and associated family relationships are fundamental rights, excluding same-sex couples from marriage not only establishes legal inequality, but also marks the excluded couples for second-class status and a loss of dignity. This subordination is a clear example of the legal and social disabilities under which gays and lesbian labor, and thus supports heightened scrutiny of the challenged law.

Shortly after *In Re Marriage Cases*, the Connecticut Supreme Court became the second state high court to find—again in a marriage equality case—that discrimination grounded in sexual orientation deserved heightened scrutiny. *Kerrigan v. Commissioner of Public Health*[60] is a direct descendant of the California case. By a similarly divided court, the Connecticut Supreme Court followed California's lead in using a heightened equal protection standard to analyze state law that permitted same-sex couples to enter into a civil union, but not to marry. Although Kerrigan relies on *In Re Marriage Cases* in part, the result is not merely additive, because the Connecticut court made more explicit the connection between the new standard it adopted and the inequality created by the then-existing civil union. Thus, the court's opinion deserves inspection.

First, although the *Kerrigan* court looked at the same factors as the California court in deciding that distinctions based on sexual orientation should be subject to heightened scrutiny, Kerrigan chose intermediate scrutiny, rather than the strict scrutiny standard adopted in California.[61] In both states, the courts followed their

---

58 The court also discussed the requirement that the characteristic defining the group be immutable, but ultimately rejected it as a poor proxy for what it took to be the more relevant inquiry: is the characteristic so important a part of one's identity that, even if it were possible to change it, members of the class should not be required to do so? (The court cited religion as an example of a characteristic of this sort.) In re Marriage Cases, 183 P.3d at 442–43. Thus, the court avoided the thorny and unanswerable question as to whether sexual orientation is innate or environmentally determined.

59 *Id.* at 400.

60 957 A.2d 407 (Conn. 2008).

61 *Id.*

own precedent for analyzing sex-based classifications, which may be most closely analogous case. As noted earlier, in these cases, intermediate scrutiny is typically used. But, as Justice George noted in *In re Marriage Cases*, the California Supreme Court, unlike the U.S. Supreme Court, does not use intermediate scrutiny.[62] Given the choice, then, between strict scrutiny and the rational basis test, application of the "suspect class" factors inexorably led the California court to the higher of the two standards. Connecticut, by contrast, follows the prevailing three-tier approach. The *Kerrigan* court acknowledged that sexual orientation might be a suspect class, but opted for the "quasi-suspect" class designation that triggers intermediate scrutiny. That standard requires that the statutory classification "be substantially related to an important governmental objective."[63]

A second, and crucial, point of interest on *Kerrigan* is that the court was clear about the connection between civil union status and its conclusion that sexual orientation classifications need heightened scrutiny. At the conclusion of the court's exhaustive analysis of the equal protection standard to apply, the court supplemented the central requirements for quasi-suspect class status by looking to economic and sociological considerations (which are factors relevant to "suspect class" status under Connecticut state law precedent).[64] As part of that discussion, the court quoted from the affidavits of the parents of young children concerned about the effect of their family's exclusion from marriage, even though civil union status is available.[65] The court then concluded its discussion of the justifications for heightened scrutiny by making the point, even more clearly than the California court had done, that the connection between civil unions and the longstanding bias against the gay community justifies heightened scrutiny:

> [B]ecause of the long history of discrimination that gay persons have faced, there is a high likelihood that the creation of a second, separate legal entity for same sex couples will be viewed as reflecting an official state policy that that entity is inferior to marriage, and that the committed relationships of same sex couples are of a lesser stature than comparable relationships of opposite sex couples.[66]

This statement was immediately followed by this vital quote from *In re Marriage Cases*, thus recognizing more explicitly than the California court the tie between virtual marriages and the need for heightened scrutiny:

> [R]etaining the designation of marriage exclusively for opposite-sex couples and providing only a separate and distinct designation for same-sex couples may well have the effect of perpetuating [the] premise that gay individuals and same-sex couples are in some respects "second-class citizens."[67]

Kerrigan is a long, thoughtful case that deserves much deeper treatment than I can give it here. Reading the decision in its entirety leaves the inescapable sense that the court fully understood both the enormous gains that civil union status achieved and the residual, discriminatory impulse thereby papered over.[68]

Shortly after *Kerrigan* was decided, the Iowa Supreme Court became the third to hold that discriminations based on sexual orientation should be subject to heightened scrutiny. But in *Varnum v. Brien*,[69] the court followed a more standard equal protection analysis (indeed, the court did not consider the fundamental rights

62 183 P.3d at 443–44.

63 957 A.2d at 423.

64 *Id.* at 473–75.

65 *Id.* at 475, n.77.

66 *Id.* at 475.

67 *Id.*, *quoting* In re Marriage Cases, 183 P.3d at 384.

68 Consider one final example of the court's appreciation of the problem. Here, the court quotes favorably and extensively from a brief submitted by Lambda Legal, where this table-turning thought experiment is proposed:

> Any married couple [reasonably] would feel that they had lost something precious and irreplaceable if the government were to tell them that they no longer were 'married' and instead were in a 'civil union.' The sense of being 'married'—what this conveys to a couple and their community, and the security of having others clearly understand the fact of their marriage and all it signifies--would be taken from them. These losses are part of what same sex couples are denied when government assigns them a 'civil union' status. *Id.* at ___.

69 763 N.W.2d 862 (Iowa 2009).

issue at all). This methodology is not surprising, because, unlike California and Connecticut, Iowa offered neither recognition nor rights to same-sex couples. Without the pure and obvious second-class citizenship conferred by civil unions and domestic partnership before it, the *Varnum* court did not engage in sophisticated braiding of the standard of review and the substantive rights infringed.

While it seems intuitive that the complete denial of rights is a purer instance of subordination than that created by "marriage lite" alternatives, that intuition may be misleading. For when a state denies all recognition to same-sex couples, it may be better able to argue that there are independent reasons for continuing to define marriage as the "union of a man and a woman" than it can once it concedes those arguments by conferring all rights and benefits of marriage on same-sex couples, but continuing to withhold the name.[70] Thus, the *Varnum* court considered and rejected these factual arguments rather straightforwardly, without any need to delve into a deeper (but more abstract) discussion about how labels confer or deny dignity, equality, and fundamental rights. As noted above, other state courts have found to the contrary, under a traditional rational basis analysis. It is not irrelevant that *Varnum* was the first case by a state supreme court since *In Re Marriage Cases* and *Kerrigan*; these ground-breaking cases seem to have inspired an evolution in thinking about the proper level of equal protection scrutiny for discrimination grounded in sexual orientation.

Windsor and the Promising (But Uncertain) Evolution of Equality

Windsor is now the third gay rights case in which the Supreme Court has engaged in analysis that rests uneasily within existing categories and doctrine. (The first two, *Romer* and *Lawrence*, were introduced during the discussion of the *Goodridge* decision.) By now, it should be clear to even a casual reader that something new has been developing; and that something appears to lie at the intersection of equal protection and due process, and to transcend the tests on which the Court had previously relied. It is the project of the remainder of this chapter to explain more clearly what the Court has so far only adumbrated. This explanation will take us back to some of the state law cases previously discussed, and tie some the decisions to the Court's own precedent, both in the previous gay rights cases and beyond. To provide further context for this discussion, it is useful to begin with Justice Scalia's overwrought dissent. For Scalia well explains the ways in which the Court's enigmatic opinion continues its departure from what had once been thought settled doctrine, and usefully distills the opinion to its essentials.

Scalia begins his dissenting opinion as to the merits with the stark statement that the majority's holding is "rootless and shifting."[71] He next notes, correctly, that many readers encountering the first few several pages of the decision would believe that the Court was headed toward a conclusion that DOMA is unconstitutional because it violates principles of federalism. Matters of family law and the definition of family relationships are usually left to state law, and DOMA inverted this federal/state balance by defining marriage for all federal law purposes as limited to the union of one man and one woman.

Then, as Scalia notes, the opinion explicitly disavows reliance on federalism as the basis for its holding, and pivots to a discussion of the guarantees of equal protection and due process. But the discussion is, from the point of view of traditional doctrine, "perplexing."

One reason the decision is puzzling cannot fairly be laid at the *Windsor* majority's door. Since *Windsor* is a challenge to a federal law, it involves the Fifth Amendment, which constrains the federal government's ability to deprive people of the liberty guaranteed by the Due Process Clause. But unlike the Fourteenth Amendment, which contains explicit protections against *state* denials of both liberty (under a separate Due Process Clause) and equality, the Fifth Amendment contains no explicit prohibition against the denial of equality. Thus, some creativity has always been required to incorporate equality analysis into a text that does not specifically contain it.[72]

70 The argument that granting civil unions but withholding marriage is unconstitutional but that withholding any recognition might not be was advanced in the Proposition 8 case; had it been adopted, the result would have been that those states with civil unions or comprehensive domestic partnerships would have been compelled to issue marriage licenses to same-sex couples. The Supreme Court's decision to dismiss the appeal for lack of standing left the issue unresolved.

71 *Windsor*, 133 S. Ct. at 2705.

72 *See* Bolling v. Sharpe, 347 U.S. 497 (1954).

A fuller discussion of the *Windsor* Court's use of precedent that drags equal protection from the Fourteenth Amendment into the Fifth is deferred for now, but in any event Scalia does not object to this exercise, at least in general.[73] Rather, his objection is to the Court's lack of clarity about whether this is an equal protection or a due process case. He also takes issue with the Court's discussion of both doctrines, finding them insufficiently faithful to precedent. Let us consider these objections in turn.

As to opacity, Scalia cites a confusing passage as muddying the equal protection/due process waters: "Near the end of the opinion, we are told that although the 'equal protection guarantee of the Fourteenth Amendment makes [the] Fifth Amendment [due process] right all the more specific and all the better understood and preserved'—what can *that* mean?—'the Fifth Amendment itself withdraws from Government the power to degrade or demean in the way this law does.'"[74] To Scalia, the "only possible interpretation of this statement" is that this a due process and not an equal protection case; so he is puzzled by the fact that all but one of the cases the Court cites in support of its holding that the law is unconstitutional were decided on equal protection grounds.

Turning then to the Court's use of both equal protection and due process, Scalia is similarly unsparing. If the decision is based on equal protection, the Court "does not resolve and indeed does not even mention" the level of scrutiny that should apply—even though this was one of the questions on which the Court had granted review and that had divided both the parties and the federal appellate court below.[75] Scalia adds that "as nearly as [he] can tell" the Court is using rational basis analysis, even though it "certainly does not *apply* anything that resembles that deferential framework."[76] In this criticism, Scalia echoes his earlier disapproval from the Court's apparent shift to "a more searching form of rational basis" analysis that has been in evidence in a few cases, and expresses agreement with the most deferential formulation of the standard—a classification can be justified by any reasonably conceivable set of facts.[77]

Scalia then trains his fire on the Court's discussion of liberty under the Due Process Clause, noting that the Court makes no mention of the two related formulations of the kind of rights that are sufficiently important to command due process protection. Rights are only entitled to such status, Scalia reminds the reader, if they are either "deeply rooted in this Nation's history and tradition"[78] or implicit in the very notion of "ordered liberty."[79] Substituted for these tests are statements dooming DOMA because it "inflicts an 'injury and indignity' of a kind that 'denies an essential part of the liberty protected by the Fifth Amendment … .'"[80]

The Court's "nonspecific hand-waving" is especially vexing to Scalia given what he thinks are the "perfectly valid—indeed, downright boring" rationales justifying the Defense of Marriage Act. Essentially, these are rooted in a "stabilizing prudence" in furthering uniformity and avoiding difficult choice-of-law issues when interpreting federal law. Tellingly, Scalia cites no Congressional sources citing either of these rationales as a reason for DOMA's enactment. But then, given the wide berth to legislation under the rational basis test he finds applicable, there is no need for such citation. Certainly DOMA furthered uniformity, as subsequent events have shown.[81] The question is whether that matters, given the Court's approach to considering the statute's constitutionality.

Scalia's hand-wringing in response to the Court's "hand-waving" is a reaction to a growing murkiness in the Court's due process and equal protection cases. While Scalia ably articulates the traditional doctrine, in practice *Windsor* represents but the next step—albeit an accelerated one—in the evolution of a doctrine of antisubordination that fuses equality and liberty, and that has as a central concern the dignity of the individual. Some effort is needed to tease out both the substance and the application of this doctrine. In this project,

73 *See Windsor* at 2706, n.5 (noting that "since the Equal Protection Clause technically applies only against the States," the Court has inferred an equal protection component to the Due Process Clause of the Fifth Amendment).

74 *Id.* at 2705–06, quoting majority opinion at 2695.

75 *Id.* at 2706.

76 *Id.* (emphasis in original).

77 *Id.*, *quoting* Heller v. Doe, 509 U.S. 312, 320 (1993).

78 *Id.* at 2707, *quoting* Washington v. Glucksberg, 521 U.S. 702, 720–21 (1997).

79 *Id.*, *quoting* Palko v. Connecticut, 302 U.S. 319 (1937).

80 *Id.*, *quoting* majority opinion at 2692.

81 *See* material discussed in notes 5–7, *supra*.

consideration of both the Court's own precedent and the approach taken in *Goodridge*, *Kerrigan*, and *In Re Marriage Cases* will be useful.

We might begin by conceding that Scalia is accurate in noting the shift in the *Windsor* majority opinion from federalism to a justification that is some unclear admixture of equal protection and due process. This bait-and-switch was even more startling given the tenor of the questions Justice Kennedy raised during oral argument on the case, which seemed highly focused on federalism. Most court watchers were convinced that, as the swing vote, he (and therefore the Court) would avoid the deeper issues of equality and liberty and seek refuge in the relative banality of separation of powers.[82] Justice Kennedy, moreover, has consistently sided with the Court's conservative wing in striking down congressional enactments thought to encroach on state sovereignty.[83]

So, what was the purpose of the federalism discussion? Apparently, to provide context for the subsequent discussion of how Congressional action in enacting DOMA was a "discrimination of an unusual character … ."[84] By going out of its way to weaken same-sex marriages, DOMA disrupted states' decisions "to give this class of persons the right to marry [and thereby to confer upon them] a dignity and status of immense import."[85] But what is the content of the "dignity and status" that the Court felt obligated to protect? Is DOMA really understandable only as an exercise of Congressional disapproval of gays and lesbians, or is Scalia right about the importance of the practical justifications for the law? And what does *Windsor* have to say about the reach of equal protection and due process, going forward? We now know that the case has set the stage for a broader decision by the Court on same-sex marriages, but how did this come to pass?

***Windsor*'s Limited Use of Precedent (and the Search for Other Antecedents)**

Given the significance of the Court's decision, the brevity of the discussion about the constitutional infirmity of DOMA is nothing short of startling. Equally arresting is the limited use of precedent. But these slender five pages open a window into a full-ranging discussion about the meaning and reach of liberty, equality, and dignity.[86] Setting aside the Court's invocation of *Bolling v. Sharpe*[87] for the proposition that the Fifth Amendment's Due Process Clause incorporates a guarantee of equal protection, the Court relies on only three cases—*Romer*, *Lawrence*, and *Department of Agriculture v. Moreno*[88]—and makes scant use of even these. Boiled down, the Court's use of these cases might be stated thus:

> Since the discrimination enacted by DOMA is "unusual," careful consideration of the law is called for. And that consideration reveals that DOMA was born of "a bare congressional desire to harm a politically unpopular

82 I was one a group of family law professors on an amicus brief in *Windsor*. *See* Brief on the Merits of Amici Curiae Family Law Professors and the American Academy of Matrimonial Lawyers in Support of Respondent Edith Schlain Windsor (Mar. 1, 2013), 2013 WL 840024. We argued that DOMA contradicted a body of federal law and the Supreme Court's own jurisprudence, which had consistently declared matters of family law to be the "virtually exclusive province of the States." *See, e.g.*, Sosna v. Iowa, 419 U.S. 393 (1975).

83 *See, e.g.*, National Federation of Independent Business v. Sebelius, 567 U.S. 132 S.Ct. 2566 (2012) (Kennedy joined a joint dissent that would have struck down the Affordable Care Act as not within Congressional power under the commerce clause).

84 *Windsor* at 2692, quoting Romer v. Evans, 517 U.S. 620.

85 *Id.*

86 My colleague Erin Daly sees in *Windsor* the rudiments of an emerging theory of dignity, which she traces back through a series of decisions (some of which are not cited in the case), and links to decisions by courts from other countries that contain more specific guarantees of dignity in their national constitutions. *See* Erin Daly, *The Dignity of* Windsor: *The Marriage of Liberty and Equality* [draft on file with the author]. *See generally* ERIN DALY, DIGNITY RIGHTS: COURTS, CONSTITUTIONS, AND THE WORTH OF THE HUMAN PERSON (U. Penn. 2012). The discussion that follows in the text is indebted to her insights.

87 347 U.S. 497 (1954).

88 413 U.S. 528 (1973).

group,"[89] and offends principles of equality in so doing. The states are entitled to further the equality and dignity of same-sex couples, a dignity that the Court recognized in Lawrence and that DOMA demeans.

Most of the discussion is an elaboration of these few simple but profound points.

The Court devotes much more ink to discussing *how* DOMA accomplishes its unconstitutional ends, and here the Supreme Court showed it was more interested in the expressive value of marriage than in its many benefits. This focus makes sense, given the Court's conclusion that DOMA imposes "a disadvantage, a separate status, and so a stigma upon all who enter into same-sex marriages made lawful by the unquestioned authority of the States."[90] It is not really the lack of benefits that demeans the couple, but the lack of *recognition*. That is why the Court emphasizes the *responsibilities* of marriage, perhaps even more than the rights. Adults assume responsibilities willingly, and by denying gay and lesbian couples the opportunity to do so, DOMA deprived them of dignity. Of course, DOMA was no statutory slouch when it came to fencing same-sex couples out of the substantial federal benefits of marriage, either, and the Court does discuss a host of these disabilities. But the opinion is clearly more concerned with the less tangible benefits of marriage; and these are also affected by DOMA, albeit indirectly.[91]

For these reasons, it is unlikely that the Court would accept any kind of "federal civil union" for same-sex couples, either, unless Congress decided to treat *all* marriages as civil unions. In an important way, the decision in *Windsor* is a close cousin to the holdings in *In Re Marriage Cases* and *Kerrigan*. By overriding states' prerogatives to grant same-sex couples the rights and dignity that only full marriage can confer, DOMA created a second-class citizenship for same-sex couples. Indeed, as Justice Kennedy is at pains to point out, that seems to have been the very reason for enacting the law: "The history of DOMA's enactment and its own text demonstrate that interference with the equal dignity of same-sex couples, a dignity conferred by the States in their exercise of their sovereign power, was more than an incidental effect of the federal statute. It was its essence."[92]

Similarly, states that have rejected the arguments against recognition of same-sex unions but offer domestic partnership or civil unions instead of marriage thereby create a parallel institution for no ostensible reason, and also demean gay and lesbian couples. Compare the following passage from *In Re Marriage Cases* to the statement from *Windsor* in the preceding paragraph: "[A]ffording same-sex couples only a separate and differently named family relationship will ... impose appreciable harm on same-sex couples and their children, because denying such couples access to the familiar and highly favored designation of marriage is likely to cast doubt on whether the official family relationship of same-sex couples enjoys dignity equal to that of opposite-sex couples."[93]

That this indignity through inequality was the paramount concern of the *Windsor* court is made clear by the fact, bemoaned by Scalia, that the Court does not even pause to examine other possible justifications for the law. It does not need to, because as Justice Kennedy notes in the final paragraph: "[N]o legitimate purpose overcomes the purpose and effect to disparage and injure those whom the State, by its marriage laws, sought to protect and personhood and dignity."[94] In short, once Congress decided to base a law on an unconstitutional infringement on equality and liberty, the Court was not going to rescue it by engaging in the exercise of considering what might have been independently legitimate reasons for the law. The loss of dignity is sufficient to the holding, because—to borrow a phrase from *In Re Marriage Cases*—even "intangible symbolic differences ... often are constitutionally significant."[95] There is no justification for *them*. We have moved far afield from the "rational basis" test that Scalia argued should have applied here.

---

89 This language is drawn from Department of Agriculture v. Moreno, 413 U.S. 538, 534 (1973).

90 *Id.* at 2693.

91 Cf. Brause v. Bureau of Vital Statistics, 1998 WL 88743, *3 (Alaska Super. Ct. 1998) (what the plaintiffs sought was "important for its public nature as much as for the ... legal consequences which attend it"), *superseded by constitutional amendment*, Art. I, § 25, Ak. Const. (amendment enacted in 1998).

92 *Id.*

93 *In Re Marriage Cases*, 183 P.3d at 401.

94 *Windsor*, 133 S. Ct. at 2696.

95 183 P.3d at 445.

Yet Scalia is correct that *Windsor* is light on precedent, and could have benefited from a fuller discussion of the connection between liberty and equality (and of the dignity principle it seemed to derive from these sources). Fortunately, *Windsor* is connected to the state law cases discussed earlier (especially *Goodridge*) through a strong filament that bears further exploration, building on our earlier discussion of these cases.

Both *Windsor* and *Goodridge* rely on the Supreme Court's two previous gay rights cases, *Romer* and *Lawrence*, but *Goodridge* enriches the discussion by citation to some of the Court's other relevant precedents; cases that went unmentioned in *Windsor*. Given that a similar spirit of equality-meets-liberty suffuses and animates both decisions, it is worth discussing at least one such case, *Loving v. Virginia*,[96] which might have fleshed out the *Windsor* opinion. (There is some of this discussion in both *In Re Marriage Cases* and *Kerrigan*, as well, but these decisions are more firmly anchored in precedents from within the state, and much of the discussion in *Kerrigan* is taken up with an exhaustive discussion of the requirements for heightened scrutiny.) A brief discussion of these precedents will be helpful.

Exploring *Windsor*'s Lineage: A Deeper Dive into the Gay Rights Trilogy, and A Fond Look at Loving v. Virginia

Windsor completes a gay-rights trilogy that began in 1996 with *Romer* and continued with the 2003 decision in *Lawrence*. Each of the earlier decisions has been criticized as enigmatic, and they are grounded in different constitutional guarantees (equal protection and due process, respectively), but taken together they can be seen as building a body of law that announces and enforces an antisubordination principle. *Goodridge* implicitly recognizes the importance of this principle. As discussed earlier, the court cites *Romer* for the admonition against singling people out for the purpose of denying them rights and (thereby) respect. The court thus drew the connection more clearly than did the *Windsor* majority; to deny equality to a class is to subordinate that class.

The *Goodridge* court also made greater use of *Lawrence*, which had been decided just five months earlier. Of greatest significance for present purposes is the court's citation of *Lawrence* for a proposition that oddly went unrepeated by the *Windsor* Court: "Equality of treatment and the due process right to demand respect for conduct protected by the … guarantee of liberty … are linked in important respects, and a decision on the latter point advances both interests."[97]

In *Lawrence*, the Court considered but rejected an equal protection rationale for striking down Texas's "gay-only" anti-sodomy law, but only because of concern that deciding on that basis would not have gone far enough to make the Court's anti-caste point crystal clear. The Court feared that, even if the law were not enforceable as drawn, it might be redrawn to prohibit the same conduct as the statute in issue as long as opposite-sex participants were also covered by the prohibition. But then the law's "stigma might remain" and constitute a continuing "invitation to subject homosexual persons to discrimination both in the public and private spheres."[98]

Thus, although *Romer* is nominally an equality case and *Lawrence* is grounded in substantive due process, they are akin. In both cases, the Court struck down laws that had the purpose and effect of conferring second-class status on gays and lesbians—either by fencing them out of laws protecting them against discrimination, or by laws singling out their private, intimate conduct for criminal sanctions. My colleague Erin Daly has persuasively argued that equal protection and due process are converging into an as-yet nascent jurisprudence of dignity.[99] *Windsor* provides a handy vehicle for furthering the collapse of the doctrinal categories that was already underway in part because of the Fifth Amendment's implied protection against inequality as an aspect of the liberty guaranteed by the Due Process Clause. Perhaps the Court's justifications for finding DOMA unconstitutional, then, were not "rootless" (pace Scalia), but rooted in a confounding, cryptic common language of dignity and antisubordination.

---

96 388 U.S. 1 (1967).

97 *Id.* at 953, quoting Lawrence v. Texas, 123 S. Ct. 2472, 2482.

98 539 U.S. 558, 575 (2003).

99 *See* Daly, *The Dignity of* Windsor, *supra* note 86.

If so, *Windsor* is only the first *gay rights* case to find purchase in this combination of constitutional sources, not the first case. Indeed, *Windsor* is in an important way the successor to *Loving v. Virginia*,[100] in which the Court struck down a Virginia anti-miscegenation law on both equal protection *and* due process grounds. Perhaps concern about tying sexual orientation and race together kept the *Windsor* Court from relying on *Loving*, but the cases are doctrinally related. The *Goodridge* court, on the other hand, had no such qualms, and cited *Loving* in several different places for interlacing reasons. Stitched together, *Loving*'s insight runs somewhat as follows:

> Marriage is a basic civil right, and that right depends for its full exercise on the ability to marry the person of one's choice, at least absent a strong reason for disqualifying certain people from marrying. And the anti-miscegenation law, which was designed to maintain white supremacy, both compromises one's liberty to choose a spouse and "violates the central meaning of the Equal Protection Clause."[101]

Along with *In Re Marriage Cases* and *Kerrigan*, then, *Goodridge* and *Loving* provided fertile soil for *Windsor*, even if these sources went unacknowledged. And the same majority of the Massachusetts Supreme Judicial Court had occasion to be even more explicit about the antisubordination principle that drove its decision in *Goodridge* shortly thereafter, when the court was asked by the Massachusetts State Senate to render an opinion as to whether its decision ordering same-sex marriages could be satisfied by enacting a civil union law. The court would have none of it:

> Because the proposed law by its express terms forbids same-sex couples entry into civil marriage, it continues to relegate same-sex couples to a different status. The holding in *Goodridge* … is that group classifications based on unsupportable distinctions, such as that embodied in the proposed bill, are invalid under the Massachusetts Constitution. The history of our nation has demonstrated that separate is seldom, if ever, equal.[102]

Note the implicit reference to *Loving*, and the court's reiteration of its repugnance to second-class status. *Windsor* could have used some "bulking up" along these lines, even though its intellectual and doctrinal provenance can, with effort, be discerned.

Beyond *Windsor*: The Future of Dignity, Equality, and Liberty

Scalia turns out to be right about a few things in his apoplectic *Windsor* dissent. In particular, it is undeniable that the Court is constructing a new jurisprudence of due process and equal protection that abandons stricter tests, in favor of … what, exactly?

As described earlier, substantive due process analysis has traditionally required that the asserted right be "deeply rooted" in the nation's history and traditions before it can be protected as "fundamental." Moreover, the right must be described with particularity. Under this formulation, the Court in *Washington v. Glucksberg* rejected a claim that there was a constitutional "right to die," on the ground that the more specific (and therefore applicable) right being advanced was a right to physician-assisted suicide, a right unknown to longstanding legal rules and traditions.[103] By contrast, the right to refuse life-saving hydration and nutrition has been found fundamental, in part because of the common law of battery that protects people from unwarranted physical contact.[104] Surely the due process analysis in *Windsor* required no such "careful description" of the right asserted.

But the *Windsor* Court's methodology is in fact typical of more recent cases relating broadly matters of the family, marriage, and procreation, and (more controversially) sexual intimacy. In this class of cases, the Court has in fact adopted a broader notion of the rights entitled to due process protection.

---

100 388 U.S. 1 (1967).

101 *Id.* at 12.

102 In Re Opinion of the Justices to the Senate, 802 N.E.2d 565 (Mass. 2004).

103 Washington v. Glucksberg, 521 U.S. 702 (1997) (describing ancient common law tradition prohibiting suicide and current state laws to the same effect).

104 Cruzan v. Director, Missouri Dep't of Health, 497 U.S. 261 (1990).

Lawrence itself is perhaps the best articulation of this broader notion of rights, because the case pointedly overruled *Bowers v. Hardwick*, where the Court had narrowly defined the issue as whether there was "a fundamental right upon homosexuals to engage in sodomy … ." Since no such right could be shown to be of long-standing, the *Bowers* Court had little trouble dismissing the due process claim. But in defiance of the supposed rule that the asserted right be defined narrowly, Justice Kennedy took a more expansive view in *Lawrence*; although stopping just short of declaring that the Constitution confers a fundamental right to engage in private sexual behavior, he wrote: "The statutes … seek to control a personal relationship that … is within the liberty of persons to choose without being punished as criminals." To hold otherwise, he wrote, would be to "demean" the claim, just as defining marriage as simply the right to engage in sex would demean the married couple. Thus, in an only-partially specified class of cases, the more exacting review to determine whether a right is sufficiently fundamental recedes in favor of a broader conception of liberty. While this approach may now be associated with the gay rights cases, because of both *Lawrence* and *Windsor*, it is not limited to them. In *Planned Parenthood of Southeastern Pennsylvania v. Casey*,[105] the Court found in the Due Process Clause a right of self-determination. *Casey* also announces an approach to liberty that is not limited to those rights protected "against government interference by other rules of law when the Fourteenth Amendment was ratified."[106] Otherwise put, "there is a realm of personal liberty which the government may not enter."[107] Decisional autonomy is to be protected in matters central to "marriage, procreation, contraception, family relationships, child rearing, and education." From this perspective, the right to choose to terminate a pregnancy is of a piece with these other rights, and the State cannot "resolve these philosophic questions in such a definitive way that a woman lacks all choice in the matter … ."[108] To do so, we might say in a way consistent with the themes of this chapter, is to consign women to second-class status.

The evolution of equal protection doctrine is also apparent in *Windsor*. As Justice Scalia points out, the issue of the standard of review is nowhere in evidence. The Court's decision effaces the already-faded "rational basis" review deployed in *Romer* in favor of a less-specific approach that casts a skeptical eye on any law the Justices think is designed to subordinate a class.

It is remarkable that courts have discovered so many ways to protect gays and lesbians as a class under equal protection law, especially in the context of marriage and sexual relations. *Romer* and *Goodridge* used a rational basis test, although admittedly one with more "bite" than is seen in the most deferential applications of the standard. *Kerrigan* and *Varnum* used intermediate scrutiny. And *In Re Marriage Cases* stands alone, using strict scrutiny to achieve the same result. Thus far it appears that the only approach to equal protection analysis that has not led to full marriage equality is the balancing approach taken in New Jersey (*Lewis v. Harris*) and Vermont (*Baker v. State*). Perhaps that is because this approach looks at tangible benefits (indeed, as stated earlier, the Vermont Constitution has a "common benefits," rather than an "equal protection" guarantee) rather than directly at the subordination that led these other courts—by whatever level of review they chose—to strike down laws singling gay and lesbian couples out for unequal treatment.

What's Next?

A side skirmish broke out among the *Windsor* dissenters over the reach of the decision. Inasmuch as the majority wrote at the very end of its opinion that the holding was "limited to those lawful marriages" that DOMA had weakened, Chief Justice Roberts and Justice Alito, in separate dissents, made essentially the same point: the logic of the opinion is limited to the case of the federal law, because the enactment of DOMA was enough to set off alarm bells telling the Court that Congress would have taken such an unprecedented step only to demean gay and lesbian marriages. There was surely support in the Congressional record for such a finding.

105 505 U.S. 833 (1992).

106 *Id.* at 847.

107 *Id.*

108 *Id.* at 850.

Justice Scalia, on the other hand, made the case that the majority had deliberately written the opinion in a way that litigants and lower courts (if so inclined) can easily read to condemn the exclusion of same-sex marriages from *state laws*.

As we now know, Scalia's prediction of the breadth of the Court's holding has been in ascendance. As this chapter has made clear, *Windsor*, although short on precedent, contains a rich vein of antisubordination language that can be mined by those seeking to upend state defense of marriage laws (whether in legislation or embedded in state constitutions). In an almost unanimous flurry of decisions, federal courts have struck down state laws barring same-sex marriages; indeed, it was the uniqueness of the Sixth Circuit's contrary decision that finally prompted the Supreme Court to step in.[109] The judges have clearly been influenced by what they see as *Windsor*'s promise of full marriage equality. (As I have written elsewhere, perhaps the most ingenious attack is directed at state non-recognition law: if Congress cannot constitutionally disrespect same-sex marriages validly entered into, then perhaps a state cannot do so, either.)[110] If the litigants currently before the Court win the day, the Supreme Court will have taken its most significant step yet in the evolving jurisprudence of antisubordination. But it won't be the final evolutionary stage, either for LGBT rights or more broadly. The dignity that the antisubordination principle instantiates is a powerful principle.

109 *See supra* note 13 and accompanying text.

110 *See* John Culhane, *The Most Ingenious Attack on Gay Marriage Bans*, Slate, Oct. 2, 2013, http://www.slate.com/articles/news_and_politics/jurisprudence/2013/10/the_pennsylvania_lawsuit_with_the_best_chance_of_toppling_state_laws_against.html.

Chapter 11
Unequal Protection for Sex and Gender Nonconformists

Julie A. Greenberg*

Introduction

The days when only women could be flight attendants and only men could be pilots are a distant memory. The Equal Protection Clause and hundreds of federal, state, and local constitutional provisions and statutes prohibit almost all facially discriminatory regulations based on a person's sex. The original goal of this legislation was to eliminate societal barriers to equal opportunities for men and women. When legislators adopted these statutes, however, they assumed that sex was binary and easy to establish. Therefore, they never felt the need to define the terms "male," "female," "sex," and "gender."

This failure is especially problematic for people who do not fall neatly into the male/female binary norm. Millions of people have an intersex condition or are transgender. Both groups suffer societal discrimination in a number of areas. First, people with an intersex condition and transgender people may find that government-created tests for determining their legal sex often rely on irrational contradictory factors. These tests could lead to invalidation of their marriages and their right to be considered legal parents. Second, transgender people and people with intersex traits may suffer discrimination in a variety of settings including employment, housing, and the provision of health care.

This chapter examines whether the government violates the Equal Protection Clause in two contexts: (1) when the government establishes an illogical "sex" test for determining who qualifies as a male or female, and (2) when the government discriminates against transgender people or people with an intersex condition by subjecting them to differential treatment. The second part of this chapter describes the people who suffer discrimination because of their failure to meet traditional sex and gender binary stereotypes. The third part provides an introduction to the Equal Protection Clause. The fourth and fifth parts analyze whether governmental treatment of people with an intersex condition and transgender people violates the Equal Protection Clause. The fourth part focuses on state-created sex classification systems and explains why current government "sex" tests do not meet the rigorous review standard mandated by intermediate scrutiny. The fifth part examines sex discrimination jurisprudence and concludes that differential governmental treatment of people with an intersex condition or transgender people constitutes impermissible "sex" discrimination. This chapter concludes that sex classification systems and other governmental acts that rely on sex and gender stereotypes violate the Equal Protection Clause.

Sex and Gender Nonconformists

Courts have relied on inaccurate sex and gender stereotypes when they have determined whether a person qualifies as a male or female or whether someone has been subjected to discrimination because of "sex." This section explains why sex-based binary classification systems based on sex and gender stereotypes do not reflect reality for the millions of people who have an intersex condition or who are transgender.

---

* Professor of Law, Thomas Jefferson School of Law. I am indebted to Marybeth Herald for her insightful comments on this chapter and for her collaboration on our joint article, Julie A. Greenberg & Marybeth Herald, *You Can't Take it With You: Constitutional Consequences of Interstate Gender-Identity Rulings*, 80 Wash. L. Rev. 819 (2005). The fourth part of this chapter is an update of the Equal Protection section of that article, which we co-authored. I want to thank my research assistant, Matt Baylot, for his excellent research support.

People with an Intersex Condition or Difference of Sex Development (DSD)

Millions of people do not have sex markers that are all clearly male or clearly female. They have what is known as an intersex condition, or DSD.[1] Although doctors and activists in the intersex community continue to debate exactly what conditions qualify as "intersex," the term is often used to include anyone with a congenital condition whose sex chromosomes, gonads, or internal or external sexual anatomy do not fit clearly into the binary male/female norm.[2]

Some intersex conditions involve an inconsistency between a person's internal and external sex features. For example, some people with an intersex condition may have a female body type, female-appearing external genitalia, no internal female organs, and testicles.[3] Other people with an intersex condition may be born with external genitalia that do not appear to be clearly male or female. For example, a girl may be born with a larger than average clitoris and no vagina.[4] Similarly, a boy may be born with a small penis or no penis.[5] Some people with an intersex condition may also be born with a chromosomal pattern that does not fall into the binary XX/XY norm.[6]

Not all intersex conditions are apparent at the time of birth; some conditions become evident as a child matures.[7] In some conditions, a child whose genitalia appeared to be female at birth will masculinize in puberty.[8] Other intersex conditions may be discovered at puberty when the adolescent fails to develop typical male or female traits. For example, the condition may be discovered when a girl reaches puberty and fails to menstruate.[9]

Because experts do not agree on exactly which conditions fit within the definition of intersexuality and some conditions are not evident until years after a child is born, it is impossible to state with precision exactly

---

1 The meaning of the term "intersex" has varied and is still a topic of debate, JULIE A. GREENBERG, INTERSEXUALITY AND THE LAW: WHY SEX MATTERS 131–32 (2012); M. Morgan Holmes, *Straddling Past, Present and Future*, *in* CRITICAL INTERSEX 1, 1 (Morgan Holmes et al. eds, 2009).

2 *Intersex FAQ*, INTERSEX INITIATIVE, http://www.ipdx.org/articles/intersex-faq.html (last updated June 29, 2008); *What Is Intersex?*, INTERSEX SOC'Y OF N. AM., http://www.isna.org/faq/what_is_intersex (last visited Nov. 6, 2012).

3 For example, women with complete androgen insensitivity syndrome (CAIS) have XY chromosomes and normal functioning testes. Because of a receptor defect, their bodies are unable to process the testosterone produced by the testes and *in utero* their bodies follow the female developmental path. External female genitalia will form but no internal female reproductive organs (uterus and fallopian tubes) will develop. *See* Melissa Hines et al., *Psychological Outcomes and Gender-Related Development in Complete Androgen Insensitivity Syndrome*, 32 ARCHIVES SEXUAL BEHAV. 93, 93 (2003). For a more detailed description of this and other intersex conditions, *see* ANNE FAUSTO-STERLING, SEXING THE BODY: GENDER POLITICS AND THE CONSTRUCTION OF SEXUALITY 52–53 (2000); Julie A. Greenberg, *Defining Male and Female: Intersexuality and the Collision Between Law and Biology*, 41 ARIZ. L. REV. 265, 281–92 (1999) [hereinafter *Defining Male and Female*].

4 For example, infants with partial androgen insensitivity syndrome (PAIS) have XY chromosomes and their bodies are able to partially process the androgens produced by their testes. Their genitalia will partially masculinize. S. Faisal Ahmed et al., *Phenotypic Features, Androgen Receptor Binding, and Mutational Analysis in 278 Clinical Cases Reported as Androgen Insensitivity Syndrome*, 85 J. CLINICAL ENDOCRINOLOGY & METABOLISM 658, 658 (2000).

5 *See, e.g.*, William G. Reiner & Bradley P. Kropp, *A 7-Year Experience of Genetic Males with Severe Phallic Inadequacy Assigned Female*, 172 J. UROLOGY 2395 (2004).

6 For example, a number of people have chromosomal patterns that vary from the typical XX and XY patterns. People have been found with XXX, XXY, XXXY, XYY, XYYY, XYYYY, and XO (signifying only one sex chromosome). In addition, some people have a mosaic chromosomal pattern, where some chromosomes are XX and some are XY. ROBERT POOL, EVE'S RIB: SEARCHING FOR THE BIOLOGICAL ROOTS OF SEX DIFFERENCES 70, 71 (1994).

7 *See, e.g.*, Julianne Imperato-McGinley et al., *Steroid 5 Alpha-Reductase Deficiency in Man: An Inherited Form of Male Pseudohermaphroditism*, 186 SCI. 1213 (1974).

8 For example, people with 5-alpha-reductase deficiency have XY chromosomes and testes but appear phenotypically female at birth. Despite a female appearance during childhood, by the onset of puberty the body will masculinize. The testes descend, the voice deepens, muscle mass substantially increases, and a penis that is capable of ejaculating develops from what was thought to be the clitoris. *Id.*

9 For example, sometimes physicians are unaware that an infant with typical female genitalia at birth has CAIS if the testes are nestled in the abdominal cavity. The condition may not be discovered until puberty, when the girl fails to menstruate. *See* Hines et al., *supra* note 3, at 93.

how many people have an intersex condition. Most experts agree, however, that approximately 1–2 percent of people are born with sexual features that vary from the medically defined norm for male and female.[10] These variations may relate to chromosomal structure, internal reproductive organs, or external genitalia. Children with ambiguous external genitalia are not as common. Approximately one in 1,500 to one in 2,000 births involve a child who is born so noticeably atypical in terms of external genitalia that a specialist in sex differentiation is consulted and surgical alteration of the external genitalia is considered.[11]

The term "intersex" itself is controversial. Many doctors favor abandoning the term "intersex" in favor of the term "disorder of sex development" (DSD). Some who support the use of DSD terminology have argued that the term "disorder" should be dropped and the initial "D" should stand for difference rather than disorder.[12]

Transsexuality and Transgenderism

Some people are confused about how intersexuality compares to transsexuality and transgenderism. Generally, intersexuality refers to a condition in which a person's biological sex markers are not all clearly male or female, while transgenderism and transsexuality are used to describe behaviors or identities of people whose gender expression, gender identity, or both, do not necessarily conform with the binary sex norm or may be different from the sex assigned to them at birth.[13] Not all communities use the terms "transgender" and "transsexual" consistently and different groups and individuals have strong feelings about which term they prefer.

One major LGBT organization, GLAAD, suggests the following definitions:

> Transgender: An umbrella term (adj.) for people whose gender identity and/or gender expression differs from the sex they were assigned at birth. The term may include but is not limited to: transsexuals, cross-dressers and other gender-variant people. Transgender people may identify as female-to-male (FTM) or male-to-female (MTF) … Transgender people may or may not decide to alter their bodies hormonally and/or surgically.
>
> Transsexual (also Transexual): An older term which originated in the medical and psychological communities. While some transsexual people still prefer to use the term to describe themselves, many transgender people prefer the term *transgender* to *transsexual*. Unlike *transgender*, *transsexual* is not an umbrella term, as many transgender people do not identify as transsexual.[14]

The University of San Francisco Medical Center defines the terms as follows:

> Transgender: literally "across gender"; sometimes interpreted as "beyond gender"; a community-based term that describes a wide variety of cross-gender behaviors and identities. This is not a diagnostic term, and does not imply a medical or psychological condition.
>
> …
>
> Transsexual: a medical term applied to individuals who seek hormonal (and often, but not always) surgical treatment to modify their bodies so they may live full time as members of the sex category opposite to their

10 Melanie Blackless et al., *How Sexually Dimorphic Are We? Review and Synthesis*, 12 Am. J. Hum. Biology 151, 161 (2000).

11 *Id.* Some experts place the number of genital anomalies at birth as 1 in 4,500. Peter A. Lee et al., *Consensus Statement on Management of Intersex Disorders*, 118 Pediatrics e488 (2006).

12 For a more detailed discussion of the debates regarding terminology, *see* Greenberg, *supra* note 1, at 118–19; Holmes, *supra* note 1, at 6–7; and Alyson K. Spurgas, *(Un)Queering Identity: The Biosocial Production of Intersex/DSD*, *in* Critical Intersex, 97, 97–111 (Morgan Holmes et al. eds, 2009).

13 *See GLAAD Media Reference Guide—Transgender Glossary of Terms*, GLAAD, http://www.glaad.org/reference/transgender (last updated May 2010).

14 *Id.*

birth-assigned sex (including legal status). Some individuals who have completed their medical transition prefer not to use this term as a self-referent.[15]

Experts differ on the prevalence of transgenderism. Numbers from recent studies range from a low of 1 in 104,000 to a high of 1 in 200.[16]

Sexual Orientation

A person's sexual orientation is determined by the person's sexual attraction. Heterosexuals are sexually attracted to the "opposite" sex. Gays and lesbians are sexually attracted to people of the "same" sex. Bisexuals are sexually attracted to people of "both" sexes.

Society and legal institutions often inappropriately conflate the distinct concepts of biological sex, gender identity, and sexual orientation. Biological sex features do not necessarily dictate a person's gender identity. Similarly, biological sex features and gender identity do not necessarily control a person's sexual orientation.

Most people meet societal sex and gender stereotypes; their sex markers are all congruent, they self-identify as the gender assigned to them at birth, and they are heterosexual. Millions of people, however, do not fit this stereotype. A person born with all male biological sex features may have a female gender identity and may live as a female. That same person, however, may be sexually attracted to women. In other words, a natal male may choose to live as a female, but may still prefer to have sex with another woman. Biological sex does not control gender identity, and neither biological sex nor gender identity can be used to predict a person's sexual orientation.

The following chart illustrates prevailing societal presumptions about men and women and the groups that directly challenge those assumptions.

	Societal Assumptions about Males	**Societal Assumptions about Females**	**Challengers**
Sexual/Reproductive Anatomy	Penis, scrotum, testicles, XY chromosomes	Clitoris, labia, vagina, uterus, fallopian tubes, XX chromosomes	People with an intersex condition
Sexual Orientation	Toward Women	Toward Men	Gays, lesbians, and bisexuals
Gender Identity	Male	Female	Transgender people
Gender Presentation	Masculine	Feminine	People who do not conform to gender stereotypes and norms

Because lesbians, gays, bisexuals, transgender people (LGBTs), and people with an intersex condition do not fit societal binary sex and gender norms, they suffer from pervasive discriminatory practices.[17] The Equal Protection Clause protects people from "invidious discrimination in statutory classifications and other

15 *Transgender Terminology*, Univ. of Cal., S.F., Ctr. of Excellence for Transgender Health, http://www.transhealth.ucsf.edu/trans?page=protocol-terminology (last visited Nov. 6, 2012).

16 For a comparison chart of various research studies, *see* A.B. Kaplan, *The Prevalence of Transgenderism-An Update*, Transgender Mental Health, (Feb. 13, 2012), http://tgmentalhealth.com/2012/02/13/the-prevalence-of-transgenderism-an-update/. Researchers report that the incidence of transgenderism is higher in cities and in more tolerant cultures. *Id.*

17 Jennifer C. Pizer, Brad Sears, Christy Mallory, & Nan D. Hunter, *Evidence of Persistent and Pervasive Workplace Discrimination Against LGBT People: The Need for Federal Legislation Prohibiting Discrimination and Providing for Equal Employment Benefits*, 45 Loy. L.A. L. Rev. 715 (2012), available at http://digitalcommons.lmu.edu/llr/vol45/iss3/3/. *See infra* notes 133–39 and accompanying text for a discussion of these discriminatory practices. Discrimination against people with an intersex condition is not as well documented because many people with an intersex condition do not share information about the fact that they have an intersex condition with other people. The major area in which people with an intersex condition suffer from sex stereotyping is in the provision of health care. *See* Julie A. Greenberg, *Health Care Issues*

governmental activity."[18] Thus, transgender people and people with an intersex condition may be able to bring equal protection claims based on government-created sex classification systems and other governmental activity that results in discrimination because of sex.

An Introduction to the Equal Protection Clause

The purpose of the Equal Protection Clause is to ensure that the government does not subject its citizens to arbitrary classifications.[19] Depending on the classification at issue, the Supreme Court will apply one of three levels of scrutiny to the government action: strict scrutiny, intermediate scrutiny, or rational basis review. Under each level, the court will apply a two-step analysis. First, it will assess the government purpose for the classification. If the government purpose is considered valid, the court will then analyze the relationship between the government purpose and the means used to accomplish the government's goal.

The Supreme Court applies strict scrutiny when the discrimination involves a suspect classification.[20] The Court has applied strict scrutiny to governmental classification systems based upon race, national origin, and sometimes alienage.[21] Under strict scrutiny analysis, the court places the burden on the government to prove that: (1) it has a compelling interest for its classification and (2) the means the government has chosen to accomplish the compelling goal are narrowly tailored for that purpose.[22] Most state actions cannot survive strict scrutiny because few government justifications qualify as compelling and the means used to accomplish the governmental goal are subject to a searching judicial inquiry.[23]

Sex classifications are subject to an intermediate level of review.[24] Sex-based classifications require that the government prove: (1) an important or exceedingly persuasive justification for its classification and (2) that the means used to accomplish the important justification are substantially related to the government's goal.[25] Although intermediate scrutiny is technically less demanding than strict scrutiny, most government sex-based classifications also fail equal protection requirements.

Courts apply the lowest level of review, rational basis review, to all other legislative classifications.[26] Under rational basis analysis, a challenger must prove that either: (1) no legitimate governmental objective for the government classification exists, or (2) rational means are not used to achieve a legitimate governmental objective.[27] It is easy to establish that a legitimate purpose exists and rational means were used to accomplish that purpose. Therefore, almost all government classifications are considered constitutional under this low level of review.[28]

Although the Supreme Court has formally recognized only three levels of scrutiny, in recent cases the Court seems to be applying a form of heightened rational basis review, often referred to as rational basis

---

Affecting People with an Intersex Condition or DSD: Sex or Disability Discrimination?, 45 Loy. L.A. L. Rev. 849 (2012) available at http://digitalcommons.lmu.edu/llr/vol45/iss3/5 [hereinafter Health Care Issues].

18 Harris v. McRae, 448 U.S. 297, 322 (1980).

19 Reed v. Reed, 404 U.S. 71, 76 (1971); Frontiero v. Richardson, 411 U.S. 677, 683 (1973); City of Cleburne v. Cleburne Living Center Inc., 473 U.S. 432, 446 (1985).

20 Mass. Bd. of Ret. v. Murgia, 427 U.S. 312 (1976). The Court has also applied strict scrutiny to government actions that limit fundamental rights, including the right to interstate travel, Shapiro v. Thompson, 394 U.S. 618 (1969), the right to vote, Reynolds v. Sims, 377 U.S. 533 (1964), and the right to marry Zablocki v. Redhail, 434 U.S. 374 (1978). The state sex classification systems discussed *infra* in the fourth part also burden the fundamental right to marry and to travel and thus should be subjected to strict scrutiny. *See* Julie A. Greenberg & Marybeth Herald, *You Can't Take it With You: Constitutional Consequences of Interstate Gender-Identity Rulings*, 80 Wash. L. Rev 819, 855–62 (2005).

21 *Cleburne*, 473 U.S. at 440; *Frontiero*, 411 U.S. at 688.

22 Gratz v. Bollinger, 359 U.S. 244, 270 (2003).

23 Fisher v. University of Texas, 133 S.Ct. 2411(2013).

24 United States v. Virginia, 518 U.S. 515, 524 (1996); Miss. Univ. v. Hogan, 458 U.S. 718 (1982).

25 *Virginia*, 518 U.S. at 524.

26 Mass. Bd. of Ret. v. Murgia, 427 U.S. 312 (1976).

27 Heller v. Doe, 509 U.S. 312, 319–20 (1993); FCC v. Beach Communications, Inc., 508 U.S. 307, 313–14 (1993).

28 Heller v. Doe, 509 U.S. 312, 319–20 (1993); FCC v. Beach Communications, Inc., 508 U.S. 307, 313–14 (1993) (classifications not involving fundamental rights or suspect classifications are accorded a strong presumption of validity).

with bite, when determining whether classifications based on sexual orientation violate the Equal Protection Clause.[29] Under a rational basis with bite analysis, the Court has struck down government classifications that are motivated by "a bare desire to harm a politically unpopular group."[30]

Transgender people and people with an intersex condition may bring an action for violation of their right to equal protection in two scenarios. First, when the government establishes tests for determining whether a transgender person or a person with an intersex condition is a male or a female and thus qualifies for a sex-based right, the government is creating a sex classification system that may violate the Equal Protection Clause. Second, when a government actor engages in discrimination against people based on their transgender or intersex status, the government may be engaged in impermissible sex discrimination under the Equal Protection Clause.[31]

Governmental Sex Classification Systems that Rely on Chromosomes, the Ability to Reproduce, Religious References, or Gender Stereotypes to Determine who Qualifies as a Male or Female Violate the Equal Protection Clause

Very few laws in the United States differentiate between men and women. The only major areas where a person's sex is legally significant is in the context of marriage and the use of gender-segregated facilities such as restrooms, locker rooms, and housing in college dormitories and prisons.[32]

Some states still define marriage as a union of one man and one woman and refuse to recognize marriages between people of the same sex.[33] Until 2013, the Defense of Marriage Act (DOMA)[34] also limited the definition of marriage for federal purposes to "one man and one woman." In 2013, the Supreme Court of the United States ruled that the portion of DOMA that denied validly married same-sex couples the same federal rights as opposite-sex married couples was unconstitutional.[35] The Court declined to rule on whether all state laws limiting the right of same sex couples to marry are unconstitutional.[36] The Court had an opportunity to review this issue again during its 2014 term, but it refused to grant certiorari in a number of cases involving same-sex marriages.[37] In 2015, the Supreme Court granted certiorari in four same-sex marriage cases.[38] If the Supreme Court fails to rule in these cases that all states must allow same-sex couples to wed, people who are considered the same sex will continue to be barred from marrying in some states.

Even if the Supreme Court mandates same-sex marriage in all states, sex determination will still be important because public spaces including restrooms, dressing rooms, and locker rooms remain segregated by sex. In addition, state universities and prisons determine housing based on a person's sex.

---

29 *See*, Romer v. Evans, 517 U.S. 620 (1996); United States v. Windsor, 133 S.Ct. 2675 (2013).

30 *See, e.g.*, U.S. Dep't of Agric. v. Moreno, 413 U.S. 528, 534 (1973); Cleburne v. Cleburne Living Ctr., 473 U.S. 432 (1985); Romer, 517 U.S. 620; United States v. Windsor, 133 S.Ct. 2675.

31 The lawsuit against the government actor would be brought as a § 1983 claim. 42 U.S.C. § 1983.

32 Until recently, the government also treated men and women differently in terms of military rights and responsibilities. The government had banned women from serving in combat positions in the military and women are excluded from selective service registration requirements. *See*, Military Selective Service Act, 50 U.S.C. §§471–73. In 2013, the Pentagon removed the combat exclusion. Elizabeth Bumiller & Thom Shanker, *Pentagon Is Set to Lift Combat Ban for Women*, N.Y. TIMES, Jan. 23, 2013 http://www.nytimes.com/2013/01/24/us/pentagon-says-it-is-lifting-ban-on-women-in-combat.html?pagewanted=all&_r=0.

33 For an updated analysis of the states that prohibit same-sex marriages, *see* Freedom to Marry, http://www.freedomtomarry.org/states/.

34 1 U.S.C. § 7 (1997).

35 United States v. Windsor, 133 S.Ct. 2675 (2013).

36 Hollingsworth v. Perry, 133 S.Ct. 2652 (2013). The Court did not address the validity of California's Proposition 8 same-sex marriage ban because it ruled that the Proposition 8 proponents lacked standing to bring the appeal to the Ninth Circuit and the Supreme Court. *Id.* at 2668.

37 Many More Same-Sex marriages Soon, but Where?, http://www.scotusblog.com/2014/10/many-more-same-sex-marriages-soon-but-where/.

38 Obergefell v. Hodges, 135 S.Ct 1039 (2015); Tanco v. Haslam, 135 S.Ct. 1040 (2015); DeBoer v. Snyder, 135 S.Ct. 1040 (2015); Bourke v. Beshear, 135 S.Ct. 1041 (2015).

As long as state laws continue to differentiate between men and women, legal institutions will be required to determine exactly what makes a man a man and what makes a woman a woman. Thus far, state legislatures have failed to include tests for determining a person's sex in their marriage statutes. Instead, they have left it to the courts to determine a person's legal sex when a marriage is challenged based upon a person's inability to qualify as a husband or wife.[39] In other areas, such as restroom use, some states have proposed specific "sex" tests for purposes of determining access to sex-segregated facilities.[40] When courts and legislatures create tests for establishing a person's legal sex, the tests must not violate the right to Equal Protection.

Government Tests that Determine whether Someone Qualifies as a Man or a Woman are Sex Classification Systems that Must Survive Intermediate Level Scrutiny under the Equal Protection Clause

When courts or legislatures establish a person's legal sex, they are creating a sex classification system. To pass constitutional scrutiny, such tests should be subjected to heightened scrutiny because the government is establishing a sex-based classification system.[41]

Since the 1970s, transgender people have argued that state sex classification systems that ignore a person's gender self-identity violate the Equal Protection Clause.[42] In the early cases, the courts inappropriately analyzed whether individuals who "change their sex" are entitled to a heightened level of scrutiny as a suspect class.[43] These courts universally determined that transsexuals were not a suspect class and thus government classifications systems that treated transsexuals as their birth sex, as opposed to the sex that accords with their gender identity, did not violate the Equal Protection Clause under rational basis review.[44]

The courts in these early cases were not focusing on the appropriate issue. The critical question to ask is not whether the discriminated-against group is suspect; it is whether the state is employing a classification

---

39 Although no state statute limiting marriage to one man and one woman addresses whether transgender people are allowed to marry in accord with their natal sex as opposed to their current gender self-identity, a majority of states have adopted statutes allowing transgender people to amend their birth records to reflect their gender self-identity. Drbecky.com, http://www.drbecky.com/birthcert.html (last visited Mar. 31, 2014). An amended birth certificate cannot necessarily be used to determine the right to marry. Some courts have looked to the sex on the birth certificate to determine a transgender person's legal sex for purposes of marriage. *See, e.g.*, Radtke v. Misc. Drivers and Helpers Union Local 638, 2012 WL 1094452 (D. Minn. 2012); *In re* Lovo-Lara, 23 I. & N. Dec. 746, 752 (2005), 2005 WL 1181062; *In re* Ladrach, 513 N.E.2d 828, 831 (Ohio Probate 1987) ("It seems obvious to the court that if a state permits such a change of sex on the birth certificate of a post-operative transsexual, either by statute or administrative ruling, then a marriage license, if requested, must issue to such a person provided all other statutory requirements are fulfilled.") *Id.* Other state courts have ruled that the sex designated on the birth certificate does not necessarily determine the person's ability to marry in that gender role. *See, e.g.*, *In re* Nash, 2003 WL 23097095 (Ohio Ct. App. Dec. 31, 2003); *In re* Estate of Gardiner, 42 P.3d 120 (Kan. 2002).

40 Proposed bills in Florida and Texas regarding bathroom and locker rooms access determine sex in terms of the sex identified at birth. http://www.myfloridahouse.gov/Sections/Documents/loaddoc.aspx?FileName=_h0583__.docx&DocumentType=Bill&BillNumber=0583&Session=2015. Texas further defines birth sex in terms of chromosomes, http://www.legis.state.tx.us/tlodocs/84R/billtext/pdf/HB01748I.pdf#navpanes=0.

41 A comparison to race classification systems illustrates why these classification systems should be subjected to heightened scrutiny. When states had statutes prohibiting mixed-race marriages, they needed to establish the race of each spouse to determine whether the marriage was of two people of the same race or of different races. If the state adopted the "one drop" rule as its race test, no one would argue that such a test was not a race-based classification system subject to strict scrutiny. Similarly, when the state adopts a test for determining whether two people are of different sexes, such a test is a sex-based classification and should be subjected to intermediate scrutiny.

42 The sex tests discussed in this section may violate other constitutional mandates as well. For a thorough discussion of all the constitutional implications of these rulings, including Full Faith and Credit, the dormant Commerce Clause and the right to travel, *see* Greenberg & Herald, *supra* note 20.

43 *See, e.g.*, Holloway v. Arthur Andersen & Co., 566 F. 2d 659, 663 (9th Cir. 1977); G.B. v. Lackner, 145 Cal.Rptr. 555, 568 (Cal. Ct. App. 1978) (Scott, J., dissenting); Terry v. E.E.O.C, No. CIV.A.80-C-408, 1980 WL 334 at *3 (E.D. Wis. 1980); Doe v. Postal Service, No. CIV.A.84–3296, 1985 WL 9446 at *4 (D.D.C. 1985).

44 *See, e.g.*, Holloway v. Arthur Andersen & Co., 566 F. 2d 659, 663 (9th Cir. 1977); G.B. v. Lackner, 145 Cal.Rptr. 555, 568 (Cal. Ct. App. 1978) (Scott, J., dissenting); Terry v. E.E.O.C, No. CIV.A.80-C-408, 1980 WL 334 at *3 (E.D. Wis. 1980); Doe v. Postal Serv., No. CIV.A.84–3296, 1985 WL 9446 at *4 (D.D.C. 1985).

system that is suspect. The appropriate level of scrutiny to apply should not be based on whether people who "change their sex" have been determined to be a "suspect group"; it should be based upon whether the state is creating a suspect classification system.[45]

For example, if a state determines that a person with female-appearing genitalia and breasts is a male because she has XY (male) chromosomes, the state is establishing a chromosomal test for determining sex. Such a test must survive heightened scrutiny under the Equal Protection Clause. An analysis of the scenario presented to the court in Kansas[46] illustrates why these determinations should be treated as sex-based classifications subject to intermediate scrutiny. J'Noel Gardiner, a male-to-female transgender person, amended her Wisconsin birth certificate and other official documents to indicate that she is a female. When J'Noel wanted Kansas to recognize her Wisconsin birth certificate and treat her as a female for purposes of determining the validity of her marriage, the Kansas court refused to do so. To reach this conclusion, the court needed to establish a test to determine whether J'Noel qualified as a male or a female.

In reaching its conclusion that J'Noel was legally a man, the court relied on Webster's dictionary to determine J'Noel's sex. According to the court:

> Webster's New Twentieth Century Dictionary (2nd ed.1970) states ... "[m]ale" is defined as "designating or of the sex that fertilizes the ovum and begets offspring: opposed to *female*." "Female" is defined as "designating or of the sex that produces ova and bears offspring: opposed to *male*."[47]

Under this test, the court determined that J'Noel was a male.[48] If instead, the Kansas court had been asked to determine the legal sex of Jennifer, a woman born in Wisconsin and identified as a female at birth, Kansas would have recognized Jennifer's status as a female, even if Jennifer had been unable to bear children. In both scenarios, Kansas would be creating rules to establish who qualifies as a woman to determine who is entitled to become a legal wife. It would thus be creating a sex-based classification system that is valid only if it satisfies intermediate scrutiny.

Under intermediate scrutiny, the state must establish an important or exceedingly persuasive justification for its classification system[49] and the chosen definition may not be based on administrative convenience or stereotypes of what it means to be a "real" woman.[50]

Rules that Bar Transgender People or People with an Intersex Condition from Marrying in the Gender Role that Comports with their Gender Self-Identity Violate the Equal Protection Clause

The state's interest in creating marriage sex tests is not important or exceedingly persuasive If states are allowed to limit marriage to one man and one woman,[51] they will also need to establish a test for determining who qualifies as a man or a woman if one of the spouses is transgender or has an intersex condition.[52] A number

45 *See, e.g.*, William N. Eskridge, *Effects of Identity-Based Social Movements on Constitutional Law in the Twentieth Century*, 100 MICH. L. REV. 2062 (2002).

46 *In re* Estate of Gardiner, 42 P.3d 120, 133 (Kan. 2002).

47 *Id.* at 135.

48 Ironically, under this test J'Noel and the millions of other people who are infertile and can neither bear nor beget would be determined to be neither male nor female. In the United States, approximately 6.1 million women, or about 10 percent of the female reproductive age population, are infertile. *Infertility Fact Sheet*, Women'sHealth.Gov, http://www.womenshealth.gov/publications/our-publications/fact-sheet/infertility.cfm#a (last visited Aug. 7, 2013).

49 United States v. Virginia, 518 U.S. 515, 524 (1996).

50 *Id.*

51 The author believes that government prohibitions against same-sex marriage should be declared unconstitutional. Although the United States Supreme Court had the opportunity to address this issue in Hollingsworth v. Perry, 133 S.Ct. 2652 (2013), it declined to do so and dismissed the case for lack of standing. The Court has agreed to address state prohibitions against same-sex marriage this term. *See*, Obergefell v. Hodges, 135 S.Ct 1039 (2015); Tanco v. Haslam, 135 S.Ct. 1040 (2015); DeBoer v. Snyder, 135 S.Ct. 1040 (2015); Bourke v. Beshear, 135 S.Ct. 1041 (2015).

52 In addition to marriage and sex-segregated facilities discussed in this chapter, a person's sex may be relevant in determining their right to participate in athletic events as a female. This issue involves Equal Protection principles if the

of courts have established tests for determining a person's sex for purposes of marriage. These cases all involved marriages in which one of the spouses was transgender.[53]

A California trial court,[54] a New Jersey Appellate Court,[55] a federal district court interpreting Minnesota law,[56] and an immigration court interpreting North Carolina law[57] ruled that the transgender spouses had legally changed their sex and that their unions were valid marriages.[58] The Supreme Court of Kansas,[59] the Court of Appeal of Florida,[60] the Court of Appeals of Texas,[61] the Court of Appeals of Ohio,[62] the Appellate Court of Illinois,[63] and two lower courts in New York[64] ruled that the sex assigned at birth had not changed and the marriages involving transgender spouses were invalid. In reaching these decisions, the courts relied on chromosomal makeup,[65] reproductive capacity,[66] and religious references[67] to determine a person's legal sex.

In the cases that refused to recognize the transgender spouses' self-identified gender as their legal sex for purposes of marriage, the courts relied on three purported state interests to justify their rulings: (1) the state's public policy against same-sex marriage,[68] (2) the inability of a post-operative transgender person to engage in procreative intercourse,[69] and (3) the inability of a state to change the sex fixed by "our Creator."[70]

Although few courts have expressly relied on their public policy against same-sex marriages, the courts that have denied the right of transgender people to marry in the role that comports with their gender self-

---

state is establishing the sex classification system for athletic events.

53 No cases in the United States have involved a spouse with an intersex condition. The validity of a marriage involving a spouse with an intersex condition has been litigated in England, W v. W, [2001] Fam. 111 (Eng.) and Australia, *In the Marriage of C. and D. (falsely called C.)* (1979) 35 F.L.R. 340, *overruled* by Attorney Gen. v. Kevin (2003) 172 F.L.R. 300. In *W v. W*, the court conducted an analysis similar to the analysis the courts have conducted in cases involving a transgender spouse. Whether courts in the United States would apply the same "sex tests" as they apply in cases involving a transgender spouse to cases involving a spouse with an intersex condition is unclear. Only two courts in the United States that had been asked to determine the legal sex of a transgender person have referred to people with an intersex condition. In both cases, the courts acknowledged that they may need to modify the "sex test" they applied to the transgender spouses if they are asked to determine the legal sex of a person with an intersex condition. The courts declined to establish a rule for people with an intersex condition because the issue had not been presented to the court. *See*, *In re* Estate of Gardiner, 42 P.3d 120, 133 (Kan. 2002); Littleton v. Prange, 9 S.W.3d 223, 232 (Tex. App. 1999) (Angelini, J., concurring).

54 Vecchione v. Vecchione, Civ. No 96D003769, reported in L.A. Daily J., Nov. 26, 1997, at 1.

55 M.T. v. J.T., 355 A.2d 204 (N.J. Super. Ct. App. Div 1976).

56 Radtke v. Misc. Drivers and Helpers Union Local 638, 2012 WL 1094452 (D. Minn. 2012).

57 *In re* Lovo-Lara, 23 I. & N. Dec. 746, 752 (2005), 2005 WL 1181062.

58 In addition to these four courts, an appellate court in Kansas and a Florida trial court also ruled that transgender people could legally change their sex and marry in the sex role that comports with their gender self-identity. These two decisions were reversed on appeal. *See*, *In re* Estate of Gardiner, 22 P.3d 1086 (Kan. Ct. App. 2001); *rev'd* 42 P.3d 120, 135 (Kan. 2002); *In re* Marriage of Kantaras v. Kantaras, No. 98–5375CA (Fla. Cir. Ct. Feb 21, 2003), *available at* http://www.transgenderlaw.org/cases/kantarasopinion.pdf *rev'd* Kantaras v. Kantaras, 884 So.2d 155 (Fla. Dist. Ct. App. 2004).

59 *In re* Estate of Gardiner, 42 P.3d 120 (Kan. 2002).

60 Kantaras v. Kantaras, 884 So.2d 155 (Fla. Dist. Ct. App. 2004).

61 Littleton v. Prange, 9 S.W.3d 223 (Tex. App. 1999).

62 *In re* Nash, 2003 WL 23097095 (Ohio Ct. App. Dec. 31, 2003). An Ohio probate court reached a similar result. *In re* Ladrach, 513 N.E.2d 828 (Ohio Probate 1987).

63 *In re* Marriage of Simmons, 825 N.E.2d 303 (Ill. App. 2005).

64 Anonymous v. Anonymous, 325 N.Y.S.2d 499 (Sup. Ct. 1971); B v. B, 355 N.Y.S.2d 712 (N.Y. Sup. Ct. 1974).

65 *See, e.g.*, Littleton v. Prange, 9 S.W.3d 223, 231 (Tex. App. 1999).

66 *See, e.g.*, *In re* Estate of Gardiner, 42 P.3d 120, 135 (Kan. 2002); Anonymous v. Anonymous, 325 N.Y.S.2d 499 (Sup. Ct. 1971); B v. B, 355 N.Y.S.2d 712 (N.Y. Sup. Ct. 1974).

67 *See, e.g.*, Littleton v. Prange, 9 S.W.3d 223, 231 (Tex. App. 1999).

68 *See, e.g.*, *In re* Nash, 2003 WL 23097095 at *5–7 (Ohio Ct. App. Dec. 31, 2003); *In re* Marriage of Simmons, 825 N.E.2d 303, 308 (Ill. App. 2005); Littleton v. Prange, 9 S.W.3d 223, 230 (Tex. App. 1999); Kantaras v. Kantaras, 884 So.2d 155, 161 (Fla. Dist. Ct. App. 2004); *In re* Estate of Gardiner, 42 P.3d 120, 135–37 (Kan. 2002).

69 *See, e.g.*, *In re* Estate of Gardiner, 42 P.3d 120, 135 (Kan. 2002); *In re* Nash, 2003 WL 23097095 at *6 (Ohio Ct. App. Dec. 31, 2003); B v. B, 355 N.Y.S.2d 712, 717 (N.Y. Sup. Ct. 1974; Anonymous v. Anonymous, 325 N.Y.S.2d 499, 500 (Sup. Ct. 1971).

70 *See, e.g.*, Littleton v. Prange, 9 S.W.3d 223, 223 (Tex. App. 1999).

identity have all cited their state's law prohibiting marriages of two people of the same sex.[71] At least one court has expressly used its view on same-sex marriage to justify denying a female-to-male transgender person the right to marry as a man.[72] In *In re Nash*, Jacob Nash's birth certificate indicated that he was a male, but the Ohio Court of Appeals concluded that the state was not obligated to issue a marriage license to Jacob and his future wife because the state would then be issuing a marriage license to a same-sex couple.[73]

In other words, the Ohio court decided to ignore the sex designation on Jacob's amended birth certificate and instead determined that Jacob was female. The Ohio court's reasoning on this matter was circular. A court cannot use a public policy against same-sex marriage to invalidate a marriage until after it determines the sex of the parties. Jacob's marriage is a same-sex marriage only if he is legally a woman. Whether Jacob is a man or a woman for purposes of marriage depends upon how the state determines a person's sex. Thus, Ohio's public policy against same-sex marriage could not be used to determine Jacob's sex.

A few courts have focused on the inability of transgender people to engage in procreative sexual intercourse.[74] The Kansas Supreme Court focused on the inability of transgender people to reproduce offspring when it invalidated a marriage in which the wife was transgender.[75] The court created a sex classification system that relied on dictionary definitions of sex. The dictionary provided that males are the sex that fertilize the ovum and beget offspring and females are the sex that produce ova and bear offspring.[76] This justification is unlikely to survive even rational relationship review under the Equal Protection Clause because no state requires proof of fertility as a condition of marriage.[77] Furthermore, because transgender people who have undergone surgery and hormonal treatment can neither bear nor beget, reliance upon the ability to reproduce implies that transgender people are neither males nor females and thus would be barred from marrying anyone. Denying transgender people the right to marry because of their infertility violates their fundamental right to marry.[78]

One state, Texas, refused to treat a male-to-female transgender person as a woman by ruling that medicine and law cannot change the sex that was "immutably fixed by our Creator at birth."[79] State actions based

71 *See, e.g., In re* Nash, 2003 WL 23097095 at *6 (Ohio Ct. App. Dec. 31, 2003); *In re* Estate of Gardiner, 42 P.3d 120, 135 (Kan. 2002); Kantaras v. Kantaras, 884 So.2d 155, 157 (Fla. Dist. Ct. App. 2004).

72 *In re* Nash, 2003 WL 23097095 (Ohio Ct. App. Dec. 31, 2003).

73 *Id.* at *5.

74 In discussing sexual intercourse, some courts focused on the procreative aspect of the marital relationship. *See, e.g., In re* Estate of Gardiner, 42 P.3d 120 (Kan. 2002). Other courts also discussed the capacity to engage in penetrative sexual intercourse. *See, e.g.,* B v. B, 355 N.Y.S.2d 712 (N.Y. Sup. Ct. 1974). Although the court in *B. v. B.* discussed the transgender husband's inability to engage in sexual intercourse, the court linked this inability to the husband's lack of procreative capacity. The court stated,

> [D]efendant "does not have male sexual organs, does not possess a normal penis, and in fact does not have a penis." Apparently, hormone treatments and surgery have not succeeded in supplying the necessary apparatus to enable defendant to *function as a man for purposes of procreation* (emphasis added). In the same way surgery has not reached that point that can provide a man with something resembling a normal female sexual organ, transplanting ovaries or a womb. Those are still beyond reach. *Id.* at 717.

The final reference to ovaries and a womb indicates that the court's key concern was procreative ability because a transgender woman with a vagina can engage in penetrative intercourse, but she is not capable of bearing children. In contrast, when the New Jersey court treated a male-to-female transgender person as the legal wife, it did consider her ability to engage in sexual intercourse unrelated to reproductive ability. M.T. v. J.T., 355 A.2d 204, 209–10 (N.J. Super. Ct. App. Div 1976).

75 *See, e.g., In re* Estate of Gardiner, 42 P.3d 120 (Kan. 2002). Courts in Florida and Ohio cited this portion of the Gardiner decision with approval in reaching the same conclusion. Kantaras v. Kantaras, 884 So.2d 155, 159 (Fla. Dist. Ct. App. 2004); *In re* Nash, 2003 WL 23097095 at *6 (Ohio Ct. App. Dec. 31, 2003).

76 *Gardiner*, 42 P.3d at 1351.

77 Although reproductive capacity is not a prerequisite to marriage, whether marriage is an institution linked to procreative capacity is still being debated. Justice Alito, in his dissenting opinion in *United States v. Windsor*, 133 S.Ct. 2675 (2013) (Alito, J. dissenting) stated his belief that the Court should not resolve whether marriage should be "viewed as an exclusively opposite-sex institution and as one inextricably linked to procreation and biological kinship" as opposed to a "consent-based institution marked by strong emotional attachment and sexual attraction." *Id.* at 2716.

78 *See, e.g.,* Zablocki v. Redhail, 434 U.S. 374, 384 (1978) (involving a prison inmate's right to marry); Loving v. Virginia, 388 U.S. 1, 12 (1967) (involving a mixed-race couple's right to marry).

79 Littleton v. Prange, 9 S.W.3d 223, 223 (Tex. App. 1999).

solely on religious justifications are unconstitutional.[80] States cannot use religion to justify their actions in the absence of a neutral secular basis for their decisions.[81] Vague religious references cannot qualify as an important government interest under the Equal Protection Clause.[82]

Refusing to recognize people's self-identified sex as their legal sex for purposes of marriage based on reproductive incapacity or religious references cannot be considered important or exceedingly persuasive justifications that can withstand equal protection intermediate level scrutiny. It is also questionable whether they would even be considered legitimate state interests under the lower level rational basis analysis.[83] Until the United States Supreme Court resolves the issue, states could continue to argue that the state's interest in limiting marriage to one man and one woman qualifies as an important state interest.[84] Courts cannot use the state's interest in limiting marriage to heterosexual unions, however, to determine that transgender people are barred from marrying in the gender role that matches their self-identity. Instead, the court must establish a "sex test" that is substantially related to the state's interest in limiting marriages to one man and one woman.

Marriage sex tests that rely on chromosomal analysis and reproductive incapacity are not substantially related to an important government interest In the event that a court finds that any of the state interests discussed above qualify as important government interests, the court must still examine the means the state uses to accomplish the government's goal.[85] To pass intermediate scrutiny, the means used must be substantially related to the important government goal and cannot be based on gender stereotypes.[86]

Courts are divided about the test to use to determine a person's legal sex. Some jurisdictions focus on gender self-identity while other jurisdictions rule that transgender people forever remain the sex assigned to them at birth.

Jurisdictions that emphasize gender self-identity as the only factor or the critical factor for determining a person's legal sex for purposes of marriage rely on scientific developments regarding sex and gender formation. These jurisdictions acknowledge that a number of factors could be used to determine a person's sex, including chromosomes, gonads, internal reproductive organs, hormones, phenotype, assigned sex, and gender self-identity.[87] In focusing on gender self-identity, these jurisdictions recognize the complex nature of sex and gender formation and their court decisions reflect current scientific knowledge on the subject.

---

80 Gillette v. United States, 401 U.S. 437, 452 (1971); Bob Jones Univ. v. United States, 461 U.S. 574, 604 (1983); Webster v. Reproductive Health Serv., 492 U.S. 490, 566 (1989).

81 *Id.*

82 McCreary County, Ky. v. ACLU of Ky., 545 U.S. 844, 881 (2005) (the Establishment Clause requires the "Government to stay neutral on religious belief, which is reserved for the conscience of the individual").

83 *See infra* notes 105–16 and accompanying text.

84 The likelihood that such arguments will be successful has diminished after the Supreme Court's ruling in *United States v Windsor*, 133 S.Ct. 2675 (2013). In *Windsor*, the Court ruled that federal laws could not grant federal benefits to opposite-sex married couples and deny legally married same-sex couples the same rights. Justice Scalia, in his *Windsor* dissent, addressed whether the Court's ruling could be used to strike down state laws prohibiting same-sex couples from marrying. *Id.* at 2709–11 (Scalia, J., dissenting). "[T]he real rationale of today's opinion … is that DOMA is motivated by a "'bare … desire to harm'" couples in same-sex marriages (citation omitted). How easy it is, indeed how inevitable, to reach the same conclusion with regard to state laws denying same-sex couples marital status. *Id.* at 2709. Since the Supreme Court's decision in *Windsor*, almost every court that has considered the issue has determined that same-sex marriage bans are unconstitutional. Freedom to Marry, http://www.freedomtomarry.org/pages/marriage-rulings-in-the-courts.

85 For purposes of this analysis, this section presumes that the state has a valid interest in engaging in sex assignment. As discussed above, it is questionable whether any state interest articulated thus far could be considered important or exceedingly persuasive.

86 United States v. Virginia, 518 U.S. 515, 524 (1996).

87 *See, e.g.,*Radtke v. Misc. Drivers and Helpers Union Local 638, 2012 WL 1094452 (D. Minn. 2012); *In re* Lovo-Lara, 23 I. & N. Dec. 746, 752 (2005), 2005 WL 1181062; M.T. v. J.T., 355 A.2d 204 (N.J. Super. Ct. App. Div 1976); *In re* Estate of Gardiner, 22 P.3d 1086 (Kan. Ct. App. 2001); *rev'd* 42 P.3d 120, 135 (Kan. 2002); *In re* Marriage of Kantaras v. Kantaras, No. 98–5375CA (Fla. Cir. Ct. Feb 21, 2003), *available at* http://www.transgenderlaw.org/cases/kantarasopinion.pdf, *rev'd* Kantaras v. Kantaras, 884 So.2d 155 (Fla. Dist. Ct. App. 2004); Attorney General v. Kevin, (2003) 172 F.L.R 300.

Studies support the finding that transgenderism has a biological basis.[88] More important, standard medical protocol recognizes that there is no "cure" for transgenderism; the appropriate treatment for transgender people is to facilitate their wellbeing in their gender self-identity. Experts recommend that transgender individuals live in their self-identified gender role.[89]

Courts and legislatures in jurisdictions that understand the nature of transgenderism have recognized the right of transgender people to have their gender self-identity legally recognized. For example, in 2002, the European Court of Human Rights ruled that states that deny transgender people the right to be recognized as their self-identified sex violate Article 8 (relating to the right to privacy) and Article 12 (relating to the right to marry and found a family) of the European Convention for the Protection of Human Rights and Fundamental Freedoms.[90] In 2004, the European Court of Justice issued a similar ruling.[91] In 2004, Great Britain, which for decades had been one of the countries that provided sparse protection to transgender people, passed sweeping legislation to provide them legal rights that recognize and protect their ability to be legally recognized as their self-identified sex.[92] A number of courts in the United States have adopted this approach.[93]

Other jurisdictions in the United States, however, have rejected gender self-identity as the test to determine a person's legal sex for purposes of marriage and instead have ruled that transgender people remain the sex assigned

88 Jiang-Ning Zhou et al., *A Sex Difference in the Human Brain and Its Relation to Transsexuality*, 378 Nature 68 (1995). Frank Kruijver et.al, *Male to Female Transsexual Individuals Have Female Neuron Numbers in the Central Subdivision of the Bed Nucleus of the Stria Terminals*, 85 J. of Clin. Endocrinology and Metabolism 2034 (2000).

89 *The Harry Benjamin International Gender Dysphoria Association's Standards Of Care For Gender Identity Disorders, Sixth Version*, World Prof. Ass'n for Transgender Health, http://www.wpath.org/documents2/socv6.pdf (last visited Aug. 7, 2013). ("The Overarching Treatment Goal … of psychotherapeutic, endocrine, or surgical therapy for persons with gender identity disorders is lasting personal comfort with the gendered self in order to maximize overall psychological well-being and self-fulfillment"). *Id.* at 1. The recently released fifth edition of the Diagnostic and Statistical Manual of Mental Disorders (DSM-V) uses the term "gender dysphoria" rather than the term "gender identity disorder" to recognize that an incongruence between people's natal sex and their gender self-identity do not indicate a disordered condition. The DSM-V and the American Psychiatric Association support medical transition for individuals with gender dysphoria. They recognize that some transgender individuals may feel distress from the incongruence between their experienced gender and their assigned gender. By adopting the term "gender dysphoria" the DSM-V clearly recognizes that transgender people do not have an identity problem that must be treated; rather if their gender identity causes them distress, it is the distress that must be addressed. Am. Psychiatric Ass'n Diagnostic and Statistical Manual of Mental Disorders 451 (5th ed. 2013).

90 *See, e.g.*, Case of I. v. United Kingdom [Eur. Ct of H.R. 2002] 36 E.H.R.R. 53; Goodwin v. United Kingdom [Eur. Ct. of H.R. 2002] 35 E.H.R.R. 18.

91 Case C-117/01, K.B. v. Nat'l Health Serv. Pensions Agency, 2004 E.C.R. I-541.

92 *See* Gender Recognition Act, 2004, Eliz. II, c. 7 (Eng.). Courts in other countries have also adopted this approach. *See, e.g.*, Attorney General v. Kevin, (2003) 172 F.L.R 300 (Australia) and Attorney General v. Otahuhu Family Court, [1991] SLR Lexis 184 (New Zealand).

93 *See, e.g.*, M.T. v. J.T., 355 A.2d 204 (N.J. Super. Ct. App. Div 1976); Vecchione v. Vecchione, Civ. No 96D003769, reported in L.A. Daily J., Nov. 26, 1997, at 1 (California); *In re* Estate of Gardiner, 22 P.3d 1086 (Kan. Ct. App. 2001); *rev'd* 42 P.3d 120, 135 (Kan. 2002); *In re* Marriage of Kantaras v. Kantaras, No. 98–5375CA (Fla. Cir. Ct. Feb 21, 2003), *available at* http://www.transgenderlaw.org/cases/kantarasopinion.pdf, *rev'd* Kantaras v. Kantaras, 884 So.2d 155 (Fla. Dist. Ct. App. 2004); Radtke v. Misc. Drivers and Helpers Union Local 638, 2012 WL 1094452 (D. Minn. 2012); *In re* Lovo-Lara, 23 I. & N. Dec. 746, 752 (2005), 2005 WL 1181062. In *Radtke*, a federal district court determined that Minnesota would allow transgender people to marry in the role that comports with their gender self-identity. The court looked at the transgender spouse's anatomical and hormonal features as well as the sex designated on the birth certificate and other official documents, which had been amended. The court concluded that "[i]t would be wholly inappropriate for this Court to invent a narrow federal definition of 'sex' based on the sex assigned at birth and impose that construction on a Minnesota statute." *Id.* at *9. Similarly, in *Lovo-Lara*, an immigration court was asked to determine whether a marriage involving a transgender spouse was a legal marriage. The court ruled that North Carolina state law controlled and held that the marriage was a legal heterosexual marriage based on scientific studies regarding sex formation as well as North Carolina's statute that allowed sex amendments on birth certificates. *In re* Lovo-Lara, 23 I. & N. Dec. 746, 752 (2005), 2005 WL 1181062.

to them at birth.[94] To reach this conclusion, the courts relied on biological factors,[95] including chromosomes,[96] the absence of internal reproductive organs,[97] and the inability to reproduce.[98] To be constitutional under the Equal Protection Clause, the state must prove that its sex text—chromosomes, the absence of internal sex organs, or the inability to reproduce—accomplishes the important interest articulated by the state.

As discussed in the previous section, courts have asserted that three interests justify their refusal to recognize people's self-identified sex as their legal sex for purposes of marriage: (1) reproductive incapacity, (2) religious references, and (3) maintaining marriage as a heterosexual union of one man and one woman. The first two articulated state interests, reproductive capacity and religious references cannot be considered important or for that matter legitimate state interests.[99]

If the Supreme Court allows states to continue to bar same-sex couples from marrying, states may continue to argue that the state's interest in limiting marriage to one man and one woman qualifies as an important state interest.[100] But the tests that the courts have used to determine a person's sex do not pass equal protection scrutiny because they are not substantially related to the articulated state interest in deterring same-sex marriages. Some jurisdictions that have ruled that post-operative male-to-female transgender people are still males for the purposes of marriage are allowing post-operative male-to-female transgender people to marry women. In other words, two individuals who both appear to be women (even when they are undressed) are now legally allowed to marry each other in these jurisdictions that otherwise ban same-sex marriages.[101]

---

94 *See, e.g.*, *In re* Nash, 2003 WL 23097095 at *5–7 (Ohio Ct. App. Dec. 31, 2003); Littleton v. Prange, 9 S.W.3d 223, 230 (Tex. App. 1999); Kantaras v. Kantaras, 884 So.2d 155, 161 (Fla. Dist. Ct. App. 2004); *In re* Estate of Gardiner, 42 P.3d 120, 135–37 (Kan. 2002). Some courts that have ruled that a transgender person remains the sex assigned at birth have stated that they do not have the power to establish a test for determining a person's legal sex. They have concluded that it is the legislature's role to make such a determination and in the absence of legislative action specifically authorizing transgender people to change their sex, the court could not act. *See*, *In re* Nash, 2003 WL 23097095 at *6 (Ohio Ct. App. Dec. 31, 2003); Littleton v. Prange, 9 S.W.3d 223, 230 (Tex. App. 1999); Kantaras v. Kantaras, 884 So.2d 155, 161 (Fla. Dist. Ct. App. 2004); *In re* Estate of Gardiner, 42 P.3d 120, 135 (Kan. 2002). When a court concludes that transgender people must remain the sex assigned on their original birth certificate because the legislature has not specifically addressed this issue, the court has established a sex test. The court's sex test is that people are the sex assigned to them at birth. Such a test must pass Equal Protection scrutiny.

95 The court in *In re* Marriage of Simmons, 825 N.E.2d 303, 308 (Ill. App. 2005) relied on biological factors, but did not state which biological factors should be used to determine sex. The court implied that the court would recognize a sex change for purposes of marriage if the person undergoes the proper medical treatment. The court stated, "while he has undergone surgeries to remove his internal female organs, he still possesses all of his external female genitalia and requires additional surgeries before sex reassignment can be considered completed." *Id.* at 309.

96 *See, e.g.*, Littleton v. Prange, 9 S.W.3d 223, 230 (Tex. App. 1999); Kantaras v. Kantaras, 884 So.2d 155, 161 (Fla. Dist. Ct. App. 2004); *In re* Estate of Gardiner, 42 P.3d 120, 135 (Kan. 2002). Some decisions do not specifically mention chromosomes; instead the court refers to "immutable traits determined at birth." *See, e.g.*, Kantaras v. Kantaras, 884 So.2d 155, 161 (Fla. Dist. Ct. App. 2004). The only immutable sex trait is chromosomes. All other sex and reproductive aspects can be surgically and hormonally altered.

97 In Littleton v. Prange, 9 S.W.3d 223 (Tex. App. 1999), the court listed seven factors that supported its conclusion that Christie Littleton, a male-to-female transgender person, was not legally a male. One of the factors was the absence of female internal sexual organs. "Through surgery and hormones, a transsexual male can be made to look like a woman, including female genitalia and breasts. Transsexual medical treatment, however, does not create the internal sexual organs of a women (except for the vaginal canal). There is no womb, cervix or ovaries in the post-operative transsexual female." *Id.* at 230.

98 *See, e.g.*, *In re* Nash, 2003 WL 23097095 at *6 (Ohio Ct. App. Dec. 31, 2003); *In re* Estate of Gardiner, 42 P.3d 120, 135 (Kan. 2002); Anonymous v. Anonymous, 325 N.Y.S.2d 499, 500 (Sup. Ct. 1971); B v. B, 355 N.Y.S.2d 712, 716 (N.Y. Sup. Ct. 1974).

99 *See supra* notes 74–82 and accompanying text.

100 The likelihood that this argument will be persuasive has diminished with recent court rulings. *See*, *supra*, n.84.

101 *See*, Todd Ackerman, *Marriage, A Changing Union? Transsexual Wedding Shows Gender Can be a Complex Issue*, Hous. Chron., Sept. 17, 2000, at 1; Chris Beam, *For Better or For Worse?*, Out, May 2000, at 60, 64; Afi-Odelia E. Scruggs, *Tying Legalities into Tangled Knot*, Plain Dealer (Cleveland), Oct. 7, 1996, at 1B. A male-to-female transsexual who identified as a lesbian and was in the process of undergoing surgical modification was allowed to marry another woman in Utah, a state that also bans same-sex marriage. See Michael Vigh, *Transsexual Weds Woman in Legally Recognized Union*, Salt Lake Trib., Feb. 5, 1999, at 1C.

These tests are also invalid because they rely on false sex stereotypes, which cannot be used to justify a state sex classification system.[102] When a state determines that it will classify only those individuals who are able to bear children, who have XX chromosomes, or who have a uterus and ovaries as women, it is engaging in impermissible sex stereotyping about what it means to be a "real" woman. These and other biologic tests effectively ignore scientific literature that clearly establishes that sex features are not binary and many people have incongruent sex attributes.[103]

Ability to reproduce, internal reproductive organs, and chromosomal structure are not more valid indicators of a person's sex than any other anatomical or physiological sex factors. For example, if a state adopted a sex determination test that defined men according to the size of their penis and women according to the size of their breasts, it would undoubtedly fail even the rational basis test. Although chromosomal make-up and ability to reproduce may be less variable than penis and breast size, courts relying on these sex indicators are still basing their determination on sex stereotypes. These stereotypes cannot be used to uphold a sex-based classification under the Equal Protection Clause. A sex classification system that rejects scientific developments in favor of stereotypes should be declared unconstitutional because the state can neither articulate an important state interest to support its system nor prove a substantial relationship between the state's interest and the means it uses to accomplish that interest.[104]

State sex classification systems that rely on chromosomal structure, the absence of internal sex organs, and reproductive incapacity to determine the validity of a marriage fail even rational basis scrutiny Even if a court were to determine that rational basis review is appropriate, states that have excluded scientific advances about sex and gender identity formation in favor of tests based solely on reproductive capacity, the absence of internal sex organs, or chromosomal structure would not pass rational basis scrutiny under recent U.S. Supreme Court equal protection jurisprudence. The United States Supreme Court's decisions in *Romer v. Evans*[105] and *United States v. Windsor*[106] suggest that, when examining laws purporting to violate the constitution under rational basis review, the Supreme Court may be moving toward affording greater protection to sexual minorities. Although the Court did not specifically rule that classifications harming sexual minorities should be subjected to heightened scrutiny, the court applied a more searching type of review in these cases. Some federal courts have interpreted the Court's decision in *Windsor* to require heightened scrutiny in cases involving classifications based on sexual orientation.[107]

In *Romer*, Colorado citizens voted to amend the Colorado Constitution to preclude all legislative, executive, or judicial action designed to protect the status of people based on their homosexual, lesbian or bisexual orientation, conduct, practices, or relationships. The Supreme Court found that this amendment violated the Equal Protection Clause because it imposed a broad and undifferentiated disability on a single group.[108] Furthermore, the Court found that the amendment was motivated by animus toward a particular group and it lacked a rational relationship to legitimate state interests. As the court stated: "[I]f the constitutional conception of 'equal protection of the laws' means anything, it must at the very least mean that a bare … desire to harm a politically unpopular group cannot constitute a legitimate governmental interest."[109]

The Court reinforced these principles in 2013, in *United States v. Windsor*, when it struck down DOMA, a federal law denying same-sex married couples federal rights granted to opposite-sex married couples. The

102 United States v. Virginia, 518 U.S. 515, 541–42 (1996) ("equal protection principles, as applied to gender classifications, mean state actors many not rely on 'overbroad' generalization to make 'judgments about people …'"). *Id.*

103 *See*, *Defining Male and Female*, *supra* note 3.

104 Even accurate stereotypes cannot be used to justify the state's interest. *See* United States v. Virginia, 518 U.S. 515, 542 (1996).

105 517 U.S. 620 (1996).

106 United States v. Windsor, 133 S.Ct. 2675 (2013).

107 *See*, *e.g.*, Smithkline Beecham Corp. v. Abbott Labs, 740 F.3d 471 (9th Cir. 2014). "*Windsor* review is not rational basis review. In its words and its deed, *Windsor* established a level of scrutiny for classifications based on sexual orientation that is unquestionably higher than rational basis review. In other words, *Windsor* requires that heightened scrutiny be applied to equal protection claims involving sexual orientation." *Id.* at 481.

108 *Romer*, 517 U.S. at 635–36.

109 *Id.* at 634.

Court found that in determining whether a law is motivated by an improper animus or purpose, the court must carefully consider "[d]iscriminations of an unusual character."[110]

Therefore, even when analyzed under the lowest standard of review, states that refuse to recognize the right of transgender people to marry in the role that matches their self-identified sex may violate equal protection guarantees. When a state defines "male" and "female" in a way that is contrary to current science and visits a broad disability on transgender people, the state's action appears to evidence a bare "desire to harm a politically unpopular group."[111] Furthermore, the state cannot justify its decision on its public policy disfavoring same-sex marriages because its sex determination ruling in effect sanctions what appears to be a same-sex marriage. For example, if J'Noel Gardiner, a male-to-female transgender person with breasts and female appearing genitalia, is legally allowed to marry another woman, to most of society it would appear to be a same-sex union.[112] Thus, no rational relationship exists between a state sex classification system that relies solely on chromosomes or ability to reproduce and its interest in limiting marriage to opposite-sex couples.

Refusing to allow transgender people to marry in the gender role in which they live indicates that the state action is based solely on an irrational animus against a discrete group. When a state denies transgender people the right to marry in their self-identified gender role, the state is inhibiting personal relationships and the denial suggests the intent to deny equal protection to a politically unpopular group. This type of animus has led the Supreme Court to strike down laws even under a rational basis level of review, concluding, for example, that the bare "desire to harm a politically unpopular group" was not a legitimate interest when it involved hippies,[113] people with a mental or emotional impairment,[114] or gays and lesbians.[115] Limiting transgender people's right to marry in accord with their gender identity appears "not to further a proper legislative end, but to make them unequal to everyone else."[116]

The rational basis test the Court applied in *Romer* and *Windsor* supports the conclusion that state classification systems that discriminate against individuals who fail to conform to chromosomal or reproductive gender norms are unconstitutional even under rational basis review. If these state classifications fail to survive rational basis review, they would clearly fail under the heightened level of scrutiny traditionally applied to sex and gender classifications.

Rules that Bar Transgender People or People with an Intersex Condition from Accessing the Restrooms, Locker Rooms, and Housing that Comports with Their Gender Self-Identity May Violate the Equal Protection Clause

Restrooms and locker rooms Recently, some states have proposed bills that would bar people from accessing single-sex facilities if the person was not born a "biological member of that sex."[117] According to a Florida bill, the state's interests in creating such legislation include protecting the public's expectation of privacy in single-sex facilities, protecting users from exposure to people of the "opposite sex," and protecting the

110 *Windsor*, 133 S. Ct. at 2692 (quoting Romer, 517 U.S. at 633).

111 *Windsor*, 133 S. Ct. at 2681 (quoting U.S. Dep't of Agric. v. Moreno, 413 U.S. 528, 534 (1973).

112 After the Texas decision in *Littleton v. Prange*, 9 S.W.3d 223 (Tex. App. 1999), two women, who to all outward appearances appear female, can now legally marry. *See, e.g.*, Todd Ackerman, *Marriage, a Changing Union? Transsexual Wedding Shows Gender Can be a Complex Issue*, Hous. Chron., Sept. 17, 2000, at 1.

113 *See, e.g.*, U.S. Dep't of Agric. v. Moreno, 413 U.S. 528, 534 (1973).

114 *See, e.g.*, Cleburne v. Cleburne Living Ctr., 473 U.S. 432 (1985).

115 *Romer*, 517 U.S. 620; *Windsor*, 133 S. Ct. 2675 (2013).

116 *Romer*, 517 U.S. at 635.

117 *See, e.g.*, Florida's proposed legislation. http://www.myfloridahouse.gov/Sections/Documents/loaddoc.aspx?FileName=_h0583__.docx&DocumentType=Bill&BillNumber=0583&Session=2015. Similar bills are also being considered in Texas, http://www.legis.state.tx.us/tlodocs/84R/billtext/pdf/HB01748I.pdf#navpanes=0, and Kentucky, http://www.lrc.ky.gov/record/15RS/sb76.htm. A comparable bill was considered in Arizona, but was withdrawn. These bills are being proposed in response to California passing a law that allows transgender students to use facilities and participate in programs that match their gender self-identity. *See*, Cal. Education Code § 221.5 (West 2015).

public in places of increased vulnerability where they could be subjected to assault, battery, molestation, rape, voyeurism, and exhibitionism.[118]

Assuming these purposes would qualify as "important" state interests,[119] the means the state is using to accomplish its goals would fail equal protection scrutiny because the means are not substantially related to the government's asserted interests. To accomplish its goal, Florida has proposed a test that establishes sex as the biological sex at birth.[120] In other words, all transgender people and people with an intersex condition whose sex was incorrectly identified at birth could be criminally and civilly liable for using the restroom or locker room that comports with their gender identity and appearance.[121] In a similar bill, Texas also proposed a "birth sex" standard, but defined birth sex in terms of chromosomes so that males include anyone with a Y chromosome and females exclude anyone with a Y chromosome.[122]

A biological birth sex test based on chromosomes or the sex indicated on the original birth certificate is not substantially related to the state's goal of protecting the public. First, such tests would mandate that some transgender and intersex people who appear male must use the women's restroom and some who appear female must use the men's restroom. It would also require transgender people who have undergone surgery so that their genitalia have a female appearance to use the men's locker room. Such results would not allay the privacy and vulnerability concerns of people who are not transgender or intersex.

More important, such legislation cannot survive equal protection scrutiny because it appears to be motivated by "a bare desire to harm a politically unpopular group." First, the legislation ignores the privacy and vulnerability concerns of the population that is most at risk; transgender people are repeatedly subjected to harassment, physical assault, and sexual violence.[123] In addition, by barring transgender people from appropriate sex-segregated facility use, it falsely implies that transgender people are more likely to engage in criminal acts such as assault, battery, molestation, rape, voyeurism, and exhibitionism. Such unsupported false stereotypes about people who fail to conform to gender norms cannot survive an equal protection challenge.

Dormitory housing College dormitory housing rules have undergone dramatic changes. Originally, males and females were housed in separate buildings. Over time, the rules were relaxed to allow men and women to share the same building, and then the same hall. Recently, some colleges have allowed students of different sexes to share the same room, but most colleges still require roommates to be of the "opposite" sex.[124]

Sex-segregated housing rules may be used to bar transgender students from living in housing that matches their gender self-identity.[125] If a state university with sex-segregated student housing refuses to allow a transgender student to choose the housing that is appropriate for the student's gender identity, the student may

---

118 http://www.myfloridahouse.gov/Sections/Documents/loaddoc.aspx?FileName=_h0583__.docx&DocumentType=Bill&BillNumber=0583&Session=2015.

119 Recently, the Equal Employment Opportunity Commission ruled that a civilian transgender employee of the army suffered employment discrimination when she was barred from using the women's restroom. The EEOC found that "supervisory or co-worker confusion or anxiety cannot justify discriminatory terms and conditions of employment … Allowing the preferences of co-workers to determine whether sex discrimination is valid reinforces the very stereotypes and prejudices that Title VII is intended to overcome." Chris Geidner, *Army Discriminated Against Transgender Civilian Worker, Federal Agency Rules*, http://www.buzzfeed.com/chrisgeidner/army-discriminated-against-transgender-civilian-worker-feder#.mrzMrYPlA.

120 http://www.myfloridahouse.gov/Sections/Documents/loaddoc.aspx?FileName=_h0583__.docx&DocumentType=Bill&BillNumber=0583&Session=2015.

121 *Id.*

122 http://www.legis.state.tx.us/tlodocs/84R/billtext/pdf/HB01748I.pdf#navpanes=0.

123 Jaime M. Grant, et al. National Center For Transgender Equality, Injustice at Every Turn: A Report of the National Transgender Discrimination Survey, Executive Summary, *available at* http://transequality.org/PDFs/Executive_Summary.pdf.

124 *See*, Larry Gordon, *Mixed-Gender Dorm Rooms are Gaining Acceptance*, http://articles.latimes.com/2010/mar/15/local/la-me-dorm-gender15–2010mar15.

125 *See, e.g.*, Emily Thomas, *Christian University Denies Transgeder Student's Request to Live in An All-Male Dorm*, http://www.huffingtonpost.com/2014/04/07/transgender-dorm-george-fox-university_n_5106075.html.

bring an equal protection challenge. If such a claim is raised, the school would likely assert the same concerns that are raised in the bathroom regulations—privacy and safety. The state's interest in protecting its citizens' rights to privacy and safety is much weaker in dormitories compared to the use of public restrooms and locker rooms. Public restrooms and locker rooms are open to all; college students, however, must agree to be housed with a person who is a different biological birth sex. Therefore, forbidding a transgender student from living with a student of the same gender identity, but different "birth" sex, does not protect anyone's interest in privacy or safety and should not survive an equal protection challenge.

Prisoner housing Prisoner housing presents a much more complicated case than housing in college dormitories. Transgender and intersex inmates have been subjected to horrific treatment, including harassment and rape, when they have been housed in a unit that does not match their gender identity. To protect them from abuse at the hands of male prisoners, some prisons place transgender and intersex prisoners in administrative segregation. Although administrative segregation is technically designed to protect the prisoner from harm that would be inflicted in the general population, conditions in administrative segregation units effectively constitute solitary confinement, a system designed to punish prisoners from misbehavior.

For example, Miki Ann DiMarco, a female who was born with an intersex condition, was convicted for check fraud and was placed on probation. When she violated the terms of the probation, she was imprisoned. Despite a security threat rating that indicated that she posed no risk to herself or others, she spent 438 days in solitary confinement in a maximum security prison. She was not allowed to interact with other inmates and she had limited access to the day room, the commissary, educational opportunities, haircuts, religious items, a radio, a lamp, or playing cards. She was forced to eat her meals alone in her cell, while sitting either on her bed or on the toilet. Miki was placed in solitary confinement because she was born with an intersex condition. Despite the fact that she had lived as a female since puberty and was not sexually functional as a male, she remained in isolation throughout her incarceration.[126]

DiMarco brought a number of constitutional claims, including an equal protection claim. The district court rejected DiMarco's equal protection cause of action. The court determined that "individuals born with ambiguous gender" are not members of a quasi-suspect or constitutionally protected class. Therefore, the court applied rational basis review and found no equal protection violation "because Defendants' actions in placing Plaintiff in segregated confinement was rationally related to the legitimate purposes of ensuring the safety of Plaintiff and other inmates and security of the facility."[127]

Similar equal protection housing challenges brought by transgender prisoners have been unsuccessful for a number of reasons.[128] First, courts have found that the government's decision to segregate prisoners by sex is "unquestionably constitutional."[129] Second, discrimination against transgender and intersex people traditionally has been analyzed under the least restrictive rational basis review.[130] Finally, even if courts are persuaded to apply intermediate scrutiny because these housing decisions constitute a sex-based classification,[131] the Supreme Court has ruled that courts should be particularly deferential to the informed decisions of corrections officials.[132]

---

126 DiMarco v. Wyoming Dep't of Corrections, 300 F. Supp. 2d 1183 (D.Wyo. 2004).

127 *Id.* at 1196–97. DiMarco did not appeal the district court equal protection denial so the Tenth Circuit did not address her equal protection claim. DiMarco v. Wyoming Dep't of Corrections, 473 F.3d 1334, 1338 (10th Cir. 2007).

128 Challenges based on violation of the Eighth Amendment guarantee to be free from cruel and unusual punishment have met with moderately greater success. *See, e.g.*, Farmer v. Brennan, 511 U.S. 825 (1994).

129 *See*, Pitts v. Thornburgh, 866 F.2d 1450 (D.C. Cir. 1989); Women Prisoners of the D.C. Dep't of Corr. v. District of Columbia, 93 F.3d 910, 926 (D.C. Cir. 1996).

130 *See infra* note 146.

131 *See infra* notes 153–69 and accompanying text.

132 Turner v. Safley, 482 U.S. 78, 90 (1987).

Differential Treatment of Transgender People and People with an Intersex Condition Constitutes Impermissible Sex Discrimination Under the Equal Protection Clause

In addition to the discrimination transgender people and people with an intersex condition experience under the sex classification systems discussed in the previous section, gender nonconforming people suffer discrimination in a number of other areas. They are subjected to harassment, physical assault, and sexual violence in the school system.[133] They experience unemployment at twice the rate of the general population.[134] Almost 50 percent have experienced job discrimination including job loss.[135] They have been subjected to housing discrimination and 20 percent have experienced homelessness.[136] More than 50 percent have been harassed or disrespected in a place of public accommodation, including hotels, restaurants, airports, and bus stations.[137] They also have suffered discrimination in the provision of health care.[138]

Discrimination against gender nonconforming people is not limited to the private sector. A recent study conducted by the Williams Institute indicates that the government discriminates on the basis of sexual orientation and gender identity as often as do private employers.[139] When the government engages in unlawful discrimination, a cause of action can be brought for violation of the right to Equal Protection.

No constitutional provisions and few state laws specifically bar discrimination against transgender people or people with an intersex condition.[140] Therefore, gender nonconforming people subjected to discrimination by a government official typically seek redress by asserting that the government violated the Equal Protection Clause by engaging in unlawful discrimination because of "sex."[141]

---

133 Jaime M. Grant, et al. National Center For Transgender Equality, Injustice at Every Turn: A Report of the National Transgender Discrimination Survey, Executive Summary, *available at* http://transequality.org/PDFs/Executive_Summary.pdf.

134 *Id.*

135 *Id.*

136 *Id.*

137 *Id.*

138 *Id.*

139 *See*, Brad Sears, Nan D. Hunter, Christy Mallory, *Documenting Discrimination on the Basis of Sexual Orientation and Gender Identity in State Employment*, The Williams Inst. (Sept. 2009), http://williamsinstitute.law.ucla.edu/research/workplace/documenting-discrimination-on-the-basis-of-sexual-orientation-and-gender-identity-in%20-state-employment/ (finding there is "a widespread and persistent pattern of unconstitutional discrimination by state governments on the basis of sexual orientation and gender identity, and there is no meaningful difference in the pattern and scope of employment discrimination against LGBT people by state governments compared to the private sector and other public sector employers.").

140 Some states, cities, and counties have adopted laws prohibiting discrimination based on gender identity or expression. *U.S. Jurisdictions with Laws Prohibiting Discrimination on the Basis of Gender Identity or Expression,* Transgender Law and Policy Inst., http://www.transgenderlaw.org/ndlaws/index.htm#jurisdictions. President Obama signed an Executive Order prohibiting discrimination against gay, lesbian, bisexual, and transgender employees by the federal government and federal contractors. https://a.next.westlaw.com/Link/Document/FullText?findType=Y&serNum=2033888258&pubNum=0001043&originatingDoc=ID989F9F0124111E4A9C8EA69610B127A&refType=CA&originationContext=document&transitionType=DocumentItem&contextData=(sc.UserEnteredCitation). Although these laws would protect people with an intersex condition who are gender nonconforming, no federal, state, or local laws specifically protect people with an intersex condition. Therefore, people with an intersex condition who are comfortable with the gender assigned to them at birth do not receive specific protection.

141 If the government engages in invidious discrimination by depriving an individual of a constitutional or statutory right or privilege, the aggrieved party can bring a cause of action against the government official under 42 U.S.C. § 1983. *See, e.g.*, Smith v. City of Salem, 378 F.3d 566, 575 (6th Cir. 2004) ("42 U.S.C. § 1983 provides a civil cause of action for individuals who are deprived of any rights, privileges, or immunities secured by the Constitution or federal laws by those acting under color of state law.") *Id.* In determining whether an action qualifies as sex discrimination in a § 1983 Equal Protection case, courts rely on court interpretations of other laws prohibiting sex discrimination, such as Title VII. *See, e.g.*, Sorlucco v. N.Y. City Police Dep't, 888 F.2d 4, 7 (2d. Cir. 1989); Back v. Hastings on Hudson Union Free School Dist. 365 F.3d 107, 122 (2d Cir. 2004); Smith v. City of Salem, 378 F.3d 566, 577 (6th Cir. 2004) ("As this court has noted several times, 'the showing a plaintiff must make to recover on a disparate treatment claim under Title VII mirrors that which must be made to recover on an equal protection claim under § 1983." *Id. at* 577.

Although hundreds of statutes prohibit sex discrimination, the meaning of the term "sex" is far from clear. During the last 40 years, courts have been asked to determine exactly what types of acts violate constitutional and statutory prohibitions against sex discrimination.

Early Sex Discrimination Cases Narrowly Construed the Meaning of Discrimination Because of Sex

When legislation prohibiting sex discrimination was first adopted, courts tended to rule that the purpose of these laws was limited to providing equal opportunities for women and men. The typical early successful sex discrimination cases involved men or women who were treated differently because of their biological sex. For example, early decisions invalidated employer rules that provided only men could be airline pilots and only women could be flight attendants.[142]

During the first three decades after sex discrimination prohibitions were first enacted during the 1960s, courts generally refused to expand the meaning of the term "sex" beyond this simple approach. Courts protected men who had been treated differently from women and women who had been treated differently from men. Typically, however, the statutory ban against sex discrimination did not protect people from discriminatory treatment based on their status as a man or woman who failed to conform to gender role stereotypes,[143] a pregnant woman,[144] a gay or lesbian person,[145] a transgender person,[146] or a person with an intersex condition.[147]

During the 1990s the Meaning of the Term "Sex" Expanded to Include Discrimination Based on Sex Stereotyping

These limited visions of the scope of sex discrimination prohibitions began to dissolve in large part due to the feminist and LGBT movements and feminist and queer theorists, who helped to educate society and the judiciary about the complex nature of sex discrimination. These scholars and activists helped courts develop a more nuanced understanding of the meaning and harm of sex discrimination.

The major expansion of the meaning of the word "sex" and the acts that encompass sex discrimination came from the Supreme Court's 1989 ruling in *Price Waterhouse v. Hopkins*.[148] In *Price Waterhouse*, an accounting firm denied a partnership to Ms Hopkins, not because she was biologically a woman, but because she failed to meet the partners' stereotyped expectations of how a woman should behave. The partners implied that her failure to conform to stereotypes of femininity blocked her path to partnership. Specifically, Hopkins was told that she overcompensated for being a woman and was too "macho."[149] She was advised to stop

142 *See, e.g.*, Diaz v. Pan Am. World Airways, 442 F.2d 385, 389 (5th Cir. 1971) (holding that Pan Am's policy of hiring only females for flight attendant positions violated Title VII).

143 *See* Joan C. Williams & Nancy Segal, *Beyond the Maternal Wall: Relief for Family Caregivers Who Are Discriminated Against on the Job*, 26 Harv. Women's L.J. 77, 103 (2003) (citing Chi v. Age Grp., Ltd., No. 94 CIV 5253 (AGS), 1996 WL 627580, at *1 (S.D.N.Y. Oct. 29, 1996); Piantanida v. Wyman Ctr., Inc., 116 F.3d 340 (8th Cir. 1997); Martinez v. N.B.C. Inc., 49 F. Supp. 2d 305 (S.D.N.Y. 1999); Bass v. Chem. Banking Corp., No. 94 Civ. 8833 (SHS), 1996 WL 374151, at *1 (S.D.N.Y. July 2, 1996); Fuller v. GTE Corp./Contel Cellular, Inc., 926 F. Supp. 653 (M.D. Tenn. 1996)).

144 Gen. Elec. Co. v. Gilbert, 429 U.S. 125 (1976); Geduldig v. Aiello, 417 U.S. 484 (1974).

145 *See, e.g.*, Williamson v. A.G. Edwards & Sons, Inc., 876 F.2d 69, 70 (8th Cir. 1989); DeSantis v. Pac. Tel. & Tel. Co., 608 F.2d 327, 330–31 (9th Cir. 1979). A number of later cases have followed this approach. *See, e.g.*, Simonton v. Runyon, 232 F.3d 33, 36–37 (2d Cir. 2000), Spearman v. Ford Motor Co., 231 F.3d 1080, 1085–86 (7th Cir. 2000); Higgins v. New Balance Athletic Shoe, Inc., 194 F.3d 252, 261 (1st Cir. 1999).

146 *See, e.g.*, Sommers v. Budget Mktg., Inc., 667 F.2d 748, 750 (8th Cir. 1982); Holloway v. Arthur Andersen & Co., 566 F.2d 659, 663–64 (9th Cir. 1977); Dobre v. Nat'l R.R. Passenger Corp., 850 F. Supp. 284, 285–86 (E.D. Pa. 1993); Doe v. U.S. Postal Serv., Civ. A. No. 84–3296, 1985 WL 9446, at *1–2 (D.D.C. June 12, 1985); Terry v. Equal Emp't Opportunity Comm'n, Civ. A. No. 80-C-408, 1980 WL 334, at *1–3 (E.D. Wis. Dec. 10, 1980); Powell v. Read's, Inc., 436 F. Supp. 369, 370–71 (D. Md. 1977); Voyles v. Ralph K. Davies Med. Ctr., 403 F. Supp. 456, 457 (N.D. Cal. 1975), *aff'd mem.*, 570 F.2d 354 (9th Cir. 1978); Grossman v. Bernards Twp. Bd. of Educ., No. 74–1904, 1975 WL 302, at *4 (D.N.J. Sept. 10, 1975), *aff'd mem.*, 538 F.2d 319 (3d Cir. 1976).

147 Wood v. C.G. Studios, 660 F. Supp. 176 (E.D. Pa. 1987).

148 490 U.S. 228 (1989).

149 *Id.* at 235.

using profanity, to take a class at charm school, and to "walk more femininely, talk more femininely, dress more femininely, wear make-up, have her hair styled, and wear jewelry."[150] The Supreme Court ruled that discrimination against a woman because she failed to conform to societal stereotypes of femininity constituted discrimination based on "sex."[151]

The Court's acceptance of sex stereotyping as a form of impermissible sex discrimination reflects a more sophisticated understanding of the harms of sex-based discriminatory conduct. Based on the *Price Waterhouse* decision, individuals who are treated differently because they fail to conform to sex-related stereotypes have been able to prove that they were subjected to impermissible sex discrimination if they appropriately frame their claims as gender nonconformity or sex stereotyping discrimination. A number of courts have embraced the concept that gender role performance, sexual orientation, and gender identity are part of a person's "sex." These courts have prohibited discrimination against people whose gender roles, gender behaviors, and gender identities fail to conform to societal norms.

The Equal Protection Clause Protects Transgender People Subjected to Discriminatory Treatment Based on Sex and Gender Stereotyping

Before the decision in *Price Waterhouse*, transgender plaintiffs consistently lost their cases when they tried to state a claim for sex discrimination. Early courts ruled that discrimination against people whose gender identity did not conform to the sex assigned to them at birth was not prohibited under statutes barring sex discrimination.[152] Since *Price Waterhouse*, however, courts in the first, sixth, ninth, and eleventh circuits have held that discrimination against transgender people because their gender identity fails to conform to their natal sex constitutes impermissible sex stereotyping discrimination.[153]

For example, in *Smith v. City of Salem*,[154] firefighting lieutenant, Jimmie Smith, had worked for seven years in the Salem Fire Department without any negative incidents. After Lieutenant Smith began transitioning to becoming a woman, coworkers began asking questions about Lieutenant Smith's appearance and commenting that the lieutenant's looks and mannerisms were not "masculine enough."[155] Smith decided to notify her supervisor about her transition and informed the supervisor that she would eventually undergo a complete physical transformation and present as a woman. After this disclosure, Smith's employer instituted a plan to fire her.[156] The court held that the fire department discriminated against Smith based on the *Price Waterhouse* sex stereotyping theory because the treatment was based on Smith's failure to conform to gender norms of how men should look and behave. The Sixth Circuit ruled that the earlier cases that had denied the ability of transgender people to recover for sex discrimination were "eviscerated" by the 1989 holding in *Price Waterhouse*.[157] The Sixth Circuit reinforced this approach one year later in *Barnes v. Cincinnati*.[158]

---

150 *Id.*

151 *Id.* at 258.

152 *See supra* note 146.

153 *See, e.g.*, Glenn v. Brumby, 663 F.3d 1312 (11th Cir. 2011) (transgender employee can state a § 1983 Equal Protection sex discrimination claim); Barnes v. City of Cincinnati, 401 F.3d 729 (6th Cir. 2005) (transsexuals are a protected class under Equal Protection and Title VII); Smith v. City of Salem, 378 F.3d 566, 575 (6th Cir. 2004) (plaintiff stated a § 1983 Equal Protection claim when he suffered discrimination because of his gender nonconforming behavior); Rosa v. Park W. Bank & Trust Co., 214 F.3d 213 (1st Cir. 2000) (transgender female could state a cause of action for sex discrimination under the Equal Credit Opportunity Act); Schwenk v. Hartford, 204 F.3d 1187, 1202 (9th Cir. 2000) (mistreatment of a male-to-female transsexual prisoner constitutes impermissible gender discrimination under the Gender Motivated Violence Act). This theory was also upheld in Schroer v. Billington, 577 F. Supp. 2d 293 (D.D.C. 2008) (withdrawal of job offer after the Library of Congress learned that the plaintiff was a male-to-female transsexual constitutes unlawful sex stereotyping discrimination under Title VII). The sex stereotyping theory has not been universally accepted in all cases involving transgender plaintiffs. *See, e.g.*, Etsitty v. Utah Transit Auth., 502 F.3d 1215 (10th Cir. 2007).

154 378 F.3d 566 (6th Cir. 2004).

155 *Id.* at 568.

156 *Id.*

157 *Id.* at 573.

158 401 F.3d 729 (6th Cir. 2005).

In 2011, the Eleventh Circuit agreed with the Sixth Circuit's approach. In *Glenn v. Brumby*,[159] the appellate court affirmed the trial court's grant of summary judgment in favor of a transgender plaintiff who brought an equal protection sex discrimination claim. Vandiver Glenn sued for sex discrimination when the Georgia General Assembly's Office of Legislative Counsel fired her from her editorial position after she notified her supervisor that she identified as a woman and was beginning her transition to living and presenting as a female. Her employer, Sewell Brumby, stated that her appearance was inappropriate, and he found it "unsettling to think of someone dressed in women's clothing with male sexual organs inside that clothing," and "that a male in women's clothing is 'unnatural.'"[160] When he fired her, he stated that her "intended gender transition was inappropriate, that it would be disruptive, that some people would view it as a moral issue, and that it would make Glenn's coworkers uncomfortable."[161] The Eleventh Circuit ruled that when the employer fired the transgender employee, the employer's actions violated the Equal Protection Clause's prohibition against sex-based discrimination because it was based on the employee's failure to conform to gender stereotypes.[162]

A number of other circuit courts have reached similar conclusions under other statutes prohibiting sex discrimination. For example, in *Schwenk v. Hartford*,[163] the Ninth Circuit ruled that discrimination against a transgender plaintiff because she failed to act like a man constituted impermissible sex discrimination under the Gender Motivated Violence Act. The First Circuit adopted a similar approach when it determined that refusing a loan to a transgender plaintiff because she failed to dress in accordance with prescribed gender roles violated the prohibition against sex discrimination in the Equal Credit Opportunity Act.[164] A number of district courts also have concluded that transgender plaintiffs who suffer differential treatment because of their failure to comply with stereotypical gender norms have been subjected to impermissible sex discrimination.[165]

The Equal Protection Clause Protects Transgender Plaintiffs Subjected to Discriminatory Treatment Because of Sex

As discussed in the previous section, many courts have allowed transgender plaintiffs to state a cause of action for sex discrimination if they properly allege that they have suffered discrimination because of their failure to conform to sex and gender stereotypes. One court has ruled that discrimination against transgender people also constitutes straightforward sex discrimination and transgender plaintiffs do not have to rely on a stereotyping theory.

In 2008, a federal district court ruled in *Schroer v. Billington*[166] that a male-to-female transgender person who had been discriminated against because of her transgender status had been subjected to impermissible sex discrimination. Diane Schroer applied for a position with the research division of the Library of Congress as a terrorism specialist providing expert policy analysis to Congress. When she applied for the job, she had not yet transitioned from male to female so she used her legal male name, David, on the application and she attended the interview in male clothing. She received the highest score of the 18 candidates and she was

---

159 663 F.3d 1312 (11th Cir. 2011).

160 *Id.* at 1314.

161 *Id.*

162 *Id.* at 1320.

163 204 F.3d 1187 (9th Cir. 2000).

164 Rosa v. Park W. Bank & Trust Co., 214 F.3d 213, 216 (1st Cir. 2000).

165 *See, e.g.*, Kaeo-Tomaselli v. Pi'ikoi Recovery House for Women 2011 WL 5572603 (D. Hawaii 2011) (natal male who self-identified as a female who was denied housing as a female stated a cause of action for violation of her right to equal protection); Lopez v. River Oaks Imaging & Diagnostic Grp., Inc., 542 F. Supp. 2d 653, 659–61 (S.D. Tex. 2008) (transgender job applicant whose job offer was rescinded after the prospective employer learned of the applicant's transgender status stated a claim under Title VII); Mitchell v. Axcan Scandipharm, 2006 WL 986971 (W.D. Pa. 2006) (transgender employee who was terminated from her job when she announced her intent to transition stated a claim under Title VII); Kastl v. Maricopa Cnty. Cmty. Coll. Dist., 2004 WL 2008954 (D. Ariz. 2004), *aff'd*, 325 F. App'x. 492 (9th Cir. 2009)(transgender employee who was discharged after she refused to use the men's restroom stated a prima facie sex discrimination case based on sex stereotyping); Tronetti v. TLC Healthnet Lakeshore Hosp., No. 03–CV-0375E(SC), 2003 WL 22757935 (W.D.N.Y. 2003) (male-to-female transsexual stated a valid cause of action for sex discrimination).

166 577 F. Supp. 2d 293 (D.D.C. 2008).

offered the job. Diane accepted the position, but before she began work, she notified the person in charge of hiring that she would begin work as a female. The job offer was revoked and Diane sued.

The court found that the Library of Congress had engaged in unlawful sex discrimination for two reasons. First, the court found that Diane was denied the job based on the sex stereotyping theory developed in *Price Waterhouse*. The court concluded that different comments by the employer indicated that Diane was viewed as "an insufficiently masculine man, an insufficiently feminine woman, or an inherently gender-nonconforming transsexual."[167] The court stated: "[T]he Library was enthusiastic about hiring David Schroer—until she disclosed her transsexuality. The Library revoked the offer when it learned that a man named David intended to become, legally, culturally, and physically, a woman named Diane. This was discrimination 'because of … sex.'"[168]

More important, the court found that, in addition to stating a sex stereotyping discrimination claim, Schroer could recover under a straightforward sex discrimination theory and did not need to rely on the stereotyping approach. The court ruled that people who "change" their sex and suffer discrimination because of the transition have suffered sex discrimination. The court continued:

> Imagine that an employee is fired because she converts from Christianity to Judaism. Imagine too that her employer testifies that he harbors no bias toward either Christians or Jews but only "converts." That would be a clear case of discrimination "because of religion." No court would take seriously the notion that "converts" are not covered by the statute. Discrimination "because of religion" easily encompasses discrimination because of a *change* of religion. But in cases where the plaintiff has changed her sex, and faces discrimination because of the decision to stop presenting as a man and to start appearing as a woman, courts have traditionally carved such persons out of the statute by concluding that "transsexuality" is unprotected by Title VII. In other words, courts have allowed their focus on the label "transsexual" to blind them to the statutory language itself.[169]

Therefore, under the reasoning of the court in *Schroer*, any government discrimination directed at transgender people based on their transgender status should be considered impermissible sex discrimination under the Equal Protection Clause.

Plaintiffs with an Intersex Condition should be able to Recover under the Equal Protection Clause Under Either a Sex or a Sex Stereotyping Discrimination Theory

Discrimination against people with an intersex condition is not as prevalent as discrimination against transgender people for two reasons. First, most people with an intersex condition self-identify as the sex assigned to them at birth and are gender conforming.[170] Second, because of fear of stigma and rejection, many people with an intersex condition are not "out"; they do not share information about their intersex condition with people in the workplace or even friends and relatives. Therefore, people with an intersex condition frequently do not suffer discrimination because their condition is not known.[171]

People with an intersex condition, who are gender nonconforming or who want to live as the sex opposite the sex assigned to them at birth, may be subjected to the same type of discrimination endured by transgender people. If so, they should be able to recover under the same sex-stereotyping theory that protects transgender

167 *Id.* at 305.

168 *Id.* at 306.

169 *Id.* at 306–07. The Equal Employment Opportunity Commission approved this approach in Macy v. Holder, 2012 WL 1435995, at *11 (EEOC Apr. 20, 2012).

170 Some women with one type of intersex condition have a higher likelihood of being bisexual or lesbian and are gender nonconforming in that they often display behavior that is stereotypically associated with males. Heino Meyer-Bahlburg, *What Causes Low Rates of Childbearing in Congenital Adrenal Hyperplasia?*, 84 J. Clinical Endocrinology & Metabolism 1844, 1845–46 (1999), *available at* http://jcem.endojournals.org/content/84/6/1844. In addition, between 5–25 percent of people with an intersex condition will ultimately reject the gender assigned to them at birth and will thus share the same concerns as the transgender community about their right to transition from one gender to the other. Peter A. Lee et al., *Consensus Statement on Management of Intersex Disorders*, 118 Pediatrics e488, e491–92 (2006).

171 People with an intersex condition do suffer from sex stereotyping in the provision of health care. *See* Greenberg, *Health Care Issues*, *supra*, note 17.

people. In addition, gender conforming people with an intersex condition should be able to recover under the straightforward sex discrimination theory adopted by the court in *Schroer*.

Thus far, only one plaintiff with an intersex condition has brought a claim alleging that she had been subjected to discrimination because of her intersex condition. In *Wood v. C.G. Studios, Inc.*,[172] an employer terminated one of its employees after learning that the employee "had undergone surgery to correct her hermaphroditic condition."[173] The federal district court refused to treat the employer's actions as unlawful sex discrimination. The court reasoned that sex discrimination prohibitions were designed to provide equal employment opportunities to women. Consequently, the court determined that the statute was not intended to remedy discrimination against individuals because they had undergone gender-corrective surgery.[174] The court limited the meaning of the word "sex" in the statute to what it considered to be the word's "plain meaning," and held that sex discrimination prohibitions do not encompass discrimination against "hermaphrodites" because of their intersex status.[175]

The holding in *Wood* is consistent with the understanding of the scope of sex discrimination prohibitions during the 1980s.[176] All the cases at that time narrowly construed the reach of statutes prohibiting sex discrimination. The holding of the *Schroer* court calls into serious question the continuing validity of this single employment discrimination case involving an employee with an intersex condition.

Just as *Price Waterhouse* eviscerated the holdings in earlier sex discrimination cases brought by gay, lesbian, transgender, and other gender nonconforming people, it should be interpreted to eviscerate the holding in *Wood*. Discrimination against people with an intersex condition should be treated similarly to the treatment of transgender people in the *Schroer* decision. If discrimination against transgender people who have transitioned from one sex to the other constitutes impermissible sex discrimination, people who have been discriminated against based on their intersex condition also have been subjected to unlawful sex discrimination.

Conclusion

Laws permitting differential treatment of men and women because of their status as males and females have almost vanished during the last 40 years. Although *de facto* gender discrimination and economic disparity still exist, outside of marriage prohibitions and jobs in which a person's sex is considered a *bona fide* occupational qualification, *de jure* sex discrimination against men and women is no longer permitted under the Equal Protection Clause.

The same is not true for sex and gender nonconformists—people with an intersex condition and transgender people. People who challenge the sex and gender binary system are still subjected to differential treatment by the government. Most of the recent cases involving sex classification have imposed arbitrary sex tests that rely on chromosomes, reproductive capacity, and sex or gender stereotypes rather than scientific developments about gender identity formation. Such sex classification systems fail the intermediate scrutiny test imposed under the Equal Protection Clause because the government's sex tests are not substantially related to an important government interest. They also likely fail the lowest level rational basis test. In addition, the government violates the Equal Protection Clause when it treats transgender people or people with an intersex condition differently from the way it treats men and women who are not transgender or intersex. Such differential treatment violates equal protection mandates prohibiting sex discrimination. People with an intersex condition and transgender people should have their right to live and work in their self-identified gender role and any infringements on this right should be considered unconstitutional under the Equal Protection Clause.

---

172 660 F. Supp. 176, 178 (E.D. Pa. 1987).

173 *Id.* At the time of this decision, people with an intersex condition were often referred to as hermaphrodites. That term "hermaphrodite" is considered pejorative and people with an intersex condition prefer the terms intersex condition or DSD.

174 *Id.*

175 *Id.* at 176–78.

176 *See* notes 143–46 *infra* and accompanying text.

Chapter 12
Bringing Equal Protection Out of the Tax Closet

Anthony C. Infanti

Constitutional arguments are notoriously difficult to win in tax cases. For example, courts considering equal protection challenges ordinarily defer to legislative classifications of taxpayers on the ground that tax legislation is "economic" legislation. Consequently, so long as the legislature refrains from blatantly classifying taxpayers on a suspect basis (for example, race or gender), the tax laws are thought to be nearly immune from attack on equal protection grounds.

This narrow focus on economics conveniently surfaces in both judicial and academic discussions of tax fairness. In both arenas, viewing taxpayers as no more than the sum of their financial transactions effectively screens out most difficult discussions of invidious discrimination in the tax laws. Though this economic lens may nicely sanitize discussions of tax fairness, it does not eliminate concerns about equal protection and fundamental fairness in the tax laws. Instead, it relegates them to the legal invisibility of the tax closet.

To bring equal protection out of the tax closet, we must recognize that, even absent blatant discrimination, the Internal Revenue Code can have a disparate impact on the basis of race, ethnicity, gender, sexual orientation, and disability. If any area of the law should be open to disparate impact analysis, it should be tax law. In tax, the idea that substance should control over form—that is, the notion that what really happens is more important than what appears to be happening—is pervasive, pervasive enough to perhaps shift equal protection analysis in other areas of the law, too.

This chapter proceeds in four sections. In the first section, I discuss the general constitutional restrictions on the power to tax and how they actually restrict the U.S. Congress hardly at all. In the second section, I discuss the application of the guarantee of equal protection of the laws to the federal tax laws. Through a series of examples, I show how this guarantee is enforced only in the most blatant cases of discrimination. In the third section, I explain how this legal schema—in tandem with academic discussions of tax fairness—relegates invidious discrimination perpetrated through the tax laws to the tax closet and explore both the nature of that closet and the rhetorical tapestry that is used to hide it from view. In the final section, I begin the task of unraveling this tapestry and removing the door to the tax closet so that we can shine a light upon—and make legally visible—the invidious discrimination that is present in the federal tax laws, as it is elsewhere in the U.S. legal system.

Restrictions on the Power to Tax

The "Power To lay and collect Taxes" is first in the list of Congress's specifically enumerated powers.[1] The priority given to the power to tax in the U.S. Constitution is no accident. After all, Alexander Hamilton observed in *The Federalist* that revenue is the lifeblood of government:

> Money is with propriety considered as the vital principle of the body politic; as that which sustains its life and motion, and enables it to perform its most essential functions. A complete power therefore to procure a regular and adequate supply of it, as far as the resources of the community will permit, may be regarded as an indispensable ingredient in every constitution. From a deficiency in this particular, one of two evils must ensue; either the people must be subjected to continual plunder as a substitute for a more eligible mode of supplying the public wants, or the government must sink into a fatal atrophy, and in a short course of time perish.[2]

1 U.S. CONST. art. I, § 8, cl. 1.

2 THE FEDERALIST NO. 30, at 188 (Alexander Hamilton) (Jacob E. Cooke ed., 1961).

As Hamilton implies, the power to tax is a double-edged sword. Though a government must have "[a] complete power" to tax at its disposal, that power must be limited because it can only extend "as far as the resources of the community will permit."[3] In other words, at the same time that the power to tax is an indispensable foundation of government, the government's abuse of the taxing power can lead to its own demise. Or, as Chief Justice John Marshall has put it, "the power to tax involves the power to destroy; ... the power to destroy may defeat and render useless the power to create."[4]

It is no wonder then that the Constitution contains several explicit restrictions on the power to tax. Congress is forbidden to impose export taxes,[5] and it was limited to a tax or duty of no more than $10 on the importation of slaves.[6] Congress must apportion direct taxes (with the exception of income taxes) by population,[7] and it must impose all indirect taxes (that is, duties, imposts, and excises) uniformly throughout the country.[8] In addition, all tax legislation must originate in the House of Representatives,[9] ostensibly "to repose the power to set the legislative agenda in the branch of the legislature that would be most accountable to the people."[10]

There are also numerous constitutional limitations that do not explicitly mention the power to tax, but that nonetheless restrict that power.[11] These include, for example, the Fifth Amendment right against self-incrimination;[12] the First Amendment prohibition against enacting laws "respecting an establishment of religion, or prohibiting the free exercise thereof";[13] and the Fifth Amendment right not to "be deprived of life, liberty, or property, without due process of law."[14] There are also a few constitutional limitations that are favored by tax protesters, but whose application to the power to tax has been met with skepticism in the federal courts (for example, the Thirteenth Amendment prohibition against involuntary servitude).[15]

The Fourteenth Amendment guarantee of equal protection of the laws, which is the subject of this book, applies only to the states and not to the federal government.[16] Nevertheless, the U.S. Supreme Court has held, through the medium of the Fifth Amendment's Due Process Clause, that the guarantee of equal protection of the law applies to the federal government as well as to the states.[17] As discussed in the next section, the federal courts have occasionally struck down a taxing statute as a violation of the equal protection component of the Due Process Clause.[18]

---

3 *Id.*

4 McCulloch v. Maryland, 17 U.S. 316, 431 (1819).

5 U.S. Const. art. I, § 9, cl. 5.

6 U.S. Const. art. I, § 9, cl. 1; see generally Robin L. Einhorn, American Taxation, American Slavery (2006) (explaining how our national tax structure is rooted in the accommodation of slavery).

7 U.S. Const. art. I, § 2, cl. 3, amended by U.S. Const. amend. XIV, § 2; U.S. Const. art. I, § 9, cl. 4, amended by U.S. Const. amend. XVI.

8 U.S. Const. art. I, § 8, cl. 1.

9 U.S. Const. art. I, § 7, cl. 1.

10 Anthony C. Infanti, *A Tax Crit Identity Crisis? Or Tax Expenditure Analysis, Deconstruction, and the Rethinking of a Collective Identity*, 26 Whittier L. Rev. 707, 775 (2005).

11 Boris I. Bittker, *Constitutional Limits on the Taxing Power of the Federal Government*, 41 Tax Law. 3, 9 (1987).

12 U.S. Const. amend. V. Issues regarding the right not to incriminate oneself can arise with respect to the filing of returns by those engaged in illegal activities. Bittker, *supra* note 11, at 6–7.

13 U.S. Const. amend. I. These First Amendment issues arise, for example, under I.R.C. § 107 (2013) (granting an exemption from gross income for the rental value of parsonages and rental allowances provided to "a minister of the gospel") and under I.R.C. § 170 (2013) (deduction for charitable contributions, but only if made to organized religions). *See* Bittker, *supra* note 11, at 7–8 (discussing both provisions); Erwin Chemerinsky, *The Parsonage Exemption Violates the Establishment Clause and Should Be Declared Unconstitutional*, 24 Whittier L. Rev. 707 *passim* (2003) (discussing I.R.C. § 107); Tracy A. Kaye & Stephen W. Mazza, *United States—National Report: Constitutional Limitations on the Legislative Power to Tax in the United States*, 15 Mich. St. J. Int'l L. 481, 490–91 (2007) (discussing I.R.C. § 170).

14 U.S. Const. amend. V. Due process issues arise, for example, when Congress enacts tax legislation retroactively. Kaye & Mazza, *supra* note 13, at 515–17.

15 Bittker, *supra* note 11, at 4–5; Kaye & Mazza, *supra* note 13, at 488–89; *see* Internal Revenue Serv., The Truth About Frivolous Tax Arguments 22–29 (Mar. 4, 2013), *available at http://www.irs.gov/pub/irs-utl/friv_tax.pdf.*

16 U.S. Const. amend. XIV, § 1.

17 Bolling v. Sharpe, 347 U.S. 497, 500 (1954).

18 Kaye & Mazza, *supra* note 13, at 500–03.

Thus, thumbing through the Constitution, the power to tax seems to be hemmed in by restrictions designed to prevent the abuse of this vital power. Indeed, Boris Bittker characterized the federal income tax as "swim[ming] in a sea of constitutional limits."[19] But, as is so often the case, the law on the books differs from the law in action. Continuing his nautical metaphor, Bittker went on to explain that

> these constitutional restraints seldom create any serious problems in the day-to-day application on the federal income tax. The tax is, in short, not like an oil tanker moving gingerly through the Straits of Hormuz, but instead resembles a freighter crossing the Atlantic, which occasionally spots an iceberg, but rarely has to make a serious change in its customary route.[20]

Equal Protection and Tax Law

Bittker's nautical metaphor is especially apt in describing the application of the guarantee of equal protection of the laws to the federal tax system. Tracy Kaye and Stephen Mazza have observed that the Supreme Court's "reluctance to second guess a legislature's decision has led it to establish a high threshold in order to find a tax provision unconstitutional on equal protection grounds."[21] In support of their assertion, they quote an illuminating passage from the Supreme Court's decision in *Regan v. Taxation With Representation*:

> [I]n taxation, even more than in other fields, legislatures possess the greatest freedom in classification. ... [T]he presumption of constitutionality can be overcome only by the most explicit demonstration that a classification is a hostile and oppressive discrimination against particular persons and classes. The burden is on the one attacking the legislative arrangement to negative every conceivable basis which might support it.[22]

Only the most blatantly discriminatory classifications will meet this standard. Or, as Leo Martinez has summarized the case law in this area, "It is clear that to be deemed harsh and oppressive, a legislature would have to border on the irrational."[23] Few aspects of the federal tax laws have openly demonstrated this level of irrationality. But that is not to say that invidious discrimination is not present in the federal tax laws:

> The racial and gender bias in the Code, while clearly present, is too subtle to be explained by any explicit discriminatory purpose—it is in the choices that Congress makes as compared to the choices it might have made. The purpose may reflect a subtle or coded gender or racial bias. Although it is unthinkable that any committee report would offer an explicitly racist or sexist reason for its legislation, some of the arguments made in debates over tax legislation can be interpreted as discriminatory rhetoric aimed at particular groups. For example, the call for protection of the traditional family through the Code, made explicitly by some legislators, can be interpreted as an argument against workplace equality for women or intolerance for homosexuals.[24]

Indeed, critical tax scholars have done important work uncovering bias in the tax laws and demonstrating the ways in which the tax laws "reflect and even reify discrimination based on race, gender, sexual orientation, class, disability, or family structure."[25]

---

19 Bittker, *supra* note 11, at 12.

20 *Id.* at 9.

21 Kaye & Mazza, *supra* note 13, at 501.

22 *Id.* at 501–02 (quoting Regan v. Taxation With Representation, 461 U.S. 540, 547–48 (1983) (quoting Madden v. Kentucky, 309 U.S. 83, 88 (1940)) (emphasis added by Kaye and Mazza omitted)).

23 Leo P. Martinez, *The Trouble with Taxes: Fairness, Tax Policy, and the Constitution*, 31 Hastings Const. L.Q. 413, 437 (2004).

24 Linda Sugin, *Tax Expenditure Analysis and Constitutional Decisions*, 50 Hastings L.J. 407, 449–50 (1999) (footnotes omitted).

25 Anthony C. Infanti & Bridget J. Crawford, *Introduction* to Critical Tax Theory: An Introduction, at xxi, xxii (Anthony C. Infanti & Bridget J. Crawford eds, 2009).

In this section, I explore concrete examples of the extraordinary deference that courts afford to tax classifications. First, I explore equal protection challenges to obvious discrimination in the tax laws on the basis of race, gender, and sexual orientation. In most of these cases, the courts have upheld the challenges; however, in one case of overt gender discrimination, the courts rejected an equal protection challenge. Then, I explore equal protection challenges to less obvious discrimination in the tax laws. In all of these cases, the courts have rejected equal protection challenges to ostensibly neutral tax classifications.

Overt Racial Discrimination

In *McGlotten v. Connally*,[26] an African-American who had been denied membership in the Benevolent and Protective Order of the Elks solely on the basis of his race brought a class action suit to enjoin the federal government "from granting tax benefits to fraternal and nonprofit organizations which exclude nonwhites from membership." A three-judge U.S. District Court denied the federal government's motion to dismiss the plaintiff's constitutional claims. The court found that the government had become involved in racial discrimination by affording tax deductions for contributions to fraternal organizations and an exemption from tax for their passive investment income. To obtain these benefits, fraternal organizations must not only engage in charitable activities but also apply for and receive government approval.[27] The court held that, "[b]y providing differential treatment to only selected organizations, the Government has indicated approval of the organizations and hence their discriminatory practice, and aided that discrimination by the provision of federal tax benefits."[28]

Overt Sex Discrimination

In *Moritz v. Commissioner*, the taxpayer challenged the constitutionality of then § 214 of the Internal Revenue Code (IRC).[29] At the time, § 214 allowed taxpayers a deduction for expenses paid to care for a dependent, "but only if such care [was] for the purpose of enabling the taxpayer to be gainfully employed."[30] (Prior to the enactment of § 214 in 1954, the courts had classified dependent care expenses as nondeductible personal expenses.[31]) On its face, § 214 limited this deduction by reference to the sex and marital status of the taxpayer. The only taxpayers eligible to claim the deduction were "a woman or widower, or ... a husband whose wife is incapacitated or institutionalized."[32] For this purpose, a "widower" was defined to include "an unmarried individual who is legally separated from his spouse under a decree of divorce or of separate maintenance."[33] Thus, a woman (whatever her marital status) was entitled to claim the deduction for dependent care expenses, but a man could claim a deduction for such expenses only if he had, at some time, been married.

As originally drafted by the House of Representatives, § 214 afforded a deduction only for child-care expenses paid by "a working widow, widower, or divorced person, or a working mother whose husband is incapacitated."[34] The deduction was to be added in recognition "that a widow or widower with young children must incur these expenses in order to earn a livelihood and that they, therefore, are comparable to an employee's business expenses."[35] The Senate liberalized proposed § 214 by extending the deduction "to a working woman or a widower for expenses paid for care of any dependent who is mentally or physically

26 338 F. Supp. 448, 450 (D.D.C. 1972).

27 *Id.* at 455–58, 459.

28 *Id.* at 459.

29 55 T.C. 113 (1970), *rev'd*, 469 F.2d 466 (10th Cir. 1972). The deduction for dependent care expenses was later converted into a credit, and it can now be found in I.R.C. § 21 (2013).

30 I.R.C. § 214(a) (1968).

31 *E.g.*, Smith v. Comm'r, 40 B.T.A. 1038, 1039 (1939), *aff'd per curiam*, 113 F.2d 114 (2d Cir. 1940); *see also* Nammack v. Comm'r, 56 T.C. 1379, 1381 (1971), *aff'd per curiam*, 459 F.2d 1045 (2d Cir. 1972).

32 I.R.C. § 214(a) (1968).

33 *Id.* § 214(d)(2).

34 H.R. Rep. No. 83-1337 (1954), *reprinted in* 1954 U.S.C.C.A.N. 4025, 4055.

35 *Id.*

incapable of caring for himself."[36] The following passage explains the rationale for the Senate's expansion of the coverage of this deduction:

> Your committee's action in extending the deduction recognizes that similar financial problems may be incurred by taxpayers who, if they are to be gainfully employed, must provide care for physically or mentally incapacitated dependents other than their children. Moreover, it is recognized that in many low-income families, the earnings of the mother are essential for the maintenance of minimum living standards, even where the father is also employed, and that in such situations the requirement for providing child care may be just as pressing as in the case of a widowed or divorced mother.[37]

The House of Representatives agreed to this liberalization of the proposed deduction.[38]

A decade later, Congress further liberalized § 214 by including husbands whose wives are incapacitated or institutionalized to the list of those eligible to claim the deduction.[39] The rationale for this extension was that a family in which the wife is incapable of caring for herself would be just as likely to incur dependent-care expenses as a family in which the husband is incapable of caring for himself.[40]

The unwritten assumption underpinning all of these decisions regarding the class of taxpayers who would be eligible to claim the deduction for dependent-care expenses was that a woman's presumptive place was working in the home as caregiver. In contrast, a man's presumptive place was in the paid workforce, freed of any worries about caregiving responsibilities. Thus, the only individuals who could claim that their dependent-care expenses were related to gainful employment were women whose families were too poor to permit them to fulfill their caregiving responsibilities; women who were on their own (that is, divorced or widowed) and could not count on a man to "provide" for them; and men whose wives were unable to fulfill their caregiving responsibilities due to death, divorce, illness, or incapacitation.

The taxpayer in *Moritz* was a single man who had never married. Though he did not fit the stereotypes underpinning § 214—as a single man he should be carefree, not a caregiver—the taxpayer did incur expenses for the care of his elderly mother.[41] The taxpayer employed a caregiver for his mother so that he could work for a publishing company in a job that required extensive travel throughout the United States.[42] The taxpayer claimed a $600 deduction for amounts paid to his mother's caregiver in 1968. On audit, the Internal Revenue Service (IRS) denied the deduction.[43]

The U.S. Tax Court upheld the IRS's decision to deny the deduction, rejecting any constitutional objection on the ground that "deductions are within the grace of Congress. If Congress sees fit to establish classes of persons who shall or shall not benefit from a deduction, there is no offense to the Constitution, if all members of one class are treated alike."[44] On appeal, the U.S. Court of Appeals for the Tenth Circuit took a different view and found this differential treatment to be based primarily on sex. Relying upon *Reed v. Reed*,[45] the Tenth Circuit sought to determine whether the classification in § 214 bore "a fair and substantial relation to the object of the legislation dealing with the amelioration of burdens on the taxpayer."[46] The court found that it did not; the classification in § 214 "did not make the challenged distinction as part of a scheme dealing with the varying burdens of dependents' care borne of taxpayers, but instead made a special discrimination premised on sex alone, which cannot stand."[47]

36 S. Rep. No. 83-1622 (1954), *reprinted in* 1954 U.S.C.C.A.N. 4629, 4666.
37 *Id.* at 4667.
38 H.R. Rep. No. 83-2543 (1954) (Conf. Rep.), *reprinted in* 1954 U.S.C.C.A.N. 5280, 5291.
39 Revenue Act of 1964, Pub. L. No. 88-272, § 212, 78 Stat. 19, 49.
40 S. Rep. No. 88-830 (1964), *reprinted in* 1964 U.S.C.C.A.N. 1673, 1741.
41 Moritz v. Comm'r, 469 F.2d 466, 467 (10th Cir. 1972), *rev'g*, 55 T.C. 113 (1970).
42 *Id.* at 468–69.
43 *Moritz*, 55 T.C. at 114.
44 *Id.* at 115.
45 404 U.S. 71 (1971).
46 *Moritz*, 469 F.2d at 470.
47 *Id.*

Rather than striking down § 214, the court chose to ignore the classification and allow the taxpayer to claim the deduction.[48]

In one case, however, overt gender discrimination avoided scrutiny in a way that seems to have effectively sanctioned that discrimination. In *Totes-Isotoner Corp. v. United States*,[49] an importer of gloves challenged the imposition of a higher tariff on men's gloves than on women's. Notwithstanding seemingly obvious gender discrimination, the U.S. Court of Appeals for the Federal Circuit concluded—with no real explanation—that the classification was not facially discriminatory.[50] Then, in considering whether the tariff provisions had a disparate impact on male glove users, the court stated that "[i]t is well established that disparate impact standing alone does not establish a violation of equal protection," though it can "support [...] a finding of purposeful discrimination."[51] The court next proceeded to heighten the pleading requirements in equal protection cases implicating the tax laws:

> [A]lthough disparate impact can be relevant to the determination of a purpose to discriminate, we think that in the area of taxation and tariffs, something more than disparate impact is required to establish a purpose to discriminate for the purposes of pleading an equal protection violation. As the Supreme Court noted in *San Antonio Independent School District v. Rodriguez*, "[n]o scheme of taxation, whether the tax is imposed on property, income, or purchases of goods and services, has yet been devised which is free of all discriminatory impact."[52]

Applying this heightened standard, the court dismissed the challenge because the plaintiff had not met "its burden to allege facts sufficient to infer a governmental purpose to discriminate."[53]

In a subsequent case, the U.S. Court of International Trade followed the *Totes-Isotoner* decision and required others challenging these tariff classifications to "allege sufficient additional facts to make plausible their claim that Congress intended to discriminate between male and female users."[54] Ultimately, the Court of International Trade found that "[t]here simply [was] nothing in the Amended Complaints that can connect the tariff provisions and congressional action in a way to suggest with plausibility the existence of a governmental intent to discriminate."[55] Unsurprisingly, the Federal Circuit easily affirmed this decision on appeal.[56] It appears that the Federal Circuit has set the bar for pleading an equal protection challenge in this area so (inexplicably)[57] high that this type of discrimination—which likewise surfaces in a number of other areas in the tariff schedule[58]—has been effectively sanctioned by the courts.

Overt Sexual Orientation Discrimination

Taxpayers challenged the constitutionality of the federal Defense of Marriage Act (DOMA) as it applied to the federal tax laws. Section three of DOMA provided:

> In determining the meaning of any Act of Congress, or of any ruling, regulation, or interpretation of the various administrative bureaus and agencies of the United States, the word "marriage" means only a legal union

---

48 *Id.*

49 594 F.3d 1346 (Fed. Cir. 2010).

50 *Id.* at 1358.

51 *Id.* at 1356.

52 *Id.* at 1357–58 (citation omitted) (quoting San Antonio Indep. Sch. Dist. v. Rodriguez, 411 U.S. 1, 41 (1973)).

53 *Id.* at 1358.

54 Rack Room Shoes v. United States, 821 F. Supp. 2d 1341, 1346 (Ct. Int'l Trade 2012), *aff'd*, 718 F.3d 1370 (Fed. Cir. 2013).

55 *Id.* at 1348.

56 Rack Room Shoes, 718 F.3d 1370.

57 Jason Lewis, Note, *Gender-Classified Imports: Equal Protection Violations in the Harmonized Tariff Schedule of the United States*, 18 CARDOZO J.L. & GENDER 171, 180 (2011).

58 *Id.* at 186.

> between one man and one woman as husband and wife, and the word "spouse" refers only to a person of the opposite sex who is a husband or a wife.[59]

This provision denied legal recognition to marriages, civil unions, and domestic partnerships entered into by same-sex couples for purposes of federal law, including federal tax laws. (The Internal Revenue Service otherwise defers to the states in defining marriage, and had even indicated a willingness to treat different-sex couples' civil unions and domestic partnerships that are the legal equivalent of marriage under state law as marriages for federal tax purposes.)[60] DOMA thus denied same-sex couples in legally recognized relationships (however denominated) the federal tax benefits (and spared the tax detriments) that are associated with marriage.

In *Gill v. Office of Personnel Management*,[61] a group of same-sex couples brought an equal protection challenge to the application of DOMA to deny them certain benefits of federal law. Among the benefits DOMA denied these couples were tax benefits associated with flexible spending arrangements and the ability to file joint U.S. federal income tax returns.[62] Applying the deferential rational basis test, the U.S. District Court in *Gill* was "convinced that 'there exists no fairly conceivable set of facts that could ground a rational relationship' between DOMA and a legitimate government objective. DOMA, therefore, violates core constitutional principles of equal protection."[63] In essence, the court found that all of the rationales for enacting DOMA—both those offered at the time of enactment and those offered in the context of litigation—were entirely implausible and that the only plausible explanation was that DOMA was borne of "irrational prejudice" and "animus" toward same-sex couples.[64]

On appeal, the U.S. Court of Appeals for the First Circuit was diffident, asserting that DOMA would actually survive the rational basis test because "Congress could rationally have believed that DOMA would reduce costs, even if newer studies of the actual economic effects of DOMA suggest that it may in fact raise costs for the federal government."[65] Ultimately, however, the First Circuit decided that "the extreme deference accorded to ordinary economic legislation" was inappropriate, and it instead applied a more searching form of rational basis scrutiny, as has been done in other cases where a classification targets a "historically disadvantaged or unpopular" group.[66] Disavowing any reliance upon antigay animus as a basis for its decision,[67] the First Circuit held that DOMA could not pass muster under this more searching form of rational basis scrutiny, stating that "[s]everal of the reasons given [in support of DOMA] do not match the statute and several others are diminished by specific holdings in Supreme Court decisions more or less directly on point."[68]

In *Pedersen v. Office of Personnel Management*,[69] another group of same-sex couples filed a similar challenge to section three of DOMA. Though the U.S. District Court concluded that sexual orientation classifications should be subject to heightened scrutiny, it ultimately concluded that section three of DOMA cannot survive even rational basis review.[70] Like the U.S. District Court in *Gill*, the *Pedersen* court found "that no conceivable rational basis exists for the provision. The provision therefore violates the equal protection principles incorporated in the Fifth Amendment to the United States Constitution."[71]

59 Defense of Marriage Act, Pub. L. No. 104-99, § 3(a), 110 Stat. 2419 (1996) (codifed at 1 U.S.C. § 7 (2006)).

60 I.R.C. § 7703 (2013); Boyter v. Comm'r, 668 F.2d 1382, 1385 (4th Cir. 1981); Amy S. Elliott, *IRS Memo Indicates Civil Unions Are Marriages for Tax Purposes*, 133 Tax Notes 794 (2011).

61 699 F. Supp. 2d 374 (D. Mass. 2010), *aff'd sub nom.* Massachusetts v. U.S. Dep't of Health & Human Servs., 682 F.3d 1 (1st Cir. 2012).

62 *Id.* at 381, 383.

63 *Id.* at 387 (citations omitted) (quoting Medeiros v. Vincent, 431 F.3d 25, 29 (1st Cir. 2005)).

64 *Id.* at 396.

65 *Massachusetts*, 682 F.3d at 9.

66 *Id.* at 10–11.

67 *Id.* at 16. DOMA's legislative history—which paints supporters of same-sex marriage as radicals on the attack and openly expresses moral disapproval of lesbians and gay men—belies the First Circuit's attempt to sanitize the motivations of DOMA's congressional supporters. H.R. Rep. No. 104-664 (1996), *reprinted in* 1996 U.S.C.C.A.N. 2905.

68 *Massachusetts*, 682 F.3d at 15.

69 881 F. Supp. 2d 294 (D. Conn. 2012).

70 *Id.* at 334.

71 *Id.* at 347.

In *Dragovich v. U.S. Department of the Treasury*,[72] a group of California public employees challenged the constitutionality of DOMA and IRC § 7702B(f) because these provisions prevented them from enrolling their same-sex spouses and registered domestic partners in California's long-term care plan, which is afforded favorable treatment under federal tax law. The U.S. District Court in *Dragovich* found that neither DOMA nor § 7702B(f) bore any rational relationship to a legitimate government interest; to the contrary, the court found that both statutes were motivated by actual or apparent antigay animus.[73] Accordingly, the U.S. District Court held that both statutes violated the plaintiffs' equal protection rights.[74]

Similarly, in *Windsor v. United States*,[75] a U.S. District Court found that DOMA violated the equal protection rights of a surviving same-sex spouse who had been required to bear the burden of more than $350,000 in federal estate taxes because she was unable to qualify for the marital deduction in IRC § 2056 that shields transfers of property from a decedent to her surviving spouse from estate tax. From among several of these challenges to DOMA, the U.S. Supreme Court decided to hear an appeal in *Windsor*, which was affirmed by the U.S. Court of Appeals for the Second Circuit after the petition for writ of certiorari was filed.[76] A sharply divided Supreme Court invalidated section three of DOMA.[77] In the majority opinion, the *Windsor* Court elided the question of the appropriate standard of review under equal protection analysis; however, it did seem to apply something more than traditional rational basis review to the taxpayer's claim.[78] In reaching its decision, the majority drew upon federalism concerns—given that questions of marital status have historically been left to the states—but relied more directly upon the antigay animus underlying DOMA's enactment.[79] Ultimately, the Court held that section three of DOMA "is invalid, for no legitimate purpose overcomes the purpose and effect to disparage and to injure those whom the State, by its marriage laws, sought to protect in personhood and dignity."[80]

Other Classifications

Aside from instances of blatant discrimination, classifications in the tax laws need only pass muster under a relaxed version of the rational basis test. Like the U.S. Supreme Court in its later decision in *Regan v. Taxation With Representation* (quoted earlier), the U.S.Tax Court has asserted that:

> A Federal income tax is only limited by the due process clause of the Fifth Amendment in those "rare and special instances" which represent "extreme and glaring" exercises of legislative discretion "fairly outside the zone of possible debate." In the absence of a suspect classification or a substantial impediment of a fundamental right, no violation of equal protection is present in a Federal income tax statute so long as there is a conceivably reasonable basis for its classification.[81]

Or as the Tax Court put it in another case:

> For economic legislation such as is involved herein, the test of constitutionality is whether the legislative action is "rationally based and free from invidious discrimination." To this test should be added the principle that,

72 872 F. Supp. 2d 944 (N.D. Cal. 2012).

73 *Id.* at 955, 959.

74 *Id.* at 959, 964.

75 833 F. Supp. 2d 394 (S.D.N.Y.), *aff'd*, 699 F.3d 169 (2d Cir. 2012), *aff'd*, 133 S. Ct. 2675 (2013).

76 Windsor v. United States, 699 F.3d 169 (2d Cir. 2012), *aff'd*, 133 S. Ct. 2675 (2013).

77 United States v. Windsor, 133 S. Ct. 2675 (2013).

78 *See id.* at 2692 (subjecting DOMA to "careful consideration"); *see also id.* at 2706 (Scalia, J., dissenting) (observing that the majority "does not *apply* anything that resembles th[e] deferential framework" of rational basis analysis).

79 *Id.* at 2690–95 (majority).

80 *Id.* at 2696.

81 Smith v. Comm'r, 77 T.C. 1181, 1188 (1981) (citations omitted) (quoting A. Magnano Co. v. Hamilton, 292 U.S. 40, 44 (1934), and Cohan v. Comm'r, 39 F.2d 540, 545 (2d Cir. 1930)), *aff'd*, 701 F.2d 807 (9th Cir. 1983).

> even where there are doubts, the usual presumption of constitutionality is "particularly strong in the case of a revenue measure."[82]

Accordingly, the courts place a firm thumb on the scale in favor of upholding tax classifications.

Given the courts' reluctance to second-guess tax classifications, the rational basis test has proved to be a nearly impossible hurdle for taxpayers to surmount.[83] A few examples will help to illustrate the ease with which the federal government is able to deflect equal protection challenges in the tax area. These examples will also set the stage for the discussion in the next section regarding the tax "closet" to which equal protection concerns have been relegated.

The high threshold that taxpayers must surmount in equal protection challenges manifests itself in different ways. In some cases, the courts' skepticism of equal protection challenges can be seen in the manifestly faulty logic used to justify their decisions. For instance, in *Beard v. Commissioner*, the U.S. Court of Appeals for the Sixth Circuit held that affording taxpayers a trial by jury only if they prepay their taxes does not violate their "equal protection rights as 'poor people.'"[84] The rational basis for this distinction: "'It is essential to the honor and orderly conduct of the government that its taxes be promptly paid.' To permit suit without prepayment might place 'the very existence of the government … in the power of a hostile judiciary.'"[85]

This rationale makes no sense at all. The question posed in the case was not whether taxpayers could access the courts without prepaying their taxes. Indeed, the taxpayers had brought suit in the U.S. Tax Court, a forum in which taxpayers contest their tax liability *without* prepaying. The taxpayers merely wished to have access to a jury trial in this forum (as they would if they had been able to afford to prepay their tax liability, request a refund, and then sue for the refund in U.S. District Court). Denying the taxpayers access to a jury trial thus had the effect of putting the government's revenue stream squarely in the hands of the judiciary (and in a court that is more likely to rule in favor of the taxpayer),[86] which is exactly what the Sixth Circuit purported to be avoiding by rejecting the taxpayer's equal protection challenge.

At other times, the high threshold manifests itself in a court's dismissal of the adverse impact of a classification. For example, in a concurring opinion in the *Totes-Isotoner* case discussed earlier, one judge would have dismissed the case because the tariff classification "distinguishes on the basis of products, not natural people."[87] Interestingly, "[t]he fact that the products are designed for use by men rather than women and children does not constitute disparate treatment of actual men."[88] Charitably put, this is a wooden interpretation of the tariff classification system; one that the judge buttressed by noting that the importer had not alleged "that the tariff results in men paying higher prices for gloves, having a more limited selection of colors and styles of gloves, or having a more limited selection of merchants for gloves than women."[89]

Likewise, in *Druker v. Commissioner*,[90] the U.S. Court of Appeals for the Second Circuit rejected an equal protection challenge to the "marriage penalty" in the federal income tax. The court acknowledged that the marriage penalty undoubtedly has "some adverse effect on marriage"; after all, it causes two-earner couples whose wages are relatively equal to pay more tax than they would have paid had they not married.[91] But the court characterized this effect as "indirect," even though the taxpayers in *Druker* had actually divorced—but continued to live together—simply to avoid the burden of the additional tax.[92] Resigned to the fact that

82 Black v. Comm'r, 69 T.C. 505, 507–8 (1977) (quoting Dandridge v. Williams, 397 U.S. 471, 487 (1970), and Nammack v. Comm'r, 56 T.C. 1379, 1385 (1971), *aff'd per curiam*, 459 F.2d 1045 (2d Cir. 1972)).

83 Lawrence v. Texas, 539 U.S. 558, 579 (2003) (O'Connor, J., concurring).

84 182 F.3d 916 (6th Cir. 1999).

85 *Id.* (quoting Cheatham v. United States, 92 U.S. 85, 89 (1875) (quoted in Flora v. United States, 357 U.S. 63, 68 (1958))).

86 Daniel M. Schneider, *Assessing and Predicting Who Wins Federal Tax Trial Decisions*, 37 WAKE FOREST L. REV. 473, 492–93, 496, 497 (2002).

87 Totes-Isotoner Corp. v. United States, 594 F.3d 1346, 1359 (Fed. Cir. 2010) (footnote omitted).

88 *Id.* at 1360.

89 *Id.*

90 697 F.2d 46 (2d Cir. 1982).

91 *Id.* at 49–50.

92 *Id.* at 50.

"[i]n the area of family taxation every legislative disposition is 'virtually fated to be both overinclusive and underinclusive when judged from one perspective or another,'"[93] the court granted Congress "wide latitude" in making classifications in this area.[94]

In yet other cases, the courts impose nearly impossible burdens of proof on taxpayers challenging an implicit tax classification. For instance, in *Black v. Commissioner*,[95] the U.S. Tax Court rejected a constitutional challenge to the former deduction for dependent-care expenses in § 214. (As discussed earlier, the *Moritz* court invalidated a portion of § 214 on equal protection grounds. Prior to the taxable year at issue in *Black*, Congress revised § 214 to be gender neutral on its face.[96]) The taxpayers in *Black* alleged that the gender discrimination that previously had been on the face of § 214 continued to be embodied in other aspects of the statute, including a requirement that married taxpayers file a joint return, a monthly cap on deductible expenses, and an adjusted gross income limitation on deductible expenses.[97] The nature of this discrimination was more clearly spelled out in an earlier equal protection challenge that the Tax Court had likewise rejected:

> Relying upon demographic and sociological data presented to this Court, petitioner has argued that most children in the United States are entrusted to the care of women; that it has traditionally been the woman's responsibility to care for her children in the home while the husband provides income for the family by pursuing an occupation; that if a woman with children works, it is almost always her responsibility to secure and maintain adequate arrangements for child care; that the costs of child care are traditionally regarded as an expense of the woman's employment when the family decides whether she should work; that even small increments in the cost of taking on a job can affect that decision; that the limitations on the deductibility of child care expenses … prevent deduction of the full amount of the expenses which most mothers must incur in order to secure child care; and that … [the] adjusted gross income [limitation] … deprives a substantial number of married women of the benefit of any deduction for child care expenses. Petitioner contends that the provisions of section 214(b) single out one class of individuals—women with children—for discriminatory treatment with regard to an expense functionally indistinguishable from other ordinary and necessary business expenses … .[98]

In rejecting the taxpayers' equal protection challenge in *Black*, the Tax Court relied upon the fact that, unlike in *Moritz*, § 214 was then "neutral on its face."[99] The court also relied upon its decision in the earlier case quoted immediately above as well as the inability of the taxpayers to provide evidence supporting their assertions that § 214 "is based on the premise that married women will not work unless it is an economic necessity … [and] operates as an economic deterrent to women who wish to work outside the home."[100]

The Tax Closet

In essence, the courts have relegated the guarantee of equal protection of the laws to the tax closet. The closet, here as elsewhere, acts as a line of demarcation between the spoken and the unspoken, the discussed and the dismissed, the visible and the invisible, the normal and the abnormal, and the voluntary and the coerced.[101] But like so many other borders that appear fixed and immovable, these lines of demarcation are, as I will now demonstrate, inherently unstable and shifting.[102]

93 *Id.* (quoting Boris I. Bittker, *Federal Income Taxation and the Family*, 27 Stan. L. Rev. 1389, 1443 (1975)).

94 *Id.* at 51.

95 Black v. Comm'r, 69 T.C. 505 (1977).

96 *Id.* at 506 n.2.

97 *Id.* at 506 & n.2, 507.

98 Nammack v. Comm'r, 56 T.C. 1379, 1382 (1971), *aff'd per curiam*, 459 F.2d 1045 (2d Cir. 1972).

99 *Black*, 69 T.C. at 509.

100 *Id.* Tucked away in a footnote, the Tax Court does acknowledge that "patent discrimination in a statute itself is not necessarily a precondition to unconstitutionality if it is clear that discrimination in fact exists." *Id.* at n.3.

101 *See* Eve Kosofsky Sedgwick, Epistemology of the Closet 11 (1990).

102 *Id.* at 9–10; *see generally* Infanti, *supra* note 10, at 747–95.

Shifting Boundaries

The federal courts have fashioned a schema in which they police only the most blatant instances of discrimination. Such a schema normalizes discrimination. It is constitutionally acceptable for Congress to discriminate against certain groups of taxpayers—even, perhaps especially, those who are routinely disadvantaged in American society—so long as that discrimination is not open and on the face of the tax laws. Thus, discrimination that would be accepted as a normal and natural part of our tax system suddenly becomes abnormal or aberrational when the legislature discriminates so overtly as to "border on the irrational."[103] (After all, if the legislature can discriminate so long as it maintains the appearance of neutrality, why would it be so irrational as to make that discrimination plain rather than hiding the discrimination in plain sight?)[104] The discrimination remains the same; the only difference between that which is normal and that which is abnormal is the degree of plausible deniability.

Aside from "the most explicit demonstration that a [tax] classification is a hostile and oppressive discrimination against particular persons and classes,"[105] the courts manifest obvious discomfort at becoming entangled in questions regarding whether the tax system is a tool for invidious discrimination.[106] The courts conveniently elide these questions by suppressing them, banishing them to the invisibility of the tax closet. But the courts do not do the work of banishment on their own. By adopting an extraordinary level of deference to the legislature's tax classifications, the courts place the metaphorical keys to the tax closet in the hands of the legislature. The two therefore work in tandem to populate the tax closet.

Though we often speak of "going into" or "coming out of" the closet as if it were a voluntary act on the part of the closeted individual, it is clear that there is nothing voluntary about closeting anyone or anything. Closeting is inherently coercive. Lesbians and gay men do not go into the closet of their own free will; they have been (and, despite remarkable gains, still are) pushed into the closet by the pressure of societal discomfort with—and, in some cases, open hostility toward—homosexuality. In the case of the tax closet, those who are the victims of invidious discrimination do not voluntarily choose to enter or exit the tax closet. Instead, the courts, with the help of the legislature, presumptively push victims of invidious discrimination into the invisibility of the tax closet. It is the choice of the legislature whether to make its invidious discrimination plain, dragging taxpayers out of the legal invisibility of the closet and into the visibility of the rare judicial opinion upholding an equal protection challenge to the tax laws. When safely locked behind the closet door, invidious discrimination perpetrated through the tax laws—no matter how real its impact—can normally be left unaddressed by the courts, summarily dismissed from their dockets, legally invisible though visible to anyone who cares to see.

This aversion to addressing invidious discrimination in our tax system, which manifested itself early in the life of the modern federal income tax,[107] is a conscious and voluntary choice on the part of the federal judiciary. Courts in other countries embrace their role as arbiters of the fairness of the tax system.[108] For example, the German Constitutional Court "has been instrumental in shaping fundamental elements of German income tax law. … [T]he German Constitutional Court has applied Germany's basic law expansively and comprehensively to tax controversies. The court aggressively limits legislative authority in tax matters."[109] Indeed, in contrast to the Second Circuit's decision in *Druker* (discussed earlier), the German Constitutional

103 Martinez, *supra* note 23, at 437.

104 Sugin, *supra* note 24, at 443.

105 Regan v. Taxation With Representation, 461 U.S. 540, 547 (1983) (quoting Madden v. Kentucky, 309 U.S. 83, 88 (1940)).

106 *E.g.*, Begay v. Comm'r, 105 T.C.M. (CCH) 1114 (2013) (rejecting an equal protection challenge to the definition of "qualifying child" brought by a Navajo elder with clan-based obligations to a child who did not fit squarely within the relationship requirements of IRC § 152(c)—a challenge that otherwise would have raised religious, cultural, and political issues).

107 Brushaber v. Union Pac. R.R. Co., 240 U.S. 1, 24 (1916).

108 Henry Ordower, *Restricting the Legislative Power to Tax: Intersections of Taxation and Constitutional Law*, *in* General Reports of the XVIIth Congress of the International Academy of Comparative Law 883, 886 (Katharina Boele-Woelki & Sjef van Erp eds., 2007).

109 Henry Ordower, *Horizontal and Vertical Equity in Taxation as Constitutional Principles: Germany and the United States Contrasted*, 7 Fla. Tax Rev. 259, 301–02 (2006).

Court struck down a similar marriage penalty in Germany's income tax and "left no opening for modification of the joint assessment that would impose a greater tax burden on a married couple than on two unmarried individuals."[110] In a subsequent decision, the German Constitutional Court held that "the deductions and exemptions available to single individuals with dependent children were inadequate to free the basic costs of caring for children from taxation" and directed the legislature to take action to redress the problem.[111] This is a far cry from the Second Circuit's choice to ignore the important effects that taxation can have on the family and to wash its hands of the issue by affording extraordinary deference to legislative decision-making.

Closeting's coercion of the victims of invidious discrimination can be witnessed in the juxtaposition of the *Moritz* and *Black* cases discussed in the previous section. Both of these cases involved equal protection challenges to former § 214. In *Moritz*, the discrimination between taxpayers on the basis of sex was clearly visible on the face of the statute. In other words, Congress had taken the keys to the tax closet, unlocked the door, and dragged the victims of its invidious discrimination out of the tax closet and into the realm of legal visibility.[112] As explained earlier, one can readily detect the motivation behind the gender classification that then appeared on the face of § 214: Woman's presumptive place was in the home acting as caregiver, and man's presumptive place was in the paid labor market. Only women whose economic or personal circumstances did not permit them to remain at home and men who lacked the caregiving aid of their wives would incur dependent care expenses to be gainfully employed.

In the later *Black* case, the court dismissed a similar equal protection challenge to former § 214. Before the taxable year at issue in *Black*, Congress had pushed the victims of its invidious discrimination back into the tax closet by revising the statute to be gender-neutral on its face. At that time, the discrimination went from being plainly visible to being hidden in plain sight (that is, through the operation of a requirement that married couples file a joint return, a cap on deductible expenses, and an adjusted gross income limitation on deductible expenses). This equal protection challenge failed because the taxpayers could not prove that § 214 was "based on the premise that married women will not work unless it is an economic necessity … [and] operate[d] as an economic deterrent to women who wish to work outside the home."[113] Turning the taxpayers away, the court futilely pointed them in the direction of Congress, which, as these two cases illustrate, is both the keeper of the keys to the tax closet and the only one with the power to redress the impact of discrimination perpetrated against those relegated to the tax closet.[114]

Covering

Though there is an oft-bemoaned disconnect between the judiciary and the legal academy in the United States,[115] the two have created a seamless rhetorical tapestry to cover and conceal the door to the tax closet (and, concomitantly, their own discomfort at the idea of addressing invidious discrimination in the tax laws). In weaving their end of this tapestry, tax academics use the principle of tax equity as their loom and economics as their yarn. Tax academics typically divide discussions of tax equity into two subcategories: horizontal equity and vertical equity. Horizontal equity demands the equal treatment of taxpayers with equal incomes, and vertical equity requires an appropriate differentiation of the tax burdens imposed on taxpayers with differing incomes (for example, through the imposition of tax at progressive, regressive, or proportional rates).[116]

Through this labeling and categorization, tax academics are able to lend an air of scientific precision to what otherwise would be a subjective inquiry.[117] Indeed, the very labels "horizontal" and "vertical" call

110 *Id.* at 320.

111 *Id.* at 322.

112 Recall that prior to the enactment of § 214, the courts had classified these expenses as nondeductible personal expenses, because they related to the "wife's services as custodian of the home and protector of its children." Smith v. Comm'r, 40 B.T.A. 1038, 1039 (1939), *aff'd per curiam*, 113 F.2d 114 (2d Cir. 1940).

113 Black v. Comm'r, 69 T.C. 505, 509 (1977).

114 *Id.* at 510.

115 Richard Brust, *The High Bench vs. The Ivory Tower*, A.B.A. J., Feb. 2012, at 50.

116 Anthony C. Infanti, *Tax Equity*, 55 Buff. L. Rev. 1191, 1193–94 (2008).

117 *See id.* at 1193–94, 1253.

to mind the *x*- and *y*-axes of mathematics. And the use of income as the coordinates in this Cartesian plane only adds to the air of neutrality or objectivity, helping to turn what would otherwise be a moral or legal debate into something akin to a study in econometrics.[118] In fact, the scientificity of tax equity "furnishes ready and plausible reasons to academics for not addressing concerns associated with race, ethnicity, gender, sexual orientation, disability, and other axes of subordination in the tax arena. In practice, it works even more effectively by rendering any mention of these subjects in a tax context immediately suspect."[119] As I have explained elsewhere, critical tax scholars often encounter difficulty articulating their equity-based concerns about the tax laws because the concept of tax equity is framed precisely to exclude them:

> [A]s defined and applied for purposes of income tax policy analysis, tax equity is solely concerned with the fair treatment of individuals who either have the same or different incomes. This represents a normative choice to consider economic differences—and only economic differences—in determining the fairness of a tax whose larger purpose is to allocate the burden of funding our government and of paying for public services. Through this insidious homogenization of the population, tax equity performs a sanitizing and a screening function; in other words, it effectively forecloses consideration of non-economic forms of difference (e.g., of race, ethnicity, gender, sexual orientation, or physical ability) when determining the appropriate allocation of societal burdens, even though these other forms of difference have served, and continue to serve, as the basis for invidious discrimination that already imposes heavy burdens on its victims.[120]

The unbending focus on the economic dimension of individuals—not to mention the tendency to transform debates over tax equity into debates over economic efficiency—is usually justified by the objectivity or neutrality of economics and the need to avoid impossible levels of complexity in an already complex area of the law.[121]

In weaving its end of the rhetorical tapestry, the judiciary uses a different loom—the constitutional guarantee of equal protection of the laws—but the same economic yarn as tax academics. When writing opinions addressing equal protection challenges to tax laws, the courts usually couch their announcement of the appropriate (that is, exceedingly low) threshold for passing constitutional muster with some reference to the fact that tax legislation is economic legislation.[122] In addition, the courts justify their extraordinary deference to Congress by pointing to the complexity of our tax system and the self-evident neutrality of its purpose.[123] Thus, as Kaye and Mazza explain, "courts tend to validate tax law provisions even when they create disparities among similarly situated taxpayers. This is due, in part, to the judiciary's treatment of tax issues as affecting property rights, which receive less constitutional protection than fundamental personal rights and liberties, and to the judiciary's willingness to defer to the legislature on tax issues."[124]

Bringing Equal Protection out of the Tax Closet

As a first step toward dismantling the door to the tax closet, let us unravel the thread that forms both the warp and weft of the rhetorical tapestry that covers and obscures that door. The courts and tax academics use the same yarn to weave this rhetorical tapestry. They both rely on the close affinity between tax and economics to justify their aversion to addressing invidious discrimination in our tax system. But tax law is, at best, only incidentally economic legislation.

---

118 *See, e.g.*, Miranda Stewart, *Global Trajectories of Tax Reform: The Discourse of Tax Reform in Developing and Transition Countries*, 44 Harv. Int'l L.J. 139, 172 (2003); Reuven S. Avi-Yonah, *Tax Stories and Tax Histories: Is There a Role for History in Shaping Tax Law?*, 101 Mich. L. Rev. 2227, 2234 (2003) (reviewing Tax Stories: An In-Depth Look at Ten Leading Federal Income Tax Cases (Paul L. Caron ed., 2003)).

119 Infanti, *supra* note 116, at 1253.

120 *Id.* at 1195–96 (footnotes omitted).

121 *See id.* at 1203–20, 1239–42.

122 *E.g.*, Knochelmann v. Comm'r, 455 F. App'x 536, 540 (6th Cir. 2011); Licari v. Comm'r, 946 F.2d 690, 692 (9th Cir. 1991); Black v. Comm'r, 69 T.C. 505, 507 (1977); *see also supra* note 83.

123 *E.g.*, Nordlinger v. Hahn, 505 U.S. 1, 11 (1992); Washington v. Davis, 426 U.S. 229, 248 (1976).

124 Kaye & Mazza, *supra* note 13, at 489 (footnotes omitted).

Pulling Back the Curtain

The tax laws do provide incentives and disincentives that shape economic behavior. For example, the federal income tax encourages charitable giving by allowing a deduction that functions as a (somewhat bizarre) matching program for charitable gifts.[125] Conversely, the federal income tax discourages the capitalization of corporate entities with equity (as opposed to debt) because dividends paid are not deductible (while interest paid on debt is).[126] Though the tax laws are, from time to time, consciously (and, more often, unconsciously) used to influence economic behavior, micromanaging the economy is far from the tax laws' primary purpose.

Rather, as the Organization for Economic Co-operation and Development has succinctly stated, "[t]ax systems are primarily aimed at financing public expenditures."[127] Or, in the words of the members of President George W. Bush's Advisory Panel on Federal Tax Reform, "[T]he interests of a few should not stand in the way of the tax code's primary goal: to raise funds efficiently for the common defense, vital social programs, and other goals of shared purpose."[128] Yet, even viewed from this perspective, the economic dimension of the tax laws—raising revenue—is not an end in itself but merely a means to an end. That is, the tax laws are designed to raise revenue not for the sake of hoarding money but so that this money can be spent. That is the true purpose of the tax laws—to fund expenditures for the common good.

With this end now in sight, it should become clear that tax is not about economics but about justice and fairness. When crafting tax laws to raise a certain amount of revenue, Congress must decide how this burden is most fairly and justly shared among the population. Whom do we ask to pay these costs? How do we determine their ability to contribute? When (and how often) should they be asked to contribute? At their core, these are not economic questions but moral ones. Thus, it should come as no surprise that, as Susan Pace Hamill has put it, "tax policy is one of the most telling indicators of the nation's true moral compass."[129]

Removing the Closet Door

Having begun to unravel the rhetorical tapestry that covers the door to the tax closet, we can now start the job of dismantling this locked door as we would any other—by removing the pins from the hinges on the door. Once the door is removed, light will be able to shine into the tax closet and reveal its (discomforting) contents. With the correct tools, this operation can be performed as easily on this figurative door as it is on the doors in your home. In place of a hammer and screwdriver, our rhetorical tool for this job will be the judicial doctrine of substance over form. As the U.S. Court of Appeals for the Fifth Circuit has stated, "[t]he principle of looking through form to substance is … the cornerstone of sound taxation."[130]

This tool is both readily available and one that should feel comfortable in the hands of the judiciary, especially following the U.S. Supreme Court's decision regarding the individual mandate in the Patient Protection and Affordable Care Act (more commonly referred to as "Obamacare").[131] In that case, the Supreme Court held that, for constitutional purposes, the label applied by Congress would not determine whether the shared responsibility payment owed by those who do not purchase health insurance under "Obamacare"

---

125 Stanley S. Surrey, *Federal Income Tax Reform: The Varied Approaches Necessary to Replace Tax Expenditures with Direct Governmental Assistance*, 84 Harv. L. Rev. 352, 384–88 (1970).

126 Boris I. Bittker & James S. Eustice, Federal Income Taxation of Corporations and Shareholders ¶ 4.01 (2013), *available at* 1999 WL 516483.

127 Org. for Econ. Co-operation & Dev., OECD Tax Policy Studies No. 20, Tax Policy Reform and Economic Growth 18 (2010).

128 Letter from the President's Advisory Panel on Fed. Tax Reform to John W. Snow, Sec'y of the Treasury (Nov. 1, 2005), *in* President's Advisory Panel on Fed. Tax Reform, Simple, Fair, and Pro-Growth: Proposals to Fix America's Tax System (2005).

129 Susan Pace Hamill, *An Evaluation of Federal Tax Policy Based on Judeo-Christian Ethics*, 25 Va. Tax Rev. 671, 747 (2006).

130 Weinert's Estate v. Comm'r, 294 F.2d 750, 755 (5th Cir. 1961).

131 Nat'l Fed'n of Indep. Bus. v. Sebelius, 132 S. Ct. 2566 (2012).

would be characterized as a "penalty" or a "tax."[132] In other words, in interpreting the Constitution, the Supreme Court disregarded the form of the exaction (that is, the "penalty" label applied by Congress) and instead focused on whether the exaction was, in substance, a tax when determining whether its imposition fell within the congressional taxing power.[133]

Contrary to established principles for applying the tax laws and interpreting the Constitution, the schema for analyzing equal protection challenges to the tax laws elevates form over substance. The courts are far more concerned with what appears to be the case (for example, is the statute neutral on its face?) than what is actually happening to taxpayers. For example, recall the difference in treatment between the *Moritz* and *Black* cases, where form played a pivotal role in determining the outcome. In *Moritz*, the deduction for dependent care expenses in § 214 discriminated on its face on the basis of gender, resulting in the court upholding an equal protection challenge to the statute. In *Black*, § 214 passed constitutional muster largely because it had changed its form—it no longer discriminated on the basis of gender on its face—even though, in substance, the taxpayer argued that § 214 continued to invidiously discriminate as it always had.

Similarly, requiring proof of congressional intent to discriminate, as in *Totes-Isotoner*, elevates form over substance and imposes an insurmountable hurdle for equal protection challenges.[134] As discussed earlier, the invidious discrimination present in the tax laws is usually subtle; indeed, the possibility of Congress articulating a discriminatory purpose in tax legislative history has been described as "unthinkable."[135] This has led one commentator to call on the courts to reconsider the need to prove intent to discriminate in tax cases:

> [E]vidence is building that the tax law is instrumental in contributing to the continued economic inequality of minorities and women. Given that the tax law is one of the most important governmental mechanisms for redistribution of societal wealth, its constitutional impenetrability behind a wall of neutrality is unfortunate. The Code's virtual immunity from equal protection analysis ... should prompt the Supreme Court to reconsider whether the intent requirement of *Washington v. Davis* fulfills the goals of equal protection.[136]

The courts' wooden approach to analyzing equal protection challenges contravenes the general principle that tax is concerned with substance and *not* with form. However a taxpayer might have cast a given transaction, the IRS and the courts are willing (and sometimes eager) to look past the form of the transaction to see what actually occurred in order to determine the appropriate tax treatment.[137] The notion of looking past form to substance is important in the area of taxation because of the relative ease with which taxpayers and their advisers can dress up a financial arrangement in the garb of one or more other arrangements merely to achieve tax savings.

Why are we not concerned about the same ease with which Congress can make the tax laws appear neutral while (wittingly or unwittingly) extending into the tax laws—and then entrenching and reinforcing there—the subordination along lines of race, ethnicity, gender, sexual orientation, class, and disability that is pervasive in our society? Why should the courts not be asked to engage in more meaningful—and less wooden—applications of the equal protection guarantee to the tax laws? In short, when considering how the burdens of funding common expenditures are distributed among the population, why does the government worry so little about imposing a disproportionate burden on those who are already carrying the burden of discrimination on their backs? Why are we not more concerned with the substance of how the tax laws operate than with their deceptive appearance of neutrality? Or, put bluntly, why does the judiciary *not* employ the same tool that it routinely uses to look through the schemes of taxpayers who shirk their duty to contribute their share of common expenditures when it must determine whether Congress has shirked its constitutional duty to afford the equal protection of the laws to all?

132 *Id.* at 2582–83, 2594–95, 2597–98.

133 *Id.* at 2593–2600.

134 *See supra* text accompanying notes 54–55.

135 *See supra* text accompanying note 24.

136 Sugin, *supra* note 24, at 456 (footnotes omitted).

137 Boris I. Bittker & Lawrence Lokken, Federal Taxation of Income, Estates & Gifts ¶ 4.3.3 (2013), *available at* 1999 WL 516483.

Out into the Light

Dismantling the door to the tax closet is not as daunting a task as it might first appear to be. By focusing our attention on the underlying purpose of the tax laws, we are able to pull back the rhetorical tapestry that has been used to obscure the closet door. We are able to see that tax is not about economics but about a just and fair distribution of the burden of funding expenditures for the common good. It is not about summing up the gains and losses from individual financial transactions but about what type of society we wish to build and whom we should ask to pay for it and how much they should be asked to pay. With clear access to the door, we have begun the job of removing that door and revealing the invidious discrimination in the tax laws hidden behind it by asking the courts to use the same approach to equal protection challenges to the tax laws as they use in analyzing and interpreting the tax laws more generally. This would be a natural extension of tax norms and one that might have a salutary effect on the application of the guarantee of equal protection to other areas of the law.

PART V
Pushing the Boundaries

Chapter 13
Equal Protection and the Immigrant: Legislating Our Way Toward Two Americas

Laura A. Hernández[1]

In what is becoming a common observation, examples of widening inequality in the United States abound. Much of the recent attention is focused on wealth inequality. This is not surprising given that monetary success serves as the American barometer of achievement. But we must dig more deeply into the root cause for the systemic reasons for this inequality, which run far deeper than the simple analogy of the "elite" top 1 percent or the "dependent" bottom 47 percent.[2] When we do, it is apparent that American federal and state legislatures have passed laws that are effectively leading to the creation of a second-class population within our borders—a population comprised of recent immigrants.

Theoretically, the Equal Protection Clause should prevent such an outcome. Indeed, a fully realized Equal Protection Clause functions more as a gatekeeper than an ephemeral expression of a constitutional ideal. It exists to counteract an uncomfortable tendency in American political life to demonize the "other," whether based on gender, race, sexual orientation or something else. Immigration status is unique in that it encompasses all of these "other" identities but adds the specter of an illegality of presence to justify what might otherwise be discriminatory legislation.

Focusing on the reduced constitutional status of the non-citizen to validate these types of laws is not an answer because their effect goes far beyond the (possibly undocumented) non-citizen. These laws harm their American-born citizen-children. This chapter will examine some of the legislation targeting non-citizens and explain why the Equal Protection Clause does not allow such discrimination.

The Non-Citizen Immigrant's Reduced Constitutional Status

Longstanding judicial precedent dictates that non-citizens are never granted the same constitutional protection as American citizens.[3] Beginning in the late 1880s, with the Chinese Exclusion Case and its progeny,[4] the

1 Laura A. Hernández is an Associate Professor at Baylor Law School. The author wishes to thank Analí Gatlin, J.D. 2014, for her invaluable assistance with this essay.

2 *Romney's Speech from Mother Jones Video*, N.Y. Times, Sept. 19, 2012, http://www.nytimes.com/2012/ 09/19/us/politics/mitt-romneys-speech-from-mother-jones-video.html?pagewanted=all (Mitt Romney's statement during a private fundraiser—"[T]here are 47 percent of the people who will vote for the president no matter what. There are 47 percent who are with him, who are dependent upon government who believe they are victims … These are people who pay no income tax; 47 percent of Americas pay no income tax."); *see also* Daniel Altman, *To Reduce Inequality, Tax Wealth, Not Income*, N.Y. Times, Nov. 18, 2012, http://www.nytimes.com/2012/11/19/opinion/to-reduce-inequality-tax-wealth-not-income.html (stating the future of the 99 percent, 47 percent, and 1 percent are threatened by wealth inequality, which is unequal access to economic opportunities).

3 *United States ex rel. Knauff v. Shaughnessy*, 338 U.S. 537, 544 (1950) (excluding the spouse of a United States citizen without a hearing as permitted by then-existing federal regulation); *Landon v. Plasencia*, 459 U.S. 21, 22 (1982) (holding permanent resident not entitled to have admissibility determined in deportation proceeding, which provided greater procedural due process protection than exclusion hearing).

4 *Chae Chan Ping v. United States*, 130 U.S. 581, 610 (1889) (upholding Chinese Exclusion Act denying re-entry of Chinese non-citizens who left the U.S. prior to the passage of the Act); *Nishimura Ekiu v. United States*, 142 U.S. 651, 664 (1892) (validating immigration inspector's detention and inspection of Japanese citizen pursuant to Immigration Act of 1882); *Fong Yue Ting v. United States*, 149 U.S. 698, 713 (1893) (upholding arrest of Chinese laborers for not carrying certificates of

United States Supreme Court has expressly left the regulation of non-citizens to Congress for two primary reasons: (1) the sovereignty of the United States government; and, (2) the political question doctrine, which renders any issue involving congressional plenary authority nonjusticiable.[5] As recently as1950, the United States Supreme Court infamously declared that the Due Process Clause of the Fourteenth Amendment was specifically delineated by federal legislative whim: "Whatever the procedure authorized by Congress is, it is due process as far as an alien denied entry is concerned."[6]

Nonetheless, more recent case law establishes that some constitutional protection is owed to non-citizens; though the scope is something of a moving target.[7] Some of the factors that courts find most dispositive are the length of the non-citizen's presence within the United States, ties to United States citizens or lawful permanent residents (otherwise described as the family unit), and good moral character.[8]

Tellingly, even while due-process protections were circumscribed, the United States Supreme Court invoked the Equal Protection Clause to protect non-citizens. The Court invalidated state legislation that discriminated against lawfully present non-citizens in employment,[9] governmental benefits,[10] land ownership,[11] and financial assistance for higher education.[12] Equal-protection concerns also led to the abrogation of a state statute that withheld access to public school education from undocumented non-citizens.[13]

At the heart of each of these decisions was a judicial concern that unequal treatment would necessarily lead to an underclass of non-citizens living within the United States. The consequences of this legally imposed stigma would then pass down to any and all of their American-born children. Current events have demonstrated that the Supreme Court's concern was not misplaced.[14]

---

residence as required by Act of May 5, 1892); *Lem Moon Sing v. United States*, 158 U.S. 538, 549–50 (1895) (holding that the Court could not review the decision of executive official in denying entry of non-citizen pursuant to the Act of August 18, 1894).

5 *I.N.S. v. Chadha*, 462 U.S. 919, 940–41 (1983); *see also* Stephen H. Legomsky & Cristina M. Rodriguez, Immigration and Refugee Law and Policy 133 (5th ed. 2009) (discussing the United States Supreme Court's holding in the *Chinese Exclusion Case*).

6 *Knauff*, 338 U.S. at 544.

7 *See Zadvydas v. Davis*, 533 U.S. 678, 693–94 (2001) (non-citizens enjoy due process protections in deportation proceedings and the government may only detain removable non-citizens for a "reasonably necessary" period, presumptively six months or less); *Clark v. Martinez*, 543 U.S. 371, 386 (2005) (extending the due process protections applied in *Zadvydas* to inadmissible non-citizens in deportation proceedings); *Demore v. Kim*, 538 U.S. 510, 523 (2003) (non-citizens are entitled to due process protection during deportation proceedings, but detention without an individualized bond hearing during removal proceedings does not violate due process).

8 *See Ikenokwalu-White v. I.N.S.*, 316 F.3d 798, 804 (8th Cir. 2003) (considering non-citizen's expunged convictions in determining moral character for purposes of removal decision); *United States v. Boliero*, 923 F. Supp. 2d 319, 333 (D. Mass., 2013) (considering the non-citizen's close family ties in her removal determination).

9 Employment cannot be denied to a lawfully present non-citizen simply because she has not naturalized. *Yick Wo v. Hopkins*, 118 U.S. 356, 373–74 (1886) (striking down city ordinance denying Chinese immigrants permits to open laundry businesses); *Takahashi v. Fish & Game Comm'n*, 334 U.S. 410, 421 (1948) (holding state could not deny commercial fishing license based on non-citizen status).

10 Similarly, government benefits cannot be denied to a lawfully present non-citizen simply because she has not naturalized. *Graham v. Richardson*, 403 U.S. 365, 376 (1971) (finding state statute violated Equal Protection Clause by denying welfare benefits based solely on non-citizen status).

11 *See Oyama v. California*, 332 U.S. 633, 635–36 (1948) (holding that California's Alien Land Law could not invalidate a citizen's right to own land simply because his parent was a non-citizen resident who could not legally naturalize).

12 *See Nyquist v. Mauclet*, 432 U.S. 1, 12 (1977) (invalidating state law discriminating against non-citizens for higher education scholarships and loans).

13 Access to primary and secondary public school education cannot be denied on the basis of lawful immigration status. *Plyler v. Doe*, 457 U.S. 202, 213 (1982) ("The Equal Protection Clause was intended to work nothing less than the abolition of all caste-based and invidious class-based legislation.").

14 The idea that pregnant immigrant women give birth to "anchor babies" in the United States in order to capitalize on U.S. benefits is a complete myth; in fact in 2006, some U.S.-born infants were denied health services because of their mother's immigration status. Priscilla Haung, *Anchor Babies, Over-Breeders, and the Population Bomb: The Reemergence of Nativism and Population Control in Anti-Immigration Policies*, 2 Harv. L. & Pol'y Rev. 385, 400 (2008) (after constitutional challenges were raised, the Centers for Medicare & Medicaid Services revoked a policy excluding immigrant women "from accessing Medicaid services for their babies until they could verify the citizenship status of their U.S.-born children").

The Optimism Inspired By *Plyler v. Doe*

In 1982, the United States Supreme Court directly addressed a polarizing issue involving undocumented immigrants.[15] *Plyler v. Doe* answered the question of whether undocumented immigrant children have the same right of access to primary and secondary public schools as citizen-children and lawfully present immigrant children.[16] Ostensibly responding to the rising cost of public education,[17] the State of Texas had legislatively denied funding to school districts that enrolled students of questionable immigration status.[18] The statute further empowered those school districts to deny enrollment to any child who was unable to prove lawful status.[19]

In *Plyler*, the Texas statute clashed with the Equal Protection Clause because it created an impermissible sub-class of residents by subjecting an individual or group to its laws while simultaneously withholding the law's protections,[20] a result that placed it squarely at odds with the Fourteenth Amendment's intent. Specifically, the Fourteenth Amendment was ratified on July 9, 1868, to counteract the rampant discrimination inflicted on this nation's newest citizens, the freed slaves.[21] The Civil War Amendments were a congressional attempt to forestall state legislatures from creating a legally imposed second-class citizenry. Reiterating the drafter's intent, the *Plyler* Court expounded "[t]he Equal Protection Clause was intended to work nothing less than the abolition of all caste-based and invidious class-based legislation."[22]

In keeping with its precedent under the Equal Protection Clause for lawfully present non-citizens, the Court expanded equal protection in the context of education to reach every individual *domiciled* in the United States, lawfully or not.[23] Interestingly, the Court declined to find that undocumented non-citizens comprised a suspect class, holding instead that the voluntary nature of their legal status precluded such a designation.[24] Nonetheless, the Supreme Court applied something more than the traditional rational basis standard of review.[25] For the statute to be constitutional despite its discriminatory nature, it would have to further some *substantial* goal of the state, as opposed to a legitimate goal.[26]

The Supreme Court appeared to be swayed by the unique situation experienced by the *Plyler* plaintiffs, minor children whose unlawful entry into the country was not within their control.[27] First, the Court refused to impute responsibility for their parents' actions onto the children: "[E]ven if the State found it expedient to control the conduct of adults by action against their children, legislation directing the onus of a parent's

15 457 U.S. 202 (1982).

16 *Plyer v. Doe*, 457 U.S. 202 (1982).

17 *Id.* at 227.

18 Tex. Educ. Code. Ann. § 21.031 (Vernon Supp. 1981); *see also* Laura A. Hernández, *Anchor Babies: something Less Than Equal Under the Equal Protection Clause*, 19:3 S. Cal. Rev. L. & Soc. Just. 346 (2010).

19 457 U.S. at 205.

20 *Id.*

21 *See Afroyim v. Rusk*, 387 U.S. 253, 262 (1967) (stating the "chief interest" of adopting the Fourteenth Amendment was to protect the citizenship rights of African Americans).

22 *Id.* at 213.

23 "[E]very citizen or subject of another country, while domiciled here, is within the allegiance and the protection, and consequently subject to the jurisdiction of the United States." 457 U.S. at 211 n.10. Therefore, undocumented aliens are clearly subject to protection, while domiciled in the state. *Id.* at 215. "That a person's initial entry into a State, or into the United States, was unlawful, and that he may for that reason be expelled, cannot negate the simple fact of his presence within the State's territorial perimeter ... And until he leaves the jurisdiction ... he is entitled to the equal protection of the laws that a State may choose to establish." *Id.* The Court concluded that the Equal Protection was applicable to all persons within the boundaries of a state. *Id.*

24 *Id.* at 219 n.19 ("Unlike most of the classifications that we have recognized as suspect, entry into this class, by virtue of entry into this country, is the product of voluntary action.").

25 *Id.* at 223–24.

26 *Id.* at 223–24. The *Plyler* Court reaffirmed its previous holding in *San Antonio Independent School District v. Rodriguez* that education was not a fundamental right. 411 U.S. 1 (1973) (analyzing the Texas public-school financing system). *Id.* at 221–22.

27 *Id.* at 220.

misconduct against his children does not comport with fundamental conceptions of justice."[28] Second, the Court held that education was an important government benefit given to all United States residents to ensure that they could beneficially participate in society by preserving the country's political and cultural heritage.[29] A wholesale denial of secondary public education to this group of resident children would necessarily result in a permanent underclass of individuals who lacked the skills and resources to better their status in American society.[30]

Implicitly, this language recognized that at least some of the undocumented immigrant children might one day become American citizens.[31] Invoking the memory of *Brown v. Board of Education*, the Court analogized the legislative discrimination against undocumented immigrant children to that experienced by Black children educated in a segregated school system.[32] By striking down the Texas statute, it appeared that the United States Constitution would not permit discriminatory legislation to act as a surrogate immigration-enforcement mechanism against those undocumented immigrants already present within the United States.

Unfortunately, the rationale of *Plyler* has not prevented recent federal and state legislation that elicits similar effects as the Texas education statute. Growing frustration over a broken immigration system and a southern border that is perceived as porous due to a lack of immigration enforcement has led state officials to fashion laws superficially aimed at the "crime"[33] of illegal presence, regardless of the Equal Protection Clause or federal immigration laws.

The Political Tide Turns Against the Non-Citizen Immigrant

Long before the United States Senate began its latest attempt at comprehensive immigration reform in 2013, various state legislatures entered the arena of immigration enforcement. States began imposing new penalties and punishments for undocumented non-citizens and anyone who interacted with them. It comes as no surprise that this form of legislation was usually enacted after an influx of Latino immigrants into communities where previously there had been minimal or no Latino presence.[34] The scope of these laws was troubling on many fronts, not least of which was the secondary effect of this discrimination on citizen-children.

The Housing Ordinances that Attempted to Convert Private Actors into ICE Agents

Beginning in 2006, three municipalities enacted ordinances designed to block access to housing by undocumented immigrants residing within their borders. The housing ordinances were a heavy-handed but slightly clever attempt to circumvent *Plyler*'s residency test while simultaneously enlisting private individuals as immigration-enforcement agents.

---

28 *Id.*

29 *Id.* at 221.

30 *Id.* at 222.

31 *Id.* at 222–23. The Court recognized the fact that undocumented immigrant children were unlikely to be deported to their country of origin. *Id.* at 230. Moreover, "undocumented children are 'basically indistinguishable' from legally resident alien children," so the savings generated by the denial of these children a public education was wholly insubstantial in light of the costs. *Id.* at 229–30.

32 *Id.* at 222–23 (citing *Brown v. Board of Education*, 347 U.S. 483 (1954)).

33 The United State Supreme Court has deemed the deportability or inadmissibility of an individual to be a *civil* matter, not a criminal one. *Harisiades v. Shaughnessy*, 342 U.S. 580, 594 (1952).

34 *See* Susan Carroll, *Small Towns Clamp Down on Illegal Immigration*, The Hous. Chronicle, Nov. 19, 2006, http://www.chron.com/news/houston-texas/article/Small-towns-clamp-down-on-illegal-immigration-1895843.php (Hazleton, Pa. Mayor believed the Hispanic population grew from 1,132 in 2000 to 8,000 by 2006); Ruxandra Guidi, *Latinos Are Majority in Escondido, But Feel Targeted by Police*, KPBS San Diego, Oct. 8, 2010, http://www.kpbs.org/news/2010/oct/08/latinos-are-majority-escondido-feel-targeted-polic/ (Escondido, Ca. was primarily white and affluent in the 1960s but today Latinos outnumber whites); Randy Kennedy, *Texas Mayor Caught in Deportation Furor*, N.Y. Times, Apr. 4, 2009, http://www.nytimes.com/2009/04/05/us/05immig.html?pagewanted=all&_r=0 (Irving, a Dallas, Tex. suburb, had an influx of undocumented immigrants and non-Hispanic whites were no longer the majority).

On October 16, 2006, the City of Escondido, California passed an ordinance entitled "Establishing Penalties for the Harboring of Illegal Aliens in the City of Escondido" (the "Escondido Ordinance").[35] The Escondido Ordinance targeted private landlords or businesses who owned and rented "dwelling units" within Escondido to tenants of undocumented status.[36] The penalties included suspension of the offender's business license, which would effectively preclude the collection of rental payments due from any of the offender's tenants whether they were legally present in the United States or not.[37] Multiple violations raised the maximum penalty to $1,000 per violation per day, a six-month jail term, or both.[38] A federal district court enjoined the Escondido Ordinance before it could be enforced.[39]

Farmers Branch, Texas was the next municipality to pass this type of legislation.[40] Ordinance 2903 ("Farmers Branch Ordinance") found it necessary "to adopt citizenship and immigration certification requirements for apartment complexes to safeguard the public. …"[41] Voters approved the Farmers Branch Ordinance on May 12, 2007.[42] As in *City of Escondido*, a federal district court enjoined the Farmers Branch Ordinance.[43] On January 22, 2008, Farmers Branch passed a revised ordinance to avoid the injunction, this time premising the ordinance on the need to "[c]ontinue to pursue strategies to address illegal immigration."[44] At the time of the revised ordinance's passage, Farmers Branch Councilman O'Hare publicly stated that his motive for introducing the law was as follows: "I saw our property values declining … what I would call less desirable people move into the neighborhoods, people who don't value education, people who don't value taking care of their properties."[45] The councilman also asserted that the undocumented immigrants were largely responsible for the decline of local schools and local retail operations.[46]

35 *Garrett v. City of Escondido*, 465 F. Supp. 2d 1043, 1047 (S.D. Cal. 2006). The ordinance stated in part: ESTABLISHING PENALTIES FOR THE HARBORING OF ILLEGAL ALIENS, 16E-1: "a. For the purposes of this section, to let, lease, or rent a dwelling unit to an illegal alien, knowing or in reckless disregard of the fact that an alien has come to, entered, or remains in the United States in violation of law, shall be deemed to constitute harboring." Escondido, Ca. Ordinance No. 2006–38R.

36 *City of Escondido*, 465 F. Supp. 2d at 1047.

37 *Id.* at 1048.

38 *Id.*

39 *Id.*

40 *Villas at Parkside Partners v. City of Farmers Branch*, 496 F. Supp. 2d 757, 762 (N.D. Tex. 2007) (citing Farmers Branch, Tex., Ordinance 2903 (2007)).

41 *Id.* Ordinance 2903 provided, in part:

> Subsection 2: "The owner and/or property manager shall *require as a prerequisite to entering into any lease or rental arrangement, including any lease or rental renewals or extensions, the submission of evidence of citizenship or eligible immigration status for each tenant family consistent with subsection* (3)."
>
> Subsection 3: "Evidence of citizenship or eligible immigration status" requires tenants to provide: (1) a signed declaration of 'eligible immigration status;' (2) a 'form designated by [United States Immigration and Customs Enforcement] as acceptable evidence of immigration status;' (3) a 'signed verification consent form.'" Farmers Branch, TX, Ordinance 2903 (2007).

42 *City of Farmers Branch*, 496 F. Supp. 2d at 761. There were no allegations of voter fraud.

43 *Id.* at 760.

44 City Council of Farmers Branch Memorandum (1–22–2008). The new ordinance provided:

> Residential Occupancy Licenses
> Prior to occupying any leased or rented single-family residence, each occupant must obtain a residential occupancy license.
> Farmers Branch, Tex. Ordinance 2952 (2008).

45 *Id.* at 9–10; *see also* Laura A. Hernández, *Anchor Babies: Something Less Than Equal Under the Equal Protection Clause*, 19:3 S. Cal. Rev. L. & Soc. Just. 346 (2010).

46 *City of Farmers Branch*, 496 F. Supp. 2d at 10. The Dallas Observer newspaper and Dallas Morning News have reported proponents of the ordinance making statements such as: (1) "They're taking our jobs, our homes. There's unemployment partly because of the Hispanics. The lady who took my job is Hispanic, and she's bilingual;" (2) "The education system is tanking, health care has gone through the roof, everybody is bilingual"; and, (3) "The schools are being overrun by non-English speaking kids … I'm tired of paying for 'anchor babies.'" *Id. See also* Laura A. Hernández, *Anchor Babies: Something Less Than Equal Under the Equal Protection Clause*, 19:3 S. Cal. Rev. L. & Soc. Just. 346 (2010).

Similarly, the City of Hazleton, Pennsylvania enacted "Illegal Immigration Relief Act" (the "IIRA") and "Tenant Registration Ordinance" (collectively, the "Hazleton Ordinances") in July 2006.[47] Again, as in *City of Escondido* and *City of Farmers Branch*, a federal district court enjoined the Hazleton Ordinances before they could be enforced. However, this court was the only one to perform an equal-protection analysis[48] because initially the IIRA allowed the city to consider race in the ordinance's enforcement as long as race was not the sole or primary consideration.[49] In response, Hazleton amended the IIRA by striking the "solely or primarily" language in an effort to create a facially neutral ordinance.[50] Based on the revised language, the *Hazleton* court declined to find an equal-protection violation because the requisite discriminatory intent was no longer present, despite the blatantly discriminatory statements within the Hazleton Ordinances' legislative history.[51] Finally, because the Hazleton Ordinances did not implicate a fundamental right or create a suspect class, the court deemed Hazleton's purpose for passing the legislation was rationally related to a legitimate state interest.[52]

Overall, each of the federal courts enjoined the municipality ordinances primarily on the basis of preemption by federal immigration laws.[53] In 2013, federal appellate courts reconsidered *City of Farmer's Branch* and *City of Hazleton* in light of the United States Supreme Court's decisions in *Arizona v. United States*[54] and

---

47 Hazleton, PA, Ordinance 2006–18 (September 21, 2006), as amended by Hazleton, Pa, Ordinance 2006–40 (December 28, 2006) and Hazleton, PA, Ordinance 2007–6 (March 21, 2007). Ordinance 2006–18 provides:

> ILLEGAL IMMIGRATION RELIEF ACT (IIRA)
>
> §4B(2): "A complaint which alleges a violation on the basis of national origin, ethnicity, or race shall be deemed invalid and shall not be enforced."
>
> §5A: "It is unlawful for any person or business entity that owns a dwelling unit in the City to harbor an illegal alien in the dwelling unit, knowing or in reckless disregard of the fact that an alien has come to, entered, or remains in the United States in violation of law, unless such harboring is otherwise expressly permitted by federal law."

Ordinance 2006–13 provides:

> TENANT REGISTRATION ORDINANCE (RO)
>
> §6a: "No person shall hereafter occupy, allow to be occupied, advertise for occupancy, solicit occupants for, or let to another person for occupancy any rental unit within the city for which an application for license has not been made and filed with the Code Enforcement Office and for which there is not an effective license."
>
> §7b(1): "Application for occupancy permits … shall specifically require the following minimum information: … (g) Proper identification showing proof of legal citizenship and/or residency"
>
> Hazleton, Pa, Ordinance 2006–13 (2006).

48 *City of Hazleton*, 496 F. Supp. 2d at 539.

49 *Id.*

50 *Id.* at 540.

51 *Id.* (*citing Personnel Administrator of Massachusetts v. Feeney*, 442 U.S. 256, 272 (1979)). "At trial, plaintiffs' attorney asked Louis Barletta, the mayor of Hazleton, whether he would 'reconsider' the ordinances if evidence appeared that they would have a 'discriminatory effect.' (N.T. 3/15/07 at 263). The mayor responded that he did 'not believe that it will have a discriminatory effect, "but would in fact" have the opposite' impact. *Id.* When asked if he would repeal the ordinances if evidence indicated that they would have a discriminatory effect, the mayor responded that 'I believe if the ordinances are legal, I believe we have the right to enforce them. As long as they're legal, that is my concern.' *Id.* When asked if he would enforce the ordinances if they were declared legal but had a discriminatory effect, the mayor declared that 'if they were legal, and I believe they had a discriminatory effect, I would not present it. If they are legal, and I believe they do not have a discriminatory effect, I would pass the ordinance.' *Id.* An opinion that the ordinances were legal from a court, despite a finding by experts that they were likely discriminatory, would not cause the mayor to change his resolve to enforce the ordinances, since '[e]ven experts have their own biases and opinions.' *Id.* at 264. Defendant also apparently passed the amendments more quickly than is usually the case for such legislation, foregoing second and third readings of the statute." *City of Hazleton*, 496 F. Supp. 2d at 540–41.

52 *Id.* at 542.

53 *City of Escondido*, 465 F. Supp. 2d at 1055 (*citing DeCanas v. Bica*, 424 U.S. 351, 354, 362–63 (1976)); *City of Farmers Branch*, 496 F. Supp. 2d at 777; *City of Hazleton*, 496 F. Supp. 2d at 518.

54 132 S.Ct. 2492 (2012) (Arizona statute making non-compliance with certain federal immigration laws a state criminal offense is preempted by federal immigration law).

Chamber of Commerce v. Whiting.[55] Still, the Farmers Branch Ordinances and Hazleton Ordinances were held to be invalid due to their conflict with federal immigration laws and congressional plenary authority.[56] The United States Supreme Court has denied *certiorari* in both cases.[57]

What is missing from these opinions is a legal analysis of the secondary effect on citizen-children when their undocumented parents are prevented from legally securing housing. While undocumented immigrants may not qualify as a suspect class *per se*, a class can be defined for their American offspring in both absolute and functional terms—minor children with full citizenship born to parents who are undocumented immigrants.[58] In 2011, the Pew Hispanic Center estimated that there were 4.5 million United States born children to parents of undocumented status.[59] According to a 2009 Pew study, over 95 percent of the children of undocumented parents under the age of five are citizen-children.[60] Further, 77 percent of the children aged 14 to 17 in this group are citizen-children.[61] Undoubtedly, the suspect class continues to grow.

It is undisputed that it would be legally impermissible for the municipalities of Escondido, Farmers Branch, and Hazleton to prevent a citizen from acquiring housing within their jurisdictions.[62] The only factual distinction here is that this class of children has not reached the age of majority so they may legally contract.[63] Children are necessarily dependent on their parents to secure housing. If, due to these types of ordinances the parents cannot provide housing, then an impermissible burden will be placed on a distinct group of citizens—a suspect class comprised of the most legally vulnerable—American children.[64]

DHS's Secure Communities Program Leads to Greater Insecurity for Immigrant Communities.

Concern over border security has also led to government programs devised to locate and remove deportable immigrants who are allegedly engaged in serious criminal activity. One of these programs is Secure Communities. Launched in 2008 by the Department of Homeland Security ("DHS"), Secure Communities aims to facilitate the goal of prioritizing the removal of criminal aliens.[65] Through this program, Immigration and Customs Enforcement ("ICE") capitalizes on an existing "information-sharing partnership" between the Federal Bureau of Investigation ("FBI") and local law enforcement jurisdictions.[66] Specifically, local law enforcement authorities commonly submit the fingerprints of all individuals who are arrested to the FBI to

55 131 S.Ct. 1968 (2011) (holding Arizona statute revoking state employer licenses for intentionally hiring undocumented employees is not preempted by federal law).

56 *Villas at Parkside Partners v. City of Farmers Branch*, 726 F.3d 524, 539 (5th Cir. 2013); *Lozano v. City of Hazleton*, 724 F.3d 297, 323 (3d Cir. 2013).

57 *Orders in Pending Cases*, 571 U.S. 1, 2 (Mar. 3, 2014), http://www.supremecourt.gov/orders/courtorders/030314zor_0971.pdf. (13 516 and 13–531).

58 *See San Antonio Indep. Sch. Dist. v. Rodriguez*, 411 U.S. 1, 19 n.49 (1973) (analyzing the Texas public school financing system).

59 Jeffrey S. Passel & D'Vera Cohn, *Unauthorized Immigrant Population: National and State Trends*, 2010, Pew Hispanic Center 1, 13 (Feb. 1, 2011), http://www.pewhispanic.org/files/reports/133.pdf.

60 Jeffrey S. Passel & Paul Taylor, *Unauthorized Immigrants and Their U.S.-Born Children*, Pew Hispanic Center 1, 7 (Aug. 11, 2010), http://www.pewhispanic.org/files/reports/125.pdf.

61 *Id.*

62 The federal Fair Housing Act, while not a fundamental constitutional right, is a comprehensive statutory scheme that forbids discriminatory rental practices by landlords. 42 U.S.C. § 3604(a)–(b) (2008).

63 Restatement (Second) of Contracts §14 (1981).

64 *Plyler*, 457 U.S. at 219–20 ("The children who are plaintiffs in these cases are special members of this underclass. … the children of these illegal entrants are not comparably situated. Their 'parents have the ability to conform their conduct to societal norms,' and presumably the ability to remove themselves from the State's jurisdiction; but the children who are plaintiffs in these cases 'can affect neither their parent's conduct nor their own status.' (citation omitted) Even if the State found it expedient to control the conduct of adults by acting against their children, legislation directing the onus of a parent's misconduct against his children does not comport with fundamental conceptions of justice.") (*citing Trimble v. Gordon*, 430 U.S. 762, 770 (1977).

65 *ICE Secure Communities*, U.S. DHS, http://www.ice.gov/secure_communities/ (last visited Mar. 30, 2014).

66 *Id.*

check for existing criminal records.[67] With the introduction of Secure Communities, the FBI now automatically forwards those same fingerprints to ICE so that it may check the prints against the immigration database. If the individual is determined to be subject to removal,[68] then "ICE generally issues a detainer, requesting that the state or local jail facility hold the individual up to an extra 48 hours (excluding weekends) to allow for an interview,"[69] after which ICE determines whether to begin removal proceedings.[70] As of January 2013, 100 percent of the 3,181 United States jurisdictions are now "activated" Secure Communities.[71]

ICE claims Secure Communities has prioritized both the removal of "aliens who pose a danger to national security or a risk to public safety, including aliens convicted of crimes, with particular emphasis on violent criminals, felons, and repeat offenders"[72] and "recent illegal entrants, individuals who have repeatedly violated immigration laws, and aliens who are fugitives."[73] There are three levels of potential criminal detainees: "Level 1: Individuals who have been convicted of major drug offenses, national security crimes, and violent crimes such as murder, manslaughter, rape, robbery and kidnapping"; "Level 2: Individuals who have been convicted of minor drug and property offenses such as burglary, larceny, fraud and money laundering"; and, "Level 3: Individuals who have been convicted of other offenses."[74]

From the inception of Secure Communities in 2008 through August 31, 2012, ICE reports "more than 166,000 immigrants convicted of crimes were removed from the United States after identification through Secure Communities."[75] Of those removed, ICE reported that "more than 61,000 immigrants were convicted of aggravated felony (Level 1) offenses."[76] In the most recent reporting period, October 2012 through November 2013, ICE identified 319,982 individuals for removal.[77] Of these, 31 percent were Level 1 offenders, 19 percent were Level 2 offenders, and 30 percent were Level 3 offenders.[78] Therefore, of all those deported, 69 percent were convicted of a crime below an aggravated felony.[79]

Yet, there is growing resistance against Secure Communities not only from pro-immigrant organizations but also from the local law enforcement jurisdictions that are the linchpin of the program. Initially, local jurisdictions were told that participation in Secure Communities was not mandatory and a jurisdiction could decide to "opt-out" of the program.[80] ICE has since clarified that although a local law enforcement agency "may choose not to receive the identifications that result from processing the fingerprints through DHS's biometric system," the jurisdiction may neither opt-out of the program nor affect whether ICE will act on the results of the fingerprint search.[81]

---

67 *Id.*

68 *Id.*

69 *Id.*

70 *Id.* ICE considers several factors in determining whether to seek removal. These include: "the person's criminal history, immigration history (such as whether the person was previously deported or has an outstanding removal order from an immigration judge), family ties, duration of stay in the U.S., significant medical issues, and other circumstances." *Id.*

71 ICE, *Activated Jurisdictions*, U.S. DHS, at 1 (Jan. 22, 2013), http://www.ice.gov/doclib/secure-communities/pdf/sc-activated.pdf.

72 ICE Office of the Director, *Protecting the Homeland: ICE Response to the Task Force on Secure Communities Findings and Recommendations*, U.S. DHS, at 5 (Apr. 27, 2012), http://www.ice.gov/doclib/ secure-communities/pdf/hsac-sc-taskforce-report.pdf.

73 ICE Office of the Director, *Protecting the Homeland: ICE Response to the Task Force on Secure Communities Findings and Recommendations*, U.S. DHS, at 5 (Apr. 27, 2012), http://www.ice.gov/doclib/ secure-communities/pdf/hsac-sc-taskforce-report.pdf.

74 U.S. Dep't of Homeland Sec., *Secure Communities Memorandum of Agreement Template*, at 2–3, http://www.ice.gov/doclib/foia/secure_communities/securecommunitiesmoatemplate.pdf.

75 ICE Secure Communities, supra note 65.

76 *Id.*

77 U.S. Immigr. & Customs Enforcement, *Secure Communities: Monthly Statistics Through November 30, 2010*, at 4, 58, http://www.ice.gov/doclib/foia/sc-stats/nationwide_interop_stats-fy2014-to-date.pdf.

78 *Id.*

79 *See id.* at 4, 58.

80 *ICE Secure Communities: Get the Facts*, U.S. DHS, http://www.ice.gov/secure_communities/get-the-facts.html (last visited Mar. 29, 2014).

81 *Id.*; *see also* Lindsey J. Gill, Note, *Secure Communities: Burdening Local Law Enforcement And Undermining the U Visa*, 54 Wm. & Mary L Rev. 2055, 2076 (2013) (jurisdictions can "opt-out" by refusing to send fingerprints to the FBI).

Nonetheless, some state and local governments are attempting to escape the mandate of Secure Communities.[82] Illinois Governor Pat Quinn, Massachusetts Governor Deval Patrick, and New York Governor Andrew Cuomo have all attempted to leave Secure Communities.[83] Governor Cuomo sent a letter to DHS stating: "The heart of the concern is that the program, conceived of as a method of targeting those people who pose the greatest threat to our communities, is in fact having the opposite effect and compromising public safety by deterring witnesses to crime and others from working with law enforcement."[84] There is also resistance among municipalities.[85] Local jurisdictions are concerned that the program has disintegrated communication between law enforcement and the immigrant community, leading to decreased security for the community as a whole.[86] Additionally, local governments and taxpayers shoulder the financial burden of the ICE detainers.[87] For instance, Los Angeles County has calculated additional costs of $26 million per year to comply with Secure Communities.[88]

There is also judicial "clarification" to the mandatory nature of Secure Communities. The Third Circuit of the United States Court of Appeals recently held that ICE immigration detainers issued pursuant to the program are not mandatory; therefore, municipalities can be held liable under section 1983 for the unconstitutional detention of a citizen pursuant to the detainer request.[89] The authority for immigration detainers is found in 8 C.F.R. § 287.7. It states in part: "A detainer serves to advise another law enforcement agency that the Department seeks custody of an alien presently in the custody of that agency, for the purpose of arresting and removing the alien. The detainer *is a request* that such agency advise the Department, prior to release of the alien ... such agency *shall maintain custody* of the alien for a period not to exceed 48 hours ..."[90]

In *Galarza v. Szalczyk*, the Third Circuit found that throughout the regulation, the term "request" is used.[91] While the regulation also contains the phrase "shall maintain custody," it does not alter the permissive nature of a detainer for three primary reasons. First, a review of case law reveals that "[a]ll Courts of Appeals to have commented on the character of ICE detainers refer to them as 'requests' or as part of an 'informal procedure.'" Second, the INA "does not authorize federal officials to command state or local officials to detain suspected aliens subject to removal." Third, ICE's policies and litigation positions are consistent with the interpretation that detainers are requests.[92] Moreover, a constitutional analysis raises Tenth Amendment concerns under the principle of anti-commandeering.[93] Perhaps in recognition of a flawed interpretation, ICE retreated from its stance of mandatory detainers with the following statement: "While immigration detainers are an important part of ICE's efforts to remove criminal aliens who are in federal, state or local custody, they are not mandatory as a matter of law."[94]

---

82 Gill, *supra* note 81, at 2077.

83 Gretchen Gavett, *Why Three Governors Challenged Secure Communities*, Frontline, Oct. 18, 2011, http://www.pbs.org/wgbh/pages/frontline/race-multicultural/lost-in-detention/why-three-governors-challenged-secure-communities/.

84 *Id.*

85 Michael Levenson, *Walsh Wants Boston out of Immigrant ID Program*, The Bos. Globe, Nov. 26, 2013, http://www.bostonglobe.com/2013/11/26/mayor-elect-walsh-says-wants-boston-pull-out-secure-communities-program/BikbYna0qIGwMWmM06uPrO/story.html (Boston mayor-elect, Martin Walsh, stated he would not enforce Secure Communities, only to find out shortly afterwards that he had no authority to exit the program).

86 Radha Vishnuvajjala, *Insecure Communities: How an Immigration Enforcement Program Encourages Battered Women to Stay Silent*, 32 B.C. J. L. & Soc. Just. 185, 186–87 (2012) (non-citizen victims of crime are reluctant to call police for help due to the risk their fingerprints processed through Secure Communities).

87 Elise Foley, *Secure Communities Costs Los Angeles County More Than $26 Million A Year: Report, The Huffington Post*, Aug. 23, 2012, http://www.huffingtonpost.com/2012/08/23/ secure-communities-los-angeles_n_1824740.html.

88 *Id.* ("Los Angeles County is spending more than $26 million a year to hold undocumented immigrants" under Secure Communities, "individuals it would otherwise release").

89 No. 12–3991, 2014 WL 815127, at *9 (3d Cir. Mar. 4, 2014).

90 *Id.* at *4 (emphasis added).

91 *Id.*

92 *Id.* at *4-*6.

93 *Id.* at *7-*8 (holding that immigration detainers require the local governments to "foot the bill," and as a result, mandating detainers would exceed federal power).

94 Letter from Daniel H. Ragsdale, ICE Acting Dir., to Mike Thompson, U.S. Rep., (Feb. 25, 2014) (on file with author), *available at* http://immigrantjustice.org/sites/immigranjustice.org/files/2014_02_25%20 Thompson-signed-response-ICE.pdf.

Once again, the zeal over border security has led to a costly program that is not serving law-enforcement purposes. Importantly, the inherent distrust between the immigrant community and police agencies only grows larger when lawfully present immigrants (including naturalized citizens) and undocumented immigrants with no criminal background are caught in the web created by Secure Communities. For example, the plaintiff in *Galarza* was an American citizen who was imprisoned for three days pursuant to an ICE detainer even after he posted a $15,000 bail.[95] The authorities simply did not believe his claim of citizenship even after he produced a social security card and a state driver's license.[96] As with the housing ordinances, the citizen-children of undocumented immigrant parents are especially vulnerable to this form of constitutional injury. If the child is ever in police detention, authorities are likely to scrutinize the child's claims of citizenship to the same degree, if not more, than that of Mr Galarza. Between distrust of the authorities and the potential for wrongful removal, programs like Secure Community effectively and impermissibly restrict citizen-children's access to local law enforcement.

The Developing Controversy over Professional Licensing for the Undocumented Immigrant

If America is a meritocracy, then the *Plyler* decision ensured access to the tool of meritocracy, education.[97] It is not implausible to believe that the Supreme Court intended to allow undocumented immigrants to participate in the American Dream.[98] Therefore, it seems inevitable that the United States would face an obvious consequence of a large undocumented population: individuals, with no legal status, who have otherwise earned all of the credentials required for a professional license. The issue has come to full fruition with respect to attorney admissions. Currently, State Bar agencies across the country are struggling with the question of whether state-licensing requirements can prevent qualified undocumented applicants from obtaining a law license.

Interestingly, the requirement of lawful immigrant status before one can be licensed as an attorney is a relatively recent occurrence.[99] Its introduction can be traced back to federal immigration reform in the late 1990s.[100] Responding to what it perceived as escalating levels of undocumented migration, Congress sought to curtail the influx of this population, especially from Mexico and Latin America.[101] Legislatures and agencies enacted severe restrictions to disincentivize those who were residents without government permission.

Congress passed two statutory schemes: the Illegal Immigration Reform and Immigrant Responsibility Act of 1996 ("IIRIRA") and the Personal Responsibility and Work Opportunity Reconciliation Act of 1996

95 *Galarza v. Szalczyk*, No. 12–3991, 2014 WL 815127, at *2.

96 *Id.*

97 The *Plyler* court stated that the Texas statute "pose[d] an affront to one of the goals of the Equal Protection Clause: the abolition of governmental barriers presenting unreasonable obstacles to advancement on the basis of individual merit." *Plyler*, 457 U.S. at 221–22.

98 *Id.*

99 *See In Fla. Bd. of Bar Examiners*, SC11–2568, 2014 WL 866065 at *1 (Fla. Mar. 6, 2014) (Florida Board of Bar Examiners adopted a policy in January 2008 requiring applicants to show evidence of their citizenship or immigration status).

100 *See* Illegal Immigration Reform and Immigrant Responsibility Act, Pub. L. No. 104–208, 110 Stat. 3009–546 (1996); *see also* Personal Responsibility & Work Opportunity Act, Pub. L. No. 104–93, 110 Stat. 2105 (1996).

101 U.S. Cong., S. Comm. on Homeland Sec. & Govt. Affairs, *The Homeland Security Department's Budget Submission for Fiscal Year 2011*, 111th Cong., 1st sess., Feb. 24, 2010 (stating that Border Patrol agent manpower assigned to the Southwest border has continued to increase rapidly since the early 1990s); *see also* Capps, R. & Passel, J.S., *The New Neighbors: A User's Guide to Data on Immigrants in U.S. Communities* (Wash.: Urban Inst., 2003) (indicating that 22 states that had relatively low percentages of immigrants saw these populations grow by more than 90 percent between 1990 and 2000); *see also* Porter, Eduardo, *Number of Hispanics Ballooned in '90s; Group Is About to Become Biggest Minority*, The Wall St Journal, Mar. 8, 2001 (explaining that the Census Bureau discovered that the Hispanic population grew by 58 percent over the 1990s to reach 35.3 million, outpacing the agency's previously issued figure by 2.5 million, along with the conclusion that the majority of that difference was attributable to an increase in undocumented immigrants during the decade).

("PRWORA").[102] The PRWORA contains a statutory provision that limits, among many, many other things, the licensing of undocumented individuals.[103] It states:

> (a) Notwithstanding any other provision of law and except as provided in subsections (b) and (d), an alien who is not—(1) a qualified alien (as defined in section 431), (2) a nonimmigrant under the Immigration and Nationality Act, or (3) an alien who is paroled into the United States under section 212(d)(5) of such Act for less than one year, ***is not eligible for any State or local public benefit*** (as defined in subsection (c)) ...[104]

> (c) (1) Except as provided in paragraphs (2) and (3), for purposes of this subtitle the term "State or local public benefit" means—(A) any grant, contract, loan, ***professional license***, or commercial license provided by an agency of a State or local government or by appropriated funds of a State or local government; and ...[105]

The PRWORA, however, provides an exception to the prohibition:

> (d) STATE AUTHORITY TO PROVIDE FOR ELIGIBILITY OF ILLEGAL ALIENS FOR STATE AND LOCAL PUBLIC BENEFITS.—A State may provide that an alien who is not lawfully present in the United States is eligible for any State or local public benefit for which such alien would otherwise be ineligible under subsection (a) only through the enactment of a State law after the date of the enactment of this Act which affirmatively provides for such eligibility.[106]

Thus, federal congressional intent statutorily bends to individual state judgment regarding the conferral of state benefits in the form of a "grant, contract, loan, professional license or commercial license."[107] While it is undisputed that the Equal Protection Clause prohibits legislation withholding these benefits from lawfully present immigrants,[108] the issue is still undecided with respect to undocumented immigrants.

In January 2014, the California Supreme Court became the first state high court to render an opinion on this matter.[109] Sergio C. Garcia applied for admission to the State Bar of California after graduating from

---

102 *See* Illegal Immigration Reform and Immigrant Responsibility Act, Pub. L. No. 104–208, 110 Stat. 3009–546 (1996); *see also* Personal Responsibility & Work Opportunity Act, Pub. L. No. 104–93, 110 Stat. 2105 (1996).

103 The congressional zeal to prohibit access to American social safety nets also led to strict curtailment on employment opportunities. As the California Supreme Court noted, the PRWORA was "primarily concerned with comprehensive welfare reform." *In re Garcia*, 315 P.3d 117, 125 (Cal. 2014). It imposed new restrictions on eligibility for "Supplemental Security Income, food stamps, child support payments, child care, child nutrition and job training." *Id.*

104 8 U.S.C.A. § 1621(a).

105 8 U.S.C.A. § 1621(c).

106 8 U.S.C.A. § 1621(d).

107 *Id.* It appears that the congressional focus on welfare benefits allowed for some laxity when it came to employment opportunities. As recent state crackdowns have demonstrated, the lack of undocumented farmworkers and factory workers creates occupational crises among documented employers. *See* Benjamin Powell, *The Law of Unintended Consequences: Georgia's Immigration Law Backfires*, Forbes, May 17, 2012, http://www.forbes.com/sites/realspin/2012/05/17/the-law-of-unintended-consequences-georgias-immigration-law-backfires/ (Georgia faced $140 million in agricultural losses due to new state immigration enforcement laws leading officials to send prisoners to Georgia farms to help harvest the 2012 crops); Editorial, *How Alabama's Immigration Law Is Crippling Its Farms*, *The Wash. Post*, Nov. 3 2011, http://www.washingtonpost.com/opinions/how-alabamas-immigration-law-is-crippling-its-farms/2011/11/01/gIQAg0JvjM_story.html (Alabama farmers "revolt against the state's over-the-top immigration law" because it threatened to deplete the farm workforce); Alfonso Serrano, *Why Undocumented Workers Are Good for the Economy*, *Bus. Time*, Jun. 14, 2012, http://business.time.com/ 2012/06/14/the-fiscal-fallout-of-state-immigration-laws/ (after conducting a fiscal study, Kentucky decided not to pass its own Arizona-like legislation because it would cost the state an estimated $89 million annually).

108 *Yick Wo v. Hopkins*,118 U.S. 356, 373–74 (1886) (striking down city ordinance denying Chinese immigrants permits to open laundry businesses); *Takahashi v. Fish & Game Comm'n*, 334 U.S. 410, 421 (1948) (holding state could not deny commercial fishing license based on non-citizen status); *Graham v. Richardson*, 403 U.S. 365, 376 (1971) (finding state statute violated Equal Protection Clause by denying welfare benefits based solely on non-citizen status); *Nyquist v. Mauclet*, 432 U.S. 1, 12 (1977) (invalidating state law discriminating against non-citizens for higher education scholarships and loans).

109 *In re Garcia*, 315 P.3d 117 (Cal. 2014).

an American high school, attending two California colleges and graduating from one, graduating from a California law school, and passing the July 2009 California bar exam.[110] Garcia is undocumented although his father, a lawful permanent resident since 1994, has filed a visa petition on his behalf.[111] At the time of this opinion, Garcia had figuratively been standing in line for over 19 years for an American visa.[112]

The California Supreme Court acknowledged that it was impermissible to bar lawfully present aliens from a license to practice law solely because of their non-citizen status.[113] In 1972, the court considered an application to practice law from Paolo Raffaelli, a lawfully permanent resident through his marriage to an American citizen. Raffaelli had graduated from the University of Santa Clara School of Law and successfully passed the California bar examination.[114] At that time, a California statute prohibited its State Bar from issuing a license to practice law to any non-citizen.[115] Reiterating the standard of review was strict scrutiny, the court held "[l]awfully admitted resident aliens" are entitled to equal protection, and classifications based on alienage are "inherently suspect and subject to close judicial scrutiny."[116] Moreover, the focus of the analysis must reflect the Fourteenth Amendment protection by tying state admission requirements not only to "a rational connection with the applicant's fitness or capacity to practice law,"[117] but also satisfy the heightened burden of proving "that the classification constitutes a necessary means of accomplishing a legitimate state interest, and that the law serves to promote a compelling state interest."[118] While California tried to meet its burden by proffering five separate governmental interests ranging from insufficient loyalty to the United States to the everyday practicalities of being an attorney, the statute could not survive the constitutional inquiry.[119] In striking it down, the court described the statute as "a lingering vestige of a xenophobic attitude which … also once restricted membership in our bar to persons who were both 'male' and 'white.' It should now be allowed to join those anachronistic classifications among the crumbled pedestals of history."[120]

Forty-two years later, the California Supreme Court considered the same question in the context of undocumented immigrants like Sergio C. Garcia. As an initial matter, the court focused on the prohibition contained in the PRWORA.[121] Acknowledging congressional plenary authority over immigration laws, the Supreme Court held that California met the exception contained within 8 U.S.C.A. section 1621(d) when it passed section 6064(b) of the California Business and Professions Code, which became effective on January 1, 2014:[122]

> (b) Upon certification by the examining committee that an applicant who is not lawfully present in the United States has fulfilled the requirements for admission to practice law, the Supreme Court may admit that applicant as an attorney at law in all the courts of this state and may direct an order to be entered upon its records to that effect. A certificate of admission thereupon shall be given to the applicant by the clerk of the court.[123]

110 *Id.* at 122. Garcia attended Butte College, California State University at Chico and Cal Northern School of Law. *Id.*

111 *Id.* at 121. In essence, Garcia had been waiting for a visa since 1994. *Id.* at 121–2. His 19-year wait is symbolic of the hurdles faced by all hopeful Mexican immigrants. American immigration laws are so dysfunctional that there is no timely path to lawful immigration absent marriage to an American citizen. As an unmarried son of an LPR, designated as a F-1 preference under the Immigration and Nationality Act, Garcia's category is only current for those who took their place in line on October 15, 1993. U.S. Dep't of State Visa Bulletin, Vol. IX, No.66 (Mar. 2003), *available at* http://www.justice.gov/eoir/vll/ qapracmanual/pracmanual/AppJ.pdf.

112 *In re Garcia*, 315 P.3d at 122.

113 *Id.* at 124–25 (citing *Raffaelli v. Comm. of Bar Exam'rs*, 7 Cal. 3d 288, 304 (1972)).

114 *Raffaelli*, 7 Cal. 3d at 291.

115 *Id.* at 291 (discussing section 6060(a) of the California Business and Professions Code).

116 *Id.* at 292 (quoting *Graham v. Richardson*, 403 U.S. 365, 371–72 (1971)).

117 *Id.* at 294 (quoting *Schware v. Board of Bar Exam'rs*, 353 U.S. 232 (1957)).

118 *Id.* at 295–96 (quoting *Purdy & Fitzpatrick v. State*, 71 Cal. 2d 566, 579 (1969)).

119 *Id.* at 296, 303.

120 *Id.* at 291.

121 *In re Garcia*, 315 P.3d at 125.

122 *Id.* at 121. Section 6064 was enacted by the California legislature in direct response to the plight of Sergio C. Garcia. *Id.* (California legislature enacted § 6064 shortly after the California Supreme Court heard oral argument in Garcia's case).

123 Cal. Bus. & Prof. Code § 6064(d) (2014).

Because section 6064 was enacted after August 22, 1996 and "affirmatively provide[d]" that an undocumented immigrant was eligible for a professional law license, the PRWORA did not prohibit an undocumented immigrant from obtaining a California law license.[124]

Then, the Supreme Court considered whether as a class California could bar otherwise qualified undocumented immigrants from obtaining a law license.[125] Tellingly, the court ruled that an immigrant's unlawful presence in the United States without more does not prevent admission to the California State Bar.[126] Unlawful presence neither constituted moral turpitude nor prevented a bar applicant from taking the necessary oath.[127] Echoing the sentiments of the United States Supreme Court in *Plyler v. Doe*, the California court reasoned that federal immigration law with respect to employment is subject to change, a fact recognized by Congress when it drafted the exception contained within section 1621(d) of the PRWORA.[128] As a result, the benefit of a professional law license should not be withheld from undocumented immigrants on the flawed erroneous presumption that the applicant must engage in unlawful employment practices to serve as an attorney.[129] Noting that Mr Garcia's application was not "entirely flawless," the California Supreme Court nonetheless held that "Garcia met his burden of demonstrating that he possesse[d] the requisite good moral character to qualify for a law license."[130]

In re Garcia stands in contrast to a recent opinion issued by the Supreme Court of Florida.[131] In response to a request for an advisory opinion by the Florida Board of Bar Examiners, the Supreme Court held that undocumented immigrants are ineligible for admission to the Florida Bar.[132] In 2008, the Florida Bar Examiners adopted a policy requiring applicants for admission to the Bar to provide proof of citizenship.[133] Unlike California, however, the State of Florida has not passed a statute that meets the standard under 8 U.S.C.A. section 1621(d) to create an exception to the PRWORA.[134] Acquiescing to the federal prohibition, the Supreme Court found it could not authorize the admission of undocumented immigrants given the lack of a viable state exception.[135]

Despite amici arguments that federal immigration law appeared to be changing with respect to undocumented immigrants who arrived in the United States as children, the Florida court was not persuaded.[136] The "Deferred Action for Childhood Arrivals" ("DACA")[137] program, the court noted, did not provide legal status to these

124 *In re Garcia*, 315 P.3d at 126.

125 *Id.* at 126.

126 *Id.* at 130.

127 *Id.* at 130. The United States Citizenship and Immigration Service defines moral turpitude as "conduct that shocks the public conscience as being inherently base, vile, or depraved, contrary to the rules of morality and the duties owed between man and man, either one's fellow man or society in general." USCIS Practice Manual, Vol. 12, Ch. 5 (Mar. 25, 2014), *available at* http://www.uscis.gov/policymanual/ HTML/PolicyManual-Volume12-PartF-Chapter5.html#S-A (citing "*Medina v. United States*, 259 F.3d 220, 227 (4th Cir. 2001) quoting *Matter of Danesh*, 19 I&N Dec. 669, 670 (BIA 1988). See Matter of Perez-Contreras, 20 I&N Dec. 615, 618 (BIA 1992). See *Matter of Flores*, 17 I&N Dec. 225 (BIA 1980) (and cases cited therein).").

128 *In re Garcia*, 315 P.3d at 132–33 (The Court noted that granting law licenses to undocumented immigrants would not alter the federal employment limitations for three reasons: (1) despite federal employment limitations, 8 U.S.C. §1621 explicitly allows states to grant professional licenses to undocumented immigrants; (2) "federal law restrictions on employment are subject to change"; and (3) law licenses should not be withheld from undocumented immigrants on an assumption that the individual will not comply with federal employment limitations).

129 *Id.* Specifically, undocumented immigrants may be precluded from handling matters before the USCIS or working for law firms, corporations, or public agencies. *Id.* at 131.

130 *Id.* at 134. Mr Garcia had used a false alien registration number when he was 17, delayed disclosing this information to the State on advice of counsel, and had been cited for driving without a license in Oregon. *Id.* at 122 n.5. The Committee of Bar Examiners investigated Mr Garcia's conduct and determined that "none of these incidents impugn[ed] Garcia's good moral character …" *Id.*

131 *In Fla. Bd. of Bar Examiners*, SC11–2568, 2014 WL 866065 (Fla. Mar. 6, 2014).

132 *Id.* at *4.

133 *Id.* at *1.

134 *Id.* at *2.

135 *Id.*

136 *Id.* at *3.

137 DACA allows for deferred prosecution of undocumented immigrants who came to the United States as children, among other eligibility requirements. *Id.* at *3.

immigrants, only legal presence.[138] Citing Arizona federal case law, the Florida court agreed that the memorandum from the Secretary of Homeland Security authorizing DACA "does not have the force of law" because it "does not purport to establish substantive rules … and it was not promulgated through any formal procedure."[139]

In his concurrence, Justice Jorge Labarga likened his personal experience to the putative Applicant who was the reason for the Florida Bar Examiners' request.[140] After citing the excellence of the applicant's overall academic and personal record,[141] Justice Labarga wrote that the only difference in their situation was the way American immigration laws treated their arrival—immigrants from Mexico are considered to be "defector[s] from poverty." On the hand, immigrants from Cuba, such as Justice Labarga, are considered "defectors from a tyrannical communist regime."[142] Indeed, the difference is enormous under American immigration laws.[143]

Case law and recent attempts at immigration reform pay much deference to the innocence of children who arrive in the United States as undocumented immigrants. Yet, once these children become adults, they are subject to the strictest interpretation of the law as demonstrated by the Florida Supreme Court advisory opinion. This outcome leads to incoherent results. An incongruous scenario exists where an individual is the product of the American educational system, possibly obtaining a graduate degree, yet is legally estopped from becoming a fully participatory member of society.

Moreover, the argument for refusing to recognize undocumented immigrants as a suspect class—a voluntary, illegal presence in the United States—is not applicable to those who arrived as children.[144] The *Plyler* Court recognized as much:

> At the least, those who elect to enter our territory by stealth and in violation of our law should be prepared to bear the consequences, including, but not limited to, deportation. But the children of those illegal entrants are not comparably situated. Their "parents have the ability to conform their conduct to societal norms," and presumably the ability to remove themselves from the State's jurisdiction; but the children who are plaintiffs in these cases "can affect neither their parents' conduct nor their own status." (citation omitted)[145]

Plyler's reasoning is still sound. When America loses the intelligence and talent of an individual like the putative Florida applicant, equal protection principles are not served, and neither is common sense.

Comprehensive Immigration Reform Should Consider the Indirect Effects of Immigration Laws on Citizen-Children to Strike the Proper Equal-Protection Balance

The insightfulness of the *Plyler* opinion is lost in today's current political climate, just as much as it was in Texas in 1975.[146] The *Plyler* Court tacitly recognized a truth about those who reside within the United

138 *Id.* at *3.

139 *Id.* at *4.

140 *Id.* at *10.

141 Indeed, the Florida applicant is almost a perfect candidate for admission to the Florida Bar apart from his immigration status. He graduated from a Tampa, Florida high school as valedictorian, attended New College of Florida, the honors college of the state, and graduated from the Florida State University College of Law "with several book awards," or awards given for academic achievement. *Id.* at *5. Law professors and lawyers, including past presidents of the American Bar Association, "strenuously supported" his admission. *Id.*

142 *Id.* at *10.

143 *Id.*; *see also Green Card for a Cuban Native or Citizen*, U.S. Citizenship & Immigr. Servs., http://www.uscis.gov/green-card/other-ways-get-green-card/green-card-cuban-native-or-citizen (last visited Mar. 30, 2014) (discussing the Cuban Adjustment Act, which provides for a "special procedure" under which Cuban native or citizens can obtain permanent residence). In a gut-wrenching conclusion, Justice Labarga wrote, "Applicant is so near to realizing his goals yet so agonizingly far because, regrettably, unlike the California Legislature, the Florida Legislature has not exercised its considerable authority on this important question." *In Fla. Bd. of Bar Examiners*, at *10.

144 *Plyler*, 457 U.S. at 219 n.19.

145 *Id.* at 220.

146 457 U.S. at 205.

States—immigration laws do not prevent the presence of a significant number of undocumented immigrants.[147] As popular attention focuses on the widening gap of opportunities available to those born to privilege versus those who are not, the additional overlay of lawful discrimination placed on the undocumented parents of citizen-children is insurmountable.

While undocumented immigrants are not a suspect class themselves, the citizen-children they bear on American soil would satisfy class requirements for purposes of the Equal Protection Clause. The reason is simple; these children suffer from the legally sanctioned discrimination imposed on their parents whether through reduced educational opportunities, lack of access to adequate housing, or lack of access to any of those governmental benefits most Americans find so important, such as police protection. While the injury could be classified as a secondary or indirect effect, it is still meaningful in a constitutional analysis.

Citizen-children bear the classic characteristics of an equal-protection violation.[148] Further, they have no recourse through the political process. They cannot vote. They are prevented from holding jobs before the age of 16, which eviscerates their economic power. Indeed, without any disposable income, minor citizen-children do not have the funds to influence policymakers through campaign contributions or registered voters through paid political advertising. Their voice is silenced. This form of disability is exactly what is envisioned in the definition of a suspect class.

Finally, citizen-children are increasingly subject to deportation if their parents/guardians are repatriated to their country of origin. While ICE regulations do carve out a deportation exception for citizen-children, the child's legal status must still be proved.[149] If they do not have relatives who are legally present in the United States, these children are placed in a difficult quandary. Their choice is either to become a ward of the State,[150] an outcome that further strains State resources in difficult economic times, or to return to their country of origin with their parents, where they face difficult assimilation because they have grown up as American children.[151] Even if the citizen-children are very young at the time of departure/deportation, they are deprived of what is typically viewed as a superior American public school education, placing them far behind their peers should they return to the United States at a later time. This Catch-22 completely and thoroughly punishes citizen-children for the "sins" of their parents, and deprives them of the full rights and privileges to which they are entitled as American citizens.[152]

Immigration policy that fails to contextualize the plight of citizen-children born to undocumented parents is a failed policy. It is constitutionally impermissible to establish a legal framework which deprives citizen-children of their American birthright, even if the effect is indirect. The Equal Protection Clause simply does not leave room for the legislative creation of "two Americas."

---

147 *Plyler*, 457 U.S. at 237. Moreover, the stronger border enforcement becomes, the more likely it is that this population will remain in the United States because the chances of apprehension at the border would make multiple crossings unfeasible. Wayne A. Cornelius, *Impacts of Border Enforcement on Unauthorized Mexican Migration to the United States*, Soc. Sci. Research Council (Sep. 26, 2006), *available at* http://borderbattles.ssrc.org/Cornelius/printable.html ("U.S. border enforcement policy has unintentionally encouraged undocumented migrants to remain in the U.S. for longer periods and settle permanently in this country in much larger numbers.").

148 The United States Supreme Court has explicitly recognized that designation of a suspect class is warranted, and worthy of strict scrutiny by the courts, if the group is "saddled with disabilities, or subject to such a history of purposeful unequal treatment, or relegated to such a position of political powerlessness as to command extraordinary protection from the majoritarian political process." *Rodriguez*, 411 U.S. at 28.

149 U.S. Dep't of Homeland Sec., *Removals Involving Illegal Alien Parents of United States Citizen Children*, OIG-09–15 at 11 (Jan. 2009).

150 Due to the increasingly level of ICE enforcement actions, this result is becoming more and more prevalent. *See* Dorsey & Whitney LLP, Report to the Urban Institute, *Severing a Lifeline: The Neglect of Citizen Children in America's Immigration Enforcement Policy*, 48–50 (2009).

151 *Id.* at 81–90.

152 The United States Supreme Court has decried unfair legislative discrimination against illegally present minor children. *Plyler*, 457 U.S. at 220 ("'Visiting … condemnation on the head of an infant is illogical and unjust. Moreover, imposing disabilities on the … child is contrary to the basic concept of our system that legal burdens should bear some relationship to individual responsibility or wrongdoing. Obviously, no child is responsible for his birth and penalizing the … child is an ineffectual-as well as unjust- way of deterring the parent.'") (citing *Weber v. Aetna Cas. & Sur.*, 406 U.S. 164, 175 (1972)). The injustice only increases when the discrimination targets minor citizen-children.

Chapter 14
Applying an Equal Protection Methodology to Speech and Religion Cases

Patrick M. Garry

Equal Protection Norms and the Bill of Rights

The currently popular view sees the First Amendment as a provision for achieving a certain vision of individual autonomy. According to this view, the Bill of Rights was included in the Constitution for the purpose of preserving individual autonomy through insulating the individual from various democratic outcomes. Under this argument, the Bill of Rights seeks first and foremost to identify particular individual freedoms and then to create a constitutional protection for those substantive freedoms, in a way that facilitates or preserves a judicially defined view of those freedoms.

Another argument looks at the Bill of Rights from a wholly different perspective. This argument sees the bill as a set of provisions designed primarily to better ensure the maintenance of limited government within the constitutional scheme. According to this argument, the Anti-Federalists, as the primary advocates for and shapers of the Bill of Rights, sought to achieve not a particular substantive protection of specific individual rights, but rather an assurance that the government being created through the new Constitution would indeed be a government of limited powers. To further secure this limited government, the Bill of Rights specified certain explicit areas in which the government would have no power to act or intrude. Whereas the rest of the constitutional scheme set out structural provisions for the overall maintenance of limited government, the Bill of Rights articulated specific substantive areas in which the principle of limited government was to prevail. The Anti-Federalists were not so concerned about identifying and protecting a finite list of particular individual rights in the new democracy; they were more concerned about alleviating fears that the original Constitution had not adequately prevented the new government from overstepping its allotted powers.

This chapter does not intend to suggest that the framers and ratifiers of the Bill of Rights did not care about individual freedoms or the constitutional protection of those freedoms. Indeed, this concern had helped inspire the Declaration of Independence and America's break with England. But it does argue that the framers and ratifiers of the Bill of Rights did not intend the preservation of individual autonomy or dignity to be the direct or primary goal of the Bill of Rights. This was because the framers and ratifiers did not know exactly how to go about that goal. To the framers, the concepts of natural and individual rights were not only vague and imprecise, but they were the subjects of substantial differences. They did not have a sufficiently clear idea of the parameters and scope of those individual rights, nor of how to protect each of those specific rights. Instead, they went about trying to protect liberty in a slightly more indirect manner—that of striving to limit the power and reach of government, which in turn would serve the cause of liberty.

It is the goal of this chapter to propose a new approach to the Bill of Rights in general and the First Amendment in particular. Instead of focusing on the particular freedoms specified in each amendment and precisely defining the scope of each freedom, this chapter seeks to arrive at a simpler, more objective and comprehensive approach. It argues that the Bill of Rights serves to protect the freedoms listed in it through the incorporation of equal protection norms. This approach may best harmonize the rights listed in the Bill of Rights with the workings of the democratic process outlined in the original Constitution. In a democracy, society governs itself according to its best judgment; but the glaring problem with any democracy is how to handle minorities and minority rights. An equal protection approach serves this concern, while at the same time allowing democratic society to govern itself—the proviso being that whatever the majority does to the minority it must do to itself.

Many current First Amendment doctrines already incorporate an equal protection approach, but a more explicit equal protection approach could eliminate much of the complexity and confusions in First Amendment doctrines, thus greatly simplifying the Court's jurisprudence in this area. The key element in a methodology for applying an equal protection approach is the identification of the proper baseline or comparison point for determining equality of treatment. But the judicial determination of appropriate baselines may be a more definable and boundaried endeavor than many of the approaches currently used by the Court in its First Amendment jurisprudence.

By viewing the Bill of Rights as a provision aimed at ensuring that government possesses only limited powers and mandating that the various listed freedoms be protected through an equal protection approach, courts would be significantly relieved of having to identify the parameters and underlying values and purposes of various individual rights and freedoms. Defining the parameters of individual rights, as well as which parameters are necessary to achieve a particular degree of individual autonomy, often puts courts into a quasi-lawmaking role. By seeking to protect individual freedoms through an equal protection approach, courts can better avoid interjecting substantive values into constitutional doctrines. Thus, their role can be both more narrow and more defined, which in turn will help preserve judicial integrity and authority.

James Madison articulated a classic concern of equal protection in *Federalist No. 10*. He worried about the potential in a democracy for "the most numerous party, or, in other words, the most powerful faction" to "trample on" the rights of minority groups.[1] For Madison, the goal was to create "a government which will protect all parties, the weaker as well as the more powerful."[2] But this has also traditionally been seen as a goal of the Bill of Rights, which then by definition must incorporate notions of equal protection. Thus, in connection with the concerns of *Federalist No. 10* and the protection of minority rights, equal protection should be a primary focus of courts in a democratic society. And it is through the Bill of Rights that the Constitution seeks to protect liberty through equal protection norms.

The Fourteenth Amendment contains an equal protection provision that exists separately and somewhat independently of the Bill of Rights. Generally speaking, equal protection norms prohibit the government from discriminating against targeted groups of people.[3] The Equal Protection Clause mandates "that all persons similarly situated should be treated alike."[4] Specifically, the clause was aimed at the newly freed slaves in the South;[5] but more generally, it was essentially aimed at tying together the rights of the minority with those of the majority, since whatever rights were given to the majority would also have to be given to the minority.[6]

Even though both equal protection and due process have been interpreted to protect fundamental rights, an equal protection approach provides for a less intrusive or arbitrary judicial review. Under this approach, courts do not need to articulate substantive individual values; they simply need to determine whether one group of individuals is being treated differently than another, similarly situated group. An equal protection approach can also often remedy improper governmental motives. Since an improper governmental motive most likely will result in some discriminatory targeting of a particular group, an equal protection approach on its own can eliminate that discriminatory treatment, even if the specific ill motive is never uncovered.

Equal Protection as a Guardian of Individual Rights in a Democracy

The Bill of Rights lays out various areas of freedoms that the ratifying generation believed important in maintaining the health and integrity of American constitutional democracy. But the problem that has

1 *See* The Federalist No. 10, at 60 (James Madison) (Jacob E. Cooke ed., 1961).

2 *See* The Federalist No. 51, at 352 (James Madison) (Jacob E. Cooke ed., 1961).

3 *See* Village of Willowbrook v. Olech, 528 U.S. 562, 564 (2000) (stating that the Equal Protection Clause secures protection against all "intentional and arbitrary discrimination").

4 Lawrence v. Texas, 539 U.S. 558, 579 (2003) (O'Connor, J., concurring).

5 *See* 6 Charles Fairman, Reconstruction and Reunion, 1864–88, at 1297 (1971); Eric Foner, Reconstruction: America's Unfinished Revolution, 1863–1877, at 258–59 (1988) (1863–77) (arguing that the Fourteenth Amendment was intended to combat violations of individual rights in the South).

6 John Hart Ely, Democracy and Distrust: A Theory of Judicial Review 84 (1980).

preoccupied generations of judges and scholars is how to protect those various freedoms in a manner consistent with the kind of political system that makes such freedoms possible in the first place—a system of democratic government. The solution offered here is that an equal protection approach is the best way to protect the individual freedoms specified in the Bill of Rights, while also respecting and upholding the workings of democratic governance.

Any equal protection approach facilitates judicial restraint and keeps the courts from usurping democratic authority. Under an equal protection analysis, government unduly expands its authority when it targets certain groups, much more so than if it happens to burden a right or activity exercised by all of society, which in turn can use its political power to eliminate that burden. Furthermore, an equal protection analysis allows courts to focus more on the exercise of government power than on the nature of individual substantive rights.

Notions of equality and neutrality, as now being applied in First Amendment jurisprudence, have had a major impact on American constitutionalism throughout the last half century. In the wake of the Supreme Court's 1954 decision in *Brown v. Board of Education*, the Court has increasingly applied equality principles, first through the Equal Protection Clause, and later extending to such individual rights areas as the First Amendment.[7] This, suggests Daniel Conkle, is not surprising "given the ever-increasing importance of formal equality under the Equal Protection Clause and in the legal culture generally,"[8] In the context of religious accommodation, for instance, "the Supreme Court defines the government's obligation in terms of neutrality."[9] As Justice Anthony Kennedy declared in *Rosenberger v. Rector and Visitors of the University of Virginia*, the Establishment Clause basically requires the government to follow "neutral criteria and even-handed policies."[10]

An equal protection approach focusing on limiting the power of government to discriminate, rather than the protection or fulfillment of individual autonomy, can be seen in the Court's decision in *Minneapolis Star and Tribune Co. v. Minnesota Commissioner of Revenue*, where the Court struck down a state tax imposed only on the ink and paper used by certain newspapers.[11] Obviously, the government could far more significantly burden individual expression and autonomy by simply imposing a high general tax on all businesses (which would be constitutional) than by imposing a lower special tax that applies only to some newspapers; but such a tax would not violate equal protection norms, and hence would probably be constitutional.

Similarly, in *R.A.V. v. City of St. Paul*, the Court held that the government could not single out certain types of fighting words to be regulated in ways that other fighting words were not regulated.[12] Thus, government cannot target certain speech for special regulation, even if that speech is generally not entitled to First Amendment protection in the first place. However, the government could heavily regulate, even to the point of censorship, all types of fighting words equally. Again, such an approach would infringe more upon individual autonomy than would a more selected approach, which was overturned in *R.A.V. v. City of St. Paul*, where equal protection norms prevailed over any kind of individual-autonomy concern. Even speech that by itself has no First Amendment protection—for example, fighting words—nonetheless has some kind of constitutional protection under the equal protection model. What is most important about the Court's decision in *R.A.V. v. City of St. Paul* is the rule that the government cannot engage in viewpoint discrimination, even with respect to speech that is not normally protected under the First Amendment.

---

7 *See* Daniel Conkle, *The Path of American Religious Liberty*, 75 Ind. L.J. 1, 26 (2000); *see also Brown v. Board of Education*, 347 U.S. 483 (1954) (outlawing formal or deliberate segregation on the basis of race in public schools).

8 *Id.* at 28.

9 *See* Gregory P. Magarian, *The Jurisprudence of Colliding First Amendment Interests*, 83 Notre Dame L. Rev. 185, 239 (2007) (arguing that "the central question in the court's free speech analysis is whether a challenged regulation is neutral as to the content of speech"). Under a neutral First Amendment analysis, "[a] principled court is simply instructing the government to treat different speakers and viewpoints in an unbiased manner." *Id.* at 235.

10 *See* Rosenberger v. Rector and Visitors of the Univ. of Va., 515 U.S. at 839 (1995).

11 460 U.S. 575 (1983).

12 505 U.S. 377, 386 (1992).

Equal Protection and the Establishment Clause

An analysis of First Amendment case law reveals how equal protection notions can govern and protect individual rights.[13] The Establishment Clause, for instance, reflects a constitutional commitment to equal treatment for all religions.[14] According to the Court, the Establishment Clause prohibits the government from preferring "one religion over another."[15] This prohibition against preferring one religion over another has been called "the clearest command of the Establishment Clause."[16]

In *Larson v. Valente*, for instance, the Court articulated the equality principle at the heart of the Establishment Clause.[17] The Court struck down a Minnesota law that exempted religious organizations from certain registration requirements imposed on groups engaged in charitable solicitations, but only if the religious entity received at least half its contributions from members or affiliated organizations. According to the Court, the law granted "denominational preferences" to certain sects but not to others.[18] And in *Board of Education of Kiryas Joel Village School District v. Grumet*, the Court ruled that New York's creation of a separate school district for a religious community violated the Establishment Clause because it "singled out a particular religious sect for special treatment."[19]

In interpreting the religion clauses of the First Amendment, courts have increasingly tended toward an equal protection approach. The effect, suggests Douglas Laycock, is that religious freedoms have changed from a substantive liberty, triggered by a burden on religious practice, to a kind of non-discrimination right, triggered by a legal treatment that is not neutral or not generally applicable.[20] Beginning in the 1980s, the Court began relying on equal treatment norms in its Establishment Clause cases, drifting away from the no-aid principle.[21] Using these norms, the Court has upheld a number of programs allowing public funds to flow to religious institutions.[22] Among the programs the Court has upheld are a voucher program in which vouchers are used to pay tuition at any school, including religious schools,[23] and long-term loans of equipment to private schools, including religious schools.[24]

As early as 1968, in *Board of Education v. Allen*, the Court upheld the state provision of secular textbooks to religious schools, noting that the statute at issue was simply conferring secular benefits neutrally among

13 Despite the criticism that modern courts have over-applied the Equal Protection Clause of the Fourteenth Amendment, there is little disagreement that it was certainly meant to apply to fundamental rights of the kind found in the First Amendment. *See* William Araiza, *Constitutional Rules and Institutional Roles: The Fate of the Equal Protection Class of One and What it Means for Congressional Power to Enforce Constitutional Rights*, 62 SMU L. Rev. 27, 42 (2009); Curtis, No State Shall Abridge 117–20 (1986) (arguing that the clause applies to fundamental rights, including those in the Bill of Rights).

14 Wallace v. Jaffree, 472 U.S. 38, 52–53 (1985).

15 Everson v. Bd. of Education, 330 U.S. 1, 15 (1947).

16 Larson v. Valente, 456 U.S. 228, 244 (1982).

17 456 U.S. 228, 231 (1982).

18 *Id.* at 246. According to the Court, the registration exemption deliberately discriminated between different religious organizations. *Id.* at 247.

19 *Id.* at 706.

20 Douglas Laycock, *Theology Scholarships, the Pledge of Allegiance, and Religious Liberty: Avoiding the Extremes but Missing the Liberty*, 118 Harv. L. Rev. 155, 156 (2004). In Establishment Clause cases, government neutrality has become a governing principle. *Id.* at 158.

21 The no-aid principle held that no government assistance, however small, should be given to any religious activities or institutions. *See* Everson v. Bd. of Education, 330 U.S. 1, 16 (1947). The non-discrimination principle, however, stated that the government could not exclude individual religious believers, because of their faith, from receiving the benefits of public welfare legislation. *Id.* According to Laycock, the no-funding tradition "is a misinterpretation of the Establishment Clause, deeply rooted in historic anti-Catholicism," at least as applied to elementary and secondary schools. *Id.* at 185.

22 *See* Zelman v. Simmons-Harris, 536 U.S. 639 (2002); Mitchell v. Helms, 530 U.S. 793 (2000); Zobrest v. Catalina Foothills Sch. Dist., 509 U.S. 1 (1993); Bowen v. Kendrick, 487 U.S. 589 (1988); Witters v. Washington Dept. of Ser. for the Blind, 474 U.S. 481 (1986).

23 *See Zelman*, 536 U.S. 639.

24 *See Mitchell*, 530 U.S. 793.

all students.[25] Later, in *Tilton v. Richardson*, the Court upheld the Higher Education Facilities Act authorizing federal grants and loans for construction by colleges and universities.[26] As the federal funds would be used to finance construction of buildings on the campuses of religiously affiliated universities, as well as secular universities, the Court found that the statute strove to equalize the governmental benefits available to all higher education students.

The Supreme Court's equality approach to the Establishment Clause has also been evident in cases involving free speech claims. In *Lambs Chapel v. Center Moriches Union Free School District*, the Court held that excluding religious speech from a designated forum violated the Free Speech Clause, despite objections from the school district that the use of such school facilities would violate the Establishment Clause.[27] After a local church was denied permission to show a film series on school property that discussed family and child-rearing issues from a religious perspective, which would clearly have been a permitted use of the building were it not for the religious content of the series, the Court ruled that the Establishment Clause could not be used to single out and exclude religious groups. Earlier, in *Widmar v. Vincent*, the Court had struck down a state university regulation prohibiting the use of university facilities for religious speech purposes.[28] The Court ruled that the university had created a designated public forum when it allowed other student groups to use its buildings for speech activities; hence, the discriminatory exclusion of the religious group was overturned.[29]

In *Rosenberger v. Rector and Visitors of the University of Virginia*, the Court again addressed the exclusion of religious speech from a state-created forum.[30] In *Rosenberger*, the University of Virginia provided funding for student publications, but specifically prohibited any religious-oriented publications from eligibility for such funds. But the Court disagreed, ruling that a denial of funding to publications with a religious perspective would constitute viewpoint discrimination in violation of the Free Speech Clause.[31] Moreover, even though *Rosenberger* essentially involved free speech issues, the Court also stated that an equal funding of both religious and nonreligious student publications did not violate the Establishment Clause.[32] In a similar vein to *Rosenberger* and *Lambs Chapel* was the Court's decision in *Good News Club v. Milford Central School*.[33] In *Good News Club*, the Court held that the exclusion of a religious group from a state-created public forum (for example, the after-hours use of public school facilities) constituted viewpoint discrimination in violation of the Free Speech Clause.[34]

In the 1985 case of *Aguilar v. Felton*, the Supreme Court in a non-neutral decision ruled against parochial school participation in a special education program that provided remedial English and mathematics assistance to economically and educationally disadvantaged students at both public and private schools. But in a later decision employing equality principles, the Court overruled *Aguilar*.[35] In *Agostini v. Felton*, the Court stressed the importance of formal neutrality in concluding that the Establishment Clause did not preclude publicly funded teachers from teaching secular, remedial courses on the premises of religious schools under a federally funded program that supported teaching at nonreligious schools as well.[36] The Court suggested that Establishment Clause invalidation would be unlikely when aid is allocated on the basis of neutral criteria.[37]

25 392 U.S. 236, 243 (1968) (stating that "the law merely makes available to all children the benefits of a general program to lend schoolbooks free of charge").

26 403 U.S. 672, 674–75 (1971).

27 508 U.S. 384, 387, 395 (1993).

28 454 U.S. 263, 265 (1981).

29 *Id.* at 277.

30 515 U.S. 819, 822–23 (1995).

31 *Id.* at 831–32.

32 *Id.* at 839–40, 843–44.

33 533 U.S. 98 (2001).

34 *Id.* at 102.

35 473 U.S. 402 (1985).

36 521 U.S. 203, 228 (1997).

37 *Id.* at 231. As an example of this no-discrimination approach, the Fourth Circuit struck down a Maryland policy that funded secular colleges and some church-affiliated colleges, but not pervasively sectarian colleges. Columbia Union Coll. v. Oliver, 254 F.3d 496, 504–8 (4th Cir. 2001).

Later, in *Zelman v. Simmons-Harris*, the Court used the neutrality doctrine to uphold Cleveland's school voucher program.[38] It ruled that the vouchers promoted private choice by giving money directly to students for their use at either religious or nonreligious schools.[39] This scheme was found neutral because it left the decision of whether to apply funds toward a religious education to the private choices of parents and their children, and not to the government.[40] According to *Zelman*, so long as the programs exhibit governmental neutrality toward religion, indirect aid programs are permissible under the Establishment Clause, regardless of whether or not tuition money is ultimately diverted for religious purposes.[41]

The requirement of denominational equality obviously demands that all religions be treated equally. However, the requirement of equality is sometimes seen as going one step further, demanding that the government neither favor nor disfavor religion in general, as compared to nonreligion.[42] Thus, the Court has often adopted a concept of religious neutrality that applies not only between different religious denominations, but also between religion and nonreligion.

This highlights a crucial issue in applying an equal protection approach—namely, that of arriving at the proper baseline to be used in determining equality of treatment. Should the baseline be a comparison of religion with nonreligion; or should the baseline only involve an inquiry into whether all religions are being treated equally? The First Amendment, concerned as it is with limiting government power to interfere with either the individual or the institutional spheres of religious observance, may not focus on drawing the same kind of limits to government intrusion into nonreligion, whatever that is.

The Free Exercise Clause

Just as neutrality and equality have become governing principles for Establishment Clause cases, they have also been applied to the Free Exercise Clause. Here the principle of equality requires that all religious believers, regardless of their beliefs, should be treated equally under the law and that the government should not have the power to single out particular individuals or religious beliefs for discriminatory treatment.

The neutrality approach was adopted in *Employment Division v. Smith*, where the Court held that a law criminalizing the use of peyote, as applied to two American Indians, did not violate the Free Exercise Clause, finding that the law was one of general applicability and was neutral regarding religious conduct.[43] The Court distinguished between laws that specifically target religion and neutral laws of general applicability, which, according to the Court, did not constitute an infringement of free exercise, no matter how substantial the burden on religious exercise.[44] With this focus on neutrality, the *Smith* Court moved its Free Exercise Clause jurisprudence in the same direction as its Establishment Clause doctrines.

The emphasis on neutrality in *Smith* marked a departure from the Court's previous free exercise "fundamental rights" jurisprudence. Prior to *Smith*, the Court's rule was that any government-imposed burden on religious practice presumptively violated the Free Exercise Clause, and that such burdens could only be justified by a compelling government interest.[45] This doctrine was articulated in *Sherbert v. Verner* and *Wisconsin v. Yoder*, where the Court held that any state action substantially burdening religious exercise had to be strictly scrutinized. But in *Smith*, the Court declared that neutral laws of general applicability burdening

38 536 U.S. 639 (2002).

39 *Id.* at 662–63.

40 *Id.* at 622.

41 In the lower court, it was found that 96 percent of the students participating in the voucher program were enrolled in religious schools. *See* Simmons-Harris v. Zelman, 234 F.3d 945, 949 (6th Cir. 2000), *rev'd*, 536 U.S. 639 (2002).

42 Conkle, *supra* note 7, at 8.

43 494 U.S. 872, 877–79 (1990).

44 *Id.* at 884–85 (1990). Thus, as long as the state does not deliberately single out a particular religious practice, any burdens on that practice will not violate the First Amendment. *See also* Church of the Lukumi Babalu Aye, Inc. v. City of Hialeah, 508 U.S. 520 (1993).

45 *See* Sherbert v. Verner, 374 U.S. 398 (1963) (holding that a state could not refuse unemployment compensation to a Sabbatarian who is unavailable for work on Saturdays. *Id.* at 403–06) and Wisconsin v. Yoder, 406 U.S. 205, 213–36 (1972) (holding that a state could not require Amish children to attend high school).

religious exercise do not require any heightened judicial review.[46] This rule—that the Free Exercise Clause prohibited only deliberate governmental discrimination against religion—rested in part on a belief that the granting to religion of exemptions from neutral laws would pose too big of a risk of discrimination between religions.[47]

The *Smith* rule of equality, however, can sometimes be a difficult rule to fulfill, particularly depending on how one measures it. Laycock has outlined two different concepts of neutrality or equality in connection with the First Amendment religion clauses. The notion of "formal neutrality" would preclude formal or deliberate discrimination either between religions or between religion and nonreligion.[48] The other form of neutrality, he suggests, is "substantive neutrality"—a principle that examines whether the government's actions, even if formally neutral, have the actual effect of promoting or discouraging religion.[49]

According to Conkle, formal neutrality is the simplest means of implementing a policy of equal treatment for religion and nonreligion, and has become the dominant theme under both the Free Exercise and Establishment Clauses.[50] This notion of formal neutrality certainly prevailed in *Smith*, where the Court upheld a formally neutral, non-discriminatory state law, even though that law resulted in a significant burden to a particular religious exercise. Thus, *Smith* changed free exercise from a substantive liberty to a comparative right, "in which the constitutionally required treatment of religious practices depends on the treatment of some comparable set of secular practices."[51] Whereas a personal-autonomy model of the Free Exercise Clause would focus on burdens caused by laws infringing on religious exercise, *Smith* changed the focus to discrimination.

The Court elaborated on the *Smith* rule in the case of *Church of the Lukumi Babalu Aye, Inc. v. City of Hialeah*, which involved a challenge to several local ordinances that prohibited animal sacrifices.[52] Although the City argued that the laws reflected a generally applicable ban on those sacrifices, the Court found that the ban was targeted at religious uses, exempting any killings of animals for secular reasons. When taking into account both the laws and all their exemptions, it became clear to the Court that only the killing of animals for religious reasons—indeed, only the ceremonies of a particular sect, the Santeria religion—was subject to penalty.[53] Consequently, because the ordinances on animal sacrifice prohibited religious but not secular killings of animals, the Court found that there was objective evidence of governmental targeting religious conduct for discriminatory treatment.[54] Thus, both *Smith* and *Lukumi* rely on the non-discrimination principle to govern the right of free exercise of religion.[55]

In *Locke v. Davey*, the Court further explained the *Smith* legacy. In *Locke*, a Washington scholarship program allowed qualified recipients to use their scholarships to pursue a degree in any course of study except a devotional theology degree.[56] Davey sued, claiming that this program violated the Free Exercise Clause because of its discriminatory purpose and effect. However, even though Washington discriminated against devotional theology students, the Supreme Court nonetheless upheld the program against a free exercise challenge.

While *Smith* banned facial discrimination against religion, *Locke* stated that, at least with respect to funding, facial discrimination against religion is presumptively unconstitutional if and only if the

46 *See Smith*, 494 U.S. at 876–90. Although the Court in *Smith* held that facially neutral statutes do not ordinarily violate the Free Exercise Clause, it also reiterated that laws imposing special burdens on targeted religions are presumptively unconstitutional. *Id.* at 877.

47 *See Smith*, 494 U.S. at 886 (stating that free exercise exemptions are "a constitutional anomaly," unlike the "constitutional norm" of "equality of treatment").

48 Douglas Laycock, *Formal Substantive and Disaggregated Neutrality toward Religion*, 39 DePaul L. Rev. 993, 999 (1990) (arguing that formal neutrality would "prohibit classification in terms of religion either to confer a benefit or to impose a burden").

49 *Id.* at 1001–06.

50 Conkle, *supra* note 7, at 10.

51 Laycock, *supra* note 48, at 202.

52 508 U.S. 520 (1993).

53 *Id.* at 535.

54 *Id.* at 535–36.

55 *Smith*, 494 U.S. 872 (1990), *Lukumi*, 508 U.S. 520 (1993).

56 Locke v. Davey, 540 U.S. 712, 717 (2004).

discrimination burdens a religious practice.[57] The *Locke* Court also held that a refusal to fund, by itself, does not burden religious exercise.[58] Thus, under the *Locke v. Davey* rule, a free exercise violation requires not only a discrimination but also a significant burden arising from that discrimination. This decision seems to move the Court away from its post-*Smith* emphasis on equality, allowing religious exercise to be targeted for special burdens, as long as those burdens are not considered significant. In *Locke*, the Court did not focus on discrimination or equal protection; it focused on the nature of the burden imposed by the program, downplaying the facial discrimination against devotional theology students. This disregard of discrimination, however, by violating the equal protection approach, may threaten free exercise rights.

The Free Speech Clause

Equal protection norms form the bedrock of the Free Speech Clause. In *Arkansas Writers' Project, Inc. v. Ragland*, the Supreme Court indicated that any law singling out certain speakers for differential treatment was suspect under the First Amendment.[59] The marketplace of ideas metaphor articulated by Justice Holmes and long used to provide a model of the First Amendment's free speech protections is essentially an expression of equal protection norms. This metaphor envisions an equality of all sovereign private citizens to participate in the speech marketplace.[60]

An equal protection approach in the free speech area is already somewhat reflected in the Court's content-neutrality doctrine. Current First Amendment doctrine requires that any content-based law be subject to strict scrutiny.[61] Although this approach theoretically indicates that content regulations might be upheld if they are narrowly drawn and supported by a compelling governmental interest, in reality it allows virtually no content-based speech restriction to survive.[62]

The Court's content-neutrality doctrine was applied in *Police Department of Chicago v. Mosley*, where the Court struck down a Chicago ordinance prohibiting all peaceful picketers, except peaceful labor picketers, from demonstrating near a school while that school was in session.[63] Although the Court's focus was on equality of treatment between all viewpoints, the determination of this equality depends on what baseline is used for measuring such equality. Should a narrow or broad baseline be used? When dealing with political speech, as broad a baseline as possible should be used.

Political Speech and the Equal Protection Approach

Political speech should be given the highest First Amendment protections, because free political speech is needed to maintain democratic control of government. As long as a democratic society has the freedom to engage in open and uninhibited political speech, that society is able to direct, control, and alter the course of its government. But if any laws infringe on political speech, those laws essentially enlarge the power of government by making it less amenable to change by a democratic society. As Justice William Douglas

---

57 *See* Laycock, *supra* note 20, at 214.

58 *See Locke* 540 U.S. at 724–25; *see also* Rust v. Sullivan, 500 U.S. 173, 192–93 (1991).

59 481 U.S. 221, 228 (1987).

60 Vincent Blasi, *Holmes and the Marketplace of Ideas*, 2004 Sup. Ct. Rev. 1, 41 (2005).

61 *See, e.g.*, Sable Commc'ns v. FCC, 492 U.S. 115, 126 (1989) (stating that content restrictions must promote a compelling government interest and be the least restrictive means of achieving that interest); R.A.V. v. City of St. Paul, 505 U.S. 377, 382 (1992) (stating the "content based regulations are presumptively invalid"); Boos v. Barry, 485 U.S. 312, 321 (1988) (stating that with content-based regulations courts will apply the "most exacting scrutiny").

62 *See, e.g.*, U.S. v. Playboy Entm't Grp., 529 U.S. 803 (2000) (overturning restrictions on cable providers of sexually explicit programming); Texas v. Johnson, 491 U.S. 397 (1989) (striking down a flag-burning law); Simon & Schuster Inc. v. Members of the N.Y. State Crime Victims Bd., 502 U.S. 105 (1991) (striking down a law regulating the earnings of convicted criminals who write tell-all books about their crimes).

63 408 U.S. 92, 102 (1972).

explained in *Terminiello v. City of Chicago*, "[I]t is only through free debate and free exchange of ideas that government remains responsive to the will of the people."[64]

A number of legal scholars have adopted this political speech theory.[65] According to Lillian BeVier, for instance, "[T]he sole legitimate First Amendment principle protects only speech that participates in the process of representative democracy."[66] Moreover, on numerous occasions, the Supreme Court has opined on the role of political speech within the First Amendment. In *Burson v. Freeman*, the Court stated that the First Amendment serves primarily "to protect the free discussion of governmental affairs."[67] And according to the Court in *FCC v. League of Women Voters*, political speech occupies the "highest rung" of constitutional concerns and is the "most protected" by the First Amendment."[68]

Despite its prominence in modern free speech theory, individual self-actualization or autonomy, which can be accomplished "through virtually all voluntary conduct, including one's choice of profession, dress, and consumer goods,"[69] cannot by themselves provide a sound basis for First Amendment jurisprudence. Not only is there absolutely no evidence that the framers of the First Amendment were at all concerned with self-realization, it is by no means clear that self-realization is even something to be constitutionally desired. To some people, the achievement of self-realization may come through ways that are damaging to society or other individuals.

Crucially, the fact that there are many areas of speech that are not protected by the First Amendment tends to support the theory that the First Amendment is not aimed at preserving individual autonomy. If it were, then defamation, fighting words, advocacy of illegal conduct, and obscene speech would be protected. Further supporting the argument that political speech was the only type of speech believed to warrant highest constitutional protection is the fact that following ratification of the First Amendment there were no attempts to challenge or question such speech restrictions as those contained in theatrical licensing acts. There was no serious discussion in the eighteenth or nineteenth century, suggesting that theater and popular entertainment were worthy of the same type of protection as political speech.[70]

In *Citizens United*, Justice Anthony Kennedy noted that "at the founding, speech was open, comprehensive, and vital to society's definition of itself; there were no limits on the sources of speech and knowledge."[71] But this statement is true only if it is confined to political speech, since at the time of adoption of the First Amendment "blasphemy was illegal in every state, and prohibitions against other forms of undesirable speech, such as pornography or other lewd material, was entirely unprotected."[72]

Opponents of the "political speech" interpretation of the First Amendment argue that it gives insufficient protection to various kinds of nonpolitical, "low-value" speech. And yet, whenever these opponents argue against any restrictions on, for instance, graphically violent video entertainment programming, they cite as their justification the need to protect controversial and unpopular political speech. They rarely argue that violent and sexually explicit entertainment are inherently as constitutionally valuable as political speech.

Judge Robert Bork has gone so far as to argue that the First Amendment should be limited to protecting only explicitly political speech.[73] He wrote that freedom of speech for literature, for instance, would depend

64 337 U.S. 1, 4 (1949).

65 *See, e.g.*, Alexander M. Bickel, The Morality of Consent 62 (1975) (declaring that "the First Amendment should protect and indeed encourage speech so long as it serves to make the political process work"); Lillian R. BeVier, *The First Amendment and Political Speech: An Inquiry into the Substance and Limits of Principle*, 30 Stan. L. Rev. 299, 358 (1978); Harry Kalven Jr, *The New York Times Case: A Note on the Central Meaning of the First Amendment*, 1964 S. Ct. Rev. 191, 208 (1964) (arguing that the First Amendment "has a central meaning—a core of protection of speech without which democracy cannot function").

66 Lillian BeVier, *The First Amendment and Political Speech*, 30 Stan. L. Rev. at 358 (1978).

67 504 U.S. 191, 196 (1992).

68 468 U.S. 364, 383, 381 (1984).

69 Stanley Ingber, *Rediscovering the Communal Worth of Individual Rights: The First Amendment in Institutional Contexts*, 69 Tex. L. Rev. 1, 19 (1990).

70 Jon M. Garon, *Entertainment Law*, 76 Tul. L. Rev. 559, 634 (2002).

71 130 S.Ct. 876, 906.

72 Darrel Menthe, *The Marketplace Metaphor and Commercial Speech Doctrine*, 38 Hastings Const. L.Q. 131, 159 (2010).

73 Robert Bork, *Neutral Principles and Some First Amendment Problems*, 47 Ind. L.J. 1, 20 (1971).

not on constitutional mandates but upon the "enlightenment of society and its elected representatives."[74] This is not as harsh a view as it might first seem. For instance, even if a book were banned because it had no First Amendment protection, there would be full constitutional protection for any protest that arose over that decision. In other words, while the book itself might not constitute political speech covered by the First Amendment, any protest over a book-banning law would certainly be protected speech.[75]

Equal Protection and Free Speech

It has been argued that the decisions in *Schacht v. United States*[76] and *Police Department of Chicago v. Mosley*[77] ushered in a new era of First Amendment jurisprudence in which the equality principle prevailed over the speech principle.[78] In both cases, the Court acknowledged that a content-neutral ban—prohibiting all soldiers from wearing their uniforms in theatrical productions, or prohibiting all protestors from picketing near schools—would be constitutional, even though such a ban would obviously be quite speech-restrictive. Professor Stone suggests that in each case "the government violated the First Amendment not because it limited Schacht's or Mosley's right to speak, but because it discriminated against them based on the content of their message."[79] The issue essentially was whether the government was treating all speakers and ideas equally, rather than whether it was restricting the marketplace of ideas.

To sustain various kinds of speech restrictions under a more permissive review than strict scrutiny, an intermediate level of scrutiny has been used for time-manner-place regulations found to be content neutral.[80] However, in its use of the content-neutrality rule as a prerequisite for employing intermediate scrutiny, the Court has often found that laws effectively singling out certain types of speech were in fact content neutral.[81] For instance, the following regulations have been found to be content neutral: laws governing the location of sexually explicit entertainment businesses;[82] laws governing the speech activities of abortion protestors;[83] regulations governing the solicitation activities of religious groups, even though those activities arise from the groups' religious beliefs;[84] and a law requiring cable television operators to carry, free of charge, the programming of local broadcast television stations.[85] Even though these laws and regulations were evaluated under the more deferential intermediate standard of review, they were effectively aimed at very specific groups of speakers. Consequently, given the subjective and inconsistent way in which the content-neutral

74 *Id.* at 28.

75 Sunstein makes a similar argument. He argues that "[r]estrictions on political speech have the distinctive feature of impairing the ordinary channels for political change." Cass R. Sunstein, Democracy and the Problem of Free Speech 306 (1993). As long as there is freedom of political speech, controls on other kinds of speech can always be protested. For instance, "[i]f the government bans violent pornography, citizens can continue to argue against the ban. But if the government forecloses political argument, the democratic corrective is unavailable. Controls on nonpolitical speech do not have this uniquely damaging feature." *Id.*

76 398 U.S. 58, 65 (1970).

77 408 U.S. 92 (1972).

78 Geoffrey Stone, *Free Speech in the 21st Century: Ten Lessons from the 20th Century*, 36 Pepp. L. Rev. 273, 280 (2009).

79 *Id.* at 282.

80 *See, e.g.*, Ward v. Rock Against Racism, 491 U.S. 781 (1989).

81 *See* Patrick M. Garry, *The First Amendment and Non-Political Speech: Exploring a Constitutional Model that Focuses on the Existence of Alternative Channels of Communication*, 71 Mo. L. Rev. 477, 485 (2007).

82 *See* City of Renton v. Playtime Theaters, 475 U.S. 41 (1986). Under the secondary-effects doctrine, a regulation is seen to be content neutral if it "serves purposes unrelated to the content of the expression … even if it has an incidental effect on some speakers or messages." Ward v. Rock Against Racism, 491 U.S. 781, 791 (1989).

83 *See* Hill v. Colorado, 530 U.S. 703 (2000).

84 *See Hefron*, 452 U.S. at 640; U.S. v. Kokinda, 497 U.S. 720 (1990).

85 *See* Turner Broadcasting System, Inc. v. FCC, 512 U.S. 622, 643 (1994) (holding that the must-carry rules were content neutral and hence subject to the intermediate level of scrutiny, even though the rules imposed a direct burden on the freedom of cable operators).

principle has been applied, its future legitimacy falls into question. For this reason, a more simplified, all-encompassing approach is needed, such as the one provided by the equal protection approach.

There has always been a tenuous connection between the Court's content-neutral approach and the secondary-effects doctrine. But this latter doctrine can be explained through an equal protection approach to the First Amendment and an identification of the proper baseline. In *City of Renton v. Playtime Theatres Inc.*, the Court upheld a zoning ordinance that on its face singled out adult movie theaters for special restrictions on location.[86] The Court ruled that the ordinance was not content based because it was justified without reference to the content of the regulated speech, but instead was justified by the government's desire to alleviate "the secondary effects of such theatres on the surrounding community."[87] However, in reality, the zoning restrictions in the ordinance applied only to theaters that engaged in a particular expressive activity. But the decision can perhaps be more clearly explained in terms of baseline comparisons. The *Renton* Court was not looking at all movie theaters as the baseline comparison, but at businesses that cause certain dilapidating effects in surrounding neighborhoods. With this as the baseline, the theaters subject to the restrictions in *Renton* were treated with equality.

In *Young v. American Mini Theatres, Inc.*, the Court upheld a Detroit ordinance that prohibited two adult theaters or bookstores from operating within 1,000 feet of one another.[88] In his concurring opinion, Justice Lewis Powell Jr argued that the City was justified in regulating adult theaters differently than other theaters "because they have markedly different effects upon their surroundings."[89] Thus, to Powell, the relevant baseline was not speech but neighborhood effects. This baseline was used in part because of the Court's recognition that pornography is not entitled to the same degree of constitutional protection as political speech, since "society's interest in protecting this type of expression is of a wholly different, and lesser, magnitude than the interest in untrammeled political debate [and] few of us would march our sons and daughters off to war to preserve the citizen's right to see 'Specified Sexual Activities' exhibited in the theatres of our choice."[90]

However, when political speech is involved, the Court does not apply the secondary-effects doctrine, and hence uses a broader baseline. For instance, in *R.A.V. v. City of St. Paul*, the Court overturned an ordinance imposing additional penalties for violent crimes that convey a racist message.[91] According to the Court, even if racial hate crimes are likely to cause violent responses, that violence does not qualify as a secondary effect. Thus, the Court will not use narrow baselines—for example, secondary effects—when political speech is involved. Similarly, in *Simon & Schuster Inc. v. Members of the New York State Crime Victims Board*, the Court overturned a law requiring convicted criminals who author books describing their crimes to share book royalties with the victims of their crimes.[92] The Court declined to review the law under the secondary-effects doctrine—for example, the effect of allowing criminals to gain an economic benefit from their crimes. This was because the speech at issue could qualify as political speech—and the law not only singled out some political speech (speech about crimes), but singled out some speakers (convicted criminals) as well.

The Court's current approach, relying as it so often does on individual autonomy considerations, treats all content-based regulations the same; it makes virtually no effort to determine whether a particular law imposes the kind of burden that threatens to drive an idea out of the marketplace of ideas. This approach—of invalidating laws found to be "content based," regardless of the actual burdens they impose—contrasts with the situation where a court determines a law to be content neutral and then sustains that law even though the burdens on speech caused by the law are readily apparent.

Contrary to the approach taken by the Court in its abortion-rights jurisprudence, there is often little consideration in current free speech jurisprudence of whether a regulation actually imposes an "undue

86 475 U.S. 41 (1986) (holding that an ordinance regulating adult theaters with the goal of reducing secondary effects "is completely consistent with our definition of content-neutral speech regulations as those are justified without reference to the content of the regulated speech.").

87 *Id.* at 41.

88 427 U.S. 50, 52 (1976).

89 *Id.* at 82 (Powell, J., concurring).

90 *Id.* at 70.

91 505 U.S. 377, 381 (1992).

92 502 U.S. 105, 115–23 (1991).

burden" on the particular speech.[93] This ignoring of the degree of actual burden has resulted in the nullification of laws providing various child-protection safeguards on commercially provided pornography,[94] as well as laws requiring fundraisers to reveal the percentage of raised money that is actually provided to the charities for whom they are working.[95]

Under traditional First Amendment jurisprudence, courts dealing with free speech issues have required an opt-out scheme rather than an opt-in one.[96] Unwilling listeners must opt out of the unwanted speech environment. But an opt-in requirement, especially with respect to nonpolitical speech, would be an attempt to balance the burdens and equalize the situations of willing and unwilling listeners. This would entail the courts' use of a receptive/unreceptive baseline in cases regarding certain new technologies and nonpolitical speech. For instance, in judicial opinions sustaining restrictions on access to dial-a-porn services, ruling that such restrictions were necessary to protect the children of parents who did not wish them to hear this particular kind of speech, the courts in *Dial Information Services* and *Information Providers* not only found that the restrictions did not amount to a complete ban on the indecent speech, but also tried to equalize the burdens of accessing and avoiding such speech.[97]

Even though as a general rule content-based regulation is strictly scrutinized by the courts, content regulation has been allowed in certain media or conduits. Under an equal protection approach, such regulation can be explained by identifying the point of comparison or baseline to be used in determining equal treatment. For instance, the Court has determined that the print media constitute a completely separate baseline than do the broadcast media, with the former receiving a higher degree of First Amendment protection than the latter. However, within broadcasting, all entities are treated the same.

Courts have used the technological differences among media to justify the differing constitutional protections for speech within each medium. As the Supreme Court proclaimed in 1969, "Differences in the characteristics of new media justify differences in the First Amendment standards applied to them."[98] Thus, in terms of an equal protection approach, courts have created different technological baselines.

Based on the notion of a scarce spectrum, the broadcast media receive the lowest degree of content protection.[99] This diminished constitutional protection was evident in *Red Lion Broadcasting Co. v. FCC*, which upheld a federal regulation called the Fairness Doctrine that forced broadcasters to give a right of reply to political figures criticized over the airwaves. Exemplifying this print/broadcast dichotomy, the Court later struck down essentially the same kind of law as applied to the print media.[100] The rationale given for the lower constitutional status of broadcasting is that a limited spectrum creates a natural monopoly, which in turn confers upon the government the need and duty to regulate it for the common good.[101]

---

93 *See* Planned Parenthood v. Casey, 505 U.S. 833, 876 (1992). In *Stenberg v. Carhart*, 530 U.S. 914 (2000), the Court struck down a Nebraska law outlawing partial-birth abortion as violating the "undue burden" test. Such a balancing approach is also used in freedom of association cases, which involve conduct that facilitates expression. *See* Barry McDonald, *The First Amendment and the Free Flow of Information*, 65 Ohio St. L.J. 249, 260 (2004).

94 *See* Ashcroft v. ACLU, 542 U.S. 656 (2004); U.S. v. Playboy Entm't Grp., 529 U.S. 803, 803 (2000).

95 *See* Riley v. Nat'l Fed'n of the Blind, 487 U.S. 781, 795–801 (1988) (imposing strict scrutiny after finding the law to be content based).

96 Courts have essentially assumed that the First Amendment requires opt-out. *See also* Cohen v. California, 403 U.S. 15, 26 (1971) (holding that, in the public square, listeners are presumed able to avert their eyes and ears from speech they find offensive and move on); Lamont v. Postmaster General, 381 U.S. 301, 305 (1965) (holding that the government may not screen out sexually offensive materials in advance and require potential recipients to opt-in); Boler v. Youngs Drug Products Corp., 463 U.S. 60, 61 (1983) (holding that the federal government could not ban the unsolicited mailing of condom ads—a law that required opt-in).

97 In *Dial Info. Svcs. v. Thornburgh*, 938 F.2d 1535 (2d Cir. 1991) and *Info. Providers' Coalition v. FCC*, 928 F.2d 866 (9th Cir. 1991), the Second and Ninth Circuits ruled that the restrictions in the so-called Helms Amendment, 47 USC § 223(b) et seq., did not violate the First Amendment.

98 Red Lion Broad. Co. v. FCC, 395 U.S. 367, 386 (1969).

99 *See* Jim Chen, *Conduit-Based Regulation of Speech*, 54 Duke L.J. 1359, 1371–93 (2005).

100 *See* Miami Herald Publishing Co. v. Tornillo, 418 U.S. 241, 258 (1974) (striking down a state right-of-reply law applied to newspapers).

101 *See* FCC v. Nat'l Citizens Comm. for Broad., 436 U.S. 775, 779 (1978).

In *Turner I*, the Court addressed the issues of whether to maintain the disparity in First Amendment treatment of the print and broadcast media, and then whether to apply the print or broadcast model to cable television.[102] The *Turner* cases tried to piece together a third model or baseline to apply to cable television. Though the Court did not want to place the same kind of content restrictions on cable that exist for broadcast, it nonetheless continued to see a difference between the print and television media, and between the impact that each medium has on its audience.

With respect to the Internet, the Court has so far decided to treat it according to the print model.[103] Nonetheless, in *Ashcroft v. ACLU*, even though conferring the highest constitutional protections on the Internet, Justice Kennedy reiterated that the "unique characteristics" of "each mode of expression" should determine the constitutional coverage of that medium.[104]

Conclusion: The Application of Equal Protection Norms

Determining the relevant baseline to be used for comparison purposes is a crucial endeavor in any equal protection approach. This baseline issue has been a longstanding issue in the Establishment Clause area. The question is often whether the measure of equality should be between religion and nonreligion, or just between different religious sects. The effect of using a secular baseline is often to prevent benefits or special accommodations from going to religious organizations or believers. In *Estate of Thornton v. Caldor*, for instance, the Court ruled that a Connecticut law giving employees the right not to work on their religious Sabbath violated the Establishment Clause.[105] The statute violated the equal protection principle, since it granted an advantage to practitioners of those religions that believe in observing a Sabbath. In fact, the law violated equal protection norms on a couple of different levels. If the baseline in *Caldor* was all secular workers, then the law clearly violated equal protection norms, since religious employees who followed Sabbath requirements were treated differently from nonreligious workers, who did not have to go against their beliefs to work any certain day of the week. But the law may also have violated equal protection norms if the baseline were changed to all religious practitioners. This is because there are some religious workers who do not have a Sabbath. Therefore, the law treated some religious workers differently than others, favoring religious workers with a Sabbath. Similarly, in *Texas Monthly v. Bullock*, where the Court struck down a sales-tax exemption for religious periodicals, the baseline used to measure equality was secular—namely, whether all secular periodicals received the same sales-tax exemption as that given to religious periodicals.

In the free exercise area, the Court's change in doctrine from *Sherbert v. Verner* to *Employment Division v. Smith* can be explained in the change of baseline used. In both *Sherbert* and *Yoder*, the baseline for determining equality was the religious freedom of religious practitioners. If a law affected some religious practitioners more detrimentally than others, then the law was unconstitutional. However, in *Smith*, the baseline changed to all members of society, including the nonreligious. So if a law affected all of society neutrally, it was not unconstitutional, even if it differentially affected the religious activities or practices of some of society's citizens.

There is an argument that the baseline established in *Smith* is the wrong baseline and does not adequately protect or consider the unique needs of religious exercise. By establishing the baseline that it did, the *Smith* Court arguably did not sufficiently consider the convictions and needs of minority religions to the same degree that those of a mainstream religion would be protected by the political process. Since *Smith* may not adequately protect the unique practices of minority religions from the burdens of generally applicable neutral state laws, it can be argued that not all religions possess equal protection of their religious practices. The argument in opposition to *Smith* is that equality among religious practitioners, rather than equality between

102 *Turner I*, 512 U.S. at 641 (addressing the disparity in First Amendment treatment as reflected in Miami Herald Publishing Co. v. Tornillo, 418 U.S. 241 (1974) (conferring the most protective First Amendment status on the print media) and Red Lion Broadcasting Co. v. FCC, 395 U.S. 367 (1969) (granting a much less protective status to broadcasters).

103 Reno v. ACLU, 521 U.S. 844, 868 (1997).

104 535 U.S. 564, 594–95 (2002) (Kennedy, J., concurring).

105 Estate of Thornton v. Caldor, 472 U.S. 703, 704 (1985).

religious practitioners and secular citizens, should be the baseline used under the Free Exercise Clause. If a different baseline had been used—namely, the ability of all religious practitioners to practice their religion equally—the case may have turned out differently.

In the free speech area, when political speech is involved, the baseline used must be that which allows for the maximum degree of protection. The search for the proper baseline in free speech cases often entails an identification of the relevant comparison group. Will it be a larger general public, or will it be a narrower, similarly situated First Amendment group? In *Minneapolis Star and Tribune Co. v. Minnesota Commissioner of Revenue*, the Court struck down a special ink and paper tax aimed at the print media (and indeed, at particular newspapers) and that was not applied to other businesses.[106] This was clearly an equal protection case, with the Court finding that the particular newspapers had been singled out for a discriminatory burden that the rest of society was not made to bear. Consequently, a broad or more protective baseline was used. In *Schneider v. State*, the Court struck down an ordinance that banned the distribution of leaflets on government property.[107] Again, a broad baseline was used, insofar as leaflets were compared with every other kind of expression that could be distributed on government property.[108]

On the other hand, in *Glickman v. Wileman Brothers and Elliott, Inc.*, the Court rejected a First Amendment challenge to marketing orders that required fruit producers to pay an assessment for generic advertising.[109] Looking at the assessment from the viewpoint of tree-fruit producers, all were asked to pay the same assessment. There was no equal protection problem from that perspective. But a broader comparison group—for example, all of society—would have shown that a special tax was placed upon a particular segment of society to pay for a speech-related purpose. This would have been a more protective comparison group, but it was not used because political speech was not involved.

Determining the proper baseline or relevant comparison group for free speech purposes depends, just as it does under the religion clauses, on the primary purpose of the Free Speech Clause. As argued previously, the Free Speech Clause serves primarily to protect political speech.[110] Therefore, when political speech is involved, the courts should use the broadest baseline that ensures the greatest speech protections. When political speech is not involved, courts can choose narrower baselines, as with so-called low-value speech.[111]

An examination of First Amendment case law reveals how the presence or absence of political speech should affect the identification of the relevant baseline. In *City of Erie v. Pap's A.M.*, the Court addressed the application to nude dancing establishments of a city ordinance forbidding public nudity.[112] The Court upheld the law's application, finding that it was a content-neutral law aimed at combating crime and other negative consequences caused by adult entertainment businesses.[113] But this holding can also be explained through an

106 *See* 460 U.S. 575, 585 (1983). In *Leathers v. Medlock*, 499 U.S. 439, 447 (1991), the Court stated that the First Amendment scrutinizes only differential-taxation schemes that threaten to target particular viewpoints or speakers. According to the Court, "differential taxation of speakers, even members of the press, does not implicate the First Amendment unless the tax is directed at, or presents the danger of suppressing, particular ideas."

107 308 U.S. 147, 148 (1939).

108 A general ban on the distribution of all materials would be acceptable, despite the fact that such a ban would have an even more restrictive effect on individual-autonomy concerns. However, such a broader ban runs much less risk of the government's singling out or discriminating against certain types of speech.

109 *See* 521 U.S. 457 (1997).

110 *See* Patrick M. Garry, *The First Amendment and Non-Political Speech: Exploring a Constitutional Model That Focuses on the Existence of Alternative Chanels of Communication*, 72 Mo. L. Rev. 477, 514–20 (2007).

111 Cass Sunstein's four-part test for whether speech qualifies as "low value" is whether: (1) the speech is "far afield from the central concerns of the First Amendment" (which is the "effective popular control of public affairs"); (2) there are important "noncognitive aspects" of the speech; (3) "the speaker is seeking to communicate a message"; and (4) the speech is in an area in which the "government is unlikely to be acting for constitutionally impermissible reasons." Cass Sunstein, *Pornography and the First Amendment*, 1986 Duke L.J. at 603–04 (1986). Stone's test states that low-value speech does not "primarily advance political discourse," is not defined in terms of "disfavored ideas or political viewpoints," has "a strong noncognitive" aspect, and has "long been regulated without undue harm to the overall system of free expression." Geoffrey Stone, *Sex, Violence and the First Amendment*, 74 U. Chi. L. Rev. 1857, 1863–64 (2007).

112 529 U.S. 277, 282–83 (2000).

113 *Id.* at 291.

equal protection approach. The issue in the case can be seen as essentially one of whether the government was treating one kind of expressive nude behavior—for example, nude dancing—differently than other kinds of nude behavior. The answer was that it was not. The City was treating all nudity, including nude dancing, in a similar fashion. The point of comparison was a very narrow and specific point—nudity. It was not the broader baseline of expressive behavior in general. This was because the type of expression at issue was not political speech.

A broad-baseline approach was applicable in *Metro Media Inc. v. City of San Diego*, where the Court overturned a law prohibiting all billboards in residential areas, even though it exempted a business's advertising at its own locations, along with other types of commercial advertising.[114] Although the law appeared to be content neutral, it obviously affected political speech. Indeed, in its operation, the ordinance gave preference to commercial over noncommercial speech. Moreover, the ordinance violated the broad baseline because it singled out billboards, as well as residential areas. And when political speech is at issue, the broadest baseline should be used, rather than some narrower baseline. Furthermore, the impact of this law may very well have had a disproportionate impact on political speech, especially if it was found that billboards were a prominent venue for political speech. In this respect, the Court should take into account not only the relative impact of the law, but the ability of speakers to shift to other means of expression.[115]

114 453 U.S. 490, 520–21 (1981).

115 *See* Stone, *supra* note 78, at 291.

Chapter 15
Equal Protection and Environmental Justice: A Matter of Unconscious Injustice?

Haydn Davies

> The IACHR recalls that the right to equal protection under international human rights law has been interpreted as prohibiting not only intentional discrimination, but also any distinction, exclusion, restriction or preference which has a discriminatory effect ...[1]

This chapter outlines the recent history of attempts by the environmental justice movement in the United States to engage constitutional equal protection provisions and analyses: (i) why these attempts have been largely unsuccessful; (ii) the jurisprudential position that has emerged in relation to environmental justice cases; (iii) the extent to which this position adequately reflects recent developments in the understanding of human cognition and decision making; and (iv) the compatibility of this position with human rights norms relating to discrimination elsewhere in the world. Finally some conclusions will be presented on the likelihood and desirability of change in the judicial attitude towards environmental justice in the United States.

Environmental Justice

Before embarking on an analysis of the activities of the environmental justice movement, the term environmental justice itself must be properly explained. Outside the United States the term would probably invoke notions of doing justice towards aspects of the environment itself such as the protection of the quality and quantity of fresh water supplies, protection of species and habitats, protection of the air and land from excessive pollution, and so forth. This is essentially an ecocentric conception of justice to the environment. However, in the United States, and increasingly elsewhere in the world, the term has a more specific meaning which is far more anthropocentric. The United States Environmental Protection Agency defines environmental justice as "... the fair treatment and meaningful involvement of all people regardless of race, color, national origin, or income with respect to the development, implementation, and enforcement of environmental laws, regulations, and policies."[2] This definition highlights very well the human-centered nature of environmental justice and is a legacy of activism, not by the environmental protection movement in the United States as such (though sections of this movement have certainly acknowledged its importance), but rather by the Civil Rights movement.

The Environmental Justice Movement

The origins and history of the environmental justice movement in the United States have been well documented and only a brief outline will be presented here.[3] The movement's origins are generally traced to events in the

---

1 *Mossville Environmental Action Now v. United States*, Petition 242–05 (2010), Inter-Am. Comm'n H.R. Report No. 43/10, ¶42, citing the Inter-American Court of Human Rights, Advisory Opinion OC-18/03 of September 18, 2003, Ser. A No 18, paras 83–96; and the UN Human Rights Committee (HRC), *CCPR General Comment No. 18: Non-discrimination*, 10 Nov.1989.

2 U.S. Envtl. Prot. Agency: Office of Envtl. Justice, Plan EJ 2014, 3 (Sept. 2011) *available at* http://www.epa.gov/environmentaljustice/plan-ej/index.html.

3 For a more detailed history of the environmental justice movement *see, e.g.*, David Schlosberg, Defining Environmental Justice: Theories, Movements And Nature 469 (2007); Gordon Walker, Environmental Justice: Concepts,

early 1980s in Warren County, North Carolina. The authorities in North Carolina discovered that a haulage company had, in 1978, progressively dumped 31,000 gallons of PCB[4]-contaminated oil along 270 miles of roadside across 14 counties (mostly at night). The contaminated soil was excavated and the decision made to "dispose" of all 600 truckloads of it in a single location, Shocco Township, where African-Americans made up 75 percent of the population, and this in a county where the average African-American population was already 65 percent. Moreover, Warren County ranked as the 97th poorest county (out of 100) in an already impoverished State.[5] A new hazardous waste landfill site was duly created there for the purpose of disposing of the PCB-contaminated soil, but a decision was made to continue to accept hazardous waste there after the initial disposal. The residents of the township, outraged by the complete lack of consultation about the siting of the waste facility, organised protests (in which local church groups took the organizational lead) along the model of the civil rights movement. In particular the residents engaged the help of the United Church of Christ Commission for Racial Justice to orchestrate a campaign of nonviolent civil disobedience. However, despite the protests and evidence that usual safety procedures were being compromised (for example the PCB-laced soil would ultimately be located only seven feet above the water table), the disposal and the operation of the new site went ahead.

Despite the ultimate failure of the protests in North Carolina, the whole question of the apparent racial targeting of the disposal of environmentally hazardous substances and the siting of environmentally hazardous activities became a high-profile issue and a series of reports followed which examined the situation across the United States as a whole.[6] The resulting political pressure gave rise to Congressional action, when Senator Al Gore and Congressman John Lewis (one of the six principal leaders of the Civil Rights Movement[7]) introduced the Environmental Justice Act 1992.[8] Though these legislative initiatives were ultimately unsuccessful, the executive action which followed in 1994 in the form of President Clinton's Executive Order 12898[9] and its accompanying memorandum[10] were to prove rather more effective. Executive Order 12898 required that "each Federal agency shall make achieving environmental justice part of its mission by identifying and addressing, as appropriate, disproportionately high and adverse human health or environmental effects of its programs, policies, and activities on minority populations and low-income populations … ."Although executive orders are not formally legally binding, they are nevertheless routinely treated as if they are. In the whole history of the United States Presidency, there are only two recorded incidences of executive orders not being observed.[11]

Evidence And Politics 78–79, 84–88 (2011); Robert D. Bullard, Dumping In Dixie: Race Class And Environmental Quality (1994); Luke Cole & Sheila R. Foster, From The Ground Up: Environmental Racism and the Rise of the Environmental Justice Movement (2001); Robert D. Bullard & Glenn S. Johnson, *Environmental Justice, Grassroots Activism and Its Impact on Public Policy Decision Making*, 56 J. Of Social Issues, 555–78 (2000); Amanda K. Frantzen, *The Time Is Now for Environmental Justice: Congress Must Take Action By Codifying Executive Order 12898*, 17 Penn St. Envtl. L. Rev. 379, 381–82 (2009); Douglas Rubin, *How Supplemental Environmental Projects Can and Should Be Used to Advance Environmental Justice* 10 U. Md. L.J. Race, Religion, Gender & Class 179,181 (2010); Alice Kaswan, *Environmental Justice and Environmental Law* 24 Fordham Envtl. L. Rev. 149 (2013).

4 A class of chemicals formerly widely in the electrical power and electronics industries and known to have a range of health effects in humans and animals. *See Polychlorinated biphenyls (PCBs) (Arochlors)*, 1336–36–3. U.S. Environmental Protection Agency, Technology Transfer Network, Air Toxics Web Site (2013) *available at* http:// epa.gov/ttnatw01/hlthef/polychlo.html (last visited Aug. 8, 2013).

5 Walker *supra* note 3 at 79.

6 *See*, e.g., U.S. General Accounting Office, Siting Of Hazardous Waste Landfills And Their Correlation With Racial And Economic Status Of Surrounding Communities. Gao/Rced 83–168 B-211461. June 1, 1983. Benjamin F. Chavis & Charles Lee, Toxic Wastes and Race in the United States: a National Report on the Racial and Socio-economic Characteristics of Communities with Hazardous Waste Sites. Comm'n for Racial Justice, United Church of Christ, Executive Summary at xiii (1987) *available at* http:// www.ucc.org/about-us/archives/pdfs/toxwrace87.pdf.

7 The others being Whitney Young, A. Philip Randolph, Martin Luther King Jr., James Farmer and Roy Wilkins.

8 H.R. 5326, 102d Cong. 2d Sess. 1992); S. 2806, 102d Cong. (2d Sess. 1992). This initiative failed to become law despite reintroduction in the 103rd Congress by Congressman Lewis and Senator Max Baucus (D-Mont).

9 59 Fed. Reg. 32 (1994).

10 See Exec. Order No. 12898, 59 Fed. Reg. 7629 (Feb. 11, 1994).

11 *See* John C. Duncan, *A Critical Consideration of Executive Orders: Glimmerings of Autopoiesis in the Executive Role*, 35 Vt. L. Rev. 333, 337 (2010).

Thus the promulgation of Executive Order 12898 was a significant victory for the environmental justice movement and to some extent represented the pinnacle of the movements' influence. Since then its success, as we shall see, has been more qualified.

Environmental Justice and Equal Protection Litigation

Given the origins of the environmental justice movement as part of the civil rights movement, it is no surprise that attempts were made to invoke the Equal Protection Clause of the Fourteenth Amendment[12] in the cause of environmental justice. However, this was always likely to be a difficult challenge given that the United States Supreme Court had decided back in 1976, in the case of *Washington v. Davis*,[13] that the engagement of the equal protection provisions of the Fourteenth and Fifth Amendments required nothing less than evidence of intentional discrimination.[14] In *Washington*, the petitioner police officers had sought to apply the standards of Title VII[15] of the Civil Rights Act 1964, previously applied in *Griggs v. Duke Power Co.*,[16] to the effect that constitutionally relevant discrimination was established through evidence of disparate impact alone. Justice White, for the court, was unequivocal in his rejection of this contention:

> We have never held that the constitutional standard for adjudicating claims of invidious racial discrimination is identical to the standards applicable under Title VII, and we decline to do so today ... our cases have not embraced the proposition that a law or other official act, without regard to whether it reflects a racially discriminatory purpose, is unconstitutional Solely (sic) because it has a racially disproportionate impact.[17]

He went on to indicate that:

> we have not held that a law, neutral on its face and serving ends otherwise within the power of government to pursue, is invalid under the Equal Protection Clause simply because it may affect a greater proportion of one race than of another. Disproportionate impact is not irrelevant, but it is not the sole touchstone of an invidious racial discrimination forbidden by the Constitution. Standing alone, it does not trigger the rule, ...[18]

The effect of this judgment was to make a distinction between the burden of proof required to engage the full constitutional protection of the Fourteenth and Fifth Amendments and that required to engage the protection of Title VII provisions. The former is engaged only where sufficient evidence is adduced of intentional racial animus; disparate impact may form a part of this evidence but it is not, in and of itself, sufficient evidence of intention. The Title VII provisions, on the other hand, do declare as unlawful "particular employment practice[s] that [cause] a disparate impact on the basis of race, color, religion, sex, or national origin"[19] if the

12 U.S. CONST. amend. XIV §1. The Fourteenth Amendment prevents the states from denying "to any person ... the equal protection of the laws." An equivalent requirement falls on the federal government by virtue of the Supreme Court's interpretation of the Due Process Clause of the Fifth Amendment (U.S. CONST. amend. V). In Bolling v. Sharpe, 347 U.S. 497,499 (1954) it was held that "the concepts of equal protection and due process ... are not mutually exclusive. This was later affirmed in Washington v. Davis, 426 U.S. 229, 239 (1976) where it was held that "... the Due Process Clause of the Fifth Amendment contains an equal protection component prohibiting the United States from invidiously discriminating between individuals or groups."

13 *Id. at* 229.

14 *Id.* at 238–42.

15 42 U.S.C. 2000e.

16 Griggs v. Duke Power Co., 401 U.S. 424 (1971).

17 426 U.S., at 239.

18 *Id.* at 242. This position was confirmed in *Village of Arlington Heights v. Metropolitan Dev. Corp.*, 429 U.S. 252 (1977) and strengthened still further in Personnel Administrator of Massachusetts v. Feeney, 442 U.S. 256 (1979) which appeared to lay down a requirement that "... the decisionmaker ... [must have] selected or reaffirmed a particular course of action at least in part "because of," not merely "in spite of," its adverse effects upon an identifiable group" *Id.* at 279.

19 42 U.S.C. 2000e-2(k)(1)(A)(i).

respondent is unable "to demonstrate that the challenged practice is job related for the position in question and consistent with business necessity."[20] The result is that disparate impact can be declared unlawful but does not necessarily offend against the Equal Protection Clause. In fact, Title VII has been successfully used in many employment cases over a long period of time to strike down employment practices that amount to disparate treatment or result in "unjustified" disparate impact.[21] Linda Krieger, in her 1995 paper on Title VII jurisprudence and equal employment opportunity, takes issue with the application of disparate impact theory to the subjective and individualistic decision-making processes that often characterize employment discrimination disputes. She raises three objections, one practical, one political and one theoretical, to the use of the disparate impact model in such cases, and prefers the disparate treatment paradigm as a more suitable mechanism.[22] Since much of what follows relates to disparate impact rather than disparate treatment, it is necessary at this point to place Krieger's objections in their proper context lest they be thought to undermine or weaken the subsequent discussion of disparate impact in the context of environmental justice.

Demonstrating disparate treatment, in the employment context, requires that the claimant demonstrate that the employer has engaged in intentional discrimination in the application of a subjective judgment about hiring, entitlements, promotion, dismissal, and so forth. Success in such cases is entirely dependent on adducing sufficient evidence of this intent. This can be a considerable challenge.[23] Disparate impact, on the other hand, does not require proof of intent, but once disparate impact is demonstrated, it transfers the burden of proof to the employer to demonstrate that the practice that led to the disparate impact is "job related" and "consistent with business necessity."[24] As Krieger points out,[25] this provision, inserted into Title VII by the Civil Rights Acts 1991,[26] does not define either of these terms. The result was that employers seeking to rely on this defense were required to statistically validate their practices in order to discharge their burden of proof. Krieger objects to the disparate impact paradigm precisely because it does require such statistical analysis. This is beyond the means of all but the largest and wealthiest employers (the practical objection) and hence is not undertaken at all, or very poorly, in most Title VII cases. This means that to reach a decision in court, a "vague, subjective, and unpredictable"[27] judicial judgment is substituted for a statistical one (the political objection.) Finally Krieger points out that the disparate impact model was formulated to deal with the adoption of "ostensibly objective, neutral selection devices which ... shielded [employers] against accusations of intentional discrimination ..." and "... was not designed to reckon with the phenomena at play in subjective, individualized interpersonal decision making, and remains ill-suited to that task"[28] (the theoretical objection.) Professor Krieger's objections are compelling but are predicated on the lack of availability of objective statistical information and the fact that disparate impact analysis is not well

20 *Id.* However, U.S.C. 2000e-2(k)(2) explicitly forbids the use of this defense in respect of intentional discrimination.

21 The "disparate treatment" line of cases is said to have begun with the case of *McDonnell Douglas Corp. v. Green*, 411 U.S. 792 (1973). For an in-depth discussion and critique of the subsequent development of Title VII jurisprudence (including a discussion of the difference between, and relative merits of, the disparate treatment and disparate impact paradigms) see Linda Krieger, *The Content of Our Categories: A Cognitive Bias Approach to Discrimination and Equal Employment Opportunity*, 47 Stan. L. Rev. 1161 (1995). Briefly, disparate treatment under Title VII requires proof that an employer has exercised discriminatory intent in respect of an employment decision directed towards an individual or class. Disparate impact, on the other hand, does not require proof of intent but does require statistical evidence that a particular employment practice disproportionately affects a protected class. Krieger was of the view that "The disparate impact paradigm as currently constructed is an inappropriate analytical tool for addressing the intergroup biases inherent in subjective decisionmaking" (*Id.* at 1231.)

22 *Id.* at 1231–37.

23 As an illustration of the magnitude of the burden of proof of intent, Krieger points to the fact that Mrs Watson, the claimant in the leading case of *Watson v. Fort Worth Bank and Trust*, 487 U.S. 977 (1988), was unable to convince the court of the requisite degree of intent on the part of her employer despite evidence that she had been told by one of her superiors "that the teller position was a big responsibility with 'a lot of money for ... blacks to have to count.'" Krieger, *supra* note 21 at 1230 (citing 487 U.S. at 990 (1988)).

24 *Supra* notes 20 and 21 and associated text.

25 Krieger, *supra* note 21, at 1219–20.

26 Pub. L. 102–66, §§ 2–3, 105 Stat. 1071 (1991) (codified at 42 U.S.C. s 2000e-2(k) (1992)).

27 Krieger, *supra* note 21, at 1236–37.

28 *Id.* at 1237.

suited to subjective individualistic decisions. By contrast, most environmental justice cases involve a much greater degree of objectivity, are nearly always related to a class or community rather than individuals, and the decisions made usually emanate from government agencies (state or federal) which are reasonably well funded, well served in technical expertise, and for whom such statistical analysis is far more feasible. Hence Krieger's objections to disparate impact analysis have less purchase in this context.

Moreover, many environmental justice situations come about as the result of a complex chain of decisions in which it would be demanding, to say the least, to demonstrate the invidious (that is, intentional or consciously motivated) racial discrimination required to engage the Equal Protection Clause or the disparate treatment paradigm. Thus the prospects for the environmental justice movement in invoking the Equal Protection Clause in their favor always appeared rather remote. Just how remote was confirmed in *Bean v. Southwestern Waste Management Corporation*,[29] the first environmental justice case to be litigated on the basis of the Equal Protection Clause. Though the federal judge in the case expressed some sympathy with the petitioners,[30] he felt bound by the *Washington* line of cases and dismissed the action as lacking sufficient evidence of intentional racial animus. The environmental justice movement was thus forced to seek redress elsewhere in the law.

The alternative legal means lighted upon was Title VI of the Civil Rights Act 1964.[31] Although employment discrimination cases founded on Title VII of the same act had failed to engage the Equal Protection Clause in the *Washington* case, described previously, the success of the disparate impact model under Title VII more generally suggested that it would be reasonable to attempt to found a similar private right of action, in seeking redress against environmental injustice, on another title in the same act, Title VI, specifically §§601[32] and 602.[33] §601 requires that "[n]o person in the United States shall, on the ground of race, color, or national origin, be excluded from participation in, be denied the benefits of, or be subjected to discrimination under any program or activity receiving Federal financial assistance." This is bolstered by §602 which provides that "[e]ach Federal department and agency which is empowered to extend Federal financial assistance to any program or activity, by way of grant, loan, or contract other than a contract of insurance or guaranty, is authorized and directed to effectuate the provisions of section 2000d of this title."

Until the decision in *Alexander v Sandoval*,[34] the case law on Title VI had been somewhat contradictory. Following *Regents of the University of California v. Bakke*,[35] it was thought that Title VI could only be engaged, like the Equal Protection Clause itself, where evidence of intentional discrimination could be adduced. However, subsequent cases seemed to suggest the possibility of a private right of redress under Title VI, §602, based on disparate impact alone.[36] In 2001 *Sandoval* settled the matter. Justice Scalia for the 5–4 majority in the United States Supreme Court left little room for doubt; nothing less than intentional racial animus was necessary to found a private right of action under Title VI:

> It is clear now that the disparate-impact regulations [that might be promulgated by an agency under § 602] do not simply apply § 601 since they indeed forbid conduct that § 601 permits—and therefore clear that the private right of action to enforce § 601 does not include a private right to enforce these regulations.[37]

Thus, although federal agencies might promulgate disparate impact regulations (and many have done so[38]) these cannot be enforced through a private right of action exercisable in federal court (though administrative

29 Bean v. Sw. Waste Mgmt. Corp., 482 F. Supp. 673 (S.D. Texas 1979).

30 District Judge McDonald questioned the siting of a landfill site so close to a non-air conditioned school. *Id.* at 679–80.

31 42 U.S.C 2000a.

32 42 U.S.C. 2000d.

33 42 U.S.C. 2000d-1.

34 Alexander v. Sandoval, 532 U.S. 275 (2001) (*Sandoval*).

35 Regents of the Univ. of Cal. v. Bakke, 438 U.S. 265, 375 (1978).

36 *See* Cannon v. Univ. of Chi., 441 U.S. 677, 694, 696 (1979); Guardians Ass'n v. Civ. Serv. Comm'n, 463 U.S. 582 (1983).

37 *Sandoval*, 532 U.S. at 285.

38 *See* the U.S. Environmental Protection Agency's regulations at 40 C.F.R. § 7.35(b) (2004), "… A recipient shall not use criteria or methods of administering its program or activity which *have the effect of subjecting individuals to discrimination* because of their race, color, national origin, or sex, …" (emphasis added). *See also* the U.S. Department of Justice regulations at 28 C.F.R. § 42.104(b)(2) (2000) and the U.S. Department of Transport regulations at 49 C.F.R. § 21.5(b)(2) (2000).

appeal, through the Office of Civil Rights, against the relevant agency, is still an option—this is further discussed *infra*[39]).

In the same case, Justice Stevens, in his dissenting judgment,[40] had alluded to the possibility of basing disparate impact cases on 42 U.S.C. §1983, a general provision which allows that:

> Every person who, under color of any statute, ordinance, regulation, custom, or usage, of any State or Territory or the District of Columbia, subjects, or causes to be subjected, any citizen of the United States or other person within the jurisdiction thereof to the deprivation of any rights, privileges, or immunities secured by the Constitution and laws, shall be liable to the party injured in an action at law, suit in equity, or other proper proceeding for redress.

However, this avenue was also closed by the U.S. Court of Appeals for the Third Circuit in *South Camden Citizens in Action v. New Jersey Department of Environmental Protection* on the grounds that §1983 did not offer a private right of action to uphold disparate impact litigation unless it could be shown that such a right could be "already found in the enforcing statute."[41] Since, following *Sandoval*, §602 (the relevant enforcing statute in the *South Camden* case) evidently did not contain such a right, this marked the end of the road for environmental justice litigants' attempts to rely successively on the Equal Protection Clause, Title VI and 42 U.S.C. §1983.

Environmental Justice and Administrative Challenges

As mentioned previously,[42] it is possible to use administrative challenges to enforce the application of disparate impact regulations promulgated by federal agencies (in this case the EPA) under Executive Order 12898. Such challenges must be brought before the Office of Civil Rights.[43] Under this procedure complainants are able to articulate disparate impact complaints directly, in a way which is likely to be more successful than using Title VI in the courts though they do not get their "day in court." Although this approach is often successful,[44] it suffers from a number of deficiencies and some significant drawbacks.[45] A report by Deloitte Consultants LLP into the EPA OCR in 2011 concluded that

> the Title VI program has struggled to develop a consistent framework to analyze complaints, resulting in a lengthy and time-consuming effort to evaluate the complaints and once accepted, to adequately investigate the cases. Only 6%, or 15 out of 247, were compliant with EPA targeted 20-day timeframe for acknowledgement. In fact, half of the complaints have taken one year or more to move to accepted or dismissed status. One case was accepted after nine years and a second case was accepted only after ten years.[46]

39 See text accompanying notes 42 to 52 *infra*.

40 "[l]itigants who in the future wish to enforce the Title VI regulations against state actors in all likelihood must only reference §1983 to obtain relief." *Sandoval*, 532 U.S. at 300.

41 S. Camden Citizens in Action v. N. J. Dep't of Envtl. Prot., 274 F.3d 771,790 (3d Cir. 2001) (cert. denied, 536 U.S. 939 (2002)) (*South Camden*). This case, in the district court, had originally relied on Title VI § 602, but this approach was undermined by the *Sandoval* decision which emerged while *South Camden* was in progress. However, Judge Orlofsky permitted the petitioners to change the basis of their claim to 42 U.S.C. §1983, *see S. Camden Citizens in Action*, 145 F. Supp. 2d 505.

42 *See* text accompanying note 39.

43 A federal body created by the EPA following President Clinton's issuance of Executive Order 12898 and its accompanying Memo.

44 *See* U.S. E.P.A. Office of Civil Rights Title VI Settlements at http://www.epa.gov/ocr/TitleVIcases/index.html.

45 Brian Crossman, *Resurrecting Environmental Justice: Enforcement of EPA's Disparate-Impact Regulations Through Clean Air Act Citizen Suits*, 32 B.C. Envtl. Aff. L. Rev. 599, 604–07 (2005).

46 Envt'l Prot. Agency, Order # Ep10h002058, Final Report: Evaluation Of The Epa Office Of Civil Rights 25 (2011) *available at* http://www.epa.gov/epahome/pdf/epa-ocr_20110321_finalreport.pdf.

Other administrative remedies and citizen suit provisions are provided by specific federal statutes, including the Comprehensive Environmental Response Compensation and Liability Act (CERCLA) of 1980 §310,[47] the Clean Air Act of 1970 §304(a)(1),[48] the Clean Water Act of 1987 §505,[49] the Resource Conservation and Recovery Act of 1976 §7002,[50] and the Safe Drinking Water Act of 1974 §1449.[51] Although much can be achieved in such actions, there are also significant drawbacks associated with them in terms of mitigating environmental injustice. Most of the citizen suit provisions make it difficult, if not impossible, to mount *preventative* challenges; establishing standing is difficult if the harm complained of will only accrue in the future. Similarly where citizen suits seek to challenge decisions related to pre-permit decisions where the permit has already been granted, the courts are unwilling to be generous.[52] These statutes permit citizens to force agencies and polluters to comply with the law. However, in cases where disparate impact has come about as a side-effect of entirely lawful activity the remedies are unavailable. Furthermore, statutory remedies do not normally permit compensatory or punitive damages. Hence those seeking compensation for decisions or activities that have disparate impact on their locality are unlikely to succeed under statutory citizen suits.

This short summary of the recent history of environmental justice litigation serves to illustrate why the ship of environmental justice so frequently founders on the rocks of intentional racial animus. One can understand why environmental justice case law in the United States has evolved in favor of a requirement for nothing less than intentional racism before a private law remedy becomes available. The successes of the Civil Rights Movement gave rise to a nation anxious to move away from attitudes of mind associated with slavery and those who sought actively to maintain such attitudes deliberately (that is, intentionally) were not to be tolerated. At the same time there emerged a perception that attempting a rebalance through social engineering, such as affirmative action, was to engage in visiting the sins of the fathers on their now more enlightened offspring. Indeed the notion of a colorblind society was, for a time, the dominant paradigm in race relations; the idea that slavery had been consigned to history, strong legislation put in place to prevent any such evil arising again, and the view that, in time, previously suppressed races would take full advantage of their emancipation and emerge into the sunshine of full equality without the need for state intervention. However, opposed to this view is the contention that the legacy of slavery cannot simply be ignored and permitted to heal itself unaided. Those whose ancestors were once considered property are still burdened with societal disadvantages accrued over centuries and these disadvantages could take just as long to be overcome. Moreover in recent times psychological evidence has accumulated which suggests that the majority of discrimination may not be conscious at all, and this suggests that an insistence on the provision of evidence of

---

47 42 U.S.C. § 9601. The citizen suit provision is limited to post-cleanup challenges by §310; other forms of challenge to EPA action *during* clean-up under CERCLA are severely limited by §130(h) and §130(i). *See* Maya Waldron, *A Proposal to Balance Polluter and Community Intervention in CERCLA Litigation*, 38 ECOLOGY L.Q. 401 (2011).

48 42 U.S.C. §§ 7604(a) (1)-(3), (f) (3, 4). Here challenges to EPA permitting decisions are limited to the postpermit era. *See* CleanCOALition v. TXU Power, 536 F. 3d 469 (5th Cir. 2008); Concerned Citizens around Murphy v. Murphy Oil USA Inc., 686 F. Supp. 2d 663 (E.D. La. 2010); Washington Envtl. Council v. Sturdevant, 834 F. Supp. 2d 1209, 2011 WL 6014664 (W.D.Wash 2011). *See also*: Jeanne Marie Zokovitch Paben, *Approaches to Environmental Justice: A Case Study of One Community's Victory*, 20 S. Cal. Rev. L. & Soc. Just. 235 (2011); Annise Katherine Maguire, *Permitting under the Clean Air Act: How Current Standards Impose Obstacles to Achieving Environmental Justice*, 14 Mich. J. Race & L. 255 (2009); Jeremy Linden, *At the Bus Depot: Can Administrative Complaints Help Stalled Environmental Justice Plaintiffs?* 16 N.Y.U. Envtl. L.J. 170 (2008).

49 33 U.S.C. §1365(a)(1). *See also* Douglas Rubin, *How Supplemental Environmental Projects Can and Should be Used to Advance Environmental Justice*, 10 U. Md. L.J. Race, Religion, Gender & Class 179 (2010).

50 42 U.S.C. §6972(a)(1)(A).

51 42 U.S.C. §300j-8.

52 *See, e.g.*, *CleanCOALition*, 536 F.3d 469. Here the U.S. Court of Appeals for the Fifth Circuit upheld the district court's interpretation of the citizen suit provisions of the Clean Air Act to the effect that "(1) section of the Act authorizing citizen suit against a person alleged to have violated or to be in violation of an emission standard or limitation under the Act does not authorize citizen suits to redress alleged pre-permit, preconstruction, or pre-operation violations, and (2) section of the Act authorizing citizen suits 'against any person who proposes to construct or constructs any new or modified major emitting facility without a permit' does not authorize preconstruction citizen suits against facilities that either have obtained a permit or are in the process of doing so."

intentional racial animus in discrimination litigation may be putting the law at odds with the realities of human cognition and motivation. It is to this evidence that I now turn.

Social Cognition Theory and Unconscious Discrimination

Professor Linda Krieger's seminal 1995 paper on Title VII employment discrimination litigation has already been referred to above.[53] Her work was principally concerned with disparate treatment and did not explicitly refer to Title VI disparate impact cases. However, the cognitive bases of the decision-making processes that she discusses are applicable to equal protection questions generally.

Krieger's paper addresses the then prevailing judicial view (arguably still the prevailing view) that apparently racist decisions must arise from consciously motivated racial animus if constitutional protections and remedies for discrimination are to be deployed. This is despite the fact that even in 1973 in *McDonnell Douglas Corp. v. Green* it was held that Title VII covered all forms of racism "subtle and otherwise."[54] Krieger's paper concludes that contemporary models used by the courts based on intentional racism "… may either fail to identify discrimination or wrongfully attribute discriminatory motive to a well-intentioned, though biased, decision-maker."[55] This contention is based on the fact that judicial decisions were premised on outmoded models no longer supported by empirical studies or contemporary theory.[56] The principal conclusions she reaches are that: (i) racism is far more likely to exert its effects through unconscious channels than through conscious ones;[57] (ii) the decision-making process is not, as had been assumed in much of the case law, a "moment-in-time" phenomenon but is mediated by much longer term influences: "stereotypes, person prototypes, and other implicit knowledge structures bias decision-making long before the 'moment of decision,'"[58] and; (iii) Title VII litigation had become infected with the notion of invidious intent on the part of the decision-maker, arising from the fact that

> people have a strong tendency to attribute emotionally relevant events to emotionally relevant causes; a profoundly negative event tends to be attributed to profoundly negative causes. Accordingly, to the extent that we see employment discrimination as a profoundly negative phenomenon, we will tend to attribute it to profoundly negative causes, such as the morally reprehensible action of an invidiously motivated decisionmaker.[59]

But Krieger demonstrates that racial bias may arise even in the absence of conscious racial animus. Indeed subconscious bias is a far more likely source of disparate treatment or impact in most decisions involving race. Thus the demand for evidence of intention does a disservice not only to the aggrieved party, who may find it immensely difficult to meet this demand, but also to the party accused of discrimination, who will face an accusation of intentional racism (since that is the only legally relevant form where equal protection or Title VII is concerned) even though their mental state will be less culpable (in the sense that the decision-maker will be unaware of their bias), though no less significant in terms of its effects. As Krieger puts it, "[t]o say that a decisionmaker lacks discriminatory motivation is not to say that his perceptions and judgments are unaffected by cognitive sources of intergroup bias."[60] Although environmental justice cases tend to involve disparate impact under Title VI, it would seem reasonable to assume that Krieger's conclusions in relation to the sources of bias would apply to environmental decision-making with equal force. As Krieger herself points out, "in the interests of normative coherence, disparate impact and social cognition-based disparate treatment should be understood and remedied in substantially similar ways."[61]

---

53 See notes 21 to 28 and associated text.
54 *McDonnell Douglas Corp. v. Green*, 411 U.S. 792, 801 (1973).
55 *See* Krieger, note 21 at 1165.
56 *Id.* 1186–217.
57 *Id.* 1212.
58 *Id.* at 1209.
59 *Id.* at 1216.
60 *Id.* at 1217.
61 *Id.* at 1244.

The fact that racism has become routinely associated with intention, and thus an accusation of racism carries with it connotations of deliberate and hostile or even malicious enmity towards racial groups, is a theme taken up by Adjoa Aiyetoro, who considers that this perception is responsible for the impoverishment of discourse on race and discrimination in contemporary America.[62] Although I have elsewhere taken issue with some of Professor Aiyetoro's other conclusions,[63] I agree with her view that the automatic association of racism with "animus" which has come to dominate discrimination jurisprudence must adversely affect the willingness of parties to engage in constructive dialogue. As Aiyetoro puts it, "[t]he association of racism with a conscious act that is ... illegal makes the accusation that race was a factor in a decision analogous to a racial slur—a disparaging remark."[64] Or put another way, most people do not like to be accused of racism and become defensive if such an accusation is made or implied.

However, although Aiyetoro occupies common ground with Krieger in her opposition to the judicial insistence on evidence of intentional racism, she robustly refutes Krieger's espousal of social cognition theory. This Aiyetoro condemns as counterproductive and tending towards the condoning of racial attitudes as "business as usual."[65]

Kang and Banaji, by contrast, enthusiastically take up Krieger's lead and embrace social cognition theory as a true reflection of the realities of bias and its role in human decision-making.[66] Like Aiyetoro, Kang and Banaji condemn the notion of a colorblind society —the keystone of much of the discrimination jurisprudence in the United States—because it is implicit within the judicial notion of "colorblindness" that race bias cannot be unconscious.[67] However, they also reject social engineering initiatives that attempt to impose diversity (like affirmative action), which is an end rather than a means when it comes to discrimination.[68] They consider that judicial recognition of social cognition theory would represent a solution to disparate impact (and treatment) cases which is free from the difficulties associated with both colorblindness and affirmative action and would enable judges to deal with such cases without the need to address directly the sins of the past or the demands of the future. In the course of their discussion, Kang and Banaji assert that society in general is "not color or gender blind and perhaps ... cannot be" and that implicit bias does indeed tend to manifest itself in discriminatory behavior.[69]

Justin Levinson's work extends that of Krieger and Kang and Banaji and attempts to consider the combined effects of both implicit social cognition and behavioral economics as simultaneous subconscious influences on decision-making.[70] Economic considerations are of central importance in many environmental justice cases, where utilitarian considerations of the impact on land values, access to transport infrastructure, value for money, and so forth often result in environmentally undesirable activities or installations being sited in locations of low socio-economic status.[71] Hence, Levinson's work in highlighting the possibly synergistic effects of race and socio-economic bias in this context is potentially of great importance. In fact it is poverty, rather than race as such, that is the better indicator of the likely destination of environmental burdens.[72] Racial minorities are often over-represented among the poor, usually a consequence of history—in the United States

62 Adjoa Artis Aiyetoro, *Can We Talk? How Triggers for Unconscious Racism Strengthen the Importance of Dialogue*, 22 Nat'l Black L.J. 1 (2009).

63 *See* Haydn Davies, *Environmental Justice and Equal Protection: Intent, Motivation and Cognition in Decision-Making*, 4(2) J. Hum. Rights & Env't. 191–214 (2013).

64 Aiyetoro, *supra* note 62, at 22–23.

65 *Id.* at 22–23. *See also* Davies, *supra* note 63 at 201–203.

66 Jerry Kang & Mahzarin R. Banaji, *Fair Measures: A Behavioral Realist Revision of "Affirmative Action,"* 94 Cal. L. Rev. 1063 (2006).

67 *Id.* at 1075.

68 *Id.* at 1075–77.

69 *Id.* at 1072–73.

70 Justin D. Levinson, *Superbias: The Collision of Behavioral Economics and Implicit Social Cognition*, 45 Akron L. Rev. 591(2011).

71 See Eileen Gauna, *The Environmental Justice Misfit: Public Participation and the Paradigm Paradox*, 17 Stan. Envtl. L J 3, 21–22 (1998).

72 Jonathan B. Forman, *Poverty: Greening the Tax and Transfer System to Create More Opportunities*, 39 Envtl. L. Rep. News & Analysis 10303 (2009).

principally owing to the legacy of slavery, or more recently because of immigration from Latin America.[73] The difficulty is that constitutional protections such as the Equal Protection Clause, and statutory provisions on equal protection such as the Civil Rights Act, do not include poverty as a criterion of discrimination, though the EPA's definition of environmental justice, given above, does take income into account[74] and poverty can in principle form the basis of administrative challenges to EPA decisions.[75]

Levinson extends the debate over subconscious bias by examining the ways in which well-known tendencies toward irrational economic decision-making in industrialized societies might interact with the implicit social cognition theory which forms the basis of Krieger's analysis. In doing so he draws on emergent system justification theory (SJT), which tends to manifest itself as "an unconscious need to maintain the social and economic status quo."[76] The essence of SJT is the idea that those in more powerful positions in the social hierarchy subconsciously seek to maintain the *status quo* such that their place in the hierarchy is not threatened. This phenomenon is thought to derive principally from the need to perpetuate feelings of self-esteem in the decision-maker. Levinson considers that the need for social dominance may be powerful enough to exacerbate the economic behaviors already alluded to: "[s]uch an implicit need could be capable of producing a powerful economic bias that wreaks discriminatory havoc."[77] Levinson summarizes the background and application of SJT but concludes that the role of subconscious bias in its manifestation may have been underestimated with many commentators in the past "rely[ing] largely on conscious factors to explain this discrimination."[78] Even more significant is Levinson's view that "SJT offers evidence that explains why even members of low-status groups may unconsciously act against their own self-interest by choosing to accept (implicitly, at least) some aspects of the discrimination and failing to oppose regimes that would improve the status quo,"[79] a situation which "may result in biased economic decision-making by consumers and service providers alike."[80] Levinson acknowledges the relative dearth of "real-world" research that confirms the role of implicit racial bias (as opposed to motivational racism) but cites a number of empirical laboratory studies that provide considerable support for the contention that at least some real-world decisions are likely to be influenced by this phenomenon.[81] He concludes that

> [a]lthough conscious discrimination undoubtedly exists and can affect all kinds of decision-making, it is unlikely that either statistical discrimination or race based animus explains all of the racial disparities revealed by the studies […]. As the reported research shows, the more likely scenario is that implicit racial bias, amplified by System Justification Theory, causes people to take economic action that perpetuates existing hierarchies.[82]

Levinson himself points out the need for more research to be undertaken to establish the extent of these effects in real-world decision-making but if his contention is confirmed, the need to take greater account of implicit bias in environmental justice cases will become even more imperative.

---

73 A phenomenon that is not restricted only to the United States of course.

74 See *supra* note 2 and associated text.

75 *See* The Shintech decision, *In the Matter of Shintech Inc. and its Affiliates' (Polyvinyl Chloride Production Facility,* Permit No. 2466-Vo No. 2467-Vo No. 2468-Vo) Order Responding to Petitioners' Requests that the Administrator Object to Issuance of State Operating Permits, 6 (1997), www.epa.gov/region07/air/title5/t5memos/shin1997.pdf. *See also* the Select Steel decision, Office of Civil Rights, U.S. Environmental Protection Agency, Investigative Report for Title VI Administrative Complaint File No. 5R-98-R5 (Select Steel Complaint), (1998), www.epa.gov/ocr/docs/ssdec_ir.pdf. More recently *see* Padres complaint, Office of Civil Rights, U.S. Environmental Protection Agency, Investigative Report for Title VI Administrative Complaint File No. 01R-95-R9 (Padres Complaint), (2012).

76 *Supra* note 70 at 596.

77 *Id.* at 621.

78 *Id.* at 622.

79 *Id.*

80 *Id.* at 624.

81 *Id.* at 627–31.

82 *Id.* at 630–31.

Of course, the notion of unconscious bias and its effects on the legal process are not new. Judicial commentary which predates the Civil Rights Movement and the Civil Rights Act by some 20 years acknowledged the existence and relevance of unconscious bias even in judges themselves:

> If … "bias" and "partiality" be defined to mean the total absence of preconceptions in the mind of the judge, then no one has ever had a fair trial and no one ever will. The human mind, even at infancy, is no blank piece of paper. We are born with predispositions; and the process of education, formal and informal, creates attitudes in all men which affect them in judging situations, attitudes which precede reasoning in particular instances and which, therefore, by definition, are pre-judices.[83]

Judge Frank went on to state that such predilections in society may "represent the community's most cherished values and ideals … which members of any given society take for granted and use as the unspoken axioms of thinking."[84] Judges, as members of society, will be subject to these axioms just as much as anyone else. The difference is that, on occasion, judges may be required to "to urge that some of them be modified or abandoned."[85]

In the intervening years judges have indeed been instrumental in modifying and abandoning social predilections which have become outdated, or even morally abhorrent, as societal attitudes have changed under new influences both conscious and subconscious. Nowhere is that better demonstrated than in attitudes to race. It seems though that where disparate impact is concerned, the judges have hitherto been prepared only to censure the conscious expression of prejudice (even though its origins in the mind are probably unconscious). The unconscious manifestations of unconscious prejudice are a different matter. This seems, at best, rather an inconsistent approach. If a widely shared predilection in the mind of society is adjudged to be outmoded and no longer acceptable, what is the difference in principle whether the effects of that predilection are manifested consciously or unconsciously? The answer of course is rooted in the concepts of culpability and just punishment. Where someone knows that they are acting with prejudice but carry on anyway, their moral turpitude is greater than where they act unconsciously, and their punishment is meted out accordingly. Any novice law student becomes familiar with this approach early in her studies. However, where disparate impact occurs as a result of unconscious racial bias that has developed over a long period of time (probably generations), surely the moral position is more nuanced. Clearly it would be absurd to treat the perpetrators of the decision that unconsciously resulted in disparate impact with the same degree of moral opprobrium as applied to consciously applied bias. But neither should the effects of that decision be treated as morally insignificant—merely an unfortunate but acceptable consequence of history, circumstance, and economics. There is undoubtedly less moral culpability in the decision-maker where the bias has occurred unconsciously, but this is not the case for society as a whole. Social inequity is a moral wrong and the legal system should offer provisions for its redress, particularly where its origins are in racial or class bias—whether conscious or unconscious.

Indeed in recent times international human rights law has begun to address the question of discrimination in the context of public health and climate change. The application of the citizens of Mossville, Louisiana, to the Inter-American Commission on Human Rights in Washington DC has subjected the disparate impact jurisprudence of the United States courts to the spotlight of international human rights norms. At the admissibility stage at least, this jurisprudence has been found wanting.

The Mossville Application to the Inter-American Commission on Human Rights

Mossville, in the state of Louisiana, has been a predominantly African-American community since well before the abolition of slavery and was originally a hunting, fishing, and agricultural community. Over the years, industrialization has impinged on the community such that the area to the south east of the community

83 Re J.P. Linahan Inc., 138 F.2d 650, 651 (9th Cir. 1943) (Opinion of Frank J.).

84 *Id.* at 652.

85 *Id.*

is now dominated by industrial enterprises that, according to the U.S. Agency for Toxic Substances and Disease Registry, the U.S. Environmental Protection Agency, and the Louisiana Department of Environmental Quality, emit a variety of toxic and hazardous substances.[86] There is a considerable body of medical evidence that the toxic load borne by the inhabitants of the 370 or so households in Mossville is well above state and national averages and there is particular concern about the higher than average exposure of the population to dioxins—a highly toxic class of organochlorine chemicals.[87] The surrounding Calcasieu Parish, comprising 72,000 households, is approximately 74 percent White, whereas the population of Mossville (which makes up around 1 percent of the Parish population) is 58 percent African-American—a classic environmental justice community. Of the 27 industrial facilities in the 1,000 square mile Parish, 14 of them are in Mossville, which occupies less than 1 percent (five square miles) of the Parish land area.[88]

The citizens have, over a number of years, sought to oppose the further industrialization of their community, citing a range of evidence on the effects on public health of the proximity of the factories[89] and employing some of the participatory procedures,[90] and administrative and legal challenges open to them under state and federal law.[91] Having failed on a number of occasions to prevent the grant of continuing and further emission permits to industrial facilities in their area, the residents, in 2010, took their case before the Inter-American Commission on Human Rights in Washington DC, claiming infringements of their rights under arts I,[92] II,[93] V,[94] IX,[95] XI,[96] and XXIII[97] of the American Declaration of the Rights and Duties of Man 1948.[98]

In fact an attempt was also made by the petitioners (in their third submission) to hold the United States accountable under the American Convention on Human Rights (1969).[99] This was rejected by the Commission on the basis that the Convention "is not binding upon the State and the IACHR is thus not competent to entertain the claims of the petitioners under this instrument."[100] Instead the basis of the Commission's jurisdiction to consider the Mossville residents' petition was that the violations alluded to were violations of rights protected under the earlier American Declaration of the Rights and Duties of Man, 1948. Since the United States did

86 *See* Mossville Environmental Action Now, Inc., Wilma Subra, The Subra Company, Advocates for Environmental Human Rights, Industrial Sources of Dioxin Poisoning in Mossville, Louisiana: A Report Based on the Government's Own Data (July 2007). http://www.loe.org/images/content/100423/mossville.pdf.

87 *See* United States Agency For Toxic Substances And Disease Registry, Toxic Substances Portal—Chlorinated Dibenzo-p-dioxins. http://www.atsdr.cdc.gov/toxprofiles/tp.asp?id=366&tid=63.

88 *Mossville Environmental Action Now v. United States*, Petition 242–05 (2010), Inter-Am. Comm'n H.R. Report No. 43/10, ¶13 (petitioners' claim). *See also supra* note 86 at ii.

89 For a summary *see* United States Environmental Protection Agency http://www.epa.gov/region6/6sf/louisiana/calcasieu/ accessed Sept 13, 2013. *See also* Jeannine Cahill-Jackson, *Mossville Environmental Action Now v. United States: Is a Solution to Environmental Injustice Unfolding?* 3 No. 6 Pace Int'l L. Rev. Online Companion 173, 175–82 (2012).

90 *See* United States Environmental Protection Agency, Summary of the Meeting of the National Environmental Justice Advisory Council, EPA 300-R-00-007B, at pp. 2–19, 9 1 to 9–9 (Nov. 2000).

91 *E.g.* Mossville Environmental Action Now v. EPA 370 F.3d 1232 (D.C. Cir. 2004).

92 O.A.S. Res. XXX, adopted by the Ninth International Conference of American States, Bogota, Colombia, Mar. 30-May 2, 1948, OEA/Ser. L./ V/II.23/doc. 2 rev. 6 (English 1979) (hereinafter *American Declaration*): Every human being has the right to life, liberty and the security of his person.

93 *Id.* article II. All persons are equal before the law and have the rights and duties established in this Declaration, without distinction as to race, sex, language, creed or any other factor.

94 *Id.* article V. Every person has the right to the protection of the law against abusive attacks upon his honor, his reputation, and his private and family life.

95 *Id.* article IX. Every person has the right to the inviolability of his home.

96 *Id.* article XI. Every person has the right to the preservation of his health through sanitary and social measures relating to food, clothing, housing and medical care, to the extent permitted by public and community resources.

97 *Id.* article XXIII. Every person has a right to own such private property as meets the essential needs of decent living and helps to maintain the dignity of the individual and of the home.

98 O.A.S., Treaty Series, Nos 1-C & 61.

99 See *supra* note 1 at ¶22 (Analysis of Admissibility).

100 The United States signed the Convention on June 1, 1977 but has never ratified it.

ratify the Organization of American States Charter on June 15, 1951, the Commission considered it bound to uphold the rights protected under the Charter.[101]

In terms of the admissibility of the claims under the various articles, the Commission dismissed the petitioners' claims under the rights to life (article I) and health (article XI) on the basis that that United States law made it possible successfully to challenge EPA permitting decisions through the federal and state courts (which the petitioners had already done[102]) but that they had not yet exhausted domestic remedies, which still had a prospect of success.[103] However, in respect of the article V and article IX claims (private and family life and inviolability of the home) the Commission found that the petitioners would not be afforded an adequate remedy in the United States courts, even if they had exhausted domestic remedies, owing to the narrow remit of privacy claims, which are limited to matters of family planning, child rearing, and abortion.[104] In the event, the article IX claim was later deemed inadmissible on the basis that no relevant facts had been adduced.[105] The article XXIII claim was dismissed as presenting no colorable claim.[106]

The most pertinent of the claims in terms of racial discrimination was that relating to the general antidiscrimination provisions of article II. The Commission interpreted this provision as a stand-alone right not to be subject to discrimination, rather than a right existing only in relation to other rights protected by the Declaration. In this respect the Inter-American Commission has departed from the approach taken in the European Court of Human Rights (ECtHR) in its interpretation of article 14 of the European Convention on Human Rights (ECHR). The latter has no independent existence and is invoked only in conjunction with one of the other "rights and freedoms set forth in [the] Convention."[107] Thus the Commission was unable to draw directly on article 14 case law since there is no stand-alone right not to be discriminated against in the ECHR. The "sting" of the petitioners' claim under article II was that the system of environmental permitting in Louisiana (which is very similar in the rest of the country) was giving rise to a disparate impact on the largely African-American Mossville community in terms of health effects. However, since only evidence of intentional discrimination would give rise to a private right of action in the United States courts (as discussed above),[108] this meant that there was no effective remedy in the United States that could be invoked to protect the rights asserted by the American Declaration, and particularly the right to the protection of the law against abusive attacks upon … honor, … reputation, and … private and family life protected by article V. In reply, the United States Government attempted to persuade the Commission that the petition was inadmissible because the petitioners had failed to exhaust domestic remedies in the state of Louisiana and through the law of tort.[109] It further pointed to the possibilities of administrative review of EPA permitting decisions and the fact that there had already been one such successful challenge.[110] The Statute of the Inter-American Commission, at article 20(c), specifically charges

101 *Supra* note 1 at ¶23. In particular, article 20 of the Statute of the Inter-American Commission on Human Rights makes explicit provision for the protection of rights "in relation to those member states of the Organization that are not parties to the American Convention on Human Rights" (which includes the United States). In particular, subsection (a) of article 20 make explicit provision for arts I, II, III, IV, XVIII, XXV, and XXVI of the American Declaration (the first two of which were invoked by the Mossville petitioners), and subsection (b) makes general provision for the Commission to make recommendations to such non-party states "in order to bring about more effective observance of fundamental human rights." Organization of American States, Statute of the Inter-American Commission on Human Rights, 1 Oct. 1979, O.A.S. Off. Rec. OEA/Ser.P/IX.0.2/80, Vol. 1 at 88.

102 *Mossville Environmental Action Now v. EPA*, 370 F.3d 1232 (D.C. Cir. 2004).

103 Note 1at ¶36.

104 *Id.* at ¶¶ 26(c), 34.

105 *Id.* at ¶43.

106 *Id.* at ¶44.

107 Eur. Conv. H. R., art. 14, 1950. U.N.T.S. I:2889 (213): "The enjoyment of the rights and freedoms set forth in this Convention shall be secured without discrimination on any ground such as sex, race, colour, language, religion, political or other opinion, national or social origin, association with a national minority, property, birth or other status." On the contingent nature of article 14 *see* Willis v. U.K. No. 36042/97 (2002) 35 E.H.R.R. 21 at ¶29.

108 *Supra* notes 12 to 41 and associated text. The Commission also summarized the position, *see supra* note 1, at ¶¶26(b), 27.

109 The requirement to exhaust domestic remedies before seeking a declaration under international human rights law is a customary requirement. *See, e.g.*, *Boyce v. Ireland* (2013) 56 E.H.R.R. SE11 at 131.

110 *Supra* note 1, at¶20.

the Commission with responsibility to ensure that domestic remedies have been exhausted before admitting a petition. However, article 31.2a of the Commission's Rules of Procedure permit it to waive this requirement if it is satisfied that "the domestic legislation [of the respondent state] does not afford due process of law for protection of the right allegedly violated."[111] Thus the Commission drew attention to the fact that:

> … both the State and the petitioners agree that it would not be possible to successfully bring an action before the domestic courts for disproportionate, discriminatory impact without a clear showing of discriminatory intent. Therefore, the IACHR is satisfied that the claims of the petitioners regarding the alleged disproportionate discriminatory pollution burden on the Mossville residents and the related consequences on the community would have no reasonable prospect of success through domestic proceedings. The petitioners are thus excused from exhausting domestic remedies on this claim … .[112]

It is notable that the Commission uses the term "discriminatory impact" rather than the more usual "disparate impact." Notable also is the fact that the petitioners' article II submission contains the term "environmental racism,"[113] a term that was originally applied to the director of the EPA during the early days of the environmental justice movement.[114] Arguably, the use of both these terms marks a return to the more condemnatory language associated with the first attempts to invoke the Equal Protection Clause itself in the cause of environmental equity.

Similarly, and specifically in relation to the article V claim, the Commission highlighted the need to

> consider [the American Declaration's] provisions in the context of the international and inter-American human rights systems more broadly, in the light of developments in the field of international human rights law since the instrument was first adopted and with due regard to other relevant rules of international law … .[115]

By way of reference to "developments in the field of international human rights law" in relation to privacy, the Commission *was* able to draw directly on the case law of the European Convention on Human Rights[116] (unlike with article II) and the expansion by the ECtHR of the interpretation of the right to privacy to include health and environmental conditions in the cases of *Lopez Ostra v. Spain* and *Fedeyeva v. Russia.*[117]

In sum, in admitting the claims under arts II and V for future consideration on the merits, the Commission implied, if not opined, that jurisprudence on disparate impact in the United States may be at odds with international norms relating to equal protection:

> The IACHR recalls that the right to equal protection under international human rights law has been interpreted as prohibiting not only intentional discrimination, but also any distinction, exclusion, restriction or preference which has a discriminatory effect and that "the notion of equality before the law set forth in the American Declaration relates to the application of substantive rights and to the protection to be given to them in the case of acts by the State or others." Without prejudging on the merits of the petition, the IACHR finds that the allegations contained in the petition, if proven, could characterize a violation of the right to equality before the law, as enshrined in Article II of the American Declaration.[118]

Though this is a strong statement from the Commission, one must bear in mind the influence which the Commission exerts within the United States itself—generally on a par with the impact of most other

111 *Id.* at ¶25.

112 *Id.* at ¶33.

113 *Id.* at ¶¶2 and 12. The Commission declaration later employs the same term, *Id.* at ¶42.

114 *See* David Schlosberg, Defining Environmental Justice: Theories, Movements and Nature, 50 (2007).

115 *Supra* note 1 at ¶ 43.

116 Council of Europe, Eur. Conv. H. R., Art. 8, 4 Nov.1950, E.T.S. 5.

117 Lopez Ostra v. Spain (1995) 20 E.H.R.R. 277; Fedeyeva v. Russia (2007) 45 E.H.R.R. 10. The Commission might also have referred to *Guerra v. Italy* (1998) 26 E.H.R.R. 357.

118 *Supra* note 1 at ¶ 42.

international human rights bodies. Even if the Commission does, in due course, uphold the Mossville petition on the merits, such a finding may have no effect at all on the availability of remedies for disparate impact in state or federal courts. Although arguments have been made that the United States should recognize international law decisions and those of the Inter-American Commission in particular,[119] the relationship of the United States with international law is paradoxical.[120] The dualist nature of the United States constitution presents particular difficulties in the implementation of international law[121] and the chimeric attitude of the Supreme Court to the question of incorporation[122] has led to the contention that the United States' attitude to human rights is "outwardly prodigious, inwardly niggardly."[123] Nevertheless, the fact remains that a highly respected international human rights commission has emphasized, albeit in anticipation of full consideration of the merits, the misalignment of disparate impact jurisprudence in the United States with international norms. The Mossville petition may yet fail on its merits of course, but, as it is difficult to see how the Commission will be able to reconcile current international legal principles on discrimination with the disparate impact jurisprudence of the United States federal courts, that part of the analysis is likely to stand.

Conclusion

Environmental justice is, at heart, a question of social equity, but one that highlights one of the negative consequences of democratic society run on capitalist principles. A measure of inequality is inevitable in such societies, and leading theories of justice applied to liberal capitalism tend to stress fairness rather than equality in recognition of this inevitability.[124] However, having accepted this limitation, it is then incumbent upon all institutions of governance and law in society to ensure that fairness is seen to be a central part of decision-making. However, fairness is a multifaceted concept and one that must take into account a wide range of competing factors. Nowhere is that more true than in the assessment of environmental injustice. On occasion, it is not sufficient simply to examine the interests of the parties involved at a particular moment in time; it may also be necessary to take account of the history and circumstances of the parties to the situation and of advances in the understanding of the exercise of human judgment. Arguably this is something that the jurisprudence of disparate impact fails to do. This failure derives in part from the understandable need in American society to distance itself from the legacy of slavery and to inculcate a truly colorblind society. The problem with this is that it assumes that this legacy can be consciously overcome, an assumption that does not appear to be supported by the scientific evidence. The fact that constitutional and statutory equal protection provisions are contingent on evidence of intentional racial animus, and nothing less, thus perpetuates an outmoded understanding of human motivation, and one, moreover, that does not appear to be consistent with discrimination jurisprudence in international law.

By the same token, the governance of the United States would grind to a halt if every environmental decision could be challenged in court and private rights engaged with every instance of disparate impact. Moreover, it is conceded that statutory and administrative challenges below the "constitutional" level do offer the possibility of real redress, but there are practical and psychological limitations with both these avenues. The practical limitations have been discussed earlier in this chapter.[125] The psychological limitation derives from the perception that disparate impact is always a "lower" form of discrimination not deserving of full constitutional protection through the courts. This in turn reflects the idea that non-intentional forms

---

119 *See* Ethan Kate, *A "Supremer" Court?: How an Unfavorable Ruling in the Inter-American Commission on Human Rights Should Impact United States Domestic Violence Jurisprudence*, 28 Wis. Int'l L.R. 430 (2010).

120 Tara J. Melish, *From Paradox to Subsidiarity: The United States and Human Rights Treaty Bodies*, 34 Yale J. Int'l L. 389 (2009). *See more generally*, Cesare P. Romano (ed.), The Sword and the Scales: The United States and International Courts and Tribunals (2009).

121 Fiona de Londras, *Dualism, Domestic Courts, and the Rule of International Law*, 3 Ius Gentium 217(2010).

122 Oona A. Hathaway, Sabria McElroy & Sara Aronchick Solow, *International Law at Home: Enforcing Treaties in U.S. Courts*, 37 Yale J. Int'l L. 51,52(2012).

123 Melish, *supra* note 120, at 391.

124 *E.g.* John Rawls, A Theory of Justice (1971).

125 *See supra* notes 42 to 52 and accompanying text.

of discrimination are less morally culpable than intentional ones. This may be a good basis in principle for dealing with situations where single individuals or institutions are making decisions on employment or educational opportunities, but it is suggested that it is a much less suitable basis for the multi-agency decision-making that characterizes most environmental situations. The consequences for the affected communities are equally serious whatever the psychological origins of the disparate impact, and at a societal level the insistence on demonstrating intentional racism before constitutional protections can be invoked represents a moral failure in terms of fairness.

Finally, where environmental justice is concerned there is even greater potential for unfairness deriving from the fact that disparate impact is far more likely to be wealth-based than race-based. Since neither the Equal Protection Clause nor the Civil Rights Act include poverty as a criterion of discrimination,[126] the potential for unfairness is exacerbated still further. In an age where the effects of climate change will have disproportionate impacts on the poor—whose contribution to the problem in the first place is likely to have been far less than the wealthy, precisely because of their poverty—it is important that legislative, executive, and judicial creativity be employed to ensure that equal protection actually means in practice what it appears to mean on paper.

126 By contrast with both article 14 of the Eur Conv. H.R. and Art. II Am. Declaration.

PART VI
Afterword

Afterword: From Identity to the Responsive State

Martha Albertson Fineman

Introduction

In a *New York Times* front page story a few years ago Adam Liptak reported the results of a study undertaken by two law professors that shows a "steep plunge" in the degree of similarity between the United States Constitution and those of other democracies in the world.[1] He notes that a 1987 article in *Time Magazine* estimated that almost all existing countries had written charters modeled directly or indirectly on the U.S. Constitution, a trend that was reversed in the 1980s and 1990s. Among the reasons offered for the declining influence by the study's authors was that "[o]ur Constitution is terse and old, and it guarantees relatively few rights." Also mentioned was the "availability of newer, sexier and more powerful operating systems in the constitutional marketplace."[2]

Offering additional authority for this point, Mr Liptak quotes Justice Ruth Ginsburg: "I would not look to the United States Constitution if I were drafting a constitution in the year 2012." She is reported to prefer the South African Constitution, the Canadian Charter of Rights and Freedoms, or the European Convention on Human Rights as potential models. Noting the difficulty of constitutional amendment in the United States and the relative malleability and short life of other countries' constitutions, Mr Liptak concludes: "[t]he rights guaranteed by our Constitution are parsimonious by international standards, and they are frozen in amber."[3]

Constitutional Innovations

There are different types or families of rights typically provided in constitutions: *security rights* that protect people against crimes; *due process rights* that protect against abuses of the legal system; *liberty rights* that protect freedoms in areas such as belief, expression, and association; *political rights* that protect political participation; *equality rights* that guarantee equality before the law and non-discrimination; and *social* (or *"welfare"*) *rights* that require protections against severe deprivation.[4] Considering the guarantees of the

1 "'We the People' Loses Appeal With People Around the World." N.Y.TIMES, Feb. 6, 2012, at 1.

2 Quoting Professor Law who also suggested "nobody wants to copy Windows 3.1."

3 He noted that other nations replaced their constitutions wholesale on an average of every 19 years, the same length of time that Thomas Jefferson suggested in a 1789 letter to James Madison marked when a constitution "'naturally expires'" because "'the earth belongs always to the living generation.'" *Id.* The United States Constitution and its first 10 amendments, known as the Bill of Rights, are well over 200 years old. There have been only 27 amendments to the Constitution. The article also includes some reflection on the declining tendency of foreign judges to cite decisions of the United States Supreme Court because of its "parochialism." Aharon Barak, when he was president of the Supreme Court of Israel, wrote in Harvard Law Review the Supreme Court was "losing the central role it once had among courts in modern democracies" and identified Canadian law as serving as a "source of inspiration for many countries around the world." Justice Michael Kirby of the High Court of Australia was reported to have stated in a 2001 interview the "America is in danger, I think, of becoming a legal backwater." Providing a counterbalance to this type of criticism, the article goes on to quote Justice Antonin Scalia's testimony before the Senate Judiciary Committee in October 2011: "Every banana republic in the world has a bill of rights" (a statement that is not true). Scalia specifically noted "The bill of rights of the former evil empire, the Union of Soviet Socialist Republics, was much better than ours … We guarantee freedom of speech and of the press. Big deal. They guaranteed freedom of speech, of the press, of street demonstrations and protests, and anyone who is caught trying to suppress criticism of the government will be called to account. Whoa, that is wonderful stuff." "Of course," he is reported to note, "it's just words on paper, what our framers would have called a 'parchment guarantee.'"

4 http://plato.stanford.edu/entries/rights-human/.

Constitution of the United States in conjunction with provisions in the constitutions of some other developed democracies reveals some interesting variations and innovations. The areas where there seem to be the most significant differences between the United States and other developed democracies are in regard to equality rights and social rights.[5]

Equality—U.S. Constitution

The equality right is typically expressed as a right to equal treatment and equal protection of law. The equality guarantee set out in the Fourteenth Amendment to the United States Constitution (which was ratified in 1868) does not specify specific groups or characteristics to be afforded equality.[6] On its face Section One applies to everyone:

> All persons born or naturalized in the United States, and subject to the jurisdiction thereof, are citizens of the United States and of the state wherein they reside. No state shall make or enforce any law which shall abridge the privileges or immunities of citizens of the United States; nor shall any state deprive any person of life, liberty, or property, without due process of law; nor deny to any person within its jurisdiction the equal protection of the laws.

The United States thus adopted a potentially radical open-text equality right under which any state classification can theoretically be challenged in federal courts.[7]

The potential avalanche of cases such an open-ended constitutional guarantee might provoke has been severely limited by Supreme Court adoption of different levels of judicial scrutiny for review of legislative classifications. The Amendment was promulgated in the wake of the Civil War and the emancipation of slaves and that legacy has directed its interpretation. Supreme Court jurisprudence clearly establishes race as the paradigmatic protected characteristic and the experience of Jim Crow exclusion of African-Americans defines the standard of discrimination against which to measure the experience of other individuals and groups. Classifications based on race or ethnicity are subjected to strict scrutiny, while gender receives intermediate review and most other classifications get only cursory rational basis scrutiny.[8]

In spite of its initial radical potential, equality as a U.S. constitutional concept is understood narrowly as the requirement of sameness of treatment or a mandate against some forms of discrimination.[9] Ironically, as a result of the differing standards of review, the equality mandate is not applied equally; only some classifications or

5 These two areas are, of course, related. As TJ Marshall pointed out long ago, it is necessary to have a certain amount of social goods before civil and political equality are meaningful. Canada and many other countries have a more developed sense of substantive equality based on provision of socio-economic rights. Those countries are also committed to international rights conferring conventions that the US has not ratified. *See* Organization of American States, American Convention on Human Rights, Nov. 22, 1969, O.A.S.T.S. No. 36, 1144 U.N.T.S. 123 (1978) (signed but never ratified by the United States); International Covenant on Civil and Political Rights, *opened for signature* Dec. 19, 1966, 6 I.L.M. 368 (1967), 999 U.N.T.S. 171 (entered into force Mar. 23, 1976) (ratified by the United States but with five reservations, five understandings, and four declarations that rendered it largely meaningless in the United States, including reserving the right to subject children to the death penalty); International Covenant on Economic, Social and Cultural Rights, *opened for signature* Dec. 19, 1966, 6 I.L.M. 360 (1967), 993 U.N.T.S. 3 (entered into force Jan. 3, 1976) (signed but never ratified by the United States).

6 The constitutional equality right in the United States Constitution arose out of the Civil War. The Thirteenth and Fourteenth Amendments to the Constitution, abolishing slavery and adding black males to those entitled to political equality.

7 The Fifth Amendment was interpreted to apply equal protection principle to the federal government.

8 There have been recent scholarly assessments that these categories are not as well defined and determinative of results as traditionally taught in law schools, but this is irrelevant to my point, which is that the categories as they have been fashioned around individual characteristics such as race, gender, ethnicity, and so on should not be employed as a limitation of the equality right.

9 Interestingly, in this catalogue, as well as in the law, class is absent as a suspect classification. *See* San Antonio Indep. Sch. Dist. v. Rodriguez, 411 U.S. 1 (1973) (rejecting the application of strict scrutiny to an education policy allegedly discriminating against students on the basis of class). Class bias would bring economic arrangements into question and, for that reason, would be incompatible with a formal equality analysis that ignores disparate underlying circumstances and economic inequality.

categories of persons receive heighted protection, leaving those outside of those categories with no realistic way to challenge arbitrary state treatment.[10] Further and leading to over-, as well as under-inclusiveness, the reliance on individual identity characteristics as proxies for disadvantage and subordination has allowed for the growing disparities in social wellbeing in American society. Formal equality leaves undisturbed—and may even serve to validate—existing institutional arrangements that privilege some and disadvantage others in American society.

Equality—Other Systems

The equality provisions in other constitutional systems are also organized around identities, but have more specifically structured equality provisions than the open-ended approach found in the Fourteenth Amendment. The objective is still equal protection of the law generally, but in recently established or revised constitutional systems, this general right is further elaborated upon by the listing of categories of persons who explicitly are to be included in the guarantee. The lists are the product of periodic amendments or revisions in these flexible systems which have been able to accommodate new claims for equal protection by individuals and groups as they arise. The nature of the characteristics reflects that equality rights arise at certain periods of history and are shaped in distinct political, cultural, and social contexts. Importantly, social welfare guarantees undergird the equal treatment of law provisions.

The post-WW II 1950s European Convention on Human Rights, article 14, requires contracting parties to secure Convention rights without discrimination based on "sex, race, colour, language, religion, political or other opinion, national or social origin, association with a national minority, property, birth or other status." The last category has allowed the European Court of Human Rights to extend article 14 protection to other grounds not specifically mentioned, including, for example, sexual orientation.[11] The Charter of Fundamental Rights of the European Union, adopted in 2000, includes the thoroughly modern and scientifically based protected category of "genetic features," along with 14 more traditional grounds.[12] The South African Constitution has 17 enumerated grounds, including the traditional race, ethnicity, religion, and sex, but adding categories addressed by legislation (if at all) in the United States, including pregnancy, marital status, social origin, sexual orientation, age, disability, and conscience.[13] The UK does not have a core constitutional

10 Julie Chi-hye Suk, *Equal by Comparison: Unsettling Assumptions of Antidiscrimination Law*, 55 AM. J. COMP. L. 295, 299 (2007) ("The unique American history of eradicating race-based slavery and the unintended consequences of this history explain these distinctive features of U.S. antidiscrimination law"). Our understanding of equality and equal protection has been profoundly shaped by their twentieth-century roots as a tool to end slavery and fight blatant forms of racial discrimination. The history of equality into protected classifications, therefore, both defines legal identities for some and also organizes us into political interest groups based on race, ethnicity, gender, and other identity characteristics.

11 Protocol No. 12 to the Convention (ETS No. 177) created an independent right not to be discriminated against and placed a duty on public authorities not to discriminate. It was adopted on November 4, 2000, in Rome and entered into force on April 1, 2005, after tenth ratification. As of 2013, it has 18 member states and 19 signatories (from 47 Council of Europe member states).

12 The preamble states that "the Union is founded on the indivisible, universal values of human dignity, freedom, equality and solidarity; it is based on the principles of democracy and the rule of law. It places the individual at the heart of its activities, by establishing the citizenship of the Union and by creating an area of freedom, security and justice." In order to achieve its goals, the community determined that "it is necessary to strengthen the protection of fundamental rights in the light of changes in society, social progress and scientific and technological developments by making those rights more visible in a Charter." Article 21 on Non-discrimination provides: 1. Any discrimination based on any ground such as sex, race, colour, ethnic or social origin, genetic features, language, religion or belief, political or any other opinion, membership of a national minority, property, birth, disability, age or sexual orientation shall be prohibited. 2. Within the scope of application of the Treaty establishing the European Community and of the Treaty on European Union, and without prejudice to the special provisions of those Treaties, any discrimination on grounds of nationality shall be prohibited.

13 Constitution of South Africa, article 9—Equality- provides: 1. Everyone is equal before the law and has the right to equal protection and benefit of the law. 2. Equality includes the full and equal enjoyment of all rights and freedoms. To promote the achievement of equality, legislative and other measures designed to protect or advance persons or categories of persons, disadvantaged by unfair discrimination, may be taken. 3. The state may not unfairly discriminate directly or indirectly against anyone on one or more grounds, including race, gender, sex, pregnancy, marital status, ethnic or social origin, colour, sexual orientation, age, disability, religion, conscience, belief, culture, language, and birth. 4. No person may

document, but enumerates protected characteristics in the Equality Act of 2010.[14] Some systems explicitly facilitate judicial expansion of the categories. The Canadian Charter sets forth enumerated grounds, but also allows judicial expansion to "personal grounds" analogous to those listed.[15]

Does it make a significant difference that many of the categories enumerated for constitutional protections or rights in other countries are instead protected by statutory law in the United States? Statutory equality reforms took place in the twentieth century and laws against discrimination now complement the Fourteenth Amendment guarantee of equal protection of law, even extending the antidiscrimination mandate to private actors in some contexts.[16] These laws are also organized around individual characteristics or identity markers, including many of the enumerated constitutional grounds found in the Canadian and European constitutional systems. These laws have not only dismantled the formal legal impediments applied to distinctions based on a wide variety of characteristics, but also provide remedies for discrimination.[17] In addition, statutory bodies such as the Human Rights and Equal Opportunity Commission play a positive role in ensuring the equal protection of law.

First, it must be noted that while the antidiscrimination measures were largely successful in improving the circumstances and prospects of many previously legally disadvantaged persons, they did not reach everyone. In addition, it has become increasingly clear that a discrimination model built around personal characteristics or identities will not be sufficient to meaningfully ensure equality of access and opportunity unless accompanied by measures that take into account structural disadvantages associated with social roles, positioning, and functioning.

In addition, there are symbolic or expressive differences between statutory provisions and constitutional rights, as well as practical reasons statutory provisions should not be considered a substitute for constitutional protection. The most important difference is that constitutional recognition entrenches the protection of a right, while legislation is subject to a majoritarian process and may not be forthcoming, can be inadequate

---

unfairly discriminate directly or indirectly against anyone on one or more grounds in terms of Subsection (3). National legislation must be enacted to prevent or prohibit unfair discrimination. 5. Discrimination on one or more of the grounds listed in Subsection (3) is unfair unless it is established that the discrimination is fair.

14 From the Home Office website: http://www.homeoffice.gov.uk/equalities/equality-act/: The Equality Act of 2010 replaced previous antidiscrimination laws with a single act to make the law simpler and to remove inconsistencies. This makes the law easier for people to understand and comply with. The act also strengthened protection in some situations. The act covers nine protected characteristics, which cannot be used as a reason to treat people unfairly. Every person has one or more of the protected characteristics, so the act protects everyone against unfair treatment. The protected characteristics are: age; disability; gender reassignment; marriage and civil partnership; pregnancy and maternity; race; religion or belief; sex; and sexual orientation. The Equality Act sets out the different ways in which it is unlawful to treat someone, such as direct and indirect discrimination, harassment, victimisation and failing to make a reasonable adjustment for a disabled person. The act prohibits unfair treatment in the workplace, when providing goods, facilities and services, when exercising public functions, in the disposal and management of premises, in education, and by associations (such as private clubs).

15 Canadian Charter of Rights & Freedoms 1984. Section 15 (1): Every individual is equal before and under the law and has the right to the equal protection and equal benefit of the law without discrimination and, in particular, without discrimination based on race, national or ethnic origin, colour, religion, sex, age, or mental or physical disability. (2) Subsection (1) does not preclude any law, program. or activity that has as its object the amelioration of conditions of disadvantaged individuals or groups including those that are disadvantaged because of race, national or ethnic origin, colour, religion, sex, age, or mental or physical disability. As "in particular" indicates, the explicitly named grounds do not exhaust the scope of section 15, additional grounds can be considered if it can be shown that the group or individual's equality rights were denied in comparison with another group that shares all of the same characteristics except for the personal characteristic at issue. A personal characteristic is considered *analogous* to the ones enumerated in section 15 if it is "immutable" or cannot be changed or can only be changed at excessive cost (constructively immutable). Thus far, several analogous grounds have been identified: sexual orientation (*Egan v. Canada* [1995], *Vriend v. Alberta* [1998], *M. v. H.* [1999] *Little Sisters Book and Art Emporium v. Canada* [2000]) This finding has led provincial courts (the Supreme Court declined in *Reference re Same-Sex Marriage* to rule on the issue as the government had voiced its intent to legalize them anyway) to find that laws against same-sex marriage in Canada would be unconstitutional. In *Halpern v. Canada (Attorney General)* (2003), the Court of Appeal for Ontario used section 15 to legalize same-sex marriage in Ontario; marital status (*Miron v. Trudel*, [1995], *Nova Scotia v. Walsh* [2002]); off-reserve aboriginal status/"Aboriginality-residence" (*Corbiere v. Canada*); and citizenship (*Lavoie v. Canada* [2000]).

16 Title 7; Age Discrimination; Americans With Disability Act;

17 On the grounds of race, gender, age, disability.

or even detrimental, and can be amended or repealed by a legislative majority for any reason, including short-term political gain. In the situation of state statutes, under applicable Supreme Court review rules the legislative majority would need only to meet the weak rational basis standard.[18]

Positive Discrimination

Another significant distinction between the constitutional systems in many other countries and that in the United States is the treatment of affirmative action or other practices that require the state to take some positive regard for the position of specific individuals or groups. During the latter part of the twentieth century it became painfully apparent to many commentators and policymakers that something in addition to an antidiscrimination agenda was necessary.

Several other countries have moved to temper the negative prohibitions against discrimination with positive duties that compel governments to proactively and vigorously promote equality. Paradoxically, such a duty may compel a government to discriminate: to draw distinctions in assessing who is deserving of special consideration or "affirmative action" in addition to, and over and above, formal equality. Redefining second order, antidiscrimination measures is necessary to allow resort to such "affirmative action."

The Canadian Charter explicitly permits affirmative action, stating in Subsection 2 that the prohibition of discrimination in Subsection 1 "does not preclude any law, program or activity that has as its object the amelioration of conditions of disadvantaged individuals or groups including those that are disadvantaged because of race, national or ethnic origin, colour, religion, sex, age or mental or physical disability."[19] South Africa's constitution specifies that "[t]o promote the achievement of equality, legislative and other measures designed to protect or advance persons or categories of persons, disadvantaged by unfair discrimination may be taken."[20]

Other countries have adopted measures that fall short of affirmative action, but nonetheless recognizing some form of positive duty on the part of the government to consider the consequences of official actions to certain groups or individuals in society. The practice of "gender-mainstreaming," for example, requires governments to consider the impact of their decisions on gender equality. This consideration goes well beyond determining if there is, or was, intentional discrimination, which is not required. Gender-mainstreaming compels the development of a process for ensuring an independent and official assessment of the gendered implications and consequences of specific plans or proposals is brought within legislative deliberation.[21] Children have been the beneficiaries of a similar approach with the establishment of Commissions on Children and Youth in the United Kingdom. The Commissioners are responsible for assessing the impact of any proposed legislation on their designated consistency and bringing that assessment to the attention of legislators.[22] Both of these mainstreaming measures are related to and rooted in United Nations

18 Of course, the states may also give greater freedom and protection than the federal Constitution provides. The United States Constitution establishes the floor below which the state may not fall. The question is whether this floor should be built a bit higher and more positive duties in regard to ensuring equality placed on federal and state governments.

19 *See* note 15, *supra*.

20 *See* note12 *supra*.

21 Mainstreaming involves ensuring that gender perspectives and attention to the goal of gender equality are central to all activities—policy development, research, advocacy/ dialogue, legislation, resource allocation, and planning, implementation, and monitoring of programmes and projects. See generally http://www.unwomen.org/en.

22 There are four Commissioners, one each for England, Northern Ireland, Scotland, and Wales. In England, the commissioner's general function is defined as "promoting awareness of the views and interests of children in England," especially as they relate to five "aspects of their well-being." There is a framework of five key outcomes in which the services are to be measured. Young people and children should: be healthy, stay safe, enjoy and achieve, make a positive contribution, and achieve economic wellbeing. The Children's Commissioner is to "use our powers and independence to ensure that the views of children and young people are routinely asked for, listened to and acted upon and that outcomes for children improve over time." They are to "do this, in partnership with others, by bringing children and young people into the heart of the decision-making process to increase understanding of their best interests."

The website of the Commissioner of Children and Youth in Northern Ireland sets forth what it does thus: "The Commissioner wants the Office to base all its work on thorough research when helping children and young people, and has been working with universities and other agencies to do this. The Commissioner has the power to undertake

Conventions these countries have ratified and the United States has not: the Convention on the Elimination of Discrimination Against Women and the Convention on the Rights of the Child.

There were some initial concessions to the need for affirmative action in cases of proven discrimination on the basis of race in the 1970s and 1980s in the United States.[23] However, recent concern with reverse discrimination and "innocent" third parties, as well as the controversy over use of strict scrutiny in such cases has raised doubts about the future of affirmative action in American jurisprudence.[24] A conscientious legislator well might be deterred by Chief Justice Roberts' words in *Parents Involved* that "[a]t the heart of the Constitution's guarantee of equal protection lies the simple command that the Government must treat citizens as individuals, not as simply components of a racial, religious, sexual or national class," as well as his concluding sentence that "the way to eliminate discrimination on the basis of race is to eliminate discrimination on the basis of race."[25]

In any case, even in the context of race and given the legacies of slavery and Jim Crow discrimination, there is no mandated duty applicable to any state or other entity in the United States to undertake such positive measures. There is also no independent body charged with making impact assessments on behalf of protected individuals and groups. The default constitutional position is that the right to equality in the United States is a right to formal equality; an antidiscrimination-sameness of treatment guarantee.

Process

Initially problematic is the fact that assessing discrimination is fundamentally a process of comparison in which it is necessary to have at least two appropriately defined individuals or groups to pose against each other. But only some characteristics receive heightened or strict review. Under Supreme Court jurisprudence, the individual or group claiming "suspect classification" status must demonstrate they are a discreet and insular minority[26] that has suffered historic discrimination analogous to race discrimination and are:

> saddled with disabilities or subjected to such a history of purposeful unequal treatment, or relegated to such a position of political powerlessness as to command extraordinary protection for the majority.[27]

general inquiries into issues where she believes children are being adversely affected. This may be an informal inquiry or a more formal investigation with the same powers of the High Court (as detailed in our legislation) that can include requesting documents or the attendance or examination of witnesses. She can also respond to requests from the Assembly and Parliament to look at issues. The Commissioner is also required to review the ways that those providing services for children listen to complaints and take account of children's views." Pursuant to this charge, the Commissioner has adopted a children's rights-based approach consistent with the Convention of the Rights of the Child, which states that children have the right to express their views on all matters affecting them. *See* Laura Lundy, Leslie McEvoy & Bronagh Byrne, *Working with Young Children as Co-Researchers: An Approach Informed by the United Nations Convention on the Rights of the Child*, 22 Early Education and Development 714, 714 (2011).

23 Franks v. Bowman, 424 U.S. 747 (1975); United States v. Paradise, 480 U.S. 149 (1988) U.S. Steelworkers v. Weber, 443 U.S. 193 (1979) Fullilove v. Klutznick, 448 U.S, 448 (1980).

24 City of Richmond v. J.A. Croson Co., 488 U.S. 469 (1989); Grutter v. Bollinger, 539 U.S. 306 (2003 narrowly tailored requirement); Parents Involved in Cmty. Schs. v. Seattle Sch. Dist. No. 1, 551 U.S. 701 (2007) (distinguishing between *de jure* and *de facto* segregation and calling into question diversity as rationale beyond higher education). In 2014 in *Schuette v. Coalition to Defend Affirmative Action, Integration and Immigrant Rights and Fight for Equality By Any Means Necessary (BAMN)*,134 S. Ct. 1623 (2014) a plurality of the Court held that Michigan voters could chose against affirmative action in upholding the state's Constitutional Amendment banning its use in public universities admissions process.

25 Parents Involved in Cmty. Sch. v. Seattle Sch. Dist. No. 1, 551 U.S. 701, 748 (2007).

26 United States v. Carolene Prods. Co., 304 U.S. 144, 152 n.4 (1938).

27 San Antonio Sch. Dist. v. Rodriguez, 411 U.S. 1, (1977) (deciding by a 5–4 majority that education was "neither 'explicitly nor implicitly' protected in the Constitution" so as to require heightened scrutiny as a fundamental right and also finding that Texas had not created a suspect class related to poverty. "Only appellees' first possible basis for describing the class disadvantaged by the Texas school-financing system—discrimination against a class of definably 'poor' persons—might arguably meet the criteria established in these prior cases. Even a cursory examination, however, demonstrates that neither of the two distinguishing characteristics of wealth classifications can be found here. First, in support of their charge that the system discriminates against the 'poor,' appellees have made no effort to demonstrate that it operates to the peculiar disadvantage of any class fairly definable as indigent, or as composed of persons whose incomes are beneath any designated

This standard undermines the development of meaningful notions of equality of opportunity and access. Under it, characteristics which are significant impediments to social and institutional inclusion for millions, such as disability and poverty (class), have not been afforded strict scrutiny.

Compounding the paucity of equality protection is the fact that the United States, unlike its peer nations, does not have a general universalized social welfare system. Our social welfare policy begins with an ideologically based premise that individuals are responsible for their own welfare and imposes expectations of self-sufficiency and independence on rich and poor, advantaged and disadvantaged alike. There is no general guarantee of housing or food, and, until recently (and perhaps not for long), no right to health care, or access to jobs or higher education. While old age assistance is virtually universal, and eligibility is based on chronological age, other social welfare programs tend to be need-based and means-tested.

Equality thus reduced to antidiscrimination has proven an inadequate tool to resist or upset persistent forms of subordination and domination and that is the case even for the individuals and groups deemed deserving of stricter constitutional scrutiny. In part, this inadequacy is the result of how assessment of discrimination under formal equality is done by focusing on the actions and motivations of individuals making decisions and determinations at specific and defined points of time. The framework is designed to capture the victims and the perpetrators of discrimination. Unless tied to individual actions, structural disadvantages and debilitating institutional and societal arrangements are left out of the picture. In fact, an assessment of formal equality largely leaves undisturbed—and may even serve to validate and facilitate—systemic inequalities that result in entrenching existing privilege and disadvantage in society.

Also significant is the fact that even in the context of well-established suspect categories, the antidiscrimination approach has not been successful in practice. For example, in the wake of legislation in the employment context, there was an arroyo of cases: in 1991 federal courts heard 8,300 employment discrimination cases and by 2000 the number exceeded 22,000. The long list of prohibited forms of discrimination represented in federal, state, and local laws and the possibility of reverse discrimination actions means that virtually everyone can fashion a discrimination claim. But fashioning a claim is not the same as winning a law suit, and at that phase of the process, the news is not good for plaintiffs. People who bring employment discrimination cases lose at trial at a greater rate than any other group of civil plaintiffs and even when they win, their victory is more likely than most other awards to be overturned on appeal.[28] Some scholars have argued that judges are ideologically predisposed to be hostile to discrimination claims.[29]

Beyond Discrimination—Beyond Identities

Curiously, the equality approach undertaken in countries such as South Africa or Canada—constitutions specifically identified by Justice Ginsburg in the *New York Times* article as being more modern and appropriate models than is the U.S. Constitution—retain the formal framework of antidiscrimination. The frame is merely expanded to encompass more and more individuals and groups. The United Kingdom even advertises the fact that under its Equality Act of 2010 "[e]very person has one or more of the protected characteristics, so the act protects everyone against unfair treatment." What should the broadly inclusive evolution of the enumeration approach do to our understanding of the concept of discrimination?

---

poverty level. Indeed, there is reason to believe that the poorest families are not necessarily clustered in the poorest property districts … . Second, neither appellees nor the District Court addressed the fact that, unlike each of the foregoing cases, lack of personal resources has not occasioned an absolute deprivation of the desired benefit. The argument here is not that the children in districts having relatively low assessable property values are receiving no public education; rather, it is that they are receiving a poorer quality education than that available to children in districts having more assessable wealth. Apart from the unsettled and disputed question whether the quality of education may be determined by the amount of money expended for it, a sufficient answer to appellees' argument is that, at least where wealth is involved, the Equal Protection Clause does not require absolute equality or precisely equal advantages … ." 411 U.S. 1, 22–24.

28 Kevin M. Clermont & Stewart J. Schwab, *How Employment Discrimination Plaintiffs Fare in Federal Court*, 1 J. Empirical Legal Studies 429, 450 (2004); *see also id.* at 449–52.

29 Samuel R. Bagenstos, *The Structural Turn and the Limits of Antidiscrimination Law*, 94 Cal. L. Rev. 1, 22–26 (2006); Michael Selmi, *Why Are Employment Discrimination Cases So Hard to Win?*, 61 La L. Rev. 555, 561–69 (2001).

If unfairness is the point and the objective is elimination of unwarranted discrimination that inhibits equality, why limit inquiry to personal characteristics such as race or gender? The affront to equality occurs not from the drawing of lines or distinctions in and of itself, but arises because of the resulting denial of access or opportunity or exclusion and isolation. The state should have a rigorous duty to ensure equal protection of the law and equal opportunity to enjoy the benefits of society to everyone, but it will only get part of the way to that objective if the monitoring is restricted to bias against or stereotyping of personal characteristics. It will be necessary to move beyond identities and beyond discrimination as it is now understood to a more universal perspective.

The Vulnerable Subject

In recent work, I develop the concepts of "dependency," "vulnerability," and "resilience" in order to argue for a state more responsive to the individual, social, and institutional circumstances in an effort to anchor the idea of equality in the human condition.[30] In particular, I have developed the concept of the "vulnerable subject," and suggested that it replace the one-dimensional, severely deformed and inadequate figure of the liberal autonomous subject that has dominated political and policy discussions, rendering pathological and deviant natural and inevitable relationships of dependency, need, and vulnerability. Appreciation of our universal and constant vulnerable subjectivity is essential if we are to successfully challenge the misleading mantras of "personal responsibility," "self-sufficiency," and "autonomy" that so pervade political and policy discourse in the United States and prevent positive social welfare measures and state responsiveness to structural and embedded inequalities.

In calling for a more responsive state in contemporary United States, the argument must begin with the observation that the choice is *not* one between an active state on one hand versus an inactive state on the other. The state is always at least a residual actor and the choice is between responsibility and neglect. Will we demand a comprehensive and just equality regime or settle for an inattentive state that fosters patronage, spoilage, and corruption on the part of powerful individuals and institutions?

An insistence that the state be restrained ignores the many ways in which the state—through law—shapes institutions from their inception to their dissolution and the ways in which those institutions produce and replicate inequalities. Society's institutions play an important role in regard to human vulnerability and everyone should have the opportunity to benefit from being part of society and its institutions. A vulnerability analysis focuses on the organization, operation, and outcomes of institutions and structures to ensure that the basic standards against which they are measured are consistent with and further the equality principles underlying the Declaration of Independence and the Fourteenth Amendment of the United States Constitution: all persons are equally entitled to the protection of law and the state is constituted for the general and common benefit, not for the benefit of a select few. In order for those principles to be realized, the state must respond when its institutions are functioning in such a way as to unduly privilege any group of citizens over others. The state must intervene in order to adjust institutional arrangements in a way that ensures equality of access and opportunity so individuals can as fully as possible live a meaningful and satisfying life.

The concept of the vulnerable subject is built around the idea of the "life-course," reflecting a perspective that encompasses all of the developmental and social stages individuals are likely to pass through. During their lives individuals will encounter a myriad of possible opportunities, frustrations, challenges, and experiences necessitating a wide range of differing and interacting abilities. We are situated beings who live with the ever-present possibility of changing needs and circumstances in our individual and collective lives. We are also accumulative beings and have different qualities and quantities of resources with which to meet these needs or circumstances, both over the course of our lifetime and as measured at the time of crisis or opportunity.[31]

---

30 *See* Martha Albertson Fineman, *The Vulnerable Subject: Anchoring Equality in the Human Condition*, 20 Yale J.L. & Feminism 1 (2008). *See also* Martha Albertson Fineman, *The Vulnerable Subject and the Responsive State*, 60 Emory L.J. 251 (2010); Martha Albertson Fineman, The Autonomy Myth: A Theory of Dependency (2004).

31 I use the term resources to encompass both material and social goods, including human capital, education, wealth, and group identification, as well as relationships in entities such as the family and other institutional arrangements. See note 35 *infra*. Resources are assets that are accumulated and dissipated over time in the process of living, making decisions,

Vulnerability and Difference

Paradoxically, while human vulnerability is universal and constant as an abstract theoretical matter, its experience is particular, varied, and unique on the individual level. This is a strength of the analysis, which allows us to see two different roles for law and policy in regard to human vulnerability. Two forms of individual difference are relevant: there are physical/mental/intellectual, and other variations and differences in human embodiment. These differences are not socially neutral; historically, reaction to some human variations has led to the creation of hierarchies, discrimination, and even violence. Individuals who have certain characteristics have been subordinated and excluded from the benefits of society, often because their differences are thought to indicate they are dangerous, or interpreted as inadequacy, inferiority, or weakness. The appropriate legal response in such instances is an improved and strengthened antidiscrimination system, perhaps complemented by affirmative action and social welfare processes to make up for past discrimination.

The second forms of relevant difference are the differences in social location that are produced as the result of institutional practices and operations. While it is the case that such differences are manifested on the individual level, attention to the functioning of institutions is the focus in this part of the analysis. We are all differently situated within webs of economic and institutional relationships that structure our options and create opportunities. All individuals are dependent on institutions, be it the family or market and state institutions, because institutions provide the primary access and pathways to gain the resources necessary to address our vulnerability. This institutional focus supplements attention to the individual subject, placing him and her in societal contexts and blurs the line between public and private. This blurring allows a reconception of the nature of state responsibility in which the state is always, already implicated in societal institutions and organizations through its monopoly on the process of legitimization.

The Responsive State

A vulnerability approach imagines societal institutions as constructs of the state, brought into existence and maintained under the legitimating authority of law and the regulatory machinery of the state. It is this connection among human vulnerability necessitating the construction of vulnerable institutions, and the role of the state in that creation and regulation that forms the foundation of the argument that the state thus has a duty to be more responsive to, and explicitly responsible for, vulnerability.[32] Vulnerability imagines that it is an integrated vision of society, not one of separate spheres and competing autonomous individuals or groups that should guide political and institutional ethics and practices. Indeed, one way to think about the formation of society is to posit that it is human vulnerability that brings individuals into families and families into communities and communities into societies, nation-states and international organizations, all such entities engaged in building

investing, and so on. At times of crisis or opportunity, our accumulated resources can limit or enhance our options. These moments can also open up different, additional resources in terms of access to institutions designed to aid or assist us at such moments, particularly the law and legal institutions.

32 These institutions in combination with the legal and governmental structures that bring them into existence and monitor their activities constitute the state as I conceive of it, as it is manifested through complex institutional arrangements. The state exercises coercive, but legitimate force in bringing these institutions into existence and regulating them through the mandate of its public authority. *See The Vulnerable Subject* (2008), *supra* note 31, at 6:

> The state [has not] wither[ed] away. Rather, it has withdrawn or been prevented by entrenched interests from fulfilling one of its traditional roles in the social compact: to act as the principal monitor or guarantor of an equal society. The fact that nonintervention has facilitated a skewed and unequal society with the distance between rich and poor growing in recent years, makes clear that some form of prevailing power is essential to counter unfettered self-interest. Understood historically as the manifestation of public authority and the ultimate legitimate repository of coercive power, the state is the only realistic contender in that regard. One pressing issue for those interested in furthering a new vision of equality must be how to modernize or refine this conception of the state and then explicitly define its appropriate relationship to institutions and individuals within contemporary society (footnotes omitted).

I picked up and continued this line of argument in *The Vulnerable Subject and the Responsive State* (2010).

the collective institutions with which to confront our shared and individual vulnerability.[33] Human beings are dependent not only on each other, but also on the institutions and political structures they build.

Significantly, it is through institutions that we gain access to resources with which to confront, ameliorate, satisfy, and address our vulnerability. Resources can come in material, social, or economic forms, including human capital, education, wealth, and group identification, as well as relationships in entities such as the family and other institutional arrangements.[34] Resources are accumulated and dissipated over time in the process of living, making decisions, and investing. At times of crisis or opportunity, our accumulated resources can limit or enhance our "autonomy" since they define what are our realistic options. Resources cannot eliminate our inherent vulnerability, but they can and do mediate, compensate, and lessen the experience of vulnerability. The institutions and political structures that allocate these resources to individuals should operate to affect the collective interest in equality of access and opportunity, but this can only be accomplished if they are designed consistent with the realities of human dependency and vulnerability.

Our experiences with institutions are often concurrent and interactive, but also can be sequential. For example, the relationship between the educational system and the employment and social security systems is sequential. Collectively they provide for the accumulation of resources, creating assets in the present and possibilities and opportunities for the future. Because they are so important both to individuals and to society, the flaws and barriers, gaps and potential pitfalls that such institutions contain must be monitored and adjusted when they are not functioning in appropriate ways. The values that should guide the judgment of appropriateness must be democratic and publicly oriented and reflect norms of equality and open access and shared opportunity.[35]

33 This notion of formation of social foundations touches on John Locke's characterization of development of familial and social bonds. According to Locke, an urge towards self-preservation, "necessity, convenience, and inclination" vested into humankind by God led him to form a society. In this sense, "the first society was between Man and Wife," to which children where thereafter added. Gordon J. Schochet, *The Family and Origins of the State* in John Locke: Problems and Perspectives: A Collection of Essays 87 (John W. Yolton, ed.) (Cambridge University Press) (2010). The familial society mentioned by Locke, however, existed in the "pre-political" state of nature. *Id.* at 88. Thereafter, however, "a certain element of necessity" (that "could hardly be avoided") caused the "transformation" of these pre-political societies to political societies and the government. *Id.* at 89.

34 I have identified at least five different types of resources or assets that societal organizations and institutions can provide: physical, human, social, ecological or environmental, and existential. Physical resources are the physical goods or material things that determine our present quality of life, such as housing, food, entertainment, and means of transportation. Physical resources also can provide us with the means for accumulating additional resources when they take the form of savings and investments. Certainly tax and inheritance laws impact the distribution of physical assets and are part of this system, but so are banking rules and regulations and credit and monetary policies. Human resources also affect material wellbeing. They are those goods that contribute to the development of a human being, allowing participation in the market and making possible the accumulation of material resources that help bolster individuals' resilience in the face of vulnerability. These resources are often referred to in terms of "human capital," primarily developed through systems that provide education, training, knowledge, and experience. Accumulation of a degree of human capital is essential in gaining access to employment systems, which themselves can provide further resources. Social assets or resources are provided by less tangible, not so easily quantifiable relationships. These include social networks from which we gain support and strength. The family is a major institution providing social resources. So too are other associations, such as political parties or labor or trade unions in which individuals bolster their resilience by joining together to address vulnerabilities generated by the market. In recent decades, a sense of community organized around identity characteristics, such as race, ethnicity, and gender, has constituted powerful networks of affiliation and belonging. Ecological resources can be conferred through our position in relation to the physical or natural environments in which we find ourselves. We live in an environment and are dependent on things like clean air and water. We experience the environment in immediate and cosmic senses. The state of our neighborhood park is important, but so too are Arctic ice flows or floods in Pakistan. A variety of external factors and physical actions can alter the environments in which we live and have profound influence over our needs and wellbeing. Existential resources are provided by systems of belief or aesthetics, such as religion, culture, or art, perhaps even politics. These systems can help us to understand our place within the world and allow us to see meaning and beauty in our existence. *See also* Peadar Kirby, Vulnerability and Violence (2006). In discussing resilience, Kirby builds on earlier definitions that understood resilience as "enabling units such as individuals, households, communities and nations to withstand internal and external shocks." *Id.* at 55 (quoting the United Nations Economic Commission for Latin America and the Caribbean).

35 The institutions may also seek efficiency and profits and operate in a market system, but equality of access and opportunity and lack of undue privilege should provide the regulatory thresholds below which their functioning must not fall.

Significantly, with sequential systems, the failures of one system, such as the provision of an inadequate education, may be impossible to undo and cannot be fully compensated for in another system later down the line, such as the workplace. In other words, society's institutions interact in ways that actually produce (or fail to produce) social, political, and economic equality. They can confer privilege or disadvantage and an initial privilege or disadvantage may determine if an individual is able to benefit from other systems. In addition, because this is true, privileges and disadvantages can be cumulative and thus have effects more profound than any single indicator of privilege or disadvantage. On the other hand, and also important is the fact that sometimes privileges conferred in one concurrent system can compensate or even cancel out disadvantages encountered in others. For example, a good early education, such as that provided by Head Start, may trump poverty as a predictor of success in school, particularly when coupled with the advantages a social or relational system can provide, such as a supportive family and progressive social network.

Some Notes on Implementation

The constructs of a vulnerable subject and the responsive state as they are articulated in this chapter set forth the guiding principles for what might be termed a political ethic or ideal. The vulnerability approach is offered as a framework or heuristic device through which to consider law and policy consistent with progressive notions of legitimization and democracy. As such, vulnerability analysis is less a blueprint for judicial review than it is a proactive model for inclusive legislative deliberation and policymaking in a pluralistic society.

Monitoring the Political: "Legislative Due Process"

A vulnerability analysis attempts to replace current paradigms in political and policy rhetoric and is aimed at changing hearts and minds, a rather elusive objective. As such, the question of how it might operate on a practical level, beyond discourse and symbolism, is often raised. Surprisingly, there have been some very practical and concrete suggestions for legal reform that might be relevant in answering that question.

As an initial matter, it seems obvious that a vulnerability approach would not be focused on the judiciary as the primary branch for its implementation, nor would it necessarily support the judicial imposition of socio-economic or other constitutional rights independent of legislative actions. The construct of the vulnerable subject and the plea for a more responsive state in the United States will have to be implemented in a political system in which the judiciary's role is limited and legislative mistakes or misconduct are assumed to be subject to correction via the election cycles. Recognizing the weakness of the assumption that our elected officials do good and careful work, Justice White wrote in his dissent in *INS v. Chadha*: "The Constitution does not and cannot guarantee that legislators will carefully scrutinize legislation and deliberate before acting. In a democracy it is the electorate that holds the legislators accountable for the wisdom of their choices."[36] Some commentators question the effectiveness of a political solution to legislative ineptness.[37] This is due both to the complexity of the legislative process and its lack of transparency, which affects both the electorate's ability to oversee the process and the functioning of the legislators. Aside from majoritarian bias, bills are often rushed to a vote before legislators have had an opportunity to review or consider them. Legislators are more familiar with the legislative history (who supported what, who added amendments, and so on) than the outcomes' impact on people.[38] Legislators generally treat constitutional issues as secondary to policy considerations, despite often

36 INS v. Chadha, 462 U.S. 919, 997 (1983) (White, J., dissenting).

37 Professor Ittai Bar-Siman-Tov suggests that "the political safeguards that scholars and judges commonly rely upon to constrain legislative behavior actually have the opposite effect: these 'safeguards' in fact motivate lawmakers to be lawbreakers." Ittai Bar-Siman-Tov, *Lawmakers as Lawbreakers*, 52 Wm. & Mary L. Rev. 805, 807 (2010).

38 Hanah Metchis Volokh, *A Read-the-Bill Rule for Congress*, 76 Mo. L. Rev. 135, 139 (2011) ("Congress sometimes rush[es] big, important bills through the legislative process without providing an opportunity for all Members to properly review the bill and consider its effects and implications.").

using constitutional rhetoric to help prevail in policy disputes.[39] There also is some speculation that the majority of the public looks at congressional votes more for symbolic value than their actual policy outcomes.[40]

Given the significance of the issues addressed by legislation, such criticisms have led to suggestions that some form of judicial oversight of the process of legislative deliberation might be warranted. Without specifically endorsing any approach, it is instructive to see how these proposals are evolving. Former Justice John Paul Stevens explored the idea of legislative due process at length in his dissent in *Fullilove v. Klutznick*: "I see no reason why the character of [the legislature's] procedures may not be considered relevant to the decision whether the legislative product has caused a deprivation of liberty or property without due process of law."[41]

In fact, in *Klutznick* Justice Stevens argued that procedural review would be *less* intrusive than substantive review.[42] The dissent relied on Terrance Sandalow's 1977 article, *Judicial Protection of Minorities*,[43] which built on Justice Stone's suggestion in *United States v. Carolene Products Co.* that the judiciary may have a heightened duty to protect discrete and insular minorities.[44] Stevens recognized that generally courts should defer to Congress to strike a balance between competing interests, but maintained that when a "special condition" exists that justifies distrust in the political process, courts should be able to engage in a more "searching judicial inquiry" for the deficiencies in the legislative process.[45]

In broad strokes, the argument for legislative due process review contends that when it is apparent that special interests have Congress's ear and minorities do not, such unequal influence should trigger judicial distrust. The resolution on review should not be that unelected judges make the ultimate determination whether the *law* is narrowly tailored, however. Rather, the courts should make a determination about the actual *processes* that Congress undertook.[46] This review of legislative history would go beyond a search for

39 Bernard W. Bell, *Metademocratic Interpretation and Separation of Powers*, 2 N.Y.U. J. Legis. & Pub. Pol'y 1, 34 (1999) ("Legislators are likely to treat constitutional issues as secondary to policy considerations and to view such constitutional considerations as useful primarily as tools to help the legislator prevail on a particular policy issue.").

40 *See* Tim Groseclose & Jeffrey Milyo, *Sincere Versus Sophisticated Voting in Congress: Theory and Evidence*, 72 J. Pol. 60, 60 (2010) (stating a commonly held belief that legislators often vote against their own policy preferences for purposes of political gain or other non-policy reasons); Nancy Marshall-Genzer, *What Is the Cost of a House Vote?*, Marketplace (July 11, 2012), http://www.marketplace.org/topics/economy/healthcare/what-cost-house-vote (exploring how the House of Representatives voted 33 times to repeal the Affordable Care Act in the preceding 18 months for symbolic reasons, despite knowing there were insufficient votes to pass the repeal in the Senate).

41 Fullilove v. Klutznick, 448 U.S. 448, 550 (1980) (Stevens, J., dissenting). Recent accounts of partisanship in the United States suggest an unwavering commitment to party ideology at the expense of compromise and necessary reform. John Avlon, *Hyper-Partisanship Dragging Down Nation*, CNN (June 7, 2012, 2:56 PM), http://www.cnn.com/2012/06/07/opinion/avlon-partisan-pew/index.html; *see also* Pew Research Ctr., Trends In American Values 1987–2012: Political Polarization Surges In Bush, Obama Years 1–4 (2012); Chris Cillizza, *Partisanship Doesn't Seem Worse. It Is Worse*, Wash. Post (June 4, 2012, 3:33 PM), http://www.washingtonpost.com/blogs/the-fix/post/partisanship-doesnt-seem-worse-it-isworse/2012/06/04/gJQAJIuzDV_blog.html. When taken to this extreme, partisanship may serve to frustrate rather than support representative governance.

42 *Klutznick*, 448 U.S. at 551 ("A holding that the classification was not adequately preceded by a consideration of less drastic alternatives or adequately explained by a statement of legislative purpose would be far less intrusive than a final determination that the substance of the decision is not 'narrowly tailored to the achievement of that goal.'").

43 *See id.* at 551 n.27 (quoting Terrance Sandalow, *Judicial Protection of Minorities*, 75 Mich. L. Rev. 1162, 1188 (1977)).

44 United States v. Carolene Prods. Co., 304 U.S. 144, 152 n.4 (1938).

45 Sandalow, *supra* note 44, at 1173–74 ("[Justice] Stone believed that the task of striking a balance among competing interests is for legislatures and that courts ought to defer to their decisions. On occasion, however, a 'special condition' might exist justifying distrust of 'those political processes ordinarily to be relied upon …' A 'searching judicial inquiry' might, in such situations, serve as a corrective for the deficiencies of the political process." (quoting *Carolene Prods.*, 304 U.S. at 153 n.4)).

46 *Id.* at 1177 ("No one supposes, for example, that fairness requires courts to substitute their judgments for those of legislatures with respect to tax rates for the wealthy, the level of welfare payments for the poor, or the content of regulations imposed upon milk producers in the interest of consumers. Such issues, it is commonly understood, are to be resolved through the political process, and that is so even though there is a risk that the majority will not fully appreciate the costs that are imposed upon the minority.").

statements clarifying the meaning of ambiguous statutory language.[47] Under such a system, "[j]udicial review is extended to an evaluation of the quality of the legislative or deliberative process."[48]

Professor Anita S. Krishnakumar has also proposed that Congress enact what she refers to as "a representation reinforcing framework" that would require all proposed legislation to be accompanied by an impact statement that outlines the legislation's expected effect on various interests.[49] This interest impact statement would set forth "who Congress intends to benefit, who it acknowledges will be harmed, who supported the bill, who opposed it and, if Congress wishes, broad instructions on which interests the statute should be construed to favor or disfavor." Her proposal calls for having a "red flag list" of societal groups that are "diffuse, politically unorganized and whose interests traditionally have gone overlooked in the legislative process."[50] These groups would be identified by a non-partisan committee. If a bill includes these groups it must have an impact statement which would be sent to the Government Accountability Office or the Congressional Budget Office, which would be responsible for assessing the qualitative and, if possible, quantitative impact the legislation will have on these groups.[51] The impact statement would also assess whether and to what extent the legislation confers benefits on other groups, such as those traditionally able to "impose their will on the legislative process by controlling the flow of information to legislators."[52]

Building on the possibility of legislative due process review, Elizabeth Garrett and Adrian Vermeule advocate a path to help Congress meet the requirements it would entail: a two-step procedure for all bills.[53] The first step would require a committee to identify potential constitutional issues in a bill and the second step would require the committee to produce a "constitutional impact statement" which would summarize the findings. To ensure Congress is equipped to carry out this process, Garrett and Vermeule suggest adding additional resources through the creation of an "Office for Constitutional Issues."

Judicial intervention might also help in cases in which strict application of the rules would fail to produce results that are compatible with the underlying purposes of legislative due process. As policymaking becomes more complex, more deliberation might be required to allow the legislature a full understanding of the issues at stake. In those cases, legislative due process rules might not provide an adequate floor for the amount of legislative deliberation required for informed and responsible decision-making. As such, the judiciary might be able to perform a supervisory (but not policymaking) role in a new framework of responsible legislative due process.

There are many criticisms of the legislative due process idea.[54] But criticism should not obscure the fact that many people are troubled by the current state of our democracy and the inability to move forward in

---

47 Spain has "systematic judicial review of internal parliamentary procedures, including legislative processes." Suzie Navot, *Judicial Review of the Legislative Process*, 39 Isr. L. Rev. 182, 188 (2006). Israel also appears to be inching toward review of process, as exemplified by Justice Matza's opinion in *Naot v. The Haifa Municipality*, in which he characterized a decision made by the city council without deliberation as an issue of voters' rights. *See* HCJ, 4733/94 Naot v. The Haifa Municipality PD 49 (5) 111, 125–26 [1996]. For a translation of the relevant portion of Justice Matza's opinion, see Navot, *supra*, at 242.

48 Philip P. Frickey & Steven S. Smith, *Judicial Review, the Congressional Process, and the Federalism Cases: An Interdisciplinary Critique*, 111 Yale L.J. 1707, 1728 (2002).

49 Anita S. Krishnakumar, *Representation Reinforcement: A Legislative Solution to a Legislative Process Problem*, 46 Harv. J. On Legis. 1, 3 (2009).

50 *Id.* at 28.

51 *Id.* at 30 ("Once a committee has submitted a legislative proposal and 'interest impact' statement to CBO/GAO, that entity then should be required to prepare an impact report evaluating: (1) the impact in qualitative and, if possible, quantitative terms, that the bill is expected to have on List groups; and (2) the benefits the bill is expected to confer on other groups.").

52 *Id.* (citing Jonathan Macey, *Promoting Public-Regarding Legislation Through Statutory Interpretation: An Interest Group Model*, 86 Colum. L. Rev. 223, 254 (1986)).

53 *See* Elizabeth Garrett & Adrian Vermeule, *Institutional Design of a Thayerian Congress*, 50 Duke L.J. 1277, 1310–11 (2001).

54 *See* Oliver A. Houck, *Things Fall Apart: A Constitutional Analysis of Legislative Exclusion*, 55 Emory L.J. 1, 8 (2006) (discussing criticisms of legislative due process by the United States Supreme Court).

solving critical problems.[55] Partisanship seems to be more important than the national good and the interests of the politically and economically disempowered are perceived as cast aside or manipulated for political advantage in a process in which money and access is increasingly unequal.[56]

In some ways, the proposals for legislative due process are reminiscent of the practice of gender mainstreaming[57] and Commissioner on Children and Youth structures found in the U.K.[58] The intention is to provide some incentives so that the legislature will engage in a comprehensive, public, and accessible harm-benefit analysis before enacting important policy legislation.[59] Perhaps such proposals are only a sign of increasing desperation, but it may be that such a structure would improve legislative transparency and allow the political process to work more effectively.

---

55 Sanford Levinson, Our Undemocratic Constitution 7–8 (2006) (pointing to polling data which indicates widespread dissatisfaction with the performance of elected officials and federal policies as evidence of "a belief that our political institutions are *not* adequately responding to the issues at hand"); Task Force On Inequality & Am. Democracy, Am. Political Sci. Ass'n, American Democracy In An Age Of Rising Inequality 5 (2004) ("According to a host of opinion surveys and other indicators, Americans are increasingly worried about disparities of participation, voice, and government responsiveness. … Between the mid-1960s and the mid-1990s the proportion of Americans who felt that 'the government is run by a few big interests looking out only for themselves' more than doubled to reach 76 percent, while the number who believed that 'public officials don't care about what people think' grew from 36 percent to 66 percent" (quoting Gary Orren, *Fall from Grace: The Public's Loss of Faith in Government*, *in* Why People Don't Trust Government 77, 81 (Joseph S. Nye, Jr et al. eds, 1997))).

56 Paul Krugman, Op.-Ed, *Plutocracy, Paralysis, Perplexity*, N.Y. Times (May 3, 2012), http://www.nytimes.com/2012/05/04/opinion/krugman-plutocracy-paralysisperplexity.html?_r=0 ("For the past century, political polarization has closely tracked income inequality, and there's every reason to believe that the relationship is causal. Specifically, money buys power, and the increasing wealth of a tiny minority has effectively bought the allegiance of one of our two major political parties, in the process destroying any prospect for cooperation."); *see also* Task Force On Inequality & Am. Democracy, *supra* note 56, at 7 ("As wealth and income have become more concentrated and the flow of money into elections has grown, campaign contributions give the affluent a means to express their voice that is unavailable to most citizens. This undoubtedly aggravates inequalities of political voice.").

57 The Report of the Council of Europe indicated that:

> "It might be useful to start with gender mainstreaming policy areas that are habitually labeled as gender-neutral. All policy areas which affect the daily life of citizens, such as transport policies, urban policies, social policies are definitely important, although this is often not recognized. The same goes for research policies, because this is an important area to generate knowledge. Mainstreaming these policy areas might be very efficient, given the eye-opening effect it will produce. This effect will be very useful for convincing policy-makers and people of the need for gender mainstreaming, even when basic gender equality seems to be achieved." For a comprehensive approach to this strategy, including reports on various governments processes *see*: *Gender Mainstreaming: Conceptual Framework, Methodology and Presentation Of Good Practices*; Final Report of the Group of Specialists on Mainstreaming; Directorate General of Human Rights, Strasbourg, 2004.

A commitment to gender-mainstreaming compels the development of a process for ensuring an independent and official assessment of the gendered implications and consequences of specific plans or proposals is brought within legislative deliberation.

This also is a forward-looking inquiry, undertaken to prevent *future* disadvantage for all members of the group. It is *not* a remedy for individual past harm.

58 *See supra* note 23.

59 There are a number of statutory precedents that would guide such a bill. *See, e.g.*, Balanced Budget and Emergency Control Act of 1985 § 221(c), 2 U.S.C. § 602(g) (2006) (allowing for the conducting of studies estimating the financial impact of legislation which includes federal mandates on states and private industries); Defense Base Closure and Realignment Act of 1990 § 2903(d), 10 U.S.C. § 2687 (2006) (requiring a committee report and hearings on the impact of such closures and a non-partisan committee to make such decisions); National Environmental Policy Act of 1969 § 102, 42 U.S.C. § 4332 (2006) (requiring environmental impact statements made after consultation with relevant agencies). Another example, although never enacted, is the Federalism Act of 1999 which would have required Congress to issue a report with every bill that: (1) identified any section of a proposed bill that expressly pre-empted state or local government authority; (2) identified the constitutional basis for pre-emption; (3) set forth reasons for the pre-emption; and (4) included a federalism impact assessment performed by the Director of the Congressional Budget Office. Federalism Act of 1999, H.R. 2245, 106th Cong. § 8(a) (1999).

Recognizing that no system is without flaws or immune from criticism, those who propose some review of legislative deliberation seek to find a mechanism through which legislators would be confronted with information about potential inequalities and distortions arising from the underlying privileges and disadvantages created by their actions. The reformers' hope lies in the possibility that if such a mechanism were in place, interest groups could organize around the findings in the reports and investigations of proposed lawmaking prepared. This would assist such groups in advocating against legislation that risks unduly privileging or unreasonably disadvantaging certain people. Voters who do not like the results of specific legislative deliberations could actually try to organize themselves and "vote the bums out."

Perhaps the prospect of such public transparency would make legislators act in more responsible and responsive ways—their own electoral vulnerability making them more responsive to the vulnerabilities of *all* their constituents, not just to those with deep pockets. The proposals for legislative due process do not diminish the legislature or its processes, nor do they seek to impose a system in which judges are making legislative decisions. While not perfect, these proposals might offer a beginning for the construction of a system with more transparency in which the implications of human vulnerability and dependency are made visible and are understood to justify some realistic checks on the ineffectiveness, bias, and ineptitude in legislative deliberations.

Vulnerability as a Political Framework

The fundamental political question a vulnerability analysis seeks to answer is simply, "What does it mean to be human?" The answer this chapter provides—it means to be constantly vulnerable and in need of resilience—necessitates an additional political inquiry as to how the United States should justly define its responsibility and channel its authority and resources (including institutions that are the product of law) in relation to the vulnerability of both individuals and the institutions in which resilience is produced?

The currently glib rhetoric of personal responsibility and self-sufficiency as the answer for poverty and other social ills will hopefully fall flat politically once the role of the state and its institutions in the production of human resilience is clearly understood. Further, universal recognition that institutions of governance are themselves susceptible to capture, decay, corruption, and decline will elucidate how these institutions can actually function to limit access and opportunity for far too many individuals. Revealing this normalization of disadvantage at the institutional level will make clear why more robust safeguards and monitors are necessary to ensure the state can be responsive to these institutional shortcomings.[60]

Ultimately, orienting law and politics around the "vulnerable subject" would emphasize a different set of values than those that have evolved around the image of a liberal subject and a restrained state. Those values would be more egalitarian and collective in nature, preferring connection and interdependence rather than autonomy and independence as the guiding visions in both the political and personal realms. In contemporary political discourse the image of the human being as both a legal reality and a political subject is reductive, diminished in both descriptive and aspirational terms. We are perversely individualized and isolated at the same time that we are cast as merely the subjects of balance sheets and statistical models, the asserted inevitability of our selfish nature captured in economic terms such as "moral hazard" and the extent of our ambition confined by the glorification of "efficiency." Further, the state is perceived as a threat to liberty and autonomy, not as one of the necessary providers or insurers of the resources whereby individual agency can be realized. These are the crabbed images that confine current political rhetoric and hobble the imagination of political and legal theorists. A vulnerability analysis asks us (and our politicians) to embrace a more complex and aspirational reality.

---

60 This is particularly problematic in the existing legislative process. See Victor Goldfeld, *Legislative Due Process and Simple Interest Group Politics: Ensuring Minimal Deliberation Through Judicial Review of Congressional Processes*, 79 N.Y.U. L. Rev. 367, 369 (2004) (describing the political impact of partisanship and congressional gridlock).

Index

For Product Safety Concerns and Information please contact our
EU representative GPSR@taylorandfrancis.com Taylor & Francis
Verlag GmbH, Kaufingerstraße 24, 80331 München, Germany